American Judicial Politics

American Judicial Politics

Second Edition

Harry P. Stumpf
University of New Mexico

with
Kevin C. Paul, Esq.

Prentice Hall
Upper Saddle River, New Jersey 07458

Library of Congress Cataloging-in-Publication Data

Stumpf, Harry P.
  American judicial politics / Harry P. Stumpf. — 2nd ed.
      p.   cm
  Includes bibliographical references and index.
  ISBN 0-13-033465-0
  1. Judicial process—United States.   2. Courts—United States.
  3. Judicial power—United States.   4. Jurisprudence—United States.
  5. Law and politics.   I. Title.
  KF8775.S78   1998
  347.73—dc21   97–12627
                                                 CIP

Editor-in-chief: Nancy Roberts
Assistant Editor: Nicole Signoretti
Acquisitions Editor: Michael Bickerstaff
Production Liaison: Fran Russello
Editorial/production supervision: Pine Tree Composition
Prepress and Manufacturing Buyer: Bob Anderson
Cover Director: Jayne Conte
Marketing Manager: Chris De John

This book was set in 9.5/11 Mallard by *Pine Tree Composition, Inc.*,
and was printed and bound by *RR Donnelley & Sons Company.*
The cover was printed by *Phoenix Color Corp.*

 © 1998, 1988 by Prentice-Hall, Inc.
Simon & Schuster/A Viacom Company
Upper Saddle River, New Jersey 07458

Printed in the United States of America
10 9 8 7 6 5 4 3 2

ISBN: 0-13-033465-0

Prentice-Hall International (UK) Limited, *London*
Prentice-Hall of Australia Pty. Limited, *Sydney*
Prentice-Hall Canada Inc., *Toronto*
Prentice-Hall Hispanoamericana, S.A., *Mexico*
Prentice-Hall of India Private Limited, *New Delhi*
Prentice-Hall of Japan, Inc., *Tokyo*
Simon & Schuster Asia Pte. Ltd., *Singapore*
Editora Prentice-Hall do Brasil, Ltda., *Rio de Janeiro*

For Bonnie

*Whose love and support throughout
my life has made all the difference*

Contents

Tables and Figures   xiii

Preface to the First Edition   xvii

Preface to the Second Edition   xix

PART I   THE JUDICIAL SETTING   1

**1   Jurisprudence Old and New: Conceptions of Law
and the Judicial Function**   3
Jurisprudence   5
   The Natural Law Tradition   6
   Analytical or Positivist Jurisprudence   8
   Sociological-Jurisprudence   11
   Legal Realism   13
   Political Jurisprudence   17
   Behavioral Jurisprudence   22
Conclusions   24
Further Reading   27

2   Political Jurisprudence Reconsidered   28
Political Jurisprudence: A Focus on Process   28
Movements and Countermovements: Post-Realism, Legal
Education, and Political Jurisprudence   31
   Critical Legal Studies   34
   Value-Enunciating Positions: The Search for a Touchstone
     of Constitutional Interpretation   36

Law and Economics (L/E) 38
Feminist Jurisprudence 40
Critical Race Theory 42
The Law and Language Movement 42
Post-Realism and Political Science 43
The New Institutionalism 44
The Princeton School 45
The Constitutive View of Law 47
The Myth of Neutrality and Formalism 48
Judicial Policy-Making 50
Courts: A Reconsideration 58
Legal Systems 61
The Common Law 61
The Civil Law 63
Further Reading 64

3 **State Judicial Organization**   **65**
Judicial Business in the States 66
State Court Systems 71
The Colonial Experience 71
State Courts Under the Constitution 74
The Politics of Structure 87
Further Reading 93

4 **The Federal Courts**   **94**
Historical Development 94
The Federal Judiciary Today 99
The District Courts 99
The United States Courts of Appeals 102
The United States Supreme Court 104
Specialized Federal Courts 115
Other Specialized Federal Courts 118
Federal Judicial Administration 119
Judicial Federalism 123
Further Reading 125

PART II JUDICIAL PERSONNEL 127

5 **The Politics of Judicial Selection: The State Experience**   **129**
The Political Culture of Judicial Selection 129
Judicial Selection Systems in the States 133
An Analysis of State Selection Systems 141
The Missouri Plan 141
Judicial Elections 147
Some Conclusions 150
State Judges: A Profile 153
A Note on Tenure and Removal 163
Further Reading 167

6 Federal Judicial Selection   **169**
  Federal District and Appellate Judges: The Force
  of Senatorial Patronage   171
    Politics   174
    Professional Competence   177
    The Carter Reforms   179
    The Reagan and Bush Legacy   183
    The Advice and Consent of the Senate   184
    Gender and Race on Federal Courts   187
  The Clinton Administration, First Term   188
  The Supreme Court   190
    The Choices of Recent Presidents   191
    Politics, Partisan, and Otherwise   197
    Professional Merit   201
    Other Factors   204
    The Senate   205
  Tenure and Turnover   208
  Further Reading   215

7 The Politics of Legal Advice   **216**
  The Attorney Role(s)   217
  The American Legal Profession: A Profile   220
  The Legal Profession to 1870   225
  Legal Education in America   230
  The Organization of the Bar   240
    The Distribution of Legal Services: The Unmet Need   244
  Professional Stratification   253
  Further Reading   258

PART III   THE JUDICIAL PROCESS   259

8 The Civil Judicial Process   **261**
  Grievances to Disputes: The Transformation Process   263
    Parties   269
    Substance of Grievance   269
    External Factors   269
  The Litigious Society?   270
  Formal and Informal Dispute Processing   276
  The Flow of Civil Litigation   278
  Civil Justice: Two Case Studies   285
    Small Claims Court: Poor Man's Justice   285
    Medical Malpractice: Obstetrics and Gynecology Cases   291
  Conclusions   297
  Further Reading   298

9 The Judicial Process in Criminal Cases   **300**
  Politics of Criminal Law   301
  Conceptualizing the Criminal Justice Process   304

Crime in America   306
Justice Without Trial: The Decision to Arrest   312
Prosecutorial Discretion and Plea Bargaining: The Heart of the
    Process   316
    Prosecutorial Discretion: The Early Stages   318
    The Work Group and Plea Bargaining   324
Trials   329
Sentencing   333
Further Reading   344

10 The State Appellate Process   **346**
Appeals: Function and Process   346
State Intermediate Appellate Courts   349
The Evolution of State Supreme Courts   356
Decision Making on State Supreme Courts   360
State Supreme Courts: The Emergence of the "New" Judicial
    Federalism   367
Conclusion   376
Further Reading   376

11 Federal Appeals   **378**
The United States Courts of Appeals   378
    Appellate Caseload: Origin and Substance   379
    Screening and Other Shortcuts at the Federal Appellate Level   382
    Circuit Court Decision Making   384
The United States Supreme Court   389
    The Setting   390
    Access and Cashflow   392
Deciding What to Decide: The *Certiorari* Process   397
    Formal Decision Making   401
Further Reading   408

SECTION IV   COURTS AND SOCIETY   409

12 Judicial Policies: Compliance, Implementation, and Impact   **411**
Impact Research: The State of the Art   411
Legislative Responses   415
    Congress and the Supreme Court   415
    State Legislative Responses   426
Executive Responses   428
The Judicial Bureaucracy   430
The Extrajudicial Bureaucracy   436
    The Exclusionary Rule   437
    School Prayers   438
Interest Groups, Public Opinion, and the Media   441
Further Reading   447

13 American Courts: An Assessment   **449**

Courts as Resolvers of Disputes   450

Judicial Policy-Making, Constitutional Democracy, and Social
    Change   458

Courts as Purveyors and Substainers of Myth   466

Further Reading   469

Name Index   **471**

Case Index   **481**

Subject Index   **485**

Tables and Figures

TABLES

2–1	Political Science Approaches to the Study of the Judiciary	27
3–1	State Court Filings, 1984, 1988, 1993, 1994	65
3–2	State and Federal Constitutional Courts Contrasted, 1994	66
4–1	Federal District Court Caseflow, 1940–1995	99
4–2	Bankruptcy Filings, 1950–1995	100
4–3	Civil Cases Commenced in U.S. District Courts, Twelve-Month Period Ending September 30, 1991, and September 30, 1995	101
4–4	Criminal Cases Commenced in U.S. District Courts, Twelve-Month Period Ending September 30, 1991, and September 30, 1995	102
4–5	United States Courts of Appeals, 1995	104
4–6	United States Courts of Appeals Caseloads, 1940–1995	105
4–7	Workload of the Supreme Court, Fall Term, 1995	110
4–8	Cases Docketed, Supreme Court, Fall Term, 1990–1995	112
4–9	Petitions for *Certiorari* Docketed and Granted and Signed Opinions Written, United States Supreme Court, 1970–1995	113
5–1	State Appellate Court Selection Plans, 1993	132
5–2	State Court of General Jurisdiction Selection Plans	133
5–3	Characteristics of State Supreme Court Judges, 1960s and 1980–1981	150
5–4	Immediate Prior Occupation of Trial Judges	154
5–5	Women Judges on State Courts, 1977–1991	155
5–6	Black Judges on State Courts, 1971–1991	156
5–7	Hispanic Judges on State Courts, 1985, 1992	156

5–8   Hispanic State Judges in States with Largest Percent
      Hispanic Population, 1985, 1992   157
5–9   Minority Judges in New York City, 1991   158
6–1   Party Relevance and Lower Court Nominations, 1884–1992   171
6–2   U.S. District Court Appointees by Administration   176
6–3   U.S. Appeals Court Appointees by Administration   178
6–4   Race/Ethnic Federal Judicial Appointments by Administration, 1969–1995 184
6–5   Minorities on the Federal Judiciary, 1976–1995   185
6–6   Gender Appointments to the Federal Bench by Administration, 1969–1995   185
6–7   Women on Federal Judiciary, 1976–1995   186
6–8   Supreme Court Nominations, 1900–1994   194
6–9   Qualifications of Supreme Court Justices   199
6–10 Characteristics of Supreme Court Justices   204
7–1   National Lawyer-Population Ratios, Selected Years, 1951–1995   217
7–2   Estimated Lawyer-Population Ratios, Selected Countries, Mid-1980s   217
7–3   Employment of Lawyers, 1980 and 1991   219
7–4   Women Lawyers: Number and Percentage, Selected Years   220
7–5   Enrollment in ABA-Approved Law Schools, Fall, 1963–1995   234
7–6   Distribution of High-Prestige Law School Graduates Among Areas of Practice   251
7–7   Distribution of Law School Graduates Among High-and Low-Prestige
      Areas of Practice   252
7–8   Prestige Scores of Legal Specialities   253
8–1   Grievances and Claims Over $1,000, Civil Litigation Research Project   260
8–2   Civil Case Filings in General Jurisdiction Courts in 29 States, 1993   273
8–3   Civil Case Types in Limited Jurisdiction Courts, 1994   275
8–4   Civil Case Filings in Federal District Courts, 1960, 1986, and 1994   277
8–5   Federal Civil Case Terminations, 1985–1994   278
8–6   Types of Tort Cases in State Courts of General Jurisdiction, 1992   286
9–1   Percentage of Crimes Reported to the Police, 1986–1995   302
9–2   Percentage of Criminal Justice Employment Expenditures
      by Level of Government, 1992   306
9–3   Estimated Police Arrests by Offense Charged, 1993   311
9–4   Disposition of Cases Involving Felony Charges
      in Five Major U.S. Metropolitan Jurisdictions, 1988   313
9–5   Goals of Courtroom Work Groups   319
9–6   Sentencing Policies in the United States, 1994   333
9–7   Mandatory Minimum Incarceration Sentencing Policies
      in the United States by Category of Offense, 1994   335
10–1 Appellate Ratio in 19 States, 1994   345
10–2 Dispositions in State Courts of Last Resort, 1994   355

10–3   Manner of Case Disposition in 26 Courts of Last Resort, 1993   356

11–1   U.S. Courts of Appeals, Appeals Filed, Terminated,
and Pending, Fiscal Years 1990–1994   374

11–2   Case Dispositions in Twelve Regional United States Courts
of Appeals, Fiscal Year 1995   378

11–3   Supreme Court Workload, 1935–1995   388

11–4   Final Disposition of Cases on the United States Supreme Court, 1991–1995   390

11–5   The Supreme Court Docket and Case Selection, 1986–1995   393

FIGURES

3–1   California Court Structure, 1994   74

3–2   Kansas Court Structure, 1994   75

3–3   Minnesota Court Structure, 1994   76

3–4   New York Court Structure, 1994   77

3–5   ABA Model for Unified State Court Systems   89

4–1   The United States Court System   98

4–2   Number and Composition of Federal Judicial Circuits   103

4–3   Federal Judicial Administration   120

8–1   Dispute Pyramid: All Disputes, Civil Litigation Research Project   262

8–2   Dispute Pyramids: Three Specific Problems   262

8–3   Tort Filings in State and Federal Courts, 1984–1993   268

8–4   Civil Cases in State General Jurisdiction Courts
in 23 States, 1984 versus 1993   274

8–5   Medical Negligence and Resulting Litigation   289

9–1   Serious Crime Flow, 1995   301

9–2   Crimes Cleared by Arrest, 1993   307

9–3   Typical Outcomes of 100 Felony Arrests Brought
by the Police for Prosecution   312

Preface to the First Edition

Since the 1940s, the study of law and the judiciary by political scientists has been in ferment, the central movement being away from "black letter" legal doctrine toward broader sociopolitical conceptions of adjudication. The jurisprudence supporting these trends—along with the new issues, research foci, and empirical findings of this movement—have constituted the central agenda of professional activity in the field. This book records and analyzes these developments, largely in the American setting.

American Judicial Politics covers contemporary judicial politics in substance as well as theory, incorporating extensive citations to the literature of the field. As such, the book is appropriate for use in upper-division and graduate courses in the social sciences, as well as in law school offerings on contemporary jurisprudential issues and social science approaches to the study of the judicial process. The book may either be adopted as the basic text in such courses (perhaps supplemented by one of several excellent readers now available) or be used in conjunction with texts or readers of quite different perspectives—those with legal doctrinal, historical, comparative, or broadly sociological (law and society) orientations—in order to present alternative approaches for the student.

The coverage begins with two chapters on modern jurisprudence, focusing on ways we think about legal institutions and how their systems and judgments affect us. Separate state and federal chapters on the politics of judicial structure and jurisdiction, the recruitment of judges, and the trial and appellate processes seek to correct the imbalance in emphasis that has existed between upper and lower courts. The tilt in favor of criminal law and courts and away from civil judicial processes likewise has been addressed, again by including separate chapters on each.

The choice of issues and materials to cover and, more importantly, their interpretation obviously reflect my own views of the extent and nature of the political character of the American judicial process—notions developed over some 35 years of teaching and research in the field. These views, constituting my own jurisprudence, so to speak, are set forth in the first two chapters, though they inevitably appear throughout the book.

Debts accumulated in writing the book are many. Acknowledgments appropriately begin with the hundreds of scholars whose tough sledding in empirical research and theory-building make a book of this genre possible. To these must be added the scores of undergraduate and graduate students at the University of New Mexico in my P.S. 415

course who assisted in a variety of research tasks over the seven-plus years the book has been aborning. Connie Harrington, Rudolph Chavez, Peter Kierst, Greg Dickson, Mary Carol Matheson, Stephanie Rowe, Houston Ross, and Anne Wood come especially to mind. In the final year of work, Kevin Paul assumed a very wide range of duties, from citation checking to editorial assistance, all accomplished at a level of skill and dedication well beyond that which an undergraduate ought to possess. He was assisted in countless ways by Melanie Lunsford.

Eulalie Brown, government documents librarian for Zimmerman Library, along with Myron Fink, Oscar Baynes, and their associates at the University of New Mexico School of Law Library were all more then helpful in locating source materials for the project. Thanks are also due Lynn Graves, Lucylle Langdon, and Robin Jones who typed major portions of the manuscript, especially in its early form. Mary Boughton and the office staff of the Department of Political Science, University of New Mexico, provided sustained assistance in a variety of tasks.

From the initial proposal to the submission of the final manuscript, several professional colleagues in the judicial field added their support and constructive criticisms. In the early stages, Jack W. Peltason, John R. Schmidhauser, Henry J. Abraham, David J. Danelski, Martin Shapiro, Joel B. Grossman, and Jerome R. Cosri lent encouragement, as did Theodore L. Becker, Sheldon Goldman, Herbert Jacob, Stuart S. Nagel, Harold J. Spaeth, Christine B. Harrington, and Albert R. Matheny. Later, several coworkers in the field agreed to read sections of the manuscript and offered sometimes extensive commentary. These were Bradley C. Canon, J. Woodford Howard, Stuart A. Scheingold, Henry R. Glick, John H. Culver, Joel B. Grossman, Henry J. Abraham, and George F. Cole. At the invitation of the publishers, Martin Shapiro (University of California, Berkeley) and Charles H. Sheldon (Washington State University) read the entire manuscript and offered numerous suggestions for improvement. Martin Shapiro deserves special thanks, not only for his early encouragement of the project, but particularly for hearing me out on a large number of issues pertinent to important parts of the manuscript.

A few special people have contributed more broadly to my thinking about courts as well as to my intellectual development generally. They include Claradine Johnson and Mildred Laughlin from too many years ago to bear revealing; my chief mentor, Victor G. Rosenblum, long a valued friend and colleague; and two of my graduate students, John H. Culver and Bernadyne Weatherford, who offered encouragement during critical stages of the book—and my life.

The volume would surely not have appeared at all for a true gentleman of the publishing world, Drake Bush, senior acquisitions editor. His facile diplomacy contributed in no small part to bringing the entire project to fruition. Johanna Schmid, associate editor; Sarah Helyar Smith, manuscript editor; Jan Duffala, production editor; and Eleanor Garner, permissions editor, all did a superb job of follow-through. Not to be forgotten are Jane E. Carey, designer; Susan G. Holtz, art editor; and Sharon Weldy, production manager. No author could ask for a more competent, pleasant, and thoroughly professional group with which to work! Of course, the customary disclaimer applies to all those whose assistance I have acknowledged: I, not they, assume responsibility for the final product.

Finally, I lovingly acknowledge the assistance of my wife, Patricia Rogers, who contributed at every stage of the project, but in particular played an indispensable role in the last year in producing a near-letter-perfect manuscript on the word processor. The quality of her work is deeply appreciated by all of us associated with subsequent stages of the project, for it made our tasks a good deal easier—and more fun—while significantly improving the overall quality of the book.

Harry P. Stumpf

Preface to the Second Edition

That this volume has been promoted to its second edition is gratifying. Whatever success *American Judicial Politics* has achieved is due in the main to that large body of scholars in law and the social sciences who continue to nudge back the frontiers of our knowledge of the roles of courts and judges in American politics and society. Thanks are also due to many of this same group who have evinced a willingness to search out and use teaching materials that not only instruct but also seriously challenge their students. It is to these teacher-scholars that this second edition is dedicated.

The book is not, and was never intended to be, a work for beginning college students. Rather, the targeted audience consists of those students and teachers who have a background in the basics of American government and constitutional law and who are ready to seriously address these questions: What roles can be ascribed to the judicial establishment in our polity and society? How is our judiciary structured, how are judicial processes played out, and what is the extent and nature of judicial outcomes that can be explained by tangential political forces? More importantly, perhaps, the book continues and expands an emphasis on jurisprudence, speaking to the question, What conceptualizations of law and courts, past and present, are most useful in helping us orient our thinking? The book is based on the belief that the best of our students are quite up to thinking conceptually about these matters. Indeed, they are clearly able, even eager, to begin the task of thinking about the *way we think about* law, politics, and society.

All chapters for the second edition have been examined in an effort to find better ways of explaining complex issues, better ways of presenting data, and better modes of covering the increasing number of politico-legal issues now surrounding the workings of American courts. The first edition's emphasis on bibliography has been continued and expanded in a persistent attempt to help achieve the impossible: a book that is authoritative and comprehensive in its coverage of the politics of American courts.

Assistance in completing the second edition has come from some usual as well as unexpected sources. Kevin C. Paul, now an established attorney and member of the Colorado Bar, increased his role in the writing of the book, such that he richly merits the "with" designation on the title page. Members of the University of New Mexico Law Library staff, particularly William R. Jacoby, Library Information Specialist and one of my former students, have continued their critical role in locating source materials. Another of my former students, David G. Richter, combed the manuscript for stylistic errors. And Ms. Dixie E. Wellborn, along with my wife, Patricia Rodgers, cheerfully suffered with me the tedium of poring over page proofs and composing the indices. Ms. Patty Sawyer of Pine Tree Composition proved a delightful and perceptive Project Manager, overseeing the main steps in the production of the book. And not to be forgotten are the scores of colleagues from coast to coast who have been touchingly generous in sharing the results of their research, often prior to publication. A list of their names rolls on and on in the chapter footnotes.

A capricious Providence has dropped into my life one Professor Walter F. Murphy, McCormick Professor of Jurisprudence Emeritus of Princeton University. Professor Murphy volunteered to read and re-read the entire manuscript, making numerous suggestions for improvement. Walter has also worked out fairly well in the role of humble research assistant as the writing progressed! As always, Professor Martin Shapiro was also at my side, particularly regarding the first two chapters, and there saved me from a number of errors. And many scholars at professional meetings and on the phone over the past several years have offered valuable suggestions for improving the work. Of course I, not they, bear responsibility for any lingering errors of commission and/or omission.

Harry P. Stumpf
Albuquerque, New Mexico

PART I
THE JUDICIAL SETTING

1

Jurisprudence Old and New: Conceptions of Law and the Judicial Function

To seek a definition of law is to set forth upon a quest for the Holy Grail. Anyone who has made this search will readily sympathize with the lament of Max Radin, "those of us who have learned humility have given over the attempt to define law."

—A.E. Hobel,
Man and the Primitive World

The movement in the subdiscipline [of public law] is toward a set of people who treat all of law and courts as interwoven with all the rest of politics.

—Martin Shapiro
"Public Law and Judicial Politics"

This is not a book about law, per se, but about courts—the judicial establishment—what Americans call the third branch of government. But to understand courts and their role in the political and social system, which is the chief aim of this book, we may logically begin with a discussion of law and different ways philosophers over time have defined and conceptualized law. The usefulness of this approach is suggested by John Saxe's well-known Hindu fable entitled "The Blind Men and the Elephant." The poem begins as follows:

> It was six men of Indostan,
>   To learning much inclined,
> Who went to see the Elephant
>   (Though all of them were blind),
> That each by observation
>   Might satisfy his mind.

The six then approach the animal from different parts of its anatomy (the side, the tusk, the trunk, the knee, the ear, and the tail). On the basis of this limited contact, they all draw definitive conclusions about the nature of the beast. Thus, the blind man who happened upon the Elephant's ear reasoned that the animal must be like a fan; while he who touched only the tusk of the beast, finding it smooth and sharp, concluded that the entire animal must be like a spear. The moral of the story, according to Saxe, is this:

> So oft in theologic wars,
> The disputants, I ween,
> Rail on in utter ignorance,
> Of what each other mean,
> *And prate about an Elephant*
> *Not one of them has seen!*

Are we not all like the blind men of Saxe's fable? We vigorously debate the "real" causes of crime, the proper stance of the United States toward the most recent of Mideast "crises," the nature and extent of the downfall of American education, or the "real" politics and personal proclivities of Supreme Court nominees—all without knowing a great deal about these subjects. The fable is especially relevant to intellectual debates on topics such as justice, conflict, law, and legal systems. This is the case because we really *are* blind as to these subjects, for the simple reason that they are *concepts*—abstractions from reality that have no known, that is to say, no empirically verifiable meaning. No one has ever seen or physically felt law or justice or jurisprudence. But this fact does not prevent us from expending enormous amounts of energy discussing and writing about the "true" meanings of these things.

That true meanings escape us, however, is not to say that it makes no difference how we conceptualize things. If, for example, we conceive of elephants as akin to snakes, we will then approach elephantology through the framework of herpetology, giving rise to questions of whether elephants are more like alligators or crocodiles or, perhaps, turtles. And if we conceive of elephants not as animals at all, but rather as some form of plant life, then an entirely different set of questions arises. Quite clearly, the ways in which we conceptualize things—the images that we compose in our heads—significantly affect the approach that we take toward the "real" world.

So it is with law and its role in society. Our perceptions of law and things legal largely shape the questions that we ask about law, our attitude toward it, and, in general, the "what" and to some extent the "how" of the study of law. We all have these perceptions: a rough theory of law consisting of a set of interrelated hypotheses purporting to depict our own "legal reality." Stated differently, we all have a sort of *jurisprudence*. To each of us, terms such as judge, jury, court, cop, lawyer, justice, and so on conjure up images pertaining to the "real" (our) meaning of things legal. Most of us also have a notion of the interrelationship of these legal entities, as well as their roles in the larger society:

- A judge wears a robe and is fair minded.
- Cops wear blue uniforms and hit people, sometimes.
- Courts have wood-paneled walls and a high bench and are places where spectators should show respect and be quiet.
- Lawyers are well dressed, talk a lot, and are dishonest.
- The law is fair to most people, but the little person gets the worst of it.
- People with lots of money can buy their way out of jail.
- The Supreme Court straightens things out and gives justice.

These are all commonplace notions about the legal process, some of which the reader will recognize as his or her own. They are conceptions of reality, indeed, bits of jurisprudence.

Our jurisprudence, or legal philosophy, like our social or political philosophy, however, is not entirely of our own making. Rather, it is an amalgam of individual and group life experiences combined with societal notions about law that are passed on to us through the home, the school, and similar social institutions.

Studies of legal socialization, the process whereby we acquire our attitudes about law, have repeatedly shown that few of us have had extensive experience with law and legal institutions. Instead, most of our beliefs are derived from extant legal theories. All social and political systems have, as an element in their substructure, a legal system and some form of legal philosophy, parts of which are passed on to the citizen through the socialization process. It is for this reason that *jurisprudence* (the philosophy of law) is an important subject of study. For thousands of years, humans have speculated about the nature and the function of law and its place in society, the sources of law, and normative and empirical roles of legal institutions in the social and political order. We are the heirs of this rich tradition of legal thought, parts of which demonstrably influence our contemporary perceptions about law.

JURISPRUDENCE

Traditionally, legal philosophy has been divided into schools of thought, each of which purports to embody a systematic, coherent, and complete set of notions about law. In reality, there is considerable overlap among schools of jurisprudence, and few systems of legal thought have succeeded in achieving the coherence and completeness suggested by their disciples. Rather, one body of thought tends to emerge largely as a reaction to the deficiencies of extant thinking, and after the social system absorbs the new "truths," yet another school of thought appears and undertakes to replace its predecessor. Thus, the history of legal thought is roughly dialectical. With all its gaps and excesses, overstatements and omissions, jurisprudence remains significant because contemporary modes of legal thought are inexplicable without reference to formal conceptualizations of the past. We need to become aware of our own jurisprudence in order to think clearly about law and legal processes. In other words, we need to look into our own heads, so to speak, and *think about the way in which we think about law.* In doing this, we need to pay particular attention to that part of a school of jurisprudence which bears on the *judicial function*—what, theoretically, courts do. This is so because, as we noted earlier, we are less concerned about law, per se, than we are about the roles and functioning of courts in society.

If we were to survey the entire course of recorded intellectual history, we could probably locate countless conceptualizations of law—nascent schools of jurisprudence. In his multivolume work on jurisprudence, Roscoe Pound identified over twenty separate schools,[1] and a more recent compendium on the American legal system listed eighteen different definitions of law, most of which suggest a more or less formal theory of law.[2] For our purposes, however, we can point to three rather distinct ways of looking at law which have been vying for ascendancy in America. (1) Natural law, (2) Analytical or Positivist Jurisprudence, and (3) Sociological-Realist Jurisprudence. It has been from the basic notions of the Sociological-Realist camp that modern social science conceptions of law and courts have emerged. Among these is what has come to be called Political Jurisprudence, adopted as the orienting conceptualization for this book. In the customary manner in which modes

---

[1]Roscoe Pound, *Jurisprudence,* 5 vols. (St. Paul, Minn.: West, 1959).
[2]Stephen D. Ford, *The American Legal System,* 2nd ed. (St. Paul, Minn.: West, 1974), 1–4.

of thought evolve, Political Jurisprudence has itself grown in a number of directions not anticipated by its founders. Due to the relevance of these developments for the modern study of judicial politics, the subject is explored more fully in Chapter 2. The description of Political Jurisprudence found in this chapter sets forth only the early development and basic tenets of this position. In considering these various ways of thinking about law, it is important to note the consequences of the theories—consequences for the legal system as a whole, for the political process in the larger social system, as well as the intellectual implications for teaching and research. As we have taken pains to make clear, theory does make a difference![3]

The Natural Law Tradition

Probably more has been written on natural law than on any other jurisprudential stance. It is one of the oldest ways of viewing law, and in some respects it has the widest appeal. Actually, it is accurate to speak not of one natural law but of several conceptions of natural law, the first being the Aristotelian notion of law as "reason unaffected by human desires." But most scholars credit the Stoics and Cicero with creating the first practical framework for natural law. For Cicero (106–43 B.C.), as well as for most natural law thinkers who followed him,

> True law is right reason in agreement with nature; it is of universal application, unchanging and everlasting; it summons to duty by its commands, and averts from wrongdoing by its prohibitions. . . . We cannot be freed from its obligations by senate or people, and we need not look outside ourselves for an expounder or interpreter of it.[4]

From Cicero, these notions of law and man's legal relationship to his fellow man and to God passed first to the Roman lawyers of the second and third centuries (particularly Gaius and Ulpian), thence to the early church fathers, and later in the elaborate conceptualization of Saint Thomas Aquinas (1225–1274),[5] to the Dutch thinker Hugo Grotius, whose *De jure belli ac Pacis* (1625) employed the concept of natural law for the development of a law of nations. To Grotius, natural law

> is a dictate of right reason, which points out that an act, according as it is not in conformity with rational nature, has in it a quality of moral baseness or moral necessity; and that, in consequence, such an act is either forbidden or enjoined by the author of nature, God.[6]

In order to relate dictates of war to some kind of jurisprudence, Grotius used the concept of basic, inherent natural rights. It was this feature of his thought, rather than his framework for international law, which turned out to be important for American thought, for it led directly to Locke's doctrine of natural rights, which is one of the cornerstones of American political philosophy.

---

[3]Or as Oliver Wendell Holmes once remarked, "Theory is the most important part . . . of law, as the architect is the most important man who takes part in the building of a house," as quoted in Edward S. Corwin, *The "Higher Law" Background of American Constitutional Law* (Ithaca, N.Y.: Cornell University Press, 1929), 1.

[4]Cicero, *De Republica*, trans. Clinton Walker Keyes (Cambridge, Mass.: Harvard University Press, 1928), 211.

[5]See his *Summa Theologica*, available in several English translations. A trenchant discussion of Aquinas's fourfold classification of law may be found in George S. Sabine, *A History of Political Theory*, rev. ed. (New York: Holt, 1950), 251–57.

[6]Hugo Grotius, *The Law of War and Peace (De jure belli ac Pacis)* (Indianapolis: Bobbs-Merrill, 1925), 38–39.

The social contract theory of the origin of government, grounded in the notions of natural law and natural rights, admirably suited the needs of the American revolutionaries. No clearer example could be cited of the impact of a rich jurisprudential tradition on current conceptions of law than that of natural law on American thought. Thomas Jefferson was clearly influenced by Locke's *Second Treatise on Government* when he penned this familiar American tract:

> When in the Course of human Events, it becomes necessary for one People to dissolve the Political Bonds which have connected them with another, and to assume among the Powers of the Earth, the separate and equal Station to which the Laws of Nature and of Nature's God entitle them, a decent Respect to the Opinions of Mankind requires that they should declare the causes which impel them to the Separation.
>
> We hold these Truths to be self-evident, that all Men are created equal, that they are endowed by their Creator with certain unalienable Rights, that among these are Life, Liberty, and the pursuit of Happiness. . . .[7]

The symbolic quality that we attribute to our Constitution as the basic organic law of the state, embodying fundamental guarantees of rights and limitations, is further evidence of the influence of natural law theory on American legal and political thought.[8] Conscientious objectors, civil rights activists, right-wing militia members—indeed, any of us who feel the heavy hand of "unjust" laws—are appealing for relief, almost without thinking, to the heritage of natural law. Thus, to some extent, we are all natural law jurisprudents, believing in the existence of "higher law," superior to positive (enacted) law which we know through our capacity to reason. A concept of justice is what we are talking about. That murder is wrong, that family life is to be highly valued, that freedom of speech and conscience exists—these are everyday notions based on natural law. For Americans, then, as for most peoples, any concept of law necessarily includes a moral element that transcends mere man-made rules. This situation is the result of the influence of the great natural law tradition.

Almost from the beginning of modern scientific thought, the natural-law school was in intellectual trouble. How can one empirically demonstrate the existence of mystical norms of behavior? People's capacity to reason can (and does) yield the most outrageously "unreasonable" notions, all of which can be defended on natural law grounds. Usury was deemed contrary to natural law in medieval Christian thought, but with the Protestants, many of whom were middle-class lenders, the doctrine changed.[9] The tendency of writers like Sir William Blackstone (*Commentaries on the Laws of England,* 1765–1768, first printed in America in 1771) to marshal natural law in defense of the status quo hastened the intellectual demise of this system of thought. But it was the Scottish philosopher and historian David Hume (1711–1776) who undertook the most systematic attack on natural law by pointing out the fallacy of reason as a discovery mechanism for law.[10] Experience, he argued, must be the only guide to moral and political issues. His sharp distinction between fact and value was fatal to a conceptualization of law grounded only in normative considerations. Hume's critique laid the groundwork for Jeremy Bentham's Utilitarianism

---

[7]The Declaration of Independence.

[8]See, for example, the excellent essay by Corwin, *Higher Law.* Another useful discussion of the influence of natural law on modern thought is Dennis Lloyd, *The Idea of Law* (Baltimore: Penguin Books, 1964). Ch. 4, "Natural Law and Natural Rights."

[9]See Bertrand Russell, *A History of Western Philosophy* (New York: Simon & Schuster, 1945), 623–24.

[10]See Sabine, *Political Theory,* 597–606.

as well as Auguste Comte's scientific study of society. Both philosophers were the intellectual forerunners of John Austin, who developed the first "scientific" jurisprudence.

In the 1990s, debate concerning uses of natural law in Supreme Court decision-making illustrates several of the points just made. Thus, with natural law somewhat in intellectual remission contrasted with earlier centuries, its role in American legal thought, though still important, tends to be surreptitious. And when brought to the surface, as it was in the 1930s New Deal era to defend the politico-economic conservatism of the "nine old men" (e.g., the use of the "substantive due process doctrine" to strike down legislation regulating working conditions), natural law became a target of bitter attack from liberal politicians. This is what happened in 1991 when Supreme Court nominee Clarence Thomas suggested that notions of natural law could be the starting place for interpreting the Constitution. That this has been so—demonstrably so—in scores of Supreme Court decisions of the past seems to have been lost on Thomas's critics. Wisely, the nominee backed away from his earlier, vocal embrace of natural law, not because it falls outside the American tradition, but because it is a two-edged sword, reminding curent liberals of the laissez-faire usage of the concept in the New Deal era. So Hume was right; the question is not natural law, per se, but rather whose natural law? This debate is older than the Constitution itself.[11]

Analytical or Positivist Jurisprudence

John Austin (1790–1859) was an English jurist whose work first appeared as a series of lectures given at University College, London, 1828–1832.[12] For Austin, law and its study had to be rescued from the vague mysticism and metaphysics of the natural-law school and conceptualized as a known and knowable body of rules. In *Lectures on Jurisprudence,* he declared this:

> Every positive law or every law simply and strictly so called, is set by a sovereign person, or a sovereign body of persons, to a member or members of the independent political society wherein that person or body is sovereign or supreme. In other words it is set by a monarch, or sovereign number, to a person or persons in a state of subjection to its author.[13]

Austin's concept of law required a clear definition of sovereignty. His definition, couched in terms of the "determinate human superior" in relation to "subject" or "dependent" members of society, reads like a modern definition of politics. This definition, however, was altered by Austin's disciples, notably T.E. Holland and J.W. Salmond,[14] such that Positivist law became simply a body of rules emanating from duly constituted legal authority and backed by the coercion of the state. As Salmond put it, law is "the body of principles recognized and applied by the state in the administration of justice."[15]

---

[11]See, e.g., Peter Steinfels, "Beliefs: Natural Law Collides with the Laws of Politics in the Squabble over a Supreme Court Nomination," *New York Times* (Aug. 17, 1991): 8. For a scholarly argument in favor of the return of natural law and natural rights, see Hadley Arkes, *The Return of George Sutherland: Restoring a Jurisprudence of Natural Rights* (Princeton: Princeton University Press, 1994). Despite such arguments, often originating in the "Princeton School" (see Ch. 2), the central thrust of current social science scholarship tends to eschew this approach.
[12]A brief but useful overview of Austinian Positivism may be found in William Seal Carpenter, *Foundations of Modern Jurisprudence* (New York: Appleton-Century-Crofts, 1958), 12–20.
[13]John Austin, *Lectures on Jurisprudence,* student's ed. (London: John Murray, 1904), 82.
[14]See Carpenter, *Modern Jurisprudence,* 18–19.
[15]Carpenter, *Modern Jurisprudence,* 19.

At any rate, analytical jurisprudence characterized law as distinct from morals on the one hand and from social and historical forces on the other. What Austin called the "science of positive law" does not hold that law has no moral content, or, for that matter, that it has no societal implications. Rather, it is conceived as a closed, self-sufficient system that is to be studied in its formal, logical content. Moral, social, and historical factors are real but are not relevant to a logical conception of law.

A logical extension of Austin's ideas may be found in the work of Hans Kelsen. In his *Pure Theory of Law,* first appearing in article form in 1934, Kelson[16] maintained that law consists of a hierarchy of norms that, level by level, culminate in the "basic norm," which is the arbitrarily chosen central premise of the whole system. Kelsen undertakes to separate law from morals absolutely: "to show the law as it is without legitimizing it as just, or disqualifying it as unjust; it seeks the real, the positive law, not the right law."[17]

Leaving aside the more formalistic versions of Austinian Positivism, this school has had a profound influence on American legal thought. And paradoxically, the baffling combination of analytical jurisprudence and natural law precepts has become the mainstay of American legal thought. Both schools found their most influential expression in America in Blackstone's *Commentaries,* which were widely read in the colonies. Indeed, Blackstone *was* American legal education through the nineteenth century. Whether we wish to take Blackstone himself as our point of departure or one of his disciples, such as John Adams or James Wilson, the endurance of Blackstone's ideas remains a prominent, if not *the* central, fact of American legal thought. As Morris Cohen wrote a half-century ago:

> The Blackstonian view of law—the confused compromise or conglomeration of law as eternal reason and law as the will of the supreme power of the state—still prevails. Blackstone with characteristic complacency juxtaposed the two elements without bothering to try to indicate how the rational and imperative elements could be combined, how the absolute supremacy could be compatible with absolute natural (individual) rights. Substitute the will of the people for the absolute power of Parliament and you have the essence of the prevalent American view.[18]

For both systems of thought, the judicial task is essentially deductive. If the judge in the natural law system declares rules derived from more general moral precepts, the *deus ex machina* of the positivist judge is the following syllogism:

> Major premise: The command of the sovereign (extant written law usually legislatively enacted)
> Minor premise: The circumstances of the present dispute
> Conclusion: The ruling emerging by force of logic.

Through this simple, almost mechanical process, the judge does little more than announce the ruling that already existed—either by virtue of preordained moral principles or by irrefutable logic. This ratiocination of the judicial function, whereby the judge merely discovers the law and then declares the discovery, became the almost universally accepted view of the judicial process in the United States. As Chief Justice John Marshall proclaimed in *Osborn v. Bank of the United States* (1824),

---

[16]Hans Kelsen, "The Pure Theory of Law: Its Methods and Fundamental Concepts," *Law Quarterly Review,* 50 (Oct. 1934): 474–535. See also Hans Kelsen, *General Theory of Law and State* (New York: Russell & Russell, 1961).

[17]Kelsen, "The Pure Theory of Law": 482. See also Edwin M. Schur, *Law and Society: A Sociological View* (New York: Random House, 1968), 27–28.

[18]Morris R. Cohen, *American Thought: A Critical Sketch* (New York: Collier Books, 1954), 171.

Judicial power, as contradistinguished from the power of the laws, has no existence. Courts are the mere instruments of the law, and can will nothing. When they are said to exercise a discretion, it is a mere legal discretion, a discretion to be exercised in discerning the course prescribed by law. . . . Judicial power is never exercised for the purpose of giving effect to the will of the judge; always for the purpose of giving effect to the will of the Legislature; or, in other words, to the will of the law.[19]

The force of Blackstone's thought was further reflected in Justice Owen Roberts' defense of the Court's decision invalidating the first Agricultural Adjustment Act passed in 1933 as a key New Deal measure to stabilize farm prices. In *U.S. v. Butler* in 1936, Justice Roberts wrote:

There should be no misunderstanding as to the function of this court in such a case. It is sometimes said that the court assumes the power to overrule or control the action of the people's representatives. This is a misconception. The Constitution is the supreme law of the land ordained and established by the people. All legislation must conform to the principles it lays down. When an act of Congress is appropriately challenged in the courts as not conforming to the constitutional mandate, the judicial branch of government has only one duty—to lay the article of the Constitution which is invoked beside the statute which is challenged and to decide whether the latter squares with the former. All the court does or can do is to announce its considered judgment upon the question. The only power it has, if such it may be called, is the power of judgment. This court neither approves nor condemns any legislative policy. Its delicate and difficult office is to ascertain and declare whether the legislation is in accordance with, or in contravention of, the provisions of the Constitution; and, having done that, its duty ends.[20]

It might be thought that the revelations attendant to the clash between president and congress during the New Deal would have laid to rest this declaratory theory of judicial decision making. To the contrary, the notion of an impersonal and impartial law remains the bedrock of American legal thinking. Examples abound; the following will suffice to make the point. When California governor Ronald Reagan, in criticizing a state supreme court ruling, suggested that "the courts, like the legislature and executive branch, are responsible to the people," he was called sharply to task by Michael L. Zeitsoff, president of the Boalt Hall (University of California, Berkeley) School of Law student body:

As students of the law . . . we must, with all due respect, call attention to the grave inaccuracy of your statement. . . . The court's first duty is to the law, and the Constitution of the United States is the highest embodiment of that law. Thus, so long as the Constitution remains unchanged, and there is a conflict between what people would have, and what the Constitution provides, the Supreme Court must inevitably follow the dictates of the Constitution, irrespective of how unpopular such a decision might be.[21]

The persistent, wide-ranging—indeed, almost desperate—search for an "objective" grounding for judicial decision making, discussed more fully in Chapter 2, is further evidence of the staying power of the Legal Formalism (as it is often called) of the Austinian-Blackstonian School of Jurisprudence in American legal thought.

---

[19]*Osborn v. Bank of the United States,* 9 Wheat. 738, 866 (1824). The implications of Blackstone's thoughts were not lost on Thomas Jefferson, who called "Blackstone Lawyers" the "ephemeral insects of the law" who, seduced by the "honeyed Mansfieldism of Blackstone . . . began to slide into Toryism." See Corwin, *"Higher Law,"* 85.

[20]*U.S. v. Butler,* 297 U.S. 1, 62 (1936).

[21]*Berkeley* (California) *Daily Gazette* (Jan. 10, 1968), 10 (Opinion Forum). For a discussion of "neutrality" in judicial decision making, see Ch. 2 of this text.

Sociological-Jurisprudence

It is a matter of dispute whether *sociological jurisprudence* can be said to stand alone as a separate school of legal thought or whether it is best seen as an extension of the historical and comparative orientations. Certainly the writings of the German jurist Frederick Karl von Savigny (1779–1861), as well as the research of Sir Henry Maine (1822–1888), both exponents of historical jurisprudence, are logically and chronologically linked to sociological thinking. Savigny, for example, insisted that law develops not by the will of the sovereign, nor by jurisprudence, but by the common consciousness or spirit of the people *(Volksgeist)*. This force, which one might call "institutionalized custom," is to be discovered through a careful study of history.[22] With an equal concern for history, the English scholar Sir Henry Maine undertook a general historical analysis of the stages of legal development in his classic work *Ancient Law,* from which he concluded that the "movement of the progressive societies has hitherto been a movement from status to contract." This insight has been rediscovered by modern sociologists in their assertion that the use of the legal contract is one of the important distinctions between informal, communal social organizations and modern heterogeneous collectivities.[23] Using quite different approaches, both writers pointed up a significant tenet of modern sociological jurisprudence—that law and legal processes are to be understood as part of the larger social order rather than in moral, ethical, or logical isolation.

This insistence on a broader view of law was shared by the Comparativists, particularly Frederick William Maitland[24] and Sir Frederick Pollock,[25] both of whom argued for the necessity of studying legal systems in a comparative framework. Historically rooted and geographically widespread legal systems, such as the common law, are difficult to compare systemically. Hence, the comparative method has been less useful in systemwide studies than in narrower foci, such as legislation. Yet, modern social science is clearly indebted to the comparative school of jurisprudence in method if not in substance.

Other intellectual forerunners of sociological jurisprudence include the Austrian Eugen Ehrlich (1862–1922),[26] and his countryman, Ludwig Gumplowicz.[27] But it was in America that sociological approaches grew to fruition, largely through the extensive writings of Roscoe Pound (1870–1964). Pound had an unusual education. He received a Ph.D. in botany from the University of Nebraska, after which he studied law at Harvard without receiving a degree. Following a stint at the practice of law and as an auxiliary judge in Nebraska, he entered academic life, serving as dean of Harvard Law School from 1916 to 1936, preceded and followed by professorships at a number of other law schools.

For Pound, law was neither a set of immutable moral principles, nor was it to be deduced from logical first principles. He denounced these conceptions as "mechanical jurisprudence." Instead, he viewed law as a social institution—in part at least, a rough set of rules reflecting society's current needs. Law exists to serve human wants rather than the reverse. Following Ehrlich's concept of "living law," Pound drew a sharp distinction between the "law in the books" and the "law in action." The former had to do mostly with

---

[22]See Schur, *Law and Society,* 32.

[23]Schur, *Law and Society,* 32.

[24]See Frederick William Maitland, *Selected Essays,* ed. by H. D. Hazeltine, G. Lapsley, and P. H. Winfield (Freeport, N.Y.: Books for Libraries Press, 1935).

[25]Sir Frederick Pollock, *Essays in Jurisprudence and Ethics* (London: Macmillan, 1882).

[26]Ehrlich's major work is *Fundamental Principles of the Sociology of Law,* trans. Walter L. Moll (Cambridge, Mass.: Harvard University Press, 1936).

[27]See Ludwig Gumplowicz, *The Outlines of Sociology,* trans. Frederick W. Moore (Philadelphia: American Academy of Political and Social Science, 1889).

the workings of appellate courts and legal principles, the latter with lower courts and "real" human needs. Fundamentally, Pound saw law as a set of societally determined rules to resolve conflicts among competing interests. As such, the judicial process obviously involved a great deal of discretion, and this discretion could be most intelligently exercised with the help of the other social sciences—psychology, history, sociology, economics, and political science. Clearly, Pound recognized the social engineering function of law. Such a conception of law obviously called for a research agenda, and this was another of Pound's contributions. He insisted on the need for the most scientific study of legal matters, calling for endowments and legal science laboratories. His emphasis on empirical research into the "realities" of the judicial process, more than any other notion, made possible the modern sociology of law.

Pound's writings had a profound effect on American legal thought, research, and practice. It was as though a fresh, cool breeze filtered through the isolated caverns of natural law and positivist jurisprudence. The property-centered ideology of laissez faire, clouded by the myopia of Austinism gave way to the socially aware, humanistically oriented tenets of sociological jurisprudence. The movement opened up the law to the findings of social science by recognizing that law in a vacuum is no law at all.

It fell to two American jurists, Justices Louis D. Brandeis (1856–1941) and Benjamin Cardozo (1870–1938), to operationalize Pound's ideas. Brandeis's work first came to public attention via the famous "Brandeis Brief," which presented as legal argument relevant social and economic data tending to support the reasonableness of legislation regulating minimum wage and maximum hour laws. For example, in *Muller v. Oregon,* 208 U.S. 412 (1908), Brandeis was able to convince a conservative U.S. Supreme Court of the reasonableness and, hence, the constitutionality, of Oregon's ten-hour workday law for women. Later, as an associate justice of the Supreme Court, Brandeis detailed the proper role for social and economic statistics. In *Jay Burns and Company v. Bryan,* he wrote in dissent the following:

> Put at its highest, our function is to determine, in light of all facts which may enrich our knowledge and enlarge our undersanding, whether the measure, enacted in the exercise of the police power and of a character inherently unobjectionable, transcends the bounds of reason. That is, whether the provision as applied is so clearly arbitrary or capricious that legislators acting reasonably could not have believed it to be necessary or appropriate for the public welfare.[28]

The contribution of Justice Cardozo to sociological jurisprudence was his candor in revealing the uncertainty, indeed the selective, creative aspects, of judicial decision making and in placing these ideas in theoretical context. Emphasizing the social element of law, he recognized that precedent or logic alone (or as Morris Cohen put it, the "phonograph theory of law") cannot get us very far in understanding the judicial process. In explaining the considerations that enter into deciding cases, Cardozo in his most celebrated work, *The Nature of the Judicial Process,* wrote:

> The directive force of a principle may be exerted along the line of logical progression; this I will call the rule of analogy or the method of philosophy; along the line of historical development; this I will call the method of evolution; along the line of the customs of the community; this I will call the method of tradition; along the lines of justice, morals and social welfare, the *mores* of the day; and this I will call the method of sociology.[29]

---

[28]*Jay Burns & Co. v. Bryan,* 264 U.S. 504a + 524 (1924), (Brandeis dissenting). For a more recent illustration of the contrast between a Sociological and Positivist view of constitutional interpretation, see the majority versus dissenting opinions in *U.S. v. Lopez,* 63 LW 4343 (1995).

[29]Margaret E. Hall, ed., *Selected Writings of Benjamin Nathan Cardozo* (New York: Fallon, 1947), 117.

Hardly a radical, Cardozo stressed that only rarely would an appellate judge break with precedent and apply the method of sociology. Yet, in recognizing the propriety of innovation in the light of social need, and with the guidance of the most reliable social scientific findings, Cardozo placed at least one foot in the sociological camp. And his standing in legal circles—his scholarly posture, indeed, his conservatism—made his writings all the more influential. Edwin Patterson nicely summarized the contributions of Justice Cardozo when he wrote,

> His continued emphasis upon pressing moral values in the law, along with the demands of reason and order and political stability, was original in its wholeness, in its recognition of inner struggle, in its mediation between the nineteenth century love of security and twentieth century love of progress. In an era of transition he was the great mediator.[30]

And in remarking on the work of both Justices Brandeis and Cardozo, Cohen wrote,

> It was these two men who, more than anyone else, gave currency to the idea that judicial decisions inevitably turn on basic questions of economics, politics and sociology, and that judges can rise above their own limitation and prejudices in these fields only by opening their minds to the progress of research and the testing of old and new theories.[31]

Legal Realism

An extension of the Sociological School came with a group of scholars, teachers, and judges known as the Legal Realists. The distinction between the Sociological and Realist positions is at best blurred. What is clear, though, is that it is at the juncture of the two positions that the contributions of Oliver Wendell Holmes, Jr. (1841–1935), are best discussed. When in *The Common Law* (his only completed book and one of the most significant volumes on American law ever written), Holmes argued that, "The first requirement of a sound body of law is that it should correspond with the actual feelings and demands of the community, whether right or wrong,"[32] thereby stating the principle closest to sociological jurisprudence. But in his definition of law as little more than a prediction of what courts will do in fact, his hope for the contribution of quantitative methodology to an understanding of the judicial process and, above all, his insistence on the demystification of the law, Holmes seems more like a Realist. Holmes had a propensity for pithy aphorisms which were illuminating and insightful, but often in need of explication. For our purposes, it should suffice to note some of the more celebrated statements. "Common Law," he said, "is not a brooding omnipresence in the sky but the articulate voice of some sovereign or quasi-sovereignty that can be identified."[33] Earlier, in *The Common Law,* he wrote:

> It is something to show that the consistency of a system requires a particular result, but it is not all. The life of the law has not been logic: it has been experience. The felt necessities of the time, the prevalent moral and political theories, intuitions of public policy, avowed or unconscious, even the prejudices which judges share with their fellow-men, have had a good deal more to do than the syllogism in determining the rules by which men should be

---

[30]Edwin W. Patterson, *Jurisprudence: Men and Ideas of the Law* (Brooklyn: Foundation Press, 1953), 529.
[31]Cohen, *American Thought,* 202–203.
[32]Oliver Wendell Holmes, *The Common Law* (Boston: Little, Brown, 1881), 41. A delightful excursion into Holmes's life is Catherine Drinker Bowen, *A Yankee from Olympus: Justice Holmes and His Family* (Boston: Little, Brown, 1944). See also Samuel J. Konefsky, *The Legacy of Holmes and Brandeis: A Study in the Influence of Ideas* (New York: Collier Books, 1961); and the very useful collection of speeches, decisions, etc., by Max Lerner, ed., *The Mind and Faith of Justice Holmes* (New York: Modern Library, 1943).
[33]*Southern Pacific Company v. Jensen,* 244 U.S. 205, 222 (1921).

governed. The law embodies the story of a nation's development through many centuries, and it cannot be dealt with as if it contained only the axioms and corollaries of a book of mathematics.[34]

And later on,

> The very considerations which judges most rarely mention, and always with an apology, are the secret root from which the law draws all the juices of life. I mean, of course, considerations of what is expedient for the community concerned. Every important principle which is developed by litigation is in fact and at bottom the result of more or less definitely understood views of public policy; most generally, to be sure, under our practice and traditions, the unconscious result of instinctive preferences and inarticulate convictions, but nonetheless traceable to views of public policy in the last analysis.[35]

His fundamental pragmatism and his insistence that judicial decisions, being policy oriented, should be based on the best available sociolegal data, are further contributions to the sociological school.

Holmes, the New England aristocrat, the soldier, the scholar-judge, contributed perhaps more than any other single person to the process that he himself described as "washing the law in cynical acid." The Holmes-Pound notions, along with the pragmatism of John Dewey and William James, clearly marked the beginning of a new era, a new direction in legal thought in America, and helped to create the basic tension that exists today between traditional jurisprudence and sociological modes of thought.[36] Holmes's aversion to the application of abstract legal principles to concrete cases, his stress upon nonlegal factors as relevant in judicial decision making, and his general pragmatic outlook made him the father of American Legal Realism.[37]

Two ways in which the Realists seem to differ from their Sociological comrades are (1) their emphasis on practical legal reforms and (2) their more radical way of conceptualizing the judicial process.[38] Moreover, unlike most sociological jurisprudents (e.g., Cardozo), who retained a significant role for doctrine—legal rules or principles—Realist writers were more willing to view law not in terms of rules at all, or at least not in the main, but simply, pragmatically, in terms of official behavior. In a controversial passage (which is probably impossible to extract briefly without changing some of the author's meaning), Karl Llewellyn, of the University of Chicago School of Law, addressed a class of first-year law students:

> *What these officials do about disputes is, to my mind, the law itself.* . . .   The main thing is seeing what officials do, do about disputes, or about anything else; and seeing that there is a

---

[34]Holmes, *Common Law*, 1.

[35]Holmes, *Common Law*, 35–36.

[36]See Patterson, *Jurisprudence*, 477–500.

[37]A useful discussion of the relation of Holmes's thought to Legal Realism may be found in Wilfred E. Rumble, Jr., *American Legal Realism* (Ithaca, N.Y.: Cornell University Press, 1968), 36–44. See also Glendon Schubert, *Human Jurisprudence: Public Law as Political Science* (Honolulu: University of Hawaii Press, 1975), especially Chs. 2 and 3.

Perhaps the best recent collection of essays representing original Realist thought is that of William W. Fisher, III, Morton J. Horwitz, and Thomas Reed, eds., *American Legal Realism* (New York: Oxford University Press, 1993). This volume makes clear the debt that the movement owed to Oliver Wendell Holmes, Jr.

[38]For an insightful discussion of the famous Realist-Sociological debate, see Grant Gilmore, *The Ages of American Law* (New Haven: Yale University Press, 1977), 77–80 and notes. See also Gilmore's "Legal Realism: Its Causes and Cures," *Yale Law Journal* 70, No. 7 (June 1961): 1037–48.

A useful discussion of some of these issues may also be found in Morton J. Horwitz, *The Transformation of American Law, 1870–1960* (New York: Oxford University Press, 1992): passim.

certain regularity in their doing—a regularity which makes possible prediction of what they and other officials are about to do tomorrow. In many cases that prediction cannot be wholly certain. Then you have room for something else, another main thing for the lawyer: the study of how to make the official do what you would like to have him. At that point "rules" loom into importance. Great importance. For judges think that you must follow rules, and people highly approve of that thinking. So that the getting of the judge to do a thing is in considerable measure the art of finding what rules are available to urge upon him, and of how to urge them to accomplish your result. In considerable measure. Rules, too, then, and their arrangement, and their logical manipulation, make up an unmistakable portion of the business of the law and the lawyer.[39]

At other times, Legal Realists maintain that rules based on precedent are but myths, clung to out of a childish need for sureness and security. A mature jurisprudence recognizes that there is no certainty in law (or in any other area of life). Judicial decisions are rendered on the basis of a judge's conception of rightness (the "right" rule), followed by an elaborate rationalization in the form of a written opinion. What deserves attention for the Realists is the empirical basis of decision making.[40]

Differences between the Realist and the Sociological schools—and the significance of those differences—have become issues of discussion among political scientists in recent years. Partly because both schools have been seen as effective attacks on the formalism of Austinism and partly because modern political scientists are primarily interested in studying courts and establishing that courts make policy—thus, are political—writers in the post–World War II era have tended to see the Sociological-Realist movement as one.

Professor Martin Shapiro, on the other hand, sees the differences as both substantial and important. He argues that at bottom, Realism is a form of social determinism. In lawmaking there is no truth, only policy preferences. Thus, Realism aims particularly at judges and their work, as clearly reflected by the thinking of Jerome Frank.

On the other hand, the Sociological school (especially Pound and certainly Cardozo), being a theory of law, not just of courts and judges, posits the lawmaker (judge, legislator, or administrator), as a social engineer, a technician reaching correct solutions to social problems rather than merely expressing personal preference. Sociological jurisprudents, more interested in legislation than in judicial policy, believed that lawmakers must engage in a rational search for truth found through experimentation—pragmatism in the strict Deweyite sense rather than logical deduction from first principles.

Shapiro sees the core of Sociological thought leading directly to the pluralism characteristic of modern political jurisprudence and to the public choice approach to the study of law, both of which will be discussed more fully. Realism, on the other hand, with its emphasis on psychological determinism, leads directly to modern behavioralism (the attitudinal model) in the study of judicial decision making, which will also be covered more fully.[41]

---

[39]Karl N. Llewellyn, *The Bramble Bush: On Our Law and its Study,* rev. ed (New York: Oceana, 1951), 12–14 (originally published in 1930). A clearer view of the Llewellyn thesis can be gained only by reading his book, particularly this edition.

[40]See Jerome Frank, *Law and the Modern Mind* (New York: Coward-McCann, 1930), especially Chs. 1 and 2.

[41]Professor Martin Shapiro, School of Law, University of California, Berkeley, has set forth these views both in conversations with the author and in correspondence extending over the summer of 1996, especially his letter of August 27. Copies of this correspondence are available on request from the author. Of closely related interest is Martin Shapiro's "Courts of Law, Courts of Politics," in Austin Ranney, ed., *Courts and the Political Process: Jack W. Peltason's Contributions to Political Science* (Berkeley: Institute of Governmental Studies Press, 1996), 99–115.

Looking at the entire body of Llewellyn's work, Shapiro views Llewellyn as more in the Sociological camp, especially in his later work, *The Common Law Tradition: Deciding Appeals.*[42] There, Llewellyn concerns himself with judicial choices made on the basis of rationally considered, pragmatic strategies for improving society—a central feature of Sociological thought—and seems to move away from some of his earlier notions.

For readers interested primarily in the study of courts and judicial decision making, these distinctions may not matter a great deal. But if one's focus is jurisprudence more broadly defined, Sociological-Realist distinctions are important, in part because they inform critical issues in contemporary legal theory.

In Llewellyn's *The Common Law Tradition: Deciding Appeals,* Professor Shapiro finds much to suggest the substantive distinction between Legal Realism and its Sociological cousin. Shapiro points out Llewellyn's focus on the phenomenon of judicial decision making founded upon rationally considered, pragmatic strategies for improving society, reflecting Llewellyn's reliance upon a central feature of Sociological jurisprudence, rather than on the behavioralist notions fundamental to Realist thinking.

More than any other school, Realism made a serious commitment to the scientific study of law, legal institutions, and legal processes—in Llewellyn's terms, "an effort at more effective legal technology." If law is essentially official behavior, the Realists sought to explain such behavior in the most rigorous scientific way, including the economic, social, political, and psychological determinants of such behavior. The short-lived Institute of Law at Johns Hopkins University, as well as later research, such as the Chicago Jury Project, were inspired by Realist thought. Finally, Realists, especially Judge Jerome Frank, make a useful contribution to a broader conception of the judicial process by focusing attention on lower courts as agencies worthy of study. Frank's critique of trial court fact-finding, including jury behavior, remains as modern today as when it was first set forth in the 1930s.[43]

If the Realists were short on original or systematic theory, they, like the Sociologists, at least inspired an enormous amount of empirical research that has influenced present-day thinking. The Sociological-Realist impact on legal education is perhaps best summed up by the fact that current law texts are commonly titled "cases and materials," rather than just "cases." In summarizing the contributions of the Realist School, Jerome Hall wrote the following:

> Most legal scholars in the United States, from the late twenties on, have been realists in important respects; . . . Legal Realism achieved a new level of critical analysis of judicial decisions, which has influenced the subsequent professional literature enormously by making American legal scholars extremely sensitive to the factual situations in the cases, as qualifiers of the *ratii decidendi.* Legal Realism also contributed much to our knowledge of the judicial process by disclosing the operation of non-legal and irrational forces more than had previously been appreciated. And it encouraged intensive socio-legal research in narrow areas, thus adding a vitally important dimension to the earlier broadly generalized discussions of a science of law.[44]

---

[42](Boston: Little, Brown, 1960).

[43]See particularly Jerome Frank, *Courts on Trial: Myth and Reality in American Jurisprudence* (Princeton: Princeton University Press, 1950).

[44]Jerome Hall, *Studies in Jurisprudence and Criminal Theory* (New York: Oceana, 1958), 136–37. For another view of Realism and its relationship to the newer movement referred to as Critical Legal Scholarship, see "'Round and 'Round the Bramble Bush: From Legal Realism to Critical Legal Scholarship," *Harvard Law Review,* 95, No. 7 (May 1982): 1669–90.

As noted earlier, it is these three basic jurisprudential positions—Natural Law, Analytical or Positivist Jurisprudence, and the Sociological-Realists—which have most heavily influenced modern (especially American) thinking about law and the role of courts. It requires but brief reflection on how our present "legal minds" work to show that contemporary legal thought of the ordinary citizen is an amalgam of all three of these orientations. Thus, we naturally, often subconsciously, find ourselves believing that something—some policy or program—is right or wrong not because the law in the formal sense so states, but because it is "simply right" (or wrong). The notion of a "higher law" is familiar to all of us, it being rooted in our Natural Law tradition. And at times we expect courts as well as other governmental bodies to inject notions of Natural Law into their decisions, though of course always without saying so.

At the same time, our immediate thought when we hear the word *law* is probably black letter law—rules devised by formal legal authority and written down for all to follow. Moreover, the Supreme Court, we believe, should and does arrive at decisions based on its reading of THE LAW. When, and to the extent this is not true—when, that is, Supreme Court justices read their own notions of policy into their decisions—many of us conclude that they are behaving improperly. We are thus very much caught up in the formulations (some would say, the myths) set forth by the Positivists.

Finally, it is not unreasonable to see law from the Sociological-Realist perspective. Do most of us really believe, for example, that the Constitution is ironbound, known as to its precise meaning, and that justices *are certain* as to how to decide cases? Or is it much more sensible to assume, believe, and support the notion that we want courts—the Supreme Court as well as other courts—to arrive at decisions based on common sense, developing legal rules that have practical applicability to the real needs of present-day society, based, consciously or unconsciously, on contemporary societal notions of right and wrong? To the extent that this position has appeal, we are adherents of the Sociological-Realist school.

Political Jurisprudence

These newer conceptualizations of law and the judicial function significantly undermined the epistemological and pedagogical orientations that grew out of natural law and Austinian Positivism. For sociology (and to a lesser extent psychology), the traditional view of law left no room for empirical exploration: the judicial process was to be understood either in terms of moral (one might say divine) revelation or through syllogistic reasoning. That was it! There was no social *process* involved in law, nothing that would be of interest to an empirically based social science. This helps to explain the traditional distance from, even alienation of, law and modern social science. They simply had nothing in common. Sociological-Realist jurisprudence turned this situation completely around so that today the most relevant and widely read research on law and courts is to be found typically in sociology and political science journals, much of it also winding up in law journals.[45] The im-

---

[45]See Schur, *Law and Society.* For trends in law and sociology see Rita James Simon, ed., *The Sociology of Law: Interdisciplinary Readings* (San Francisco: Chandler, 1968); also William M. Evan, ed., *Law and Sociology: Exploratory Essays* (New York: Free Press of Glencoe, 1962); "Law and Society," *Social Problems,* Summer 1965; and Roman Tomasic, *The Sociology of Law* (London: Sage Publications, 1985). See also Kim Lane Scheppele, "Legal Theory and Social Theory," *Annual Review of Sociology, 1994,* 20: 383–406.

The state of research in psychology and law is reflected in the volume by June L. Tapp and Felice J. Levine, eds., *Law, Justice and the Individual in Society: Psychological and Legal Issues* (New York: Holt, Rhinehart & Winston, 1977). See also Shari Seidman Diamond, "Growth and Maturation in Psychology and Law," *Law and Society Review* 17, No. 1 (1982): 11–20. This entire issue of *Law and Society Review* gives a status report on research in law and psychology.

pact of Sociological-Realist jurisprudence on political science was similar, if not even more far-reaching, and since we are most directly concerned with the law-politics nexus, the gradual unfolding of an empirically based "political jurisprudence" should be detailed.

Political science, much more than the other social sciences, has always retained a significant role for legal studies, perhaps because the discipline had its roots in history, philosophy, and law, with a strong emphasis on the latter. In the mid-nineteenth century and even extending into the twentieth century, the study of politics was legally and constitutionally oriented. Indeed, as Herman Pritchett reminds us, the Columbia University political science department was, in the period around the turn of the century, entitled the Department of Public Law and Jurisprudence. Early leaders in political science (who were also, incidentally, members of the Columbia department) were as often as not scholars trained in law as well as the social sciences and held joint appointments in the law school. John W. Burgess, Frank Goodnow, Monroe Smith, and John Bassett Moore come readily to mind.[46]

Gradually the gap between legal education and political science widened as the latter began to orient its legal studies branch more to social science concerns. Helping this trend along was the Princeton School, led by scholars such as Woodrow Wilson, who was succeeded in the McCormick Chair of Jurisprudence by Edward S. Corwin, Alpheus T. Mason, and Walter F. Murphy. These scholars, most of whom accepted the central thinking of sociological and Realist jurisprudence, were less interested in the uniquely legal dimension of courts and justice and more interested in the political, historical, and constitutional aspects. Thus it was that the great Public Law Tradition in political science (consisting of the subfields of international law, administrative law, constitutional law, and jurisprudence), at one time the heart of the young discipline, began to dissipate. Administrative law was folded into and eventually all but swallowed up by public administration; international law, now hardly mentioned in political science, was subsumed under international politics and organization; and jurisprudence as a subdiscipline fell into disrepute in the face of the general advance of empirical social science. This left little but traditional constitutional law which, for reasons not entirely clear, remained the chief representative of legal studies in modern political science.

For nearly a century, constitutional law has been taught in political science departments, usually employing the case method of instruction borrowed from the law schools. The nation's law schools, in turn, borrowed it from Harvard Law School where the method was first introduced by Harvard's dean, Christopher Columbus Langdell. Dean Langdell believed that a few general principles were the basis of all law and that one could deduce these central tendencies through the careful study of a relatively few appellate decisions. The method was Analytic, the general approach Positivistic, and the result myopic (see Chapter 7).[47]

---

[46]A brief, useful essay on the development of public law in political science is C. Herman Pritchett, "Public Law and Judicial Behavior," in Marian D. Irish, ed., *Political Science: Advance of a Discipline* (Englewood Cliffs, N.J.: Prentice-Hall, 1968), 190–219. The Irish volume was first published as the 30th anniversary issue of the *Journal of Politics,* May 1968. For a more detailed treatment of the development of public law, see Walter F. Murphy and Joseph Tanenhaus, *The Study of Public Law* (New York: Random House, 1972). For a slightly different view of these developments, see Schubert, *Human Jurisprudence,* especially Ch. 2, "The Future of Public Law."

Some materials in the latter sections of this chapter were originally published in Harry P. Stumpf, et. al., "Whither Political Jurisprudence: A Symposium," *Western Political Quarterly* 36, No. 4 (Dec. 1983).

[47]One of the most interesting discussions of Langdell's ideas may be found in Gilmore's *The Ages of American Law,* 42 ff. Gilmore writes that "Langdell seems to have been an essentially stupid man who . . . hit upon one great idea to which . . . he clung with all the tenacity of genius. . . . Langdell's idea was that law is a science" (42). Gilmore seems to argue that nineteenth century legal formalism was much more Langdellism than it was Austinianism, although one is of course closely related to the other.

Although the case method usually involved a polite nod in the direction of history, economics, and politics, as well as an occasional reference to lower courts, the heart of the study of the judicial branch of government was the appellate decision. The underlying jurisprudence of such an approach is clearly Austinian. Since the judicial *process* was essentially mechanical, there really was no *process* to study; only the outcome, the decision, the principle of law was important. In this way, several generations of American college students were introduced to the legal system. And the pedagogy continues to the present day.

In 1963, on the occasion of the publication of a newer text on the judicial process written by a political scientist, a reviewer remarked as follows:

> I suspect that most political science teachers who offer courses in American constitutional law to undergraduates have had to face up to the problem of giving them some preliminary background information about courts and processes of justice before starting with the cases. It is simply impossible to take up the first case until students learn something about the nature of courts and of the judicial process, and particularly about the American judicial system. Since the study of constitutional law usually centers upon the work of the United States Supreme Court, the student must first try to understand the nature of this interesting and complex institution. . . .
>
> Inasmuch as a great deal of time cannot be devoted to this matter the book must be a short one, and preferably an inexpensive one.[48]

Such was—and is—the tenacity of the case method of instruction (not to forget its underlying jurisprudence) in constitutional law in American political science departments.

For a growing number of post–World War II "public law" political scientists, however, something was missing in the old formulation. Not only had the Sociologists-Realists had their say, but the events of the New Deal era removed any remaining doubt as to the nature of judicial politics in America.

In the first major realigning election since 1860, the American voters of 1932 endorsed a new coalition of interests that promised to restore economic and social progress to the nation. Following his election, President Franklin D. Roosevelt proposed a series of far-reaching measures for dealing with the Great Depression—far-reaching, at least, for American political and legal thought, though hardly novel for most modern industrial societies. Relying chiefly on the commerce and taxing clauses of the Constitution, Roosevelt sought from Congress the power to establish fair codes of competition in American industry and regulatory powers to stabilize the oil and coal industries, as well as agriculture, banking, and so forth. In a series of decisions beginning in 1935 and extending into the 1936 term, the Supreme Court struck down eight of ten Roosevelt proposals brought before it, thereby gutting the New Deal and setting the stage for a major constitutional crisis between the executive and judicial branches of government.[49]

---

[48]David Fellman, "The Judicial Process," *American Political Science Review* 57, No. 2 (June 1963): 476.

A glimpse of the undergraduate case method of instruction in political science is found in the experience of a young man from Hot Springs, Arkansas, in his sophomore year at Georgetown University under the professorship of one Walter I. Giles. See David Maraniss, *First In His Class: The Biography of Bill Clinton* (New York: Simon & Schuster, 1996): 70–71.

[49]For a useful coverage of the New Deal court crisis, see Robert H. Jackson, *The Struggle for Judicial Supremacy* (New York: Knopf, 1949); and Joseph W. Alsop and Turner Catledge, *The 168 Days* (Garden City, N.Y.: Doubleday, Doran, 1938). An excellent recent account is William E. Leuchtenburg, *The Supreme Court Reborn: The Constitutional Revolution in the Age of Roosevelt* (New York: Oxford University Press, 1995). See also Howard Gillman's insightful paper pointing up the importance of this shift in jurisprudential perspective: "State Building and the Collapse of Constitutional Originalism," delivered at the Annual Meeting of the American Political Science Association, San Francisco, Aug. 29–Sept. 1, 1996.

Fresh from the landslide electoral victory of 1936, President Roosevelt submitted to Congress a plan to reorganize the federal courts (popularly called the "court-packing plan"), whereby voluntary retirement was provided for the justices of the U.S. Supreme Court at seventy years of age. For justices of that age not wishing to retire, an additional justice could be appointed up to a total court complement of fifteen. Although couched in terms of more efficient administration of justice, the ill-disguised plan was obviously designed to alter the course of judicial policy-making. The reaction of Congress, as well as that of the press and the general public, ranged from lukewarm to a feeling of outrage that the president would dare lay hands on an independent judiciary. From the outset the proposal was doomed to failure.

The Court, whose decisions so infuriated the President and Congress, consisted of nine justices reflecting a curious blend of liberal and conservative views. Justices Pierce Butler, James McReynolds, George Sutherland, and Willis Van Devanter represented the nearly impregnable conservative bloc. Committed to an economic policy of laissez-faire and convinced that such a philosophy was mandated by the Constitution, these four justices could be counted upon to haul out one or more of the three chief legal barriers ordinarily used to negate governmental regulation of the economy: (1) a narrow, localized definition of the congressional power to regulate commerce; (2) a similarly restrictive view of the taxing and spending power of Congress; or (3) strangely enough, a *substantive* interpretation of the Fifth and Fourteenth Amendments due process clauses—that the "liberty" referred to in these clauses included the liberty of employer and employee to bargain together freely without governmental interference. Hence, minimum wage and maximum hour legislation would be an unconstitutional interference with such liberty. Justices Louis D. Brandeis, Benjamin Cardozo, and Harlan Stone, on the other hand, were equally adamant in their view that the realities of modern economic life made governmental regulation of the economy necessary, and, in any case, it was not the business of the Court to substitute its policy preferences for those of the executive and legislative branches. In the center stood Chief Justice Charles Evans Hughes, often joined by Associate Justice Owen Roberts. When voting with the conservatives, as they usually did, these two justices spelled doom for New Deal measures. Their occasional swing to the liberal side, however, changed constitutional history. Indeed, these two justices, in a sudden shift of votes following the defeat of the FDR court-packing plan but prior to a single change in court personnel, reversed the course of American constitutional law. On March 29, 1937, in a dramatic about-face, the Court, in *West Coast Hotel v. Parrish,* dropped its use of the liberty of contract doctrine to strike down wages and hours legislation. Speaking for a majority of the Court in upholding a minimum wage statute for women in the state of Washington, Chief Justice Hughes wrote:

> The principle which must control our decision is not in doubt. The constitutional provision invoked is the due process clause of the Fourteenth Amendment governing the States, as the due process clause invoked in the *Adkins Case* governed Congress. In each case the violation alleged by those attacking minimum wage regulation for women is deprivation of freedom of contract. What is this freedom? The Constitution does not speak of freedom of contract. It speaks of liberty and prohibits the deprivation of liberty without due process of law. In prohibiting that deprivation the Constitution does not recognize an absolute and uncontrollable liberty. Liberty in each of its phases has its history and connotation. But the liberty safeguarded is liberty in a social organization which requires the protection of laws against the evils which menace the health, safety, morals, and welfare of the people. Liberty under the Constitution is thus necessarily subject to the restraints of due process, and regulation which is reasonable in relation to its subject and is adopted in the interest of the community is due process.[50]

---

[50]*West Coast Hotel v. Parrish,* 300 U.S. 379, 391 (1937).

And on April 12, 1937, the chief justice again spoke for the same majority in setting forth a broad, nearly all-encompassing view of congressional power over interstate commerce which reads more like a statement from Chief Justice John Marshall or even a dictum of Oliver Wendell Holmes:

> When industries organize themselves on a national scale, making their relation to inter-state commerce the dominant factor in activities, how can it be maintained that their in-dustrial labor relations constitute a forbidden field into which Congress may not enter when it is necessary to protect interstate commerce from the paralyzing consequences of industrial war? We have often said that interstate commerce itself is a practical concep-tion. It is equally true that interferences with that commerce must be appraised by a judg-ment that does not ignore actual experience.[51]

Such was the response of the Court to the New Deal electoral landside of 1936, even prior to the enunciation of Roosevelt's Court packing plan. Thus, experience joined with theory to produce a new conceptualization of judicial studies for political science, an ap-proach which came to be called "political jurisprudence." Political scientists of this hue, writing in the 1950s and 1960s, accepted most or all assumptions of the Sociologists and Realists, adding little other than a translation of these ideas into political terms. That judges are human, not robots; that their personal and social ideas of rightness enter into, indeed probably dictate their decisions; that law and courts must be understood and stud-ied in their larger social context—such were (and are) the building blocks of political ju-risprudence.

If one were to point to one modern scholar whose work set the stage for an entire gen-eration of political research on courts, it would probably be Jack Peltason. In his essay *Fed-eral Courts in the Political Process,* published in 1955, Peltason wrote this:

> The purpose of this essay is to describe federal judges as participants in the political process. It is an attempt to do in a small way for federal judges what Bertram Gross and others have done more exhaustively for Congress. *The concern is with process rather than product.* The orientation is Bentleyan, behavioristic, actional, and nonmotivational.[52]

Peltason then proceeds to analyze the federal courts as part and parcel of the interest group struggle.

In the same year (1955), Victor Rosenblum of Northwestern University set forth the now-familiar argument that became the linchpin for political jurisprudence: that since (1) politics consists of activities of influencing, formulating, and administering public policy, and since (2) experience as well as current jurisprudence make it clear that courts fashion public policy, then (3) courts are clearly political agencies and are to be understood as subinstitutions in the larger political process.[53]

---

[51]*National Labor Relations Board v. Jones and Laughlin Steel Corporation,* 301 U.S. 1, 41 (1937). But see *U.S. v. Lopez,* 115 S. Ct. 1624 (1995), suggesting retrenchment on this issue by members of the Rehnquist Court.

[52]Jack W. Peltason, *Federal Courts in the Political Process* (New York: Doubleday, 1955), 1 (emphasis added).

[53]Victor G. Rosenblum, *Law as a Political Instrument* (New York: Doubleday, 1955). This is not to imply that Peltason and Rosenblum wrote on a clean slate. As David J. Danelski pointed out and as the foregoing discussion should make clear, "There was a political jurisprudence long before Martin Shapiro first used the term in the 1960s." Though Danelski specifies the prior work of Arthur F. Bentley and C. Herman Pritchett, he might well have begun the family album with Edward S. Corwin, Charles Grove Haines, and company. See David J. Danelski, "Law from a Political Perspective," *Western Political Quarterly* 36, No. 4 (Dec. 1983): 548–51. Even more pertinent is C. Herman Pritchett, "Public Law and Judicial Behavior."

Neither Peltason nor Rosenblum deny the uniqueness of the judicial process. Their point is simply that one gets a good deal closer to reality by conceptualizing courts as political agencies than was the case in the old jurisprudential view, which idolized courts as purely legal agencies. As Martin Shapiro writes in summing up political jurisprudence as it was understood in the mid-1960s:

> The difficulty in examining the Supreme Court through constitutional law or public law or constitutional history is that such an approach tends to obscure the nature of the Court as one governmental agency among many. In the last few years, a body of scholarship has begun to develop that seeks to take the Court out of the context of law and place it in the context of politics, to treat the Supreme Court as an agency of government. It is this movement that I call the "new" or "political" jurisprudence.[54]

Behavioral Jurisprudence

Growing through and out of these developments was a strand of research and theory known as "behavioral jurisprudence." Whereas political jurisprudence was an extension of sociological-Realist notions via Dewey, Bentley, and Truman—all of whom emphasized the significance of interest group theories in studying legal phenomena—the behavioral approaches sprang more from the psychology of the Realist school via scholars such as Jerome Frank, Felix Cohen, Charles Grove Haines, Underhill Moore, and in the 1940s, the quantitative attitudinal studies of C. Herman Pritchett.[55] By the 1950s and early 1960s, it was clear to even the casual observer that the study of "public law" in political science was undergoing a transformation and that the trend was in the direction of the behavioral revolution characterizing the entire discipline. Not until a few years later, however, did it become apparent that the public law metamorphosis was developing in two directions. Though both branches were negative reactions to traditional constitutional law, the political jurisprudents moved somewhat cautiously in the direction of reconceptualizing judicial studies as a social science in the Bentleyan-Peltason sense, whereas the behavioralists moved a bit more sharply into a human-oriented approach to the study of legal phenomena.

Essentially, the judicial behavioralists seemed somewhat closer to the disciplines usually labeled the behavioral sciences (particularly psychology) than were their fellow scholars. Whereas political jurisprudents are oriented toward the sociological dimensions of the adjudicative process—with a heavy reliance on group theories—and whereas traditional scholars tend to interest themselves in a speculative study of legal norms (bringing them somewhat closer to the humanistic approaches characteristic of philosophy, history, and Austinian conceptions of law), behavioralists are more interested in studying judges as human beings and relating their behavior to the more general body of theory about human decision making (see Table 2–1). There was thus a tendency among behavioralists to deemphasize both the peculiarly legal as well as the political aspect of adjudication in an attempt to relate judicial behavior to broader psychological theory presumably applicable to all human beings.

Writing in the mid-1970s, Glendon A. Schubert explained the difference between what he called the conventional and the behavioral approaches in terms of the gap between his work and that of Jack Peltason:

---

[54]Martin Shapiro, *Law and Politics in the Supreme Court: New Approaches to Political Jurisprudence* (New York: Free Press of Glencoe, 1964), 6. A relevant essay briefly tracing the development of political jurisprudence from the Corwin era through Peltason to the present is Shapiro, "Courts of Law, Courts of Politics."

[55]See Glendon Schubert, ed., *Judicial Behavior: A Reader in Theory and Research* (Chicago: Rand-McNally, 1964), especially Ch. 1, "Jurisprudence and Judicial Behavior." The pioneering research of Professor Pritchett appeared in *The Roosevelt Court* (New York: Macmillan, 1948).

To Peltason political meant interest group interaction. . . . To me political meant not abstract institutional fallacies such as "groups," but rather people—discrete, usually identifiable, humans acting in roles that directly affect the making or carrying out of public policy choices.[56]

To employ the behavioral perspective, warns Schubert, requires that political scientists climb off their "ramparts" and involve themselves in the "life sciences: anthropology, psychology, social psychology, and modern sociology." Later, biology, ethnology, population genetics, and ecology were stressed by Schubert as "essential components of a behavioral approach to the study of politics (including judicial politics)."[57]

Whatever the merits of the judicial behavioral wing of political jurisprudence, it is fair to say that the movement never really took root as the mainstay in classroom approaches to the study of the judiciary, nor did its research arm ever come to dominate the work of the subfield. For the modern student, a prime example of the once widely discussed judicial behavioral movement may be found in the continuing work of scholars associated with the "Attitudinal Model" in the study of appellate court decisions.[58]

Hence, although many of the substantive findings of behavioral scholarship were and are relevant in current teaching and research activities, the focus of courses now being offered (and textbooks used) is closer to the central ideology of political jurisprudence. This focus has a long, strong root reaching back into traditional constitutional law (where most political science classroom teaching regarding things legal still takes place). Furthermore, its branches extend into criminal law (an explosive area since the 1960s), into the everbroadening interest in civil judicial processes, and into studies of implementation processes, the sociology and politics of the legal profession, public opinion and interest groups as related to courts, judicial recruitment, the details of the work of appellate courts, and so on, across the broad expanse of the "judicial process" in all its dimensions.

In sum, the culmination of some forty years of ferment in teaching and research of things judicial in political science has been the development of a rich diversity of substantive concerns within the subfield, linked by an overarching ideological consensus (currently more implicit than explicit) centering on political jurisprudence.[59]

---

[56]Schubert, *Human Jurisprudence*, 6.

[57]Schubert, *Human Jurisprudence*, 6.

[58]See Jeffery A. Segal and Harold J. Spaeth, *The Supreme Court and the Attitudinal Model* (Cambridge: Cambridge University Press, 1993), along with some responses to that research found in "Symposium: The Supreme Court and the Attitudinal Model," *Law and Courts,* Newsletter of the Law and Courts Section of the American Political Science Association 4, No. 1 (Spring 1994): 3–12. A good example of behavioral judicial research in a comparative context is Glendon Schubert, *Political Culture and Judicial Behavior,* 2 vols. (Lanham, Md.: University Press of America, 1985).

[59]For a useful survey of work in the field, see Martin Shapiro, "Public Law and Judicial Politics," in Ada W. Finifter, ed., *Political Science: The State of the Discipline II* (Washington: American Political Science Association, 1993), 365–81. See also Shapiro's "Courts of Law, Courts of Politics." Some professional reaction to the Shapiro assessment may be found in the papers of a roundtable chaired by Harry P. Stumpf: "Author Meets Critics: Martin Shapiro and the Study of Public Law and Judicial Politics," Annual Meeting, American Political Science Association, Chicago, Aug. 31–Sept. 3, 1995.

Modern approaches and concerns in the political study of courts are illustrated in Lee Epstein, ed., *Contemplating Courts* (Washington: Congressional Quarterly Press, 1995); and John B. Gates and Charles A. Johnson, eds., *The American Courts: A Critical Assessment* (Washington: Congressional Quarterly Press, 1991). It is interesting to note that both of these readers rather explicitly adhere to an empirical social science model of research on law and courts based, at least implicitly, on the logical positivism of the 1960–1990 "behavioral" revolution in political science. Some detractors of this orientation are discussed in Ch. 2 of this text. Also noteworthy is the rather explicit political jurisprudential (judicial policy-making) grounding of these readers.

CONCLUSIONS

Research and teaching of the political jurisprudential movement, especially in the early years, tended to be characterized by two unfortunate tendencies. First, and not surprisingly, work leaned rather sharply in the direction of the United States Supreme Court, almost as though that were the only court worthy of political analysis. Peltason; Rosenblum; Robert Dahl's influential piece[60]; early Schubert and Schmidhauser texts[61]; indeed, even Shapiro's early work—all of these and many other once mainline materials were oriented to federal courts if not the U.S. Supreme Court alone. In other words, these materials all suffered in varying degrees from what Jerome Frank called the "Upper Court Myth" (actually, "Supreme Court Myth"). As Shapiro himself pointed out, the debate coming out of the 1930s and 1940s concerning the policy-making role of the Supreme Court, as well as the rich scholarship of the Corwin-Pritchett-Mason variety, again on the Supreme Court, produced a result in which

> It is little wonder . . . that the Supreme Court should be the point at which sociological jurisprudence, judicial realism, and political science come together and that study of the Supreme Court has so far been the principal vehicle for political jurisprudence. The Supreme Court is the first political court of the nation and the first to be examined in political terms.[62]

In the three decades since Shapiro first summed up the lineaments of political jurisprudence, a tilt in favor of federal and appellate courts has continued, though less so, as scholars in the subfield, perhaps hemmed in by the almost invariable demand to teach American Constitutional Law, have continued to place strong emphasis on the work of the United States Supreme Court.[63] This orientation has been strengthened in recent years by a renewed interest in constitutional theory and interpretation (see Chapter 2), along with continuing work in judicial behavioralism or the "scientific" approach to the study of courts, which has always carried a heavy emphasis on the decision making of appellate courts, especially the "Highest Court in the Land."[64] In recent years there has been consid-

---

[60]*Journal of Public Law* 6, No. 2 (1957): 279–95.

[61]John R. Schmidhauser, ed., *Constitutional Law in the Political Process* (Chicago: Rand-McNally, 1963); Glendon A. Schubert, *Constitutional Politics* (New York: Holt, Rinehart & Winston, 1960).

[62]Shapiro, *Law and Politics,* 16–17.

[63]See Shapiro, "Public Law and Judicial Politics," 377. In *The Transformation of American Law,* xii, Morton J. Horwitz points up the disadvantages of the overstudy of constitutional law from the viewpoint of the historian; much of this analysis would apply equally to political science.

[64]Harold J. Spaeth, "Different Strokes for Different Folks: A Reply to Professor Shapiro's Assessment of the Subfield," in Stumpf, "Roundtable."
In a very useful survey of judicial articles published in the four main American political science journals (*American Political Science Review, Journal of Politics, American Journal of Political Science,* and *Political Research Quarterly,* representing respectively, the American, Southern, Midwest, and Western Political Science Associations), Thomas R. Hensley found that in the period 1988–1995 (a follow-up of his earlier 1960–1987 survey), 56 percent of published articles focused primarily on the Supreme Court, and, writes Hensley, "this has not varied significantly across the 36-year period." Moreover, articles devoted to the "conversion process" (judicial decision making), along with doctrinal (substantive decisional) analysis together made up 60 percent of all judicial politics articles. See Thomas R. Hensley, "Studying the Studies: An Assessment of Judicial Politics Research of Four Major Political Science Journals, 1960–1995," *Law and Courts: Newsletter of the Law and Courts Section of the American Political Science Association,* 7, No. 1 (Winter, 1996–97): 14–15.

erable movement toward other courts and other settings, to be sure, but the growth along the leading edge of the subfield, discussed in recent survey articles[65] and covered in its theoretical dimensions in Chapter 2, has had a somewhat delayed and reduced impact at the center of professional activities.

Secondly, political jurisprudence has perhaps taken too seriously the judicial process approach. That is, in moving away from the absurdities of Austinian jurisprudence and the narrower confines of traditional constitutional law, scholars, on the one hand, happily recognized that the judicial decision-making process is hardly mechanical. Rather, the process involves a complex set of personal, social, and political as well as institutional variables. On the other hand, the preponderance of research and text writing, again particularly in the early years, tended to focus on the internal dynamics of judicial decision-making processes, especially at the appellate level, giving relatively less attention to the broader sociopolitical context in which the judicial process operates. Courts, after all (as political jurisprudents stressed), do not function in a vacuum any more than do the executive or legislative branches. As previously suggested, the *judicial process* in its broader meaning ought to include the *entire* range of politically relevant activities that influence decisional outcomes. Hence, the subfield that we are discussing is perhaps best labeled *judicial politics* rather than the *judicial process,* in order to suggest the real and legitimate interests of political scientists, which include the decisional process itself in addition to all the forces and influences that impinge on that process. However, work in the subfield has been rather slow in encompassing the widest reaches implied in the political jurisprudential orientation.[66]

These points can easily be overemphasized. There is, to be sure, an ever-growing body of research and teaching focusing on pre- and post-litigation activities. And the politics of trial courts, lawyers, private as opposed to purely public law issues, along with a strong comparative and even international law research movement—all of these and other foci are leading to a considerable enrichment of work in the field.[67] But it remains the case that political scientists now at work in public law, joined too often by scholars *not* within the subfield itself, tend to conceptualize the field in terms of good ole' "con-law," offered up to undergraduate students headed for law school. And whatever one might say as to current movements in public law (covered in Chapter 2), the frontiers of our activities still remain some distance from our central, day-to-day work ways.

Stepping back for a somewhat broader look, it is apparent that political science is but one discipline significantly affected by the empirical rejuvenation of the study of law. Sociological-Realist jurisprudence has vastly enriched legal studies across the spectrum of the social and behavioral sciences, with the empirical study of legal phenomena now prospering as a subfield in (and around) most social science disciplines. Research and teaching approaches are unabashedly interdisciplinary, with psychologists and sociologists now having common intellectual concerns with the political scientist and the anthropologist. The formation in 1964 of the Law and Society Association, and the accompanying publication of the *Law and Society Review,* has hastened these developments. Concern over differ-

---

[65]The rich diversity of work in the field is illustrated by Shapiro, "Public Law and Judicial Politics." See also various scholarly responses in Stumpf, "Roundtable."

[66]The aforementioned Hensley survey results also support this second point. Thus, only 9 percent of judicial articles published in the four leading American political science journals from 1988 through 1995 dealt with impact or feedback processes, and only 9 percent focused on inputs to the judicial system. See Hensley, "Studying the Studies": 15.

[67]Again, the Shapiro essay, "Public Law and Judicial Politics," is useful here.

ences in methodology, or research foci pall in contrast with the common ground found in the social and behavioral sciences since the 1960s.[68]

Scholars from the law schools have formed an increasingly important segment of this joint enterprise, but their numbers have been relatively small and they represent an even smaller, though some have argued leading, portion of the nation's total law faculties. In the main, the Realist movement to the contrary notwithstanding, the central thrust of legal education has remained largely isolated from this social science rejuvenation.[69] In teaching, the case method, with its emphasis on the appellate decision and the legal principle to be derived therefrom, still predominates. There is much talk of Pound, Llewellyn, and new conceptualization, but underneath, little has changed from the long-standing vocational orientations of legal instruction.[70] In research, the outlook is somewhat more promising, with large social scientific projects now commonly based in law schools and law journals frequently reporting the best of recent empirical research.

As for political science itself, one finds general acceptance of Pritchett's admonition to "Let a hundred flowers bloom."[71] The impact of Sociological-Realist jurisprudence, through the development of political jurisprudence, has had a shattering (or better, scattering) effect on the activities of political science practitioners. For reasons of inertia, if nothing else, traditional constitutional law has remained at center stage in teaching. But now center stage is shared by other regularly offered courses such as "The Judicial Process," "Judicial Politics," "Judicial Behavior," or some similar titles. From these, course offerings fan out in many directions, following the fads or the research orientation of the individual professor. Broadly conceived law and society courses are common, as are courses in criminal law, jurisprudence, offerings on various aspects of state and local judicial politics, topics on the legal profession, and so on.

Research in political science has followed jurisprudential trends more closely than has teaching. Most political scientists would label themselves political jurisprudents and, together with their behavioral colleagues, have produced a large number of empirical studies of legal phenomena which now fill the syllabi of upper-division and graduate courses on the judiciary. Work is moving not only "down and out" in domestic judicial politics, but materials are increasingly available within a comparative and international context.[72]

Conceptually, problems remain for political jurisprudence. Beyond an agreement that courts make policy and are therefore political, the departure point for virtually all current

[68]A helpful overview of these developments may be found in Lawrence M. Friedman, "The Law and Society Movement," *Stanford Law Review* 38, No. 3 (Feb. 1986): 763–80. See also Richard Lempert and Joseph Sanders, *An Invitation to Law and the Social Sciences* (New York: Longman, 1986). One scholar has suggested that these developments have, in fact if not in name, brought about a new discipline—Legal Studies—which stands apart from disciplines such as Sociology, Political Science, Psychology, and Law. See Kim Lane Scheppele, "Political Science and Legal Studies: A Case for Dualism," in Stumpf, "Roundtable."
[69]Friedman, "Law and Society Movement," has a set of explanations for this (773–78). But see Martin Shapiro, "Recent Developments in Political Jurisprudence," in Stumpf et al., "Whither Political Jurisprudence," 541–48. See also the comments of Derek Bok, former dean of Harvard Law School, in "A Flawed System of Law Practice & Training," *Journal of Legal Education* 33, No. 4 (Dec. 1983): 570–85.
[70]An interesting account of law school instruction is Stephen C. Halpern, "On the Politics and Pathology of Legal Education (Or, Whatever Happened to that Blindfolded Lady with the Scales?)," *Journal of Legal Education* 32, No. 3 (Sept. 1982): 383–94. But consider the developments of Post-Realism, discussed in Ch. 2.
[71]See Pritchett, "Public Law and Judicial Behavior," 219.
[72]For some examples, see John R. Schmidhauser, ed., *Comparative Judicial Systems: Challenging Frontiers in Conceptual and Empirical Analysis* (London: Butterworths, 1987); Douglas Greenberg, et al., eds., *Constitutionalism and Democracy: Transitions in the Contemporary World* (New York: Oxford University Press, 1993); and Neal C. Tate and Torbjorn Vallinder, eds., *The Global Expansion of Judicial Power* (New York: New York University Press, 1994).

work,[73] contemporary political scientists are not clear exactly what all the teaching and research ramifications are, nor what the parameters, not to mention the emphases, of the subfield should be. Of late, there has been a return to square one in an attempt to clarify the political conception of law and courts. What is policy? Is policy-making the central function of courts? Do courts at all levels perform this function? To what extent should public law scholars include legislative and administrative law-making in their ambit? What are the adjudicative (versus the nonadjudicative) roles, and so on? These and similar issues will be addressed in subsequent chapters.

FURTHER READING

Baum, Lawrence, "Judicial Politics: Still a Distinctive Field." In Ada F. Finifter, ed., *Political Science: The State of the Discipline,* 189–215. Washington: American Political Science Asssociation, 1983.

Frank, Jerome, *Law and the Modern Mind,* New York: Coward-McCann, 1930.

Gates, John B., and Charles A. Johnson, eds. *The American Courts: A Critical Assessment.* Washington: Congressional Quarterly, 1991.

Gilmore, Grant. *The Ages of American Law.* New Haven: Yale University Press, 1977.

Holmes, Oliver W. *The Common Law.* Boston: Little, Brown, 1881.

Llewellyn, Karl N. *The Bramble Bush: On Our Law and Its Study* (rev. ed.). New York: Oceana, 1951.

Murphy, Walter F., and Joseph Tanenhaus. *The Study of Public Law.* New York: Random House, 1972.

Patterson, Edwin W. *Jurisprudence: Men and Ideas of the Law.* Brooklyn: Foundation Press, 1953.

Pound, Roscoe. "Law in the Books and Law in Action." *American Law Review* 44 (1910): 12–36.

Pritchett, C. Herman, "Public Law and Judicial Behavior." In Marian D. Irish, ed., *Political Science: Advance of a Discipline,* 190–219. Englewood Cliffs, N.J.: Prentice-Hall, 1968.

Rumble, Wilfred E., Jr. *American Legal Realism.* Ithaca, N.Y.: Cornell University Press, 1968.

Schubert, Glendon A. *Human Jurisprudence: Public Law as Political Science.* Honolulu: University of Hawaii Press, 1975.

Shapiro, Martin, *Law and Politics in the Supreme Court: New Approaches to Political Jurisprudence.* New York: Free Press of Glencoe, 1964.

————. "Public Law and Judicial Politics," in Ada W. Finifter, ed. *Political Science: The State of the Discipline, II.* Washington: American Political Science Association, 1993, 365–81.

Stumpf, Harry P., Martin Shapiro, David J. Danelski, Austin Sarat, and David M. O'Brien. "Whither Political Jurisprudence: A Symposium," *Western Political Quarterly* 36 (Dec. 1983): 533–69.

---

[73]This point is made more fully in Harry P. Stumpf, "Conceptions of 'Court' in Contemporary Judicial Research: The Politics of A-Historical Jurisprudence," paper presented at the XVIth World Congress of the International Political Science Association, Aug. 21–25, 1994, Berlin.

2

Political Jurisprudence Reconsidered

It is high time for general acceptance of the fact that the Emperor has no clothes. . . . One cannot be both a legal realist and a mechanist.

—Arthur S. Miller,
"A Note on the Criticism of Supreme Court Decisions"

[T]he settlement of disputes is the primordial internal function which a political order has to perform, antedating the making of rules and the application of such rules in administrative work.

—Carl J. Friedrich,
Man and His Government

POLITICAL JURISPRUDENCE: A FOCUS ON PROCESS

As a point of departure, it is useful to characterize jurisprudential perspectives in contemporary political science by the shorthand trichotomy seen in Table 2–1.[1] Of course the table is an oversimplification of reality and merely suggestive of the different approaches. It does serve, however, as a starting point for the reader in becoming oriented to the subfield. Further, it includes a point not raised in the previous chapter having to do with the foci of study. That traditional scholars study only the law, conventionalists only courts, and behavioralists only judges, as suggested in the third category in the chart, is of course not completely true, for it is hardly possible to focus on one without also discussing the other two. But understood as a broad generalization, this statement is helpful in further

---

[1]This table was suggested by the writings of Glendon Schubert, especially his "The Future of Public Law," *George Washington Law Review* 34, No. 4 (May 1966): 593–614; his "Ideologies and Attitudes, Academic and Judicial," *Journal of Politics* 29, No. 1 (Feb. 1967): 3–44; and his "Academic Ideologies and the Study of Adjudication," *American Political Science Review* 61, No. 1 (Mar. 1967): 106–29.

Table 2–1   Political Science Approaches to the Study of the Judiciary

	Traditional	**Conventional**	**Behavioral**
Jurisprudential grounding	Austinian Positivism	Sociological-Realist-Political Jurisprudence	Realist-Behavioral Jurisprudence
Cognate disciplines	History, law, philosophy—the humanities	Modern empirical social, especially sociology	Behavioral sciences, especially psychology; also biology and statistics
Focus of study	The law—legal rules and principles, appellate decisions	The adjudication process—courts and their accoutrements	Judges—human behavior in the judicial setting
Method of study	Te⸱	Social science research techniques—systematic observation ⸱f the judicial process; ⸱vey research, etc.	Quantitative analysis of judicial behavior, empirical theory-building as applied to small groups
Current status discipline		ideological ⸱⸱ity position, ⸱⸱st research	Declining, represented by a minority of practitioners

clarifyir   in explicating the thrust of political
jurispri   particularly as that stance was originally f

of ar   ·inciples emanating from the decisions
spe·   alue, for it fails to account for a broad
de·   ·der the rule—the gap between what is
w   gh a course in American foreign policy
J·   y decisions of the International Court of
                                                                ·n the basis of readings and analyses of

                                                                ·nd, seems equally narrow to the political
jurisprudent, ···   aspect of a much larger arena of activity
which is clearly relevant to ··· ·   ·ary in the political and social system as a
whole.² To continue our analogy, the foreign policy process involves a good deal more
than the decisions of the president. Similarly, while legislative committee chairpersons are

²For a more extensive discussion of these matters, see Walter F. Murphy and Joseph Tanenhaus, *The Study of Public Law* (New York: Random House, 1972). In the preface (p. viii), these scholars write:

> A word about the title of this volume: one noted scholar (Glendon Schubert, *Judicial Decision Making* (New York: Free Press of Glencoe, 1963), has said that the study of judicial behavior is replacing the study of public law. Although we choose the older characterization for descriptive rather than ideological reasons, we think that political scientists who study courts and judges are concerned with much more than how judges vote and write opinions and how they make up their minds. We believe that most of our colleagues who call themselves behavioralists would agree with that judgment. In our view the study of judicial behavior is only one segment, although a major one, in the larger study of public law.

of considerable importance in understanding the legislative process, they are hardly the whole story.

Political jurisprudence recognizes the importance of rule as well as judge, but it tends to include both in a broader conception of the subject summed up in the word *process*.[3] The initial focus of a process orientation is the *court*, but that is by no means the sole subject of study. Rather, court and judge are seen as the centerpieces of a system which begins with (1) the *problem*—the felt need or grievance of an individual or group in society—then moves to (2) a consideration of alternative dispute processing mechanisms, then (3) is screened by the professional cadre (lawyers and others) surrounding courts, and passes on to (4) an appropriate judicial body, resulting in a disposition which (5) has an impact upon the individual or group in society, whose reaction may in turn feed back into the legislative, executive, and judicial mechanisms of government.[4] Viewing the judicial function in this way—as a complex process involving the interaction of problem, judge and company, rules, impacts, and feedback—is taken by the political jurisprudent as more inclusive, more realistic, and more likely to provide broad insight into the role of adjudication in the larger society. Clearly, rules are important, for they establish the parameters of the system and help predict outcomes. Rules are prized by actors in the system, for they are a form of power. Legality is an important political resource. Judicial decisions, appellate and otherwise, are significant too, not only for the rule of law they emit, but even more for the feature or features of the judicial process they exemplify. Thus, as we shall see, decisional materials are not excluded by the political jurisprudent; they are merely used differently than is the case with the traditional approach.[5] Judges obviously are central in the system, and their behavior must come under close scrutiny. But they are not the only significant judicial personnel. Bar association presidents, prosecutors, law enforcement officials, defense attorneys, and litigants are also important actors in the system.

---

[3]The term *process* as used here is far different from its usage in many jurisprudential writings. In works of and about the Critical Legal Studies movement, the term usually connotes a sort of "Neo-Positivism" associated with the work of Henry Hart and Albert Sacks in the 1950s. See Elizabeth Mensch, "A History of Mainstream Legal Thought," in David Kairys, *The Politics of Law: A Progressive Critique,* rev. ed. (New York: Pantheon Books, 1990), 13–37.

[4]Compare this schema with that of Grossman and Wells. Accompanied by an elaborate diagram, the schema of these two political scientists is stated as follows:

> The five components of the judicial system are (1) the environment in which it operates; (2) the inputs from other systems; (3) the conversion process, by which inputs are transformed into outputs . . . ; (4) the outcomes of the policy outputs; and (5) the feedback as a result of these outputs and outcomes.

Joel B. Grossman and Richard S. Wells, *Constitutional Law and Judicial Policy-Making,* 2nd ed. (New York: Wiley, 1980), 44.

Two other works that use the system approach in studying the judiciary are Glendon Schubert, *Judicial Policy-Making,* rev. ed. (Glenview, Ill.: Scott, Foresman, 1970); and Sheldon Goldman and Thomas P. Jahnige, *The Federal Courts as a Political System,* 3rd ed. (New York: Harper & Row, 1985).

[5]In fact, there are several texts published by political jurisprudents in which the decisions of the Supreme Court are arranged not by the dictates of doctrinal development per se, but by the aspects of judicial policy-making the decisions illustrate. See, e.g., Martin Shapiro and Douglas S. Hobbs, *American Constitutional Law: Cases and Analyses* (Cambridge, Mass.: Winthrop, 1978); and Victor G. Rosenblum and A. Didrick Castberg, eds., *Cases on Constitutional Law: Political Roles of the Supreme Court* (Homewood, Ill.: Dorsey Press, 1973). See also, e.g., the manner in which decisional materials are used in Walter F. Murphy and C. Herman Pritchett, eds., *Courts, Judges, and Politics: An Introduction to the Judicial Process,* 4th ed. (New York: Random House, 1986).

Two additional casebooks that organize cases in other than doctrinal fashion are Sheldon Goldman, *Constitutional Law and Supreme Court Decision-Making* (New York: Harper & Row, 1982); and John

In short, political jurisprudence takes the judiciary out of legal isolation and places it in the mainstream of politics. It conceptualizes the judicial system as a subsystem within a larger political structure and proposes to study the process as one would study legislative or administrative politics—that is, as a *process* rather than a single event.

MOVEMENTS AND COUNTERMOVEMENTS: POST-REALISM, LEGAL EDUCATION, AND POLITICAL JURISPRUDENCE

The departure point for political jurisprudence, as we have attempted to make clear, is a particular conception of the judicial function and the role of law in the political and social system. Laws—legal rules and court decisions—are seen as political resources rather than neutral guidelines to promote an objective social good. If politics can be viewed as the process of who gets what, when, and how,[6] or those activities having to do with the allocation of societal values,[7] then the legal system, in its on-going task of rendering decisions in countless cases, is in the business of daily granting and withholding advantages and disadvantages, rewards and deprivations—including wealth, power, security, and general well-being—for thousands of individuals, groups, and interests. That this is political activity in its clearest sense seems patent, and it would hardly be necessary to state, let alone elaborate, the point were it not for the persistence of the contrary view so prevalent among members of the legal profession and the public at large.[8]

As seen, this contrary conceptualization is based on Austinian positivism, if not, at times, precepts of natural law. In more contemporary dress, it reappeared in the 1960s in the debate over "neutral" principles of constitutional adjudication. In 1959, Herbert Wechsler of Columbia Law School published a piece in which he called for Supreme Court decision making on the basis of "neutral principles."[9] The Court's justices, Wechsler argued, should make their decisions purely on grounds of reason, logic, and consistency, regardless of the social interests involved or the impact of the decision on those interests. No political, economic, or social preference should be exhibited by the Court. Rather, the Court's role is to be one of strict impartiality, with the exception of its allegiance to principles. De-

---

R. Schmidhauser, *Constitutional Law in American Politics* (Monterey, Calif.: Brooks/Cole, 1984). Two more texts that in different ways combine decisional excerpts with unusually heavy doses of judicial process materials are David O'Brien, *Constitutional Law and Politics,* 2 vols. (New York: W.W. Norton, 1991); and Paul Brest and Sanford Levinson, *Processes of Constitutional Decisionmaking: Cases and Materials,* 3rd ed. (New York: Little, Brown, 1992).

A very useful overview of constitutional law texts available in the early 1990s may be found in *Law and Courts Newsletter,* Law and Courts Section of the American Political Science Association, Spring, 1993.

[6]As in Harold D. Lasswell, *Politics: Who Gets What, When and How* (New York: Peter Smith, 1950).

[7]David Easton, *The Political System* (New York: Knopf, 1953), Ch. 5.

[8]See Glendon Schubert, *Human Jurisprudence: Public Law as Political Science* (Honolulu: University of Hawaii Press, 1975), Chapter 3; "Behavioral Jurisprudence," 43. This chapter, "Behavioral Jurisprudence," first appeared as an article in *Law & Society Review* 2; No. 3 (May 1964): 407–28.

[9]Herbert Wechsler, "Toward Neutral Principles of Constitutional Law," *Harvard Law Review* 73, No. 1 (Nov. 1959): 1–35. The "neutrality" debate is analyzed in Martin Shapiro's *Law and Politics in the Supreme Court: New Approaches to Political Jurisprudence* (New York: Free Press of Glencoe, 1964), 17–32. A fascinating account of the intellectual history and jurisprudential implications of the "neutral principles" concept may be found in Gary Peller's "Neutral Principles in the 1950's," *University of Michigan Journal of Law Reform"* 21, No. 4 (Summer 1988): 561–662.

cisions must be "principled," insists Wechsler, in order to be differentiated from mere exercises in naked power:

> A principled decision . . . is one which rests on reason with respect to all the issues in the case, reasons that in their generality and their neutrality transcend any immediate result that is involved.[10]

And who decides what the relevant issues in the case are, not to mention whose reasoning is to apply? The judge, of course. And on what grounds? We are not told. Henry Hart as well as Dean Griswold, both of Harvard Law School, joined in the plea, expressing concern that critical sectors of the public were losing respect for the judiciary, thanks to its errant decision making. This was particularly true of the Court's most outspoken critics, "first-rate lawyers."[11]

Rebuttals were not long in coming. Thurman Arnold ridiculed the concept of neutrality and principled decisions as "pompous generalizations dropped on the Court from the heights of Olympus."[12] He scoffed at criticism from "first-rate lawyers," whom he took to mean corporate lawyers representing established economic interests who were out of sympathy with the rulings of the Warren Court. Miller and Howell published a somewhat more systematic critique of the Hart-Griswold-Wechsler thesis. After demonstrating through a history of Supreme Court decisions that the high bench has never adhered to a value-free jurisprudence, these scholars argued that

> In the interest-balancing procedure of constitutional adjudication, neutrality has no place, objectivity is achievable only in part, and impartiality is more of an aspiration than a fact—although certainly possible to some degree. In making choices among competing values, the Justices of the Supreme Court are themselves guided by value preferences. Any reference to neutral or impersonal principles is, accordingly, little more than a call for a return to a mechanistic jurisprudence and for a jurisprudence of nondisclosure as well as an attempted denial of the teleological aspects of any decision, wherever made. The members of the high bench have never adhered to a theory of mechanism, whatever their apologists and commentators may have said, in the judicial decision-making process.[13]

To call for judicial decision making to be reasoned means little, Miller and Howell argue, "for reason is a tool, not an end; the results of a process of reasoning depend entirely on what premises (i.e., values) are used in the process.[14] In a subsequent article, Miller rather impatiently concludes that

> The upshot is that it is high time for general acceptance of the fact that the Emperor has no clothes. We should not beguile ourselves with the attractive but un-attainable quest for realization of the rule of law above men and above society. All of us now know that the Emperor is striding around in his birthday suit, and while it may be possible, it serves no useful or desirable purpose to act as if he were fully clothed. More than verbal acceptance

---

[10]Wechsler, "Toward Neutral Principles," 19.
[11]See Henry M. Hart, Jr., "The Supreme Court, 1958 Term—Forward: The Time Chart of the Justices," *Harvard Law Review* 73, No. 1 (Nov. 1959): 84–240; and Irwin N. Griswold, "The Supreme Court, 1959 Term—Forward: Of Times and Attitudes: Professor Hart and Judge Arnold." *Harvard Law Review* 74, No. 1 (Nov. 1960): 81–211.
[12]Thurman Arnold, "Professor Hart's Theology," *Harvard Law Review* 73, No. 7 (May 1960): 1298–1317.
[13]Arthur S. Miller and Ronald F. Howell, "The Myth of Neutrality in Constitutional Adjudication," *University of Chicago Law Review* 27, No. 1 (Summer 1960): 671.
[14]Miller and Howell, "Myth of Neutrality," 682.

must be given to that view of the judicial process; one cannot be both a legal realist and a mechanist.[15]

Old myths die hard, however (or more accurately, they do not die at all), for we have witnessed a return to the barricades of judicial independence and our "true" constitutional values. In another article appearing in the *Harvard Law Review,* entitled "The Forms of Justice," the claim is once again vehemently asserted and reasserted, this time by Owen Fiss of Yale Law School:

> The task of the judge is to give meaning to constitutional values, and he does this by working through the constitutional text, history, and social ideals. He searches for what is true, right, or just. He does not become a participant in interest group politics.[16]

In the landmark policy-making decision of *Brown v. Board of Education,* wherein the Supreme Court held racial segregation in public education unconstitutional, as well as later when the Court outlawed various forms of torture used in the Arkansas prison system, Fiss insists that the justices were not reading into the Constitution their own views of social policy. Rather, in each case, they were giving a "true account" of our constitutional values.[17] Fiss claims that judges are enabled—indeed, forced—to be "objective" because of two central facets of adjudication: (1) the judges' obligation to take cases, listen to the arguments, and respond (what Fiss calls dialogue); and (2) the judges' independence.[18] The judicial response—the reasons given for a judge's decision—must be "good reasons," and we can all agree on at least two facts as to what might be considered in determining "good reasons":

> The first is that the reason cannot consist of a preference, be it a preference of the contestants, or of the body politic, or of the judge. The statement "I prefer" or "we prefer" in the context of a judicial, rather than a legislative decision, merely constitutes an explanation, not a justification. Second, the reason must somehow transcend the personal, transient beliefs of the judge or the body politic as to what is right or just or what should be done. Something more is required to transform these personal beliefs into values that are worthy of the status "constitutional" and all that it implies—binding on society as a whole, entitled to endure, not forever but long enough to give our public morality an inner coherence, and largely to be enforced by courts.[19]

If there remains any doubt that this is essentially the Wechsler plea, a return to the old, timeworn, declaratory theory of jurisprudence, note the following:

> We have lost our confidence in the existence of the values that underlie the litigation of the 1960s, or, for that matter, in the existence of any public values. *All is preference.* That seems to be the crucial issue, not the issue of relative institutional competence. Only once we reassert our belief in the existence of public values, that values such as equality, liberty, due process, no cruel and unusual punishment, security of the person, or free speech can have a true and important meaning, that must be articulated and implemented—yes,

---

[15]Arthur S. Miller, "A Note on the Criticism of Supreme Court Decisions," *Journal of Public Law* 10, No. 1 (Spring 1961): 148.

[16]Owen M. Fiss, "The Supreme Court 1978 Term—Forward: The Forms of Justice," *Harvard Law Review* 93, No. 1 (Nov. 1979): 1–58.

[17]Fiss, "Supreme Court 1978 Term": 12.

[18]Fiss, "Supreme Court 1978 Term": 12–13.

[19]Fiss, "Supreme Court 1978 Term": 13–14.

discovered—will the role of the courts in our political system become meaningful, or for that matter even intelligible.[20]

What can one say, except perhaps to cite Thurman Arnold's critique of the Hart thesis, "Legal theorists like Professor Hart designed the clothes which concealed the person of the king and which give him his authority and public acceptance."[21] "I refuse to accept a world where 'all is preference,'" Fiss is saying, "There simply must be *Truth* somewhere!" A world without truth or objectivity, a dismal world where "all is preference," is simply too much.

Actually, the Wechsler-Fiss position is more usefully viewed as a spur of a larger movement that, for lack of a better term, has been dubbed "Post-Realism."[22] To the extent that important segments of this highly disparate "movement" take an anti-Realist posture, "Neo-Positivism" would be a better term. And at the opposite end of the spectrum, where the Critical Legal Studies scholars are found, the movement might better be described by the term "Neo-Realism." At any rate, as used here, Post-Realism is meant to designate the major currents of legal thought that have impinged on legal scholarship, particularly in the law schools—though to some extent in political science—in the 1960s and especially in the 1970s and 1980s. To briefly summarize these developments, it is perhaps best to begin with the Critical Legal Studies (CLS) movement, for it is with the "Crits," as they are sometimes called, that most of the other strains of thought can be juxtaposed.

Critical Legal Studies

Launched in the late 1970s, CLS took as its central article of faith a denial of the rational determinacy of the traditional model of judicial decision making. Legal reasoning is bunk. *Law is politics,* and its agencies and agents (lawyers, courts, legislatures), are part of the push and pull of the political process.[23] So-called objective legal rules, like the dictates of natural law of old, "can be manipulated to justify an almost infinite spectrum of possible

---

[20]Fiss, "Supreme Court 1978 Term": 16–17 (emphasis added).

[21]Arnold, "Professor Hart's Theology": 1310.

[22]The first use of this term that this writer has been able to locate was by Mark Tushnet of the University of Wisconsin School of Law. See his "Post-Realist Legal Scholarship," *Journal of the Society of Public Teachers of Law* 15 (Mar. 1980): 20–32. But Peter Sperlich may have invented the term. See his "Post-Realism: Should Ignorance Be Elevated to a Principle of Adjudication?" *Judicature* 64, No. 2 (Aug. 1980): 93.

[23]The literature on the Critical Legal Studies movement is immense, and no attempt is made here to survey the field. The items found most useful in the writing of this section are the following: "Critical Legal Studies Symposium," *Stanford Law Review* 36, Nos. 1 & 2 (Jan. 1984), especially Allan C. Hutchinson and Patrick J. Monahan, "Law, Politics, and the Critical Legal Scholars: The Unfolding Drama of American Legal Thought," 199–245; David Kairys, ed., *The Politics of Law: A Progressive Critique,* rev. ed. (New York: Pantheon Books, 1990); and a lengthy review essay of the Kairys book by Wythe Holt, "A Law Book for All Seasons: Toward a Socialist Jurisprudence," *Rutgers Law Review* 14, No. 4 (Summer 1983): 915–49. See also "'Round and 'Round the Bramble Bush: From Legal Realism to Critical Legal Scholarship," *Harvard Law Review* 95, No. 7 (May 1982): 1669–90; and several items by Mark Tushnet, such as his "Post-Realist Legal Scholarship"; his "Truth, Justice, and the American Way: An Interpretation of Public Law Scholarship in the Seventies," *Texas Law Review* 57, No. 8 (Nov. 1979): 1307–59; and his "Critical Legal Studies: A Political History," *Yale Law Journal* 100, No. 5 (March 1991): 1515–44.

In addition to the Kairys volume, cited above, four other useful books are Roberto Mangabeira Unger's *The Critical Legal Studies Movement* (Cambridge: Harvard University Press, 1983); Mark Kelman, *A Guide to Critical Legal Studies* (Cambridge: Harvard University Press, 1987); a collection of individual essays edited by Allan C. Hutchinson, *Critical Legal Studies* (Totowa, N.J.: Rowman & Littlefield, 1989); and Andrew Altman, *Critical Legal Studies: A Liberal Critique* (Princeton: Princeton University Press, 1990).

Finally, pieces attempting to interpret the Critical Legal Studies movement to and for political scientists include Rogers Smith, "All Critters Great and Small: Critical Legal Studies and Liberal Political Theory,"

outcomes."[24] There is no middle ground; if law is politics, it is little else. All is indeed preference—the policy choices of those in positions to make or influence legal decisions.

So far, so good. The political jurisprudent can read most of critical legal thought with a big yawn, concluding that law professors, or at least a vocal minority of them, have finally joined the club. These notions have been commonplace in political science since Peltason.[25] As one scholar put it (and as occurred in political science in the late 1950s), "The uneasy marriage of Formalist and Realist traditions has finally been prodded to a reluctant self-awareness that is compelling a reappraisal of basic approaches to legal scholarship."[26] But CLS goes further. Although it takes sociological-realist-political jurisprudence seriously (as opposed to the lip service given it in legal education and scholarship in law schools since the 1930s), it expressly rejects the liberal assumptions of these modes of thought. In fact, CLS has a decided neo-Marxist tone; it maintains that liberalism, in its faith in an enlightened hierarchy as a road to social progress, overlooks the inherent contradictions between real individual freedom and community. And the Crits further argue that the concept of the Rule of Law, passively accepted by both Realists and political jurisprudents, tends to rationalize fundamental social inequities inherent in the modern bureaucratic state. Thus,

> Under this ideal [the Rule of Law], outcomes are said to be the product of impersonal, neutral methods of choice rather than the imposed preferences of an illegitimate hierarchy. Moreover, the rule of law is presented as the only buttress against a descent into an anarchical world in which all moral claims would be equally subjective and therefore equally devoid of authority. By obscuring the value choices inherent in the application of rules, the liberal model of adjudication makes it possible to believe that existing social hierarchies are not just the result of interrupted fighting. In the process, a world of deals begins to be transformed into a world of rights.[27]

In this dual critique of traditional legal thought, CLS raised a hornet's nest of opposition, particularly in the law schools. Leaving aside the most serious shortcoming of CLS thought (the absence of any satisfactory set of alternatives), the attack on the integrity of Legal Formalism was itself sufficient to evoke widespread condemnation. In one critique, the Crits were advised to "love it or leave it," so to speak. Dean Paul D. Carrington of Duke Law School, in a widely cited Mark Twain allegorical essay, "Of Law and the River," reasoned that

> What it [the profession of law teaching] cannot abide is the embrace of nihilism and its lesson that who decides is everything, and principle nothing but cosmetic. . . . The nihilist teacher threatens to rob his or her students of the courage to act on such professional judgment as they may have acquired. . . . Nihilist teachers are more likely to train crooks

---

Newsletter, Law, Courts and Judicial Process Section, American Political Science Association 3 (Summer 1986): 1–9; and Austin Sarat, "Critical Legal Studies Outside the Law School," *Focus on Law Studies,* American Bar Association, IV (Spring 1989): 1, 10–11.

[24]Hutchinson and Monahan, "Law, Politics, and the Critical Legal Scholars": 206.

[25]See Jack W. Peltason, *Federal Courts in the Political Process* (New York: Random House, 1955).

[26]"'Round and 'Round the Bramble Bush," 1669. See also Smith, "All Critters Great and Small," where he asserts that "Public Law scholars in political science frequently protest that little of this [CLS thought] is original, all of . . . [their arguments being] more or less anticipated by . . . the legal realists" (p. 2).

[27]Hutchinson and Monahan, "Law, Politics, and the Critical Legal Scholars": 210. For an elaboration of the CLS attack on liberalism in Realism, see Mark Tushnet, "Legal Scholarship: Its Causes and Cure," *Yale Law Journal* 90, No. 5 (Apr. 1981): 1205–23. This issue of the *Yale Law Journal* contains a symposium on contemporary legal scholarship.

than radicals. If this risk is correctly appraised, the nihilist who must profess that legal principle does not matter has an ethical duty to depart the law school, perhaps to seek a place elsewhere in the academy.[28]

And in another face-off between Crits and their critics, Richard Posner of the University of Chicago School of Law wrote that

> Some of these [CLS] scholars belong to . . . the "anti-law" or "anti-society" bloc in law school faculties. The "anti-law" people do not want to train practicing lawyers, at least not practicing business lawyers. They do not like practicing lawyers. They do not like the traditional modes of legal analysis and training. They do not respect their conventional colleagues. . . . The "anti-law" people do not speak or comport themselves like lawyers. They are, in short, unassimilable and irritating foreign substances in the body of the law school.[29]

Not surprisingly, Professor Fiss weighed in with his own critique of Critical Legal Studies in an essay appropriately entitled "The Death of Law." Decrying the rejection by CLS of the notion of law as generative of public values (morals), Fiss sees the movement as entirely negative: "This will mean the death of law," he writes, "as we have known it throughout history, and as we have come to admire it."[30]

Such acrimony in academic debate is not new; it reminds the political scientist of similar exchanges in the 1960s over the issue of behavioralism in that discipline. The response of the legal educational establishment is understandable, because taken seriously, the CLS critique leaves traditional modes of legal analysis no place to hide. As one of the more vocal members of CLS, Mark Tushnet has argued, "Current legal scholars may be . . . aware that legal rules have no objective content. They cannot bring this personal insight into their scholarly work, however, because their acceptance of fundamental principles of liberal political theory requires them to proceed as if legal rules do have objective content."[31] This helps to explain another large body of Post-Realist thought, that which has been dedicated to the task of locating and defending some middle ground between legal formalism of old and the "law is politics" datum.

Value-Enunciating Positions: The Search for a Touchstone of Constitutional Interpretation

Much of this middle ground has been claimed by a rather large group of scholars who continue to search for a "constant" or a bedrock departure point for the study of law. In place of *Stare Decisis* and the now discredited traditional Austinian model of judicial decision making, this group maintains that it is possible to locate and defend alternative means of developing a rational, predictable datum for law, usually found either in inherent constitu-

---

[28]Paul D. Carrington, "Of Law and the River," *Journal of Legal Education* 34, No. 2 (June 1984): 227. Not surprisingly, the Carrington comments evoked a number of responses. See also his "Of Nihilism and Academic Freedom" in *Journal of Legal Education* 35, No. 1 (Mar. 1985): 1–26. One respondent (Paul Brest) remarked that "I thought that the sort of Red-baiting Carrington is engaging in had disappeared once and for all in the 1950s" (17).

[29]Richard A. Posner, "The Present Situation in Legal Scholarship," *Yale Law Journal* 90, No. 5 (Apr. 1981): 1128.

[30]Owen M. Fiss, "The Death of Law," *Cornell Law Quarterly* 72, No. 4 (Nov. 1986): 16.

[31]Tushnet, "Legal Scholarship": 1206.

tional values or in societal norms.[32] This value-enunciating school, housing an impressive array of writers, is well illustrated in our previous discussion of Wechsler's "neutral principles" and Fiss's insistence on the presence and relevance of public or constitutional values. Others who in varying degrees take this position include Guido Calabresi[33] and Harry Wellington,[34] who maintain that although American society is pluralistic, there are certain underlying values attendant to our history and that it is the task of the judge to use these as a basis of decision making.

Another version of the value-enunciating school points to the presence of certain constitutional values (such as equality) that exist independent of societal agreement and maintains that such values can become standards by which we may critique contemporary judicial decision making. In different ways, Ronald Dworkin,[35] Lawrence Tribe,[36] and Kenneth Karst[37] are of this persuasion.

John Ely[38] has taken a more procedural perspective, arguing that constitutional law must be based on a "participation-oriented, representation-reinforcing" standard.[39] Using this benchmark, Ely argues, courts should measure legislation as to whether it restricts a political process that promises to repeal undesirable policies or conversely, a process that is prejudiced against discrete minorities. Of course such procedural standards actually rest on substantive values, here the value of participation within the specified representative arrangement as well as the value of a prejudice-free polity.[40]

A more widely publicized view of constitutional interpretation that is also part of the eternal search for a "constant" in adjudication is the Bork-Meese argument for a jurisprudence of original intent. Here, the key assertion is that the only legitimate path to interpreting the constitution is marked by the original intent of the framers, upon which current de-

---

[32]Useful readings on the "jurisprudence of values" include Martin Shapiro "Fathers and Sons: The Court, the Commentators, and the Search for Values," in Vincent Blasi, ed., *The Burger Court: The Constitutional Revolution That Wasn't* (New Haven: Yale University Press, 1983), 218–38; Hutchinson and Monahan, "Law, Politics and Critical Legal Scholars": 207–08; and Mensch, "The History of Mainstream Legal Thought": 31–33. See also Martin Shapiro's "Recent Developments in Political Jurisprudence," *Western Political Quarterly* 36, No. 4 (Dec. 1983): 541–48.

[33]Guido Calabresi, *A Common Law for the Age of Statutes* (Cambridge, Mass.: Harvard University Press, 1982).

[34]Harry H. Wellington, "Common Law Rules and Constitutional Double Standards: Some Notes on Adjudication," *Yale Law Journal* 83, No. 2 (Dec. 1973): 221–311.

[35]Ronald Dworkin, *Taking Rights Seriously* (Cambridge, Mass.: Harvard University Press, 1977).

[36]Lawrence Tribe, *American Constitutional Law* (Mineola, N.Y.: Foundation Press, 1978). But see a biting critique of this work by Mark Tushnet, "Dia-Tribe," *Michigan Law Review* 78, No. 5 (Mar. 1980): 694–710.

[37]Kenneth Karst, "Forward: Equal Citizenship Under the Fourteenth Amendment," *Harvard Law Review* 91, No. 1 (Nov. 1977): 1–68. The grandfather, if not great-grandfather of the value-enunciating school is often said to be John Rawls; see his *A Theory of Justice* (Cambridge, Mass.: Harvard University Press, 1971). In "Fathers and Sons," Shapiro lists the following additional scholars as among the new generation representing the value-enunciating school: Vincent Blasi, Paul Brest, Jessie Choper, John Ely, Thomas Grey, Frank Michelman, Henry Monaghan, and William Van Alystyne.

[38]John Ely, *Democracy and Distrust: A Theory of Judicial Review* (Cambridge: Harvard University Press, 1980).

[39]See Mensch, "A History of Mainstream Legal Thought": 32. Mensch asserts that the "paradigmatic" standard of the value-enunciating school was Frank Michelman's "Forward: On Protecting the Poor through the Fourteenth Amendment," *Harvard Law Review* 83, No. 1 (Nov. 1969): 7–59. This suggests that the motivation of this movement is a resurrection of liberalism, with its faith in the rule of law, in the face of the Realist and Post-Realist attack.

[40]Mensch: 32.

cisions can and must be founded.[41] Two questions usually occur in response to this argument: (1) Is it possible to determine the intent of the Constitution's framers and ratifiers, and (2) is it desirable—even if possible—to base current decision making on that foundation? Most observers—certainly most of those subscribing to a political view of law—would answer both questions in the negative. Former Supreme Court Justice William Brennan,[42] along with a number of other commentators,[43] have roundly criticized the original intentionalists as being out of touch with reality.

Law and Economics (L/E)

Another way of escaping the abjectness of the Political Jurisprudence–Critical Legal Studies position is through the Law and Economics movement. Often labeled as the rightist or conservative alternative to CLS, and equally controversial, this school points to yet another underlying constant in the law—one that judges and legislatures should and do use as a point of departure in lawmaking—namely, utilitarianism. In place of moral-societal-constitutional values, one may posit the standard of allocative *efficiency* as the touchstone not only to explain the growth and development of law but also to serve as a neutral benchmark by which we may judge judging.[44]

The Law and Economics position is most closely identified with the work of Judge Richard A. Posner, Milton Friedman, and the Chicago School,[45] although a number of off-

---

[41]See the speech of Attorney-General Edwin Meese, III, before the American Bar Association, July 9, 1985, Washington, D.C., in *The Great Debate: Interpreting the Written Constitution* (Washington: The Federalist Society), 1–10. The writings of Robert Bork have appeared in a variety of places. See his "Neutral Principles and Some First Amendment Problems," *Indiana Law Journal* 47, No. 1 (Fall 1971): 1–35; *Tradition and Morality in Constitutional Law* (Washington, D.C.: American Enterprise Institute, 1984); and Speech of Robert H. Bork at the University of San Diego School of Law, Nov. 18, 1985, in *The Great Debate,* 43–52. This debate is sometimes couched in terms of "Interpretivism" vs. "Noninterpretisism." See, e.g., Traciel V. Reid, "Interpretism and the Burger Court: A Closer Examination," paper presented at the American Political Science Association Meeting, Chicago, Sept. 3–6, 1987.
Some have argued that a better representative of "originalism" is Justice Antonin Scalia. See his "Originalism: The Lesser Evil," *University of Cincinnati Law Review* 57, No. 3 (1989): 849–65. More broadly, see Jack N. Rakove, *Original Meanings: Politics and Ideas in the Making of the Constitution* (New York: Knopf, 1996). That "originalism" died with the New Deal Court–President crisis of 1936 is persuasively argued by Howard Gillman in "State Building and the Collapse of Constitutional Originalism," paper presented at the Annual Meeting of the American Political Science Association, San Francisco, Aug. 29–Sept. 1, 1996.
[42]See the speech by Justice William J. Brennan, Jr., at Georgetown University, Oct. 12, 1985, in *The Great Debate,* 11–25.
[43]See, e.g., Judith A. Baer, "The Fruitless Search for Original Intent," in Michael W. McCann and Gerald L. Houseman, *Judging the Constitution: Critical Essays on Judicial Lawmaking* (Glenview, Ill.: Scott, Foresman, 1989), 49–71. Two books that take opposing views on original intent are Walter Berns, *Taking the Constitution Seriously* (New York: Simon and Schuster, 1987); and Leonard W. Levy, *Original Intent and The Framers' Constitution* (New York: MacMillan, 1988).
That "originalism" or "intentionalism" is more talk than action is suggested in a recent research report by John Gates and Glenn Phelps. These scholars empirically examine the use of intentionalism in Supreme Court decision making and find that the doctrine is essentially a cover-up for justices' ideology; at least this is the case for Justices Rehnquist and Brennan. See "Intentionalism in Constitutional Opinions," *Political Research Quarterly* 49, No. 2 (June 1996): 245–61.
[44]Hutchinson and Monahan, "Law, Politics, and the Critical Legal Scholars": 208. As with most jurisprudential movements, the Law and Economics position is represented by a broad and diverse set of writings. For a brief overview see Gary Minda, "The Jurisprudential Movements of the 1980's," *Ohio State Law Journal* 50, No. 3 (1989), especially 604–14 and the sources cited therein. See also Robert Cooter and Thomas Ulen, *Law and Economics* (New York: Harper Collins, 1988).
[45]See Richard A. Posner, *Economic Analysis of Law,* 2nd ed. (Boston: Little, Brown, 1977); and his *The Economics of Justice* (Cambridge: Harvard University Press, 1981).

shoots have now developed that render this general stance increasingly diverse and diffi-cult to characterize.[46] Lewis Kornhauser has set forth four claims that to a greater or lesser extent encompass the core thought of the movement: (1) the claim that economic theory is a useful way to predict how people behave under law; (2) the normative claim that "law ought to be efficient"; (3) the factual assertion that under the common law system, law is in fact efficient; and (4) the so-called "genetic claim," that the common law, left to its own natural development, *will* generally settle on rules of law that maximize the value of effi-ciency.[47] Some observers, however, argue that in the throes of constant revision, the only point on which all, or most, Law and Economic scholars agree is that *law is rational* and thus subject to analysis by basic concepts of economics.[48]

In its contemporary dress, some of the work of Law and Economics shares common ground with the public choice approach in political science.[49] Thus, in an interesting work, Susan Rose-Akerman attempts to develop a new economic approach to the study of administrative law based in part on social choice theory.[50]

The extreme positions taken by early members of this general movement, combined with its close association with conservative politics, have invited a good deal of criti-cism—criticism similar to that met by the early utilitarianism of the Benthamites. Over-simplification, the failure to account for nonrational but nonetheless strongly held soci-etal beliefs, and an alleged lack of understanding of economics—these are frequent points made. Fiss, for example, has argued that the L/E position flies in the face of real-ity: judges do not, in fact, see their role as promoting efficiency in a raw economic sense. Rather, their decisions embody the values that they find in the law.[51] CLS writers, of course, find little to their liking in the L/E position. If law is indeterminate, it is certainly not amenable to analysis through the rationality of economics. Such an approach serves only to mask further the hierarchy and rank *injustices of law* as it reflects corporate capi-talism.[52]

---

[46]See Minda, "The Jurisprudential Movements": 605–606.

[47]Lewis A. Kornhauser, "The Great Image of Authority," *Stanford Law Review* 36, Nos. 1 & 2 (Jan. 1984): 349, 353–55.

[48]See Kornhauser, "The Great Image": 610–11.

[49]See, e.g., "Symposium on the Theory of Public Choice," *Virginia Law Review,* 74, No. 2 (Mar. 1988): 167–518.

[50]Susan Rose-Akerman, "Progressive Law and Economics—and the New Administrative Law," *Yale Law Journal* 98, No. 2 (Dec. 1988): 341–68. Shapiro has argued that, leaving aside its methodology, the public choice stance involves asking extremely relevant questions about law and politics—questions not being asked by those caught up in the ". . . esoterica of constitutional law." See Martin Shapiro, "From the Sec-tion Chair," *Newsletter,* Law and Courts Section, American Political Science Association 5, No. 1 (Spring 1995): 1. Shapiro further believes that the law and economics-public choice movement has now evolved into something like the familiar pluralist theory of democratic policy-making. As applied to legislation, outputs are and should be the product of group bargains. As for judges, one group within this camp holds that judges act properly when they honor group bargains struck by the legislature, while a second group urges courts to correct legislation where it did not provide adequate access to all groups. See Martin Shapiro, "Courts of Law, Courts of Politics," in Austin Ranney, ed., *Courts and the Political Process: Jack W. Peltason's Contributions to Political Science* (Berkeley: Institute of Governmental Studies Press, 1996): 103–104.

A general perusal of the journal *International Review of Law and Economics* will help keep the reader abreast of many of the developments in this field. Political scientists may be particularly interested in the Symposium on Constitutional Law and Economics 12, No. 2 (June 1992).

[51]Fiss, "The Death of Law": 8.

[52]Much of Kornhauser's piece, "The Great Image," is a critique of Law and Economics. See also Mark G. Kelman, "Misunderstanding Social Life: A Critique of Core Premises of Law and Economics," *Journal of Legal Education* 33, No. 1 (Mar. 1983): 274–87.

Feminist Jurisprudence

Law and Economics and Critical Legal Studies are often discussed in conjunction with the emergence of Feminist Jurisprudence, that branch of general feminist theory that addresses the "maleness," or paternalistic coloration, of law, legal institutions, and legal processes.[53] Feminist Jurisprudence, as with all other approaches discussed, is difficult to describe accurately, largely because of the diversity and disputatiousness of the movement.[54] There probably is no universally agreed-upon set of propositions that can be set forth to describe Feminist Jurisprudence. Generally, however,

> Feminist jurisprudence attempts to tell the woman's story of law—what it *feels* like to be a woman living in a legal and social world that is defined and manipulated by male attitudes and *experiences.* The goal is to show how the prevailing conceptions of the rule of law fail to respect the experiences and harms of women by objectifying women under allegedly *gender-neutral norms.*[55]

Certain terms are italicized in the preceding passage to suggest some of the main themes of contemporary feminist writings on law. One of these is the "deconstructionist" aspect of the movement, whereby liberal, traditionalist scholarship, thought, and practice is assailed as appearing to be neutral but is actually heavily male-dominated. In this respect the movement has borrowed from the methodology as well as some of the substantive arguments of Critical Legal Studies. Indeed, some feminist writers on law call themselves "Fem-Crits," denoting their general orientation to CLS but rejecting the "male-constructedness" of that movement.[56]

Another feminist theme is "consciousness-raising" wherein "stories" become a way for women to share the actual *experience* of discrimination in a male-oriented world. To the extent that experiential-based ways of knowing contradict the epistemological assumptions of modern social science, Feminist Jurisprudence sometimes takes on the hue of Post-Modernism, as does some of the Critical Legal Studies work.[57]

Feminist Jurisprudence is unwilling to take any major aspect of a legal system as gender-neutral. From scholarship to modes of legal training, practice arrangements, and of course, the substance as well as the *language* of the law—all is seen as dominated by the "assumed-neutral" patriarchy, defined as "that ubiquitous phenomenon of male domination and hierarchy . . . that men have the bulk of the power and have used that power to subordinate women, . . ."[58]

---

[53]In "Jurisprudential Movements" Gary Minda does a reasonably thorough job of comparing and contrasting the three movements.

[54]Leslie Bender writes that Feminism itself ". . . is not a monolothic concept but an ongoing conversation about women's subordination—a conversation that is enriched by each contributing voice and strengthened by its internal debates." See Leslie Bender, "A Lawyer's Primer on Feminist Theory and Tort," *Journal of Legal Education* 38, Nos. 1 & 2 (Mar./June 1988): 5, note 5.

[55]This useful summarization is by Minda, "Jurisprudential Movements": 630.

[56]In general, see Carrie Menkel-Meadow, "Feminist Legal Theory, Critical Legal Studies, and Legal Education, or The Fem-Crits Go to Law School," *Journal of Legal Education* 38, Nos. 1 & 2 (Mar./June, 1988): 61–85; and Tushnet, "Critical Legal Studies: A Political History": 1517.

[57]On Post-Modernism generally, see Pauline Marie Rosenau, *Post-Modernism and the Social Sciences: Insights, Inroads, and Intrusions* (Princeton: Princeton University Press, 1992), especially 86, 115. See also Patricia A. Cain, "Feminism and the Limits of Equality," *Georgia Law Review* 24, No. 4 (Summer 1990): 803–47. The Cain piece is part of a very useful Symposium on Feminist Jurisprudence. Cain divides approaches to the concept of equality into four categories, one of which is the Post-Modern position. See also Dennis Paterson, "Postmodernism/Feminism/Law," *Cornell Law Review* 77, No. 2 (Jan. 1992): 254–317.

[58]Bender, "A Lawyer's Primer:" 6. Regarding the thesis that American law is a source of and perpetuates patriarchy, see Kevin C. Paul, "Private/Property: A Discourse on Gender Equality in American Law," *Law*

Feminist critiques have taken varying approaches to the problem of the law's inequality. One strand of thought, often labeled the "equal treatment" approach, insists on the factual equality of men and women and calls for equal treatment in the workplace and elsewhere.[59] Another view, labeled "difference jurisprudence," sees significant gender differences and argues for recognition of those differences within the law.[60] And yet a third and more radical view, often labeled *dominance* theory, maintains that gender inequality in the law is not merely casual discrimination but is grounded in the systemic social deprivation of women. Thus, sexuality itself is so structured in society as to create a *gender hierarchy*. Gender is really a question of power, and to accede to the status quo in these matters, say in the law and social customs of heterosexual relations (or pornography), is for women to partake in their own diminution. Thus, Catherine MacKinnon suggests that

> It may be worth considering that heterosexuality, the predominant social arrangement that fuses this sexuality of abuse and objectification with gender in intercourse . . . organizes women's pleasure so as to give us a stake in our own subordination.[61]

To be "anti-sex," then, may be "to refuse to affirm loyalty to this political system of inequality whose dynamic is male control and use and access to women. . . ."[62]

For MacKinnon, the "dominance" approach in feminist legal thought

> centers on the most sex-differential abuses of women as a gender, abuses that sex equality law in its difference garb could not confront. It is based on a reality about which little of a systematic nature was known before 1970, a reality that calls for a new conception of the problem of sex inequality. This new information includes not only the extent and intractability of sex segregation into poverty . . . but the range of issues termed violence against women. . . .[63]

Because of the diversity of its adherents as well as of its call for a fundamental reordering of the American legal and social system, Feminist Jurisprudence has been called "the most powerful" of the contemporary jurisprudential movements.[64] Whether it succeeds in its goal of a complete rethinking and restructuring of American law, only time will tell.

---

and Inequality: A Journal of Theory and Practice," 7, No. 3 (1989): 399–439. See also Christine A. Littleton, "Reconstructing Sexual Equality," *California Law Review,* 75, No. 4 (July, 1987): 1279–80.

[59]These various "strands" of feminist thought, as he calls them, are discussed in Minda, "Jurisprudential Movements," 626–29. For a somewhat different view of the diversity of Feminist Jurisprudence, see Cain, "Feminism and the Limits of Equality," 829 ff., where the movement is divided into Liberal, Cultural, Radical, and Post-Modern Feminism.

[60]See Judith A. Baer, "Nasty Law or Nice Ladies? Jurisprudence, Feminism, and Gender Difference," *Women and Politics* 11, No. 1 (1991): 10–31, where "difference" jurisprudence is critiqued. One approach to the "difference" view is that of Carol Gilligan, *In a Different Voice* (Cambridge: Harvard University Press, 1982). For other ways of conceptualizing "difference," see Martha Minnow, "Justice Engendered," *Harvard Law Review* 101, No. 1 (Nov. 1987): 10–95; and Robin West, "Jurisprudence and Gender," *University of Chicago Law Review* 55, No. 1 (Winter 1988): 1–72.

[61]Catherine A. MacKinnon, *Feminism Unmodified: Discourses on Life and Law* (Cambridge: Harvard University Press, 1987): 7. MacKinnon carries this argument further in *Only Words* (Cambridge: Harvard University Press, 1993).

[62]MacKinnon, *Feminism Unmodified,* 7–8. See also MacKinnon's *Toward a Feminist Theory of the State* (Cambridge: Harvard University Press, 1989), especially Ch. 13.

[63]MacKinnon, *Feminism Unmodified,* 40–41. Another writer often associated with the radical perspective (which MacKinnon regards as the only feminism) is Christine Littleton. See her "Reconstructing Sexual Equality."

[64]Minda, "Jurisprudential Movements": 623. For empirical evidence on gender discrimination in the legal profession, see American Bar Association, Commission on Women in the Profession, *Unfinished Business: Overcoming on Sisyphus Factor* (Chicago: ABA, 1995).

Critical Race Theory

A jurisprudential movement closely allied with both Critical Legal Studies and Feminist Jurisprudence is the now much-discussed Critical Race Theory.[65] Launched in the mid-1970s, the movement is based on the early writings of Guido Calabresi,[66] but to an even greater extent on the work of Derrick A. Bell, Jr.[67] Like feminist theorists, critical race scholars rely heavily on the methodology of the personal narrative to make their point, the best example being *The Rodrigo Chronicles,* by Richard Delgado of the University of Colorado School of Law, which first appeared as a series of law journal articles but now is in book form.[68] Other themes important to critical race thought are set out in a useful annotated bibliography by Prof. Delgado. These themes include a critique of liberalism not unlike that of Critical Legal Studies; a revisionist (actually, deconstructionist) interpretation of American civil rights law and history; attention to the racial minority issue in law school instruction; a willingness to explore sex, class, and other intersections with the critical racial movement; a form of structural determinism similar to the constitutive view, discussed later; and a strain of separatism, in which scholars argue the advantages of preserving diversity and separateness of the races.[69] As with other jurisprudential viewpoints discussed herein, Critical Race Theory is largely law-school based, though causing less disturbance in the traditional legal academy than was the case with Critical Legal Theory. Still, there are dissenters, the epistemology of "storytelling" being one of the more controversial aspects of Critical Race Theory, as well as Feminist Jurisprudence.[70]

The Law and Language Movement

Finally, what has come to be called the "Law and Language" movement may also be seen as an attempt to escape the logical conclusions of the sociological-Realist critique. Through a careful study and development of legal language, law may be rendered more exact and a more compelling force in society. Of course, those who learn to speak the newly refined language will be "experts" in the law, which turns the study of law inward, rendering it once again "special" and quite separate from political discourse.[71] In critiquing Christo-

---

[65]A brief overview of the scholars and ideas of this movement is by Anna Snider, "New Trend Hits Legal Education," *Los Angeles Daily Journal* (Aug. 7, 1996): 1. Some scholars associated with this orientation, all professors of law, are Richard T. Ford (Stanford), Richard Delgado (Colorado), Patricia Williams (Columbia), Robert S. Chang (California Western), and of course Derrick Bell, sometimes seen as the founder of the movement, who is Professor of Law at New York University.

[66]See Guido Calabresi and A. Douglas Melamed, "Property Rules, Liability Rules, and Inalienability: One View of the Cathedral," *Harvard Law Review* 85, No. 6 (Apr. 1972): 1089–1128.

[67]See especially Bell's early work, such as "Forward: The Civil Rights Chronicles," *Harvard Law Review* 99, No. 1 (Nov. 1985): 4–83. See also his *Confronting Authority: Reflections of an Ardent Protester* (Boston: Beacon Press, 1994).

[68]Richard Delgado, *The Rodrigo Chronicles: Conversations About America and Race* (New York: New York University Press, 1995). Another of his works, also a series of his previously published articles, is coauthored with Jean Stefancic, *Failed Revolutions: Social Reform and the Limits of Legal Imagination* (Boulder, Col.: Westview Press, 1994).

[69]See Richard Delgado and Jean Stefancic, "Critical Race Theory: An Annotated Bibliography," *Virginia Law Review* 79, No. 2 (Mar. 1993): 461–516.

[70]See the critique by Arthur Austin, "Evaluating Story Telling as a Type of Nontraditional Scholarship," *Nebraska Law Review* 74, No. 3 (1995): 479–528.

[71]On the Law and Language movement, see Christopher D. Stone, "From a Language Perspective," *Yale Law Journal* 90, No. 5 (Apr. 1981): 1149–92. See also John Brigham, *Constitutional Language: An Interpretation of Judicial Decisions* (Westport, Conn.: Greenwood Press, 1978).

pher Stone's argument for a language perspective in the study of law, political scientist Martin Shapiro argues that

> Law as language is aimed principally at reasserting the autonomy of law—at returning law to lawyers by claiming that law is a specialized language that only lawyers can speak. It is indicative that Stone turns to musical notations and mathematics, esoteric languages that allow their masters to claim that others cannot understand, let alone contribute to, their disciplines. . . . Is this more than a prologue to yet another round in the endless search for the holy grail of neutral principles or reasoned elaboration or the law working itself clear?[72]

POST-REALISM AND POLITICAL SCIENCE

Most of these jurisprudential themes, now common to the dialogue heard in America's law schools, are now spilling over into political science. Some writers, straddling the two disciplines, have become translators of these intellectual currents in the law schools, deciphering and critiquing this vast literature for their political science colleagues.[73] Others on the social science side with normative theoretical inclinations have recently entered the fray, sometimes acting as critics, at other times setting forth their own agenda, and sometimes doing both.[74]

The resurgence of a "jurisprudence of values" among legal scholars finds enthusiastic adherents among a number of political scientists, for many of them, like their counterparts in the law schools, never abandoned the barricades of Formalism. With little taste for, and even less training in, modern empirical social science methodology, ensconced in the comfortable pedagogy of the case method, and still attracted to the appealing idea of a neutral or objective rule of law—of law and courts as serving "justice"—a few such scholars have engaged in public displays of impatience with contemporary politico-Realist jurisprudence. One of these is David O'Brien, who has rather vociferously lambasted Realism and its reliance on social science evidence in judicial decision making. In his denunciation of the use of social science in courts, O'Brien sets forth a defense of "principled" judicial decision making which reads much like Owen Fiss and sounds more like the debate of the 1960s than it does the discourse of the mid-1980s.[75] Peter Sperlich was led to reply in an article whose title rather accurately suggests its content: "Post-Realism: Should Ignorance Be Elevated to a Principle of Adjudication?"[76]

Despite Sperlich, O'Brien and many other scholars of his persuasion may hold the future, for there does appear to be something of a counterrevolution under way in the subfield, with an increasing amount of normative work in progress. Thus, Martin Shapiro has argued that

---

[72]Martin Shapiro, "On the Regrettable Decline of French Law: Or Shapiro Jettet le Brickbat," *Yale Law Journal* 90, No. 5 (Apr. 1981): 1200. Depending on how the work is interpreted, Lief Carter's *Contemporary Constitutional Lawmaking* (New York: Pergamon Press, 1985) may be seen as a variant of the "Law and Language" school of thought. If Shapiro is right—that there is some significance in Stone's use of musical metaphors—perhaps it is also worth noting that Carter has expressed interest in studying the interaction between politics and music.

[73]The best example is probably Martin Shapiro of the University of California, Berkeley (Boalt Hall) School of Law. See his work cited throughout this chapter.

[74]The work of John Brigham and Lief Carter, for example cited in fns. 71 and 72, above, are certainly contributions to the Post-Realist Debate.

[75]See David M. O'Brien, "The Seduction of the Judiciary: Social Science in the Courts," *Judicature*, 64, No. 1 (June–July 1980): 8–21. The O'Brien argument is directly counter to that of CLS.

[76]See Sperlich, "Post-Realism."

For better or worse, the kind of old-fashioned con law presented by the work of David O'Brien ... is, thanks to the new emergence of the jurisprudence of values, no longer old-fashioned. ... The danger is, of course, that much of the work will contain no distinctive political analysis—that the new jurisprudence of values will serve as a cover for slipping back into playing "little law professor" for undergraduates, writing traditional case law doctrinal analysis of the same sort that the less-bright academic lawyers do and engaging in seat-of-the-pants social judgment.[77]

The New Institutionalism

Other political scientists, speaking more from the subfield of political philosophy than "Public Law," has suggested that political jurisprudence can escape these needless feuds by taking a page from the "New Institutionalism," first set forth by March and Olsen in 1984.[78] Rogers Smith argues that conventional (that is, post-1950s) political science has analyzed politics chiefly in terms of the pluralistic interplay of individuals and groups engaging in rational calculations of self-interest.[79] This basic model of politics assumed that these various players, including government officials, acted on the basis of established policy preferences, somewhat independent of the pull of existing institutions and structures, including not only formal governmental structures but also the forces (structures) of economic, social, and legal change. Thus, in moving away from the old institutionalism of traditional political science, the "behavioral revolution" in the discipline has all but overlooked the importance of institutions and structures in shaping preferences and ultimate outcomes in the political process.

The "New Institutionalism" would reintroduce variables emanating from structural and institutional norms as potentially important if not determinative in the overall political equation. Thus, writes Smith,

... [A] full account of an important political event would consider both the ways the context of "background" institutions influenced the political actions in question, and the ways in which those actions altered relevant contextual structures or institutions.[80]

In this way, Smith hopes to bring together the normative and the empirical wing of public law. This could be done, he says, if both would focus on what Theda Skocpol called "the dialectic of meaningful actions and structural determinants."[81]

---

[77]Shapiro, "Recent Developments in Political Jurisprudence": 543. Shapiro specifically referenced O'Brien's two works: *Privacy, Law and Public Policy* (New York: Praeger, 1979); and *The Public's Right to Know: The Supreme Court and the First Amendment* (New York: Praeger, 1981). Probably the clearest statement reflecting a normative jurisprudence in political science is Carter's *Contemporary Constitutional Lawmaking*. And an equally clear example of the continuation of "old-fashioned" constitutional law may be found in the several editions of Alpheus T. Mason and Donald Grier Stephenson, Jr.'s, *American Constitutional Law* (Englewood Cliffs, N.J.: Prentice Hall).

[78]James G. March and Johan P. Olsen, "The New Institutionalism: Organizational Factors in Political Life," *American Political Science Review* 78, No. 3 (Sept. 1984): 734–49.

[79]The argument is admittedly a bit more complex and extended than this. See Rogers M. Smith, "Political Jurisprudence, the 'New Institutionalism,' and the Future of Public Law," *American Political Science Review* 82, No. 1 (Mar. 1988): 89–108. See also a recent return to the "New Institutionalism" debate: Howard Gillman, "The New Institutionalism, Part I: More or Less Than Strategy: Some Advantages to Interpretive Institutionalism in the Analysis of Judicial Politics," *Law and Courts: Newsletter of the Law and Courts Section of the American Political Science Association*, 7, No. 1 (Winter, 1996–97): 6–11.

[80]Smith, "Political Jurisprudence": 91.

[81]Smith, "Political Jurisprudence": 90.

Is the "New Institutionalism" really new? Some have suggested that it is not, pointing to a number of studies of the judiciary which clearly take into account the institutional factor(s). Shapiro notes that the message to Public Law political scientists might be written as follows: "Process analysis ought to be given a place of equal honor with behavioral analysis in the study of law and judges."[82] That the notion of process is central to political jurisprudence has been noted earlier. Smith's program might better fit the behavioral wing of the subfield, but there too, there are problems.

John B. Gates, for example, has cautioned that Smith's approach might well take us away from the behavioral pluralistic perspective from which we have learned so much. Also, when one explores the "deep structures" influencing politico-judicial outcomes, one is almost calling for lengthy, descriptive studies reminiscent of old, traditional political science. Explanation—the generation of testable hypotheses—must be the core aim of the subfield.[83]

Underlying these debates is clearly a concern for accommodation—the bridging of empirical and normative scholarship. For Shapiro, who, I suspect, speaks for a good many other political scientists, values—that is, ethics—are best left to the field of moral philosophy, whereas public law–political jurisprudential scholarship and teaching have a full agenda of their own in the continuing and ever-expanding study of judicial politics in its multifarious dimensions.[84]

The Princeton School

A well-established movement within public law whose practitioners feel quite at home with normative concerns is the so-called Constitutionalist, or "Princeton School" (also variously labeled constitutional theory or constitutional studies).[85] As with other "schools" or movements discussed herein, membership is loose and extends far beyond its seedbed,

---

[82]Martin Shapiro, "Political Jurisprudence, Public Law, and Post-Consequentialist Ethics: Comment on Professor Barber and Smith," *Studies in Political Development,* 3 (New Haven: Yale University Press, 1989), 89. For a somewhat different view, see Susan R. Burgess, "What's New About the 'New Institutionalism'? Legal Rhetoric and Judicial Supremacy," paper delivered at the American Political Science Association meeting, Washington, D.C., 1991.

[83]John B. Gates, "Theory, Methods, and the New Institutionalism in Judicial Research," in John B. Gates and Charles A. Johnson, eds., *The American Courts: A Critical Assessment* (Washington: Congressional Quarterly Press, 1991): 479–81. The Gates essay is a very useful overview and assessment of research, methodology, and theory in the subfield.

[84]Shapiro, "Political Jurisprudence": 96–102. For the view that the "New Institutionalism" leaves little room for normative concerns, see Sotirios A. Barber, "Normative Theory, the New Institutionalism, and the Future of Public Law," in *Studies in American Political Development* 3 (New Haven: Yale University Press, 1989), 56–73.

In the Barber-Smith-Shapiro debate, the Barber position might be seen by some readers as the most appealing alternative. His approach, which he terms "constitutionalist," eschews the need for unity in the subfield, speaks strongly of the importance of saving normative theory in the study of law and courts, and posits *The Federalist* and Aristotle's *Politics* as models. See Barber's essay, "Normative Theory," especially 71–73, for an elaboration of this position.

[85]See, for example: Sotirios A. Barber, *On What the Constitution Means* (Baltimore: Johns Hopkins University Press, 1984); Barber, *The Constitution of Judicial Power* (Baltimore: Johns Hopkins University Press, 1993); Mark E. Brandon, *Free in the World: American Slavery and Constitutional Failure* (Princeton: Princeton University Press, 1997); John E. Finn, *Constitutions in Crisis: Political Violence and the Rule of Law* (New York: Oxford University Press, 1991); Robert P. George, *Making Men Moral: Civil Liberties and Public Morality* (Oxford: The Clarendon Press, 1993); William F. Harris II, *The Interpretable Constitution* (Baltimore: Johns Hopkins University Press, 1993); Stephen Macedo, *Liberal Virtues: Citizenship, Virtue, and Community in Liberal Constitutionalism* (New York: Oxford University Press, 1990); Macedo, *The New Right v. The Constitution* (Washington, D.C.: Cato Institute, 1987); Wayne D. Moore, *The Constitutional Rights and Powers of the People* (Princeton: Princeton University Press, 1996); and Jennifer Nedelsky, *Private Property and the Limits of American Constitutionalism* (Chicago: University of Chicago Press, 1991).

and ideas are diverse, with internal disagreements frequent. But rather than trying to detail this diversity, the discussion here relies heavily on the writings of Walter F. Murphy, who helped bring many of these theorists to Princeton.[86]

In the tradition of Woodrow Wilson, Edward S. Corwin, and Carl J. Friedrich, these "constitutionalists" have been concerned with jurisprudence not merely as orienting law, courts, and judges, but more broadly, as ordering norms and political institutions for an entire political system. Although their writings have tended to concentrate on the American polity, a great deal of comparative research and publication has also been part of this large and influential body of work.[87]

At least two distinctions are often made by this school. The first is that between democracy—the norms ordaining that the people should govern through freely chosen representatives—and constitutionalism—the norms decreeing that all government, even government by the people, must be limited so as to respect certain fundamental rights of citizens. These scholars contend that most nations of the Western world and Asia, which journalists call democracies, are more accurately described as constitutional democracies, with political systems that uneasily blend the sometimes conflicting principles of constitutionalism and democracy.

The second distinction, one that Murphy and his colleagues stress more than other theorists, is between a constitutional text—the formal document that proclaims itself to be fundamental law—and a larger constitution. The latter extends beyond the written words to include certain understandings, practices, and underlying political principles, which give meaning to those words. It is not the constitutional text alone that creates a constitutional democracy (or any other kind of political system), but rather that document as embedded in the broader constitution.

The first task that many of these constitutional scholars set is to determine exactly what principles, practices, and understandings are included in the term "the constitution." This search is important, theorists assert, because, when public officials and/or citizens engage in constitutional interpretation, they typically construe not merely the text but also the more comprehensive "constitution" as well.

[86]Among others are "Constitutions, Constitutionalism, and Democracy," in Douglas Greenberg, et al., eds., *Constitutionalism & Democracy* (New York: Oxford University Press, 1993), 1–25; "The Right to Privacy and Legitimate Constitutional Change," in Shlomo Slonim, ed., *The Constitutional Bases of Political and Social Change in the United States* (New York: Praeger, 1990), 213–35; "Civil Law, Common Law, and Constitutional Democracy," *Louisiana Law Review* 52, No. 1 (Sept. 1991): 91–136; "Staggering Toward the New Jurisprudence of Constitutional Theory," *American Journal of Jurisprudence* 37 (1992): 337–57; "Exclusing Political Parties," in Donald P. Kommers and Paul Kirchhof, eds., *Constitutionalism in the Federal Republic of Germany* (Baden-Baden: Nomos, 1993), 173–205. "Merlin's Memory," in Sanford Levinson, ed., *Responding to Imperfection* (Princeton: Princeton University Press, 1995), 163–190; and, with James E. Fleming and Sotirios A. Barber, *American Constitutional Interpretation,* 2nd ed. (Westbury, N.Y.: Foundation Press, 1995) (the first edition's authors/editors included William F. Harris II).

[87]For instance, Henry Abraham, *The Judicial Process* 6th ed. (New York: Oxford University Press, 1993); Lawrence W. Beer, ed., *Constitutional Systems in Late Twentieth Century Asia* (Seattle: University of Washington Press, 1992); Mauro Capelletti, *The Judicial Process in Comparative Perspective* (Oxford: The Clarendon Press, 1989); Martin Edelman, *Courts, Politics, and Culture in Israel* (Charlottesville: University of Virginia Press, 1994); Daniel J. Elazar and John Kinkaid, eds., *Covenant, Polity and Constitutionalism* (Lanham, Md.: University Press of America, 1980); Jon Elster and Rune Slagstad, eds., *Constitutionalism and Democracy* (New York: Cambridge University Press, 1988); Douglas Greenberg et al., *Constitutionalism and Democracy;* Finn, *Constitutions in Crises;* Gary J. Jacobsohn, *Apple of Gold: Constitutionalism in Israel and the United States* (Princeton: Princeton University Press, 1993); Donald P. Kommers, *The Constitutional Jurisprudence of the Federal Republic of Germany,* 2nd ed. (Durham: Duke University Press, 1996); Walter F. Murphy and Joseph Tanenhaus, *Comparative Constitutional Law* (New York: St. Martin's, 1977); Alec Stone, *The Birth of Judicial Politics in France* (New York: Oxford University Press, 1992); C. Neal Tate and T. Vallinder, eds., *The Global Expansion of Judicial Power* (New York: New York University Press, 1995).

A second task for many constitutional theorists concerns *who* authoritatively interprets the constitution. In most constitutional democracies, judges have a formal and important role in this process, but in no country do they have a monopoly. They share authority with legislators, executives, and perhaps the electorate as a whole. As do notions about the substantive content of a "constitution," proposed designations of the specific persons who share—and the precise ways in which they share—interpretive authority have enormous political consequences. Authority to interpret the "constitution" entails authority to define both the general principles and the more particular rules that undergird the political system. Thus those definitions frequently determine what political structures and public policies are legitimate.

Constitutional theorists often divide the study of political life into three analytic categories: creating a constitution, maintaining a constitution, and changing a constitution. It is important to understand that these categories refer to operations, not to discrete events occurring one after the other in neat sequence. Indeed, some scholars contend that the latter two categories sometimes collapse into the first. Although most constitutional theorists believe that interpretation is a pivotal part of constitutional maintenance, they divide over exactly how central it is to life under a constitution. To interpret a constitution, some, but not all, theorists reason, is often to change it; and occasionally those changes are of such magnitude as to create, piecemeal, a new constitution. This flow of functions from "maintenance through interpretation" to "change," and even "creation through interpretation," underlines the centrality to a political system of answers to questions such as *who* can authoritatively interpret a constitution and *what* it is those authoritative interpreters construe.

The Princeton School links the political science subfields of normative political theory and comparative politics with the study of law and courts (more accurately, constitutions), such that their work seems to some scholars somewhat far afield of the center of judicial politics as presently practiced. A comparison, say, of the three "how-to" appendices in Lee Epstein's reader, *Contemplating Courts,*[88] with the major lineaments of the Constitutionalist position, illustrates the point—and, incidentally, the wide variety of flowers now blooming in the public law subfield of political science.

The Constitutive View of Law

A final strand of Post-Realist Jurisprudence now receiving increasing attention in political science centers on the notion that law and the judicial function are neither politically instrumental, per se, nor matters of fundamental discoverable norms. Rather, this position, associated with the late "Amherst Seminar," sees law as a *constitutive* act or practice. That is, law is actually made as the legal process unfolds through what we say about it—what we (judges, lawyers, litigants, and even scholars) say or do about it in and out of courts. Hence, a statement from our ongoing legal discourse is always both descriptive and prescriptive. And when, and to the extent that such statements become imbedded in such discourse, we "make" law simply by talking about it.

This situation means that legal discourse itself is political activity, moving toward the essential political act of allocating values in Eastonian parlance. Moreover, "law talk" points to what we want out of government (and what we are willing to pay for it—discourse) and what the authoritative rules of society are and ought to be. In this sense the constitutive view attempts to move beyond the old dichotomy between fact (formalism) and value (political jurisprudence), because "law statements" are necessarily statements of both *is* and *ought*—making language real. And since this "law talk" moving toward law-

---

[88]Washington: Congressional Quarterly Press, 1995.

making (policy-making) is engaged in not only by practitioners but also by scholars, we who study law have a responsibility for what the law is—and ought to be. Law, then, is not a mere instrument of politics; law *constitutes* (is) politics.[89]

The extent to which the Constitutive School has succeeded in giving us a new point of departure in legal studies, the reader may decide. However, it is interesting to note the overlap of this position with Critical Legal Studies. Thus, in the very introduction to the second edition of THE BIBLE (my term for Kairys's *The Politics of Law*), one finds the following:

> ... [L]aw is not simply an armed receptacle for values and priorities determined elsewhere; [a political instrument, in other words] it is part of a complex social totality in which it *constitutes* as well as is constituted, shapes as well as is shaped. ... [T]he law consists of people-made decisions and doctrines, and the thought processes and modes of reconciling conflicting considerations of these people (judges) are not mystical, inevitable, or very different from the rest of ours [including presumably, scholars and teachers of the law].[90]

THE MYTH OF NEUTRALITY AND FORMALISM

A common thread running through much of American legal thought, of both the Pre- and Post-Realism variety, is a seemingly endless search for neutrality, for the philosopher stone of law—anything to avoid the black pit of "law is politics."[91] The persistence of this famous American myth seems astonishing. On reflection, however, it becomes more understandable. We have long used myths and their outward manifestation, symbols, to explain the unexplainable, to bridge that discomforting gap between what is and what is desired, thereby creating the illusion of security and stability. As R. M. MacIver insightfully wrote,

---

[89]The "Constitutive" position is presented and discussed in a widely scattered body of literature. Shapiro, in "Courts of Law, Courts of Politics," especially 108–113, offers the best brief overview of the movement, dividing it into three strands. The first is based on the thought of Niklas Luhmann, especially as interpreted in such works as Gerald Teubner and Alberto Febbjajo, eds., "State, Law and Economy as Autopoietic Systems," in *European Yearbook of the Sociology of Law* (Milan: Giuffre, 1992). A second strand, asserts Shapiro, springs from Richard Rorty's *Philosophy and the Mirror of Nature* (Princeton: Princeton University Press, 1979), while a third dimension of this movement, more directly linked with the Amherst group, may be found in the works of Michael McCann, John Brigham, and Christine Harrington, among others. The most recent pieces from these three scholars, containing cites to much previous work, are Michael McCann, "It's Only Law and Courts, But I Like It," paper presented at the annual meeting of the American Political Science Association, Chicago, Aug. 31–Sept. 3, 1995; Christine B. Harrington, "Constitutive Sociolegal Theory and Empirical Practice," paper presented at the annual meeting, Western Political Science Association, San Francisco, March 14–16, 1996; and John Brigham, "Professions of Realism as Institutional Form," paper presented at the Western Political Science Association Meeting, Mar. 14–16, 1996. Earlier work includes John Brigham and Christine B. Harrington, "Realism and Its Consequences: An Inquiry into Contemporary Sociological Research," *International Journal of the Sociology of Law* 17: 41–62; David M. Trubek and John Esser, "'Critical Empiricism' in American Legal Studies: Paradox, Program, or Pandora's Box," *Law and Social Inquiry* 14, No. 1 (1989): 3–52; and Christine B. Harrington and Barbara Yngvesson, "Interpretive Sociolegal Research," *Law and Social Inquiry* 15, No.1 (1990): 135–48.

A presentation of a constitutive (as opposed to instrumental—political jurisprudential) interpretation of Supreme Court decision making is found in Ronald Kahn, *The Supreme Court and Constitutional Theory, 1953–1993* (Lawrence: University of Kansas Press, 1994). His constitutive approach is explained in Ch. I.

[90]Kairys, *The Politics of Law* 6, emphasis added. The argument here is carried a step further in Stumpf, "Conceptions of 'Court'": 17–18.

[91]A useful critique of the idea of neutrality in the law is H. N. Hirsch, *A Theory of Liberty: The Constitution and Minorities* (New York: Routledge, 1992), especially Ch. 1

> Every society is held together by a myth-system, a complex of dominating thought-forms that determines and sustains all its activities. All social relations, the very texture of human society, are myth-born and myth-sustained. . . .
>
> Every civilization, every period, every nation, has its characteristic myth-complex. In it lies the secret of social unities and social continuities, and its changes compose the inner history of every society.[92]

The situation of one person or a group having authority over others cannot be maintained without the use of myth and symbols.[93] In the case of the American political system, we use a host of myths to bridge the yawning "is–wish" gap. The concepts of freedom and equality are two such myths, justice is another. It makes us comfortable to say "We are a government of law, not of men," for it conjures up the notion of a higher (divine), impersonal law.[94] With symbols such as law degrees, robes, walnut-paneled courtrooms, elevated benches, a special language, and the like, we help sustain the myth of an impersonal judiciary divining decisions based on some objective truth contained in the Constitution (another symbol), and knowable only by a select few. It is all a very reassuring view of policy-making (or rather, rule divining), for after the tumult, greed, and indecisiveness of the legislative process—not to mention the excesses, embarrassments and dissonance of the executive policy process—we quickly weary of the frustrations and disappointments of plain old POLITICS and wish to repair to the serenity, the sureness, indeed the utter sublimity of JUSTICE, which the LAW and its purveyors promise. Judges, for their part, are more than anxious to tout the salutary qualities of their medicament. They can hardly be faulted for packaging and marketing a product that is in such large demand by the public. And with the ever-present support of intellectual respectability proffered by the law schools, the whole enterprise is buoyed up, and a cadre of legal experts issues forth to proclaim the myth: they support it, for after all, it supports them. Thus, the ingrained need of the people for assurance, security, stability—a need to know all is well—sustains the myth; the myth, in turn, functions to fulfill the need. It has always been so in all forms of social groupings.[95]

One can no more dispel the myth by pointing it out and describing it than one can destroy faith in a supreme being by discouraging religious practices.[96] Courts, law, judges, the concept of justice—these are America's gods in secular form. Faith in an invisible god comes hard; secular deities are our substitute. Point it out, even deride it, and one's listen-

---

[92]R. M. MacIver, *The Web of Government* (New York: Macmillan, 1947), 4, 39. Another way of stating this is Martin Shapiro's delightful little essay, "Judges as Liars," *Harvard Journal of Law and Public Policy"* 17, No. 1 (Winter 1994): 155–56.

Also of direct relevance here is the useful essay by Glenn A. Phelps and John B. Gates, "The Myth of Jurisprudence: Interpretive Theory in the Constitutional Opinions of Justices Rehnquist and Brennan," *Santa Clara Law Review* 31, No. 3 (1991): 567–96.

[93]See, e.g., Robert Paul Wolff, *In Defense of Anarchism* (New York: Harper & Row, 1970).

[94]See Edward S. Corwin, *The "Higher Law" Background of American Constitutional Law* (Ithaca, N.Y.: Cornell University Press, 1955).

[95]On the significance of symbols and myths in law and politics, see Thurman W. Arnold, *The Symbols of Government* (New Haven: Yale University Press, 1935); and Murray Edelman, *The Symbolic Use of Politics* (Urbana: University of Illinois Press, 1976). Other explanations of the persistence of the judicial myth may be found in Spaeth, *Supreme Court Policy-Making*, 1–8; and Grossman and Wells, *Constitutional Law and Judicial Policy-Making*, 5–6.

[96]Some scholars argue the contrary, that too much candor can bring harm to the bench. See, e.g., Theodore L. Becker, "On Science, Political Science and Law," *American Behavioral Scientist* 7, No. 4 (Dec. 1963): 11–15; Shapiro, *Law and Politics in the Supreme Court,* 27; and Miller, "Criticism of Supreme Court Decisions": 151, n. 21.

ers nod in agreement, only to depart quickly in order to return to their old idols. As Professor (later Judge) Arnold reminds us,

> Thus "realists" insist that the principles on which society thinks it operates are a species of hokum. They cry out at the foolishness of a society which thus "deceives itself." The fact that rational or moral principles do not lead to rational or moral conduct is taken as proof that they have no effect on conduct, or else they have a "bad" effect on conduct. The human race appears under this attack as a group of "unconscious hypocrites," or "dupes." . . . Such realists sit on pillars and laugh or weep (according to their temperaments) at the human race because it is what it is, instead of something which it isn't. They are in the same intellectual position as the naturalist who insists on writing on the foolishness of animals or as a beekeeper who discourses on the "empty and meaningless" buzz of a bee. The probability of such a point of view producing competent biologists is small. . . .
>
> The trouble with their [improvement] schemes is that they violate currently important symbolism. Therefore even if the reform is accomplished it is apt to find itself twisted and warped by the contradictory ideas which are still in the background in spite of the reform. A people will never accept an institution which does not symbolize for them the simultaneously inconsistent notions to which they are at various times emotionally responsive.[97]

Thus, courts and other things legal continue to be important symbols of government, undergirding the wish-fulfilling notions we have of impartial decision making. At the same time, one can hardly deny that courts are political, for in construing statutes, executive orders, or constitutions, they inevitably weigh competing arguments, interests, and philosophies in arriving at decisions that cannot be neutral. Each and every judicial decision rewards some interest or viewpoint and deprives another. Decisions are thus allocative of society's scarce resources, making them, by definition, political. This is the great paradox of the judicial role.

JUDICIAL POLICY-MAKING

For many observers, social scientists and lawyers alike, it is relatively easy to accede to the political conceptualization of courts if one is talking about the United States Supreme Court. All would presumably agree that this unique body makes law (or policy), and hence is political (it is also, by the way, our most important institutional symbol of JUSTICE and of LAW impartially applied).[98] How else can one explain the fortunes of Elsie Parrish, chambermaid in the West Coast Hotel, whose claim to her full minimum wage of $14.50 (48-hour week) was surprisingly upheld by the Supreme Court in 1937 when that same Court had been holding the contrary for so many years? How, indeed, can one claim the existence of neutral principles of adjudication in light of *Brown v. Board of Education* decision (1954) which overturned the old "separate but equal" doctrine based upon the Equal Protection Clause of the Fourteenth Amendment, whose text remains unchanged since its ratification in 1868? And if these examples are unconvincing, consider the decision of the Court in *Baker v. Carr,* 369 U.S. 186 (1962), wherein the Court held, for the first time in American constitutional history, that the manner in which state legislatures were apportioned was a justiciable issue (susceptible to judicial scrutiny), again on grounds of the Equal Protection Clause; or *Roe v. Wade,* 410 U.S. 113 (1973), in which the

---

[97] Arnold, *The Symbols of Government,* 7, 9–10.
[98] See the insightful piece by Max Lerner, "Constitution and Court as Symbols," *Yale Law Journal* 46 (June 1937): 1290–1319.

United States Supreme Court—nine *legally* trained men—established a profound and far-reaching *medical* policy in the area of *women's* health.

The point seems clear enough, and we need not go on, unless one wishes to brandish the old argument that while the Supreme Court does indeed behave in this fashion, it has done so only fairly recently—particularly since the advent of the Warren Court—and that we would all be better off with a return to the safer,. saner posture characteristic of the "good old days." This argument, so frequently set forth by present-day political conservatives (often couched in terms of returning the Court to the control of "strict constructionists," or "Interpretivists") is easy to rebut.[99]

Some of the most profound policy-making decisions were enunciated by the Supreme Court under the tutelage of Chief Justice John Marshall, who presided over the Court from 1801 to 1835. Among the most far-reaching of the Marshall edicts was the decision in *Marbury v. Madison* 1 Cranch 137 (1803), wherein the Court held that the judiciary had the authority—indeed, the duty—to rule on the constitutionality of the acts of the other branches of government. Thus, the great American doctrine of judicial review was born. Add to this perhaps Marshall's greatest decision, that of *McCulloch v. Maryland* (1819), in which the Court held that congressional power extended not only to those powers specifically enumerated in the Constitution, but also to those powers and duties, as the text itself states, which could be reasonably inferred from the constitutional enumeration. Wrote Marshall:

> Let the end be legitimate, let it be within the scope of the Constitution, and all means which are appropriate, which are plainly adapted to that end, which are not prohibited, but consistent with the letter and spirit of the Constitution, are constitutional. . . .[100]

Equally significant policy decisions came under Marshall's successor, Chief Justice Roger B. Taney. Indeed, one need not embark upon a recitation of American constitutional history to conclude that the Supreme Court has been a policy-making body all along, and that there really are no "good old days" to return to.

That the Supreme Court has always acted as a policy-making, hence a political, body is apparent. Whether the Court *should* behave as such is, however, an entirely different matter. Here again, though, little reflection on the nature of adjudication is required in order to answer the question. The Constitution is a relatively brief document which outlines the leading principles of government in terms of structure and powers. A perusal of almost any of its sections will raise any number of questions as to precise meaning. For example, the document contains this seemingly clear passage:

> Congress shall have Power . . . To regulate Commerce with foreign Nations, and among the several States, and with the Indian Tribes.

But what does the word "commerce" include? And what is involved in "to regulate"? Does "to regulate" include an actual prohibition of certain kinds of commerce? If so, what kinds? Can Congress prohibit the shipment from one state to another of goods produced under labor conditions that it deems detrimental to the health, morals, safety, and good

---

[99]"Strict constructionist" judges are what President Nixon sought for the Court. See James F. Simon, *In His Own Image: The Supreme Court in Richard Nixon's America* (New York: David McKay, 1973). For a corresponding view from the academic community, see Philip B. Kurland, "Forward: Equal in Origin and Equal in Title to the Legislative and Executive Branches of Government," *Harvard Law Review* 78, No. 1 (Nov. 1964): 143–76.

[100]*McCulloch v. Maryland,* 4 Wheat, 316, 420 (1819). A brief but penetrating account of the life and jurisprudence of Chief Justice John Marshall has recently been published. See Charles F. Hobson, *The Great Chief Justice: John Marshall and the Rule of Law* (Lawrence: University of Kansas Press, 1996).

order of its citizens (e.g., products of child labor)? Or, if it can prohibit at all, can it prohibit only items that are themselves detrimental to the health, morals, and so on, of our citizens (such as prostitutes, fireworks, certain toxic chemicals)? Indeed, are these items "commerce" at all?

All of this leads to this fundamental question: On what grounds does one interpret the Constitution? If in the light of the intent of the Founding Fathers, how does one determine what that intent was? Most scholars in fact agree that if interviewed today, the Founding Fathers would sharply disagree with us and one another as to the meaning of various clauses of the Constitution. In any case, interpretation in light of "the intent of the framers," even if determinable, freezes the Constitution into an eighteenth-century mold. So unless one is willing to permit an interpretation of the document such that it may be "adapted to the various crises of human affairs,[101] as Chief Justice Marshall put it, the document must be amended frequently in order to tackle present-day problems. If the reader is willing to grant the argument set forth thus far, then the problem becomes one of agreeing on contemporary standards of interpretation.

Probably the most frequently mentioned method of contemporary interpretation is *stare decisis*—follow the precedent. There we have it. Neutrality through precedent. We simply search through the precedent, find existing and relevant principles of law, apply these principles to the instant set of facts, and out comes the decision. But it is hardly that simple. The bulk of controversies that reach the Supreme Court are by definition difficult cases, wherein there is no precedent (or rather, there is good precedent on both sides). As the first Justice Harlan has reminded us, "If we don't like an act of Congress, we don't have much trouble to find grounds for declaring it unconstitutional.[102] Or, take the testimony of Felix Frankfurter, who, before his appointment to the Court, wrote that

> The words of the Constitution . . . are so unrestricted by their intrinsic meaning or by their history or by tradition or by prior decisions that they leave the individual Justice free, if indeed they do not compel him, to gather meaning, not from reading the Constitution, but from reading life. . . . Members of the Court are frequently admonished by their associates not to read their economic and social views into the neutral language of the Constitution. But the process of Constitutional interpretation compels the translation of policy into judgement. . . .[103]

And as Chief Justice Charles Evans Hughes was said to have told William O. Douglas:

> You must remember (that) at the Constitutional level where we work, 90 percent of any decision is emotional. The emotional part of us supplies the reasons for supporting our predilections.[104]

Surely, enough has been said to convince anyone that there exists no philosopher's stone of constitutional interpretation. Rather, it is a human process undertaken by human beings with human desires, motivations, feelings and failings. It is inevitable, then, that the Constitution will be read in the light of the philosophy of the reader, including his or her view of right and wrong, sound and unsound policy. It can be no other way.

If these conclusions regarding constitutional interpretation are convincing, what we have said is even more true of statutory interpretation, also a common activity of the

---

[101]*McCulloch v. Maryland,* 413.
[102]Quoted in Walter F. Murphy and C. Herman Pritchett, *Courts, Judges and Politics: An Introduction to the Judicial Process* (New York: Random House, 1961), 7–8.
[103]See Felix Frankfurter, *Law and Politics,* ed. Archibald McLeish and E. F. Prichard, Jr. (New York: Capricorn Books, 1962), 30.
[104]William O. Douglas, *The Court Years* (New York: Random House, 1980), 8.

United States Supreme Court. The problems of statutory interpretation are manifold. In addition to the well-known difficulty of conveying meaning through the symbols of words, there is the added fact that statutes emerge from a decisional process fraught with compromise and confusion. At times, legislators pass intentionally vague statutes, leaving to the courts the problem of finding meaning—meaning not at all clear to the legislators themselves. Even if the statutory language is reasonably clear, legislative intent might go well beyond the words themselves. The search for intent often leads to the conclusion that the answer one receives depends almost entirely upon which legislator one asks. It is not that there are no guidelines to statutory construction. The point is simply that *clear* guidelines are nonexistent, leaving the Court, once again, in the position of making law.[105]

The inevitability of policy-making by the Supreme Court in both constitutional and statutory construction, past and present, is a fact of life. But what of lower courts, of other judicial bodies? As the story goes, a Texas lawyer, asked to distinguish between the role of the United States Supreme Court and that of lower courts, replied, "The Supreme Court is a policy court; the others are law courts."[106] A similar dual formulation of the judicial function is extant in the literature of contemporary political science. Herbert Jacob, for example, has set forth a fairly elaborate set of distinctions between judicial policy-making and what he terms "judicial norm-enforcement," a formulation that seems to have been rather uncritically adopted by other political scientists.[107] Of the thousands of cases handled by the American judiciary in a single year, Jacob argues, only a small percentage are really policy decisions; the vast majority involve only norm enforcement. Essentially, he makes what amounts to a fourfold distinction between the two based on (1) the judges' intent, (2) the form the decision takes, (3) decisional impact, and (4) the spread of litigants. Policy-making is conscious, in that the judge renders a decision that sets forth a new departure in norms. The judge intends to set a new precedent.[108] Second, policy-making usually produces opinions to which lawyers and others can later refer for guidance, whereas norm enforcement decisions are usually unwritten, or at least unpublished. Third, the policy decision becomes a guidepost for future action, whereas the norm enforcement decision is limited to the case at hand. Finally, writes Jacob,

> Judicial policymaking is not distinguished from other court actions only by the intent of the judges, the form of their decisions, and the impact of their actions. It is also characterized by a different array of participants. Whereas norm-enforcement decisions usually concern only the immediate litigants, policy decisions draw a wider group of participants to the court room. They especially attract the concern of organized interest groups.[109]

In general, policy-making is reserved for appellate courts, argues Jacob; only rarely does the opportunity arise for trial courts to make policy.

---

[105]See e.g., Murphy and Pritchett, *Courts, Judges and Politics,* Ch. 11.

[106]See Richard S. Wells and Joel B. Grossman, "The Concept of Judicial Policy-Making: A Critique," *Journal of Public Law* 15, No. 2 (1966): 286. Also see the treatment given the concept of norm enforcement in Henry R. Glick, *Courts, Politics and Justice,* 3rd ed. (New York: McGraw-Hill, 1993): 355–57.

[107]See Herbert Jacob, *Justice in America: Courts, Lawyers and the Judicial Process,* 4th ed. (Boston: Little, Brown, 1984), Ch. 2. See also Howard Ball, *Courts and Politics: The Federal Judicial System,* 2nd ed. (Englewood Cliffs, N.J.: Prentice-Hall, 1987), 19–23. An excerpt from the Jacob book on the norm enforcement–policy-making distinction is to be found in Grossman and Wells, *Constitutional Law and Judicial Policy-Making,* 36–42.

[108]Ball, in *Courts and Politics,* holds that "conscious intent" is "the essential difference between norm-enforcement and policy-making," 20.

[109]Jacob, *Justice in America,* 39.

The norm enforcement–policy-making dichotomy does not hold up under analysis. To begin with, to suggest intent as a distinction between policy-making and non–policy-making implies the necessity of a rational planning element in policy-making. This is nothing more than the restoration of the old *stare decisis* argument, which is that there are guiding principles hidden in the corpus of the law and that the job of the judge is to sift through past decisions in order to discover these principles and apply them to the present case. Policy-making, legislative as well as judicial, is perhaps more realistically viewed as incremental in nature, wherein decisional bodies move in small steps—often not consciously—in the direction of significant policy shifts.[110] The notion of intent really feeds back into traditional jurisprudence, whereby we take the judge at his/her word: if they insist they did not intend to make policy (and most judges do so insist), then we must conclude that they did not. At least a part of a definition of public policy must be its impact on the policy recipient. If there is a change in impact, that is surely some indication that policy has been made. Intent has nothing to do with it. As James Anderson notes in his analysis of the concept policy-making,

> Policy is what governments actually do in regulating trade, controlling inflation, or promoting public housing, not what they intend to do or say they are going to do. If a legislature enacts a law requiring employers to pay no less than the stated minimum wage but nothing is done to enforce the law, and consequently no change occurs in economic behavior, then it is fair to contend that public policy in this instance is really one of non-regulation of wages. It seems nonsensical to regard an intention as policy without regard for what subsequently happens.[111]

The norm enforcement–policy-making distinction also depends significantly on a new departure in policy. Writes Jacob:

> Opportunities for judicial policy making arise less frequently than occasions for enforcing norms. Every case affords the chance to enforce a norm. Only when a norm itself is challenged can the courts engage in policy making.[112]

A moment's reflection will reveal, however, that neither intent nor evidence of a new departure provides a particularly useful criterion for determining when courts are engaged in policy-making. As Wells and Grossman write,

> [It] makes no sense to say that policy cannot be made through the application of settled law, for the mere decision to apply that law—or to depart from it—is a policy decision. Furthermore, if policy is seen as a process of which implementation and feedback are important parts, and not just as the initial choice between competing values, and if the entire judicial system in any one jurisdiction is seen as a piece of complex but essentially unified policy machinery, then this distinction falls.[113]

Had the United States Supreme Court, in 1954, declined to hold racial segregation in education unconstitutional, instead of issuing the decision that it did in *Brown v. Board of Education,* law (policy) would still have been made.[114] Or, as Schur notes in his discussion of the interaction of Realists' notions of policy-making with modern sociological views,

---

[110]Martin Shapiro, "Stability and Change in Judicial Decision Making: Incrementalism or Stare Decisis," *Law in Transition Quarterly* 2, No. 3 (Summer 1965): 134–57.

[111]James E. Anderson, *Public Policy Making* (New York: Praeger, 1975), 3–4.

[112]Jacob, *Justice in America,* 37.

[113]Wells and Grossman, "Concept of Judicial Policy-Making," 294.

[114]This is a point made by Ronald Dworkin, *Taking Right Seriously* (Cambridge, Mass.: Harvard University Press, 1977), 132.

The Realist thesis that policy issues are central to legal disputes, and that every outcome constitutes a form of policy, is generally consistent with sociological views. For example, sociologists, at least since Max Weber, would insist that "non action" is itself a form of social action; this point comes across nicely in the realist analysis, with the realization that following past precedent is as much a policy act as rejecting it—in neither case can the need to make policy be avoided.[115]

Finally, to suggest that policy-making is restricted to appellate courts is to understate the role of trial courts in the political process. The degree of political independence of federal district judges is considerable, as is their capacity for individual policy-making, even, at times, in outright defiance of the United States Supreme Court.[116] State trial courts are in some ways even more significant. It is at this level that the vast majority of litigants begin (and end) their experience with the judiciary. As with appellate tribunals, these local courts inevitably engage in the weighing of competing community interests (social, political, legal, economic, and otherwise) in arriving at decisions. The process can hardly be said to be mechanical. Rather, it calls for the exercise of considerable discretion. which, by the slow process of accretion, amounts to the fashioning of significant community policy. The low appeal rate, combined with the low visibility of these courts, has the effect of maximizing the judges' discretionary powers, resulting in an enhancement of their policy-making capacity. Even the most "inferior" of courts have not been reluctant to affix their stamp of approval or disapproval on many dimensions of individual and group behavior within the community.[117]

A few examples should suffice to underline the argument. Several years ago, a student newspaper announced that possession of small amounts of marijuana, or its use on campus, would not be penalized. Campus police had an "understanding" (unwritten, of course) with local (city) police, prosecutors, and local judges that in spite of the letter of the law (which provides rather stiff penalties for use of marijuana, possession, and distribution on-campus) peaceful use and possession would be accepted. This clearly constitutes significant policy for the student body. Yet, it was neither written nor published, in any official sense, nor was it fashioned by an appellate court. To this day, as far as anyone can determine, this remains community policy.

The decisions of municipal traffic courts are yet other examples of judicial policy-making. When municipal judges generally agree that DWI offenders will be ordered to traffic school in lieu of a jail sentence, or when particular judges consistently offer a one-month jail term or a period of compulsory treatment to previously convicted drunk drivers, significant community policy is clearly being established.

---

[115]Edwin M. Schur, *Law and Society: A Sociological View* (New York: Random House, 1968), 48.

[116]See, for example, Jack W. Peltason, *Fifty-eight Lonely Men: Southern Federal Judges and School Desegregation* (New York: Harcourt, Brace & World, 1961). See also Richard J. Richardson and Kenneth N. Vines, *The Politics of Federal Courts: Lower Courts in the United States,* (Boston: Little, Brown, 1970), 4–7, and passim; and Walter F. Murphy, "Lower Court Checks on Supreme Court Power," *American Political Science Review* 53, No. 4 (Dec. 1959): 1017–1031.

[117]This argument was made in an earlier work by the author. See Harry P. Stumpf, "Law and Poverty: A Political Perspective," *Wisconsin Law Review,* No. 3 (1968): 717–18. For a similar conceptualization of the local judiciary as having a policy-making function, see Kenneth M. Dolbeare, *Trial Courts in Urban Politics* (New York: Wiley, 1967); and James R. Klonoski and Robert I. Mendelsohn, "The Allocation of Justice: A Political Approach," in their *The Politics of Local Justice* (Boston: Little, Brown, 1970), 3–19.

For a more recent analysis of policy-making in trial courts, see Lynn Mather, "Policy Making in State Trial Courts" in Gates and Johnson, *The American Courts;* 119–57; and Mather, "The Fired Football Coach (Or, How Trial Courts Make Policy)," in Epstein, *Comtemplating Courts:* 170–202.

The realities of judicial politics in America suggest a conception of the judicial function that involves policy-making from top to bottom. No one denies that there are differences between appellate and trial courts, but the differences are not those suggested by the norm enforcement–policy-making distinction. Indeed, that distinction appears to add up to a difference without a difference—one which tends to becloud more than enlighten our understanding of the judicial function.[118]

We need go no further than David Easton in clarifying our understanding of politics: it is "a web of decisions and actions which allocate values."[119] We are, of course, speaking of authoritative values—those about which there is a widespread feeling that they must be or ought to be obeyed. Easton continues:

A decision alone is, of course, not a policy: to decide what to do does not mean that the thing is done. A decision is only a selection among alternatives that expresses the intention of the person or group making the choice. Arriving at a decision is the formal phase of establishing a policy; it is not the whole policy in relation to a particular problem. A legislature can decide to punish monopolists; this is the intention. But an administrator can destroy or reformulate the decision by failing either to discover offenders or to prosecute them vigorously. This failure is as much a part of the policy with regard to monopoly as the formal law. When we act to implement a decision, therefore, we enter the second effective phase of a policy. In this phase the decision is expressed or interpreted in a series of actions and narrower decisions which may, in effect, establish new policy.[120]

The creation of policy may be accompanied by a blast of trumpets, as when the president signs a congressional bill. More frequently, however, policy just *is*. That is, there are rules on the books that most people feel ought be obeyed. And, indeed, most do obey them most of the time. There are exceptions, however. In short, a wide gap exists between the LAW (POLICY) and the law (policy), or as Roscoe Pound would say, "law in the books" and "law in action." In reference to this example, the LAW as written might read thus:

And littering of any public place, street, sidewalk, or thoroughfare with foreign matter is a misdemeanor and shall be punished by a fine of not less than Fifty Dollars ($50.00) nor more than One Hundred Dollars ($100.00) and imprisonment for not more than fifteen days, and for the second and subsequent offenses, one guilty of a misdemeanor shall be punished by a fine of not less than One Hundred Dollars ($100.00) nor more than One Thousand Dollars ($1,000.00) or by imprisonment for a definite term less than one year, or both.

But the latter—the law in action—reads more like the following:

It makes the city ugly to litter; we all have to live in the city; you shouldn't litter. If you do, however, there is not likely to be a penalty unless (1) you're Black or Chicano, (2) you're young, (3) you toss stuff out of the car window on Central Avenue while cruising on Friday or Saturday night. If you do this you might get a ticket. The word is out; people

[118]A partial critique of the norm enforcement–policy-making dichotomy may be found in Wells and Grossman, "Concept of Judicial Policy-Making," 289–93. See also Glendon Schubert's review of the Jacob book, *American Political Science Review* 59, No. 4 (Dec. 1965): 1038–40, wherein Schubert argues that "the use of this kind of conceptualization [norm enforcement–policy-making] by political scientists today does not advance political science one whit beyond the understanding of judicial decision making made possible by [Ernst] Freund's work over half a century ago" (p. 1039). Finally, see the critique by Mather, "Policy Making in State Trial Courts," especially 120–21.
[119]Easton, *Political System,* 130.
[120]Easton, *Political System,* 130. Other useful (and not inconsistent) definitions of policy are those of James E. Anderson, *Public Policymaking: An Introduction* (New York: Houghton Mifflin, 1990), 4–8; and Grossman and Wells, *Constitutional Law and Judicial Policy Making:* 36.

are mad about kids cruising Central. They'll get you. If this happens, hope you get Judge Ryan—he's usually sympathetic to kids. The other judges are harder; you'll probably get probation the first time, then a $50.00 fine after that, or worse.

If you're White (Anglo) and live in the Heights, it's usually OK to litter. Tossing stuff on the school ground is OK. So is dropping stuff out of your pickup when you're hauling trash to the dump on Saturday, so long as you don't overdo it. Nobody can remember anyone getting a ticket for littering up in the Heights. If you do, the judge will let you off unless you give him a hard time. Tell him you're guilty; judges don't like you to waste their time fighting small things like that.

So the law—the policy in action—is a good deal more complex, more uncertain, more class oriented (or one might say a good deal more idiosyncratic) than the POLICY that was enacted. What accounts for the change? Clearly, it is the interaction of law enforcement policy-making and citizen attitudes and behavior. As is evident, the decisions (i.e., "policy") of courts, cops, and even citizens are every bit as significant as those arrived at by city officials in determining what is to be. As David Easton puts it, "Political science is concerned with every way in which values [policy] are allocated for a society, whether formally enunciated in a law or lodged in the *consequences of practice*.[121] Note, too, that "the consequences of practice" take effect whether or not a judicial decision has been made, which reminds us of Holmes's aphorism, "The prophesis of what the courts will do in fact, and nothing more pretentious, are what I mean by the law."[122]

James Eisenstein carries the point one step further. In using a similar example (street littering) to distinguish between law on the books and what he calls "law-as-applied," he writes as follows:

> There is another dimension to law-in-action that must be recognized. In addition to the behavior of participants in the legal process who enforce or fail to enforce statutes, a comprehensive survey of the law-in-action regarding littering must also examine the behavior of potential litterbugs. Some people refrain from littering because they wish to avoid official punishment, or because they feel it is morally wrong to violate an ordinance prohibiting such action. Others may deliberately litter because they know it is formally prohibited. In both instances, the behavior of private citizens is modified by perceptions of the legal process and law, and is an integral component of the law-in-action.[123]

The reader may object that we are confusing policy-making with policy implementation and enforcement. The city council or the legislature made the policy; the courts and police, respectively, interpret and enforce it. But as we have seen, the significance of policy (to the extent a policy is to have any significance at all) lies in what is actually done, not in what is intended. To view policy as a single discrete act is next to useless, for a single act often produces nothing. This point was made in a somewhat different way many years ago by Luther Gulick, who had cause to reflect on the role of the administrator in policy-making:

> Discretion, the use of judgement, is the essential element in the determination of policy: If any government employee, any one of our "rulers," has discretion, he not only has power, but is by circumstances compelled to determine policy.

---

[121]Easton, *Political System,* 131 (emphasis added).

[122]Oliver W. Holmes, "The Path of the Law" (address delivered by Justice Holmes of the Supreme Judicial Court of Massachusetts at the dedication of the Boston University School of Law, January 8, 1897), *Harvard Law Review* 10, No. 8 (Mar. 25, 1897): 461.

[123]James Eisenstein, *Politics and the Legal Process* (New York: Harper & Row, 1973), 11.

It is impossible to analyze the work of any public employee from the time he steps into his office in the morning until he leaves at night without discovering that his every act is a *seamless web of discretion and action.*[124]

In conclusion, then, the courts, through their interpretation of administrative orders, statutes, and constitutions, are necessarily rendering decisions that have significant allocative effects upon the community involved, be that community Buttermilk, Kansas, or the United States of America. Resources are inevitably redistributed in the form of rights, privileges, freedom, money, status, and so on. This is clearly policy-making, hence political activity.

Much attention has been focused on judicial functions, because everything else we say or do not say about courts depends on this initial conceptualization. If judicial functions are prospectively allocative of societal values, this in turn makes courts the center of a wide range of activities that are also political. For example, because values are allocated, it matters a great deal who does the allocating, who exercises discretion. This explains the intense political activity that swirls about the selection of judges. It also explains the perennial struggle over the form and structure of courts, for all believe that if courts are organized one way rather than another, certain values are thereby served (or depreciated). Because judges as political decision-makers function in a professional context, it becomes important to ask about the nature of the legal profession and the values it brings to bear on judicial behavior. This alone suggests a host of research topics, from recruitment of law students to the effectiveness of codes of professional responsibility. Because the policies courts make or do not make obviously depend upon the disputes brought into the judicial arena, the series of forces, influences, and patterns of behavior which determine what issues do and do not reach courts also become significant. And because, as we have seen, the initial judicial policy decision may constitute an empty gesture unless it has impact in terms of altering individual, group, or societal behavior, the nature and extent of the political struggle surrounding court decisions also become relevant to our understanding of courthouse government. These are but a few of the topics to be taken up in the ensuing chapters. There is, however, at least one further conceptualization of the judicial function that warrants comment.

COURTS: A RECONSIDERATION

On reflection, the foregoing discussion postulates but two conceptions of judging. One is that of the neutral, objective judge discovering an inner, higher (correct) meaning to our societal (constitutional) values, whereas the other is that of courts, peopled by human beings and having discretionary power, rendering decisions that are obviously allocative of societal values, hence political. The presentation thus seems to cast the debate into a dichotomy, an either-or situation. The essence of "courtness" is either neutral judging or is an allocative, political process. A third view suggests that it may be useful to call a halt to the present debate, at least momentarily, step back a few paces, and consider anew the nature of adjudication. This is the approach taken by Martin Shapiro in his essay entitled "Courts" in the *Handbook of Political Science.*[125]

---

[124]Luther Gulick, "Politics, Administration and the New Deal," *Annals* 169 (Sept. 1933): 61, (emphasis added).

[125]Martin Shapiro, "Courts," in Fred I. Greenstein and Nelson W. Polsby, eds., *Handbook of Political Science,* Vol. 5: *Governmental Institutions and Processes* (Menlo Park, Calif.: Addison-Wesley, 1955), 321–72. The Shapiro essay may also be found in his *Courts: A Comparative and Political Analysis* (Chicago: University of Chicago Press, 1981), Ch. 1, "The Prototype of Courts," 1–64.

Shapiro begins by noting that political jurisprudence has rested its case largely on findings which show that courts do not act like courts. That is, the judicial archetype, consisting of (1) an independent judge (2) applying established legal rules (3) in an adversarial proceeding to achieve (4) a dichotomous decision in which legal right is assigned to one party and legal wrong to the other, has rarely, if ever, existed across the range of our experience. Thus, to found a jurisprudence either on the basis of a prototype that never existed, or to attack such a straw man, is equally unsatisfactory. Better that we should begin with the basic concept of conflict resolution, or dispute settlement, and with no prior notions about what courts actually do, but mindful of the caveat that we should not tax ourselves in attempting to discover the "true essence" of the judicial function (as such may not exist in the real world), let us move to a basic reconsideration of the judicial role in society.

Beginning, then, with the classic conflict resolution triad, which is based on mutual consent (to resolve their dispute, A and B seek out C, who will recommend a solution acceptable to all), Shapiro makes the following observations:

1. In order to increase the probability of acceptance of their decision, courts frequently approach the disputing parties in a mood of mediation or arbitration, which suggests that the boundary between these forms of dispute resolution and formal adjudication is not as clear-cut as we might have thought.
2. With the growth of societal complexity, simple consent of the parties is replaced by law and the trappings of judicial office. The adjudicative outcome must now be accepted, not because the parties agree to the procedure in advance, but because society has imposed a mechanism that assures fairness and impartiality (the myth, supported by symbols).
3. When laws (rules) are imposed to help in the dispute settlement, courts engage in social control, which of course threatens the stability of the classic triad, based as it was on spontaneous consent.
4. In the course of performing both conflict resolution and social control, courts inevitably make law (public policy), which further involves them in the political thicket and upsets the triadic balance.
5. Casual empirical observation also reveals a very significant administrative role that courts play in most societies. This is obvious at the appellate level, for one of the clearer functions of appellate courts is administration. But it also is true at the trial court level, where courts often put into effect policies created in other sectors of the political system.

Whether or not this brief presentation adequately summarizes Shapiro's argument, enough has been said at least to call into question the conventional political jurisprudence just outlined. Our "political" conception of "courtness" has probably been too narrowly drawn, for in insisting on an either-or view, we have tended to overlook the possibility (probability) that the adjudicative function is multifaceted, playing several societal roles.

When we focus upon conflict or dispute resolution, or at least dispute-processing, we find that in a complex society, the role of courts involves social control as well as policymaking, and both roles are closely associated with regime maintenance. Courts also play an administrative role almost as often as (or more accurately, in the course of) dispute resolution, and the distinction between adjudication on the one hand and arbitration-mediation on the other, so sharply drawn in most modern societies, is equally questionable.

What we have, then, is a much more fluid view of judicial functions, a view much closer to Gulick's "seamless web," and we probably need not argue over which are the right or "true" judicial roles. This is not to say that courts play all roles equally well, or that it makes no difference which roles courts adopt at a particular time in a particular society. Socially and politically assigned roles are, of course, easiest to play; courts frequently get themselves into trouble with the regime by playing roles neither politically assigned nor societally accepted. What we are saying, then, is that from the perspective of conventional political jurisprudence, it does not matter a great deal whether we *initially* perceive courts to be conflict resolvers, policy-makers, arbitrators, or administrators. On reflection, all of these roles will be found to be political, for it is hardly possible to arbitrate, administer, or settle disputes without allocating general societal values; and as we have repeatedly said, this is obviously political activity.[126]

The chief contribution of Shapiro's reconsideration has been to remind us of the flexibility of judicial roles. This is especially useful in a social-academic setting characterized by (1) increased complexity, (2) the doctrine of separation of powers, and (3) a scholarship grown accustomed to conceptualizing courts as policy-makers only. It is useful to recall that in colonial America, courts at both the trial and appellate level customarily and consciously performed the multiple functions discussed by Shapiro (see Chapter 3). But, with the strictures of the American doctrine of separation of powers (with its attendant practice of a rather rigid system of checks and balances), we came to view the judicial function as dictated by theory; courts neutrally interpret the law, or alternately, with a more realistic jurisprudence, courts make public policy. Actually, they perform both functions, and a good many more.

What might be termed "political jurisprudence, updated," however, suggests a considerably wider range of research and teaching concerns than even that very large agenda set forth by the conventional sociological-Realist-political jurisprudential school, and in this respect it does shed new light on old issues. It is instructive, for example, to explore the extent to which adjudication, as traditionally viewed, is in fact administration, mediation, or arbitration, the boundaries between and among these functions being much less fixed than before. What are the conditions under which courts are likely to perform one function rather than another? And how do courts compare with other social institutions in these roles? If we posit the judicial role as essentially policy-making, we are likely to compare judicial bodies with other policy-making entities. But if we begin with a conflict resolution, dispute-settling role, we are led to compare courts with a different set of institutions and processes.[127] This is not the place to set forth a new research desideratum, but it is important to note, once again, that different conceptualizations of judicial functions can lead to a different (and in this case, expanded) set of questions for teaching and research. Even so, beginning at a different place in thinking about courts has not moved the subfield of judicial studies away from the central political conceptualization discussed earlier.

Incorporating these revisions into political jurisprudence does not change another of our earlier conclusions—namely, that the contemporary jurisprudential problem re-

---

[126]That conflict resolution is what politics is all about has been a position commonly held by political scientists, and it is becoming fashionable to use the concept to orient judicial studies. See, e.g., Austin Sarat and Joel B. Grossman's significant article, "Courts and Conflict Resolution: Problems in the Mobilization of Adjudication," *American Political Science Review* 69, No. 4 (Dec. 1975): 1200–17. See also the implications of a dispute-processing (or conflict-resolution) focus for public law in political science as seen by Adelaide Villamoare, "What Is the Conceptional Future of the Analysis of Public Law?" paper presented at the American Political Science Association meeting, Denver, Sept. 2–5, 1982.

In "Conceptions of 'Court,'" 19–24, Stumpf expands the argument for a dispute-processing orientation to the study of courts, based on earlier writings of Shapiro, Villamoare, Carl Friedrich, and others. Friedrich, for example, maintains that policy-making is eclipsed in significance by dispute resolution as the core political act. "[T]he settlement of disputes," writes Friedrich, "is the primordial internal function which a political order has to perform, antedating the making of rules and the application of such rules in administrative work." Carl Friedrich, *Man and His Government: An Empirical Theory of Politics* (New York: McGraw-Hill, 1963), 57. For yet another exponent of the dispute processing orientation, see Peter H. Russell, *The Judiciary in Canada: The Third Branch of Government* (Toronto: McGraw-Hill Ryerson, 1987), especially Ch. 1.

[127]See, e.g., Richard L. Abel, "A Comparative Theory of Dispute Institutions in Society," *Law & Society Review* 8, No. 2 (Winter 1973): 217–347.

mains that of reconciling the traditional view of adjudication as an independent, objective search for truth, with that of the Sociological-Realist view, which sees law as a social-political instrument used to allocate values. If any single current piece of literature makes this point clear, it is the Fiss article discussed earlier.[128] Conceptualizations of the judicial function as policy-making or dispute settling are equally objectionable to Fiss; to him, the heart of the matter is, and of necessity must be, an independent judiciary that remains above the battle of competing interests in its pristine search for "what is true, right, or just." Drawing a sharp distinction between adjudication and other public decisional processes (administration, arbitration), Fiss insists that politics is not the realm of the judge. The judicial realm is a very special one, that of discovering the true meaning of our public (constitutional) values. The legitimacy of courts rests on their competence to perform this lofty function, never on the consent of the people, their needs and desires, nor the "felt necessities of the time."[129]

The lines could not be more sharply drawn. Courts are either in society or above it, and adjudication either is political or is not. Whether one conceptualizes the judicial function as principled, objective, neutral, independent, or a process by which one discovers true constitutional values, the jurisprudential position is the same, that old timeworn view of law as existing above the individual and society—a brooding omnipresence in the sky. Given the manner in which the debate is currently framed, choice is inescapable. As Miller reminded us, "One cannot be both a legal realist and a mechanist."[130] This is precisely why certain strains of Post-Realism, particularly the Critical Legal Studies movement, evoke such hostile response.

LEGAL SYSTEMS

The reason underlying our lengthy discussion of jurisprudence is the belief that concepts of law and of courts influence actual judicial and legal systems—indeed, that theory informs practice in real and observable ways. This is not to say, however, that legal philosophy is the only antecedent worthy of attention. Rather, some understanding of the two overarching legal systems—*common law* and *civil law*—that have shaped American government is also critical to the study of judicial politics.[131]

The Common Law

The world has known many legal systems (taken here to mean overarching, enduring systems of rules), but those that have had significant lasting impact on contemporary norms and practices are few. The two great legal systems that have influenced Western society are the *Common Law* system and the *Civil Law.* The system of the Common Law originated in medieval England. Following the Norman conquest in 1066, the problem arose of uniting under a single kingdom the diverse tribes that roamed Britain. William the Conqueror could have imposed his will in the fashion of the Roman emperors, thereby making London the seat of ultimate authority. He chose, instead, to send his representatives, who acted as itinerant royal judges, into the countryside, assuming that such judges were likely

---

[128]Owen M. Fiss, "Forward: The Forms of Justice," *Harvard Law Review* 93, No. 1 (Nov. 1979): 1–58.
[129]Fiss, "Forward": 38.
[130]Miller, "Criticism of Supreme Court Decisions": 148.
[131]On the nature of "legal systems," see Lawrence M. Friedman, *Law and Society: An Introduction* (Englewood Cliffs, N.J.: Prentice-Hall, 1977), 5–9.

to settle disputes using the principles of law found to exist in the local medieval courts. The decisions of these traveling justices, along with those of the central courts in London, gradually molded a system of rules "common" to the realm, in contrast to the established ecclesiastical law.[132] Thus, Common Law developed as essentially case- or judge-made law (indeed, it is often referred to as "unwritten" law), and through a slow process of accretion, a fairly elaborate body of legal principles eventually emerged. The doctrine of *stare decisis* was the mechanism that evolved over five or six centuries, the principle being that once a higher court settled a case in a certain way, all other disputes with a similar set of facts were to utilize that decision as precedent. The genius of the Common Law has been its capacity to promote stability yet at the same time to maintain adaptability. Further, it developed something of an osmotic quality, a capacity to infuse into legal rules the practical element of real-life problems. This quality has been nowhere better stated than in Holmes's famous statement, "The life of the law has not been logic; it has been experience. The felt necessities of the time." Holmes reiterated this notion in his opinion in *Gompers v. the United States,* in which we wrote that

> The provisions of the Constitution are not mathematical formulas having their essence in their form; they are organic, living institutions transplanted from English soil. Their significance is vital, not formal; it is to be gathered not simply by taking the words of the dictionary, but by considering their origin and the line of their growth.[133]

In addition to these qualities, the Common Law is also notable for its emphasis on procedure, which has led to a special sensitivity for the rights of the individual. Due process of law is a Common Law concept and may be roughly defined as the requirement for basic fairness in governmental actions involving the individual. The jury and the adversary system are also derived from the Common Law.

In the early centuries of the Common Law, access to courts was restricted and rules were often narrowly drawn and rigid, leading to a close observance of the letter of the law often resulting in basic unfairness. The king responded to special petitions for relief from these perceived wrongs by referring them to his Chancellor, who became *Keeper of the King's Conscience.* The office of Chancellor eventually evolved into a Chancery Court, which heard petitions not in law but in *equity.* Such tribunals could issue subpoenas, injunctions, and the like, with a view to bringing "extralegal" standards of fairness to the resolution of disputes. In the main, equity has long since merged with Common Law and is normally administered by the regular courts.[134]

By the close of the seventeenth century, the Common Law had developed a fairly sophisticated body of doctrine in most substantive areas. This was most clearly the case in the fields of criminal law, property, and torts.[135] However, the development of commercial legal doctrine had to await the growth of commerce and industry toward the end of the century.

The spread of the Common Law accompanied the growth of the British empire. Today the nations that base their legal systems on the Common Law include not only the

---

[132]Perhaps the best readily available treatment of the development of the Common Law is Sir Frederick Pollock and Frederick W. Maitland, *The History of English Law* (Cambridge: University Press, 1923). See also Theodore F. T. Plucknett, *A Concise History of the Common Law,* 5th ed. (Boston: Little, Brown, 1956).

[133]*Gompers v. the United States,* 233 U.S. 604, 610 (1914).

[134]A useful review of the development of equity may be found in C. Gordon Post, *An Introduction to the Law* (Englewood Cliffs, N.J.: Prentice-Hall, 1963), Ch. 3. See also T. F. T. Plucknett, *Statutes and Their Interpretation in the First Half of the 14th Century* (Cambridge, Mass.: Harvard University Press, 1922).

[135]Torts are offenses (other than a breach of contract) that give rise to legal actions though not necessarily criminal in nature: If my tree falls on your house, I may be liable for damages.

United States, but Canada, Australia, Ireland, and New Zealand, as well as most of the nations of Africa formerly under British rule. Indeed, the worldwide influence of the Common Law serves to illustrate its capacity to adapt to diverse cultures and regions.

The Civil Law

The second great system of law of considerable influence in the Western World is the Civil Law, sometimes called Statutory Law or Roman Law.[136] As its name implies, this legal system traces its origin to Rome. One of the earliest legal codes was that of the XII Tables of 450 B.C., engraved in bronze and placed in the Roman Forum. Actually, neither this code nor that of Hammurabi, King of Babylon (800 B.C.), were legal systems as we are using the term, but rather they were early codifications that provided the basic framework of later Roman law.

One of the great contributions by Rome to the modern world was its legal system. The first law books as we know them today were Roman, as were the first professional schools of law and the development of the legal concept to solve practical problems. In about A.D. 535, Emperor Justinian I directed that Roman law be completely codified. Passed on to us as the *corpus juris civilis,* this important codification was lost to scholarship until the twelfth century, when it was reintroduced into legal studies at Bologna University. Civil law is, as suggested, codified law. It is written in statutory language and interpreted by judges or administrators, but unlike the Common Law, it is supposedly not judge-made. Rather, it depends on the sustained study and interpretation of legal scholars. Upon its rediscovery, it quickly spread throughout medieval Europe so that today the Civil Law system forms the basis of the legal systems of continental Europe, and through colonization Civil Law was brought to French Africa, Québec, and Louisiana. Even in the Scandinavian countries, the Civil Law system has had significant influence.[137] Important modern codifications of the Civil Law tradition have included the *Code Napoléon,* published in 1804 and still of considerable importance in modern France, and the German *Bürgerliches Gesetzbuch* of 1901.[138]

It is easy to overemphasize the difference between civil and common law systems in contemporary society. It is true that the codification of law has a centralizing effect, and the law in civil systems is somewhat more precise and clear-cut than in common law systems. At the same time, codes contain general legal principles as well as mere rules, which must be interpreted by judicial bodies that use decisional approaches not totally unlike those employed in common law systems. Remember also that the two systems have touched and overlapped throughout history, resulting in "mixed" practices in many countries. For example, the concept of equity, so clearly associated with common law systems, seems to be Roman in origin. The common law as currently practiced can hardly be said to be purely judge-made, for it has been heavily supplemented by statutes passed by legislatures in response to the needs of modern industrial society. Thus, today we have common law courts following the legislative lead, rather than the other way around, a characteristic traditionally associated with civil law systems.

---

[136]The term "civil law" is used in two senses, a fact that is often the source of confusion to the student. Here, we are of course referring to an historic legal system. But the term is also used in contrast to criminal law when referring to the *substance* of the law itself. In this sense, civil law usually applies to issues that arise between private citizens or organizations (e.g., divorce, landlord-tenant issues), whereas criminal law involves actions brought by the public (government) against an individual (e.g., homicide, perjury).

[137]Friedman, *Law and Society,* 73.

[138]Fannie J. Klein, *Federal and State Court Systems: A Guide* (Cambridge, Mass.: Ballinger, 1977), 261.

There are, of course, other legal systems in the modern world, such as those in the socialist countries, that of the Peoples Republic of China, the religious systems of canon law, Muslim law, and the like. But enough has been said to alert the student to the significance of substantive legal systems in understanding modern judicial processes.

FURTHER READING

Arnold, Thurman W. *The Symbols of Government.* New Haven: Yale University Press, 1935.

Cooter, Robert, and Thomas Ulen. *Law and Economics.* New York: Harper Collins, 1988.

"Critical Legal Studies Symposium." *Stanford Law Review* 36, Nos. 1 & 2 (Jan. 1984): 1–674.

Delgado, Richard, and Jean Stefancic. "Critical Race Theory: An Annotated Bibliography." *Virginia Law Review* 79, No. 2 (Mar. 1993): 461–516.

Fiss, Owen. "Forward: The Forms of Justice." *Harvard Law Review* 93, No. 1 (Nov. 1979): 1–58.

Gates, John B. "Theory, Methods, and the New Institutionalism in Judicial Research," in John B. Gates and Charles A. Johnson, eds., *The American Courts: A Critical Approach.* Washington: Congressional Quarterly Press, 1991, 469–89.

Kairys, David, ed. *The Politics of Law: A Progressive Critique.* Rev. ed. New York: Pantheon Books, 1990.

Kelman, Mark. *A Guide to Critical Legal Studies.* Cambridge: Harvard University Press, 1987.

Lerner, Max. "Constitution and Court as Symbols." *Yale Law Journal* 46 (June 1937): 1290–1319.

MacKinnon, Catherine A. *Feminism Unmodified: Discourses on Life and Law.* Cambridge: Harvard University Press, 1987.

Minda, Gary. "The Jurisprudential Movements of the 1980s." *Ohio State Law Journal* 50, No. 3 (1989): 599–662.

Murphy, Walter F., James E. Fleming, and Sotirios A. Barber, *American Constitutional Interpretation,* 2nd ed. Westbury, N.Y.: Foundation Press, 1995.

Peller, Gary. "Neutral Principles in the 1950s." *University of Michigan Journal of Law Reform* 21, No. 4 (Summer 1988): 561–662.

Rawls, John. *A Theory of Justice.* Cambridge: Harvard University Press, 1971.

Shapiro, Martin. *Courts: A Comparative and Political Analysis.* Chicago: University of Chicago Press, 1981.

———. "Fathers and Sons: The Court, The Commentators, and the Search for Values," in Vincent Blasi, ed., *The Burger Court: The Counter-Revolution That Wasn't.* New Haven: Yale University Press, 1983, 218–38.

———. "Public Law and Judicial Politics," in Ada W. Finifter, ed., *Political Science: The State of the Discipline, II.* Washington: American Political Science Association, 1993, 365–381.

Smith, Rogers M. "Political Jurisprudence, the New Institutionalism, and the Future of Public Law." *American Political Science Review* 82, No. 1 (Mar. 1988): 89–108.

"Symposium on Feminist Jurisprudence." *Georgia Law Review* 24, No. 4 (Summer 1990): 759–1044.

Tushnet, Mark. "Critical Legal Studies: A Political History." *Yale Law Journal* 100, No. 5 (Spring 1991): 1515–44.

3

State Judicial Organization

It is . . . a mistake to speak of a judicial "system" or "hierarchy," for neither . . . exists [in state court organization]. Although dozens of courts (in some instances hundreds) exist side by side in a city or metropolitan area, they remain uncoordinated except in the crudest way.

—Herbert Jacob
"The Courts as Political Agencies"

Most readers are cognizant of the storm of political controversy that can erupt over judicial decisions. When the United States Supreme Court upholds capital punishment, strikes down racial discrimination, or restricts access to abortion, waves of intense public debate are sure to follow. The same can be said of decisions of state and local courts. When a local judge upholds a zoning variance that permits developers to construct a hotel in a former all-residential neighborhood, voids a state constitutional amendment adopted by ballot initiative, or suppresses key evidence in a criminal prosecution, the media and public are likely to take notice.

Less prominent, but hardly less intense, are conflicts surrounding issues of judicial organization. From the volleys heard in the First Congress over the proposed Judiciary Act of 1789, to more recent debates concerning the workload of the United States Supreme Court,[1] to a state legislative bill to change the boundaries of state judicial districts, a veritable war has ensued over issues of the structure and jurisdiction of federal and state courts. To create a system of lower federal courts at all was a matter of sharp conflict in the First Congress, for some congressmen feared that a national system of courts might usurp state rights and lead to a dangerous growth in the power of the central government. Instead, some suggested that state courts already in existence should adjudicate federal matters, allowing for the possibility of direct appeal to the United States Supreme Court.[2] And, if courts were to be

---

[1]Among the many works addressing the caseload of the Supreme Court, see Gerhard Casper and Richard A. Posner, *The Workload of the Supreme Court* (Chicago: American Bar Foundation, 1976); and Richard L. Pacaelle, Jr., *The Transformation of the Supreme Court's Agenda* (Boulder, Colo.: Westview Press, 1991).

[2]These issues are discussed from a political perspective in Richard J. Richardson and Kenneth N. Vines, *The Politics of Federal Courts: Lower Courts in the United States* (Boston: Little, Brown, 1970), Chs. 2–3.

created inferior to the United States Supreme Court, what was their jurisdiction to be, and over what geographical area? If federal judicial districts include more than one state, would not federal judicial power eventually supersede state judicial prerogatives? Such structural issues at both the federal and state level have constituted an important chapter in the history of American judicial politics—and of American federalism.

To understand the politics of court structure in the United States, two preliminary facts must be stressed. Both are obvious to the professional student of American courts, but somewhat obscured by that widely held view of the American judiciary mentioned in Chapters 1 and 2, namely "The Upper (especially federal) Court Myth."[3] First, the great, overriding fact of judicial organization in the United States is that two separate and distinct systems of courts exist, one state, the other federal.[4] There are overlaps, confusion over jurisdiction, and so on (which will all be discussed later). But the notion that somehow the average citizen is entitled to begin his or her case in the lowest of magistrate courts, then to proceed up the ladder of appeals to the United States Supreme Court, is almost entirely mythical.

This leads us to the second important reality of American courts, namely that the great majority of cases filed in American courts in a given year are begun—and ended—in *state courts,* particularly state trial courts. The statistics are convincing, if not astounding.

JUDICIAL BUSINESS IN THE STATES

In 1990, for the first time in history, there were in excess of 100 million cases (civil, criminal, traffic, and juvenile) filed in state trial courts. Although the total had dipped a bit by 1993 and 1994, the long-term trend has been decidedly up, up, up, with cases in most categories increasing over the decade 1984 to 1994. These data are presented in Table 3–1. In that decade, state court civil case filings rose some 24 percent, criminal filings 35 percent (felony filings alone increasing 70 percent), domestic relations nearly 60 percent, and juvenile case filings about 59 percent. As noted, case filings for *all* levels of state courts in 1994 totaled some 86.7 million. The decline since 1990 is due almost entirely to redefinitions of traffic cases, with several jurisdictions moving to decriminalize minor traffic violations. This situation, of course, leaves these courts with the more serious traffic offenses to process.[5]

By way of contrast, there were but 281,864 civil and criminal cases filed in federal district courts in the year ending September 30, 1994. When we add the 48,322 cases commenced in the United States Courts of Appeals and 7,787 matters of all types found on the docket of the United States Supreme Court in 1993–1994, we have a total federal figure of only some 338,000 cases, giving us a federal-state case filing ratio of roughly 1:308 (see

---

[3]The term is, of course, Judge Jerome Frank's. See his *Courts on Trial: Myth and Reality in American Jurisprudence* (Princeton: Princeton University Press, 1950), Ch. 15.

[4]Of course the word *federal* is being used in its usual "misnomeric" sense, because the term properly applies to the entire governmental system in the United States, national and state. Hence, we really mean "national" or "central" rather than "federal."

[5]The best state court caseload data may be found in National Center for State Courts, *State Court Caseload Statistics: Annual Report* (Williamsburg, Va.: National Center for State Courts, Annual) (hereinafter referred to as *State Court Caseload Statistics*). Data for 1994 are summarized in a useful publication by the National Center for State Courts, *Examining the Work of State Courts, 1994* (Williamsburg, Va.: National Center for State Courts, 1996).

Dr. Brian J. Ostrom, Director of the Court Statistics Project of the Center, along with members of the statistics research team, has been extremely helpful in providing the author with data used throughout this book.

Table 3–1   State Court Filings, 1984, 1988, 1993, 1994

	1984	1988	1993	1994
Appellate Courts				
Courts of Last Resort	55,977	67,203	75,953	81,738
Intermediate Appellate Courts	119,021	154,590	179,050	181,955
Total	174,998	221,793	255,003	263,693
Trial Courts				
Civil*	13,580,067	16,919,204	19,348,322	19,014,662
Criminal	7,367,219	11,961,285	12,987,604	13,481,778
Traffic**	39,847,432	68,186,467	55,583,666	52,072,396
Juvenile	1,172,750	1,435,857	1,664,409	1,897,469
Total	61,967,468	98,502,813	89,584,001	86,456,305
Total All State Courts	62,142,466	98,724,606	89,839,004	86,719,998

*Includes domestic relations

**Includes ordinance violations

Source: National Center for State Courts, *State Court Caseload Statistics: Annual Report, 1984, 1988, 1994* (Williamsburg, Va.: National Center for State Courts, 1986, 1996); National Center for State Courts, *Examining the Work of State Courts, 1993, 1994* (Williamsburg, Va.: National Center for State Courts, 1995, 1996).

Table 3–2).[6] Even if we include the 517,397 matters handled by the United States magistrates assisting the U.S. district court judges in 1994, plus the 837,797 federal bankruptcy petitions filed that year, one may still conclude that for every piece of federal judicial business filed in 1994, there were some fifty filings in state courts.[7] To put this all another way, there were well over six times as many cases filed in a single state (California) in 1994 as there were in the entire federal judical system that year.[8]

True, one of the most important factors explaining the sharp contrast between federal and state judicial business is the large number of traffic cases handled by the states, for

[6]Data on the workload of the federal courts for years ending September 30, 1994, and 1995, may be found in abbreviated presentations by the Administrative Office of the U.S. Courts entitled simply *Judicial Business of the United States Courts, 1994, 1995* (Washington, D.C.: Administrative Office of the U.S. Courts, n.d). For many years, more extensive reports of federal caseload and management statistics, including detailed appendix tables, have also been published by the Administrative Office of the U.S. Courts under the triple title *Reports of the Proceedings of the Judicial Conference of the United States, Activities of the Administrative Office of the United States Courts,* and *Judicial Business of the United States Courts,* annual (Washington, D.C.: Administrative Office of the U.S. Courts, n.d). Throughout this book the former will be cited as *Judicial Business,* Abbrev., and the latter as *Judicial Business of the United States Courts.*

[7]On the work of federal magistrates and bankruptcy judges, see *Judicial Business,* Abbrev., 17–19. See also Christopher E. Smith, *United States Magistrates in the Federal Courts: Subordinate Judges* (New York: Praeger, 1990); and Christopher E. Smith, "From U.S. Magistrates to U.S. Magistrate Judges: Developments Affecting the Federal District Courts' Lower Tier of Judicial Officers," *Judicature* 75, No. 4 (Dec.–Jan. 1992): 210–15.

[8]*Examining the Work of State Courts, 1994,* 20–21, and passim. These federal-state comparisons admittedly ignore important differences in the work of the two levels of courts. For a discussion of this issue, which is part of the larger matter of shifting cases from federal to state courts, see *State Court Caseload Statistics, 1990,* 42–43, and the tables contained therein. Also see Brian J. Ostrom and Geoff Gallas, "Case Space: Do Workload Considerations Support a Shift from Federal to State Court Systems?" *State Court Journal* 14, No. 3 (Summer 1990): 15–22.

Table 3–2   State and Federal Constitutional Courts Contrasted, 1994

	Number of Courts		Number of Judgships		Number of Case Filings	
	Trial	Appellate	Trial	Appellate	Trial	Appellate
Federal	94	13	649[a]	176	1,637,058[b]	56,109
State	16,387	95	27,194	1,200	86,456,305	263,693
California Only	187	7	1,554[c]	95	10,524,903	28,171

[a]In addition, there were 494 Federal Magistrates and 326 Bankruptcy Judgships authorized in 1994.

[b]Figure includes 281,864 Federal District Court filings, 837,797 bankruptcy petitions, and 517,397 Federal Magistrate matters.

[c]Includes 789 judges of general jurisdiction courts and 670 limited jurisdiction judges, not including commissioners and referees.

Source: For state courts: National Center for State Courts, *State Court Caseload Statistics, 1994* (Williamsburg, Va.: National Center for State Courts, 1996); and National Center for State Courts, *Examining the Work of State Courts, 1994* (Williamsburg, Va.: National Center for State Courts, 1996). For federal courts: United States, Administrative Office of the U.S. Courts, *Judicial Business of the United States Courts 1994* (Washington: Administrative Office of the U.S. Courts, n.d.); and U.S., Administrative Office of the U.S. Courts, *Judicial Business* (Abbrev.) *1994* (Washington: Administrative Office of the U.S. Courts, n.d.).

which there is no federal counterpart. This means that approximately *98 percent* of American judicial business is handled by state courts. But if one excludes this enormous volume of traffic and local ordinance matters and simply compares civil and criminal cases handled by state courts of general jurisdiction with those cases processed in federal district courts; and further, if one uses filings per judge as a more direct means of comparing relative caseloads, we may still conclude, in the words of the National Center for State Courts, that

> With only 14 times as many judges as the federal judiciary, the state general jurisdiction judiciary handles 90 times as many criminal cases and 26 times as many civil cases. On average, a judge in a state court of general jurisdiction handles six times as many criminal and three times as many civil cases as a U.S. District Court judge.[9]

Yet another way of contrasting the federal and state judicial systems is by numbers of courts and judges. Although we do not have completely reliable data on all state courts and judges, the National Center for State Courts (NCSC) places the figure for state trial courts at 16,387 in 1994, with 27,164 trial judges.[10] Similar figures for state appellate courts, federal courts, and the California figures are presented in Table 3–2. Thus, for example, for every federal constitutional judge, there were 34 state judges, and for every federal court there were 155 state courts.

Not only can we ill afford to dismiss state courts and judges on grounds of their numbers and workload, but the nature of state court decision making referred to in the previous chapter must also be taken into account in assessing the significance of our fifty state judicial systems. Let us recall that state courts, particularly police courts, magistrate courts, and trial courts of general jurisdiction are, for all practical purposes, the courts of last resort for the great majority of American citizens involved in litigation each year. It is at this lower level that the elusive product we like to call "justice" is usually experienced by the

---

[9]*Examining the Work of State Courts, 1994,* 21.
[10]*Examining the Work of State Courts, 1994,* 14–15.

average citizen. If general and limited state trial courts processed some 86.5 million matters in 1994 (with some states not reporting), whereas state appellate courts heard only about 255,000 cases, this suggests an appeal ratio of only about 1 out of every 350 cases (.29 percent), which makes our most "inferior" of courts, in fact, courts of last resort for the vast majority of litigants. An ecclesiastical analogy further illustrates the point:

> A certain Bishop of Paris known through Europe for his great learning and humility, came to the conclusion that he was unworthy of his high place in the Church and successfully petitioned the Pope for reassignment to service as a simple parish priest. . . . After less than a year of parish work, the former Bishop was back in Rome with another petition, this one praying for his restoration to episcopal status, and for good and sufficient reason. "If I am unworthy to be Bishop of Paris," he said, "how much more unworthy am I to be priest of a parish. As Bishop I was remote from men and women of lowly station, my shortcomings and weaknesses concealed from them by distance and ecclesiastical dignity. But as parish priest, I move intimately each day among the members of my flock, endeavoring by comfort, counsel and admonition to make their hard lot on earth seem better than it is. I am the Church to them; when my faith flags or my wisdom fails or my patience wears thin, it is the Church that has failed them. *Demote me,* Your Holiness, and make me Bishop again, for I have learned how much easier it is to be a saintly bishop than to be a Godly priest."[11]

As Victor Rosenblum reminds us, these courts

> serve more often than not as courts of last resort as well as first resort. Exercise of the right of appeal takes time and money, and the average traffic offender, barroom scuffler, or delinquent debtor rarely has both. Judicial discretion reaches maximum proportion in these low-visibility cases. Whereas public awareness of and interest in the disposition of suits may be aroused in murder trials or occasional spicy divorce actions, the day-in, day-out drabness of the great majority of local court proceedings limits the public's range of concern and enhances, in effect, the judge's discretionary powers.[12]

If the state trial court is worthy of our attention, so much more so are state appellate courts. William J. Brennan, Jr., former associate justice of the United States Supreme Court and himself once a state supreme court justice (New Jersey), points out that

> The composite work of the courts of the fifty states probably has greater significance [than the United States Supreme Court] in measuring how well America attains the ideal of justice for all. The state courts of all levels must annually hand down literally millions of decisions which determine vital issues of life, liberty, and property of human beings of this nation. Even the yearly total of decisions handed down by the highest courts of the fifty states must run into the tens of thousands. We should remind ourselves it is the state court decisions which finally determine the overwhelming aggregate of all legal controversies in this nation.[13]

State supreme courts are and always have been the ultimate arbiters in a wide variety of politico-legal-economic matters of vital concern to the state and nation. Examples abound:

---

[11]The story is told by Harry W. Jones in "The Trial Judge: Role Analysis and Profile" in Harry W. Jones, ed., *The Courts, the Public, and the Law Explosion* (Englewood Cliffs, N.J.: Prentice-Hall, 1965), 25.

[12]See the excellent pair of essays on the politics of state courts by Victor G. Rosenblum, "Courts and Judges: Power and Politics" and "Judicial Reform: Needs and Prospects" in James W. Fesler, ed., *The Fifty States and Their Local Governments* (New York: Knopf, 1966), 411. This same point was made by Associate Justice Byron R. White in "The Special Role of State Judges," *Judges' Journal,* 30, No. 6 (Spring 1991): 7.

[13]William J. Brennan Jr., "State Supreme Court Judge vs. United States Supreme Court Justice: A Change in Function and Perspective," *University of Florida Law Review* 29, No. 2 (Fall 1966): 236.

1. In 1939, the state of New Mexico, at the behest of the state's liquor industry, passed a "fair trade" pricing law on liquor, and for nearly thirty years an interesting alliance of conservative Protestant clergymen and liquor interests defeated over three dozen attempts to overturn this law. As the industry reaped untold millions of dollars from the rigged, mark-up pricing system on liquor sales, the chief liquor lobbyist boasted that he "owned" the legislature.[14] In 1965, the state's leading political columnist reported that it was the "driest" legislature in many years, thanks to the refusal of the industry to stock the closets of legislators' hotel rooms with cases of their favorite booze, as they had always done in the past. Finally, on November 7, 1966, the state supreme court, in a unanimous opinion, held the law unconstitutional, concluding that "The fair trade contract and mark-up provisions of the Liquor Control Act are manifestly unreasonable legislation, and are not an appropriate exercise of the state's police power. . . ."[15]

2. The old common law rule that private hospitals owe no duty to the public to accept patients was altered by the Delaware Supreme Court in 1961 in an opinion which reasoned that when emergency facilities are maintained, the person severely hurt has a legal right to hospital access, and refusal of aid in a clear emergency renders the hospital liable for damages.[16]

3. The California Supreme Court, often cited as a highly innovative state court, has frequently shown in its decisions the creative capacity of the state appellate bench. Perhaps the best example is its decision on public school financing. In 1971, in *Serrano v. Priest,* the California Supreme Court held that the state's school financing formula, deriving some 55 percent of public school revenue from local taxes, discriminated against children in poorer school districts by depriving them of the equal protection of the laws guaranteed in both the state and national constitutions.[17] The circumstances that gave rise to the suit were exemplified by the Beverly Hills and Baldwin Park financing plans. Wide disparities in the tax bases of these two communities led to vast differences in per pupil expenditures. Indeed, in 1968–1969 the per child expenditure in Beverly Hills was $1,230 annually, whereas in neighboring Baldwin Park, it stood at $580 per year.[18] Despite the fact that the United States Supreme Court, in *San Antonio Independent School District v. Rodriguez,* 411 U.S. 1 (1973), declined to hold such financing plans in violation of the Federal Equal Protection Clause, the *Serrano* holding was followed by several other state supreme courts (notably Arizona, Kansas, Michigan, Minnesota, and New Jersey) and has tended to nudge state legislatures across the country to revise school funding programs.[19]

[14]A portion of the story is related in Harry P. Stumpf and T. Phillip Wolf, "New Mexico: The Political State: in Frank H. Jonas, ed., *Politics in the American West* (Salt Lake City: University of Utah Press, 1969), 281–82. The 1939 state liquor legislation was not fundamentally changed until the state legislative session of 1981.

[15]*Drink, Inc. v. Babcock,* 421 P.2d. 798 (1966).

[16]Rosenblum, "Courts and Judges": 408. Rosenblum's analysis includes several other excellent examples of state appellate court policy-making. Further examples in addition to useful information on the role of state supreme courts may be found in G. Alan Tarr and Mary Cornelia Aldis Porter, *State Supreme Courts in State and Nation* (New Haven: Yale University Press, 1988). On the current activism of state supreme courts, see Harry P. Stumpf and John C. Culver, *The Politics of State Courts* (New York: Longman, 1992), especially Ch. 7, and the sources cited therein.

[17]*Serrano v. Priest,* 487 P.2d. 1241, 96 Cal. Rptr. 601 (1971). The literature on the public school financing issue is voluminous. As an introduction, *see* John E. Coons, William H. Clune, and Stephen Sugarman, *Private Wealth and Public Education* (Cambridge, Mass.: Harvard University Press, 1970).

[18]See Robert B. Keiter, "California Educational Financing System Violates Equal Protection," *Clearinghouse Review* 5, No. 6 (Oct. 1977): 287–88, 297–300. See also James Flanigan, "Taxing for Schools, Investing in the Future," *Los Angeles Times* (June 3, 1990): D-1; and Stumpf and Culver, *The Politics of State Courts,* 149–157.

[19]See Richard Lehne's *The Quest for Justice: The Politics of School Finance Reform* (New York: Longman, 1978). Through a detailed case study of the New Jersey Supreme Court's school financing decision of 1973 (*Robinson v. Cahill*), Lehne provides an excellent analysis of the policy role of state supreme courts. Lehne argues that the *Serrano* and like cases were more "agenda-setting" than they were decision-making cases.

Examples of significant judicial policy-making could be multiplied along the entire range of state courts. The point is that for most purposes, it is time to stop viewing the state judiciaries as inferior country cousins. Actually, they are the great, but barely visible, nine-tenths (or ninety-eight one hundredths) of the iceberg. Moreover, the influence of state court lawmaking was considerably enhanced by the United States Supreme Court in the 1938 decision of *Erie Railroad v. Tompkins,* 304 U.S. 64. Prior to that time, under the old rule of *Swift v. Tyson,* 16 Pet. 1 (1842), the Court held that when federal courts heard cases involving citizens of different states ("Diversity of Citizenship") the law applied should be based on whatever general legal principles seemed proper. This often led to two sets of rules governing the resolution of disputes in diversity cases: one set applied by federal courts and based on a sort of federal common law, the other fashioned by state courts interpreting state law. Disputants thus "court shopped," filing diversity cases either in federal or state courts depending on which body of law offered the best probability of upholding their particular claim. *Erie* ruled that, at least in matters of substance, federal courts were to apply state law to state claims.[20] One of the effects of this holding has been to render state court rulings important not only for state policy but also as they impact on federal judicial decision making. The growing importance of state courts of last resort is discussed more fully in Chapter 10. Having argued the general case for the significance of state courts, let us now turn to the structure of the courts themselves.

STATE COURT SYSTEMS

The Colonial Experience

As with most other human organizations, state judicial systems are to be understood not as a static, rigid hierarchy existing for all times, but rather as a set of human institutions created and modified over time to meet constantly changing needs. The states that were colonies inherited their judicial systems directly from their colonial structures. Each colonial judiciary was a reflection of the legal, historical, economic, and social characteristics of that particular colony. One must also remember that the systems evolved over a period of some 180 years (the settlement at Jamestown to the writing of the Constitution). We can gain some perspective by considering that this is approximately equal to the time span between the ratification of the Constitution and the first inauguration of Richard Nixon!

Colonial judicial records are sparse, forcing historians to fill in the gaps with secondary evidence and supposition. But it seems clear that colonial law and courts were, in a very broad sense, rough approximations of the seventeenth- and eighteenth-century English judiciary. Most colonies had local judges, called justices of the peace or magistrates, usually appointed by the colonial governor for the processing of minor disputes. Above these were general trial courts, often called county courts, and finally, at the apex, was a court consisting of the governor and his council, or later, a specially appointed appellate body which acted as a court of last resort. A lack of institutional specialization was a characteristic of colonial justice, so that at times the colonial legislature itself would sit as an appellate tribunal, while local justices of the peace were often administrative as well as judicial officers.[21] Grand and petit juries were also introduced and became common.

---

[20]But see Note, *"Swift v. Tyson Exhumed," Yale Law Journal* 79, No. 2 (Dec. 1969): 284–310.

[21]A useful piece of research on colonial judiciaries is Francis R. Aumann, *The Changing American Legal System: Some Selected Phases* (Columbus: Ohio State University Press, 1940). See also Stephen Botein, *Early American Law and Society: Essays and Documents* (New York: Random House, 1980); and Kermit L. Hall, *The Magic Mirror: Law in American History* (New York: Oxford University Press, 1989), especially Chs. 1 and 2.

The colonial county courts, usually having both original and appellate jurisdictions, exemplify the nondifferentiation existing in colonial governmental structure and function. Lawrence Friedman explains their role in seventeenth-century Maryland:

> The county courts were at the heart of colonial government. As more and more of their records are published, a picture of colonial justice vividly unfolds. For example, one can now look in on the county court of Prince Georges County, Maryland, meeting "att Charles Towne the twenty fourth day of November in the Eight yeare of the Reigne of our Sovereigne Lord William the third" (1696). . . . At Small's [Inn], the court discharged its business—judicial, administrative, quasi-legislative. . . . Benjamin Berry and Robert Gordon were found to have been drunk at an inn, "profanely Cursing and Swareing"; they were ordered to be put in the stocks. A number of citizens recorded marks for their animals; [branding]. . . . A grand jury met and made presentments: "Elizabeth Pole Servant woman . . . for haveing a bastard."[22]

It is easy to assume that the corpus of American colonial law was a transplanted version of English common law. Several factors make that assumption questionable, however. First, the common law system of seventeenth-century England was in such low repute that its wholesale importation into colonial life would have met with stiff opposition. The bench and bar under Stuart England were both thoroughly corrupt, giving rise to bitter resentment in the colonies toward all things legal. Colonial laws against the practice of law itself were not uncommon, there being a widespread assumption that the average person could conduct his or her legal business without the aid of an attorney.[23]

Second, the common law of that era was complex, technical, and tedious, hampered in some respects by an excessive formalism held over from the Middle Ages. In its style as well as content, it often simply did not fit into the raw colonial life. Finally, in the absence of professionally trained lawyers, the obvious vehicle for transferring the ways of the common law into everyday colonial life was lacking. Thus, through at least the early decades of colonial history, law consisted of a rough-and-ready frontier justice based on the political and social philosophies of the settlement leaders, frequently founded upon a biblical ethic. As one historian put it, "the 'word of God' played a greater part in the progress and practise of the law than the words of Brackton, Littleton or Coke. . . . [T]here was more need of clever clergymen than of trained lawyers."[24]

Outside of the major port cities, adjudication tended to deal mostly with matters of morals, family problems, agriculture, and personal property issues. The Pynchon court record of western Massachusetts of 1671–1672 is illustrative:

February 2, 1670 (1671)

> Richard Barnard examined concerning his getting Sarah Clarke (the daughter of John Clarke) with child acknowledged it and finding none that would become Bound for him was Commuted: till he should find suertys for his appearance at the County Cort to answer for his said fornication: and John Clarke Ingaged for his daughter Sarah to be then forthcoming: who by her owne Confeshion is above halfe gon with child: Richard Barnard having had carnall knowledge of her Body last English harvest at the very beginning of Reaping Ry: and she saith for which there fornication they are both to appeare at

---

[22]Lawrence M. Friedman, *A History of American Law,* 2nd ed. (New York: Simon & Schuster, 1985), 43. Friedman is quoting from Joseph H. Smith and Philip A. Crowl, eds., *Court Records of Prince Georges County, Maryland, 1696–1699* (Indianapolis: Bobbs-Merrill, 1966), 59 ff.

[23]Charles Warren, *A History of the American Bar* (Boston: Little, Brown, 1911), 3–19. More generally, see the insightful analysis of the eighteenth century transformation of the common law in Morton J. Horwitz, *The Transformation of American Law, 1780–1860* (Cambridge: Harvard University Press, 1977).

[24]Warren, *History of the American Bar,* 8.

next Court in Northhampton on the last Tuesday in March next, and so the whole case and examinations taken I Transmit thither. [They were married February 13th, though they were each later fined 40 shillings for their transgression.]

July 27, 1671

Obadiah Cooly makes complaint against 2 Indians for getting into his Howse and stealing from him wampam and some other small things: The Indians Missahump and Mahamatap: appeared (being brought by the Constable) who owne That last Saturday they went into Obadiah Coolys howse at the window noebody being at hom and tooke thence a knife: and a long Indian Jewel: 7 hands of white wampam and 2 hands of black wampam and a fine workt Basket. . . . [Missahump was sentenced to be whipped 10 stripes and Mahamatap with 8 stripes] . . . well laid on the naked Body. . . .[25]

By the early decades of the eighteenth century, colonial judicial systems were beginning to look more English. The needs of commercial and industrial interests invited growth of the legal profession.[26] The familiar three-tiered judicial structure did not change significantly (except for increased specialization of function, such as admiralty and chancery), but judicial procedures grew more sophisticated as lawyers trained in the English Inns of Court became more numerous and slowly replaced colonial procedure with that of the English common law. Appeals from the colonies' highest court could be taken to the Privy Council in London, though that was rare. When it did occur, the Privy Council was found to be an ineffective royal governing device.[27] Thus, colonial and English legal practices grew more similar, not because of effective policy-making from London, but because of common commercial needs, a common language, and common legal background.

As the colonies moved toward independence, the adoption of the common law quickened. This was due, in part, to the dramatic growth of the English common law itself, and in part to the pressing colonial need for legal concepts to serve the twin needs of commercial growth and the political requirements of the move toward independence. Thus, economics joined with politics to help create a period of intense legal development in America, only modestly slowed by the Revolutionary War. Isaac Parker, then chief justice of the Massachusetts Supreme Court, explained the political side of the equation:

Without doubt, the approaching dismemberment of the colonies from the parent country, had enlarged the minds and invigorated the faculties of the lawyers of the day, for we always find that a great political crisis produces extraordinary efforts of the human understanding. The constant claim of prerogative on one side, and privilege on the other, required a knowledge of the rights and duties of the subject in those who presented themselves for royal patronage or popular favor. Profound discussions of the principles of free government, the duty of submission and the right of resistance, sharpened the faculties and exercised the wits of the most distinguished lawyers, to which class of the community these discussions were almost entirely left. . . . [I]t cannot be doubted that the law was then deemed a science, worthy of the most enlightened minds to learn, and honorable for the most dignified institution to teach.[28]

---

[25]Joseph H. Smith, ed., *Colonial Justice in Western Massachusetts (1639–1702), The Pynchon Court Record* (Cambridge, Mass.: Harvard University Press, 1961), 272, 274–75.

[26]Friedman, *History of American Law*, 48.

[27]Friedman, *History of American Law*, 49.

[28]Isaac Parker, *North American Review* 3 (May 1816): 16–17, as quoted in Aumann, *Changing American Legal System*, 70–71.

Legal principles, concepts, organization—in short, a legal system—was needed. The reworked English common law lay readily at hand, and in a relatively short time—between 1760 and 1820—a rather backward colonial legal framework was transformed into a very English common law system. To be sure, colonial experience forced significant modifications, but with nearly two centuries of fits and starts, the English common law was growing on American soil.[29]

State Courts Under the Constitution

With the ratification of the Constitution in 1789 came a new set of issues for state courts. At the outset these tribunals were the heirs apparent of the evolving common law—that is, the American legal system *was* the state court system, and many of the most distinguished lawyers of the day sat on these courts. Only gradually did the federal judiciary eclipse state courts in prestige and power.

One noted scholar of American legal institutions has seen state judicial structure characterized by three interdependent features: (1) localism, (2) hierarchy, and (3) emphasis on the right of appeal.[30] We might add two additional features that stand out: (4) a strong and enduring resistance to basic organizational change, and (5) the paradox of unity in diversity.

First, from the earliest (even colonial) times, Americans have viewed courts as local institutions created for local needs. The "lowest" of courts (justices of the peace) were created almost, as James Willard Hurst says, "on a neighborhood basis." Even the trial courts of general jurisdiction (civil and criminal) were initially located in districts laid out according to the distance a person could travel on horseback in a day. State law, or the state constitution, usually established jurisdiction, venue, and certain details of practice, whereas local courts saw themselves as semiautonomous in matters of case flow, finance, and general judicial administration. This tradition of localism spurred by economic factors led to other (sometimes peculiar) features of judicial structure in the states. For example, as caseloads increased, states and communities responded by piling court upon court. This process brought about a rash of courts and court systems in some metropolitan areas with no logical interaction between and among them. For example, in the 1930s there were over 500 separate courts in the Chicago metropolitan area alone.

Second, the American tradition of judicial structure always dictated the creation of courts in a hierarchical fashion, giving rise to sharp differences in rank, salary, tenure, and status among judges. "Lower" and "inferior" courts are American terms which imply that judges in such courts need not be selected by criteria applicable to "superior" courts. Thus, the American concept of court structure tends to depict trial judges as inferior, demeaning perhaps the most important of our judicial institutions. At the same time, appellate courts are considered to be "superior." It is interesting to note that although the 1873 reform of English courts awarded a higher status to its trial courts, American practice has yet to follow suit.

Third, perhaps more than any other nation, we have insisted on a judicial organization characterized by multiple rights of appeal. This has led to enormous waste, duplication of effort, and general inefficiency in litigation in the United States. Much of the his-

---

[29]Aumann, *Changing American Legal System,* 71–93. But see the important changes in conceptualization of law described in Horwitz, *The Transformation of American Law, 1780–1860.*

[30]James Willard Hurst, *The Growth of American Law: The Lawmakers* (Boston: Little, Brown, 1950), 85–107.

tory of reform in American courts has had to do with a reduction, by various means, in an almost inexhaustible appeals route.

Typically, American court organization has been set out in great specificity in state constitutions or in elaborate legislative enactments. This has been in sharp contrast to federal practice. The U.S. Constitution provides for only one Supreme Court, leaving to Congress the existence, character, and jurisdiction of other federal courts. The state approach of careful constitutional-legislative control, combined with entrenched localism, as well as the myth of judicial independence, all help explain the fourth overall characteristic of American state judicial organization, namely its surprising resistance to change.[31] Basic court structural patterns have been with us since colonial times, and not until the beginning of the present century was there a serious move for reform.[32] To be sure, structural modification has been frequent, but it has seldom upset the basic organizational philosophy of the system.

Finally, American state courts are the source of a paradox. As the following discussion will show, the tradition of localism, inherited from our colonial experience, has helped to produce fifty seemingly distinct judicial systems. Yet, beneath the surface there emerges a basic similarity of judicial organization and procedure that must not escape our attention. It is this tension between unity and diversity that produces the paradox of state court organization. With these general considerations as a backdrop, let us look at some of the specifics of contemporary state judicial structure.

Fundamentally, the courts of our fifty states are organized in three tiers: a variety of limited or special jurisdiction tribunals at the bottom, the state's trial courts of general jurisdiction in the middle, and the appellate courts on top. However, with the growth of industrialization and urbanization, along with the vastly increased judicial workload, state courts have tended to expand into a structural form having a five-tiered appearance. At the bottom is the old justice of the peace (JP) system (often rural and frequently replaced by a somewhat modernized magistrate system, but not considerably reformed). Next are metropolitan or municipal courts, also of limited and specialized jurisdiction. Third, there are state trial courts of general jurisdiction handling both criminal and civil cases. With the workload of state supreme courts growing out of control, most states have created intermediate appellate courts. Finally, at the apex, are state courts of last resort. Collapsing the JP-magistrate and metropolitan courts into one category, entitled trial courts of limited jurisdiction, provides a four-tiered state court system, as illustrated in the California and Kansas court organization charts circa 1994 (Figures 3–1 and 3–2). Each of these structural models may be contrasted, on the one hand, with a more "unified" two-tier system exemplified by the Minnesota state courts (Figure 3–3), and on the other hand, with the relatively unreformed, confusing and complex New York structure (Figure 3–4). The basic four-tiered structure of state courts is detailed in these figures.

Courts of Limited Jurisdiction.   These tribunals go by various names: municipal court, police, justice of the peace, juvenile, magistrate, and so on. They represent approximately 85 percent of all courts in the United States and normally hear some 75 percent of

---

[31]See Herbert Jacob, "The Courts as Political Agencies: An Historical Analysis," in Herbert Jacob and Kenneth N. Vines, eds., *Studies in Judicial Politics,* Tulane Studies in Political Science, Vol. 8 (New Orleans: Tulane University, 1962), 46–50, for further reasons for state court resistance to reform.

[32]A speech by Roscoe Pound in 1906, entitled "The Causes of Popular Dissatisfaction with the Administration of Justice," is generally credited with launching the reform movement in American courts. The speech is reprinted in the *Journal of American Judicature Society* 20, No. 5 (Feb. 1937): 178–87. The speech was an address delivered at the Annual Convention of the American Bar Association.

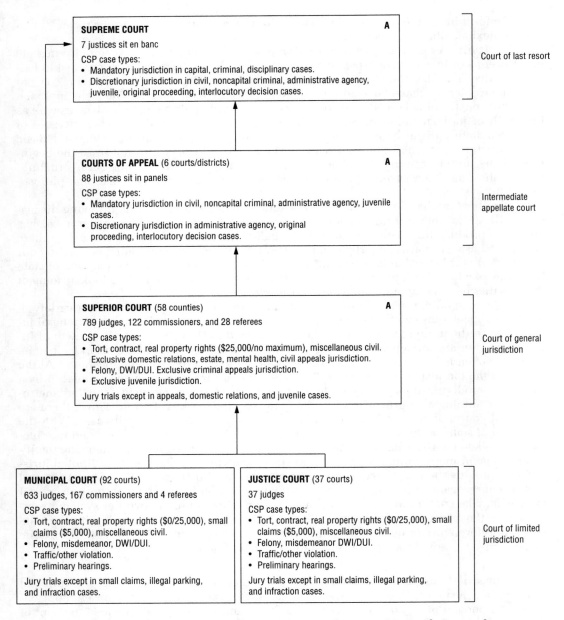

Figure 3–1 California Court Structure, 1994 (SOURCE: National Center for State Courts, *State Court Caseload Statistics, 1994* (Williamsburg, Va.: National Center for State Courts, 1996): 12.)

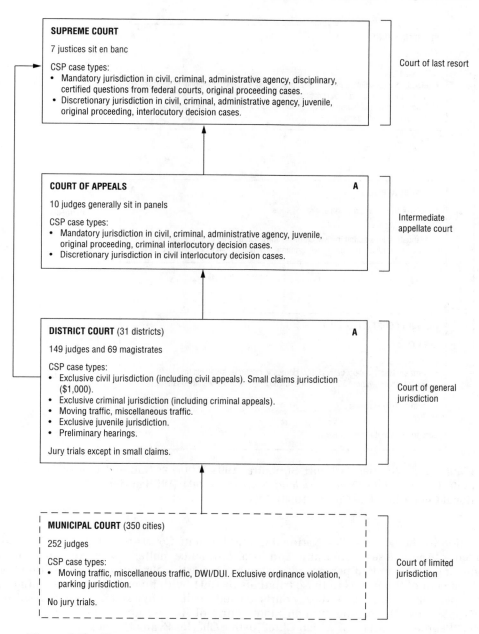

Figure 3–2   Kansas Court Structure, 1994 (SOURCE: National Center for State Courts, *State Court Caseload Statistics, 1994* (Williamsburg, Va.: National Center for State Courts, 1996): 24.)

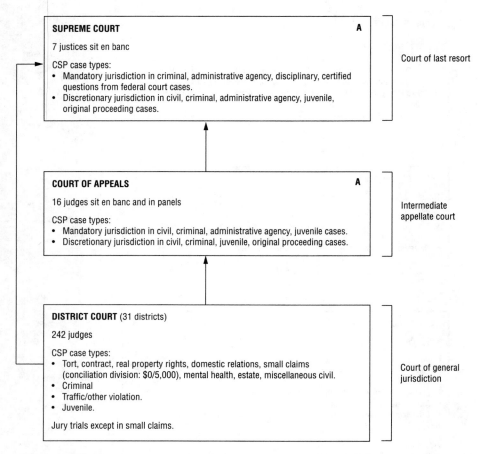

Figure 3–3 Minnesota Court Structure, 1994 (SOURCE: National Center for State Courts, *State Court Caseload Statistics, 1994* (Williamsburg, Va.: National Center for State Courts, 1996), 31.)

all litigation in state courts. The National Center for State Courts reports that in 1994 some 70 percent of these cases were traffic and local ordinance matters, with civil and criminal cases making up 15 and 13 percent respectively. Domestic relations cases constituted only about 2 percent of the filings in these tribunals in 1994, with juvenile issues weighing in at only one percent.[33] As of 1994, these courts existed in all but five states, these five subsuming all trial courts under one system. State courts of limited jurisdiction remain, if you will, the "People's Courts," of which Chief Justice Charles Evans Hughes spoke:

> A petty tyrant in a police court, refusals of a fair hearing in minor civil courts, the impatient disregard of an immigrant's ignorance of our ways and language will daily breed Bolsheviks who are beyond the reach of your appeals. Here is work for lawyers. The Supreme Court of the United States and the Court of Appeals will take care of themselves. Look

---

[33]*Examining the Work of State Courts, 1994,* 13.

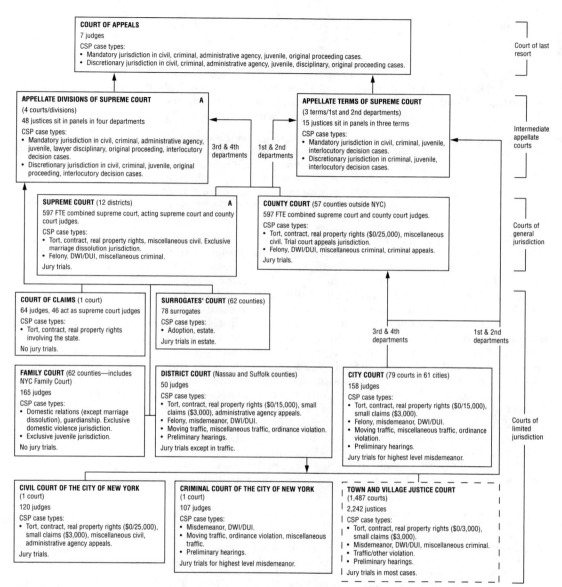

Figure 3–4   New York Court Structure, 1994* (SOURCE: National Center for State Courts, *State Court Caseload Statistics, 1994* (Williamsburg, Va.: National Center for State Courts, 1996): 40.)

after the courts of the poor, who stand most in need of justice. The security of the Republic will be found in the treatment of the poor and the ignorant; in indifference to their misery and helplessness lies disaster.[34]

It seems ironic that while commentators are in agreement as to the significance of these courts, they are also in agreement that the courts constitute the weakest part of the American judicial structure. Indictments of limited jurisdiction courts fill the pages of the literature on state court organization, the following critique being representative:

> Courts of limited and special jurisdiction have come to mirror their position on the bottom rung of the judicial ladder. The sheer volume of cases in relation to personnel, the generally poor quality of judicial and non-judicial personnel, low salaries, inadequate facilities, weak administration, the fragmentation of jurisdiction, along with the inefficient and archaic trial *de novo* system, simply underscore the shortcomings of courts of limited jurisdiction and the myriad problems which must be overcome to compensate for generations of neglect.[35]

The jurisdiction of these courts is limited in one of two ways, and sometimes both. First, in criminal matters in most states, they may judge only the lesser offenses (misdemeanors, traffic violations, and so forth) and may impose only limited fines (most may not impose fines in excess of $1,000, nor impose jail terms of more than 12 months). Second, they are often limited to certain kinds of substantive matters (traffic, domestic relations, juvenile), rather than being open to all types of controversies.

America's state courts of limited and special jurisdiction are noted for additional characteristics. First, they are often not courts of record; their proceedings, more often than not, go unrecorded, and their general procedures tend to be informal, haphazard, and unpredictable. Absent a record, either tape-recorded or transcribed, of the cases they resolve, appeals from these courts must be heard anew (*de novo*) in the next highest court, creating duplication of court effort. The American Judicature Society's survey of courts of limited jurisdiction revealed that lack of record keeping is largely a function of lack of funding, which leads us to a second feature of these courts: woeful underfunding. In fact, a few of these courts have no funding at all; they operate essentially on the fees collected. Many others are only partially funded.[36]

Third, the presiding judges of these courts (some 14,000 courts in 1994) are often not required to have formal legal training.[37] Many are part-time judges who may well have an-

---

[34]As quoted in John A. Robertson, ed., *Rough Justice: Perspectives on Lower Criminal Courts* (Boston: Little, Brown, 1974), vii–viii.

[35]American Judicature Society, *Courts of Limited Jurisdiction: A National Survey* (Chicago: American Judicature Society, 1975), 10. A similar indictment of these courts was made by the National Advisory Commission of Criminal Justice Standards and Goals, *Courts* (Washington: GPO, 1973), 164–67.

[36]American Judicature Society, *Courts of Limited Jurisdiction,* 15–19. See also Carl Barr, *Separate but Subservient: Court Budgeting in the American States* (Lexington, Mass.: Heath, 1975). Funding patterns for state courts are reported in U. S., Dept. of Justice, Office of Justice Programs, *State Court Organization, 1993* (Washington: Bureau of Justice Statistics, 1995): Table 17, 136–165. Hereinafter referred to as *State Court Organization.*

[37]In 1976 in *North v. Russell,* 427 U.S. 382, the Supreme Court refused to require state courts to have legally trained judges, so long as litigants could appeal to higher courts presided over by lawyer-judges. The most recent survey of state courts in this regard (1993) reveals that approximately two-thirds of the states have at least one limited jurisdiction court in which lay judging is permitted. See *State Court Organization,* Table 7, 70–77.

An excellent, though dated, review of lay judging is Linda J. Silberman, *Non-Attorney Justice in the United States: An Empirical Study* (New York: Institute of Judicial Administration, 1979). See also Doris Provine, *Judging Credentials: Non-Lawyer Judges and the Politics of Professionalism* (Chicago: University of Chicago Press, 1986).

other position in local government. At the same time, it is not unusual to find these local judicial figures serving in a number of nonadjudicative roles—as family counselors, officials who perform marriages, ex officio coroners, and so on.

Fourth, many of these courts are not courts at all in the sense of having a permanent residence. They may meet in any number of settings hardly conducive to the serious allocation of justice.[38] No clerk, no courtroom, little or no training, underfunding—it is easy to understand the low esteem in which these tribunals are held. In addition, these courts are noted for the assumption of guilt, rather than innocence, that they place on the defendant. Lacking legal training and other resources for fair trials, many of these judges presume guilt, focusing their attention not on guilt or innocence but on the sentence to be imposed.

Finally, a general lack of supervisory influence creates an anomaly in these courts relating to caseloads. Some limited jurisdiction tribunals, chiefly in the metropolitan areas, have outrageously heavy caseloads, whereas others, often rural courts, are peopled by judges having little or nothing to do—ten cases per month, perhaps. These general characteristics have led to the following specific experiences with limited jurisdiction courts:

- A 1966 study of the Virginia Justice of the Peace system revealed that only 4 out of 411 past and present JPs had law degrees, 71 percent had never attended college, and 18 percent had not graduated from high school.[39] Similar proportions emerge in data from the Oregon and Pennsylvania JP or magistrate systems.
- One New Mexico JP (before the state adopted the magistrate system) testified, "I know a lot of Justices of the Peace that are not qualified. . . . They can't even sign their name and can't read or write."[40]
- The American Judicature Society's study of courts of limited jurisdiction revealed "Courtrooms that are dirty, crowded, noisy, or makeshift . . . (such as the Oddfellows Hall)."[41] JP, magistrate, or municipal court is often held in private homes. New Mexico JP courts were known to have been held in bars, a coal mine, a curio shop, or a café; much the same pattern is apparent in the operation of the new magistrate system in New Mexico.
- 150 municipal courts in Texas collected fees amounting to five times the actual operating expense of their courts, while most of these same courts lacked adequate courtrooms. Some New Mexico JPs were reported to have grossed $45,000 and $65,000 per year (in 1980 dollars) through that state's fee system, usually involving collusion with state police in arrests and fines.[42]
- It is not difficult to find lower court judges in some states who never recall having found a defendant innocent. A study of the JP system in New Mexico uncovered the following testimony:

  Q: *You have had cases in every instance, you have found them guilty?*
  A: Well, it depended according to the evidence. I go by the charges and the evidence. I can't recollect one that I found not guilty.
  Q: *I want you to answer the question. You have had cases where they have pled not guilty?*
  A: Yes.

---

[38]See New Mexico, State Judicial Systems Study Committee, *The Courts of New Mexico* (Santa Fe: State of New Mexico, 1961); and Provine, *Judging Credentials,* 171–72.

[39]As reported in Henry J. Abraham, *The Judicial Process,* 6th ed. (New York: Oxford University Press, 1993), 139.

[40]*Courts of New Mexico,* 1.

[41]American Judicature Society, *Courts of Limited Jurisdiction,* 35.

[42]*Courts of New Mexico,* 11–12.

Q: *What do you do?*
A: I find them guilty.

- A New Mexico JP headed an inquest in which, according to the evidence, the man was shot "three times in the heart and once in the head" and a verdict of "suicide" was rendered.[43]
- Conviction rates reported in Michigan, Mississippi, and Tennessee run from 95 to 99.5 percent,[44] and a lay judge in Kern County, California, was quoted as openly admitting that in his court "a defendant is often presumed guilty until proven innocent."[45]

The culmination of the leading characteristics of these courts can often resemble the following:

- In California, "justice courts" consisted of 156 nonattorney judges who handled approximately 90,000 criminal proceedings per year. Some of the results were:

  A. Judge "H," Santa Barbara County, attempted to pronounce a defendant guilty without waiting to hear the defense. When defense counsel objected, he was allowed to put on a defense. Judge "H" then found the defendant guilty again and tried to impose a sentence five times greater than the statutory maximum.

  B. Lay Judge "I" of Sacramento County learned of a recent United States Supreme Court decision prohibiting the imposition of jail terms upon convicted persons who are financially unable to pay their fines. The judge applied the decision by imposing jail terms on all persons convicted in his court, upon indigents and nonindigents, in serious cases and in traffic cases alike.

  C. Courtroom practice for one nonattorney judge was to conduct an informal poll for the "verdict" of the courtroom audience prior to announcing his own decision in a case.

  D. "I don't know anything more about the law than a hog does about the 4th of July," admits Judge "A" of Riverside County, "but I know what's right and wrong."

  E. One lay judge stated he always practiced "sniffing" each witness from the bench because he believed he would *[sic]* tell the witness's veracity by the witness's scent.

  F. Lay Judge "A" stated, "If a nigger comes in here and doesn't have any money for a $10 fine, that doesn't bother me just because he's black. I'm not prejudiced. . . . I don't have anything against the black bastards even though they lie and steal all the time."[46]

In *Gordon v. Justice Court,* 525 P.2d 72 (1974), the California Supreme Court held the use of lay judges to be a violation of due process, and this was repeated in a number of other states. Some state supreme courts, however, have moved in the opposite direction, resulting in non-lawyer judging remaining alive and well in various forms in most states.[47]

Within the last two or three decades, courts of limited jurisdiction, viewed from a national perspective, have undergone considerable reform, though some of the changes are more apparent than real. For example, at the time of *Gordon v. Justice Court,* there were

---

[43]*Courts of New Mexico,* 11–12.

[44]Abraham, *Judicial Process,* 139.

[45]Migrant Legal Action Program, *Monthly Report* 3, No. 2 (Feb. 1974): 4.

[46]Migrant Legal Action Program, *Monthly Report,* 4. These examples are taken from a writ of prohibition of *Gordon v. Justice Court of Yuba City, California, et al.,* seeking to require all judges to have legal training.

[47]Silberman, *Non-Attorney Justice,* 24–25; Appendix A, 253–260. Similar examples may be found in Provine, *Judging Credentials.*

156 judges in California without law degrees, but in 1976 non-lawyer judging was abolished. Moreover, via Proposition 191, overwhelmingly approved by California voters in November 1994, California's Justice Courts were incorporated into the state's municipal court system.[48] In New Mexico, the old Justice of the Peace courts were abolished in the mid-sixties; however, the magistrate court system that replaced it retains many of the JP court characteristics, especially in the state's rural areas. Indeed, this seems to be the pattern throughout the nation, wherein court reform tends to result in change in name and form, though not always in the actual character of the courts.[49]

A thorough study of non-attorney judging by Doris Marie Provine in the mid-eighties, concluded that differences between lawyer and non-lawyer judges were minimal. Lay judging might be seen as an important link between an otherwise distant legal system and the people, especially in small-town and rural America. In such environs, there are often no practicing attorneys, and people-to-people disputes are perhaps best handled by local officials knowledgeable about local conditions and concerns. This is in the best tradition of American judicial history. In any event, the case against lay judges should not be seen as conclusive.

The reader should also bear in mind that the category "courts of limited jurisdiction" constitutes a wide spectrum of tribunals located in major metropolitan areas. These courts though heavily overworked, handle large volumes of cases (often traffic matters along with minor neighborhood disputes, petty larceny, prostitution, and drunkenness), with reasonable dispatch, if not careful consideration. Again, the presumption of guilt may lie just beneath the surface—assembly-line "justice" being the rule—but they are at least courts of record with modern recording equipment, a trained judge, and adequate physical facilities, all leading to a decent courtroom decorum.[50] Municipal courts of a specialized nature also include juvenile courts, small claims courts, domestic relations courts, and probate courts. As their names imply, these courts have been established in various states to achieve the advantage of subject-matter specialization and to relieve the workload of courts of more general jurisdiction. The latest development in this regard is the drug court, sometimes a court, per se, at other times simply a diversion option for drug treatment.[51]

Several states have created separate statewide juvenile courts, although the general state pattern is to handle juvenile cases either in special municipal courts or in the state trial court of general jurisdiction. Americans continue the long-standing debate over their judicial philosophy toward juveniles, the issue sooner or later always coming down to whether to treat juvenile offenders in a paternalistic manner or as adults. In *In re Gault,* 387 U.S. 1 (1967), the Supreme Court held that the Fourteenth Amendment due process safe-

---

[48]Matthew Heller, "It's a Nightmare: Elevation of Justice Courts Causes Fiscal Problems," *Los Angeles Daily Journal* (July 6, 1995): 1, 5. Some of the advantages of the old Justice Courts are discussed by David D. Minier, "Proposition 191 Sweeps Away a Tradition in Rural California Justice," *Sacramento Bee* (Nov. 3, 1994): B-7.

[49]Provine, *Judging Credentials,* 25. On the pros and cons of reforming courts of limited jurisdiction, see an insightful piece by Julia Lamber and Mary Lee Luskin, "Court Reform: A View from the Bottom," *Judicature* 75, No. 6 (Apr.–May, 1992): 295–99.

[50]For a graphic description of such courts, see Howard James, *Crisis in the Courts,* rev. ed. (New York: David McKay, 1971). Ch. 3, "Courts for the Common Man."

[51]See *State Court Organization, passim.* For a brief discussion of the drug court development, see "New Drug Court Resource Center," *State Court Report* 1, No. 2 (Winter 1995): 1, 11. A more comprehensive view of the drug issue as related to state courts is found in "Special Issue: Swift and Effective Justice: New Approaches to Drug Cases in the States," *Justice System Journal* 17, No. 1 (1994). For a description of the workings of the Miami Drug Court, see Mireya Navarro, "Special Courts Use New Tactics in Battle Against Drug Addiction," *New York Times,* Oct. 17, 1996: A-1.

guards must be applied to juveniles, including adequate notice, representation by counsel, and the privilege against self-incrimination. Still, the debate ensues as to how best to fulfill these requirements in dealing with the juvenile offender.[52]

Small claims courts have been created in many municipalities to provide quick, inexpensive processing of relatively minor civil suits. Although originally intended for the easy access of the common person, research has repeatedly shown that the vast majority of actions in small claims courts are brought not by individual consumers but by physicians, hospitals, utilities, department stores, and collection agencies *against* individual citizens (see Chapter 8). A study of these courts by Consumers Union in 1970 observed that their gravest defect is the perversion of their original purpose as far as the poor are concerned.[53] A small claims judge in Washington, D.C., said of his clientele (usually black), "It is a miracle they don't burn down the courthouse. All they see is white people enforcing white law designed to do them in."[54]

Trial Courts of General Jurisdiction.   When most Americans conceptualize the term *court,* it is more than likely the trial court of general jurisdiction that they have in mind. It is not that these courts are the most numerous (there are far more courts of limited jurisdiction), but probably because this is the court most frequently projected by the media. This is the "Perry Mason" court, or, if you will, the O. J. Simpson court, which typically hears serious cases, both criminal and civil in nature, as well as probate, if that is not handled at the lower level. This is also where jury trials are most common, if the state uses juries at all.

The diversity of forms existing in the fifty states makes it difficult to generalize as to the structure of general jurisdiction courts. Most states are divided into judicial districts composed of one or more counties. A few states maintain a system of dual courts, with courts of equity existing alongside courts of general jurisdiction.[55] Although state legislators frequently give in to pleas for state court reorganization, the basic organizational philosophy remains relatively unchanged.

---

[52]A useful, brief overview of juvenile courts and the issues surrounding them may be found in H. Ted Rubin, *The Courts: Fulcrum of the Justice System,* 2nd ed. (New York: Random House, 1984), Ch. 4, 79–117. See also Robert H. Mookin et al., *In the Interest of Children: Advocacy, Law Reform and Public Policy* (New York: Freeman, 1985); and Ira M. Schwartz, ed., *Juvenile Justice and Public Policy: Toward a National Agenda* (Lexington, Mass.: D. C. Heath, 1992). The topic is also intelligently addressed by Mark D. Jacobs in *Screwing the System and Making It Work: Juvenile Justice in a No-Fault Society* (Chicago: University of Chicago Press, 1990).

[53]See "Buyer v. Seller in Small Claims Court," *Consumer Reports* 36, No. 10 (Oct. 1971): 324–31. American small claims courts have been a popular subject of study. The best research has been recorded, summarized, and analyzed in Barbara Yngvesson and Patricia Hennessey, "Small Claims, Complex Disputes: A Review of the Small Claims Literature," *Law and Society Review* 9, No. 2 (Winter 1975): 219–74. See also John C. Ruhnka and Stephen Weller, *Small Claims Courts: A National Examination* (Williamsburg, Va.: National Center for State Courts, 1978). But for a different view, see Neil Vidmar, "The Small Claims Court: A Reconceptualization of Disputes and an Empirical Investigation," *Law and Society Review* 18, No. 4 (1984): 515–50.

An extensive study of the Iowa small claims court produced findings very similar to studies in the 1970s such as that of Consumers Union. See Suzanne E. Elwell and Christopher D. Carlson, "The Iowa Small Claims Court: An Empirical Analysis, *Iowa Law Review* 75, Nos. 1 & 2 (Jan. 1990): 433–558. But a different and more positive use of small claims courts in San Francisco is reported in Andrew D. Freeman and Juli E. Farris, "Grassroots Impact Litigation: Mass Filing of Small Claims," *University of San Francisco Law Review* 26, No. 2 (Winter 1992): 261–81.

[54]See James S. Campbell, Joseph R. Sahid, and David P. Stang, *Law and Order Reconsidered, Report of the Task Force on Law and Law Enforcement to the National Commission on the Causes and Prevention of Violence* (New York: Bantam Books, 1970), 36.

[55]See *State Court Organization,* and *Caseload Statistics, 1994.*

General trial courts typically hear appeals from limited jurisdiction courts in addition to functioning as courts of original jurisdiction. Most state judicial statutes provide for an overlap of jurisdiction between general jurisdiction and limited jurisdiction courts. Some states divide jurisdiction (for example, civil and criminal) into two courts at this level. These courts go by several names: superior court; circuit court; district court; court of common pleas; and even, in New York, the supreme court! General trial court judges in all states are required to have law degrees, the absence of at least minimal clerical help for recorded proceedings is almost unknown, and facilities as well as procedures in these courts are (with several notable exceptions) both modern and professional. Judges' salaries range from $62,000 to $113,000 per year, the 1995 mean being about $86,000.[56]

State Appellate Courts.   The organization of appellate courts in the fifty states is hardly less complex than that of trial courts. Basically, states have two types of appellate courts: (1) *courts of last resort,* called the supreme court in most states, though also known as courts of appeals (in Maryland, New York, and the District of Columbia), the supreme judicial court (in Maine and Massachusetts), and the supreme court of appeals (West Virginia); and (2) *Intermediate Appellate Courts,* variously called courts of appeals, appellate division of supreme court, and so on.[57]

All states have, and have always had, courts of last resort. However, intermediate appellate courts are of fairly recent origin. Only thirteen intermediate appellate courts existed in 1911, whereas thirty-one states had created such courts as of 1980, and by 1995, thirty-eight states had established these courts. The essential purpose of the intermediate appellate court is obvious: to relieve the workload of the state's supreme court without expanding the size of that body. State statutes or constitutions usually provide for the structure and jurisdiction of these courts. Most states have one such court, with jurisdiction extending statewide. However, some states (for example, Ohio) have created appellate "districts," with appeals being processed within each geographic district. In other states, intermediate appellate jurisdiction is given to an appellate division of the state's general trial courts, while still other states have separate intermediate appellate courts for civil and criminal matters.

The jurisdiction of these courts is usually limited by statute to certain dollar amounts, to certain types of cases or to appeals from specified lower courts. Their size varies widely, from three judges in Alaska to eighty judges sitting (in panels) on the Texas Court of Civil Appeals. Intermediate appellate judges' salaries ranged from $76,000 to $123,000 in 1995.

State supreme courts, however titled are composed of from three to nine judges (called justices), sit at the state capital, typically have jurisdiction in all matters pertaining to state law, and, of course, are the final arbiters in matters of state constitutional interpretation, subject on rare occasion to contrary interpretation by federal courts in matters involving federal questions. Also typical is the practice of insisting that parties to an action exhaust all remedies at lower judicial and administrative levels prior to bringing their case to the highest court. In addition to the appellate functions, state supreme court justices in many states have considerable administrative burdens in overseeing the work of lower courts in matters of finance, caseload, judicial discipline, and so on. As one might expect, salaries of state supreme court justices are generally quite substantial, ranging from about $62,500 to $131,000 annually in 1995.

---

[56]See "Survey of Judicial Salaries—Winter, 1995," *State Court Report* 1, No. 2 (Winter 1995): 4–9.
[57]*State Court Organization,* Tables 1 and 2, 13–19.

A Note on Juries. A brief overview of juries is appropriate at this point, for they are best viewed as adjuncts of the regular court system. Although the Sixth and Seventh Amendments to the Constitution provide for jury trials in civil and criminal cases respectively, the United States Supreme Court had long held that the Bill of Rights applied as a set of restrictions and requirements only upon the federal government, not upon the states. Gradually, after the adoption of the Fourteenth Amendment, this doctrine changed such that most of the significant items in the Bill of Rights were interpreted as applicable to the states.[58] Not until 1968, however, did the Court in *Duncan v. Louisiana,* 391 U.S. 145, get around to holding that in serious criminal cases states must accord defendants the right to trial by jury. Wrote Justice White:

> Because we believe that trial by jury in criminal cases is fundamental to the American scheme of justice, we hold that the 14th Amendment guarantees a right of jury trial in all criminal cases which—were they to be tried in a federal court—would come within the 6th Amendment's guarantee.[59]

The decision, later interpreted to mean that a jury was required if the penalty imposed is in excess of six months in jail, did not change the crazy patchwork of jury practices in the states. Several states have, by leave of the United States Supreme Court, permitted juries to reach verdicts by less than unanimous vote; others often used juries of fewer than twelve members. Such deviations from the traditional requirement of unanimity of "twelve good men and true" are quite frequent in civil trials and not at all uncommon in criminal trials as well.[60]

Issues surrounding the selection of juries have become prominent in recent years. Methods of selection vary widely from city to city and state to state. Random selection from voter lists is a common state practice, and this, along with lenient provisions for excusing "busy" people (doctors, lawyers, teachers, and the like) often leads to juries quite unrepresentative of the community as a whole. The Supreme Court has been anything but consistent and specific in what the Constitution requires as to jury representativeness. In general, the Court has held only that certain categories of citizens (essentially racial minorities or women) cannot be kept off juries.[61]

The use of juries is clearly on the decline, not only in the United States but throughout the world. Henry Abraham reports that in England, the common law birthplace of the modern jury, they are used in only 1 percent of civil cases and only about 4 percent of criminal trials.[62] In the United States, the figures are not radically different: only about 5 percent of felony cases are processed by juries; and in civil cases, only about 1 percent of state cases are resolved using jury trials.[63] The frequency of jury use, however, may not be a perfect gauge of the institution's significance. In his survey of jury politics, for example, James Levine concludes that

---

[58]This constitutional development is described in most works on American constitutional law. See, e.g., Gerald Gunther, *Constitutional Law,* 12th ed. (Westbury, N.Y.: Foundation Press, 1991), 413–31. See also a useful work on issues surrounding juries: James P. Levine, *Juries and Politics* (Pacific Grove, Calif.: Brooks-Cole, 1992).

[59]*Duncan v. Louisiana,* 391 U.S. 145, 149 (1968).

[60]See Levine, *Juries and Politics,* 27–29.

[61]Levine, *Juries and Politics,* Ch. 3.

[62]Abraham, *The Judicial Process,* 100.

[63]Levine, *Juries and Politics,* 34–35. A very valuable collection of essays on the civil jury has been edited by Robert E. Litan, *Verdict: Assessing the Civil Jury System* (Washington: Brookings Institution, 1993). See especially the essay by Marc Galanter, "The Regulatory Function of the Civil Jury," 61–102.

. . . [T]he jury's importance today lies not in the number of cases it hears but in the types of cases it decides and the impact their decisions have. Not only does jury power remain substantial [in the United States], but jury politics remains live and well.[64]

So far, our reference has been to the trial or "petit" jury, which is the type most readers will recognize. However, a few words on the grand jury are in order. This is a group of citizens whose job it is to determine whether there is sufficient evidence to bring formal charges (indictment or "true bill") against an individual. Grand juries are even more frequently empowered to investigate alleged wrongdoing of public officials, and if the evidence warrants, to bring criminal charges. Ideally, the institution is intended to protect citizens—private and public alike—from having false charges brought against them. In practice, however, grand juries can become *instruments* for the exercise of prosecutorial discretion.

The Fifth Amendment to the United States Const' ation provides that "no person shall be held to answer for a capital or otherwise infamous crime, unless on presentment or indictment of a grand jury." Unlike jury trials in serious criminal matters, however, the grand jury guarantee has been held by the Supreme Court not to be of such significance as to be "essential to our concept of ordered liberty,"[65] and thus not applicable to the states. Most states have replaced the use of the grand jury with the device of "information" whereby the prosecutor makes the critical decision of when to bring charges.

THE POLITICS OF STRUCTURE

From the ratification of the Constitution in 1789 to the present, state courts have struggled for recognition and status. Their conflicts with state legislatures for independence, power, and funds is one story; their competition with the growing prestige and prerogatives of federal courts (discussed in Chapter 4) is yet another; and, in this century, their struggle for organizational modernization—largely, though not entirely, an intercourt struggle—has come to the fore. Powerful interests align themselves along both sides of issues of court organization, for they perceive matters of where, how, and to what extent judicial powers are organized as vitally important to the attainment of their goals: economic, political, professional, or otherwise.

State legislatures have long been aware that the process of judicial selection carried with it tremendous potential for control. Hence, it was not uncommon for legislatures (most of which were given constitutional powers of judicial appointment in the first place) to simply refuse to reappoint wayward judges. Limiting judicial tenure to short terms, or periods of "good behavior," was also a popular disciplinary device.[66] Early state legislatures were also given to the use of brisk removal tactics (though impeachment was more often threatened than implemented) in order to rein in recalcitrant state judges.

Much of this legislative strong-arming was highly popular, growing as it did from a general colonial distrust of courts as institutions wielding arbitrary and coercive power. Laws were passed forbidding even the citation of English decisions. And in Pennsylvania,

---

[64]Levine, *Juries and Politics*, 25. See 34–38 for an expansion of Levine's argument.

[65]See *Hurtado v. California*, 110 U.S. 516 (1884); and *Gyuro v. Connecticut*, 393 U.S. 937, (1968). The concept of "ordered liberty" is from Justice Cardozo's majority opinion in *Palko v. Connecticut*, 302 U.S. 319 (1937).

[66]See Jacob, "Courts as Political Agencies": 16–20. See also William S. Carpenter, *Judicial Tenure in the United States* (New Haven: Yale University Press, 1918).

three justices of the Supreme Court were impeached for jailing a defendant for contempt of court, the view being that "punishment for contempt was a piece of English common law barbarism, unsuited to this country."[67] Clearly, the warm embrace of the common law was not universal in the new nation. Clearly, too, with the sharp decline of state executive authority following the adoption of the new Constitution, legislative rather than judicial power was in the ascendancy. Another practice growing out of colonial experience that worked to the advantage of the legislature was the lack of differentiation of governmental functions. Many state legislatures continued the practice of acting as appellate tribunals themselves. They set aside judicial decisions, heard appeals, and otherwise performed functions that today we would call judicial.

It was probably the growing acceptance of the doctrine of judicial review which, more than any other factor, contributed to a redress in the balance of power between state legislatures and judiciaries. Prior to the Revolution, the acts of colonial legislatures and courts alike were subject to review by the Privy Council in England, and the power to strike down legislative acts had been exercised in at least five colonies prior to the writing of the Constitution. Between 1789 and 1803, several other states followed suit, either by actually declaring legislative statutes unconstitutional or by claiming the power to do so.[68]

But it was the enunciation of the principle by Chief Justice John Marshall in *Marbury v. Madison,* 1 Cranch 137 (1803), that seemed to provide the catalyst for general acceptance of the doctrine. By 1818, reports historian Aumann, the doctrine had been recognized in virtually every state, although only ten years earlier, two Ohio supreme court justices were impeached for exercising the power.[69] Gradually, as the flow of litigation increased in all levels of courts, and as the need for more complex legal doctrine emerged, the work of state courts became more specialized, adding to their aura as apolitical agencies, and incidentally, adding to their independence. The state court exercise of the power of judicial review (defined here in the narrow sense wherein legislative acts are actually declared unconstitutional) grew very slowly, and in the era before the Civil War was limited to relatively few states. However, as popular opinion gradually shifted from distrust of state courts to distrust of state legislatures (as reflected in newly revised and highly restrictive state constitutions enacted around the turn of the century), judicial review became more common. One survey indicates that between 1903 and 1908 some 400 state laws were declared unconstitutional by state courts; in New York alone, from 1906 to 1938, 136 state laws were struck down.[70] These data may be a bit misleading, however, for the vast majority of issues of state judicial review have been of a detailed, technical nature rather than basic policy conflicts. Overall, most studies of the subject have concluded that state judicial review has had but slight impact on long-term state public policy. Still, as with most aspects of the politics of state courts, more research is needed on this important question.[71]

---

[67]Aumann, *Changing American Legal System,* 80.

[68]Aumann, *Changing American Legal System,* 190. A useful discussion of the early usages of judicial review may be found in Charles Grove Haines, *The American Doctrine of Judical Supremacy,* 2nd ed. (Berkeley: University of California Press, 1932).

[69]Aumann, *Changing American Legal System,* 191.

[70]See William J. Keefe and Morris S. Ogul, *The American Legislative Process: Congress and the States,* 8th ed. (Englewood Cliffs, N.J.: Prentice-Hall, 1993): 433.

[71]Recent research is discussed in Keefe and Ogul, *The American Legislative Process,* 432–33. See also an insightful discussion of judicial review in state courts in Charles H. Sheldon, "Judicial Review and the Supreme Court of Washington: 1890–1986," *Publius* 17, No. 1 (Winter 1987): 69–90. A particularly interesting perspective on legislative-judicial relations in the states is set forth by Hans A. Linde, Associate Justice of the Oregon Supreme Court, in "Observations of a State Court Judge," in Robert A. Katzmann, ed., *Judges and Legislators: Toward Institutional Comity* (Washington: Brookings Institution, 1988), 117–28.

The creation of a federal judicial system via the Judiciary Act of 1789 posed a further series of threats to state judicial power. It was clear to most observers, even to delegates of the Constitutional Convention, that a federal judiciary was a potentially effective device in centralizing the power of the national government. Constitutional delegates, as well as later "states' rights" congressmen, urged the defeat of proposals to create a federal judiciary inferior to the Supreme Court, arguing that state courts could interpret federal law. But the courts were established, and, as predicted, a slow growth of federal judicial power (related in the next chapter) became a crucial nationalizing force.[72]

Perhaps the most striking political conflict state court systems have joined has been a struggle with themselves, so to speak. With the enormous growth of societal complexity brought about by industrialization and urbanization, along with our mass system of production and distribution of goods and services, there has not been a corresponding growth in the sophistication of judicial organization and processes. In general, American courts—especially state courts—are outmoded organizations attempting to deal with increasingly complex issues. The problems are many, from insufficient and unstable funding to antiquated and inefficient procedures leading to chronic delays. But aside from the matter of judicial selection (to be discussed in Chapter 5), the issues of court modernization have tended to coalesce into one overriding concern, that of *court unification.* Speaking of the organizational status of state judiciaries at the outset of the twentieth century, Herbert Jacob has succinctly summarized the problems. And if we may take the liberty of changing his past tenses to the present tense, we have a roughly accurate present-day critique:

> Within each state various courts operate autonomously from each other. As in early rural America, the judiciary consists of justice or magistrate courts for petty cases, various courts of general jurisdiction for more serious criminal cases and for civil suits involving larger sums of money, appellate courts for intermediate appeals and a state Supreme Court for the final decision. Although the courts of lesser jurisdiction are obliged to follow the legal rulings of appellate courts, there are no disciplinary proceedings available if they fail to do so. Moreover, the courts are supervised in no other way. The hours and days judges sit, the way in which they preside over their courtrooms, the manner in which they hire and fire assistants, the quality of subordinate personnel, the speed with which they handle cases, and dozens of other details are subject to the whim of each individual judge and no one else. It is, therefore, something of a mistake to speak of a judicial "system" or "hierarchy," for neither system nor hierarchy exists. Although dozens of courts (in some instances hundreds) exist side by side in a city or metropolitan area, they remain uncoordinated except in the crudest way.[73]

All of this stands in sharp contrast to a *"unified" court system,* a term having almost as many definitions as users. The National Advisory Commission on Civil Justice Standards and Goals once defined the term in this way:

> All State courts should be organized into a unified judicial system financed by the State and administered through a statewide court administrator or administrative judge under the supervision of the chief justice of the State supreme court.
> All trial courts should be unified into a single trial court with general criminal as well as civil jurisdiction. Criminal jurisdiction now in courts of limited jurisdiction should be placed in these unified trial courts of general jurisdiction, with the exception of

[72]A recent and careful reexamination of the importance and implications of the Judiciary Act of 1789 is Maeva Marcus, ed., *Origins of the Federal Judiciary: Essays on the Judiciary Act of 1789* (New York: Oxford University Press, 1992).
[73]Jacob, *Courts as Political Agencies,* 43–44 (as revised).

certain traffic violations. The State supreme court should promulgate rules for the conduct of minor as well as major criminal prosecutions.

All judicial functions in the trial court should be performed by full-time judges. All judges should possess law degrees and be members of the bar.

A transcription or other record of the pretrial court proceedings and the trial should be kept in all criminal cases.

The appeal procedure should be the same for all cases.

Pretrial release services, probation services, and other rehabilitative services should be available in all prosecutions within the jurisdiction of the unified trial court.[74]

Ashman and Parness have argued that there are three basic ingredients of a unified court structure on which most observers would agree: a simplified court structure, the need for centralized supervision and centralized funding. Geoff Gallas, however, concludes that court unification consists of four elements: elimination of overlapping and conflicting jurisdictional boundaries, centralized administrative responsibility vested in the state's chief justice, centralized budgeting and financing, and a separate judicial personnel system centrally administered.[75] A modified model of a unified state judicial system (that of the American Bar Association, appears in Figure 3–5. This simplified structure can be compared with or contrasted to other state court organizational charts presented earlier.[76] Unification is defined as consolidation and simplification of court structure, centralized management, centralized rule-making, and centralized budgeting and state financing.

Considering that the movement for court reform began with the famous Pound address in 1906, if not, indeed, in the mid-nineteenth century, the pace of structural reform seems agonizingly slow, at least to reformers.[77] Recall, however, that we are discussing a political process, and any reform proposal involves winners and losers who may be expected to engage in a sometimes fierce struggle to advance or defeat the various proposals. At first glance we might ask how or why anyone would be opposed to streamlining our state court system. However, students of the process point to the following factors as relevant in understanding the politics of unification. To begin with, certain interests, particularly those of regular participants in the process itself, have important investments in the status quo and are often in the forefront of attempts to frustrate change. This is particularly true of judges, for one can hardly expect them to be critical of a system that has so generously rewarded them. In fact, judges as a group are the entity most opposed to change. Not only is this situation due to normal institutional inertia, based on nearly three-hundred years of local judicial institutional autonomy, but judges by training tend to see a problem in a case-by-case format, only infrequently seeing the systemic impact of their position. Professionally, they are highly individualistic and parochial.

[74]National Advisory Commission on Criminal Justice Standards and Goals, *Courts,* 164.

[75]The Ashman and Parness conceptualization may be found in Allan Ashman and Jeffrey A. Parness, "The concept of a Unified Court System," *DePaul Law Review* 24, No. 1 (Fall 1974): 1–41. These writers omit any reference to methods of judicial selection as an element in court unification. Also omitted is any reference to intermediate appellate courts, an institution that is often included in definitions of unified court systems. The Gallas definition may be found in Geoff Gallas, "The Conventional Wisdom of State Court Administration: A Critical Assessment and an Alternative Approach," *Justice Systems Journal* 2, No. 1 (Spring 1976): 35–55.

[76]The ABA model is discussed in *Standards Relating to Court Organization* (Chicago: American Bar Association, 1974).

[77]An indication of the pace of reform may be found in Larry Berkson, Susan Carbon, and Judy Rosenbaum, *Court Unification: History, Politics and Implementation* (Washington: National Institute of Law Enforcement and Criminal Justice, Law Enforcement Assistance Administration, Department of Justice, 1978).

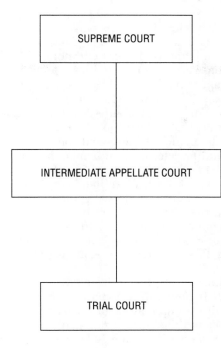

Figure 3–5   ABA Model for Unified State Court Systems (SOURCE: Larry Berkson, Susan Carbon, and Judy Rosenbaum, *Court Unification: History, Politics and Implementation* (U.S. Dept. of Justice, Law Enforcement Assistance Administration, 1978), 7).

Court clerks, attorneys, and even public participants are often found to be equally opposed to change, because they are reluctant to accept a disruption of the pattern of behavior to which they have become accustomed. Attorneys regularly practicing before a certain court can hardly be expected to push for structural changes, particularly if "their judge" is opposed to it. Clerks, occupying a critical and powerful position in the judicial system, often oppose change for fear of losing jobs or of having a higher authority impose changes on their routine or increasing their responsibilities. When one adds to this a general paucity of information—largely a result of the lack of empirical research on state courts—as well as the frequent necessity of achieving structural change only through state constitutional amendments, it becomes clear how institutional factors alone can frustrate, if not defeat, repeated attempts at reform.

State executive and legislative leaders might be expected to be in the forefront of reform, but they too may have interests in retaining the status quo. After all, they seldom hear a coherent, unified voice for change coming from the courts. There are always financial considerations involved in proposals for court unification, and perhaps most important, court unification often results in enhanced power for state judiciaries, often at the expense of state legislatures or executives.[78]

---

[78]Berkson, Carbon, and Rosenbaum, *Court Unification,* 71–87, contains a useful rundown on groups likely to oppose reform. On court reform in general, see Malcolm M. Feeley, *Court Reform on Trial: Why Simple Solutions Fail* (New York: Basic Books, 1983). For an empirical study of court unification in one county, see Josef M. Broder, John F. Porter, and Webb M. Smathers, "The Hidden Consequences of Court Unification," *Judicature* 65, No. 1 (June–July 1981): 10–17.

A more recent single state study focused on legislative attitudes toward court reform. See Mark C. Miller, "Lawmaker Attitudes toward Court Reform in Massachusetts," *Judicature 77*, No. 1 (July–Aug. 1993): 34–41. Miller emphasizes the low interest most state legislatures have in the issue.

The literature on court reform contains two persistently held notions. One, a widely held belief of reformers themselves, is that inasmuch as judges often constitute the chief barrier to unification, attempted administrative changes will not be successful until judges themselves are free from the influence of electoral politics. Hence, "merit" selection of judges (the Missouri-plan arrangement to be discussed in Chapter 5) must precede general court unification. A second hypothesis is familiar to students of state policy processes. It is that reorganization of state courts is a function of broader features of state government politics and economics. The states with a higher level of urbanization, with more complex, mixed socioeconomic systems, which tax more heavily and spend more, are more likely to be innovative in policy-making, including reforms in judicial administration.

Henry Glick has examined both of these notions and found that neither one goes very far in explaining why the core of the court unification plan is or is not adopted in states.[79] The adoption of merit selection has very little to do with broader court unification measures, while the latter hypothesis carries some weight only insofar as it concerns centralized judicial management, which is but one feature of court unification. Glick reasons that much of the court unification program implies a significant shift in the locus of state political power and that to understand this requires a "sensitive political analysis of why change occurs."[80]

Given the stalemate now characterizing the movement for court unification some have concluded that the whole issue is now a dead letter and that we should move on to what has been termed the "Post-Unification" approach.[81] This would include ". . . statewide cohesiveness and coordination without heavy reliance on command and control mechanisms."[82] In general, this approach seeks a balance between rigid centralization and local autonomy and creativity.

Although the movement toward court unification as an overarching, multifaceted concept has been slow, progress toward certain specific segments of that goal has moved along rather rapidly. As caseloads of state courts at all levels have increased, the *office of court administrator* has become a virtual necessity. As of 1979, every state had a court administrator or at least administrative officers who performed this function. This is a relatively recent phenomenon, largely of the 1960s and 1970s. Although these entities vary widely in power, level of activity, budget, and other resources, the data gathered and compiled by these administrative offices, mostly of a statistical nature, have proven quite helpful not only in moving the court system along toward a more centralized posture but also in furthering research on state court systems. The office of court administrator at both the statewide and trial court level is clearly moving toward a more professional mode. Qualifications of personnel are being upgraded, and the field of judicial administration is coming

---

[79]Henry R. Glick, "State Government and Judicial Administration: A Political Analysis," *State Government* 53, No. 1 (Winter 1980): 46. Glick presents a somewhat more extended version of his research in "Innovations in State Judicial Administration: Effects on Court Management and Organization," *American Politics Quarterly* 9, No. 1 (Jan. 1981): 49–69.

[80]Glick, "State Government": 49.

[81]Some have argued that the movement is now dead because it has achieved its prime objectives, while others have said the opponents to unification have triumphed. See Robert D. Lipscher and Samuel D. Conti, "A Post-Unification Approach to Court Organizational Design and Leadership," *The Justice System Journal* 15, No. 2 (1991): 667–76; and Lamber and Luskin, "Court Reform: A View from the Bottom": 295–96.

[82]Lipscher and Conti, "A Post-Unification Approach . . .": 668. Victor E. Flango has found that as measured by demand for the use of state courts in diversity cases, the "quality" of state courts is, on the whole, not improved through unification. See his "Court Unification and Quality of State Courts," *Justice System Journal* 16, No. 3 (1994): 33–55.

into its own as a significant area of both practice and research. Again, these developments are of fairly recent origin, most of them taking place since the 1960s.[83]

Another administrative entity at the state level of at least potential significance is that of the *judicial council.* The judicial council movement grew out of the proposals of the National Municipal League in the 1920s, and in the post–World War II period the movement spread to most states. These councils, usually comprised of judges with a scattering of legislators, practicing attorneys, and academics, are typically only advisory in nature. This limitation plus their meager funding has robbed them of the administrative and managerial clout they might have had. One notable exception is in California, where that state's judicial council works closely with the administrative office of the court in exercising significant administrative authority over the state's judicial system.[84]

FURTHER READING

Aumann, Francis R. *The Changing American Legal System: Some Selected Phases.* Columbus: Ohio State University Press, 1940.

Friedman, Lawrence M. *A History of American Law,* 2nd ed. New York: Simon & Schuster, 1985.

Glick, Henry R., and Kenneth N. Vines. *State Court Systems.* Englewood Cliffs, N.J.: Prentice-Hall, 1973.

Hurst, James Willard. *The Growth of American Law: The Lawmakers.* Boston: Little, Brown, 1950.

Jacob, Herbert. "The Courts as Political Agencies: An Historical Analysis." In Herbert Jacob and Kenneth N. Vines, eds., *Studies in Judicial Politics,* Tulane Studies in Political Science 8: 9–50. New Orleans: Tulane University, 1962.

National Center for State Courts, *State Court Caseload Statistics, Annual Report, 1994.* Williamsburg, Va.: National Center for State Courts, 1996.

Provine, Doris Marie. *Judging Credentials: Non-Lawyer Judges and the Politics of Professionalism.* Chicago: University of Chicago Press, 1986.

*State Court Journal.*Williamsburg, Va.: National Center for State Courts, quarterly.

Stumpf, Harry P., and John H. Culver, *The Politics of State Courts.* New York: Longman, 1992.

Tarr, G. Alan, and Mary Cornelia Aldis Porter, *State Supreme Courts in State and Nation.* New Haven: Yale University Press, 1988.

---

[83]For a useful overview of the court management movement, see the entire issue of *The Justice System Journal* 15, No. 2 (1991).

[84]For the effectiveness of judicial councils, see Russell Wheeler and David W. Jackson, "Judicial Councils and Policy Planning: Continuous Study and Discontinuous Institutions," *Justice System Journal* 2, No. 2 (Winter 1976): 121–40. There is some evidence (in Georgia, for example) of renewed interest in state judicial councils.

4

The Federal Courts

The Judicial Power of the United States shall be vested in one Supreme Court, and in such inferior Courts as the Congress may from time to time ordain and establish. . . .

This Constitution and the Laws of the United States which shall be made in Pursuance thereof and all Treaties made, or which shall be made, under the Authority of the United States, shall be the supreme law of the Land; and the judges in every State shall be bound thereby, any Thing in the Constitution or Laws of any State to the Contrary notwithstanding.

— United States Constitution,
Articles III and VI

HISTORICAL DEVELOPMENT

The delegates attending the Constitutional Convention of 1787 readily agreed that the nation they were forming needed one supreme national court.[1] Dissent arose, however, over the formation of a system of federal trial and appellate courts. States' rights advocate John Rutledge vehemently argued:

> the State tribunals might and ought to be left in all cases to decide in the first instance, the right of appeal to the supreme national tribunal being sufficient to secure the national rights & uniformity of Judgmts: that it was making an unnecessary encroachment on the jurisdiction of the States, and creating unnecessary obstacles to their adoption of the new system.[2]

---

[1]*See* Daniel Farber and Suzanna Sherry, *A History of the American Constitution* (St. Paul, Minn.: West Publishing, 1990): 51.

[2]Paul M. Bator, Daniel J. Meltzer, Paul J. Mishkin and David L. Shapiro, *Hart and Wechsler's The Federal Courts and the Federal System,* 3rd ed. (Westbury, N.Y.: The Foundation Press, 1988) (with 1992 Supplement), 10–11 (hereafter *"Hart and Wechsler"*).

Rutledge eventually persuaded his fellow Conventioners to forgo mandating a federal court system.[3] Instead, the Convention adopted a compromise position, authorizing, but not requiring, Congress to create such courts.[4]

Almost immediately, however, the First Congress acted to exercise this authority, proposing "an Act to Establish the Judicial Courts of the United States," which was adopted on September 24, 1789.[5] The debate over this legislation reflected the ongoing struggle between national unity and localism that has characterized much of American Federalism.

Thus, the student of current American politics will detect a familiar ring in the following exchange in the House of Representatives in August 1789. In opposition to the creation of federal courts inferior to the Supreme Court, some declared: "State courts were fully competent to the purposes for which these courts were to be created and that they [federal courts] would be a burdensome and useless expense," and "I think I see a foundation laid for discord, civil wars, and all its concomitants." And there were further objections: "An offender is dragged from his house, friends and connections, to a distant spot, where he is deprived of every advantage of former character, of relations and acquaintance." In support of the federal judiciary, others argued: "Suppose a State Government was inimical to the Federal Government, and its judges were attached to the same local policy . . . where would be your redress. Shall we apply to the State Legislatures that patronize them?" State courts "cannot be trusted with the execution of Federal laws. . . . Laws dependent on them would throw us back into all the embarassments that characterized our former situation."[6]

Felix Frankfurter and James Landis, in their classic work on the history of the federal judiciary, maintained that the Judiciary Act of 1789 is a notable piece of legislation for at least three reasons:

> It devised a judicial organization which, with all its imperfections, served the country substantially unchanged for nearly a century. Through supervision over state courts conferred upon the Supreme Court by its famous Section Twenty-five, the Act created one of the most important nationalizing influences in the formative period of the Republic. But the transcendent achievement of the First Judiciary Act is the establishment for this country of the tradition of a system of inferior courts.[7]

The Act specified a Supreme Court composed of five associate justices and a chief justice. Below this were two further tiers of courts: district courts and circuit courts. The country was divided into thirteen federal judicial districts, each presided over by one federal district judge, and each corresponding to state lines. The infant nation was further divided into three circuits, but separate judges were not provided for this level of court. Rather, each circuit court was to be composed of two justices of the Supreme Court riding circuit (that is, periodically traveling to specified locations in the district to hold court) and one district judge. The circuit courts were to meet twice a year in each district within the circuit.

---

[3]*Hart and Wechsler*, 11.

[4]Max Farrand, *The Records of the Federal Convention* (New Haven, Conn.: Yale University Press, 1911); 1:124–25, quoted in *Hart and Wechsler*, 11.

[5]*Act To Establish The Judicial Courts of the United States, Statutes at Large*, Vol. 1, Sec. 73 (1789).

[6]These excerpts are reported in Richard J. Richardson and Kenneth N. Vines, *The Politics of Federal Courts: Lower Courts in the United States* (Boston: Little, Brown, 1970), 20.

[7]See Felix Frankfurter and James M. Landis, *The Business of the Supreme Court* (New York: Macmillan, 1928). See also Maeva Marcus, ed., *Origins of the Federal Judiciary: Essays on the Judiciary Act of 1789* (New York: Oxford University Press, 1992).

The district courts were tribunals of original jurisdiction over relatively minor matters. The circuit courts, which were the important trial courts, had original jurisdiction along with some appellate powers. In general, the jurisdiction of both courts was extremely limited, much less than that outlined in the Constitution.[8] This limitation was due in large part to the necessity for compromise in winning congressional approval of the measure. Thus, although it is true that the very creation of a federal court structure below the Supreme Court proved to be a strong nationalizing influence (and, incidentally, a victory for the Federalist Party of Adams, Washington, and Hamilton), the provisions of the act itself have a surprisingly strong state and local flavor.

First, and quite important, the circuit and district court boundaries were drawn coterminous with state lines, ensuring a strong local coloration in district court personnel and decisions. These courts were, as Richardson and Vines point out, "state-contained".[9] Second, district judges were to reside in their districts, and although nominated by the president, their final approval was dependent upon confirmation by the Senate (translated, senators of their home states). Thus, district judges were to be (and are today) local appointees with local political lineage, often locally educated and subject to the continuing political and social influences of their locale and region. This orientation has proven to be of the utmost importance in understanding the politics of federal courts. Federal district judges are, and always have been, hybrid federal-state officials with potential for severely undermining federal judicial policies.[10] When we add to these two localizing forces the limited jurisdiction of the new federal courts as well as the state-local orientation of the work of the new circuit courts (their caseload in volume and content was essentially dictated by the determinations of the district courts), we can clearly detect a ring of political compromise in the Judiciary Act of 1789 between nationalist and antinationalist forces.

The history of our federal courts from 1789 to the present is marked with often successful attempts to manipulate the structure and jurisdiction of the federal judicial system for political advantage: to force out judicial decisions favorable to a given legislative majority, to forestall undesired judicial policies, to punish courts and judges for past wrongdoing, or to adjust the system for purposes of patronage—all with the underlying theme of competing theories of federalism. The Federalists, who were unhappy with some of the compromises forced upon them in 1789, led the way.

One of the most obvious weaknesses of the 1789 structure was that of circuit riding. In 1838, the nine Supreme Court justices reported having traveled an average of 2,975 miles; Justice McKinley of the then Ninth Circuit (Alabama, Louisiana, Mississippi, and Arkansas) traveled 10,000 miles that year! Yet, he confessed:

> I have never yet been at Little Rock, the place of holding the court in Arkansas; but from the best information I can obtain, it could not be conveniently approached in the spring of the year, except by water, and by that route the distance would be greatly increased.[11]

Despite the obvious hardships, some justices and legislators found benefit in the travel. James Buchanan, for instance, argued in the Senate in 1826 that

---

[8]The details of the jurisdiction of these courts can be found in *Hart and Wechsler,* 31–35.

[9]Richardson and Vines, *Politics of Federal Courts,* 21. Ch. 2 of this volume is a brief but insightful overview of the politics of federal court organization. The instant discussion draws heavily on this useful summary.

[10]John Minor Wisdom, "The Friction-Making Exacerbating Political Role of the Federal Courts," *Southwestern Law Review* 21 (1967): 411.

[11]Quoted in Frankfurter and Landis, *Business of the Supreme Court,* 49–50.

The importance of a full knowledge of the local law is greater in the Western States, than in the rest of the Union. . . . By compelling the Judges of the Supreme Court to hold the Circuits, the knowledge they have acquired of the local laws will be retained and improved, and they will thus be enabled, not only the better to arrive at correct results themselves, but to aid their brethren of the Court who belong to different Circuits, and are, of course, deprived of an opportunity to acquire such information, except in that manner.[12]

On the other hand, Gouverneur Morris, as early as 1802, concluded that

I am not quite convinced that riding rapidly from one end of this country to another is the best way to study law. I am inclined to believe that knowledge may be more conveniently acquired in the closet than in the high road.[13]

Competing factions advanced proposals to end or to maintain the circuit riding system. Federalists labored to eliminate the practice in an effort to reduce local influence over federal courts while Jeffersonians fought to preserve it as a way to monitor the work of federal judges.

In 1793, Congress reduced the number of circuit-riding justices from two to one for each federal circuit. Then, in the so-called "Midnight Judges Act" of 1801, a Federalist Congress abolished circuit riding altogether, expanded the federal district and circuit court systems, provided for circuit judges, and vastly increased the scope of federal jurisdiction.[14]

While these changes were profound, the Jeffersonians repealed them as soon as they wrested power from the Federalists in the early 1800's. They restored circuit riding and revived the assignment of Supreme Court justices to each federal circuit. Despite its popularity with the Jeffersonian Republicans, however, circuit riding rapidly began to die under its own weight, with trail weary justices balking at the task of traveling through the nation's rapidly expanding territory.[15]

Between 1802 and 1891, the history of federal judicial organization and jurisdiction was one of minor, piecemeal change within the context of general agreement on the inadequacy of the whole system—an era suggestive of the current politics of state judicial organization. With both district and circuit courts effectively "localized," the development of federal law lacked a strong nationalizing influence. The Supreme Court, to be sure, provided a centralizing voice, but its reach was still limited, whereas the forces of regional and local interests were strong. As population and societal complexity increased, so did the appellate workload. Indeed, the whole system was so overburdened (there being no effective barrier to appeals directly to the Supreme Court) that selective policy articulation by the Supreme Court was quite difficult.

In 1875, Congress took important steps both forward and back. First, as part of its Reconstruction strategy, it expanded federal jurisdiction to include almost all of the potential judicial authority granted by the Constitution. This step represented a victory for "centralist" forces, overcoming the earlier "localization" efforts of the Jeffersonian Republicans. This change, however, also unleashed a torrent of new federal cases that nearly paralyzed the entire judicial system.

---

[12]Frankfurter and Landis, *Business of the Supreme Court,* 16
[13]Frankfurter and Landis, *Business of the Supreme Court,* 17.
[14]This infamous Federalist court-packing plan led to the celebrated decision in *Marbury v. Madison,* 1 Cranch 137 (1803).
[15]*Hart and Wechsler,* 35.

In 1870, the Supreme Court docketed 630 cases. By 1880, that number expanded to over 1,200. Likewise, the district and circuit courts saw their caseloads explode from about 29,000 cases in 1873 to 38,000 in 1880, and 54,000 in 1890.[16] These tremendous increases spawned loud protests from those who favored a severely limited role for the federal judiciary. However, the die appeared to have been cast, and the move toward even broader federal jurisdiction seemed irreversible.

Having gained the upper hand in the struggle over the scope of federal jurisdiction, the nationalist forces remained desperately in need of a screening mechanism for cases appealed to the Supreme Court. Thus, from 1860 until the mid-1920s, the center of attention became the creation of a free-standing, intermediate appellate court that would afford the Supreme Court some breathing room to concentrate on key policy issues. The Federalists put such a system into place, in embryonic form, in 1801, only to have it almost immediately nullified by the Republicans in 1802. By the late 1800s, however, circumstances favored another attempt.

In 1891, Congress passed the "Evarts Act," which established circuit courts of appeal with at least two judges apiece in each of nine circuits.[17] The third seat on these courts could still be filled by a district judge or a Supreme Court justice. As to jurisdiction, perhaps the most important innovation of the 1891 act was to make circuit court decisions final (subject to discretionary review by the Supreme Court) in a vast array of judicial matters. Thus, the Supreme Court was given an enormous boost toward the role it plays today as final arbiter on issues of genuine significance, leaving to lower but now "federalized" judges the task of judicial implementation.[18]

Two further steps were taken in the post-1890 period to bring the federal judicial system into modern focus. One was the enactment of the Judicial Code of 1911, which finally abolished the old 1802 circuit courts themselves, transferring their power to the district courts.[19] The 1911 legislation also expanded and clarified the jurisdiction of district courts and the courts of appeal. Then in 1925, in the so-called Judges' Bill, all federal court jurisdiction was realigned and clarified, and in effect, the three-tiered system of courts we know today was created. First, the Act, which was drafted by a committee of Supreme Court justices,[20] further narrowed litigants' rights of appeal, replacing this with a very wide measure of discretionary review via the writ of *certiorari*. Second, the legislation clarified the role of district courts as basically general trial courts of original jurisdiction.

As these events make clear, the modern structure and jurisdiction of federal courts is the result of diverse political forces that have been locked in an intermittent struggle for some two hundred years. The outcome must not be seen as a series of conflicts over efficient management as a professional value, reducing and redistributing caseload and so on. Rather, it has been an important chapter in the continuing struggle for power between the states and their diverse interests, on the one hand, and those who saw the desirability, if not necessity, of a strong central government, on the other. This struggle, of course, predates the writing of the Constitution. The leading edge of the legal profession, for its part, wavered between these two camps for much of our history, but in the twentieth century it gave the nationalist forces a boost by supporting an intermediate appellate court as well as the adoption of the judicial code.

---

[16]*Hart and Wechsler*, 37.
[17]*The Circuit Court of Appeals Act of 1891, Statutes at Large*, vol. 26, sec. 826 (1891).
[18]Richardson and Vines, *Politics of Federal Courts*, 31.
[19]*Act of March 3, 1911, Statutes at Large*, vol. 36, sec. 1087 (1911).
[20]*Hart and Wechsler*, 39.

THE FEDERAL JUDICIARY TODAY

The District Courts

The federal courts are presently organized in a familiar three-tiered system (see Figure 4–1). At the base are 94 district courts—at least one in each state—with the most populous states having four. Six hundred thirty-six permanent and 13 temporary federal district court judges serve for life after having been appointed by the President and confirmed by the Senate.[21] Each is paid $133,600 annually[22] and can continue hearing cases as a "senior" judge following retirement.[23]

Federal district court jurisdiction is bounded by Article III of the Constitution. In a nutshell, the district courts may hear cases where a matter of federal law is at issue,[24] where the federal government is a party, where two or more state governments are parties, where a state government is suing the citizens of another state, where a citizen of one state is suing a citizen of another state and more than $50,000 is in dispute, where a foreign government or foreign citizen is a party, or where an ambassador or consul is a party. Litigation to which the U.S. government is a party provides the bulk of the district courts' work, followed by cases involving citizens from different states.[25]

Table 4–1 presents a statistical profile of the workload of U.S. district courts. It indicates that the bulk of the cases in district courts are civil—civil rights disputes, attempts by the federal government to recover overpayments, and so on. Bankruptcy filings are presented separately in Table 4–2, as these cases are handled by special bankruptcy judges, who serve as officers of the district courts but do not have the same tenure and salary protections as district judges.[26] As indicated, civil filings grew by over 700 percent between 1940 and 1995. During the same period, criminal cases increased by only about a third, while bankruptcy filings exploded from just under 30,000 in 1950 to nearly 900,000 in 1995.

Tables 4–3 and 4–4 provide a more detailed look at the types of civil and criminal cases filed in federal trial courts during 1990 as contrasted to 1995.

In 1968, Congress created the Federal Magistrate system to address increasing federal caseloads. Magistrate judges are appointed by district judges to either four-year or eight-year terms.[27] They are authorized to hear most pretrial matters and may preside over civil trials where the parties agree to the arrangement. In general, decisions rendered by a federal magistrate judge may be appealed to a federal district court.[28]

---

[21]*Judgeship Act of 1990,* 28 U.S.C. §133 (a) (1991).

[22]See 28 U.S.C. §135, Ex. Ord. No. 12984, Dec., 28, 1995, 61 F.R. 237.

[23]See U.S., Administrative Office of the U.S. Courts, *Judicial Business, 1995* (Abbrev.) (Washington, D.C.: Administrative Office of the U.S. Courts, n.d.): 25.

As head of the Judicial Conference (discussed later), the Chief Justice issues an annual report on the state of the federal judiciary. The 1996 message by Chief Justice William Rehnquist decried the lack of cost of living increases for federal judges, whose salaries have not changed since 1993. In general, federal judicial salaries are far below what these men and women could earn in private practice. See Linda Greenhouse, "Rehnquist Criticizes Congress on Raises," *New York Times,* Jan. 1, 1997: 52.

[24]With respect to federal question jurisdiction, *See Hart and Wechsler,* 960–66.

[25]Federal jurisdiction is an extremely complex subject and no attempt is made here to provide more than the broadest sense of its scope. Particularly with respect to litigation between citizens of different states—so-called "Diversity Jurisdiction"—see Delores K. Sloviter, "Diversity Jurisdiction Through the Lens of Federalism," *Judicature* 76, No. 2 (Aug.–Sept., 1992): 90–93.

[26]*U.S.C.,* vol. 28, §151–53 (Supplement 1992).

[27]*Federal Magistrates Act,* 28 U.S.C. §636.

[28]*See* Christopher E. Smith, *U.S. Magistrates in the Federal Courts: Subordinate Judges* (New York: Praeger Publishers, 1990); see also Smith, "From U.S. Magistrates to U.S. Magistrate Judges: Developments Affecting the Federal District Courts' Lower Tier of Judicial Officers," *Judicature,* 75, No. 4 (Dec.–Jan., 1992), 210–15.

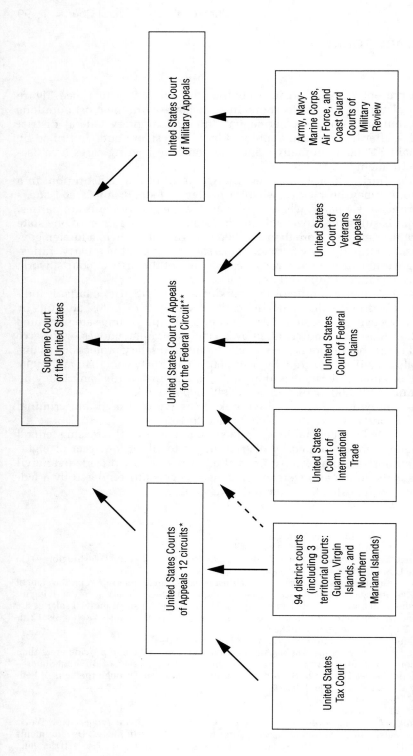

Figure 4–1 The United States Court System (SOURCE: U.S., Administrative Office of the United States Courts, *Understanding the Federal Courts* (Washington, D.C.: Administrative Office of the U.S. Courts, n.d.): Fig. 1.)

* The 12 regional courts of appeals also review cases from a number of federal agencies.
**The Court of Appeals for the Federal Circuit also receives cases from the International Trade Commission, the Merit Systems Protection Board, the Patent and Trademark Office, and the Board of Contract Appeals.

Table 4–1   Federal District Court Caseflow, 1940–1995

Year Ending June 30*	Authorized Judgeships	Civil Cases Commenced		Criminal Cases Commenced	
		No.	Cases per Judgeship	No.	Cases per Judgeship
1940	190	34,734	183	33,401	176
1945	193	60,965	316	39,427	204
1950	215	54,662	254	37,720	175
1955	244	59,375	243	37,123	152
1960	245	59,284	242	29,828	122
1965	307	67,678	220	33,334	109
1970	401	87,323	218	39,959	100
1975	400	117,320	293	43,282	108
1980	516	168,789	327	28,932	56
1985	575	273,670	476	39,500	69
1990	575	217,879	379	48,904	85
1994	649	236,391	364	45,473	70
1995	649	248,335	383	45,788	71

*Or for 1994–95, September 30.

Source: United States Administrative Office of the U.S. Courts, *Judicial Business of the United States Courts, 1980, 1985, 1990, 1994, 1995* (Washington: Administrative Office of the U.S. Courts).

In addition to these specified aspects of the work of U.S. district courts—the regular civil and criminal caseloads, bankruptcies, and matters handled by the U.S. magistrates—the system also involves at least three additional areas of significant activity:

1. An elaborate federal probation system exists with over 85,000 persons under supervision in 1995. In that year federal probation officers prepared nearly 170,000 investigative reports, with presentence reports and those having to do with supervised release (which has largely replaced federal parole) being the most common.[29]

2. A system of 59 federal public defender organizations has been created nationwide. In the twelve-month period ending September 30, 1995, this system opened 45,912 new cases. Of these, 28,405 were representations of criminal defendants before magistrate or district judges. The remainder included handling appeals for federal prisoners as well as representation in probation/parole revocation hearings and motions to correct or reduce sentences.[30]

3. U.S. District Courts still use both grand and petit (trial) juries quite frequently. In the year ending September 30, 1995, 9,822 trial juries (civil and criminal) were selected from over 372,000 potential jurors called. In addition, 960 federal grand juries were impaneled in 1995. These juries met in over 10,500 sessions, utilizing the services of over 208,000 citizens.[31]

---

[29]*Judicial Business 1995* (Abbrev.): 35–37.
[30]*Judicial Business 1995* (Abbrev.): Table S–23.
[31]*Judicial Business 1995* (Abbrev.): Tables S–17 and S–18.

Table 4–2 Bankruptcy Filings, 1950–1995

Year Ending June 30*	Filings
1950	33,392
1955	59,404
1960	110,034
1965	180,323
1970	194,399
1975	254,484
1980	360,960
1985	364,536
1990	725,484
1994	837,797
1995	883,457

*Or for 1994–95, September 30.

Source: United States, Administrative Office of the U.S. Courts, *Judicial Business of the United States Courts, 1980, 1990, 1994, 1995* (Washington: Administrative Office of the U.S. Courts).

One can easily understand, then, why the District Courts are called the workhorses of the federal judicial system. Including bankruptcies and cases heard by magistrate judges, these 94 courts each year handle some 97 percent of the total federal judicial caseload.

The United States Courts of Appeals

Because the United States Courts of Appeals are, by a circuitous route, the successors of the old circuit courts, and since they exist in geographic subdivisions called circuits, the term "circuit court" has stuck, although it has been a misnomer since 1948. The United States Courts of Appeals were actually created in 1891, in part to screen the Supreme Court from the avalanche of appeals it had been obliged to hear, and in part, of course, to move toward a nationalization of the federal judiciary.

As indicated in Figures 4–1 and 4–2, and Table 4–5, the nation is divided into 13 federal judicial circuits: 11 in the states, 1 in the District of Columbia, and a 13th (called the Federal Circuit) created in 1982 by combining the existing Court of Claims with the United States Court of Customs and Patent Appeals. The creation of the new Federal Circuit added 12 new judges. This, in addition to the 24 new positions added in the 1984 bankruptcy legislation, brought the total number of judges of the United States Courts of Appeals to 168. Eleven more judges were added via the Federal Judgeship Act of 1990, for a total in 1995 of 179. The number of judges per circuit varies, as shown, from 6 to 28, again, as with the district courts, depending primarily on caseflow.

The Courts of Appeals typically handle cases in three-judge panels. Sometimes, however, all of the judges in a particular circuit will participate in a case, sitting *en banc*. This procedure usually occurs in high profile appeals or in cases in which a losing party can persuade a majority of the judges that the three-judge panel made a wrong decision.

Table 4–3   Civil Cases Commenced in U.S. District Courts, Twelve-Month Period Ending September 30, 1991, and September 30, 1995

Action	Year	
	1991	1995
Contract Actions	45,418	31,182
Real Property	10,049	6,869
Tort Actions	35,945	53,986
Antitrust	654	781
Bankruptcy	5,050	5,046
Banks and Banking	771	432
Civil Rights	19,892	36,600
Commerce (ICC Rates, etc.)	1,900	580
Environment	1,080	1,081
Deportation	54	106
Prisoner Petitions	42,316	63,550
Forfeiture and Penalty	5,525	2,517
Labor Laws	14,917	14,954
Copyright, Patent and Trademark	5,186	6,866
Securities, Commodities, and Exchanges	2,084	1,906
Social Security Laws	8,491	9,354
Other	11,558	12,525
Total Cases	210,890	248,335

Source: United States Administrative Office of the U.S. Courts, *Judicial Business* 1995 (Abbrev.) (Washington: Administrative Office of the U.S. Courts, n.d.), Table C–2A.

A Chief Judge presides over each circuit and is statutorily defined as the judge in the circuit who is not yet age 65 and has the longest continuous period of service as a circuit judge. Each circuit judge is nominated by the president and must be confirmed by the Senate. The annual salary of a "circuit" judge was $141,700 in 1995.

As its name implies, the work of the United States Courts of Appeals is almost entirely appellate and consists primarily of appeals from federal district courts. Excluding the U.S. Court of Appeals for the Federal Circuit (explained later), these 12 courts in 1995 handled 50,072 filings, 89 percent of which originated with the district courts. The remainder arrived at the courts of appeals from the federal administrative agencies (about 7 percent) and the bankruptcy courts (3 percent), the final 1 percent being original proceedings.[32]

As indicated in Table 4–6, the caseloads of the circuit courts have grown dramatically in recent years—some three-fold between 1975 and 1995. During this same period, the number of circuit judgeships increased at a much lower rate, from 97 to the present 167 (again, excluding the 12 judges sitting on the U.S. Court of Appeals for the Federal

---

[32]*Judicial Business, 1995* (Abbrev.): 20, Table 2. See also a useful recent analysis of the work of these courts by Thomas E. Baker, *Rationing Justice: The Problems of the U.S. Courts of Appeals* (St. Paul, Minn.: West Publishing Co., 1994); and Michael C. Gizzi, "Examining the Crisis of Volume in the U.S. Courts of Appeals," *Judicature,* 77, No. 2 (Sept–Oct, 1993): 96–103.

Table 4–4　Criminal Cases Commenced in U.S. District Courts, Twelve-Month Period Ending September 30, 1991, and September 30, 1995

Action	1991	1995
Homicide	208	295
Robbery	1,573	1,240
Assault	553	561
Burglary—Breaking and Entering	134	63
Larceny and Theft	3,420	3,432
Embezzlement	1,929	1,368
Fraud	7,049	7,416
Auto Theft	212	267
Forgery and Counterfeiting	1,213	1,001
Sex Offenses	460	412
Drug Laws	11,954	11,520
Miscellaneous General Offenses**	12,948	11,113**
Immigration Laws	2,167	3,960
Liquor, Internal Revenue	4	3
Miscellaneous Federal Statutes***	2,513	2,402***
Total Cases	46,337*	45,053*

*Excludes transfers.

**Largest categories are drunk driving and weapons/firearms violoation.

***Such as Food and Drug Act, migratory bird laws, customs and postal laws, etc.

Source: United States Administrative Office of the U.S. Courts, *Judicial Business, 1995* (Abbrev.) (Washington: Administrative Office of the U.S. Courts, n.d.): Table D–2.

Circuit). Presently, assuming that each appeal heard by a three-judge panel is then assigned to one of the three judges for an opinion, and further assuming, purely for descriptive purposes, that no judge ever authors a concurring or dissenting opinion, each circuit judge appears to resolve some 300 appeals per year, a rate of more than one appeal per workday.

Given the extremely small number of cases heard by the Supreme Court, the U.S. Courts of Appeals are for all practical purposes the federal courts of last resort in most instances. Because of their heavy caseloads, these courts rarely grant the opportunity for oral argument. Rather, they decide most cases on the basis of the trial records and appellate briefs submitted by attorneys.

The United States Supreme Court

Although there was strong opposition among delegates to the Constitutional Convention to the creation of lower federal courts, the proposition that there should be at least one national judicial body as part of a triumvirate of governmental entities met with near unanimous approval. Oddly, it was often those delegates associated with a "states' rights" philosophy—generally opposed to the creation of lower federal courts—who were most insistent on the creation of a Supreme Court and on giving that Court power to review actions of state courts. This situation was due to the needs of commerce, which, according

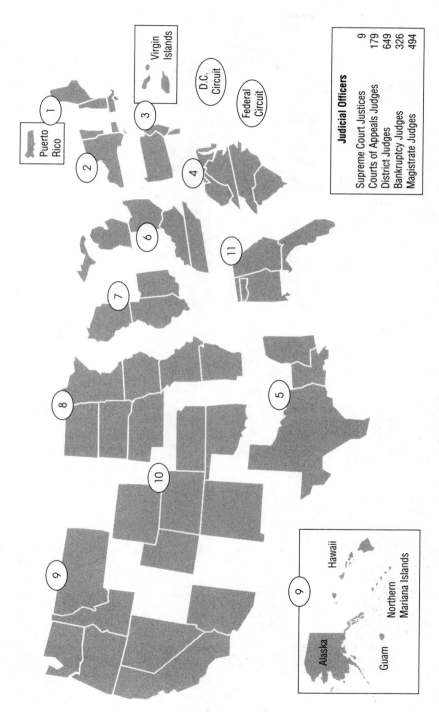

Judicial Officers	
Supreme Court Justices	9
Courts of Appeals Judges	179
District Judges	649
Bankruptcy Judges	326
Magistrate Judges	494

Figure 4–2 Number and Composition of Federal Judicial Circuits (SOURCE: U.S., Administrative Office of the U.S. Courts, *Understanding the Federal Courts* (Washington: Administrative Office of the U.S. Courts, n.d.): 8.)

Table 4–5 United States Courts of Appeals, 1995

Courts of Appeals	Number of Judgeships	Location and Postal Address
Federal Circuit (United States)	12	Washington, DC 20439
District of Columbia Circuit (District of Columbia)	12	Washington, DC 20001
First Circuit (Maine Massachusetts, New Hampshire,Rhode Island, and Puerto Rico)	6	Boston, MA 02109
Second Circuit (Connecticut, New York, and Vermont)	13	New York, NY 10007
Third Circuit (Delaware, New Jersey, Pennsylvania, and the Virgin Islands)	14	Philadelphia, PA 19106
Fourth Circuit (Maryland, North Carolina, South Carolina, Virginia, and West Virginia)	15	Richmond, VA 23219
Fifth Circuit (Louisiana, Mississippi, and Texas)	17	New Orleans, LA 70130
Sixth Circuit (Kentucky, Michigan, Ohio, and Tennessee)	16	Cincinnati, OH 45202
Seventh Circuit (Illinois, Indiana, and Wisconsin)	11	Chicago, IL 60604
Eighth Circuit (Arkansas, Iowa, Minnesota, Missouri, Nebraska, North Dakota, and South Dakota)	11	St. Louis, MO 63101
Ninth Circuit (Alaska, Arizona, California, Hawaii, Idaho, Montana, Nevada, Oregon, Washington, Guam, and the Northern Mariana Islands)	28	San Francisco, CA 94101
Tenth Circuit (Colorado, Kansas, New Mexico, Oklahoma, Utah, and Wyoming)	12	Denver, CO 80294
Eleventh Circuit (Alabama, Florida, and Georgia)	12	Atlanta, GA 30303

Source: United States Administrative Office of the U.S. Courts, *Understanding the Federal Courts* (Washington: Administrative Office of the U.S. Courts, n.d.), 18.

Table 4–6   United States Courts of Appeals Caseloads, 1940–1995

Year Ending June 30	Authorized Judgeships	Appeals Commenced	Cases per Three-Judge Panel
1940	57	3,446	184
1945	59	2,730	139
1950	65	2,830	131
1955	68	3,695	163
1960	68	3,899	172
1965	78	6,766	260
1970	97	11,662	361
1975	97	16,658	515
1980	132	23,200	527
1985	156	33,360	642
1990	156	40,858	786
1994[a]	167	48,322	868
1995[a]	167	50,072	899

[a]Year ending September 30.

Source: United States, Administrative Office of the U.S. Courts, *Judicial Business of the United States Courts, 1980, 1990, 1994, 1995* (Washington: Administrative Office of the U.S. Courts).

to many delegates, required the uniformity and guarantees that only a national court could provide. As stated by James Wilson in the Pennsylvania debates on the Constitution,

> But when we consider the matter a little further, is it not necessary, if we mean to restore either public or private credit, that foreigners as well as ourselves, have a just and impartial tribunal to which they may resort? I would ask how a merchant must feel to have his property lay at the mercy of the laws of Rhode Island? I ask further, how will a creditor feel who has his debts at the mercy of tender laws in other states? It is true, that under this constitution these particular inequities would be restrained in future; but Sir, there are other ways of avoiding payment of debts. There have been installment acts, and other acts of a similar effect. Such things, Sir, destroy the very sources of credit.
>
> Is it not an important object to extend our manufacturers and our commerce? This cannot be done unless a proper security is provided for the regular discharge of contracts. This security cannot be obtained, unless we give the power of deciding upon those contracts to the general governments [sic].[33]

As earlier noted, the Constitution itself is notoriously brief and vague as to the precise structure of the Supreme Court. Neither its size nor the qualifications of its members are specified.[34] The Judiciary Act of 1789 fixed the number of justices at six: five associate justices and one chief justice. The Congress has changed this seven times since then. The membership of the Court was decreased to five by the Judiciary Act of 1801, restored to six by the Judiciary Act of 1802, and increased to seven in 1807, and then to nine in 1837. In 1863, Congress expanded the number of seats on the Court to ten, reduced the number

---

[33]Frankfurter and Landis, *Business of the Supreme Court*, 39.
[34]See a discussion of this point by John R. Vile and Mario Perez-Reilly, "The U.S. Constitution and Judicial Qualifications: A Curious Omission," *Judicature* 74, No. 4 (Dec.–Jan., 1991): 198–202.

to seven in 1865, and finally, in 1869, increased the number again to nine where it has remained since. Some of these alterations (for example, those of 1807 and 1837) were in response to increases in population in the West and the resultant caseload increases. However, all were, to some extent, policy motivated—to reduce the influence of the president's political philosophy on the Court by denying the president appointments, or to directly encourage some policies or discourage others on the part of the Court itself.

Supreme Court justices are appointed in the same manner as all federal judges—that is, nominated by the president with the advice and consent of the Senate. They serve, as the Constitution states, "during good behavior," which means, in effect, life tenure.[35] In 1996 the Chief Justice's salary was $171,500; for associate justices it was $164,100.

In contrast to the popular perception that service on the Supreme Court is the most prestigious position to which a member of the bar may aspire, the first presidents actually had difficulty persuading qualified people to serve. Of the six original appointees selected by President Washington, one declined in order to accept a state government post; another accepted but never attended a Court session; and one, John Jay, resigned his position as Chief Justice to become governor of New York. Only with the tenure of Chief Justice John Marshall, from 1801 to 1835, did the Court begin to achieve the level of prestige that it now enjoys.

Although circuit riding by the justices has long since disappeared, each justice is still assigned one or two circuits to oversee. The role each justice plays with respect to her or his circuits is largely ceremonial. There are, however, instances of emergency pleadings that the justices must act upon, such as a request for a stay of execution upon a death sentence filed while the Court is in recess.[36]

In contrast to other branches and agencies of government whose personnel rosters have burgeoned with the increase in the size of government generally, the Supreme Court operates on a relatively modest annual budget of some 29 million dollars (fiscal year 1996) and employs, in all, only about 350 people. These include, in addition to maintenance workers, the Clerk of the Court (the Court's chief administrative officer responsible for the administration of the smooth flow of the Court's business, the assignment of cases to dockets, and similar duties), the Court's Marshal (responsible for security and protocol), and the Court's Reporter (who edits and supervises the printing and publication of the Court's decisions). The Court also has a press officer and a librarian. These 5 officials with their respective staffs, in addition to about 15 messengers who work for the Court, constitute the bulk of the Court's employees.[37]

Bearing a closer relationship to actual Supreme Court decision making are the law clerks to the justices themselves. These numbered 34 in 1995. Seven of the associate justices work with 4 clerks each (the maximum authorized), while Chief Justice Rehnquist and Justice Stevens have only 3 clerks. Clerks are typically selected on the basis of their academic record, largely from prestige law schools.[38] Each justice makes the selection in

---

[35]No Supreme Court justice has been removed from the Court by process of impeachment. Associate Justice Samuel Chase was impeached by the House of Representatives in 1804 but was acquitted by the Senate in 1805.

[36]See William O. Douglas, *The Court Years, 1939–1975* (New York: Random House, 1980), 78–85, detailing his grant of a stay of execution in the cases of Ethel and Julius Rosenberg, pending review by the full Court.

[37]These data were drawn from Kermit L. Hall, et. al., eds., *The Oxford Companion to the Supreme Court of the United States,* (New York: Oxford University Press, 1992), 817–18; and Lee Espstein, et. al., *The Supreme Court Compendium: Data, Decisions and Developments,* 2nd ed. (Washington: Congressional Quarterly, Inc., 1996), 41–42, 49–54, updated by data from the Court's budget office.

[38]Based on data from the Supreme Court's Public Information Office, Prof. Lawrence Baum reports that in the Court's 1993 Term, three-fourths of the law clerks hailed from but four law schools: Harvard, Stanford, Chicago, and Yale. See Lawrence Baum, *The Supreme Court,* 5th ed. (Washington: Congressional Quarterly, 1995), 18.

his or her own way; some tilt toward a particular geographic region and some toward the law school they attended.[39] Before assuming their positions on the Court, many clerks spend at least a year clerking in one of the lower federal courts, sometimes even in a state supreme court.

After a year (in a few instances, longer) with the Supreme Court, law clerks typically move on to extraordinarily high-paying positions in the nation's most prestigious law firms, or immediately accept positions on law school faculties. Some have even found their way back to the Supreme Court as appointed justices. Justice Byron White, for instance, had clerked for Chief Justice Fred Vinson; Justice John Paul Stevens for Justice Wiley Rutledge; Chief Justice Rehnquist for Justice Robert Jackson; and Justice Stephen Breyer had clerked for Justice Goldberg.[40]

With respect to the Court's actual workload, the Constitution defines two types of Supreme Court jurisdiction: original and appellate. The Court's original jurisdiction accounts for only a tiny portion of its total caseload. Although Article 3, Section 2 of the Constitution mandates that the Court shall have original jurisdiction—that is, jurisdiction to act as a trial court—in "all cases affecting ambassadors, other public ministers and consuls, and those in which a state shall be a party," the Court itself has interpreted this provision as providing it discretion to determine which cases falling within the Constitutional parameters of its original jurisdiction it must actually hear. The Court has decided only about 175 cases in this category over its more than two-hundred-year history. In recent years, these cases have primarily involved disputes between states over boundaries and water rights. In order to deal with such cases, the Court often appoints a "special master" to carry out the day-to-day duties of a trial judge and to recommend a disposition to the justices.[41]

For all practical purposes, then, the Supreme Court is an appellate body. After specifying the Court's original jurisdiction, the Constitution provides that "in all the other Cases before mentioned, the Supreme Court shall have appellate Jurisdiction, both as to Law and Fact, with such Exceptions, and under such Regulations as the Congress shall make." Congressional control over the Court's appellate jurisdiction—in reality, control over what the Court will hear—has worked both to enhance and to threaten the efficacy of Supreme Court policy-making. The Judiciary Act of 1891, in conjunction with the Judges Bill of 1925, gave the Court virtually total control of its docket. As noted earlier, the result of this legislation was to sharpen and enhance the ability of the Court to articulate policy in critical areas almost entirely of its own choosing if a case is brought. On the other hand, in the frequent clashes between Congress and the Court, the congressional power to control the

---

[39]Justice William O. Douglas, for example, developed the practice of selecting his clerks from the Ninth Circuit in the West, an area of the nation up to that time not well represented in the Court's clerk pool. As to the other justices, Douglas reports,

> While each of the other justices had his own circuit, no one else followed my practice of giving the patronage of their prized law clerkships to graduates of schools in their respective circuits. Hugo Black usually chose a southerner, but there were no restrictions of the law school from which he came. Earl Warren, while taking one clerk from the University of California Law School at Berkeley, took the rest from wherever he could find them. Felix [Frankfurter] always had Harvard graduates. Harlan did the same, but his clerks [had] always first served for a term with a judge in the Second Circuit.

Douglas, *The Court Years*, 171.

[40]More extensive coverage of the Court's law clerks, along with their selection and role in decision making, may be found in Henry J. Abraham, *The Judicial Process*, 6th ed. (New York: Oxford University Press, 1993), 239–44; David M. O'Brien, *Storm Center: The Supreme Court in American Politics*, 4th ed. (New York: W.W. Norton, 1996): 171–75; and Bernard Schwartz, *A History of the Supreme Court* (New York: Oxford University Press, 1993), 369–72 and passim.

[41]*Hart and Wechsler*, Ch. 3, provides a useful summary of the Supreme Court's original jurisdiction.

Court's jurisdiction has rendered the judicial branch vulnerable to intense pressures. Indeed, the last major time that Congress significantly restricted the Court's jurisdiction was in the Habeas Corpus Act of 1867, with which Congress prevented the Court from holding the post-Civil War Reconstruction Acts unconstitutional. In *Ex Parte McCardle,* 7 Wall. 506 (1869), the Court acknowledged Congress's constitutional prerogative to so act (even though arguments had already been heard in the case), holding that it was powerless to rule on the constitutionality of the acts. Inasmuch as over a century and a quarter have passed since the exercise of this ultimate congressional power, many scholars presume that the power has slipped away. But the threat is always there, as a potential device to keep the Court in line. (See Chapter 12 on Court and Congress relations.)

Current statutes, along with Supreme Court practice, mean that cases for review come to the Supreme Court in one of three ways: certification, appeal, and *certiorari.* Certification is a seldom-used mode of access. If an appellate court needs instructions on a matter of law, it may *certify* questions to the Supreme Court. Federal law permits the Court either to give instructions or to reject the request.

Time was when the second-listed method of reaching the Supreme Court, *Writ of Appeal,* accounted for a substantial portion of the Court's workload. Even up to 1988, Congress had "required" the Court to grant appeals in certain categories of disputes (e.g., when a state supreme court held a treaty or a federal statute unconstitutional), though the Court could ignore the request, citing lack of a "substantial Federal question." But the Act to Improve the Administration of Justice of June 27, 1988 (P.L. 100-352), removed virtually all mandatory appellate review, leaving the justices with almost complete discretion as to what cases to hear.[42]

The overwhelming majority (some 99 percent) of cases on the Supreme Court's docket at any given time now arrive there via a writ of *certiorari,* a Latin term meaning "to make more certain." After receiving an adverse decision from a federal court of appeals, from the highest appellate court in a particular state, or in very limited instances from a federal district court, one of the parties in a case can submit a petition to the Court asking it to review that decision. The petition must explain the facts of the case, the actions taken by the lower court or courts, the legal issues that the case raises, and the reasons why those issues are important enough to merit Supreme Court review. If four of the nine justices agree that the case should be heard, the Court issues a writ of *certiorari*—it "grants cert" in the legal jargon—and orders the records and documents that the case has generated transferred for review.

Once the Court grants a petition, the lawyers involved prepare and submit briefs outlining the case and their arguments. Typically, the Court schedules an oral argument in which each side has 30 minutes to present its position and, perhaps most important, to field the questions of individual justices. The Court then prepares and releases an opinion or a set of opinions that explain its decision. A more detailed explanation of the Court's work is set forth in Chapter 11.

All matters brought before the Supreme Court are placed on one of two dockets, Original or Appellate. Most statistical presentations of the work of the Court, however, divide cases on the Appellate Docket into paid cases and those matters filed *in forma pauperis,* sometimes called the Miscellaneous Docket. This division is illustrated in

---

[42]The few remaining "mandatory" appeals (which the Court can still avoid if there is no substantial federal question involved) include appeals in reapportionment cases, suits under the Civil Rights and Voting Rights Acts, antitrust matters, and issues under the Presidential Election Campaign Fund Act. See Epstein et. al., *The Supreme Court Compendium,* 27. See also "New Law Eliminates Court's Mandatory Jurisdiction," *Judicature* 72, No. 2 (Aug.–Sept. 1988): 138.

Table 4–7, which presents the work of the Court for its Fall 1994 Term (calendar 1994–1995).

In that term, a total of 7,565 matters were presented to the Court. Of these, however, only 6,611 cases were disposed of, (mostly by denying review), and of this number, only 227 cases were addressed "on the merits" (actually decided). Among this small number of cases (which was only 3.4 percent of cases disposed of) only 92 were dealt with by full written opinions, the treatment that is usually associated with the work of the Court. Since the justices often combine cases that present similar issues, the actual number of conventional full written opinions that term was only 75, with four more decided *per curiam*— that is, for the entire Court without a particular justice identified as author of the opinion—but with legal reasoning sufficiently lengthy to be tabulated as full written opinions (see Table 4–7). The remaining 135 cases (plus the four *per curiam* opinions just mentioned) were resolved without oral argument via summary rulings of not more than a sentence or two.

These data should not be taken to suggest that the workload of the Court is light. Virtually every case that the Court takes on raises significant questions of constitutional or statutory interpretation. Weighing these matters as a member of the nation's supreme judicial body is both important and time-consuming work.

Further, the Court must wade through a tremendous number of petitions for review, approximately 98 percent of which it denies or dismisses, or the petitioner withdraws. This fact suggests both the care and the extraordinary discretion the Court exercises in deciding what to decide.

In keeping with the pattern of providing caseload data over time, Table 4–8 presents figures for the Supreme Court since 1810. Those figures reflect an enormous increase in the number of petitions for review over the past two centuries, and particularly in recent decades. In the October 1980 term, for example, the Court's docket was approximately five times larger than it was in 1930. And just since 1985, that number has again leaped by over 45 percent.

Such increases gave rise to a nationwide debate in the 1970s and early 1980s as to whether the Court's workload is too heavy, leading to a lowering of the quality of its decisions and a lessening of its effectiveness as the nation's key judicial policy-making body. In 1971, Chief Justice Warren Burger appointed a seven-member commission, called a study group, on the Supreme Court's caseload problem, headed by Paul A. Freund of Harvard Law School. A short time later, Congress created a similar group called the Commission on Revision of the Federal Court Appellate System, chaired by Senator Roman Hruska (R-Neb.). Both groups recommended the creation of a national court of appeals. Freund's group would have created a court that would screen all cases, sending some on to the Supreme Court, rejecting others, and deciding some for itself. The Hruska court would work in reverse, receiving certain cases sent down to it by the Supreme Court.[43]

A 1976 study by the Justice Department recommended that these proposals be rejected. Several Supreme Court justices also joined in opposition to a new court. Nevertheless, a number of factors, including a heavy 1981–1982 caseload, caused a few of the justices to rethink their positions. With the constant prodding of Chief Justice Burger, a more modest proposal was developed, looking to the creation of a tribunal to resolve conflicts among the circuits. According to the Chief Justice, this could decrease the Supreme Court's

[43]A useful summary of the arguments for and against the proposal for a new national court of appeals may be found in American Enterprise Institute, *Proposals for a National Court of Appeals* (Washington, D.C.: American Enterprise Institute for Public Policy Research, 1977).

Table 4–7 Workload of the Supreme Court, Fall Term, 1995

	Disposed of	Remaining on Docket
Original Docket	5	6
Appellate Docket[a]	2099	357
On Merits	154	
Review Granted[b]	92	
(Percent Granted: 4.4%)[c]		
Summarily Decided[d]	62	
Appeals and Petitions for Review		
Denied, Dismissed, or Withdrawn[e]	1945	
Miscellaneous Docket[f]	4507	591
On Merits	68	
Review Granted	13	
(Percent Granted: 0.3%)		
Summarily Decided	55	
Appeals and Petitions for Review		
Denied, Dismissed, or Withdrawn	4439	
Total	**6611**	**954**

Method of Disposition			
By Written Opinion[g] *(Number of Written Opinions: 79)*[h]	92	By Denial, Dismissal, or Withdrawal of Appeals or Petitions for Review	6384
By Per Curiam or Memorandum Decision	114		
Total			**6590**

Disposition of Cases Reviewed on Writ of Certiorari			
	Reversed[i]	**Vacated**[j]	**Affirmed**	**Total**
Full Opinions	47 (56.0%)	10 (11.9%)	27 (32.1%)	84
Memorandum Orders	0 (0.0%)	106 (96.4%)	4 (3.6%)	110
Total	**47 (24.2%)**	**116 (59.8%)**	**31 (16.0%)**	**194**

[a]The appellate docket consists of all paid cases.

[b]This category includes cases in which review was granted that were carried over to a subsequent Term, but not cases summarily decided.

(*continued*)

caseload by one-third. Legislation to create the new court was introduced in Congress, but considerable opposition emerged, and with the resignation of Chief Justice Burger in 1986, agitation for legislative caseload relief eventually subsided.

A central point in this long-simmering debate—an argument often made by opponents to the creation of a new court—is simply that (1) by far the most time-consuming and onerous task performed by the justices is the drafting of opinions, and (2) that particular aspect of their work is well within their own power to control—and limit. Thus, under the stewardship of Chief Justice Rehnquist, the Court moved from a plea for outside help to a self-help mode, simply by granting fewer petitions for *certiorari,* scheduling fewer oral arguments, and writing fewer full-dress opinions. The data presented in Table 4–9 make the point.

Enthusiasm for the Court's new-found efficiency has not been universal, however. Justice Byron White, for example, before he left the Court, complained that the justices seemed intent upon subordinating their obligation to resolve important legal issues (particularly those involving conflicts among the circuits) to an irrational concern for docket management.[44] Be that as it may, and whatever their rationale, the justices, by the end of

---

[44]Linda Greenhouse, "Rehnquist Urges Curb on Appeals of Death Penalty; calls for Bill's Passage" *New York Times* (May 16, 1990): 1; Mark Hansen, "Limiting Death Row Appeals: Final Justice", *ABA Journal* 78 (Mar. 1992): 64–68 (noting that a majority of the justices, led by Rehnquist, is making strides to limit death penalty appeals despite congressional unwillingness to do so). Another possible explanation for the Court's decreasing caseload is that the U.S. Justice Department is itself filing fewer appeals on behalf of the federal government, having virtually abandoned civil rights litigation under Presidents Reagan and Bush and finding lower courts disproportionately filled with Reagan and Bush appointees who are receptive to Justice Department positions. Linda Greenhouse, "As Its Workload Decreases, High Court Shuns New Cases," *New York Times* (Mar. 7, 1982): 1.

See also Hart and Wechsler, "Federal Habeas Corpus," Ch. XI, and 1992 Supplement, 166–94.

In an insightful article in the *New York Times Magazine* (Oct. 6, 1996), David J. Garrow covers some additional factors which may explain the Court's reduced opinion-writing. See "The Rehnquist Reins," especially the quotations from Justice Souter, 71. Justice Souter's detailed remarks on the Court's workload are contained in Shannon P. Duffy, "Inside the Highest Court: Souter Describes Justices' Relationship, Caseload Trend," *Pennsylvania Law Weekly* (Apr. 17, 1995): 10, 28–30. (The author is indebted to Prof. James Eisenstein of Pennsylvania State University for locating and sharing this item.)

---

[c]In the computation of the percentage of cases granted review last Term, the divisor is the number of cases docketed during last Term plus the number of cases not acted upon in prior Terms minus the number of cases not acted upon last Term. Past versions of this table inflated the number of cases granted review by including cases in which review was granted in prior Terms.

[d]Including cases summarily affirmed, reversed, or vacated.

[e]This category primarily includes dismissals of appeals and denials of petitions for certiorari. It also includes withdrawals of appeals and denials of other applications for review, such as petitions for writs of habeas corpus or mandamus.

[f]This miscellaneous docket consists of all cases filed in forma pauperis.

[g]Including five cases decided per curiam containing legal reasoning sufficient to be considered full written opinions rather than per curiam opinions. These cases are *Pennsylvania v. Labron,* 116 S. Ct. 2485 (1996) (per curiam); *Leavitt v. Jane L.,* 116 S. Ct. 2068 (1996) (per curiam); *Lawrence v. Chater,* 116 S. Ct. 604 (1996) (per curiam); and *Wood v. Bartholomew,* 116 S. Ct. 7 (1996) (per curiam). The opinion for *Pennsylvania v. Labron* decided two cases.

[h]Including four per curiam opinions containing legal reasoning substantial enough to be considered full written opinions rather than per curiam opinions.

[i]Including cases reversed in part and affirmed in part.

[j]Including cases affirmed in part and vacated in part.

Source: "The Supreme Court, 1995 Term," *Harvard Law Review,* Vol. 110, No. 1 (Nov., 1996): 371–372.

Table 4–8   Cases Docketed, Supreme Court, Fall Terms, 1900–1995

Fall Term	Number
1900	723
1905	794
1910	1,116
1915	1,093
1920	975
1925	1,309
1930	1,034
1935	1,092
1940	1,109
1945	1,460
1950	1,321
1955	1,849
1960	2,296
1965	3,256
1970	4,212
1975	4,761
1980	5,144
1985	5,158
1990	6,316
1991	6,770
1992	7,245
1993	7,786
1994	8,100
1995	7,565

Source: Lee Epstein, Jeffrey A. Segal, Harold J. Spath, and Thomas G. Walker, *The Supreme Court Compendium: Data, Decisions and Developments* (Washington: Congressional Quarterly, Inc., 2nd ed., 1996), Table 2–2.

their 1995 term, had significantly lightened their workload through a rather dramatic reduction in both the absolute number and the percentage of petitions they granted, formally heard, and decided.

Matters of caseload aside, the student of judicial politics should not lose sight of the abject political considerations driving proposals for major structural change in federal appellate courts. Should a new national court ever be created, such a body might well—indeed, some have said was intended to—undercut the power and prestige of the Supreme Court, thereby lessening its political clout. In like manner, a significant lowering of the number of issues that the Court addresses clearly constitutes a political statement about the proper functions of the Court and its decisions in our polity. Fewer cases bring clear advantages to some interests, disadvantages to others. At bottom, the matter of "whose ox might be gored" is the real issue around which debate swirls, although for over two hundred years, the "rules of the game" have dictated that we approach the topic via discus-

Table 4–9   Petitions for *Certiorari* Docketed and Granted and Signed Opinions Written, United States Supreme Court, 1970–1995

Fall Term	Petitions for *Certiorari*			Signed Opinions
	Docketed	Granted	Percent	
1970	4,192	255	6.0	109
1971	4,515	299	6.6	129
1972	4,619	252	5.5	140
1973	5,065	259	5.1	141
1974	4,756	263	5.5	123
1975	4,747	272	5.7	138
1976	4,722	267	5.7	126
1977	4,690	248	5.3	129
1978	4,714	244	5.2	130
1979	4,758	231	4.9	130
1980	5,120	184	3.6	123
1981	5,289	210	4.0	141
1982	5,062	179	3.5	151
1983	5,037	149	3.0	151
1984	4,991	185	3.7	139
1985	5,148	186	3.6	146
1986	5,111	167	3.3	145
1987	5,252	180	3.4	139
1988	5,643	147	2.6	133
1989	5,732	122	2.1	129
1990	6,302	141	2.2	112
1991	6,758	120	1.8	107
1992	7,233	97	1.3	107
1993	7,774	99	1.3	84
1994	8,089	93	1.1	82
1995	7,554	105	1.4	75

Source: Lee Epstein, Jeffrey A. Segal, Harold J. Spaeth, and Thomas G. Walker, *The Supreme Court Compendium: Data, Decisions and Developments.* 2nd ed. (Washington: Congressional Quarterly Inc., 1996): Tables 2–6 and 2–7.

sions of burdensome caseload, administrative efficiency, and other euphemisms of judicial diplomacy.

Specialized Federal Courts

The Constitution empowers Congress to establish courts both in Article III, the judicial article, and in Article I, which authorizes Congress "to constitute Tribunals inferior to the Supreme Court." Legislators have relied on the latter provision several times in creating what have come to be known as Article I "legislative" courts. The Supreme Court, however, has disagreed with this interpretation. In its 1962 *Glidden v. Zdanok* decision, the Court concluded that the "inferior tribunals" authority of Article I spoke to the "inferior courts" mentioned in Article III.[45] In other words, the Article I provision did not extend congressional authority beyond that enumerated in the judicial article.

Despite this conclusion, the Supreme Court has recognized Congress's authority to create "legislative" courts pursuant to its power to act as is "necessary and proper" in exercising its other enumerated powers. Thus, because Congress is empowered to tax and spend, it may create a tribunal of sorts to handle monetary issues; because it has authority to raise a military force, it can create a military "court."

In the past, the Supreme Court has distinguished Article I legislative courts from their Article III constitutional counterparts.[46] More recently, however, that distinction has become somewhat blurred. In 1978, for example, the federal statute establishing a system of bankruptcy courts was challenged as unconstitutional. The basis of the challenge was that Congress exceeded its authority by empowering bankruptcy courts, created pursuant to Article I, to hear the same sorts of "cases or controversies" as Article III courts. Although the Supreme Court agreed and held the bankruptcy court system unconstitutional, its reasons for doing so were not clear. A prominent concern of the Court, however, was that permitting Congress to create legislative courts without Article III protections and then to empower those courts with jurisdiction over the "cases and controversies" expressly included in Article III jurisdiction would undermine the independence of the judiciary.[47]

Since its bankruptcy court decision, the Court has looked somewhat more favorably upon legislative courts, tending toward a loose, multifactor analysis of their constitutionality. Given that Congress seems likely to continue creating legislative tribunals to handle increasingly specialized categories of disputes, one would expect challenges to their constitutional legitimacy to continue as well. Following is a brief description of several prominent legislative courts, past and present.

United States Court of Military Appeals. The United States Court of Military Appeals came into existence by virtue of the congressional enactment in 1950 of the Uniform Code of Military Justice, itself an extensive revision and liberalization of the old Articles of War under which the armed forces had functioned throughout much of our history. The creation of the Court of Military Appeals constituted a significant departure in military law in that it was a *civilian* body, calculated to bring some of the constitutional rights civilians have long enjoyed to military personnel. The court consists of a chief judge and two associate judges appointed by the president with the advice and consent of the Senate, for staggered fifteen-year terms. They may be reappointed. Not more than two judges may be from the same political party. The court, by law, must review cases involving military officers of flag rank (admirals and generals), all capital cases, and all cases certified by the judge advocate general. In other cases, which of course involves the vast majority of courts martial, the court has discretionary review.

The court has not been shy in reversing court martial convictions on constitutional grounds. Its work, along with the enactment of the 1968 Ervin Military Justice Act, has considerably liberalized military law. To date, the court has reversed about half of all cases heard, a record rare for appellate bodies. At the same time, the influence of military com-

---

[45]*Glidden v. Zdanok,* 370 U.S. 530 (1962).
[46]*Ex Parte Bakelite Corp.,* 279 U.S. 438 (1929). A detailed discussion of case law on the issue of legislative versus constitutional courts may be found in *Hart and Wechsler,* 425–73, and the 1992 Supplement.
[47]*Northern Pipeline Construction Co. v. Marathon Pipe Line Co.,* 458 U.S. 50 (1982).

manders, particularly over lower level military trials (summary and special courts martial) such as to raise serious questions about the impact of the Court of Military Appeals, its record to the contrary notwithstanding.[48]

United States Tax Court. Closer to an administrative agency than a court, the United States Tax Court began its work in 1924 as the United States Board of Tax Appeals in the Executive Branch under the Internal Revenue Service. In 1942, it became officially known as the Tax Court of the United States, and in 1969 its name was changed to its present label. The chief function of this court is to rule on taxpayers' challenges to deficiency judgments made by the commissioner of internal revenue. It consists of nineteen judges appointed, as are many other federal judges, for staggered terms of fifteen years. One of the nineteen is elected by the judges themselves to serve a two-year term as chief judge. As with the Court of International Trade, the Tax Court does its work in divisions, each of which is headed by a judge. Although the court is located in Washington, D.C., sessions are typically conducted throughout the United States. Decisions of the Tax Court are appealable to the United States Courts of Appeals and are, of course, subject to final review on writ of *certiorari* to the United States Supreme Court. In the fiscal year ending September 30, 1992, the Tax Court received 30,345 new filings. In that year, 34,823 cases were disposed of, but 44,376 were still pending.[49]

The Court of Veterans Appeals. This court was created by Congress in 1988 to review decisions by the Board of Veterans Appeals. Disability issues, in addition to loan eligibility and educational benefits matters, are the mainstay of the docket of this court. In 1992 it reviewed nearly 2,000 cases. The court has seven judgeships, appointed by the president with the advice and consent of the Senate. The court is based in Washington, but may sit elsewhere.[50]

The U.S. Court of Federal Claims. This court was one of the earliest legislative courts created. Claims against the federal government arising out of war debts and similar matters were being brought to Congress under the First Amendment's provision for the right to "petition the Government for redress of grievances." Although Congress could—and did—deal with such matters through private bills, this procedure was quite time-consuming as well as inequitable, since Congress had delineated no guidelines for the adoption of such legislation. Thus, by an act of February 24, 1885, Congress created a seven-member Court of Claims. In addition, fifteen commissioners performed trial functions by sitting in different locations throughout the country to take evidence and prepare findings of fact and recommendations for the court itself. Except for tort cases and tax refund cases (wherein the district courts had exclusive and concurrent jurisdiction, respectively), claims against the federal government in excess of $10,000 go to the Court of Claims. The Court

---

[48]More extensive studies of the work of the United States Court of Military Appeals are Luther C. West, *They Call It Justice: Command Influence in the Court Martial System* (New York: Viking Press, 1977); Robert Sherrill, *Military Justice Is to Justice as Military Music Is to Music* (New York: Harper & Row, 1970); and Harold F. Nufter, *American Service Members' Supreme Court: Impact of the U.S. Court of Military Appeals on Military Justice* (Washington: University Press of America, 1982). An overview of the work of this court is presented by Abraham, *The Judicial Process,* 145–49.
[49]See United States, Administrative Office of the U.S. Courts, *Understanding the Federal Courts,* 2nd ed. (Washington: Administrative Office of the U.S. Courts, n.d.), 17.
[50]*Understanding the Federal Courts,* 16.

also has appellate jurisdiction over the Indian Claims Commission. Holdings of the Court of Claims are subject to review by the U.S. Court of Appeals for the Federal Circuit.

Currently, the court's sixteen judges are appointed by the president with the advice and consent of the Senate for fifteen-year-terms. The court's headquarters are in Washington, D.C., but it sits in numerous sites throughout the country.

The constitutional position of the old Court of Claims has changed twice since it was created. It began as a legislative court, but its status was altered by Congress in 1953 to an Article III tribunal when its judges were given the constitutional protections of tenure and salary. In 1982, however, Congress (96 Stat. 25) provided for limited terms for the judges of the court, returning it to Article I status, and in 1992 its name was changed to the Court of Federal Claims. In the fiscal year ending September 30, 1995, 1,151 new cases were filed before this court, with 1,449 cases terminated that year.[51]

Territorial Courts.　Territorial courts can be categorized as specialized federal tribunals with Article I status even though they are part of the federal district court system. This is because they perform functions that are unique to federal courts. From the beginning of our history as a nation, the governing of territories has been an ever-present problem. The Constitution's framers, in Article IV, made provisions for such governments, empowering Congress to "make all needful Rules and Regulations respecting the Territory or other Property belonging to the United States." The mechanism Congress has usually employed for the adjudicative needs of the territories has been a hybrid federal district court. Today, with the exception of the Commonwealth of Puerto Rico, which has its own United States District Court with exclusive jurisdiction over matters of federal law, as well as a separate set of local courts, all U.S. territories have a federal court having both federal and local jurisdiction. Currently such tribunals exist in Guam, the Virgin Islands, and, since 1978, the Northern Mariana Islands. Not only are these courts multipurpose entities, but also their judges have limited terms of office (10 years), and their procedures and doctrines tend to be oriented somewhat to local territorial needs. Such courts are included as federal district courts for statistical purposes, but they are better characterized and categorized as specialized federal tribunals.

Other Specialized Federal Courts

Finally, a word must be said concerning legislative (Article I) judicial bodies which have been reconstituted into Article III constitutional courts. Central among these are the old-line Court of Claims (previously discussed), which has again been converted back to a legislative court; the Customs Court; and the Court of Customs and Patent Appeals. The old Customs Court (now titled the *U.S. Court of International Trade*) has existed in altered form since the earliest days of the nation. It now has nine judges appointed in the usual manner but with the proviso that not more than five may be drawn from the same political party. As its name implies, this court deals with controversies regarding the classification of imports and duties thereon. The court sits in panels of three judges, and though based in New York City, it convenes at port cities throughout the states and territories. This court

---

[51]*Judicial Business, 1995* (Abbrev.), Table G–2A. The Court of Claims, as well as its successor, the Court of Federal Claims, is discussed in Abraham, *The Judicial Process,* 150–51. On specialized federal courts, see also Louis Fisher, *Constitutional Structures: Separated Powers and Federalism* (New York: McGraw-Hill, 1995), 150–58; and *Understanding the Federal Courts:* 11–18. See also the useful coverage of the history and constitutional status of the Court of Claims in Hart and Wechsler, passim.

currently terminates around five hundred to six hundred cases annually, although it may have three or four times that number of cases pending each year.[52]

The Court of Customs and Patent Appeals had also been a well-known tribunal among America's specialized federal courts, ultimately designated an Article III court. Congress created this court in 1909 to hear appeals from the Board of General Appraisers (later the Customs Court), and enhanced its jurisdiction in 1929 (adding "Patent Appeals" to its title) by assigning to it appeals from the patent office. It also heard appeals from the Tariff Commission as well as from findings of the Secretary of Commerce. Its caseload was always small, involving, in its latest years, primarily patent and trademark issues, along with matters of customs, commerce, and international trade.[53]

By the Federal Court Improvement Act of 1982, this court was abolished and its work transferred to a new "13th Circuit Court," formally entitled the United States Court of Appeals for the Federal Circuit. The new court also assumed the appellate portion of the work of the old Court of Claims; and in the same legislation, the latter court was converted back to a legislative entity, as previously mentioned.

The jurisdiction of the new twelve-judge court, unlike the regular United States Courts of Appeals, is by subject matter rather than by geographic region. It receives appeals from a wide variety of federal entities: the Court of Federal Claims, the Court of International Trade, the Court of Veterans Appeals, the International Trade Commission, the Board of Contract Appeals, the Patent and Trademark Office, and the Merit Systems Protection Board. Certain decisions of the Secretaries of Agriculture and Commerce are also appealable to the Court of Appeals for the Federal Circuit. Currently, this court receives some 1,500–2,000 filings per year.[54]

FEDERAL JUDICIAL ADMINISTRATION

Until 1922, the administration of the federal courts had been as haphazard as that existing at the state level. Judicial independence and localism reigned supreme. As described by Frankfurter and Landis, the United States had created a hierarchy of courts but not of judges. Judicial independence had come to mean not only independence from undue political influence; the judges were, to a considerable degree, independent of each other. Little or no federal authority existed to move judges with light dockets into districts with heavier caseloads. In short, the federal judicial structure resulted in loose-jointed unprofessional standards:

> The system was without direction and without responsibility. Each judge was left to himself, guided in the administration of his business by his conscience and his temperament. The basis for informed public judgment and self criticism were wanting, since adequate judicial statistics were unknown. The types and volume of litigation, the charac-

[52]Caseload data on the Court of International Trade are found in *Judicial Business, 1995* (Abbrev.), Table G-2A. See also Abraham, *The Judicial Process*, 152–53.

[53]Social scientists seldom study specialized federal courts, but see Lawrence Baum's interesting work, "Judicial Specialization, Litigant Influence, and Substantive Policy: The Court of Customs and Patent Appeals," *Law and Society Review* 11, No. 5 (Summer 1977): 823–50.

[54]The reorganization of specialized federal courts is briefly described in "New Federal Appeals Court," *Congressional Quarterly Almanac, 1982* (Washington, D.C.: Congressional Quarterly Publishing, 1983), 396. The law itself is found at *Statutes at Large,* vol. 96, sec. 25, 37–38, or at *United States Code,* vol. 28, U.S.C. §1295. A useful study of this court is Rochelle Cooper Dreyfus, "The Federal Circuit: A Case Study in Specialized Courts," *New York University Law Review* 64, No. 1 (Apr. 1989): 1–77. Current caseload data for the Court of Appeals for the Federal Circuit may be found in *Judicial Business, 1995* (Abbrev.), Table B–8.

ter of issues, the duration of trials, the speed of disposition, the delay of appeals—these and kindred data must be known in order to determine competence or laxity in judicial administration. Such information is particularly indispensable for any fruitful scrutiny of the workings of a single system of courts extending over so vast an area as that of the United States. Without it, the demands of different districts for more judges have to be decided in the dark. Nor will statistics gotten up for the occasion serve the purpose. There must be recognized standards of interpretation and continuity of observation. Thus only can the system be subjected to scientific accountability.[55]

The forces unleashed or stimulated by the Civil War—industrialization, increased centralism, the ethic of business efficiency, combined with a more highly organized and vocal bar association—all helped to bring about change. But the leadership of Chief Justice Taft during the 1920s was the most immediate catalyst for administrative reform. He, more than any other single individual, was responsible for persuading Congress to have a new look at the organization of the federal judiciary. By the Act of September 14, 1922, two significant steps were taken for change. First, the legislature expanded the power of the chief justice to assign district judges where they were needed. Second, the Act created an administrative mechanism for centralized administration in the courts, namely the Judicial Conference. The first such conferences consisted only of the senior circuit judges annually convened by the chief justice to gather information about the needs of the courts and to provide leadership in the formulation of proposals to Congress for the better functioning of the courts. The conference was empowered to

> make a comprehensive survey of the condition of business in the courts of the United States and prepare plans for assignment and transfer of judges to or from circuits or districts where the state of the docket or condition of business indicates the need thereof, [and to] submit such suggestions to the various courts as may seem in the interest of uniformity and expedition of business.[56]

The device of the administrative conference was significantly strengthened by Congress in 1939. By giving the conference a secretariat, so to speak, in the administrative office of the courts, the means was finally provided for the amassing of reliable data on court operations, on which any effective administrative action must be based. The 1939 legislation made three other important improvements in federal judicial administration: it centralized the judicial budget in the new administrative office under control of the judicial conference, it created a judicial council in each circuit, and it required the convening of an annual conference in each circuit of district and circuit judges as well as requiring members of the bar to plan the work of the circuit and make suggestions for improvement in judicial processes.[57] The 1939 legislation, especially the section creating the administrative office of the courts, was a highly important step, for it provided the judicial conference with some of the administrative tools necessary for effective centralized administration of the courts. The *Annual Report* of the administrative office of the courts is deemed basic to research and administration of the federal judicial system.

Today, the Judicial Conference of the United States, renamed from the old Senior Circuit Conference, includes not only the chief justice and the chief judge in each circuit but also a district judge elected for a three-year term from each of the twelve geographic circuits, and the chief judge of the International Court of Trade. This group meets semiannually at the Supreme Court in Washington, and reports of its proceedings are now being reg-

---

[55]Frankfurter and Landis, *Business of the Supreme Court,* 220–21.

[56]*Statutes at Large,* vol. 42, sec. 837, as cited in *Hart and Wechsler,* 61.

[57]James Willard Hurst, *The Growth of American Law: The Law Makers* (Boston: Little Brown, 1950), 115.

ularly published by the administrative office of the courts in conjunction with the caseload and management statistics. The key task of the Judicial Conference and its committees is to study problems and make recommendations to Congress for the improvement of the federal courts. Frequent requests of the conference for increases in the number of district and appellate judgeships, as well as for budgetary increases, are examples of the work of the conference.

> In addition to the judicial conference and its administrative arm, the administrative office of the courts, Congress in late 1967 created what could be called the third branch of federal judicial administration in the establishment of the Federal Judicial Center. The center is essentially a research and training institute directly related to federal judicial matters. Advocated by Chief Justice Earl Warren, the judicial conference, and eventually supported by President Johnson and the American Bar Association, the center was created with four purposes in mind: (1) to conduct research on the federal judiciary, (2) to make recommendations to the judicial conference on improvements in the federal courts, (3) to organize training programs for judges and other court personnel, and (4) to bolster the research and planning arm of the judicial conference.[58]

The center, located in the historic Dolley Madison House on Lafayette Square in Washington, is controlled by a seven-member board headed by the chief justice. Also on the board are three U.S. district judges and two judges from the Courts of Appeals (all selected by the members of the judicial conference) as well as the director of the administrative office of the courts. The staff of about one hundred, headed by a director, sponsors some one hundred educational and training sessions each year, bringing in sitting judges and other judicial personnel for orientation to new approaches to court operations. The creation of the Federal Judicial Center, along with the establishment of the National Center for State Courts in 1972 in Williamsburg, Virginia, have proven to be significant steps forward in augmenting the research and training segments of federal and state judicial administration. A chart depicting the administrative organization of the federal courts is set forth in Figure 4–3.

It would be naive, of course, to assume that these administrative changes have been wrought without struggle. Equally naive would be the assumption that the creation of this triumvirate of federal administrative entities has, in and of itself, brought significant change in the locus of power within the federal judiciary. We still have a federal system of government, federal district courts remain what has been called "state contained," and strong centrifugal forces at work over a century ago are still with us. Speaking of the new machinery, Peter Fish, in his study of the politics of federal judicial administration, noted that

> Emergence of these institutions occurred simultaneously with the growth of professionalism among court officers and supporting personnel. Over a period of time and in response to felt needs, these developments have imposed a degree of administrative integration on the federal courts. In the same vein, the rules of civil and criminal procedure have produced nationalizing tendencies in lieu of former federal attachment to state procedures. Yet, . . . changes wrought have been changes in degree rather than kind. As former Senator Joseph D. Tydings, Jr., observed: "Our courts are administered today in essentially the same way that they were two centuries ago."
>
> [Future] reform prospects are dim, given the low visibility of courts and court reform legislation in the American scheme of government. The political clout enjoyed by local magistrates standing securely on their geographical basis renders the prospects even darker. Consequently, reforms in court and administrative organization have been

---

[58]*Hart and Wechsler,* 63.

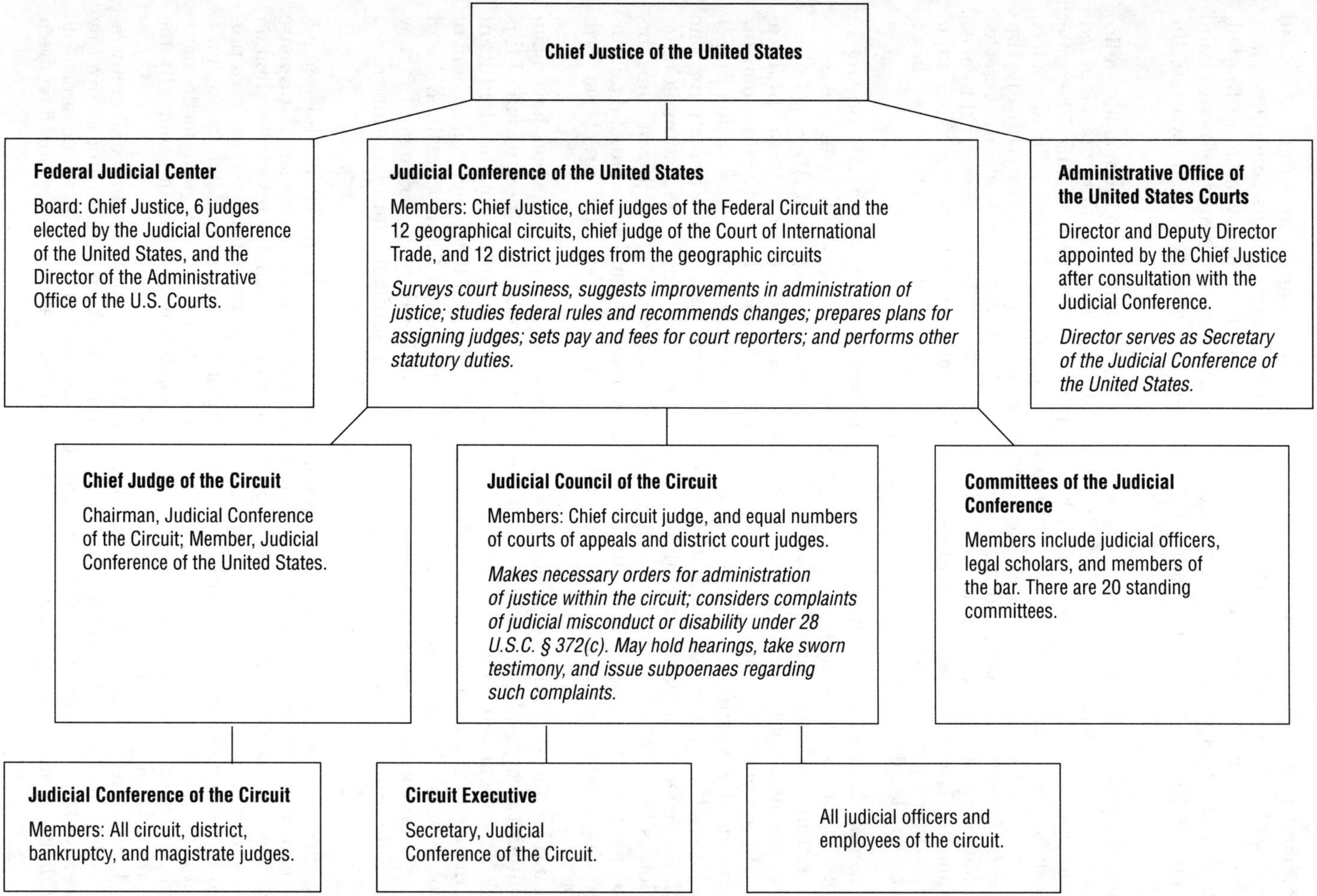

Chief Justice of the United States

Administrative Office of the United States Courts

Director and Deputy Director appointed by the Chief Justice after consultation with the Judicial Conference.

Director serves as Secretary of the Judicial Conference of the United States.

Federal Judicial Center

Board: Chief Justice, 6 judges elected by the Judicial Conference of the United States, and the Director of the Administrative Office of the U.S. Courts.

Judicial Conference of the United States

Members: Chief Justice, chief judges of the Federal Circuit and the 12 geographical circuits, chief judge of the Court of International Trade, and 12 district judges from the geographic circuits

Surveys court business, suggests improvements in administration of justice; studies federal rules and recommends changes; prepares plans for assigning judges; sets pay and fees for court reporters; and performs other statutory duties.

Committees of the Judicial Conference

Members include judicial officers, legal scholars, and members of the bar. There are 20 standing committees.

Chief Judge of the Circuit

Chairman, Judicial Conference of the Circuit; Member, Judicial Conference of the United States.

Judicial Council of the Circuit

Members: Chief circuit judge, and equal numbers of courts of appeals and district court judges.

Makes necessary orders for administration of justice within the circuit; considers complaints of judicial misconduct or disability under 28 U.S.C. § 372(c). May hold hearings, take sworn testimony, and issue subpoenaes regarding such complaints.

All judicial officers and employees of the circuit.

Judicial Conference of the Circuit

Members: All circuit, district, bankruptcy, and magistrate judges.

Circuit Executive

Secretary, Judicial Conference of the Circuit.

Figure 4-3 Federal Judicial Administration (SOURCE: United States, Administrative Office of the United States Courts, *Understanding the Federal Courts* (Washington: Administrative Office of the U.S. Courts, n.d.), Figure 5.)

and will likely continue to be in the realm of "minor adaptations rather than basic changes."[59]

JUDICIAL FEDERALISM

The First Congress took a groundbreaking step in creating a national system of trial and appellate courts. And although at the time, that system represented perhaps the only one appropriate for the young nation, it has remained the root of controversy.

Despite the clarity of the Constitution's supremacy clause, the scope of federal judicial review was disputed from the outset. Indeed, between 1789 and 1860, seven state courts declared the U.S. Supreme Court powerless to review their decisions. Several state legislatures as well as the U.S. Congress also attempted to divest the Court of jurisdiction to review state court decisions.[60]

Nevertheless, the Court itself has consistently asserted its role as supreme arbiter of cases falling within its jurisdiction. As Chief Justice Roger B. Taney, hardly a nationalist, wrote in *Ableman v. Booth,*

> The powers of the General Government, and of the State, although both exist and are exercised within the same territorial limits, are yet separate and distinct sovereignties, acting separately and independent of each other, within their respective spheres. And the sphere of action appropriated to the United States is as far beyond the reach of the judicial process issued by a State judge or a State court, as if the line of division was traced by landmarks and monuments visible to the eye.[61]

Striking a similar chord, the Court in 1958 boldly stated in *Cooper v. Aaron,*[62] an Arkansas school desegregation dispute,

> Article 6 of the Constitution makes the Constitution the "supreme Law of the Land." [*Marbury v. Madison*] . . . declared the basic principle that the federal judiciary is supreme in the exposition of the law of the Constitution, and that principle has ever since been respected by [the Supreme Court] and the Country. . . . It follows that the interpretation of the Fourteenth Amendment enunciated by (the Supreme Court) in the *Brown* case is the supreme law of the land, and Art. 6 of the Constitution makes it of binding effect on the States. . . .
>
> No state legislator or executive or judicial officer can war against the Constitution without violating his undertaking to support it.[63]

Opposition to federal judicial supremacy is definitely not a relic of the past. In early 1981, Louisiana state Judge Richard E. Lee made three public school students wards of his court and threatened a school principal with arrest if he refused to enroll them in an effort to undermine a federal court order mandating school busing as a means to correct racial segregation.[64] And even the Supreme Court itself has occasionally questioned unre-

---

[59]Peter G. Fish, *The Politics of Federal Judicial Administration* (Princeton: Princeton University Press, 1973), 431, 432–33. But see the numerous recommendations for change contained in the *Report of the Federal Courts Study Committee, Apr. 2, 1990* (Washington: GPO, 1990).

[60]Charles Warren, "Legislative Attacks on the Supreme Court of the United States: A History of the 25th Section of the Judiciary Act," *American Law Review,* 47 (1913), 1.

[61]12 Howard 506, 516 (1859).

[62]358 U.S. 1.

[63]358 U.S. 1, 18.

[64]"The New Contempt for Civil Rights," *New York Times* (Jan. 11, 1981): Sec. E, 22.

strained expansion of federal authority. As Justice Potter Stewart wrote in *City of Greenwood v. Peacock*,[65] another important decision on civil rights appealed from the state courts of Mississippi,

> [A federal civil rights statute] does not require and does not permit the judges of the federal courts to put their brethren of the state judiciary on trial. . . . The vindication of the defendant's federal rights is left to the state courts except in the rare situations where it can be clearly predicted by reason of the operation of a pervasive and explicit state or federal law that those rights will inevitably be denied by the very act of bringing the defendant to trial in the state court.[66]

More recently, the Rehnquist Court significantly limited the scope of federal jurisdiction over the posttrial claims of those convicted in state courts. In *Coleman v. Thomas*,[67] the Rehnquist-led majority concluded that an attorney's error in calculating a filing deadline stripped his client of all right to federal review of his conviction even though the issues on appeal turned on questions of federal law. Irrespective of the Court's rhetoric regarding its concern for "leaving undisturbed" the reasoned decisions of state tribunals, *Coleman* clearly signaled a considered attack on federal judicial supremacy.

Along the same lines, the 104th Congress adopted and President Bill Clinton signed into law the Anti-Terrorism and Effective Death Penalty Act of 1996. At the heart of this legislation is a substantial restriction on the availability of *habeas corpus*—perhaps the most extreme since President Lincoln suspended the writ during the Civil War.[68] The Act requires federal judges to defer to state judges as to whether a criminal conviction violates the U.S. Constitution, creates stringent new time limits, and adds restrictions to those already imposed on successive petitions.[69]

Although five justices agreed to hear a challenge to the Act almost as soon as it became effective, the Supreme Court hastily affirmed its constitutionality.[70] Critics of the Act have pointed out that those most directly injured by its mandates are not the terrorists it was allegedly crafted to punish, but indigent, primarily African American inmates, particularly those under sentence of death.

Assaults on national judicial supremacy can also originate in the executive branch. Thus, in the fall of 1986 former Attorney General Edwin Meese, III argued that "a Supreme Court decision does not establish a 'supreme law of the land' that is binding on all persons and parts of government." Only the parties to a case, Meese said, are bound by the Court's decision. Taking aim at *Cooper v. Aaron,* Meese contended the notion of federal judicial

---

[65]384 U.S. 808 (1966).

[66]384 U.S. 808. The *Peacock* decision is discussed at length in Peter W. Low and John Calvin Jeffries, Jr., *Federal Courts and the Law of Federal-State Relations,* 2nd ed. (Westbury, N.Y.: Foundation Press, 1989): 553-590.

[67]111 S. Ct. 2546 (1991).

[68]*See* "Terrorism Bill is Headed to President's Desk," *Congressional Quarterly Weekly Report,* 54, No. 16 (April 20, 1996), 1044–46; and Stephen Labaton, "Bars on Death Row," *New York Times* (April 15, 1996): C-15.

[69]*See* Garrow, "The Rehnquist Reins."

[70]See *Felker v. Turpin,* 64 LW 4677, June 28, 1996. The *Felker* decision turned entirely on the question of whether Congress had unconstitutionally restricted the Supreme Court's appellate jurisdiction in its habeas corpus legislation. See also David M. O'Brien, *Supreme Court Watch, 1996* (New York: W.W. Norton, 1996): 212, 215; and Linda Greenhouse, "How Congress Curtailed the Court's Jurisdiction," *New York Times,* Oct. 27, 1996: E-5. Greenhouse argues that congressional restrictions on attorneys of the Legal Services Corporation (detailed in Ch. 7) together with the habeas corpus legislation and the Illegal Immigration Reform and Immigrant Responsibility Act, add up to very significant limits on the ability of federal courts to protect "immigrants, prisoners and the poor—people who don't vote or can't vote."

supremacy was "at war with the Constitution, at war with the basic principles of democratic government, and at war with the very meaning of the rule of law."[71]

Understood as something more than political hyperbole, Meese's concept of federalism would restrict the principle of desegregated, integrated public education affirmed in *Brown v. Board of Education* to the particular school district involved in that historic case. Few scholars have adopted this unworkably restricted view of our federal system. However, the extremely large number of federal judges selected by the Reagan and Bush administrations after unprecedented ideological screening suggests that such notions may linger on the federal bench for some time.[72]

That the federal judiciary is and will remain a source of heated debate comes as no surprise. Unfortunately, that debate is often encrypted in legalese, rather than carried on as an open and honest political struggle. Nevertheless, issues of jurisdiction and judicial selection, of administration and of structure, are issues of power—who has it and who can exercise it. Even if those involved in the federal judicial system cannot say so themselves, politics is the common thread woven throughout the "third branch" of American government.

FURTHER READING

Abraham, Henry J. *The Judicial Process: An Introductory Analysis of the Courts of the United States, England, and France.* 6th ed. New York: Oxford University Press, 1993.

Bator, Paul M., et. al. *Hart and Wechsler's The Federal Courts and the Federal System.* Third Edition. Westbury, New York: The Foundation Press, 1988, with supplements.

Congressional Quarterly, *Guide to the United States Supreme Court.* 2nd ed. Washington: Congressional Quarterly, 1990.

Epstein, Lee, et. al. *The Supreme Court Compendium: Data, Decisions and Developments.* 2nd ed. Washington: Congressional Quarterly, 1996.

Fish, Peter G. *The Politics of Federal Judicial Administration.* Princeton: Princeton University Press, 1973.

Frankfurter, Felix, and James M. Landis. *The Business of the Supreme Court.* New York: Macmillan, 1928.

Hellman, Arthur D., ed. *Restructuring Justice: The Innovations of the Ninth Circuit and the Future of the Federal Courts.* Ithaca, N.Y.: Cornell University Press, 1990.

Marcus, Maeva, ed. *Origins of the Federal Judiciary: Essays on the Judiciary Act of 1789.* New York: Oxford University Press, 1992.

McLaughlin, William P. *Federal Court Caseloads.* New York: Praeger, 1984.

---

[71]Stuart Taylor, Jr., "Meese Says Court Doesn't Make Law," *New York Times* (October 23, 1986): Sec. A, 1, 20.

[72]Another interpretation of the Meese comments is possible, of course. For the view that Reagan's Attorney-General was merely stating the unremarkable idea that there is a difference between the Constitution and judicial enforcement of its provisions, see "The Irrepressible Mr. Meese, *Wall Street Journal* (Oct. 29, 1986). These issues are intelligently discussed by Laurence H. Tribe in his *American Constitutional Law,* 2nd ed. (Mineola, New York: Foundation Press, 1988), 32–36. See also Gerald Gunther, *Constitutional Law,* 12th ed. (Westbury, N.Y.: The Foundation Press, 1991), 21–28.

For an inside perspective of the Reagan administration's early attempts to alter fundamentally the direction of the federal judiciary, see William French Smith, *Law and Justice in the Reagan Administration: The Memoirs of an Attorney-General,* especially Ch. 4, "Judicial Activism and the Search for Sandra Day O'Connor" (Stanford, Calif.: Hoover Institution Press, 1991), 58–73. Another insightful essay on the Reagan judicial nominees is Walter F. Murphy, "Reagan's Judicial Strategy," in Larry Berman, ed., *Looking Back on the Reagan Presidency* (Baltimore: Johns Hopkins University Press, 1990), 207–37.

Richardson, Richard J., and Kenneth N. Vines. *The Politics of Federal Courts: Lower Courts in the United States.* Boston: Little, Brown, 1970.

Smith, Christopher E. *United State Magistrates in the Federal Courts: Subordinate Judges.* New York: Praeger, 1990.

United States, Administrative Office of the U.S. Courts, *Judicial Business of the United States Courts, 1994, 1995* (Washington: Administrative Office of the U.S. Courts, n.d.).

PART II
JUDICIAL PERSONNEL

5
The Politics of Judicial Selection
The State Experience

Oh, the Old Missouri Plan,
Oh, the Old Missouri Plan,
When Wall Street lawyers all judicial candidates will scan
If you're not from Fair Old Harvard,
They will toss you in the can. . . .

Oh, the Old Missouri Plan,
Oh, the Old Missouri Plan,
It won't be served with sauerkraut nor sauce Italian.
There'll be no corned beef and cabbage,
And spaghetti they will ban;
There'll be no such dish
As gefilte fish
On the Old Missouri Plan.
   —Judge James Garrett Wallace,"The Old Missouri Plan"

THE POLITICAL CULTURE OF JUDICIAL SELECTION

No decision is more important in determining the nature of the judicial establishment, nor more clearly illustrates "judicial politics," than the selection of judges. The issues around which both federal and state courts are organized—including centralization of judicial power, the nature and extent of jurisdiction, the process of appeals, and the geographic boundaries of judicial districts—have all become matters of intense interest and the foci of incessant political strife for the simple reason that structural arrangements are widely believed to play a significant role in determining substantive policy outcomes. By the same token, the relationship between *who* is to be judge and *what* judicial decisions are made is clear to the professional politician and casual political participant alike. Hence, both the manner in which judges are chosen and the actual decision as to who is to sit on the bench serve to evoke the highest level of political activity and the greatest expenditure of political resources that one is likely to encounter in the game of judicial politics. From the nomination and confirmation of United States Supreme Court justices to the selection of local justices of the peace, principal actors in the struggle for judicial power and influence keep an ever-watchful eye on court vacancies in the hope of improving the likelihood of judicial outcomes favorable to their interests.

Political parties are especially concerned with judgeships inasmuch as these prestigious positions constitute an important source of patronage needed to oil the machinery of party politics. Not only are judgeships important political plums, but in turn, state and federal judges themselves become important dispensers of patronage, thereby multiplying party influence. For party leaders of the executive or legislative branch, whether they are office-holders at the national, state, or local level, influence over judicial selection provides a potential handle on numerous substantive policy outcomes in almost all areas of government. Courts, as we have shown, are important agencies for governing, and judges friendly to the regime may help carry out party policy. Beyond policy outcomes, parties have more long-range interests in judicial posts. Respectable, if not distinguished, judges enhance the party's image in the eyes of the voter. The party's philosophy in the broad sense is advanced, and party loyalists are more likely to survive short-term electoral challenges. For these reasons, among others, party fortunes are inextricably linked with the politics of judicial selection.[1]

Major political interest groups have more sharply focused interests at stake in judicial appointments and removals. The business community wants judges with "free enterprise" orientations; trade unions, conversely, push for judges sympathetic to labor concerns. "Law and order" interests work for the "right" kind of judges; environmental groups do the same. Thus, most selection decisions become entangled in interest-group politics. Examples abound of otherwise politically qualified candidates for judicial office going down to defeat at the hands of particularly determined interest groups that are able to bring sufficient pressure to bear on appropriate legislative or executive decision makers. Conversely, pressure groups can successfully advance and champion judicial nominees.[2] Similar results in the negative or positive vein can be attributed to the influence of politi-

---

[1]The role of party politics in judicial selection is nicely illustrated in the study by Martin A. Levin, *Urban Politics and the Criminal Courts* (Chicago: University of Chicago Press, 1977), especially 54–59. Also see an earlier study, now almost a classic, by Wallace S. Sayer and Herbert Kaufman, *Governing New York City* (New York: Russell Sage Foundation, 1960). For a brief overview of party influence on judicial selection, see Paul Allen Beck and Frank J. Sorauf, *Party Politics in America,* 7th ed. (Boston: Little, Brown, 1992), 420–24. Finally, see the examples discussed in Harry P. Stumpf and John H. Culver, *The Politics of State Courts* (New York: Longman, 1992), especially 39–41.

[2]Such campaigns by various interest groups have become the databases for some insightful case studies on the politics of judicial selection. See, for example, an early illustrative description of the Brandeis and Parker nominations to the United States Supreme Court in Jack W. Peltason, *Federal Courts in the Political Process* (Garden City, N.Y.: Doubleday, 1955), 34–35. Another study is David J. Danelski's *A Supreme Court Justice Is Appointed* (New York: Random House, 1964). The Danelski work is a case study on the appointment of Pierce Butler to the United States Supreme Court. Another useful work is Richard Harris, *Decision* (New York: Dutton, 1971), on the nomination of G. Harrold Carswell to the Supreme Court. See also the work by John H. Culver and John T. Wold on the controversy surrounding the reconfirmation of California Chief Justice Rose Elizabeth Bird, "Rose Bird and the Politics of Accountability in California," *Judicature* 70, No. 2 (Aug.–Sept. 1986): 81–89; and "The Defeat of the California Justices: The Campaign, the Electorate, and the Issue of Judicial Accountability," *Judicature* 70, No. 6 (Apr.–May 1987): 348–55. A brief but fascinating account of the intense efforts of Texas business interests to influence the selection of that state's Supreme Court justices is Wayne E. Green, "Texas Businesses Play Judicial Politics," *Wall Street Journal* (Sept. 12, 1988): Sec. 2, 21; and Peter Applebome, "Rubber Stamp Is Gone in Texas Judicial Election" *New York Times* (Oct. 21, 1988): B-17.

cal parties. Historian James Willard Hurst reported some examples regarding the selection of justices to the United States Supreme Court:

> The enemies of Andrew Jackson in 1835 defeated Taney's nomination as Associate Justice; a Democratic Senate in 1852, for purely partisan reasons rejected three nominations sent to it by the Whig President Fillmore; in 1861 the Republicans as a party matter rejected Buchanan's nomination of Jeremiah Black; in 1866 the Senate would not even consider the nomination of Henry Stanbery, and Congress passed legislation which in effect barred further nominations by President Andrew Johnson. Such were but a few of many incidents and these merely from one thirty-year period.[3]

Bar associations are particularly prominent in the struggle for judicial posts. In fact, the impetus for the formal organization of bar associations was a deep concern among lawyers over the "political" domination of the judicial selection process. The American Bar Association, organized in 1878, has always claimed a special expertise in the matter of judicial selection, arguing that the legal profession is best equipped, by training and experience, to select judges. Indeed, the organized legal profession has been so successful in winning special influence over the selection process that the political history of judicial selection in the United States since 1878 could be written largely in terms of the struggle between legal professionals and political professionals, with the public, organized in terms of specific economic and social interests, being courted by both sides.

The struggle over the selection of judges is usually couched in euphemistic terms of structure and "principles of sound government and administration," or the substantive merit of the candidate, rather than party patronage, personalities, and substantive issues. Thus, although members of the legal profession speak of "merit" selection, professional standards, and qualifications as well as the importance of "the law," seasoned politicos are more likely to emphasize the public accountability of judges, judicial sensitivity to the needs of "the little guy," the necessities of "democracy," and so on. Each, of course, publicly claims that it is best qualified to select the best judges. Privately, however, both press for representation on the bench of viewpoints consistent with their own policy values. This subterfuge of doublespeak is nicely illustrated by Jack Peltason's description of President Wilson's campaign in 1916 to place Louis Brandeis on the Supreme Court:

> By 1916 Brandeis was a well-known campaigner for vigorous governmental regulation of utilities, for savings-bank insurance, against bigness, and for conservation. He had been active before the Supreme Court and had successfully persuaded the judges to sustain laws limiting hours of work. Quite clearly Brandeis's nomination presented a threat to those interests that had been most successful in securing judicial representation from the 1890's.
>
> Opposition to Brandeis was phrased not in terms of his views but of his supposed lack of judicial temperament. On the other hand, Brandeis's supporters also played down his values since they did not want to lose the support of the southern Democrats on the

If one wishes to study the role of interest groups in judicial selection, the massive literature describing and analyzing the struggle over the nomination and nonconfirmation of Robert Bork to the U.S. Supreme Court can be recommended, especially Ethan Bronner, *Battle for Justice: How the Bork Nomination Shook America* (New York: W.W. Norton, 1989). A different view of the Bork episode is Patrick B. McGuigan and Dawn M. Weyrich, *Ninth Justice: The Fight for Bork* (Washington: Free Congressional Foundation, 1990). Finally, for a view that interest group activity surrounding judicial appointments has if anything increased in recent years, see Gregory A. Caldeira and John R. Wright, "Lobbying for Justice: The Rise of Organized Conflict in the Politics of Federal Judgeships," in Lee Epstein, ed., *Contemplating Courts* (Washington: Congressional Quarterly Press, 1995), 44–71.

[3]James Willard Hurst, *The Growth of American Law: The Law Makers* (Boston: Little, Brown, 1950), 143–44.

Judiciary Committee. Each side sought testimonials from distinguished members of the bar. Each side accused the other of representing a selfish special interest.[4]

Just beneath the surface of the politics of judicial selection are the philosophical cleavages as to conceptions of judicial roles. Still enamored with notions of mechanical jurisprudence, leaders of the legal profession maintain that a high level of expertise is required for faithful interpretation of the Constitution and statutes. This being so, they argue, the task of judging demands well-qualified professionals best selected by other well-qualified professionals, namely attorneys. On the other hand, politicos are likely to see the judicial function largely in terms of policy-making (though they seldom say so openly) and to emphasize the significance of a judge's political acceptability. Given this conception of the judicial role, the best method of judicial selection is that which most enhances the political accountability of those on the bench. Appointment by a politically responsible executive (or even the legislature) or selection by popular election would thus be the favored method of recruitment. It is perhaps for this reason—the existence of the still unresolved cleavage in American jurisprudence—that the debate over the proper method of selecting judges has raged in the United States for over two hundred years and shows little sign of moving toward resolution.

This is not to say that as a people, we lack agreement on every aspect of the judicial recruitment and retention process. From the time of the writing of the Constitution, a consensus has grown regarding certain of its aspects. From English constitutional history, Americans have borrowed, and generally adhered to, two basic principles regarding judicial tenure: (1) that the salaries of judges are not to be reduced or withheld during their term of office, and (2) that a judge might be removed from office only for cause, to be established only through formal proceedings. When one adds to these two principles a third notion, also drawn from our English common law heritage, that judges are to be immune from suit as regards their official duties, the result is a trio of principles that have provided judges with a degree of insulation from the more direct influences of partisan politics. To be sure, adherence to these principles has not been perfect, but Hurst is undoubtedly correct in his view that, through trial and error, these tenets of judicial independence have "received little attention, . . . [but] probably [have] had more effect on the quality of our courts than the more prominent questions of selection and tenure" currently in dispute.[5] The two principles are closely related, however; since the rules of the game make it difficult to "get at" a sitting judge, the process whereby judges are initially selected becomes all the more important.

The foregoing considerations may be seen as the parameters within which the politics of judicial selection are played out. Summarizing, they include (1) agreement on some essentials of tenure and removal that translates into a measure of judicial independence; (2) an agreement to disagree on specific methods of selection, and of course, on specific

---

[4]Peltason, *Federal Courts,* 34. The case of Daniel Manion, nominated to the United States Courts of Appeals by President Reagan in 1986 (more fully discussed in Ch. 6), also underscores the politics of doublespeak in judicial selection. Senators both favoring and opposing the nomination were at pains to defend their stand on the basis of "merit" rather than the real politics of the nominee. See, e.g., Philip Shenon, "Senate, Ending Judicial Fight, Gives Manion Final Approval," *New York Times* (July 24, 1986): 1. Finally, perhaps the most notorious modern example of the use of the artifice of "merit" in camouflaging the politics of a judicial nomination is that of President George Bush, who denied that race had anything to do with his nomination of Clarence Thomas to the Supreme Court. Rather, he insisted that ". . . I kept my word to the American people and to the Senate by picking the best man for the job on the merits." See "Excerpts from News Conference Announcing Court Nominee," *New York Times* (July 2, 1991): A-10.

[5]Hurst, *Growth of American Law,* 128.

candidates, reflecting both a normatively and an empirically based disagreement on the nature of judicial roles; and (3) an agreement to keep the waters muddied with double-speaking (providing lip service to the myth of judicial objectivity), reflecting America's fundamental jurisprudential confusion which, it will be recalled, is rooted in the Blackstonian admixture of Natural and Positivist notions of law. Against this background, we shall discuss the politics of judicial selection, tenure, and removal, first from the state perspective. Then, in Chapter 6, we shall take up judicial recruitment at the federal level.

This division seems appropriate, since the mechanisms of judicial selection are fundamentally different for the two levels of courts. This is not to say, however, that the sources and nature of political influence at work in the process (nor the outcomes) necessarily differ in basic ways, for a fourth general feature of the politics of judicial selection in the United States has been the deceptiveness of form. More often than not, formal differences in selection and removal procedures belie an underlying sameness in the lineaments of political influence and often in the outcomes as well.

JUDICIAL SELECTION SYSTEMS IN THE STATES

In the century preceding the American Revolution, the extent and nature of judicial independence in England was a hotly contested issue. The blatant use of judicial office for short-term political gain by the Stuart kings played no small part in the Glorious Revolution in 1688.[6] Pitifully incompetent men were elevated to high judicial office, while able but determined judges were removed by the king at will. Such practices resulted in a grossly inequitable application of the law itself, dependent almost entirely upon the monarch's whim. Again and again Parliament protested. In December, 1680, it petitioned the king:

> That from henceforth, such Persons only may be judges . . . as are men of Ability . . . And they hold both their Offices and Salaries *quan diu se bene gesserint*.[7]

But the king dissolved Parliament, and it took the short and judicially corrupt reign of James II to add the final catalyst to spark the revolution. The Act of Settlement of 1701 hardly settled everything, but it did provide that

> Judges' commissions be made *quan diu se bene gesserint,* and their salaries ascertained and established; but upon the address of both houses of parliament it may be lawful to remove them.[8]

Even so, judges continued to be removed for making decisions repugnant to the Crown, and it was not until 1761 that Parliament decreed that

> Commissions of the Judges . . . shall . . . remain in full force and effect during good behavior notwithstanding the demise of his Majesty . . . or of any of his heirs and successors.[9]

---

[6]See generally Edward Foss, *The Judges of England* (London: John Murray, 1864), Vol. 7 (1660–1714) and Vol. 8 (1714–1820).

[7]Evan Haynes, *The Selection and Tenure of Judges* (New York: National Conference of Judicial Councils, 1944), 72.

[8]Haynes, *Selection and Tenure of Judges,* 78.

[9]Haynes, *Selection and Tenure of Judges,* 78–79.

The experience of English judges at the hands of the monarchy was not lost on the American colonists, who insisted that control over judicial appointments and removals be lodged in other than executive hands. Hence, in the early years of the republic, state judicial appointments were usually placed under legislative control. Specific methods of selection varied, but in the case of nearly all the original thirteen states, executive appointment of judges was modified either by placing the power entirely in legislative hands or by insisting on a legislative veto. The few states that retained gubernatorial selection required the concurrence of executive councils.

Nevertheless, once state judicial bodies began to compete in policy areas deemed judicial, state legislatures began behaving in a manner reminiscent of the House of Stuarts. Statutes limiting the tenure of judges from life to specified terms, or during good behavior, were commonly enacted. Legislatures also attempted to remove judges for other than cause. Judicial decisions unpopular with legislative leaders often constituted grounds for attempted removal. Though the practice resulted in the dismissal of relatively few judges (Judge Alexander Addison in 1802 in Pennsylvania, several Ohio judges in 1808 and 1809, for example), such tactics soon lost favor partly because of the growing belief that tenure during good behavior was a sound principle of judicial politics.[10] This is not to say that either state judicial policy-making or attempts to rein in growing judicial power in the states ceased to be controversial. What changed were tactics. The new approach was dictated in large part by a nationwide intensification of the drive for popular government, often lumped under the term "Jacksonian Democracy."

The second quarter of the nineteenth century witnessed a greater concern for popular sovereignty than at any time in our history. Indeed, forces for reform in public policy-making—from absolutism to radical democracy—swept most of the world. Tangible signs included the English Reform Bill of 1832 and the Radical Revolt in England of 1848, the adoption of popular constitutions in Spain and Italy, the end of Bourbon rule in France, the Belgian Revolution of 1880, and the chronic unrest in the smaller German states.[11]

In the United States, dominance of the long-standing aristocracy was threatened by the growing economic, demographic, and political power sparked by continued westward expansion. Writes Haynes:

> It was inevitable that there should be an assault everywhere on the political monopoly of the old upper class. The assault can be said to have begun with the election of Jefferson in 1801. In the years after 1815 substantial progress was made in New York and Pennsylvania; and in 1829 the new democratic spirit swept into national power with Andrew Jackson.[12]

Changes in the mechanics of popular government were but a part of this much broader reform movement. Along with the extension of the franchise, a reduction in public floggings, and the elimination in some states of capital punishment, many appointive posts, including judgeships, were transformed into elective offices, often with brief terms. Thus, in a movement unique among judicial systems of the world, American state legislatures and delegates to state constitutional conventions jumped on the bandwagon favoring an elective judiciary.[13]

Some states adopted elective selection mechanisms for at least a portion of their judges early in their history (Vermont in 1777, Georgia in 1812, Indiana in 1816, and Mis-

---

[10]Kenneth N. Vines and Herbert Jacob, *Studies in Judicial Politics,* Tulane Studies in Political Science, Vol. 8 (New Orleans: Tulane University, 1963), 16–17.

[11]Haynes, *Selection and Tenure of Judges,* 83–85.

[12]Haynes, *Selection and Tenure of Judges,* 88.

[13]Other reasons proffered by Haynes for the movement toward popular election of the judiciary include (1) the continuing general American hostility toward law and lawyers; (2) the adoption of a largely unwritten common law system, giving rise to the widespread belief that American judges, more than most, were of

sissippi for all of its judges in 1832), but such moves were exceptions to the general pattern of legislative dominance of judicial selection. But in 1846, after prolonged political conflict, New York adopted an elective judiciary and, as Haynes explains,

> Within ten years, fifteen of the twenty-nine states existing in 1846 had by constitutional amendment provided for the popular election of judges; and of the states which have entered the Union since 1846, every one has provided that most or all judges shall be popularly elected for terms of years.
>
> In the year 1850 alone, seven states changed to popular election of judges; and thereafter, year by year until the Civil War, others followed.[14]

Following the Civil War, several states returned to appointive judgeships, but, in general, the popularity of electing judges remains high in state politics. Today, despite the intrusions of "merit selection," as well as the persistence in a few states of executive or legislative selection, election of judges is the single most common method of state judicial selection.

Specifically, using data drawn from the National Center for State Courts and the Bureau of Justice Statistics for 1993, state judges of appellate and general trial courts in the fifty states, 7,602 (7,025 general trial and 577 appellate), or 70.5 percent of the total, are ostensibly elected on either partisan or nonpartisan ballots for their full terms.[15] Indeed, if one asks the question a little differently, namely, how many judges of these same courts face election at least once in their careers, the proportion jumps to approximately 75 percent. This higher figure is explained by a number of states requiring their judges to face real, i.e., contested, or at least contestable, elections in order to retain their seats. New Mexico, for example, moved in 1988 to what is usually called "merit" selection, but the state's constitution requires that all state judges must fight to retain their seats in the first round of retention via partisan elections. Maryland, Nebraska, and Wyoming are other states that employ this device, albeit in a nonpartisan format, for some or all of their judges.

Popular election, executive appointment, legislative election, and various combinations thereof—what we are clearly painting is a rather unclear patchwork of selection systems in the states. Certainly no other governmental official is selected by so many different methods. Since each reform era seems to have produced its own judicial selection mechanism, it would follow that the partisan election of judges would eventually give way to new, more modern approaches. To some extent, this has been the case.

As the selection of state judges through partisan elections melded into actual selection by party leaders, the opposition of the legal profession grew. This led to the formal organization of bar activities (the first being the formation of the Bar of the City of New York in 1870), followed by a push for nonpartisan elections—a trend also supported by the Progressives around the turn of the century. The many nonpartisan judicial selection plans presently existing in the states (Tables 5–1 and 5–2) are remnants of this movement. If any

---

necessity imbued with legislative function; and (3) a growing class consciousness of American industrial workers. Haynes, *Selection and Tenure of Judges,* 95–98.

For a somewhat different view by a contemporary historian, see Kermit L. Hall, "Progressive Reform and the Decline of Democratic Accountability: The Popular Election of State Supreme Court Judges, 1850–1920," *American Bar Foundation Research Journal,* 2 (Spring 1984): 345–69.

[14]See Henry J. Abraham, *The Judicial Process: An Introductory Analysis of the Courts of the United States, England and France,* 6th ed. (New York: Oxford University Press, 1993), 34.

[15]See United States, Dept. of Justice, Bureau of Justice Statistics, *State Court Organization, 1993* (Washington: National Center for State Courts and Conference of State Court Administrators, 1995): Tables 2, 3, 4, and 5. A comparison of these data with those published in Council of State Governments, *The Book of The States, 1994–95* (Lexington, Ky.: Council of State Governments, 1995), Tables 4.1, 4.2, 4.3, and 4.4, illustrates different methods of counting state judges and tabulating methods of judicial selection.

Table 5–1   State Appellate Court Selection Plans, 1993

Partisan Election	Nonpartisan Election	Merit Selection	Gubernatorial Appointment	Appointment by Legislature
Alabama	Georgia	Alaska	California[e]	South Carolina
Arkansas	Idaho	Arizona	Maine[c]	Virginia
Illinois	Kentucky	Colorado	New Hampshire	
North Carolina	Louisiana	Connecticut	New Jersey[c]	
Pennsylvania	Michigan	Delaware[c]		
Tennessee[a]	Minnesota	Florida		
Texas	Mississippi	Hawaii[c]		
West Virginia	Montana	Indiana		
	Nebraska	Iowa		
	Nevada	Kansas		
	North Dakota	Maryland[c]		
	Ohio	Massachusetts		
	Oklahoma[b]	Missouri		
	Oregon	Nebraska		
	Washington	New Mexico[d]		
	Wisconsin	New York[c]		
		Oklahoma[b]		
		Rhode Island		
		South Dakota		
		Tennessee[a]		
		Utah[c]		
		Vermont[c]		
		Wyoming		

[a]Split system, with Supreme Court using partisan elections, IAC using merit plan.

[b]Split system: Supreme Court using merit selection, IAC using nonpartisan elections.

[c]Consent of senate required.

[d]First retention election is a partisan race.

[e]Gubernatorial nominees approved by a judicial appointments commission—a reverse "Merit" plan.

Source: American Judicature Society, *Judicial Selection in the States: Appellate and General Jurisdiction Courts, 1986* (revised 9/1/94) (Chicago: American Judicature Society, 1995). See also 8/9/95 *Summary of Initial Selection Methods.*

valid generalization can be made concerning nonpartisan elections, it is that they are *not* nonpartisan. From the starting gate (nomination), through the campaign itself, such races are shot through with partisan influences.

From the point of view of the legal profession, then, "nonpartisan" elections were no better than partisan elections, for the voice of party politics continued to dominate the selection decision. Bar leaders despaired of any improvement as long as traditional electoral mechanisms remained in use. This view was substantiated by Roscoe Pound. In his famous 1906 address before the American Bar Association, he asserted that "putting courts into

Table 5–2   State Court of General Jurisdiction Selection Plans

Partisan Election	Nonpartisan Election	Merit Selection	Gubernatorial Appointment	Appointment by Legislature
Alabama	Arizona[b]	Alaska	Maine[e]	Connecticut[d]
Arkansas	California[c]	Arizona[b]	New Hampshire[h]	South Carolina
Illinois	Florida	Colorado	New Jersey[e]	Virginia
Indiana	Georgia	Connecticut[d]		
Kansas[a]	Idaho	Delaware[e]		
New York	Kentucky	Hawaii[e]		
North Carolina	Louisiana	Iowa		
Pennsylvania	Michigan	Kansas[a]		
Tennessee	Minnesota	Maryland[e]		
Texas	Mississippi	Massachusetts		
West Virginia	Montana	Missouri[f]		
	Nevada	Nebraska		
	North Dakota	New Mexico[g]		
	Ohio	Rhode Island		
	Oklahoma	Utah[e]		
	Oregon	Vermont[c]		
	South Dakota	Wyoming		
	Washington			
	Wisconsin			

[a]Merit selection in most judicial districts; partisan election in seven districts; county electoral option every eight years.

[b]Merit selection in the two most populous counties; nonpartisan election in the others.

[c]Unless county electors opt for merit selection.

[d]Legislative appointment from gubernatorial recommendations from lists furnished by judicial nominating commission.

[e]Senate confirmation required.

[f]Merit selection in five counties; partisan election in the others.

[g]Partisan election at next general election following selection.

[h]Nominees approved by popularly elected councils.

Source: American Judicature Society, *Judicial Selection in the States: Appellate and General Jurisdiction Courts, 1986* (revised 9/1/94) (Chicago: American Judicature Society, 1995). See also 8/9/95 *Summary of Initial Selection Methods.*

politics, and compelling judges to become politicians, in many jurisdictions has almost destroyed the traditional respect for the bench."[16] And in 1913, former president William Howard Taft echoed this sentiment, arguing that even persons with little political, let alone professional, standing could be elected to the bench under the nonpartisan selection sys-

---

[16]Pound's famous address of 1906, entitled "The Causes of Popular Dissatisfaction with the Administration of Justice," was reprinted in the *Journal of the American Judicature Society* 46, No. 3 (Aug. 1962): 55–66. The statement quoted may be found on p. 66.

tem.[17] The bar, it was believed, needed a new mechanism if the growing force of the legal profession was to be meaningful in the selection of judges.

The year 1913 brought the establishment of the American Judicature Society. Although its declared purpose was the general "improvement of justice," it was more specifically concerned with the search for a system of judicial recruitment superior to popular selection. In 1914, Albert Kales, one of the founders and the director of research of the society, set forth a combination elective-appointive scheme of judicial selection that provided for an elected chief judge to fill vacancies on the bench with his own appointments. The plan called for the judge to make at least every other appointment from a list of well-qualified nominees drawn up by a judicial commission, itself composed of judges. Periodically, the names of the judicial appointees were to be submitted to the electorate for retention or rejection on the basis of their records.[18] In 1926, the British social scientist Harold Laski suggested a similar mechanism for judicial selection. Instead of a presiding judge, Laski proposed that the chief nominating official be the governor of the state. In addition, Laski's plan placed the attorney general and the president of the bar association on the nominating commission.[19]

This compromise plan was discussed, modified, and reproposed by various bar leaders in several states in the 1920s and 1930s. Alternately termed the ABA Plan (endorsed by that body in 1937), the Missouri Plan (adopted in that state in 1940 for some of its courts), the Merit Plan, and the Nonpartisan Court Plan (suggesting its "nonpolitical" essence), the device in all its forms and variations has three chief features: (1) establishment of a commission (usually consisting of members of the bar, the bench, and lay persons) that nominates candidates for judicial vacancies, (2) selection of one of the nominees by an elected official (usually the governor) to serve for a short term, after which the judge faces the electorate in (3) an unopposed referendum consisting of the simple question, "Shall Judge X be retained in office?"[20]

The first state to adopt a variation of the plan was California in 1934. California, often classified as a "Missouri Plan state," has a system of selection for its appellate bench that essentially reverses the Missouri Plan, however. Instead of a nominating com-

[17]Sari S. Escovitz, Fred Kurland, Nan Gold, *Judicial Selection and Tenure* (Chicago: American Judicature Society, 1975), 8.

[18]The Kales plan was initially set forth in his article "Methods of Selecting and Retiring Judges in a Metropolitan District," *Annals of the American Academy of Political and Social Science* 52 (Mar. 1914): 1–12.

[19]See Harold J. Laski, "The Technique of Judicial Appointment," *Michigan Law Review* 24, No. 6 (Apr. 1926): 529–43.

[20]The literature on the Missouri Plan is overwhelming and often polemic. For a history of the plan by one of its leading proponents, see Glen R. Winters, "The Merit Plan for Judicial Selection and Tenure: Its Historical Development" in Glen R. Winters, ed., *Selected Readings on Judicial Selection and Tenure* (Chicago: American Judicature Society, 1973), 29–41. For a standard political analysis and good bibliography, see Richard A. Watson and Rondal G. Downing, *The Politics of the Bench and the Bar* (New York: Wiley, 1969). See also Henry R. Glick, "The Promise and the Performance of the Missouri Plan: Judicial Selection in the Fifty States," *University of Miami Law Review* 32, No. 3 (June 1978): 509–41; and Henry R. Glick and Craig F. Emmert, "Selection Systems and Judicial Characteristics," *Judicature* 70, No. 4 (Dec.–Jan., 1987): 228–35. A reasonably complete overview of the history and issues surrounding "merit selection," though somewhat focused on one state, is John M. Roll, "Merit Selection: The Arizona Experience," *Arizona State Law Journal* 22, No. 4 (Winter 1990): 837–94.

The polemical literature is exemplified by Norman Krivosha, "In Celebration of the 50th Anniversary of Merit Selection," *Judicature* 74, No. 3 (Oct.–Nov., 1990): 128–32 (pro); and William Cousins, Jr., "A Judge's View of Judicial Selection Plans," *Illinois Bar Journal* 76, No. 2 (Oct. 1987): 790–99 (con). A direct response to the latter is Kathleen M. Sampson, "A Reply to Judge Cousins," *Illinois Bar Journal* 76, No. 5 (Jan. 1988): 260–61. Krivosha is former Chief Justice of the Nebraska Supreme Court, and Cousins is a trial judge in Cook County, Illinois. Sampson is Director of Information of the American Judicature Society.

mission submitting names to the governor, the governor recommends candidates to a three-member commission on judicial appointments (the state's chief justice, the attorney general, and a judge of the court of appeals), after which the commission essentially ratifies the governor's choice. The nominee sits on the bench until the next gubernatorial election, at which time his or her name is submitted to the voters in a referendum. The plan, in effect, constitutes executive appointment, since the committee seldom rejects a governor's choice.[21]

The generic "Merit Plan" is probably that established in Missouri. In that state, three separate nominating commissions were created: one for the state's appellate courts and one each for the trial courts (called circuit courts) of Jackson County (Kansas City) and St. Louis. Each of the circuit court commissions consists of five members—two lawyers elected by attorneys practicing in the relevant court's jurisdiction, two lay members appointed by the governor who reside in the court's jurisdiction, and the presiding judge of the court of appeals of the area (who is ex officio chairman of the commission).[22] Missouri's appellate nominating commission has seven members and nominates judges to fill vacancies on the Missouri Supreme Court and on the state's three courts of appeal, one each in Kansas City, St. Louis, and Springfield. On the commission are three lawyers elected by attorneys residing in each of the state's appeals jurisdictions, three laypersons residing in those jurisdictions, and the state's chief justice acting as ex officio commission chairperson. Upon the occasion of a judicial vacancy, the relevant commission nominates three candidates from which the governor selects one. After serving for one year, the judicial selectee's name appears on the ballot of the next general election with the question, "Shall Judge X be retained in office?" If approved by the electorate, the judge serves a regular term (six years on the trial bench, twelve years for the appellate post). Failing voter approval, the judge steps aside and the process begins anew.[23]

So-called merit selection did not immediately sweep the country. By 1954, forty years after the initial Kales plan was set forth, Missouri stood alone in having adopted it. The voters in several states (and several times in some states) both prior to and since that time have rejected proposals to adopt the mechanism. In 1956, Alaska enacted the essential features of the plan for all of its courts, and in 1958 Kansas applied the plan to select its supreme court justices. In the 1960s and 1970s, the plan spread to several other states, at least for some levels of courts, so that by 1978 Henry Glick could write that

> The non-partisan, reformist Missouri Plan is currently the most popular [state judicial selection plan], winning acceptance in more and more states. . . . In the past thirty years, every state which has changed its method of judicial selection has adopted some version of the Missouri Plan. No state has moved to any other judicial selection procedure. . . . The chances for the continued adoption of the Missouri Plan are excellent and we can expect to see it used in more states.[24]

The various selection mechanisms used in the states as of 1993 are presented in Tables 5–1 and 5–2. Many states have followed the practice of adopting a dual or even triple selection system. New York typifies this practice, with its appellate judges being appointive but its trial judges selected in partisan elections. States with mixed systems usually divide

---

[21]For an analysis of the California plan, see John H. Culver, "Governors and Judicial Appointments in California," *State Government* 54, No. 4 (1981): 130–34.

[22]See Watson and Downing, *Politics of the Bench and the Bar*, 13–14.

[23]Watson and Downing, *Politics of the Bench and the Bar*, 13–14.

[24]Glick, "Promise and the Performance," 509–10. For an update on adoption of the plan, see Jona Goldschmidt, "Merit Selection: Current Status, Procedures and Issues," *University of Miami Law Review*, 49, No. 1 (Fall 1994): 1–25.

selection mechanisms along lines of court level, one method of selection being used for appellate courts, another for trial courts. Another division is drawn along urban-rural lines (for example, Arizona). With such a hodgepodge of selection mechanisms it is difficult to classify state judicial selection systems as a whole. Tables 5–1 and 5–2 set forth an approximate classification for state appellate courts and general trial courts, respectively.

The tendency of states to lean toward one selection system rather than another is probably not random, although it is difficult to point to precise variables to help explain the phenomenon. Certainly legislative and in some cases gubernatorial selection mechanisms are holdovers from colonial history. States such as New Hampshire, Rhode Island, and Virginia are examples of this phenomenon.

Expanding this point a bit, researchers have been impressed with regionalism as an important correlate to types of judicial selection mechanisms. Thus, a study by the American Judicature Society in the late 1970s argued that the partisan election of judges tended to be limited to the South (except Florida) plus several of the larger Northeastern states. With some exceptions, these states are part of what could be called "old" America.[25] In contrast, the use of nonpartisan ballots to select judges was more likely to be found in "new" America, such as the border states, the upper Midwest, and the West Coast. Conversely, the various forms of "merit" selection tend to be concentrated in the Rocky Mountain West in states such as Colorado, Utah, Wyoming, and Alaska. There are many exceptions to the "regionalism" hypothesis, to be sure; nevertheless, the borrowing of ideas about judicial selection (as well as judicial structure) from neighboring states, combined with the popularity of a given selection mechanism when states came into the union, gives us a hint as to why states fashion their selection mechanisms as they do.[26]

Moving away from geographic/historical factors, other research has suggested a multiple explanation for the adoption of merit selection plans in the states. Judith Haydel tested a multivariate explanatory model that included as hypothesized explanatory factors (1) changes in the partisan balance of power in the state, (2) a state's moralistic political culture, (3) innovative tendencies within the state, (4) concern for increasing professionalism and efficiency in state government, and (5) the level of activity and support by the state bar association. This model correctly predicted just under 90 percent of cases in which states did or did not adopt merit judicial selection. The findings, however, were

[25]These findings are taken from John Paul Ryan, Allan Ashman, and Bruce D. Sales, "Judicial Selection and its Impact on Trial Judges' Background, Perceptions and Performance," paper presented at the Western Political Science Association meeting, Los Angeles, Mar. 16–18, 1978: 5. The regionalism hypothesis has been cited by a large number of scholars. For one example, see Henry R. Glick and Craig F. Emmert, "Selection Systems and Judicial Characteristics," *Judicature* 70, No. 4 (Dec.–Jan. 1987): 230. See also Lawrence Baum, *American Courts: Process and Policy,* 3rd ed. (Boston: Houghton Mifflin, 1994), 116.

[26]The geographic or regional explanation quickly melds into the concept of "political culture," which has also been cited as correlating with the choice of selection mechanisms. Early research testing the political culture hypothesis turned up negative results, but more recent evidence linking these two variables is set forth by Philip L. Dubois, "Voter Responses to Court Reform: Merit Judicial Selection on the Ballot," *Judicature* 73, No. 5 (Feb.–Mar. 1990): 245–46.
Another offshoot of the geographic explanation is the urban-rural hypothesis. For some time it was held that rural interests, seeking to counter the growth of urban power in the wake of legislative reapportionment, would more likely support merit selection. See, e.g., Marsha Puro, Peter J. Bergerson, and Steven Puro, "An Analysis of Judicial Diffusion: Adoption of the Missouri Plan in the American States," *Publius* 15, No. 4 (Fall 1985): 85–97. However, in "The Politics of Innovation in State Courts: The Merit Plan of Judicial Selection," *Publius* 20, No. 1 (Winter 1990): 23–42, Dubois finds otherwise—that the plan is more apt to be supported in urban areas. In contrast, Mr. R. G. Henley, Staff Attorney for the Office of Judicial Administration, State of Kansas, has observed that rural counties in that state seem more likely than urban areas to opt for merit selection. Henley cites the emergence of political/professional leadership as perhaps a better explanation for the choice of judicial selection mechanisms in that state. Phone interview, Dec. 28, 1992.

heavily weighted in favor of the political explanations previously given, especially state bar association involvement. Concludes Haydel,

> While bar association influence is [most] important to adoption of merit selection, so are the political and socioeconomic characteristics of state populations. Legal groups appear to have more chance for success in influencing adoption of merit selection in states in which the governor is organizationally weak and in which the legislature is more professionalized. It appears, then, that adoption of merit selection is more complex than was previously supposed.[27]

Of perhaps greater interest are the actual consequences of the various selection mechanisms used in these states. The two basic questions inevitably raised are (1) what are the actual influences at work in the different plans, and (2) what are the real differences, if any, in outcome—that is, in the types of judges selected? Contemporary research has been oriented to these questions because it has tended to follow the polemics of judicial selection in an attempt to bring empirical evidence to bear on the alleged advantages and disadvantages of each selection plan.[28] We might do well to follow a similar pattern in our discussion, looking first at the alleged advantages of merit selection.

AN ANALYSIS OF STATE SELECTION SYSTEMS

The Missouri Plan

"Merit" selection, by whatever name, has been marketed since 1913 as a preferred method of recruiting judges. Those favoring the plan (the American Judicature Society in company with a host of reformist organizations and sizable elements of the bench and bar) argue that the chief advantage of the plan is that it takes the business of selecting judges *out of politics,* rendering the process free—or at least freer—of the evils of partisan political influence. Instead, professional considerations are to hold sway in the recruiting of judges. Given the disdain with which Americans seem to view "politics," promises of a nonpolitical selection process are inherently appealing. But what does the evidence show?

In 1969, Watson and Downing of the University of Missouri undertook a comprehensive study of the origin, operation, and consequences of the Missouri Plan in that state, gathering data from the entire twenty-five years that the plan had been in operation. Regarding the claim that the plan takes judicial selection out of politics, they wrote,

> It is naive to suggest . . . that the Plan takes the "politics" out of judicial selection. Instead, the Plan is designed to bring to bear on the process of selecting judges a variety of interests that are thought to have a legitimate concern in the matter and at the same time to discourage other interests. It may be assumed that these interests will engage in the "politics" of judicial selection, that is, they will maneuver to influence who will be chosen as judges (1) because such judgeships constitute prestigious positions for aspiring lawyers, and (2)

---

[27]Judith Ann Haydel, "Explaining Adoption of Judicial Merit Selection in the States, 1950–1980: A Multivariate Test," Ph.D. Dissertation, Dept. of Political Science, University of New Orleans, August 1987: 100. See also same author and title, paper at the Annual Meeting of the Southwestern Political Science Association, Dallas, Tex., Mar. 18–21, 1987.

[28]Sheldon and Lovrich read the research record somewhat differently, arguing that the two chief foci have been (a) the backgrounds of judges selected by the various plans, and (b) the behavior, i.e., decisional tendencies of the judges selected under the different plans. See Charles H. Sheldon and Nicholas P. Lovrich, Jr., "State Judicial Recruitment," in John B. Gates and Charles A. Johnson, eds., *The American Courts: A Critical Assessment* (Washington: Congressional Quarterly Press, 1991), 170.

because, in the course of making decisions, judges inevitably affect the fortunes of persons and groups involved in the litigation process.[29]

These researchers found that in the process of selecting lawyer members of the nominating commissions, attorneys tended to split into two groups, much in the manner of a traditional two-party system. Far from bringing "professional" values to bear on the selection process, the attorneys tended to focus on more tangible selection criteria, in particular the socioeconomic interests of their clients. Thus, "plaintiff" attorneys (usually Democrats, in solo or small-firm trial practice who tend to be graduates of the less prestigious law schools and have relatively low incomes) pressed for "have-not" economic interests in the selection of judges. "Defendant" attorneys (more often Republicans with corporate practices, having graduated from the more prestigious law schools and who enjoy a substantially higher income), however, worked for the selection of judges sympathetic to "have" economic interests—banks, corporations, insurance companies, and so on.[30] Hence, each group struggled to secure a position on the nominating commissions for its representatives, who, in turn, could be relied upon to vote for the "right" judicial nominee when a vacancy occurred. As it turned out, these competing plaintiff and defendant bar interests were about equally successful in obtaining commission seats, the result being a rather well-balanced two-party competition in the Kansas City and St. Louis bars.

Thus, far from taking judicial selection out of politics, the Missouri Plan actually tended to replace Politics, wherein the judge faces popular election (or selection by a popularly elected official), with a somewhat subterranean politics of bar and bench involving little popular control. There is, then, a sense in which merit selection does operate to enhance the weight of professional influence in the selection process (one of its stated goals), in that lawyers and judges are given a direct, indeed official, role in the nominating process. On close examination, however, one finds raw political considerations masquerading as professionalism via attorney representation of the socioeconomic interests of their clients. This result is even more in evidence when one observes the behavior of lay and judicial members of the nominating commissions.

Although lay commission members ostensibly represent "the people," in practice they are strongly oriented to the wishes of the governor. Typically, they are prominent individuals who have been (and are) political supporters of the governor and are in tune with his or her values. In short, they serve as "the governor's man (or woman)" on the commissions and are often open to direct pressure, if not actual instructions, from the executive branch regarding specific nominees.[31]

This avowedly partisan input into merit selection is even clearer in the case of the judges who preside over the nominating commissions. Those judges are, in most cases, former politicians who obtained their positions through the same highly politicized process over which they now preside. They, more than most, understand the rules of the game and, due to their position, tend to dominate the deliberations of the selection commissions. Even more than the lay commissioners, they are quite likely to push for the selection of judicial nominees favored by the governor and the governor's party.[32]

---

[29]Watson and Downing, *Politics of the Bench and the Bar,* 331–32.

[30]This basic cleavage in bar politics is also revealed in a seminal piece by sociologist Jack Ladinsky, "Careers of Lawyers, Law Practice and Legal Institutions," *American Sociological Review* 28, No. 1 (Feb. 1963): 47–54. See also Ch. 7 of this text.

[31]For the backgrounds of members of these commissions, see Beth M. Henschen, Robert Moog, and Steven Davis, "Judicial Nominating Commissioners: A National Profile," *Judicature* 73, No. 6 (Apr.–May, 1990): 328–34, 343, along with the sources cited therein.

[32]This argument may be found in Glick, "Promise and Performance," 522, and throughout the literature.

The conclusion is inescapable: "merit" selection has little or no merit, if by merit we mean that nonpolitical (that is, professional) considerations dominate the selection process. "Professional" considerations turn out to be next to meaningless when applied in the real world. They are ideals that no one has succeeded in translating into tangible, workable guidelines.[33] As a result, the more concrete, understandable criteria of political qualifications emerge as the dominant force in the selection process.

Supporters of the "merit" system have often argued that although merit selection admittedly fails to eliminate politics, it at least substitutes a somewhat more lofty form of politics (that of professional considerations) for the less desirable forms of partisan politics endemic in other selection systems. But even this is unfounded, for if we have learned anything about the operation of merit selection, it is that bar and bench politics *is* partisan politics; there is no other game in town. As more fully discussed in Chapter 7, lawyers act primarily as surrogates for the interests of their clients. That is their function, their *raison d'être.* And while a separate set of "professional" values may be said to exist, the claim that such values have on the loyalty of an attorney is clearly submerged by the much more pressing claims of client representation.

It is contradictory to attempt to remove politics from the process of selecting political decision makers. The considerations that dominate the process are precisely those that dominate the judicial decisional process. Hence, as long as judges decide cases in part on the basis of socioeconomic and political values—their own and those they share with their fellow citizens—those who choose judges will understandably insist that like value considerations weigh heavily in the selection process. It can be no other way, although reformers will continue in their attempt to lead us in the search for the philosopher's stone by perpetuating the myth, the internal contradiction, of nonpolitical selection.

A second argument frequently made by proponents of "merit" selection (one already implied), is that in replacing partisan political considerations with professional criteria, the selection process inevitably produces "better" judges—that is, judges with superior professional and personal qualifications. This is the import of the song that opens this chapter. One problem in empirically testing this proposition is the near impossibility of operationalizing the concepts "good" and "better." Beyond a consensus that judges ought to be "judicious," have proper "judicial temperament," be objective, and perhaps have prior judicial experience (terms that lead into tautologies, for example, "A good judge is one who thinks and acts like a judge"), there remains no direct measure of what a "good" judge is. Even so, there are some empirically verifiable factors that at least point to quality on the bench, even if indirectly. At the very least, one can determine whether different selection mechanisms tend to produce different types of individuals as measured by these variables. Thus, presumably, educational attainments, prior judicial experience, the absence of parochialism, and so on, would tell us something, at least inferentially, about the quality of judicial nominees. And if the Missouri Plan is supposed to produce decidedly superior judges, these results might be expected to show up in such data. However, the research reported thus far does not lend much support to this claim.

Not only is there little evidence of the superiority of judges selected by the "merit" system (although there is some evidence to the contrary), but also there is little to show that judicial selection mechanisms make any difference at all. In an early study (1964) examining trial judges in twelve states with different types of selection systems, Herbert Jacob found that if judicial quality can be measured by the extent of prelaw college education (in that era, it was common to attend law school without having first received one's

[33]See Allan Ashman and James J. Alfini, *The Key to Judicial Merit Selection: The Nominating Process* (Chicago: American Judicature Society, 1974), 60–69.

baccalaureate degree) or attendance at a prestigious law school, the Missouri Plan judges were no better than, and in some cases actually inferior to, judges selected by other methods.[34] A later (1972) study of supreme court judges in all fifty states by Bradley Canon discovered that although background characteristics of judges do differ widely from state to state, *regional factors* appear to be as important as selection systems in explaining the difference. And neither educational backgrounds nor prior judicial experience set Missouri Plan judges apart from judges selected by other mechanisms.[35]

Similar results were obtained from a study in 1971 of all appellate judges in the history of the states of California and Iowa. In these states, popular election of judges was superseded, after several decades, by modified merit plans. But whether measured by quality of legal education or by degree of parochialism (whether or not the judge was born in the state), there is little evidence that the way judges were selected made any significant difference.[36]

Finally, Glick and Emmert have reported data on the education, legal experience, and judicial experience, as well as on the religion, race, and gender of state supreme court justices selected under different mechanisms in all the fifty states in 1980 to 1981. Again, the findings were essentially the same as those just reported. These scholars conclude that

> Our research confirms previous studies which find little evidence that selection systems produce judges with markedly different or superior judicial credentials or that they vary on most other background characteristics. Differences in localism, type of education, type of law practice, and previous experience are due mainly to region, not selection system.[37]

Thus, reformers' claims that Missouri-type plans improve the quality of judicial personnel are not borne out by the evidence, at least to the extent that quality can be measured by such factors as prior judicial experience, prestige legal education, years of legal practice, and so on. Or, the other way around, if merit selection produces better judges, social science and legal research has thus far failed to substantiate the claim.

In addition to claims of taking judicial selection "out of politics" and of choosing superior judges, advocates of the Missouri Plan have long maintained that "merit" selection has the unique advantage of balance. That is, it incorporates equitable portions of partisan political consideration (through the governor's influence), and professional legal factors (the influence of bar and bench as represented on the selection commissions), as well as lay opinion. Lay opinion, in fact, has a dual input: (1) lay persons are part of the selection commissions, and (2) the public participates in retention elections. We have already seen

---

[34]Herbert Jacob, "The Effects of Institutional Differences in the Recruitment Process: The Case of State Judges," *Journal of Public Law* 13, No. 1 (1964): 104–19.

[35]Bradley Canon, "The Impact of Formal Selection Processes on the Characteristics of Judges: Reconsidered," *Law and Society Review* 6, No. 4 (May 1972): 579–93.

[36]See Larry L. Berg, Justin J. Green, John R. Schmidhauser, and Ronald S. Schneider, "The Consequences of Judicial Reform: A Comparative Analysis of the California and Iowa Appellate Systems," *Western Political Quarterly* 28, No. 2 (June 1975): 263–80.

[37]Henry R. Glick and Craig F. Emmert, "Selection Systems and Judicial Characteristics": 235. One possible exception to these conclusions is religion. These researchers found that ". . . merit selection appears to limit the recruitment of [judges from religious] minorities" (234).

A related question, though one not usually raised in the debate over methods of judicial selection, is, Do different selection plans used in the states tend to produce judges exhibiting different *behavior,* that is, different decisional propensities? Again, the answer is largely negative. Past research and recent findings on this point are summarized in Jerome O'Callaghan, "Another Test for the Merit Plan," *Justice System Journal* 14, No. 3, and 15, No. 1 (1991): 477–85. The O'Callaghan study addresses the issue of differences in judicial behavior of trial judges in two counties in two Eastern states in their sentencing of drunk drivers. He concludes that judges' responsiveness to public concern for drunk driving is indistinguishable in the two counties, even though one county has an elected judiciary, the other a merit plan.

the actual working out of lay influence on the commissions, but what of the operation of retention elections?

The Watson-Downing study of these elections in Missouri found that in 179 separate judicial ballots over a 25-year period, only 1 judge was ever turned out of office, and this under highly unusual circumstances.[38] In a more recent study of 353 judges (32 appellate, 321 trial) who stood for retention elections, only 3 trial judges were rejected.[39] This finding indicates a rejection rate so low (an average of about seven-tenths of 1 percent) as to be inconsequential, tantamount to guaranteeing life tenure for Missouri Plan judges![40]

A still more recent study of retention elections for general trial court judges in ten states during a period of twenty years (1964–1984) reveals that in 1,864 separate "elections," only 22 judges were defeated, a scant 1.2 percent! Nearly half of these were in but one state, Illinois, which requires a minimum 60 percent affirmative vote for retention. Had Illinois fallen in line with most other states in allowing 50 percent vote for confirmation, the overall percentage of defeats would have been only .06 percent. The mean affirmative vote for these judges was 77.2 percent, with only 45 of these races (2.4 percent) falling below a 60 percent affirmative vote.[41]

These conclusions do not gainsay the possibility of occasional defeats of incumbent merit plan judges at the hands of determined interests, especially those able to mount well-financed campaigns. Such was the fate of three justices of the California Supreme Court who, on November 4, 1986, were soundly defeated in a retention referendum following an intense campaign which attracted national attention.[42] The three defeated justices—Chief Justice Rose Elizabeth Bird and Associate Justices Cruz Reynoso and Joseph Grodin—were liberal judges caught in a public opinion swing to the right. In particular, these justices were punished—"slam dunked out of business," as one of their opponents put it—for their strong voting records against capital punishment, which the California public favored by a 75 percent margin.[43] Yet, this electoral outcome does not provide sufficient evidence to contradict our chief generalizations regarding retention elections. In the California case, for example, we should not forget that the events of 1986 marked the first time in fifty-two years that appellate judges were turned out of office by the voters.

It is not difficult to understand why retention elections do not work. The old political saw, "You can't beat somebody with nobody," clearly applies. Indeed, as one observer put it, "in political combat, as in speed contests among horses, the outcome becomes doubtful only after the entry of the second contestant.[44] Overall, "merit" plan judges are retained by strong voter majorities (although turnout is usually quite low), and this obtains almost

---

[38]Watson and Downing, *Politics of the Bench and the Bar,* 345.

[39]See William Jenkins, Jr., "Retention Elections: Who Wins When No One Loses?" *Judicature* 61, No. 2 (Aug. 1977): 80.

[40]This is not to imply that state trial judges do in fact remain on the bench for life, only that they usually leave for reasons other than defeat in retention elections.

[41]See William K. Hall and Larry T. Aspin, "What Twenty Years of Judicial Retention Elections Have Told Us," *Judicature* 70, No. 6 (Apr.–May 1987): 340–47. This and similar research on judicial elections is usefully summarized by Elliot E. Slotnick in "Review Essay on Judicial Recruitment and Selection," *Justice System Journal* 13, No. 1 (Spring 1988): 109–124.

Since 1994 the constitution of the state of New Mexico requires 57 percent for the retention of judges. See Mike Taugher, "Keeping Jobs Gets Harder for Judges," *Albuquerque Journal,* Oct. 5, 1996: A-1. A recent note on the Illinois situation is Larry T. Aspin and William K. Hall, "Campaigning for Retention in Illinois," *Judicature,* 80, No. 2 (Sept.–Oct., 1996): 84–87.

[42]See Culver and Wold, "Rose Bird" and "Defeat of the California Justices."

[43]See Los Angeles *Times* (Aug. 18, 1985), I: 3, 26.

[44]Warren Burnett, "Observations on the Direct Election Method of Judicial Selection," *Texas Law Review* 44, No. 6 (June 1966): 1099.

without regard to the judges' party, age, ability, or any other known variable. Typical retention elections will produce about a 20 percent negative vote, again regardless of supposed factors denoting judicial performance. In no way can it be said that these referenda have the effect of eliminating poor judges, except under highly unusual circumstances. As an Arizona political commentator noted—in seemingly harsh but probably accurate and realistic terms—in reference to Arizona's merit plan:

> Short of committing incest at high noon at Central and Van Buren, it would appear our honorable judges now have lifetime sinecures. Which may be reading too much into the first retention election (in which all sixteen jurists on the ballot were kept on the job by monstrous margins) under Arizona's new merit selection system, but the history in other states with similar plans is not one to give a judge pangs of job insecurity. Illinois, for example, adopted such a system in 1962, and 10 years later, not a single one of some 300 judges on the bench—including more than a few notorious drunks and softballs—had been junked by the voters. For some reason that defies logical analysis, "voters are reluctant to pierce the aura of infallibility that judges don with their robes and expose them for what they are—normal human beings. And not only that, but lawyers to boot."
>
> Maybe now you understand why the judges pushed so hard for merit selection two years ago.[45]

In response to continued criticisms of the plan, local and state bar associations have undertaken various forms of bar polls in an attempt to inform the public of the legal community's "expert" opinion on judges' competence. Typically, data from such polls provide information to the voters as to the number and kinds of lawyers polled, lawyer ratings of judges along several dimensions of performance, and perhaps an overall rating. The impact of such polls in improving the discriminatory power of the voters has generally been minimal to negative. An unfavorable bar poll might lower a judge's margin of victory (by about 10 to 15 percent), but it may also have the opposite effect. It is not uncommon to find judges with low bar poll ratings being reelected by margins greater than—sometimes much greater than—judges who have received much higher ratings in similar polls.[46]

Where are we, then? If the lay, the professional, and even the political inputs built into the Missouri Plan, do not work as advertised, and if the plan in general cannot be shown to produce superior judges, what is left of the argument? The answer is, not much. In a thorough examination of the Missouri Plan undertaken by Henry Glick, other avenues of analysis were pursued, but the results in no instance reveal redeeming support for the claims made

---

[45]John Kolbe, "Results of Arizona's Election '76 Defy Any Logical Interpretation," Phoenix *Gazette* (Nov. 8, 1976): 6. See also James D. Cameron, "Merit Selection in Arizona: The First Two Years," *Arizona State Law Journal* 1976, No. 3 (June 1976).

[46]Jenkins, "Retention Elections," 83–84. Paul Lermack of Bradley University reports that bar polls in Illinois have been similarly unsuccessful:

> Between 1970 and 1978 the ISBA [Illinois State Bar Association] recommended against the retention of thirty-three sitting judges. Thirty-one of these were retained. In 1972, they recommended against ten, all of whom were retained. In 1978, the Chicago Council of Lawyers, one of two Chicago area bar associations which rate incumbent judges, recommended against retaining thirteen judges. Twelve were retained.

See Paul Lermack, "The Retention-Election System: Some Generalizations and a Case Study," paper presented at the Southern Political Science Association meeting, Gatlinburg, Tenn., November 1979, p. 8. On bar polls generally, see Dorothy L. Maddi, *Judicial Performance Polls* (Chicago: American Bar Foundation, 1977).

A zero to negative correlation between bar poll rankings and the selection of judges in election systems is also common. See, e.g., "Victors in Bar Association Poll Beaten in Election for Judge," Albuquerque *Tribune* (June 4, 1986), A-4. For similar results, see John M. Scheb, II, "Is Anyone Listening? Assessing Bar Influence in Merit Retention Elections in Florida," *Judicature* 67, No. 3 (Sept. 1983): 112–19.

for merit selection.[47] Why, then, does bar, bench, and general public support for the plan continue, and why is the plan being adopted in more and more states? The specific reasons are many, but they ultimately boil down to the aggrandizement of national and state bar associations. Already powerful as political interest groups, bar associations have grown in power and influence partly because of large increases in the number of lawyers and in the pervasiveness of their role in society. The volume of litigation in America is at an all-time high, as is the ratio of attorneys to population (see Chapter 7). In short, the entire judicial process, dominated as it is by legal professionals, plays a larger role in society than ever before. Although we must be cautious against seeing the bar and bench as a monolithic entity, the ideology of what might be called "neutral professionalism" among members of the bar is, if not unanimous, at least very widespread. Thus, despite the lack of empirical evidence supporting the superiority of merit selection, the *idea* of professional neutrality in judicial recruitment is both appealing and consistent with general professional ideology.[48]

Aside from this important ideological dimension, there is a practical political reason for such widespread professional support for merit selection: control, or at least increased influence, over the machinery of judicial selection itself. As earlier noted, judgeships are highly valued policy-making positions, sought after both for their own sake as well as for the expected policy outcomes. The legal profession desires a larger voice in judicial selection for the same reason that other interest groups do—to advance their cause through judicial policy-making. "Merit" selection gives them that added leverage. All the better if they can sell their old line of increased political influence over the courts by using the attractive, but phony, label of "neutral professionalism." After all, there is no law against false advertising in the game of American judicial politics.

Judicial Elections

If merit selection, along those dimensions examined, has so little merit, what are the alternatives? All things considered, is it preferable to elect judges, or is legislative or, perhaps, executive selection the best system? Our answer must depend on the perceived consequences of these alternative plans and upon how we would weigh such consequences.

The familiar argument usually set forth in favor of electing judges is that (1) whereas America purports to be a democracy, (2) whereas democracy is usually defined as a governmental arrangement wherein policy-makers are held *accountable* to policy recipients, (3) whereas judges are policy-making officials, and (4) whereas elections are the usual method for ensuring or at least promoting political accountability, election is the preferred method of judicial selection, because such a system best assures accountability and, hence, is the most consistent with principles of democratic government. Granting Points 1 through 4, recent research on the actual operation of judicial elections raises considerable doubt as to their efficacy in ensuring accountability.

The central point to be made about judicial elections is that they are *not* "elections," at least as that term is generally understood. This is true on several counts. First, in states providing for the election of at least some judges, aside from judges of limited jurisdiction courts, either on a partisan or nonpartisan ballot (and by 1994 that included 23 states with a

---

[47]For example, Glick examined whether or not Missouri Plan judges have a better record of ethical behavior on the bench and whether or not they may be shown to exhibit a greater degree of dispassionate or detached decision making. The results were negative on both counts. See Glick, "Promise and the Performance," 530–39. See also Glick and Emmert, "Selection Systems and Judicial Characteristics," especially p. 235.

[48]Glick, "Promise and the Performance," passim. The arguments by Glick have guided much of the discussion herein. The reader is also referred back to our earlier discussion of the factors associated with the adoption of "merit" selection in the states.

total of 7,602 appellate and general trial judges), a large proportion of these judges initially obtain their seats by executive appointment. This practice has been fairly widespread since states first began electing judges, but it was not well documented until the publication of James Herndon's research in 1962. In a nationwide study of state supreme courts, drawing data from 1948 through 1957, Herndon found that 56 percent of those who became judges during that period had been appointed by governors to replace judges who had retired, resigned, or died while in office. Indeed, in 18 of the 36 state supreme courts studied, a majority of the justices were initially appointed to the bench. And Maryland, South Dakota, and Wyoming, despite claiming "elective" judiciaries, were found to have 100 percent appointed supreme court benches! Herndon concluded that the less partisan a state's judicial election system, the greater the percentage of initially appointed judges one could expect to find.[49]

Another study generally confirmed these findings and supported Herndon's chief conclusion. In all state supreme courts in non-Southern states from 1948 to 1974, 53 percent of the 436 justices studied were initially appointed. Sixty-seven percent of "elective" judges were appointed in nonpartisan election states, whereas 42 percent were so selected in partisan states.[50]

The American Judicature Society undertook a nationwide study of the same phenomenon regarding trial judges. Their 1977 survey found that 30 percent of the sitting trial judges in partisan states were initially appointed, whereas some 57 percent were appointed in nonpartisan states.[51] It is true that in situations of initial gubernatorial appointment, the judges must face the voters, usually in the next election. But by that time, the strength of incumbency has taken hold and the chances of defeat are small.

This brings us to a second general reason judicial elections are often criticized as something less than meaningful: the very low incidence of electoral turnover of judicial seats. A host of factors relating to the rules of the game of judicial elections and voter behavior help to explain why this is so. In the first place, the level of competition is typically very low. An early Texas study found that in the period 1940 to 1962, 66 percent of the supposedly "elected" judges were actually appointed. So important was incumbency in these judgeships that in the first election following gubernatorial appointments, 96 percent of the judges were reelected, 86 percent without opposition.[52] Other states report a similar pattern: incumbency, once established, strongly discourages competition; and where there is a contest, the challenger is usually unsuccessful. Typically, if competition emerges, it is more likely to occur against judges who were originally elected than those who received their seats through appointment. Furthermore, competition is more likely in the first election than in subsequent races.[53]

The unwritten rule is that once an attorney has given up his or her practice for the bench, that person is to be treated with some deference. It is usually considered dirty pool to attempt his or her defeat, particularly early on. There is yet another reason that potential

---

[49]James Herndon, "Appointment as a Means of Initial Accession to Elective State Courts of Last Resort," *North Dakota Law Review* 38, No. 1 (Jan. 1962): 71–73.

[50]Philip L. Dubois, *From Ballot to Bench: Judicial Elections and the Quest for Accountability* (Austin: University of Texas Press, 1980), 105–106.

[51]Ryan, Ashman, and Sales, "Judicial Selection," 25–26.

[52]Bancroft C. Henderson and T. C. Sinclair, *The Selection of Judges in Texas: An Exploratory Study* (Houston: Public Affairs Research Center, University of Houston, 1965), 21.

[53]In North Dakota between 1950 and 1970, district judges' races went uncontested about 80 percent of the time. See note, "Judicial Selection in North Dakota: Is Constitutional Revision Necessary?" *North Dakota Law Review* 48, No. 2 (Winter 1972): 333. And Glick reports that:

> Of the total number of judicial elections held in the fifty states, closely contested, partisan "unjudicial" judicial elections probably constitute no more than five to seven percent of the total. Figures from other research show that few judges are ever challenged, and almost never face a close, hard-

judicial contestants are reluctant to challenge an incumbent: such candidates are typically attorneys practicing in the community in which the judge sits. Who wants to incur the wrath of a judge before whom one must practice?

A second set of factors helping to explain the infrequent turnover of elective seats is that even with competition, the incumbent usually has the advantage. The "judge" can usually beat the nonjudge; the judge's name is frequently in public view, whereas his or her challenger's is not. Consistent with well-entrenched professional ideology, undergirded by state and national canons of professional ethics, judicial campaigns are usually low-key, with candidates often refusing to discuss judicial issues. In general, the races have a low visibility, voter knowledge is scanty, and turnout is almost always light. These factors, too, usually work to the advantage of the incumbent, although incumbents with little name recognition can occasionally be defeated by candidates with popular names.[54] Conversely, it is not unknown for dead incumbents to be reelected.[55] Hence, barring a major scandal, an unusual shift in partisan voting patterns, some other notable disturbance of the system, or a fluke, the incumbent judge, whether selected by the governor, the electorate, or the mixed merit system, and whether challenged or unopposed, is usually assured a long term in office, typically until retirement or resignation. There are exceptions, to be sure, and they provide interesting data for insightful case studies.[56] But they *are* exceptions. Judicial elections, then, though we have hardly covered all facets of the process,[57] appear to fall short of their ideal

---

fought campaign. Even after the election is over, no matter how it was fought, the incumbent usually comes out the winner.

See Glick, "Promise and the Performance," 519.

[54]A notable example was the 1990 defeat of Chief Justice Keith M. Callow of Washington's Supreme Court by an unknown candidate who did not campaign in the nonpartisan race but whose name, Charles W. Johnson, apparently sounded more friendly to voters. See Robb London, "For Want of Recognition, Chief Justice Ousted," *New York Times* (Dec. 28, 1990): B-10; and John Balzar, "Washington State Puzzled as Voters Oust Chief Justice," *Los Angeles Times* (Oct. 3, 1990): A-5. See also Robb London, "What Is in a Familiar Name Could Well be a Judgeship," *New York Times* (Oct. 19, 1990): B-11.

[55]See "Few Upsets Among Judges," *National Law Journal* 13, No. 11 (Nov. 19, 1990): 6, where an Oklahoma incumbent judge, Frank Ogden, III, who had died, was reelected; and in 1971 a dead Tennessee judge, Beverly Boushe, finished second in a three-way race, forcing the third-place finisher out of the runoff. See James Chisum, "Selection of Judges in Shaky Balance," *Commercial Appeal* (Memphis, Tenn., May 27, 1990).

On voter awareness generally, see Anthony Champagne and Greg Thielemann, "Awareness of Trial Court Judges," *Judicature* 74, No. 5 (Feb.–March, 1991): 271–76, and the sources cited therein; Lawrence Baum, "Judicial Election and Appointment at the State Level: Voters' Information in Judicial Elections: The 1986 Contests for the Ohio Supreme Court," *Kentucky Law Journal* 77, No. 3 (1988–89): 645–670; Philip L. Dubois, "Voting Cues in Nonpartisan Trial Court Elections: A Multivariate Assessment," *Law and Society Review* 18, No. 3 (1984): 395–436; Charles H. Sheldon and Nicholas P. Lovrich, Jr., "Knowledge and Judicial Voting: The Oregon and Washington Experience," *Judicature* 67, No. 5 (Nov. 1983): 235–45; and Nicholas P. Lovrich, Jr. and Charles H. Sheldon, "Is Voting for State Judges a Flight of Fancy or a Reflection of Policy and Value Preferences?" *Justice System Journal* 16, No. 3 (1994): 57–71.

[56]Exceptions can be found in most states at some point in their history. See, e.g., The defeat of the California Supreme Court Justices in Culver and Wold, "Rose Bird"; the defeat of Chief Justice Frank D. Celebrezze of Ohio and Chief Justice Rhoda B. Billings of North Carolina, both in 1986, are also notable. Too, the high-stakes race for Supreme Court posts in Texas the same year was also an exceptional judicial selection event. See Anthony Paonita, "Voters in 3 States Reject Chief Justices," *National Law Journal* (Nov. 12, 1986): 3, 16. The Celebrezze case is discussed in a number of pieces, including Lawrence Baum, "'Voters' Information." Still, Lovrich and Sheldon remind us that we should not develop our perception of judicial voting on the basis of the uncommon. See Lovrich and Sheldon, "Is Voting A Flight of Fancy," 58.

[57]The most thorough study of judicial elections is by Dubois, *From Ballot to Bench;* see also the review of recent research by Slotnick, "Review Essay." Another useful set of references to recent research on judicial elections is found in Marie Hojnacki and Lawrence Baum, "'New Style' Judicial Campaigns and Voters: Economic Issues and Union Members in Ohio," *Western Political Quarterly* 45, No. 4 (Dec. 1992): 921–48. Finally, for an excellent current study of judicial selection generally, see Charles H. Sheldon and Linda Maule, *Judicial Recruitment: Choosing Federal and State Judges* (Chicago: Nelson-Hall, forthcoming).

function, which is to ensure popular choice of policy-makers and accountability of judicial behavior. At least this is so as they are presently conducted.

Some Conclusions

What can we conclude from our analysis of the politics of judicial selection in the states? The most persistent finding that emerges is that the forces and influences at work in the process have a way of making themselves felt irrespective of the specific selection mechanism. While the debate rages as to form, the underlying reality remains the same: neither those who influence the process nor the substantive outcomes are much affected by a change in method of selection. Glick makes this point concerning the Missouri Plan, but it may justifiably be extended to the other selection systems as well:

> It is abundantly clear . . . that the selection process in . . . [Missouri] is dominated by the Governor and the Democratic Party. This and other research demonstrates that it probably is impossible to alter the dominant features of a state political system by creating a new method of judicial selection. Instead, well established patterns of party politics and the action of political officials will adapt to the new method of selection and, in turn, find ways of making the new method operate within the context of existing political conditions. The Missouri Plan has not taken judicial selection out of partisan politics. It has created a new and distinctive way of selecting judges, but in an established partisan setting where the governor and his allies in the dominant political party continue to have considerable influence in the appointments. In this way, the Missouri Plan does not operate very differently from formal gubernatorial appointment or the interim appointment of judges in elective states.[58]

Viewing the process from the perspective of gubernatorial appointment, with or without legislative concurrence, produces a similar result. Political professionals are reluctant to make final judicial appointments without serious (and often semiformalized) consultation with relevant bar groups.[59] It is politically dangerous to do so; bar associations have too much power to be ignored. What we have, then, is merit selection significantly modified in practice by partisan political influences, while at the same time deep inroads are being made into political selection mechanisms by professional interests. Hence, the closer we examine the process, the more the selection mechanism turns out to be the same! Actual selection is inevitably the result of an amalgam of politically and professionally relevant influences, the nominee ultimately being drawn from the same politically and professionally approved pool of candidates. It would be difficult to find any aspect of our judicial system that more clearly illustrates the interaction of law and politics, the close interdependence of the political and legal systems.

The conclusions we have drawn concerning the influences at work in judicial selection also help us to understand why researchers are able to find so little difference in the characteristics of judges selected irrespective of the mechanism used. The answer to the riddle is that the mechanisms are not that different; in fact, at bottom, they are about the same. Hence, the exaggerated claims for one system, as well as criticisms, by opponents of another, are equally without foundation. If one mechanism fails to produce measurably better judges than another, it is also true that competing selection systems also fail to produce the disastrous results predicted. Neither the professional politician nor the

---

[58]Glick, "Promise and the Performance," 522–23.

[59]Many governors, in making appointments, interim or otherwise, frequently insist on a process of consultation with relevant bar leaders, which results in a de facto Missouri-type selection process. See R. Stanley Lowe, "Voluntary Merit Selection Plans," *Judicature* 55, No. 4 (Nov. 1971): 161–68.

professional legal practitioner has anything to gain through the appointment of incompetent persons to the bench. As already explained, political parties have a good deal riding on judicial performance, not only in terms of substantive policy outcomes but also in the favorable reflection on the party brought about by the work of competent judges. Even more, legal professionals are concerned with selecting candidates with reputations for intelligence and skill, both political and legal. Both sides, then, usually select well-qualified people who in turn perform the task of judging with decorum, skill, and a sincere commitment to doing justice. Mistakes crop up, to be sure, but they are not systemic.

Having said this, it is still necessary to adopt some selection system. Choice cannot be avoided. So what should that system be? As noted earlier, the answer depends primarily on one's view of the judicial functions as well as on the nature of the political system as a whole. On the face of it, selection via popular elections (or alternately, selection by popularly elected officials) is most consistent both with a political conceptualization of the judiciary and with the dictates of democracy. Simply put, if judges make policy, democratic governmental arrangements require that they be held accountable, and elections are the best (though by no means perfect) means of ensuring this accountability. The principles of merit selection, on the other hand, seem more in keeping with a mechanical or Blackstonian view of the judicial function, and, one could argue, more consonant with an elitist view of society: we—the professionals—know best who would make good judges; the ordinary voter lacks the expertise to make that choice, though we will permit ratification of our selections as long as no real threat is posed to professional domination of the process.

But if we can accept the logic of the argument thus far—that the political selection of judges is, on the grounds stated, to be preferred—what of the accountability problem? Such accountability is ill-served by an electoral system that is to a large extent appointive, and that, in addition, lacks competitiveness and meaningful, informed voter participation.

One answer might be that the trouble with elections is not with the elections themselves but with their underlying jurisprudence. It is the myth of a nonpolitical judiciary, fostered by bench and bar through quasi-professional rules and expectations, that turns otherwise spirited campaigns for judicial office into boring, nonissue tea parties. The belief that a frank discussion of issues compromises judicial independence (or the view that there really are no issues to discuss, that judicial matters must be handled in a neutral manner) are the building blocks of judicial noncompetitiveness and noncampaigning that seriously reduce the effectiveness of the ballot box in bringing the judiciary to account.[60] A more realistic appraisal of the judicial roles reveals a host of matters that could constitute legitimate campaign issues. It is little wonder, then, that voters perform so poorly, so indiscriminately, in judicial elections, for such contests (or rather noncontests) give them precious little to sink their teeth into. As noted by Atkins,

> The process of conducting judicial elections produces and perpetuates ignorance among the electorate. Jurisprudence assumes that judicial decision-making is qualitatively different from decision-making processes within other governmental institutions. Moreover, the hallmark of the judicial role is that of the neutral judge adjudicating disputes unencumbered by political liaisons. This drive toward defending the integrity of the judicial

---

[60]This point has been made by several writers over the years. See, e.g., two early pieces by Larry L. Berg and Leo J. Flynn, "Judicial Elections and Accountability: Conventional Wisdom Reexamined," *Southern Review of Public Administration* 2, No. 1 (June 1978): 44–45; and Joel B. Grossman, "A Political View of Judicial Ethics," *San Diego Law Review* 9, No. 4 (June 1972): 809–11; See also Glick, "Promise and Performance," 541; and Charles H. Sheldon and Nicholas P. Lovrich, Jr., "Knowledge and Judicial Voting," 245.

process has meant, in reality, that the kinds of information needed to evaluate judges' performances are not made available to the electorate, particularly the judges' view of issues which might be relevant to pending or future litigation. . . . The manner in which relevant information concerning issues and candidates is made virtually inaccessible to the electorate establishes tremendous hurdles which supporters of judicial elections must overcome. Naturally, such a system would tend to produce poor results, at least from the perspective of voter participation.[61]

But even taking judicial elections as they are, rather than as they could be, we can conclude that as instruments of accountability they have not totally failed. When compared with elections for other officeholders, rather than with a democratic ideal that has never been achieved, they do not come off so badly. On this crucial point of the effectiveness of partisan elections (since there really are no other kind) as instruments of accountability in the judiciary, Dubois has concluded that

Though elections are blunt instruments of accountability, they are effective in maintaining popular control over the outer limits of governmental decision-making. As long as voters can know within such wide limits the general ideological and political orientations of those individuals they put in policy-making positions, they will be able to exercise effective indirect control over their own affairs.

In the context of judicial elections, therefore, since it appears that a certain amount of judicial decision-making will necessarily have a partisan base regardless of the formal selection system, voters can achieve maximum control over the broad outlines of judicial policy through partisan elections (at least as much as they currently seem to have with respect to controlling policy-making in the other two branches of government).[62]

Since Dubois penned these conclusions, there is an accumulating body of evidence that judicial elections of a contested, meaningful variety are growing in number and intensity. Reports from California, Ohio, Texas, New York, North Carolina, Wisconsin, and other states point to what Baum cautiously calls "New Style" judicial campaigns that resemble more closely state and national legislative races.[63] Moreover, recent research has pointed to new, or at least newly discovered, voter discernment of judicial issues and candidates.[64] Taken together, these developments provide hope, though hardly a promise, that judicial elections might perform one of their intended purposes, that of enhancing the ac-

---

[61]Burton M. Atkins, "Judicial Elections: What the Evidence Shows," *Florida Bar Journal* 50, No. 3 (March 1976): 155. A similar argument may be found in Charles H. Sheldon and Nicholas P. Lovrich, Jr., "Judicial Accountability vs. Responsibility: Balancing the Views of Voters and Judges," *Judicature* 65, No. 10 (May 1982): 470–80.

[62]Dubois, *From Ballot to Bench*, 238–39.

[63]Hojnacki and Baum, "'New Style' Judicial Campaigns" and the sources cited therein, particularly Roy Schotland, "Elective Judges' Campaign Financing: Are State Judges' Robes the Emperor's Clothes of American Democracy?," *Journal of Law and Politics* 2, No. 1 (Spring 1985): 57–167. See also, for example, "Statement of Roy A. Schotland before the Joint Select Committee on the Judiciary of the Texas Legislature, Austin, Texas, Mar. 25, 1988," *Judicature* 72, No. 3 (Oct.–Nov. 1988): 154–57; Jane Ruffin, "Rancorous Politics May Bolster Move to Halt Judicial Elections," *News and Observer* Raleigh, North Carolina (Feb. 10, 1991): G-2-3; Applebome, "Rubber Stamp," and Slotnick, "Review Essay."
Concern is growing over the inequity in judicial campaign financing, with candidates from, or backed by, large firms receiving the bulk of funds. In Los Angeles, a federal suit was filed on these grounds. See "Lawsuit Seeks to Change Financing of Judicial Campaigns," *New York Times* (May 19, 1996): A-9.

[64]See Dubois, "Voting Cues"; Dubois, "Accountability, Independence, and the Selection of State Judges: The Role of Popular Elections," *Southwestern Law Journal* 40, Special Issue (May 1986): 31–52; Nicholas Lovrich, Jr., and Charles H. Sheldon, "Assessing Judicial Elections: Effects upon the Electorate of High and Low Articulation Systems," *Western Political Quarterly* 38, No. 2 (June 1985): 276–93; and Lovrich and Sheldon, "Is Voting a Flight of Fancy," and the sources cited therein.

countability of state judicial policy-makers. In any case, there is certainly no evidence of the superiority of alternative means of selecting judges, such as "merit" plans, at least as measured by democratic principles of government.

STATE JUDGES: A PROFILE

Although formal state selection systems have attracted a good deal of both scholarly and political attention, we must remember that such mechanisms operate only at the final stages of the recruiting process. Decisions made long before the formal selection mechanisms are actuated—decisions at both the individual and societal level, and rooted in our political culture—probably have more bearing on who becomes a judge than does the formal process itself. As the preceding analysis indicates, the attorneys who are ultimately selected as judges tend to have the same general characteristics over time and across the different selection systems, though such characteristics do vary somewhat with state or region. This fact strongly suggests the existence of a rather persistently held set of norms about the "proper" qualifications for judicial office that must be taken into account if we are to understand fully the politics of state judicial selection. So the appropriate question is, What factors seem to be most important in choosing state judges?

We are provided with broad insight into these criteria through research that examines the socioeconomic backgrounds and career routes of sitting judges. Not only do such data on judges' background characteristics give us the best evidence available regarding the criteria thought important in the initial selection decision, but also we are able to understand better certain decisional tendencies on the part of state courts—tendencies to be discussed more fully in subsequent chapters.

Bradley Canon undertook a nationwide study of all justices of state supreme courts sitting in the 1961–1968 period. Of the 479 judges, data were gathered and tabulated on 441—about 91 percent.[65] Henry Glick and Craig Emmert gathered similar data on 85 percent (about 300) of the same set of judges who were sitting in 1980–1981.[66] A summary of the findings from both studies, where comparable data existed, is presented in Table 5–3.

The first point that stands out in this table is the overpowering dominance of these courts by white males. In spite of the recent upsurge in the number and percentage of women in the legal profession (see Chapter 7), there were only 10 women serving as justices of state supreme courts in 1980–1981, 3 percent of those polled. There were, however, only 3 women (less than 1 percent) in the Canon survey of 441 judges; and according to a count taken from the regional reporters (which lists state supreme court justices by name), there were 23 serving on these courts in 1985. This fact tends to support the contention of political scientist Beverly Blair Cook, who maintains that the proportion of women judges will follow (with a time lag) the proportion of women lawyers (13.1 percent of the legal profession were women in 1985, at a time when about 6 percent of state supreme court justices were women—23 out of some 361 judges).[67] The fact that but two

---

[65]See Bradley C. Canon, "Characteristics and Career Patterns of State Supreme Court Justices," *State Government* 45, No. 1 (Winter 1972): 34–41. See also Canon's "Impact of Formal Selection Processes."

[66]See Henry Glick and Craig Emmert, "Stability and Change: Characteristics of Contemporary State Supreme Court Judges," *Judicature* 70, No. 2 (Aug.–Sept. 1986): 107–12.

[67]See Beverly Blair Cook, "Women Judges: The End of Tokenism," in Winifred L. Hepperle and Laura Crites, eds., *Women in the Courts* (Williamsburg, Va.: National Center for State Courts, 1978), 84–105. See also *Judicature* 65, No. 6 (Dec.–Jan. 1982). This entire issue is devoted to the subject of women in the judiciary.

Table 5–3 Characteristics of State Supreme Court Judges, 1960s and 1980–1981

	1961–1968 (percentage, N = 441)	1980–1981 (percentage, N = 300)
Race and Sex		
Female	—[a]	3.1
Nonwhite	—	0.6
Religious Affiliation		
High-status Protestant[b]	38.8	29.9
Low-status Protestant	41.5	30.3
Catholic	16.1	23.9
Jewish	3.6	11.6
Other	—	4.2
Localism		
In-state birth	74.6	78.1
In-state undergraduate school	73.9	69.5
In-state law school	64.6	69.0
Possesses Bachelor's Degree	57.8	80.0
Democratic Party Affiliation	57.4	67.0
Government Career Experience		
Prosecutor	51.5	21.5
Legislator	19.3	20.2
Previous judicial	57.8	62.9
Other	—	39.2
Average No. Years Practiced Law	—	14.5

Note: Missing data are excluded from the calculations in this table.

[a]Dashes indicate that no data are available.

[b]High-status Protestant denominations include Episcopalian, Congregationalist, Presbyterian, and Unitarian. These are conventional categories and were used by Canon.

Sources: Data for the 1960s are based on a recalculation of data reported in Bradley C. Canon, "The Impact of Formal Selection Process on the Characteristics of Judges: Reconsidered," *Law and Society Review* 6, No. 4 (May 1972): 575, 579–93. The table is reprinted from Henry R. Glick and Craig F. Emmert, "Stability and Change: Characteristics of State Supreme Court Judges," *Judicature* 70, No. 2 (Aug.–Sept. 1986): 107–12.

black state supreme court justices sat in the 1980–1981 period is even more shocking in this era of supposed racial justice. This, in addition to the proportion of women, clearly underscores the tokenism of such representation on state appellate courts. Table 5–3 reveals a significant increase in the number of Catholic and Jewish state supreme court justices, but it is clear that Protestants still dominate these positions (over 60 percent in 1980–1981) and, together with the race and sex profile, lends a decidedly WASPish hue to the personnel of these courts.

Moving down the column of figures presented in Table 5–3, we find that the long-standing tendency to localism on these courts continues. Briefly stated, these judges are mostly home-grown products. Nearly 8 out of 10 were born in the state in which they serve, and few (less than one-third) journeyed out of state for their undergraduate degrees, or even for their law degrees. This pattern tends to be repeated in all background studies of state judges and is also reflected in the patterns of work experience these justices bring to the bench. Whatever the particular career path taken, it is almost inevitably at the state level. As Glick and Emmert remark,

> Only 13 per cent of the judges had any form of prior federal experience, whereas 93 per cent had some form of prior state experience. Only 7 per cent reached the state supreme court without some form of previous involvement in state government.[68]

The political party affiliation of these judges is also to some extent suggestive of their localism. That the Democratic Party label predominated on state supreme courts is probably a result of that party's electoral victories in several states in the mid-1970s.

Finally, the prior work experience of state supreme court justices tends to follow a rather predictable pattern. A typical, though not invariable, route would begin with prosecutorial or state legislative experience, thence to a trial judgeship (nearly two-thirds—63 percent—had previous judicial experience), and from there to the state supreme court, with stopover service on the intermediate appellate court (if one existed in the state) or perhaps in the state attorney general's office. Canon's data, which are somewhat richer on this point than are the results of the Glick survey, indicate that about 85 percent of the justices held at least one of the following positions prior to being appointed to the supreme court: prosecutor (51 percent), state legislator (19 percent), and trial judge, (58 percent). The comparable percentages from the 1980–1981 data are presented in Table 5–3. Almost half (about 40 percent) had served in two of these slots, and a few had served in all three.[69] As to the two other frequently held positions, Canon reports that 19 percent of the justices served in their state's office of attorney general, usually as attorney general, while 13 percent had had service on the state's intermediate appellate court.

Forty-one (9.3 percent) of the justices studied by Canon had held none of these five key offices. Most of these had won a seat on their state's highest appellate court on the strength of their record in private practice (often including extracurricular political activity), while for the remainder, state executive or federal legislative experience was common. Thus, a small group of justices could be found who were former governors, U.S. senators, or U.S. representatives.[70] With the exception of a sharp decline in state prosecutorial experience, this career path did not change significantly for the early 1980s. The average age of appointment to state supreme courts in the 1980–1981 period, by the way, was found to be 53.

The overall pattern of background characteristics suggests a relatively narrow politicolegal career path to the state supreme court bench, as well as a painfully restricted socioeconomic pool from which the justices are selected. These informal norms of recruitment painted a portrait of the typical state supreme court justice as likely to be a well-educated, professionally mature male with a good deal of previous experience in responsible policy-making positions. Also easily discernible in the portrait is a staid, middle-of-the-road (or perhaps somewhat to the right) "establishment-type" with a strong local—one might even say provincial—orientation. Thus, while we are likely to find a good deal of professional competence on our state supreme courts, this is hardly a group of people who could be looked upon

---

[68]Glick and Emmert, "Stability and Change," 110.
[69]See Canon, "Impact of Formal Selection Processes," 583.
[70]Canon, "Characteristics and Career Patterns," 41.

as innovative public policy-makers. Rather, they would seem more likely to be oriented to the maintenance of the status quo in politics, economics, and general social concerns.

Somewhat more limited and dated data are available on the background characteristics of state trial judges. In a national survey undertaken in 1977 by the American Judicature Society, some 5,000 judges serving on trial courts of general jurisdiction in the 50 states were studied on a variety of matters pertaining to their backgrounds and work patterns. Sixty-three percent (over 3,000) responded, providing a rich set of data not heretofore available.[71]

Not surprisingly, state trial judges in 1977 were, like their brethren at the appellate level, overwhelmingly white and male. No data were gathered on their religion, but we can surmise that it was about as WASPish as we would find on state supreme courts. Ninety-six percent were white, almost 98 percent were male. Only 80 black judges were found, while 12 were Native American and 12 Asian. Women judges numbered 73, although, had there been a 100 percent response, more could probably have been identified. Both black and women judges were found to be disproportionately located in metropolitan areas where blacks, though not women, were concentrated.[72]

State trial judges came to the bench at a somewhat younger age than appellate judges (46 years old as compared with 53 for state supreme court justices in the Glick-Emmert survey), while the average age of trial judges was found to be about 53 years as against 62 for supreme court justices in Canon's survey. At the time of the American Judicature Society surveys, the trial judges questioned had served an average of eight years. Typically, then, a state trial judge will be in his or her 50s, whereas only a very small percentage were under 40 (7.3 percent), or 70 or over (2.6 percent). Thus, unlike the federal bench, especially the United States Supreme Court, rarely does it appear that state trial courts are plagued with problems of superannuation.

The party affiliation of state trial judges was quite similar to that of supreme court justices. Fifty-five percent of the trial judges said they were Democrats, 36 percent Republicans, and 9 percent indicated they had no political affiliation. As with the pattern found among state supreme court justices, the Democratic majority was due to then preponderance of that party's representation on state trial courts in the South (82 percent); elsewhere, a fairly even balance was found to exist. Even more than with state supreme court justices, the partisan distribution of trial judges in the various states was closely tied to recent state electoral fortunes. Even a one- or a two-term change in party in the governor's mansion could have quite significant effects on party balance on trial courts, not to mention the impact on other judicial background characteristics.[73] Although no direct questions were asked on the extent of political activity of the judges either prior to or during their service on the bench, we can infer from other research that there is a high level of such activity among this group of political decision makers. As earlier noted, such involvement is often crucial to being selected for judicial service.

The American Judicature Society's research gave us the first national data on the career routes of state trial judges. Although the questions asked did not extend very far beyond the positions held immediately prior to appointment to the bench, the data are

---

[71]The research is reported in John Paul Ryan et al., *American Trial Judges: Their Work Styles and Performance* (New York: Free Press, 1980). The methodology of the American Judicative Society research is discussed in Ch. 1 and App. B.

[72]Ryan et al., *American Trial Judges,* 128. Beverly Blair Cook reported 135 women trial judges in 1977, though the percentage of women on the trial bench according to the American Judicature Society survey (2.4 percent) was essentially the same as that reported by Cook (2.5 percent). See Ryan et al., *American Trial Judges,* 143; and Cook, "Women Judges," 100–101.

[73]See, for example, the experience in Wisconsin under Governor Patrick Lucey, reported in Ryan, Ashman, and Sales, "Judicial Selection and Its Impact," 28–33.

nonetheless instructive. As indicated in Table 5–4, private practitioners constituted the chief occupational pool from which trial judges were recruited (nearly 54 percent), while about one-quarter of the general trial judges serving in 1977 were elevated from a lower court judgeship. A wide variation existed among the states in this respect. With notable exceptions, the larger states tended to draw their trial judges from lower courts, whereas the smaller states had a tendency to appoint practicing attorneys to the trial bench.[74] The type of private practice from which the judges were drawn is of more than passing interest. Well over half reported a general practice without specialization, whereas most of the rest had worked in civil practice. Only a few (3 percent) had come from criminal practice.

More than 20 percent of the judges were recruited either from the ranks of district attorneys (this was especially true in the South and the border states) or from other types of public or political service. The research revealed that Rhode Island (where judges are appointed by the governor for life) and South Carolina (where the legislature selects the state's trial judges) were two states in which trial judges tended to be drawn directly from the ranks of former or practicing politicians.

General trial judges, then, like their appellate brethren, represented a comparatively narrow group of legal professionals. White, middle-aged male lawyers in private practice (or sitting on lower courts or working in district attorney's offices) constitute the bulk of the pool. If you are young, female, a member of a racial minority, are of the wrong political party, or presumably have few contacts within the organized legal-political community in your state, the chances of making it to the trial bench are slight. Considering the background characteristics of state judges in general, it is hardly surprising that so many Americans feel a sense of alienation from legal institutions and processes. Both the formal and informal norms of judicial recruitment in the states are clearly slanted toward a professional-political elite; "have-not" interests are grossly underrepresented and can hardly fail to perceive this in contact with the legal system.

Since these judicial profile data were gathered, national concern has intensified for achieving a more representative state (and federal) judiciary. Depending on one's perspective, the most notable progress may be found in the area of gender, largely because of the increasing number of women lawyers. In 1970 one could identify only some 150 women attorneys serving on state, county, or municipal courts nationwide, whereas a count of women judges on the state bench in 1980 indicated that 46 were serving at the appellate level (12 on courts of last resort and 34 on intermediate appellate courts), with a balance of 545 found at the trial level. By 1991 these figures had jumped to a total of approximately 1900 women judges on all state courts.[75] As seen in Table 5–5, although the rapid increases in the percentage of women attorneys is the direct feeder for larger percentages of women judges on state courts, the latter continues to considerably lag the former. Even so, by 1991 both the total number and the percentage of women state judges stood as impressive testimony to the celebrated gender shift in the bar that had begun in the 1970s (see Chapter 7).[76]

---

[74]Ryan et al., *American Trial Judges,* 125–26.

[75]One should read figures on women, Black, and Hispanic judges with some caution. Sources seldom specify how the count was made, and data published in one source seldom agree with that found in another. For early (1970, 1977) figures on women judges, see Martha Gossblat and Bette H. Sikes, eds., *Women Lawyers: Supplemental Data to the 1971 Lawyer Statistical Report* (Chicago: American Bar Foundation, 1973); Table 18; Cook, "Women Judges"; and *Judicature* 65, No. 6, especially Larry Berkson, "Women on the Bench: A Brief History": 289–93.

[76]Basic data pointing to the explosion in the number of women law students and bar admittees may be found in Barbara A. Curran, "American Lawyers in the 1980's: A Profession in Transition," *Law and Society Review* 20, No. 1 (1986): 19–52, along with the American Bar Foundation statistical reports of 1980, 1985, 1988, and 1992 cited in Ch. 7.

Table 5–4   Immediate Prior Occupation of Trial Judges

	Percentage	No.
Private legal practice	53.8	1,616
Lower court judges	24.0	720
District attorney's office	10.1	303
Federal or local government lawyer	2.5	76
Other public official	8.9	268
Other	.7	22
	100.0	3,005

Source: John Paul Ryan et al., *American Trial Judges: Their Work Styles and Performance* (New York: Free Press, 1980), 125.

As for increased racial minority representation on state courts, progress has been, in some respects, less impressive. The American Judicature Society's survey of state judges in late 1971 and early 1972 indicated that there were but 255 Blacks on the state bench (including auxiliary or part-time judges), or about 1.3 percent of all such state judges. Of these, 86 percent sat on trial courts, with only token representation on state appellate bodies. By 1986, the next time that such statistics became available, a considerable increase had taken place in the numbers and percentages of Black judges serving at the state level; and by 1991, those numbers had again increased, though much less impressively (Table 5–6). Hence, by 1991, there was a total of 822 Black judges on state courts at all levels, though again the vast majority (nearly 94 percent) served at the trial level, including quasi-judicial positions.[77]

Data on the numbers of Hispanic state judges have been more difficult to obtain. Still, the Fund for Modern Courts and the Hispanic National Bar Association have published figures for 1985 and 1992 respectively, as presented in Table 5–7. Examining the seven states with the largest percentage of Hispanic population, we see in Table 5–8 that New Mexico is well ahead of all other states in its willingness to place Hispanics on the bench. Not only does that state have the largest percentage of Hispanic population, but it also leads all other states in the representation of its Hispanic citizens on state courts.[78]

A number of factors have been cited as possible explanations for the small number of Blacks and Hispanics on state courts, but undoubtedly the most immediate cause is the small percentage of these minorities in the practice of law, that figure now running only about 3.3 percent for Blacks and no more than 2.0 percent, perhaps less, for Hispanics. Inasmuch as the national percentage of Black and Hispanic state judges seems to approximate their national percentages in the bar, it might be argued that their judicial representation is currently running somewhat ahead of gender representation on the bench, at least as measured by this criterion.

---

[77]The best single source for the number of Black judges is Joint Center for Political and Economic Studies and the Judicial Council of the National Bar Association, *Elected and Appointed Black Judges in the United States, 1991* (Washington: Joint Center for Political and Economic Studies, 1991). On pp. 5–7 of this report may be found a useful quantitative summary of the changes in the numbers of Black judges in federal and state courts from 1986 to 1991.

[78]The same is true of Hispanics in the New Mexico legislature. See F. Chris Garcia, Christine Marie Sierra and Margaret Maier Murdock, "The Politics of Women and Ethnic Minorities," in Clive S. Thomas, ed., *Politics and Public Policy in the Contemporary American West.* (Albuquerque: University of New Mexico Press, 1991), 216.

Table 5–5   Women Judges on State Courts, 1977–1991

Year	Courts of Last Resort	Inter-mediate Appellate Courts	General Trial Courts	Courts of Limited Jurisdic-tion[a]	Totals	Percent All State Judges[b]	Percent of Women in the Bar
1977	9	18	130	317	474	2.6	7.0 (est)
1980	12	34	195	350	591	2.9	8.1
1985	23	46	426	377	872	5.7	13.1
1991[c]	35	71	932	874	1912	9.7	20.0 (est)

[a]These figures must be regarded as estimates and are known to be understated.

[b]Courts of Limited Jurisdiction are deleted from this computation because of the uncertainty of the data.

[c]By January 1996, the American Judicature Society had identified 227 women serving on state appellate courts. See "Women Judges Currently Serving on State Courts of Last Resort and Intermediate Appellate Courts, January, 1996" (Chicago: American Judicature Society, 1996).

Source: Beverly Blair Cook, "Women Judges: The End of Tokenism," in Winifred L. Hepperle and Laura Crites, eds., *Women in the Courts.* (Williamsburg, VA.: National Center for State Courts, 1978), 87–88; Larry C. Berkson and Donna Vandenberg, *National Roster of Women Judges* (Chicago: American Judicature Society, 1980); Fund for Modern Courts, *The Success of Women and Minorities in Achieving Judicial Office: The Selection Process* (New York: Fund for Modern Courts, 1985), and Marie T. Hough, Nancy L. Jellison, and James R. Hoffman, eds., *The American Bench: Judges of the Nation,* 6th ed., 1991–1992 (Sacramento, Ca.: Forster-Long, Inc., 1991). The methods used to count women judges from this volume are available from the author.

Data on the percentages of women in the bar were taken from the various lawyer statistical reports of the American Bar Foundation, while totals for state judges, on which column 7 percentages are based, were supplied by Brian Ostrom of the National Center for State Courts.

One must recall, however, that the large numbers of women lawyers are mostly young. In 1991 two-thirds were under 40 years of age; 93 percent were under 50.[79] This leaves a rather small base from which to select women judges and suggests that as measured by their percentage of the total bar, women of "judge-age"—presumably at least 40 years old—are well represented on state courts. Hence age may have replaced gender as the discriminatory factor. Taking a broader view, however, it is clear that the modest numbers of both women and racial minorities now seated on state courts is the product of long years of social discrimination against these groups, particularly as reflected in historic attitudes and policies within the bar itself (see Chapter 7).

Another important ingredient in the long-standing underrepresentation of racial minorities on the state bench is the electoral mechanisms by which these judges are chosen. If one includes courts of limited jurisdiction, there are now 41 states that use elections (excluding "merit" plan retention elections) to select at least some of their judges.[80] A common practice is to elect judges at large in county or multicounty judicial districts where a

---

[79]Barbara A. Curran and Clara N. Carson, *The Lawyer Statistical Report: The U.S. Legal Profession in the 1990s* (Chicago: American Bar Foundation, 1994), 5.

[80]This is the figure reported by Linda Greenhouse in "Supreme Court Hears Arguments on Election of Judges" (*New York Times,* Apr. 23, 1991): A-12. A careful reading of the *Book of the States, 1994–95,* Table 4.4, and the descriptions of judicial selection provisions in *State Court Organization, 1993,* Tables 4 and 6, produces the same number. Hence, according to this tabulation, the nine states which elect no judges (excepting merit plan retention elections) as of mid-1994 were Alaska, Colorado, Hawaii, Iowa, Massachusetts, New Jersey, New Hampshire, Rhode Island, and Virginia.

Table 5–6   Black Judges on State Courts, 1971–1991

Year	Courts of Last Resort	Intermediate Appellate Courts	Trial Courts (inc. Quasi-Officers)	Total	Percent of all State Judges	Percent of Blacks in the Bar
1971	2	7	246	255	1.3	1.2
1986	11	28	675	714	3.8	3.8
1991*	19	34	769	822	2.8	3.4

*The American Judicature Society reported that as of January 1996, 81 African-Americans were serving on state appellate courts. See "African-American Judges Currently Serving on State Courts of Last Resort and Intermediate Appellate Courts, January, 1996" (Chicago: American Judicature Society, 1996).

Sources: "The Black Judge in America: A Statistical Profile," *Judicature* 57, No. 1 (June–July, 1973): 18–25; Barbara Luck Graham, "Judicial Recruitment and Racial Diversity on State Courts: An Overview," *Judicature* 74, No. 1 (June–July, 1990): 28–34: Ellen Joan Pollock and Stephen J. Adler, "Legal System Struggles to Reflect Diversity, But Progress Is Slow," *Wall Street Journal* (May 8, 1992): A-1, 6; Joint Center for Political and Economic Studies and The Judicial Council of the National Bar Association, *Elected and Appointed Black Judges in the United States, 1991* (Washington: Joint Center for Political and Economic Studies, 1991), 5–7.

majority of white voters can easily swamp the vote of racial minorities, even though the percentage of such minority voters may be quite large. The same result can be achieved by old-fashioned gerrymandering, namely drawing judicial voting-district lines in such a way as to slice up geographic concentrations of minority voters, thereby diluting their strength. Such practices have been common, though hardly limited, to Southern states.

In New York City, for example, 146 judges of the supreme court (the title of that state's general trial courts) are elected in the five boroughs of the city according to the distribution in Table 5–9. As seen, in each borough, including the combined boroughs of Brooklyn and Staten Island, the percentage of racial minority judges (African-American and Hispanic) does not even approximate the percentage of minority voters. Similarly, from the First Supreme Court District of Louisiana, consisting of the four parishes (counties) in and around New Orleans, two state supreme court justices are elected at large. No Black justice has ever won a seat from that district in its history, despite the fact that in Orleans Parish itself, well over half of the registered voters are Black. These Black voters are

Table 5–7   Hispanic Judges on State Courts, 1985, 1992

Year	Courts of Last Resort	Intermediate Appellate Courts	Trial Courts	Totals	Percent of all State Judges	Percent of Hispanics in the Bar
1985	3	10	142	155	1.2	1.7
1992	5	14	625	644	2.3	2.0 (est.)

Source: Fund for Modern Courts, *The Success of Women and Minorities in Achieving Judicial Office: The Selection Process* (New York: Fund for Modern Courts, 1985); Hispanic National Bar Association, "Nationwide Summary of Hispanics on the State Judiciary" (Melville, N.Y.: Hispanic National Bar Association, 1992). Percentages of Hispanics in the bar are drawn from various newspaper sources in the 1988–1990 period, all of which use the 1.7 percent figure.

Table 5–8   Hispanic State Judges in States with Largest Percent Hispanic Population, 1985, 1992

State	1985		1992	
	Percent of Hispanic Population	Percent of State Judges who are Hispanic	Percent of Hispanic Population	Percent of State Judges who are Hispanic
New Mexico	37.8	24	38.2	35.8
California	22.1	5	25.8	4.9
Texas	22.8	7.9	25.5	9.4
Arizona	16.8	6.8	18.8	12.1
Colorado	11.9	2.8	12.9	3.2
New York	10.6	1.5	12.3	.7
Florida	9.8	0	12.2	3.4

Sources: Fund for Modern Courts, *The Success of Women and Minorities in Achieving Judicial Office: The Selection Process.* New York: Fund for Modern Courts, 1985; Hispanic National Bar Association, "Nationwide Summary of Hispanics on the State Judiciary." Melville, N.Y.: Hispanic National Bar Association, 1992; and U.S., Bureau of the Census. 1990 Census Profile, "Race and Hispanic Origin," No. 2, June, 1991: 8.

easily counterbalanced by the white voting majorities in the remaining parishes. The same is true of Houston (Harris County), Texas, where the 20 percent Black population has been able to elect but three Black judges out of 59 judgeships in the district, or only 5 percent.[81]

In the Voting Rights Act of 1965, Congress broadly mandated the cessation of racially discriminatory schemes in voting, with a wide presumption that the language of this important Act applied to judicial elections.[82] However, the Supreme Court in *Mobile v. Bolden* 446 U.S. 55 (1980) held that only intentional discrimination was banned by the Act. In 1982, Congress reversed this interpretation by making it clear that proof of intent was not required to attack racial discrimination in voting arrangements. However, the now-famous Sec. 2 of the 1982 Amendments injected new language that raised the question of whether the Act now applied to judicial elections. The amendment states that whether a voting scheme is lawful is to be determined by "the totality of circumstances" as to whether minority voters are afforded "less opportunity than other members of the electorate to participate in the political process and to elect *representatives* of their choice" (emphasis added).[83]

---

[81]The Texas and Louisiana data are taken from *Chisom v. Roemer; U.S. v. Roemer* and *Houston Lawyers' Association v. Attorney-General and League of United Latin American Citizens, et. al., v. Attorney-General,* 111 S.Ct. 2345 (1991) at 2358 and 2379. On the New York malapportionment of judicial seats, see Ronald Smothers, "Challenges to Judicial Elections Revived" *New York Times* (June 22, 1991): 9; and Kevin Sack, "Panel Faults Method of Electing Justices," *New York Times* (Feb. 12, 1992): B-12-13.

[82]For an extensive analysis of the original Act in which the Supreme Court upheld its constitutionality, see *South Carolina v. Katzenbach,* 383 U.S. 301 (1966).

[83]*Chisom v. Roemer, et. al.,* at 2364. For useful background and broader-ranging analyses of these issues, see Judith Haydel, "Section 2 of the Voting Rights Act of 1965: A Challenge to State Judicial Election Systems," *Judicature* 73, No. 2 (Aug.–Sept., 1989): 68–73. An edited transcript of an AJS-sponsored panel on this topic in Denver in 1989 follows the Haydel article. See also Barbara Luck Graham, "Federal Court Policy-making and Political Equality: An Analysis of Judicial Redistricting," *Western Political Quarterly* 44, No. 1 (Mar. 1991): 101–117; and Richard Saks, "Redemption or Exemption? Racial Discrimination in Judicial Elections Under the Voting Rights Act," *Chicago-Kent Law Review* 66, No. 1 (Winter 1990): 245–98.

Table 5–9 Minority Judges in New York City, 1991

Borough	Number of Judges	Percent of Minority Voters	Percent of Minority Judges
Manhattan	38	51	26.5
Bronx	23	77	33
Queens	37	52	14.7
Brooklyn–Staten Island	48	54	14.9

Source: Ronald Sullivan, "Lawsuit Challenges Process for Election of Judges," *New York Times,* Feb. 19, 1992: C-14; and Kevin Sack, "Panel Faults Method of Electing Justices," *New York Times,* Feb. 12, 1992: B-12.

Whether the injection of the word *representative* precluded judges was answered by the Court in the twin rulings of *Chisom v. Roemer; U.S. v. Roemer* and *Houston Lawyers' Association v. Attorney-General; League of United Latin American Citizens et. al. v. Attorney-General,* 111 S.Ct. 2345, both decided June 20, 1991. In these landmark decisions, Justice Stevens wrote for the Court in making clear that the Voting Rights Act, as amended, did indeed apply to judicial elections. Reasoned Stevens;

> If executive officers, such as prosecutors, sheriffs, state attorneys general, and state treasures, can be considered "representatives" simply because they are chosen by popular election, then the same reasoning should apply to elected judges. . . .
> It is difficult to believe that Congress, in an express effort to broaden the protection afforded by the Voting Rights Act, withdrew, without comment, an important category of elections from . . . protection. Today we reject such an anomalous view and hold that state judicial elections are included within the ambit of Sec. 2 as amended.[84]

The opinion has been hailed as the *Brown v. Board of Education* and/or *Baker v. Carr* of judicial elections, so potentially important is the doctrine for improving racial minority representation on state courts. Since the decision, litigation has sprung up, or has been revived, in over a dozen states, including New York, the test states of Texas and Louisiana, Alabama, Florida, Tennessee, Arkansas, Georgia, Illinois, Ohio, and others. Not only are straight elective systems under legal attack, but also merit plans are being hauled into court as embodying selection commissions that are allegedly racially discriminatory.[85] Ironically, it is possible that such legal assaults on partisan or nonpartisan electoral districting arrangements could persuade state officials to switch to "merit" plans. Such was the case in Georgia in 1992, where an out-of-court settlement of *Chisom*-based litigation resulted in the

[84] *Chisom v. Roemer,* at 2366, 2368.
[85] For developments subsequent to the *Chisom* ruling, see Nancy J. Smith and Julie Garmel, "Judicial Election and Selection Procedures Challenged Under the Voting Rights Act," *Judicature* 76, No. 3 (Oct.–Nov., 1992): 154–156; Brenda Wright, "The Bench and the Ballot: Applying the Protections of the Voting Rights Act to Judicial Elections," *Florida State University Law Review* 19, No. 3 (Winter 1992): 669–91; and Anthony Champagne and Judith Haydel, eds., *Judicial Reform in the States* (Lanham, Maryland: University Press of America, 1993). This book covers judicial reform (mostly the recent politics of judicial selection) in North Carolina, Ohio, Louisiana, Texas, Pennsylvania, California, and Washington. Finally, see Ann M. Scruggs, Jean-Claude Mazzola, and Mary E. Zaug, "Recent Voting Rights Act Challenges in Judicial Elections, *Judicature* 79, No. 1 (July–August 1995): 34–41. In this piece, challenges to state judicial electoral procedures in fifteen states are discussed: Alabama, Arkansas, California, Florida, Georgia, Indiana, Mississippi, Missouri, New Mexico, New York, Ohio, Oklahoma, Tennessee, Texas, and Wisconsin.

adoption of a "merit" selection system, though with special provisions for initial increases in the number of Black judges selected for general trial courts.[86]

No sooner had the potential of *Chisholm et al.* been presented to hopeful Black and Hispanic judicial candidates, however (Arkansas, for example),[87] than the Supreme Court began to question whether, and if so how and to what extent, race could be a constitutionally acceptable basis for drawing electoral districts. In the lead case of *Shaw v. Reno,* 509 U.S. 630 (1993), the Court, speaking through Justice O'Connor, held that legislative apportionment schemes producing "bizarre" shaped districts, apparently using race as the guiding factor, could be challenged on Equal Protection grounds.

In 1995 and 1996 the Court tightened and somewhat clarified its *Shaw* holding. In *Miller v. Johnson,* 63 LW 4726 (1995), Justice Kennedy spoke for the Court in a 5–4 ruling, maintaining that the Georgia legislature had unconstitutionally used race as the predominant factor in the creation of its Eleventh Congressional District. Moreover, in twin rulings in 1996, one from Texas, the other from North Carolina, the Court continued its scrutiny of alleged racial gerrymandering of legislative districts. In the key case from Texas, *Bush v. Vera,* 64 LW 4726, the Court invalidated three congressional districting schemes on grounds that the apportionment was subject to the "strict scrutiny" set forth in the *Miller* ruling. While the districts were reapportioned on the basis of many factors, the fatal flaw, according to Justice O'Connor, was that race was seen as predominating. And in *Shaw v. Hunt,* 64 LW 4437, in an extension of the *Shaw v. Reno* case, the Court, through Chief Justice Rehnquist, again stuck to its "strict scrutiny" test in determining that the state's reapportionment of its Congressional District 12 was not narrowly tailored so as to serve a "compelling state interest," but rather was clearly drawn on racial grounds to create a Black congressional district and is thus in violation of the 14th Amendment's Equal Protection Clause.[88]

These rulings, though pertaining to legislative apportionment, cast into grave doubt the ability of state officials to redraw electoral district lines in such a way as to achieve greater representation of racial minorities on state courts, thus rendering empty the promise of *Chisholm* and related decisions. Still, the racial gerrymandering rulings from *Shaw, I* forward have hinged on 5–4 splits, which could of course be reversed should President Clinton appoint the next justice(s) to the Court.

A NOTE ON TENURE AND REMOVAL

Selecting judges is but one side of the coin of the politics of recruitment. The other side has to do with tenure, turnover, and removal. For reasons already explained, the tenure of

---

[86]See Steve Harvey and Rhonda Cook, "Accord on State Judges Settles Major Rights Case," *Atlanta Journal/Atlanta Constitution* (June 19, 1992): A-1. These and related materials were generously shared by Prof. Barbara Luck Graham of The University of Missouri-St. Louis.

[87]In Arkansas, where all of the state's 105 trial judges ran at large in expansive judicial districts, few Blacks were ever elected. In 1992, a federal district court, following *Chisholm* et. al., upheld a reapportionment plan with subdistricts, making it easier for Blacks to win. Now, however, on the strength of *Miller v. Johnson,* not to mention the 1996 reaffirmations, the redistricting is being challenged. The same "on again, off again" phenomenon is now under way in other states. See Ronald Smothers, "Arkansas Plan to Promote Election of Black Judges Brings a Familiar Challenge," *New York Times* (Apr. 8, 1996): A-8.

[88]These decisions are summarized in 65 LW 3080–3082, August 8, 1996. See also Linda Greenhouse, "High Court Voids Race-Based Plans for Redistricting," *New York Times* (June 14, 1996): A-1. The process continued into the fall of 1996. On the strength of the North Carolina and Texas opinions, a combined panel of federal district and appellate judges on Sept. 24, 1996, held several South Carolina legislative districts unconstitutional. See "9 Legislative Districts Ruled Unconstitutional by Judges," *New York Times* (Sept. 25, 1996): A-13.

most state judges, as with that of federal judges, is lengthy: life terms are virtually guaranteed under all existing selection plans. One result has been superannuated judges, especially at the highest appellate level where judging is often regarded as the capstone of a person's career.[89] As earlier noted, however, superannuation at the state level has been less a problem than in the federal judicial system, and this fact has been due in large part to state mandatory retirement systems. Over two-thirds of the states have such plans. State minimum ages for retirement range from 65 to 75, with the typical mandatory age set at 70. State judicial retirement plans are relatively generous, usually 50–80 percent of salary. Some states go a step further by actually reducing or eliminating these benefits for judges who refuse to retire by age 70.[90]

Retirement systems, regardless of how attractive, are not always effective in luring aging or incompetent judges off the bench, nor are they effective in meeting the more common problem of inappropriate, unethical, or outright corrupt behavior of sitting judges. From the beginning, state governments recognized this problem by providing mechanisms of removal, usually in their constitutions. Impeachment is the most frequent provision, though recall and/or concurrent resolution of the state legislature may also be found.[91] Such methods, however, are usually ineffective, both because they are cumbersome and time-consuming and because they are politically difficult to put into operation. One result has been a system of state courts that has, at times, suffered from the embarrassment of judges who are alcoholic, senile, corrupt, or simply ineffective. The following examples will illustrate the problem.

- The Chief Judge of New York's Court of Appeals was arrested on federal extortion charges in connection with a woman who had broken off an affair with him.[92]
- Three Miami, Florida, trial judges and one former judge were indicted for taking cash bribes in exchange for granting favors to fictitious drug dealers.[93]
- A New Mexico Magistrate (lowest state court) was convicted for multiple offenses of driving while intoxicated.[94]
- A New York trial judge, presiding over a sentencing hearing, opined that "I know that there is another nigger in the woodpile, I want that person out, is that clear?"[95]
- In a sting operation, a number of Chicago judges, lawyers, and police were caught in acts of mail fraud, tax violations, and racketeering by taking bribes to fix cases. Nine former or sitting judges were convicted.[96]

---

[89]The Canon data indicate an average age upon leaving the supreme court bench of seventy-two, with a range of forty-two to ninety-one. Canon reported that five supreme court justices had been appointed at or over the age of seventy, while several octogenarians could be found on supreme courts in the states. See Canon, "Characteristics and Career Patterns," 36–37.

The problem of superannuation of state judges is illustrated in the charges against Nevada Supreme Court Chief Justice John Mowbray. Fellow justices accused Mowbray of "diminished legal abilities," stemming in part from his glaucoma, which has rendered him nearly blind. See Sue Morrow, "A Row Among Nevada Justices Gets Bitter," *National Law Journal* (Feb. 17, 1992): 10.

[90]These retirement plans are summarized in Thomas Pyne, *Judicial Retirement Plans* (Chicago: American Judicature Society, 1984). Compulsory retirement of state judges was upheld by the Supreme Court in 1991 in *Gregory v. Ashcroft,* 111 S.Ct. 2395, as against the claim that it violates the federal Age Discrimination in Employment Act.

[91]See *Book of the States, 1994–95,* Table 4.5.

[92]Josh Barbanel, "Top Judge Quits New York Court over a Scandal," *New York Times* (Nov. 11, 1992): A-1.

[93]Mike Clary, "Miami Court Scandals Reveal Tarnish on the Scales of Justice," *Los Angeles Times* (May 18, 1992): A-5.

[94]Kathy Haq, "Judicial Panel Urges Magistrate's Suspension," *Albuquerque Journal* (Aug. 16, 1988): D-2.

[95]Yvette Begue and Candice Goldstein, "How Judges Get Into Trouble," *Judges' Journal* 26, No. 4 (Fall 1987): 11.

[96]Martha Middleton, "Chicago Courts Reel from Corruption Probe," *National Law Journal* (March 2, 1987): 1.

- A Minnesota judge admonished a woman attorney for not wearing a tie, calling her a "lawyerette." Years later, the same judge addressed a woman employee of the attorney-general's office as an "attorney-generalette."[97]
- A New Jersey judge had sexual relations with his secretary, and exchanged sexual-related gifts with her in chambers. He later fired her, and she brought suit for wrongful discharge.[98]
- A Mississippi trial judge collected $21,000 in criminal fines and in litigant trust funds, and then converted the money to his own use.[99]
- A Missouri circuit judge developed a relationship with a former go-go dancer who was in his court in a divorce proceeding. He wrote several letters to her, detailing how she could gain advantage in the matter of custody and child support.[100]
- A Texas trial judge was accused of improper off-bench remarks, such as "These two guys . . . wouldn't have been killed if they hadn't been cruising the streets picking up teenage boys. . . . I don't much care for queers. . . . I put prostitutes and gays at about the same level."[101]

In order to meet the need for more flexible disciplinary processes, the state of California in 1960 created an entity entitled the Commission on Judicial Performance. The Commission consists of 9 members—5 judges appointed by the state Supreme Court, 2 attorneys selected by the bar, and 2 laypersons chosen by the Governor. This body receives and reviews complaints against judges, and investigates, holds hearings, and recommends disciplinary action to the Supreme Court.[102] Since 1960, virtually all states have created similar bodies. Most states followed California's unitary arrangement whereby the commissions themselves are responsible for all steps in the process, from the filing of a complaint through the recommendation of final action. A few states have divided the investigatory and adjudicative function, and in three states a special court was created to make final disciplinary decisions.[103]

A new (1990) ABA Model Code of Judicial Conduct has been proffered as a guide for state disciplinary proceedings, and the bench and bar in most states have adopted the new Code, though at times in modified form. The revised rules update the old canons, particularly on such matters as membership in socially discriminatory private clubs, gender-neutral speech and behavior, confidentiality of judicial proceedings, disqualification for conflict of interest, and behavior in judicial campaigns and fund raising.[104]

Early experience with the California commission system pointed up basic problems with such disciplinary mechanisms—problems which have never been seriously addressed in most states. A principal shortcoming is that those most likely to be familiar

[97]Begue and Goldstein: 11.

[98]Begue and Goldstein: 12.

[99]Begue and Goldstein: 39.

[100]Charles R. Ashman, *The Finest Judges Money Can Buy* (Los Angeles: Nash Publishing, 1973), 120–21.

[101]Jeffrey M. Shaman, Steven Lubet, and James J. Alfini, *Judicial Conduct and Ethics* (Charlottesville, Va.: Michie Co., 1990), *1991 Supplement,* at 33.

[102]An early study of the California Commission is John H. Culver and Randal L. Cruikshanks, "Judicial Misconduct: Bench Behavior and the New Disciplinary Mechanisms," *State Court Journal* 2, No. 2 (Spring 1978): 3–6, 30–38.

[103]The structure and jurisdiction of these commissions is covered in Irene A. Tesitor and Dwight B. Sinks, *Judicial Conduct Organizations,* 2nd ed. (Chicago: American Judicature Society, 1980). Case law on judicial discipline is covered in the *Judicial Conduct Reporter* and Yvette Begue, ed., *Judicial Discipline and Disability Digest* (Chicago: American Judicature Society).

[104]See American Bar Association, *Model Code of Judicial Conduct* (Chicago: American Bar Association 1990); and Jeffrey M. Shaman, Steven Lubet, and James J. Alfini, "The 1990 Code of Judicial Conduct: An Overview," *Judicature* 74, No. 1 (June–July 1990): 21–27.

with errant judicial behavior—judges themselves—are the least likely to initiate complaints; it is the familiar problem of professionals closing ranks to protect their own. Attorneys are equally reluctant to bring charges of judicial misconduct, especially in situations where they may involve judges before whom they must appear. The result is simple cover-up of many, perhaps even most, instances of judicial misconduct. An anonymous example not only illustrates the point but also underscores the professionally and socially sanctioned practice of enabling alcoholics to continue down the deadly spiral of their disease:

> We all know he's on the bottle and the [chief court] administrator no longer assigns him any real cases. . . . The tragedy is that he was a great man and a very good judge before he turned to drink. . . . [N]o one wants to be . . . the mean bastard who went public with what we know. We . . . just cover for him and hope he will either lay off all the booze or resign.[105]

This leaves primarily the lay litigant to bring charges of improper conduct on the bench, the chief problem there being the inability of many such citizens to separate their disappointment with the outcome of the case from actual judicial misconduct. Nonetheless, thousands of such complaints are filed annually in the states. In 1987, for example, 5,827 complaints were brought against state judges. Ninety-two percent were dropped as frivolous or ill-based (the public, as here, is usually not told of the content of such complaints, only the number). However, over 450 cases were investigated, resulting in the censure of 126 judges in 27 states, with 21 of these judges being removed from office.[106] Frequently, investigation of charges of improper conduct leads to voluntary retirement, as was the case with 112 state judges in 1987. Even so, the closed-door approach to state judicial discipline, combined with the refusal of members of bench and bar to take a lead in rooting out behavior that they know to be improper, makes state judicial disciplinary processes themselves questionable.

By and large, the commission system now in existence may have the effect of protecting errant judges more than the often unsuspecting public. With notable exceptions, judges have little to fear from disciplinary procedures in most states. In Illinois, for example, judicial disciplinary figures for 1988–1989 show that of 155 complaints brought, in only 29 instances was there more than token investigation, and 148 of the 155 complaints were dismissed without formal adjudication. Only two cases led to public discipline of any sort.[107] As is the case in virtually all states, the public is never told of the disposition, or even of the existence, of the vast majority of complaints. In Connecticut, that state's legislature, searching for ways to save money, saw the judicial disciplinary board as a lost cause and stripped it of its budget. The council had censured only two judges since its creation in 1977 and recently had become the target of at least two federal lawsuits challenging its secret procedures and weak disciplinary decisions. Said one state senator, "there is probably

---

[105]Robert A. Carp and Ronald Stidham, *Judicial Process in America,* 3rd. ed. (Washington: Congressional Quarterly Press, 1996), 284. For a comparative study of judicial discipline, see Mary L. Volcansek, *Judicial Misconduct: A Cross-National Comparison* (Gainesville, Fla.: University of Florida Press, 1996). This study includes France, Italy, England, and the United States, with an extensive bibliography.

[106]See Anne Lawton, "AJS Surveys JCO Complaint Dispositions for 1987–88," *Judicial Conduct Reporter* 11 (Fall 1989): 1, 4.

[107]Benjamin K. Miller, "Assessing the Functions of Judicial Conduct Organizations," *Judicature* 75, No. 1 (June–July 1991): 19.

no better example of an inefficient, do-nothing program than the activities of the Judicial Review Council."[108]

FURTHER READING

Begue, Yvette, and Candice Goldstein. "How Judges Get Into Trouble." *The Judges Journal* 26, No. 4 (Fall 1987): 8–13, 37–41.

Canon, Bradley C. "The Impact of Formal Selection Processes on the Characteristics of Judges: Reconsidered." *Law and Society Review* 6, No. 4 (May 1972): 579–93.

Champagne, Anthony, and Judith Haydel, eds. *Judicial Reform in the States.* Lanham, Md.: University Press of America, 1993.

Dubois, Philip L. *From Ballot to Bench: Judicial Elections and the Quest for Accountability.* Austin: University of Texas Press, 1980.

———. "The Politics of Innovation in State Courts: The Merit Plan of Judicial Selection. *Publius* 20, No. 1 (Winter 1990): 23–42.

Fund for Modern Courts. *Success of Women and Minorities in Achieving Judicial Office: The Selection Process.* New York: Fund for Modern Courts, 1985.

Glick, Henry R., and Craig F. Emmert. "Stability and Change: Characteristics of Contemporary State Supreme Court Judges." *Judicature* 70, No. 2 (Aug.–Sept. 1986): 107–112.

Graham, Barbara Luck. "Judicial Recruitment and Racial Diversity on State Courts: An Overview. *Judicature* 74, No. 1 (June–July 1990): 28–34.

Hall, Kermit L. "Progressive Reform and the Decline of Democratic Accountability: The Popular Election of State Supreme Court Justices, 1850–1920." *American Bar Foundation Research Journal* 2, No. 2 (Spring 1984): 345–69.

Hall, William K., and Larry T. Aspin. "What Twenty Years of Judicial Retention Elections Have Told Us." *Judicature* 70, No. 6 (Apr.–May 1987): 340–47.

Haydel, Judith. "Section 2 of the Voting Rights Act of 1965: A Challenge to State Judicial Election Systems." *Judicature* 73, No. 2 (Aug.–Sept. 1989): 68–86, 118.

Haynes, Evan. *The Selection and Tenure of Judges.* New York: National Conference of Judicial Councils, 1944.

Lovrich, Nicholas P., and Charles H. Sheldon. "Is Voting for State Judges a Flight of Fancy or a Reflection of Policy and Value Preferences? *Justice System Journal* 16, No. 3 (1994): 57–71.

Roll, John M. "Merit Selection: The Arizona Experience." *Arizona State Law Journal* 22, No. 4 (Winter 1990): 837–94.

Ryan, John Paul. *American Trial Judges: Their Work Styles and Performance.* New York: Free Press, 1980.

Saks, Richard. "Redemption or Exemption? Racial Discrimination in Judicial Elections Under the Voting Rights Act." *Chicago–Kent Law Review* 66, No. 1 (Winter 1990): 245–98.

Sheldon, Charles H., and Nicholas P. Lovrich, Jr. "State Judicial Recruitment," in John B. Gates and Charles A. Johnson, eds., *The American Courts: A Critical Assessment.* Washington: Congressional Quarterly Press, 1991, 161–88.

Sheldon, Charles H., and Linda Maule, *Judicial Recruitment: Choosing Federal and State Judges.* Chicago: Nelson-Hall, forthcoming.

---

[108]Thomas D. Williams, "Connecticut First to Abolish Judge Panel," *National Law Journal* (Oct. 28, 1991): 6. The ineffectiveness of state judicial conduct commissions is also illustrated in the New York experience. See Joyce Purnick, "Low Priority for Judging of the Judges," *New York Times,* March 7, 1996: A-20.

Slotnick, Elliot E. "Review Essay on Judicial Recruitment and Selection," *Justice System Journal* 13, No. 1 (Spring 1988): 109–124.

United States, Bureau of Justice Statistics. *State Court Organization, 1993.* Washington: Bureau of Justice Statistics, 1995.

Watson, Richard A., and Rondal G. Downing. *The Politics of the Bench and the Bar.* New York: Wiley, 1969.

6

Federal Judicial Selection

A President who sets out to "pack" the Court seeks to appoint people to the Court who are sympathetic to his political or philosophical principles.
There is no reason in the world why a President should not do this.
—Chief Justice William H. Rehnquist,
Speech at the University of Minnesota School of Law

Any differences existing between the politics of state judicial selection and federal judicial selection are differences in form more than in substance, for the underlying forces of partisan politics dominate the selection process at both levels. In contrast to the variety of mechanisms employed by the states, the founding fathers struck a compromise between the sharply competing proposals of exclusive congressional selection and independent presidential selection by adopting a relatively simple method of choosing federal judges, that of appointment by the president, with the advice and consent of the Senate. The pertinent section of the Constitution reads,

> [The President] . . . shall have Power, by and with the Advice and Consent of the Senate, to . . . appoint Ambassadors, and other public Ministers and Consuls, Judges of the Supreme Court, and all other Officers of the United States, whose appointments are not herein otherwise provided for, and which shall be established by Law: but the Congress may by Law vest the Appointment of such inferior Officers, as they think proper, in the President alone, in the Courts of Law, or in the Heads of Departments. (Article II, Section 2)

Thus, the Constitution clarifies the manner of selecting Supreme Court justices, but leaves peculiarly unclear how other federal judges are to be chosen. Were federal judges to be considered "other Officers," or were they in the category of "inferior Officers"? If the latter, then presumably Congress could determine the method of their selection. From the outset, it was simply assumed that federal district and appellate judges were, indeed, "other Officers," and thus to be selected in the same manner as Supreme Court justices. Finally, in 1891, Congress formally specified presidential appointment of circuit judges; and in 1948, for the first time, Congress elaborated by providing that circuit and district judges were to be appointed by the president with the advice and consent of the Senate.[1]

Other than the two principles noted earlier—those of tenure during good behavior and the prohibition against the reduction of judges' salaries while in office—the Constitution contains little on the subject of the appointment and tenure of judges. Nothing whatever is said of qualifications for federal judicial office; there is not even the requirement that judges be lawyers.[2] Nevertheless, a number of informal qualifications have been created through custom and tradition over the past two hundred years. One of these is, obviously, that a person must be an attorney (though the meaning of that title has changed substantially over the years) to be appointed to the federal bench. Even so, it has often been suggested that nonlawyers could add an important dimension to judicial decision making, especially on the Supreme Court. The late Justice Hugo Black often advanced this idea. And Justice William O. Douglas, in his autobiography, *The Court Years: 1939–1975*, published after his death, recalls the following conversation that took place late in the presidency of Franklin D. Roosevelt:

> FDR did have a lingering grudge against the Court as an institution. He never really got over the defeat of his Court-packing plan. He mentioned it again when I proposed that the Court move to Denver. This time he asked why lawyers were so conservative, why they turned out to be stodgy judges. He mentioned no names, but he obviously had been disappointed at some of his own judicial appointees. I told him that there was nothing in the Constitution requiring him to appoint a lawyer to the Supreme Court.
>
> "What?" he exclaimed. "Are you serious?"
>
> I answered that I was.
>
> He lit a cigarette, leaned back and after a moment's silence said, "Let's find a good layman." He became expansive and enthusiastic and held forth at length, going over various names.
>
> "You'll have to pick a member of the Senate," I said. "The Senate will never reject a layman as a nominee who is one of their own."
>
> His face lit up and he said excitedly, "The next Justice will be Bob LaFollette." There was no vacancy then, and none occurred before FDR died. But a plan had been laid to shake the pillars of tradition and make the Establishment squirm by putting an outstanding, liberal layman on the Court.[3]

Thus, while the mechanics of federal judicial selection can be described briefly, the forces, influences, and traditions endemic to the process will require a more extended explanation. Although the Constitution, by presumptive interpretation, specifies one mechanism for the selection of all federal judges, political practice has dictated the evolution of two somewhat different processes, one for the selection of federal district judges and another for the selection of Supreme Court justices. The process of presidential nomination and Senate confirmation of judges of the United States Courts of Appeals as well as judges of the more specialized federal courts is something of a hybrid of these two more basic approaches. The differences among these federal selection processes, unlike those differences earlier noted between state and federal selection systems, and among the various state

---

[1]See Harold W. Chase, *Federal Judges: The Appointing Process* (Minneapolis: University of Minnesota Press, 1972), 4–5. An early account of the role of the Senate in the appointing process can be found in Joseph P. Harris, *The Advice and Consent of the Senate* (Berkeley: University of California Press, 1955).

[2]For a discussion of possible reasons for these constitutional omissions, see John R. Vile and Mario Perez-Reilly, "The U.S. Constitution and Judicial Qualifications: A Curious Omission," *Judicature* 74, No. 4 (Dec.–Jan. 1991): 198–202.

[3]William O. Douglas, *The Court Years: 1939–1975* (New York: Random House), 1980, 281.

mechanisms, point less to form than to content: the formal system of federal judicial selection looks the same for all federal judges, but the underlying influences at work—the informal norms involved—are somewhat different as between the selection of district judges and justices of the United States Supreme Court.

FEDERAL DISTRICT AND APPELLATE JUDGES: THE FORCE OF SENATORIAL PATRONAGE

So enamored are we with the upper court myth, particularly as reflected in the splendor of the United States Supreme Court and its justices, that scholarly research on judicial selection has been turned on its ear, so to speak. One result has been that our knowledge of processes and outcomes of recruitment to the United States Supreme Court is broad, comprehensive, and rich in detail, while available data on judicial selection of "inferior" federal judges are just now beginning to approach adequacy. Not until 1972 did anyone in the discipline of political science publish a careful and systematic study of the recruitment of federal judges below the Supreme Court.[4] Since then, we have made considerable though slow progress in filling gaps in our knowledge.

The process of selecting federal district judges is one of bargaining among key people: the president (or actually the attorney general and deputy attorney general, or alternately any other official the president might designate); the senators of the president's party from the state in which the vacancy occurs, along with the senators on the Senate Committee on the Judiciary; local and state political figures who have bargaining clout with the senators; members of the bar, both those representing local and state interests as well as members of the American Bar Association's Committee on the Federal Judiciary; and the FBI.

On the occasion or anticipation of a vacancy on a federal district court, the attorney general, usually through his deputy, undertakes a search for possible nominees. At this early stage, the senators of the president's party are usually brought into the process. They may have their own nominee or slate of nominees, or they may elect at this point to reserve judgment, preferring to react to the deputy attorney general's nominees. In any case, their role is crucial, some say determinative. Through the custom of senatorial courtesy, the relevant senators may exercise a virtual veto over the president's choice. The extent and nature of the exercise of this power varies considerably with the senator: some prefer wide consultation with state and local interests, giving those interests in effect the power of choice (in return, of course, for favors rendered); others jealously fight for this power to

---

[4]The study referred to is Chase, *Federal Judges.* Subsequent research on the process and outcomes of the selection of lower federal judges is presented in a wide variety of articles, essays, and book chapters as indicated in the sources cited below, but no recent comprehensive book-length study is available. Most recent work focuses on but one aspect of the process, or one presidential administration. For essays on the "state of the art" in this sub-subfield of judicial politics, see Elliot E. Slotnick, "Federal Judicial Recruitment and Selection Research: A Review Essay," *Judicature* 71, No. 6 (Apr.–May 1988): 317–24; and Sheldon Goldman, "Federal Judicial Recruitment," in John B. Gates and Charles A. Johnson, eds., *The American Courts: A Critical Assessment* (Washington: Congressional Quarterly Press, 1991), 189–210. See also David M. O'Brien, *Judicial Roulette: Report of the Twentieth Century Fund Task Force on Judicial Selection* (New York: Priority Press, 1988); and a useful overview much broader than its title would suggest by Walter F. Murphy, "Reagan's Judicial Strategy," in Larry Berman, *Looking Back on the Reagan Presidency* (Baltimore: Johns Hopkins University Press, 1990), 207–37, and the sources cited therein.

The reader will want to look for the arrival of Sheldon Goldman's *Picking Federal Judges: Lower Court Selection from Roosevelt to Reagan* (New Haven: Yale University Press, 1997, forthcoming), which should fill several gaps in the literature on the subject.

virtually dictate the choice of a particular nominee.[5] If political conflicts are on the horizon, it makes sense for all parties to seek compromise at an early stage. With both the president and the relevant senators having ultimate veto power over the nomination, it ill behooves either side to risk a long and drawn-out fight in the Senate.

No particular sequence of events transpires in every case, but the usual process involves a letter from the attorney general to the president offering a short list of nominees. When the list has been narrowed to a somewhat smaller group of "finalists," the names are given to the FBI for loyalty-security checks. It is usually at this point that the Committee on the Federal Judiciary of the American Bar Association is given the list of nominees; then, after deliberating, the committee issues a rating of "well qualified," "qualified," or "not qualified" for each nominee.[6]

The name of the final nominee then goes to the Senate Judiciary Committee. The committee chair sends to both senators of the nominee's home state a "blue slip" asking for their views. Time was when the failure to return this critical blue slip was tantamount to a personal senatorial veto of the nominee. This custom changed with the chairmanship of Senator Edward Kennedy in 1979–1981. The current practice is that hearings and quite possibly a favorable committee vote may now follow a senator's negative blue slip, but the latter is still used as an important bargaining chip in the process. The success of a senator in blocking a nomination is now more likely to depend on his political muscle, the stance of the chair of the Senate Committee on the Judiciary and extant congressional-presidential relations.[7]

Following these steps, a subcommittee holds hearings, although they are often little more than perfunctory. In the early 1970s, John Duffner, executive assistant to the Deputy Attorney General under President Nixon, provided the following description of these proceedings:

> I can write the script for the hearing. I tell them [the judicial nominees] that the only senators likely to be there are Eastland, McClellan, and Hruska. I tell them to volunteer nothing, that it's like the Army—the longer you keep the first sergeant from knowing your last name, the better off you are. I suggest that they answer questions only and don't bring any witnesses.
>
> The committee will refer to the ABA report, and then they'll recognize the senator or whoever the man's sponsor is. Then Eastland asks if the biographical sketch they have is accurate, and he'll ask the nature of the man's practice—I tell them to hold it down to a minute and emphasize their trial experience. Then McClellan will give a lecture about how judges have to think of protecting society as well as the individual. I tell them to listen politely and to watch for a question at the end of it, but don't volunteer anything unless there's a question. Hruska will ask if he's an officer or director in a profit-making corporation and point out that he's supposed to resign if he is.
>
> Then Eastland will ask if the candidate has anything to say. I suggest that they say thanks and that they'll do their best. The senators get impatient if a man brings his family and friends along—one did one time and Eastland got irritated. They don't go into the judge's philosophy. It's all over in about ten minutes.[8]

---

[5]For an example of a federal judge being handpicked by a senator, see the circumstances surrounding the selection of Judge Thomas Meskill. Sheldon Goldman and Thomas P. Jahnige, *The Federal Courts as a Political System*, 3rd ed. (New York: Harper & Row, 1985), 44–45.

[6]The standard study of the role of the ABA in the selection of federal judges is Joel B. Grossman, *Lawyers and Judges: The ABA and the Politics of Judicial Selection* (New York: Wiley, 1965). See also Elliot E. Slotnick, "The ABA Standing Committee on the Federal Judiciary: A Contemporary Assessment," *Judicature* 66, Nos. 8 and 9 (Mar. and Apr. 1983): 348–62 and 385–93. The official ABA document describing the composition and work of their 15-member committee is American Bar Association, *Standing Committee on the Federal Judiciary: What It Is and How It Works* (Chicago: American Bar Association, 1991).

[7]O'Brien, *Judicial Roulette,* 71–72.

[8]Donald Dale Jackson, *Judges* (New York: Atheneum, 1974), 260.

Confirmation hearings have changed little since the 1970s. Thus, following President Clinton's nominations of Martha Vazquez to the Federal District Court for New Mexico, the proceedings on September 23, 1993, were similarly lacking in drama. Vazquez, appearing before the subcommittee with three other Clinton nominees, was questioned briefly by Senator Dianne Feinstein (D-Cal) about the use of cameras in the courtroom and about her views on limiting habeas corpus appeals. Senator Orrin Hatch (R-Utah) extracted a promise from the candidate that she would adhere to Supreme Court and Courts of Appeals precedents in deciding cases. A few other questions were asked of the candidates, but other than preliminary courtesies, the proceedings for the four were over in about an hour or so.[9]

Given the prior agreements reached by the principal parties involved, there is seldom any hitch in the selection process from the subcommittee stage forward. The full committee endorses its subcommittee report, followed by a vote of the entire Senate. Certain nominees to the federal courts have met with a good deal more than perfunctory opposition (as explained later), but the long history of the Senate confirmation process has been one of general acquiescence. For example, in an early study of Senate confirmations between 1951 and 1962, Prof. Joel Grossman reported that some 98 percent of the President's nominees were approved by the committee, in most cases with little more than pro forma investigation.[10] Recent years have brought little change in this pattern. Thus, for the Reagan nominations of 1981–1988, the confirmation rate for federal district and appellate courts was about 97 percent. Indeed, it was not until mid-1986—over five and one-half years into the Reagan presidency—that the Senate Judiciary Committee showed any life at all by staging its first open resistance to a nomination. President Bush likewise experienced few outright defeats (actually, only one), although in anticipation of winning the White House in the 1992 election, senate Democrats were slow to take action on his nominations; and this, in combination with the slow pace of the Bush administration itself in filling vacancies, awarded President Clinton the fat prize of 109 vacancies on the federal district and appellate courts at the time he was sworn into office on January 20, 1993.[11]

The mechanics of the process for the selection of judges to the United States Courts of Appeals is essentially the same as for federal district judges with the important substantive difference that since appellate court appointments involve several states, senatorial courtesy is less efficacious, the preferences of the president thereby having relatively greater weight. Essentially the same consultative process takes place, but with the senators of the state represented by the departing appellate judge often claiming the new post as their own.

According to a study of 84 appellate judges sitting in the Kennedy and Johnson years, 70 percent hailed from the same state as their immediate predecessors.[12] Subsequent presi-

---

[9]Richard Parker, "Key Senator Backs Vasquez for Seat on Federal Bench," *Albuqurque Journal* (Sept. 24, 1993), D-3; phone interview with Judge Vazquez, Oct. 20, 1993.

[10]Grossman, *Lawyers and Judges,* 170. O'Brien, *Judicial Roulette,* Ch. 4, contains a useful discussion of the Senate's "rubber stamp" confirmation process.

[11]The record of the Bush administration in federal judicial appointments is described in some detail by Sheldon Goldman, "Bush's Judicial Legacy: The Final Imprint," *Judicature* 76, No. 6 (Apr.–May, 1993): 282–96. Some difficulties faced by the Clinton administration in obtaining Senate confirmation of judicial appointments are discussed in David M. O'Brien, "Clinton's Legal Policy and the Courts: Rising from Disarray or Turning Around and Around," in Colin Campbell and Bert A. Rockman, eds., *The Clinton Presidency: First Appraisals* (Chatham, N.J.: Chatham House, 1996), 126–62. See also Neil A. Lewis, "Partisan Gridlock Blocks Senate Confirmations of Federal Judges," *New York Times* (Nov. 30, 1995): A-13; and Neil A. Lewis, "Clinton Judicial Nominee Is Focus of G. O. P. Attack," *New York Times* (Apr. 9, 1996): A-12.

[12]Sheldon Goldman, "Judicial Appointments to the United States Courts of Appeals," *Wisconsin Law Review* 1967, No. 1 (Winter 1967): 202. A feel for the importance of state representation in the selection of federal appellate judges may be gleaned from the work of Elliot E. Slotnick, "Federal Appellate Judge Selection During the Carter Administration: Recruitment Changes and Unanswered Questions," *Justice System Journal* 6, No. 3 (Fall 1981): 283–304.

dential eras have witnessed similarly high percentages, because of the unwritten rule that each state shall have at least one representative on the federal appellate bench of the circuit in which the state is located. Thus, when a vacancy occurs, senators of the home state of the ex-judge have a very strong argument for a replacement from their state, particularly if a senator is of the same political party as the president. With the growth of the federal appellate bench, it is possible for states to have more than one representative on these courts; in addition, there may be a prior agreement among the competing senators for rotating these seats among the states, taking into consideration such factors as the relative population of the states, court caseloads, and other relevant factors. The overall result is that although senatorial courtesy, seen as a virtual veto over the choice of judges, is not in operation at the federal appellate level, senatorial consultation is still quite important in the process, again depending on the power of the individual senator and his or her relation with the White House.

As we have learned from our survey of state judicial recruitment, it is well to look beyond the formalities of the process to the actual forces and influences at work. Of prime importance to the student of politics are the factors that are associated with becoming a federal judge. What criteria do presidents, senators, fellow lawyers, citizens, and interest groups apply in the selection process? In a study of the recruitment of judges for the United States Courts of Appeals, J. Woodford Howard, Jr., reported that the judges themselves list four ingredients in the recipe for their appointment: political participation, professional competence, personal ambition, and luck.[13] Richardson and Vines, in their discussion of the politics of federal judicial recruitment, emphasized roughly parallel factors, especially partisan politics and the political significance of localism, along with professional training and experience.[14] A third view, that of Goldman and Jahnige, listed competence, party, and ideology as the three important factors in federal judicial selection.[15] Leaving aside random variables such as luck, the two common ingredients in these three formularizations are (1) politics, including ideological and geographic factors, and (2) professional competence.

Politics

If the three most important factors determining the value of real estate are location, location, and location, we might conclude from a study of federal judicial selection that the three most important ingredients in becoming a federal judge are party, party, and party. Presidents rarely cross party lines in selecting their nominees to the trial and intermediate appellate federal bench. In a study of appointments to these courts between 1884 and 1962 (the presidencies of Cleveland through Kennedy), it was found that an average of 93 percent of the judges were selected along partisan lines—that is, the judges were of the same party as the appointing president.[16] Partisanship would have been even higher in these appointments were it not for the Republican presidencies of Taft and Hoover. These two presidents were virtually forced into appointing at least some Southern Democrats, since

---

[13]J. Woodford Howard, Jr., *Courts of Appeals in the Federal Judicial System* (Princeton: Princeton University Press, 1981), 90.

[14]Richard J. Richardson and Kenneth N. Vines, *The Politics of Federal Courts* (Boston: Little, Brown, 1970), Ch. 4.

[15]Sheldon Goldman and Thomas P. Jahnige, *The Federal Courts as a Political System,* 3rd ed. (New York: Harper and Row, 1985), 43–49. An interesting historical study of the varying emphasis of these factors in different presidential administrations is Rayman L. Solomon, "The Politics of Appointment and the Federal Courts' Role in Regulating America: U.S. Courts of Appeals Judgeships from T. R. to F. D. R.," *ABF Research Journal* 1984, No. 2 (Spring 1984): 285–343.

[16]Richardson and Vines, *Politics of Federal Courts,* 68.

Table 6–1   Party Relevance and Lower Court Nominations, 1884–1992

President	Percentage of Nominations from Party of President
Cleveland	100
Harrison	90
McKinley	96
T. Roosevelt	97
Taft	82
Wilson	99
Harding	97
Coolidge	94
Hoover	86
F. Roosevelt	96
Truman	93
Eisenhower	95
Kennedy	93
Johnson	95
Nixon	93
Ford	86
Carter	92
Reagan	95
Bush	87

Sources: Evan A. Evans, "Political Influence in the Selection of Federal Judges," cited in Richard J. Richardson and Kenneth N. Vines, *The Politics of Federal Courts* (Boston: Little, Brown, 1970) (updated with Truman through Kennedy). For appointments of Johnson through Carter, see Sheldon Goldman, "Carter's Judicial Appointments: A Lasting Legacy," *Judicature* 64, No. 8 (Mar. 1981): 344–55. For the Reagan appointments, see Sheldon Goldman, "Reagan's Judicial Legacy: Completing the Puzzle and Summing Up," *Judicature* 72, No. 6 (Apr.–May 1989): Table 2 and p. 323; and for the Bush record see Sheldon Goldman, "Bush's Judicial Legacy: The Final Imprint," *Judicature* 76, No. 6 (Apr.–May, 1993): Tables 1 and 3. President Bush's non-Republican appointees were mostly political independents.

there were so few Southern Republicans available. For the last six presidencies—Johnson, Nixon, Ford, Carter, Reagan, and Bush—the percentages, which run roughly the same as those of their predecessors, are presented in Table 6–1.

These data tell only part of the story of partisanship, however. To be a party member is hardly enough. Aspirants to judicial office have again and again found that active, intelligent, persistent, and successful party service is what counts.[17] And it certainly helps to know one's senators personally (or better, the president himself), or to have worked actively for the election of these officials. But even this may not be enough. Beyond being a loyal party member, a person must be the "right kind" of party member. Liberal Democrats are hardly likely to select judicial nominees from the conservative wing of the party, and

---

[17]For example, Howard found that of the federal appellate judges he studied, over 70 percent had either been candidates for office or party activists at some point in their career prior to their appointment to the bench. See Howard, *Courts of Appeals,* 91.

likewise, conservatives look first to members of their own camp. Indeed, political ideology is probably more significant than either party label or partisan activism in the judicial selection process. Thus, with President Kennedy making the appointments, it became important to have a moderate to liberal coloration similar to that of the president.[18] Under Richard Nixon, it was essential to have a strong "law and order" orientation; otherwise, one was classified as "soft headed." As one Washington lawyer put it,

> You can't be a federal judge today . . . unless you believe the whole hardnose line. It's like getting ahead in the FBI—you have to be for the death penalty, you have to regard all the criminal decisions of the Warren Court as wrong. I've never seen such stereotypes. Any background of liberalism or orientation toward the Bill of Rights is a disqualifier. Or a philosophical kinship with Learned Hand, say, the idea that better one guilty man go free than an innocent man be hanged—if you feel that way, you don't make it.[19]

The Reagan administration provides the best example of the concern presidents have for choosing the "right kind" of judges. Perhaps no other president so carefully developed and managed the judicial selection process. Once the province of the deputy attorney general's office, the selection of judges was shifted almost entirely to the Office of Legal Policy. In addition, the post of Special Counsel for Judicial Selection was created in 1984, enhancing the administration's capacity to scrutinize potential nominees. Most significant, however, was the formation of the President's Committee on Federal Judicial Selection. Composed of high-ranking administration officials, the committee formalized White House control of the selection process, helping to ensure that the federal bench would reflect the political ideology of Ronald Reagan for many years to come. As one careful student of federal judicial selection wrote,

> Arguably, the Reagan administration . . . engaged in the most systematic judicial philosophical screening of judicial candidates ever seen in the nation's history, surpassing Franklin Roosevelt's administration.[20]

One dimension of political ideology of particular significance in federal judicial recruitment, especially at the district level, is the element of localism ("regionalism" at the appellate level). That is, it is not enough to be a loyal and successful party activist of the right stripe; it is also important to be identified with the values, the political and social culture of the relevant locale or region. As we saw in the politics of federal court structure, the local and regional pull—the centrifugal forces at work on the federal courts—are still quite strong, the tradition being that lower federal judges should, not unlike congressmen, represent local interests. "Regard for local representation is one of the most obstinate characteristics of American politics," argued Frankfurter and Landis in their classic work on American courts. This sentiment for localism was well expressed by Congressman John Sharp

---

[18]For an extended discussion of the criteria for judicial selection in the Kennedy presidency, see Chase, *Federal Judges,* 48–119.

[19]See Jackson, *Judges,* 270.

[20]Sheldon Goldman, "Reagan's Judicial Legacy: Completing the Puzzle and Summing Up," *Judicature* 72, No. 6 (Apr.–May 1989): 319. President Reagan's judicial appointments have become the subject of more commentary than perhaps that of any other president since Franklin D. Roosevelt. For example, see Murphy, "Reagan's Judicial Strategy"; Sheldon Goldman, "Reaganizing the Judiciary: The First Term Appointments," *Judicature* 68, Nos. 9–10 (Apr.–May 1985): 313–29; Timothy B. Tomasi and Jess A. Velona, "All the President's Men? A Study of Ronald Reagan's Appointments to the U.S. Courts of Appeals," *Columbia Law Review,* 87, No. 4 (May 1987): 766–93; and Herman Schwartz, *Packing the Courts: The Conservative Campaign to Rewrite the Constitution* (New York: Scribner's, 1988).

Williams of Mississippi, who, in opposition to a congressional proposal of 1921–1922 to assign federal judges with lighter caseloads to busier districts in other states, said,

> I'm frankly opposed to a perambulatory judiciary, to carpetbagging Nebraska with a Louisianian, certainly to carpetbagging Mississippi or Louisiana with somebody north of Mason and Dixon's Line, which will almost certainly happen if this bill passes.[21]

That localism is still an important factor in the selection of federal district judges is clear in that well over half such posts are customarily filled by men and women who either were born in the state of the court on which they sit or were educated at law schools in the state, or both.[22] As already noted, the importance of local representation is also felt in the selection of judges to the United States Courts of Appeals. In such selection decisions, writes Goldman, "Justice officials readily acknowledge in interviews that state claims for 'representation' are usually accepted.[23] Politics, then, whether defined in terms of ideology, geography, or party label, has always been, and continues to be, the prime qualification for selection to the federal bench.[24]

Professional Competence

Seldom do political considerations weigh so heavily in judicial selection that professional competence is entirely ignored. Party and group interests can ill afford the political costs of selecting judges who turn out to be professionally embarrassing. On the contrary, all political decision makers actively seek candidates who have legal as well as political qualifications.

A definition of "legally qualified" would include a good many factors, but ultimately it is the opinion of a candidate's legal colleagues that weighs most heavily. An operational definition—that is, the actual professional profile of the candidates selected—gives us the best indication of the professional factors that are most highly valued by those making this judgement. The possession of a law degree has become, of course, fundamental; but the quality of legal education varies. Federal judges, particularly those at the appellate and Supreme Court level, tend to be disproportionately drawn from the ranks of lawyers who were fortunate enough (or had the foresight) to have attended one of the *prestige* law schools.

Some 40 percent of the judges of the United States Courts of Appeals studied by Howard in 1969–1971 received their law degrees from Harvard, Yale, or Columbia, whereas another 15 percent were educated at the so-called national law schools of Cornell, George Washington, Georgetown, Michigan, and Northwestern. In the Second Circuit alone, 9 of the 10 judges had Harvard, Columbia, or Yale law degrees.[25]

Moving to more recent years, an examination of the total field of Courts of Appeals judges selected by Presidents Reagan and Bush in the 1981–1992 period reveals that of 115 selectees, 29, or 25 percent, carried Ivy League law school banners. If one includes the non–Ivy League but "near-prestige" national law schools such as Michigan, New York Uni-

---

[21]Felix Frankfurter and James M. Landis, *The Business of the Supreme Court* (New York: Macmillan, 1927), 239. Also see Goldman, "Reaganizing the Judiciary," 315.

[22]See Richardson and Vines, *Politics of Federal Courts,* 72.

[23]Goldman, "Judicial Appointments," 201.

[24]One view of federal judicial appointments divides political factors into the president's *policy agenda* and his *partisan agenda*. See Sheldon Goldman, "Judicial Appointments and the Presidential Agenda," in Paul Brace, Christine B. Harrington, and Gary King, *The Presidency in American Politics* (New York: New York University Press, 1989), 19–47.

[25]Howard, *Courts of Appeal,* 93–94.

versity, Texas, Northwestern, Stanford, and Virginia, the figure rises to 45 percent for these two presidents, each weighing in with almost exactly the same percentage.[26]

It is true that for the federal trial courts, prestige legal education is eclipsed by the predominance of state law schools (again, the intrusion of localism); however, even at this level, one finds prestige and near-prestige law school graduates represented far out of proportion to their numbers, the proportion of such appointees in the twelve years of the Reagan and Bush presidencies being nearly one-third. Considering Ivy League legal education alone, the average of such appointees to federal district courts through the six presidencies of Johnson through Bush was about 17 percent, this figure rising to an average of about 30 percent for Courts of Appeals appointees for these six presidents.[27]

In addition to legal education, other aspects of a candidate's career path are also pertinent to the determination of legal qualifications for judicial office. Of particular interest is prior experience, either as a judge, a prosecutor, or another significant functionary in the judicial process. Again relying on Goldman's research:

> Since 1963, through five administrations (Johnson, Nixon, Ford, Carter, and Reagan through 1982), less than one-third of the district judge appointees had neither judicial nor prosecutorial experience (federal, state, or local) in their career profiles. At the appeals level, only about one-fourth of the appointees had neither judicial nor prosecutorial experience. By contrast, about 60 percent had judicial experience and close to 40 percent (including some with judicial experience) had prosecutorial experience.[28]

As it turned out, President Reagan's overall record of prior judicial experience for his trial court nominees was almost identical to that of President Carter's, and Bush's record in this regard is a carbon copy of his presidential predecessor: exactly 46.6 percent of both the Reagan and the Bush trial court appointees had prior judicial experience. For Courts of Appeals nominees, the figures for Presidents Bush and Reagan were also similar; only about a third of their appointees had neither judicial nor prosecutorial experience, a pattern not radically dissimilar from that of most recent presidents (Tables 6–2 and 6–3).

Perhaps the most frequently cited indicator of professional qualifications is the rating given each nominee by the Committee on the Federal Judiciary of the American Bar Association. These ratings for the nominees of the last four presidents are shown in Tables 6–2 and 6–3. As the data indicate, although presidents by no means limit their selections to "well-qualified" candidates, at least by ABA standards, neither are they likely to select candidates who are rated "not qualified."[29] Out of 555 federal district judges selected by the four presidents prior to Ronald Reagan, only six nominees were rated by the ABA as not qualified (three of Carter's nominees and three of Johnson's nominees). Of 153 appellate judges selected by these four presidents—Carter, Ford, Nixon, and Johnson—only one judge was ultimately selected who was rated "not qualified" by the American Bar Association, that one being nominated by President Johnson.

During the Reagan and Bush presidencies, *no one* was placed on the federal bench who was rated "not qualified" by the American Bar Association, and both administrations turned in exceptionally strong records of appointing federal judges with the highest or sec-

---

[26]These data are taken from the two articles by Sheldon Goldman: "Reagan's Judicial Legacy," 325; and "Bush's Judicial Legacy: The Final Imprint," *Judicature* 76, No. 6 (Apr.–May 1993): 294.

[27]See Goldman, "Reagan's Judicial Legacy," 322; and "Bush's Judicial Legacy," 290.

[28]Goldman and Jahnige, *Federal Courts as a Political System,* 56.

[29]Early in the Bush administration, the bar dropped its "Exceptionally Well-qualified" rating, making it necessary to meld this category with the "Well Qualified" rating in Tables 6–2 and 6–3 for purposes of comparing presidential administrations.

ond highest ABA ratings.[30] Ironically, however, both these presidents placed a high percentage of judges on the bench whose ABA ratings were in the lowest ("qualified") category. Moreover, many of these judges, particularly in the Reagan administration, went on the bench with split votes, that is, with a minority of committee members ranking the candidate "not qualified." The willingness of presidents to accept less than the highest ABA-rated nominees reflects the dominance of party and ideology in the selection process. This situation was especially true in the Reagan, and to a lesser extent, the Bush administrations.

The Carter Reforms

Upon taking office, President Carter was determined to improve the process of federal judicial selection. His thinking was generally along the lines of the merit selection plan used in the states. On February 14, 1977, by Executive Order 11972, he announced the creation of the Circuit Court Nominating Commission.[31] The commission was divided into 13 panels, 1 for each judicial circuit (2 for the larger Fifth and Ninth Circuits). Once a vacancy occurred, the panel was to give public notice of the vacancy, then recruit and screen candidates, and ultimately submit its recommendation to the president. Although there was much ado regarding the selection of commissioners, most panels included a cross section of Americans—women, men, whites, and nonwhites, lawyers, nonlawyers, and so on. Nearly all panelists, however, were Democrats.[32]

The panels were given detailed instructions regarding criteria of selection. Summarized, they were as follows:

> Applicants must be members in good standing of at least one state bar or the District of Columbia bar, and must be in good standing in all other bars of which they are members. They must possess reputations for integrity and good character and be of sound health. They must have demonstrated outstanding legal ability and a commitment to equal justice under law. Candidates must possess a demeanor, character, and personality which indicate that they would exhibit a favorable judicial temperament if appointed to the bench. Additionally, when selecting the persons whose names will be sent to the President, a panel must consider whether the applicants' training, experience, or expertise will help to meet a particular need when a vacancy exists.[33]

Despite this heavy emphasis on professional merit, broadly defined, the criterion that ultimately became most important was that of affirmative action. As expressed by Michael J. Egan, associate attorney general, "The Carter administration is determined to broaden the bench and add a significant number of women and minorities . . . , the types that traditionally have not been on the bench."[34] This goal was repeated several times by the president

---

[30]During the Reagan administration, the ABA still used the "Exceptionally Well-qualified" category. The percentage of federal district judges selected by Reagan who ranked in the top two ABA categories was the highest of all administrations tabulated by Prof. Goldman, while the percentage of President Reagan's nominees to the Courts of Appeals who were ranked "Exceptionally Well-qualified" was the highest since the Johnson administration. See Goldman, "Reagan's Judicial Legacy," 322, 325.

[31]This was later superseded by Executive Order 12059 of May 11, 1978.

[32]Complete (one might say nearly exhaustive) data on the work of the commission may be found in Larry C. Berkson and Susan B. Carbon, *The United States Circuit Judge Nominating Commission: Its Members, Procedures and Candidates* (Chicago: American Judicature Society, 1980). The major findings of the Berkson and Carbon research are summarized in Larry C. Berkson, Susan B. Carbon, and Alan Neff, "A Study of the U.S. Circuit Judge Nominating Commission: Findings, Conclusions and Recommendations," *Judicature* 63, No. 3 (Sept. 1979): 105–29.

[33]Berkson and Carbon, *United States Circuit Judge Nominating Commission,* 24. For detailed criteria see 24–35.

[34]Berkson and Carbon, *United States Circuit Judge Nominating Commission,* 34.

Table 6–2 U.S. District Court Appointees Compared by Administration

	First Term Clinton % (N)	Bush % (N)	Reagan % (N)	Carter % (N)
Occupation				
Politics/government	10.7% (18)	10.8% (16)	13.4% (39)	5.0% (10)
Judiciary	44.4% (75)	41.9% (62)	36.9% (107)	44.6% (90)
Large law firm				
100+ members	8.3% (14)	10.8% (16)	6.2% (18)	2.0% (4)
50–99	5.3% (9)	7.4% (11)	4.8% (14)	6.0% (12)
25–49	3.6% (6)	7.4% (11)	6.9% (20)	6.0% (12)
Moderate size firm				
10–24 members	8.3% (14)	8.8% (13)	10.0% (29)	9.4% (19)
5–9	8.3% (14)	6.1% (9)	9.0% (26)	10.4% (21)
Small firm				
2–4	5.3% (9)	3.4% (5)	7.2% (21)	10.9% (22)
solo	2.4% (4)	1.4% (2)	2.8% (8)	2.5% (5)
Professor of law	2.4% (4)	0.7% (1)	2.1% (6)	3.0% (6)
Other	1.2% (2)	1.4% (2)	0.7% (2)	0.5% (1)
Experience				
Judicial	49.7% (84)	46.6% (69)	46.2% (134)	54.0% (109)
Prosecutorial	37.9% (64)	39.2% (58)	44.1% (128)	38.1% (77)
Neither	31.4% (53)	31.8% (47)	28.6% (83)	30.7% (62)
Undergraduate Education				
Public	44.4% (75)	44.6% (66)	36.6% (106)	56.4% (114)
Private	40.8% (69)	41.2% (61)	49.7% (144)	33.7% (68)
Ivy League	14.8% (25)	14.2% (21)	13.8% (40)	9.9% (20)
Law School Education				
Public	42.6% (72)	52.7% (78)	42.4% (123)	50.5% (102)
Private	37.3% (63)	33.1% (49)	45.9% (133)	32.7% (66)
Ivy League	20.1% (34)	14.2% (21)	11.7% (34)	16.8% (34)
Gender				
Male	69.8% (118)	80.4% (119)	91.7% (266)	85.6% (173)
Female	30.2% (51)	19.6% (29)	8.3% (24)	4.4% (29)
Ethnicity/Race				
White	72.2% (122)	89.2% (132)	92.4% (268)	78.7% (159)
African American	19.5% (33)	6.8% (10)	2.1% (6)	13.9% (28)
Hispanic	6.5% (11)	4.0% (6)	4.8% (14)	6.9% (14)
Asian	1.2% (2)	—	0.7% (2)	0.5% (1)
Native American	0.6% (1)	—	—	—
Percentage White Male	47.3% (80)	73.0% (108)	84.8% (246)	68.3% (138)
ABA Rating				
EWQ/WQ	63.9% (108)	57.4% (85)	53.5% (155)	51.0% (103)
Qualified	34.3% (58)	42.6% (63)	46.6% (135)	47.5% (96)
Not qualified	1.8% (3)	—	—	1.5% (3)
Political Identification				
Democrat	91.1% (154)	5.4% (8)	4.8% (14)	90.6% (183)
Republican	1.8% (3)	88.5% (131)	91.7% (266)	4.5% (9)
Other	0.6% (1)	—	—	—
None	6.5% (11)	6.1% (9)	3.4% (10)	5.0% (10)

Table 6–2   (*Continued*)

	First Term Clinton % (N)	Bush % (N)	Reagan % (N)	Carter % (N)
Past Party Activism	53.9% (91)	60.8% (90)	59.0% (171)	60.9% (123)
Net Worth				
Less than $200,000	17.2% (29)	10.1% (15)	17.6% (51)	35.8%* (53)
$200–499,999	22.5% (38)	31.1% (46)	37.6% (109)	41.2% (61)
$500–999,999	28.4% (48)	26.4% (39)	21.7% (63)	18.9% (28)
$1+ million	32.0% (54)	32.4% (48)	23.1% (67)	4.0% (6)
Average Age at Nomination	48.7	48.1	48.7	49.6
Total Number of Appointees	169	148	290	202

*These figures are for appointees confirmed by the 96th Congress for all but six Carter district court appointees (for whom no data were available).

Source: Sheldon Goldman and Elliot Slotnick, "Title," *Judicature,* Table 3, forthcoming.

himself. On the occasion of the signing of the Omnibus Judgeship Bill on October 20, 1978, for example, the president said, "This act provides a unique opportunity to redress . . . [a] disturbing feature of the federal judiciary: the almost complete absence of women or members of minority groups."[35]

The commission did its work in two phases: in the first round, from February 1977 to October 1978, the panels submitted the names of 74 candidates to fill 17 vacancies; in the second round, October 1978 to April 1979, they submitted 146 names for 38 vacancies—vacancies created by the Omnibus Judgeship Bill of 1978. At the urging of President Carter, similar, but of course voluntary, nominating commissions were created in 30 states to advise senators on the selection of district judges.[36]

The impact of the Carter reforms is difficult to assess. Certainly partisanship was not eliminated from judicial selection, but the federal practice of merit selection, even if by one president, established a precedent that could prove significant for the future. The work of the nominating commissions had the effect of considerably widening the recruitment net, turning up a much broader spectrum of candidates than had previously been available. As a result of the enactment of the Omnibus Judgeship Bill during his presidency, Carter, though denied the opportunity to name a Supreme Court justice, chose more federal district and appellate judges than had any previous president. He nominated 202 district judges and 56 judges of the United States Courts of Appeals. The impact of his emphasis on affirmative action, combined with the large number of judges he was able to name, is indicated by the following rather telling statistics:

> The number and proportions of women, black Americans, and Hispanic (or Spanish ancestry) Americans placed by Carter on the bench are an historic first and a dramatic contrast with previous presidents. . . . In total, President Carter appointed twenty-eight black Americans, twenty-nine women (including six black women), and fourteen of Hispanic origin (including one woman) to lifetime federal district court posts. By the end of the

[35]Berkson and Carbon, *United States Circuit Judge Nominating Commission,* 34.

[36]The work of these commissions is assessed in Alan Neff, *The United States District Judge Nominating Commissions: Their Members, Procedures and Candidates* (Chicago: American Judicature Society, 1981).

Table 6–3 U.S. Appeals Court Appointees Compared by Administration

	First Term Clinton % (N)	Bush % (N)	Reagan % (N)	Carter % (N)
Occupation				
Politics/government	3.4% (1)	10.8% (4)	6.4% (5)	5.4% (3)
Judiciary	58.6% (17)	59.5% (22)	55.1% (43)	46.4% (26)
Large law firm				
100+ members	13.8% (4)	8.1% (3)	5.1% (4)	1.8% (1)
50–99	—	8.1% (3)	2.6% (2)	5.4% (3)
25–49	3.4% (1)	—	6.4% (5)	3.6% (2)
Moderate size firm				
10–24 members	3.4% (1)	8.1% (3)	3.9% (3)	14.3% (8)
5–9	6.9% (2)	2.7% (1)	5.1% (4)	1.8% (1)
Small firm				
2–4	—	—	1.3% (1)	3.6% (2)
solo	—	—	—	1.8% (1)
Professor	10.3% (3)	2.7% (1)	12.8% (10)	14.3% (8)
Other	—	—	1.3% (1)	1.8% (1)
Experience				
Judicial	69.0% (20)	62.2% (23)	60.3% (47)	53.6% (30)
Prosecutorial	37.9% (11)	29.7% (11)	28.2% (22)	32.1% (18)
Neither	20.7% (6)	32.4% (12)	34.6% (27)	39.3% (22)
Undergraduate Education				
Public	51.7% (15)	29.7% (11)	24.4% (19)	30.4% (17)
Private	27.6% (8)	59.5% (22)	51.3% (40)	51.8% (29)
Ivy League	20.7% (6)	10.8% (4)	24.4% (19)	17.9% (10)
Law School Education				
Public	41.4% (12)	29.7% (11)	41.0% (32)	39.3% (22)
Private	31.0% (9)	40.5% (15)	35.9% (28)	19.6% (11)
Ivy League	27.6% (8)	29.7% (11)	23.1% (18)	41.1% (23)
Gender				
Male	69.0% (20)	81.1% (30)	94.9% (74)	80.4% (45)
Female	31.0% (9)	18.9% (7)	5.1% (4)	19.6% (11)
Ethnicity/Race				
White	72.4% (21)	89.2% (33)	97.4% (76)	78.6% (44)
African American	13.8% (4)	5.4% (2)	1.3% (1)	16.1% (9)
Hispanic	10.3% (3)	5.4% (2)	1.3% (1)	3.6% (2)
Asian	3.4% (1)	—	—	1.8% (1)
Percentage White Male	44.8% (13)	70.3% (26)	92.3% (72)	60.7% (34)
ABA Rating				
EWQ/WQ	82.8% (24)	64.9% (24)	59.0% (46)	75.0% (42)
Qualified	17.2% (5)	35.1% (13)	41.0% (32)	25.0% (14)
Political Identification				
Democrat	86.2% (25)	5.4% (2)	—	82.1% (46)
Republican	3.4% (1)	89.2% (33)	96.2% (75)	7.1% (4)
Other	—	—	1.3% (1)	—
None	10.3% (3)	5.4% (2)	2.6% (2)	10.7% (6)

Table 6–3   *(Continued)*

	First Term Clinton % (N)	Bush % (N)	Reagan % (N)	Carter % (N)
Past Party Activism	48.3% (14)	70.3% (26)	65.4% (51)	73.2% (41)
Net Worth				
Less than $200,000	6.9% (2)	5.4% (2)	15.6%* (12)	33.3%** (13)
$200–499,999	10.3% (3)	29.7% (11)	32.5% (25)	38.5% (15)
$500–999,999	44.8% (13)	21.6% (8)	33.8% (26)	17.9% (7)
$1+ million	37.9% (11)	43.2% (16)	18.2% (14)	10.3% (4)
Total Number of Appointees	29	37	78	56
Average Age at Nomination	51.3	48.7	50.0	51.8

*Net worth was unavailable for one appointee.

**Net worth only for Carter appointees confirmed by the 96th Congress with the exception of five appointees for whom net worth was unavailable.

Source: Sheldon Goldman and Elliot Slotnick, "Title," *Judicature*, Table 6, forthcoming,

Carter administration, the proportion of women judges on the federal bench had risen from one percent to close to seven percent, and for blacks from four percent to close to nine percent.[37]

President Carter thus appointed more blacks, more Hispanic Americans, and more women to the bench than had been chosen by all previous presidents combined![38]

A study of Carter's appointments to the district courts also reveals a strong emphasis on prior judicial experience. Of the four administrations—Johnson, Nixon, Ford, and Carter—Carter appointed the lowest percentage of district judges who had neither judicial nor prosecutorial experience. This was clearly a major step toward professionalizing the federal judiciary by promoting the most experienced state judges and federal magistrates. The combination of these innovations in procedures, affirmative action, and professionalization may, indeed, have constituted what Goldman called President Carter's major domestic achievement.[39]

THE REAGAN AND BUSH LEGACY

Upon relinquishing power on January 20, 1989, President Reagan had appointed a total of 372 federal appellate and trial judges. After subtracting the 18 appointments that were elevations from trial to appellate courts, the figure is reduced to 346, representing 47 percent of the then existing judgeships of Article III courts having general jurisdiction (including the Supreme Court).[40] In the four years of the Bush administration, an additional 148 trial and 37 appellate judges were chosen by a Republican president. Given the expansion by

---

[37]See Goldman, "Carter's Judicial Appointments," 349.

[38]See Stuart Taylor, Jr., "Carter Judge Selection Praised, But Critics Discern Partisanship," *New York Times,* (Oct. 3, 1980): A-1, A-20.

[39]Goldman, "Carter's Judicial Appointments," 349, 355.

[40]Goldman, "Reagan's Judicial Legacy," 318–19.

85 judgeships (74 trial and 11 appellate) via the Federal Judgeships Act of 1990, President Bush himself nominated a net total of some 15 percent of the newly expanded federal judiciary. When one considers the sheer numbers of Republican appointees in this era in combination with the heavy emphasis placed on conservative ideology in the selection process, the Reagan-Bush years represent the most far-reaching shift in the political orientation of the federal courts since the administration of Franklin D. Roosevelt.

As might be expected, President Reagan significantly altered the selection process instituted by Jimmy Carter. As previously discussed, the selection commission concept was replaced by a highly centralized, White House–directed effort, spearheaded by the President's Committee on Federal Judicial Selection. Indeed, with the appointment of Edwin Meese to the post of Attorney-General, it is arguable that the entire selection process was brought under direct executive control to an extent unknown in history.

In the main, President Bush continued Reagan's emphasis on careful, centralized screening and selection of candidates. Judicial selection under President Bush was centered in the office of the attorney-general rather than that of the deputy attorney general. The Justice Department's Office of Legal Policy of the Reagan years was discontinued, but the President's Committee on Federal Judicial Selection was retained, maintaining White House domination of the process.[41] Even so, the Bush administration stressed the importance of judicial selection somewhat less than it was stressed in the Reagan years, leading to increased delays in choosing judges and failure to capitalize on the 85-judge increase in federal judiciary. As a result, scores of nominations that might have been pushed through under George Bush were left hanging when his administration ended.

As for the characteristics of the judges selected under these two presidents, trends that stand out (in addition to those already discussed) seem to be (1) an inordinate emphasis on youth, (2) a small number of appointments from the academic community, (3) a tendency to draw from large law firms, (4) a perhaps unexpected emphasis on gender balance, and (5) for President Bush, a stronger than expected effort to select African Americans (again, see Tables 6–2 and 6–3). Overall, however, the outstanding feature of the judges selected by these two presidents was the political ideology of the people chosen. This factor is difficult to gauge and tabulate in graphic form. Nevertheless, research has rather convincingly shown that in a number of policy areas, these judicial selectees have moved the nation's judicial decisions in a decidedly conservative direction, which of course is making use of one of the benefits of winning the White House.[42]

The Advice and Consent of the Senate

Few presidents have completed their terms of office without major controversy in the game of judicial selection, and the Reagan and Bush administrations were no exceptions. In addition to the struggle over the Bork and Thomas nominations to the Supreme Court, discussed further on, lower court selection politics also brought frustration to the door of the White House for these two presidents.

---

[41]Goldman, "The Bush Imprint on the Judiciary: Carrying on the Tradition," *Judicature* 74, No. 6 (Apr.–May 1991): 296–98; and Goldman, "Bush's Judicial Legacy," 285.

[42]For example, see C. K. Rowland, Donald Songer, and Robert A. Carp, "Presidential Effects on Criminal Justice Policy in the Lower Federal Courts: The Reagan Judges," *Law and Society Review* 22, No. 1 (1988): 191–200. The impact of judicial selection on judicial policy-making is discussed more fully in Robert A. Carp and Ronald Stidham, *Judicial Process in America,* 3rd ed. (Washington: Congressional Quarterly Press, 1996, 262–274.

As if to underscore the perfunctory character of the Senate's role of "advice and consent," its judiciary committee approved 262 nominations to the federal district and appellate bench (plus one to the Supreme Court—Sandra Day O'Connor) before it turned down a Reagan choice. But finally, on May 8, 1986, by a tie vote of 9–9, the committee refused to recommend confirmation of Daniel A. Manion, a conservative Indiana lawyer, to take a seat on the United States Court of Appeals for the Seventh Circuit. The committee then voted 11–6 to send Manion's name to the floor without a recommendation. One month later, on June 5, the same committee rejected outright (10–8) the nomination of Jefferson Beauregard Sessions, III, a Mobile, Alabama, U.S. attorney, for a seat on the United States District Court in that state.[43]

These actions, especially that in the Manion case (the Sessions vote was accepted by the Reagan administration without a fight), served to renew the ongoing national debate on the right of the president to his choice of judges against the prerogative of the Senate to review and veto these selections. Both of these nominees appeared to moderate Republicans as well as to Democrats on the Senate Judiciary Committee as weak, if not embarrassing. Sessions's past statements on the subject of race (for example, he called the NAACP and the American Civil Liberties Union "un-American" and "communist-inspired") would seem to have placed him beyond the pale, rather in the category of G. Harrold Carswell (see later). Manion's nomination appeared to be especially weak on professional grounds, suggestive of the mediocrity with which Carswell was labeled. He had had no experience in federal court litigation, no prior judicial experience, and no record of scholarship whatever. Moreover, the briefs he submitted in support of his own confirmation were characterized as weak in spelling and grammar and poorly organized.[44]

Although the Sessions candidacy was quietly withdrawn, the Reagan administration decided to fight for the confirmation of Manion. Deans of more than thirty law schools as well as representatives of over fifty labor unions and allied organizations (e.g., the Leadership Conference on Civil Rights, the American Jewish Congress, and the National Organization for Women) wrote the Senate in opposition to the Manion confirmation. In response, President Reagan, in his weekly radio address of June 21, 1986, denounced the opposition to Manion as a "partisan use of the confirmation process." The president said his judicial appointees were people of "proven ability and the finest character," and he argued that the Senate "should consider only a nominee's qualifications and character, not his political views."[45] The notion that the president may employ political criteria for judicial selection, but the Senate may not, was widely criticized by the press and by senators opposed to Manion.

On June 26, 1986, in a rare parliamentary maneuver, the Senate approved the Manion nomination by a vote of 48–46, but Democratic Senator Robert Byrd switched his vote to favor the nomination in order to be able to move for reconsideration after the July 4 recess. The ploy did not succeed, however, for on July 23, 1986, the Senate, addressing the reconsideration of its earlier approval of Manion, voted 49–49 against, effectively reapproving the nomination. Vice president and Senate president pro tem George Bush cast the 50th

---

[43]See "Senate Judiciary Ties over Manion Nomination," *Congressional Quarterly Weekly Report* 44, No. 19 (May 10, 1986): 1073; and Lena Williams, "Senate Panel Turns Down Nominee" *New York Times* (June 6, 1986): 9. Of the Sessions vote, Williams notes that this was the first judicial nominee in six years to be rejected by the committee, and only the second in the last 48 years!

[44]"Senate Confirms Texas Judge by Close Vote," *Congressional Quarterly Weekly Report* 44, No. 12 (Mar. 22, 1986): 670. See also Philip Shenon, "Law Deans Oppose Naming of Judge" *New York Times* (June 24, 1986): 1.

[45]Bernard Weintraub, "Reagan Defends His Nominations to Federal Bench," *New York Times* (June 22, 1986): 1.

vote against reconsideration, although it was neither needed nor valid, since under Senate rules, a motion to reconsider fails unless it has a majority vote.[46] The vote could not have been closer, but in the end the White House was able to win approval of a judicial nominee considered weak even by some of his supporters.

The Manion and Sessions cases illustrate a number of points concerning the process of federal judicial selection: (1) the intensely political nature of the process, (2) the continued use of euphemisms to cloak the raw policy preferences on all sides of the struggle, (3) the deep concern of presidents to appoint the "right" judges in order to extend their political influence beyond their term of office, and (4) the informal norm that although there is a line beyond which the president may not go in selecting judges, his or her choices are normally honored in the Senate.

President Bush, too, experienced difficulty with some of his nominations, chief among these being his choice of Kenneth L. Ryskamp and Edward E. Carnes, both for the U.S. Court of Appeals for the Eleventh Circuit. Even after eight years of Republican rule, the Eleventh Circuit, covering the civil-rights-sensitive states of Florida, Alabama, and Georgia, still lacked a true Reagan majority, making nominees for that circuit especially controversial. Ryskamp, originally selected by President Reagan for U.S. District Court for the Southern District of Florida, was tapped by the Bush White House for elevation to the Eleventh Circuit on April 26, 1990. During the 101st Congress, the Senate Judiciary Committee took no action, and upon Ryskamp's renomination in the 102nd Congress, the Committee rejected the nomination by a vote of 8–6 and refused to send his name to the floor.

Civil rights groups were especially offended by Ryskamp because of his record of insensitivity to racial issues. In a case in which Blacks had been mauled by police dogs in a search, he intimated that such treatment was not so bad, considering that some societies cut off people's hands for wrongdoing. The judge wondered aloud from the bench whether it might be good for these suspects to "carry around a few scars" as a reminder of their offenses.[47] The judge was also heavily criticized for his membership in an all-white country club that had a clear history of discrimination against Blacks and Jews.

The Carnes case was resolved in favor of the administration, but not without considerable opposition. Carnes had long served as Alabama's Assistant Attorney-General with authority over death penalty cases. He rewrote that state's death penalty statute and fought for many years to increase the application of capital punishment in Alabama as well as nationally. Before the Senate Judiciary Committee, Carnes categorically denied that capital punishment is applied in a racially discriminatory manner, either in Alabama or nationally. Following a 10–4 approval by the Senate Judiciary committee, on September 9, 1992, the nominee was approved by the Senate 62–36 to take his seat on the Eleventh Circuit Court of Appeals. Civil rights groups saw the vote as a major defeat,

[46]The initial June 26 vote came as a surprise to Senate Democrats. Apparently, the White House was able to pressure (or buy) a vote or two in one case by promising support for a federal judicial nominee from the state of Washington it had previously opposed. This was enough to convince Senator Slade Gorton of that state to support Manion. For some reaction in Seattle to this "buying of judgeships," see "Appointing Judges," *Seattle Times* (July 8, 1986), A-7. In general, see "Controversy Surprises Manion, But Nominee Won't Withdraw," *Congressional Quarterly Weekly Report* 44, No. 27 (July 5, 1986): 1541–42; and two items by Philip Shenon in the *New York Times,* "Byrd Maneuver Stalls Selection of a U.S. Judge (June 27, 1986): 1; and "Senate, Ending Judicial Fight, Gives Manion Final Approval" (July 24, 1986): 1. Senator Slade Gorton's (R-Wash.) defeat for reelection in November 1986 has been attributed, at least in part, to the bad publicity surrounding this bit of presidential patronage.

[47]See Neil Lewis, "Committee Rejects Bush Nominee to Key Appellate Court in South," *New York Times* (Apr. 12, 1991): A-1; and Goldman, "Bush's Judicial Legacy," 291.

whereas the Bush administration needed the win as a symbol to its efforts to fill the federal judiciary with genuine conservative voices.[48]

As seen, outright Senate rejections of Reagan and Bush nominations to the lower federal courts were quite rare, but for President Bush the most significant loss, it might be argued, was his failure to move quickly in filling vacancies. This failure lead to 42 district and 10 appeals court nominees being left at the altar as Bush's administration came to a close. Because of the administration's anger over alleged leaks of FBI reports on judicial nominees, growing out of the fight over the Clarence Thomas nomination (to be discussed later), President Bush ordered that access to these sensitive reports by congressional staff be strictly limited. This action was taken by Senate Democrats as a major affront, and by the time that the matter was resolved, delays in scheduling confirmation hearings put pending nominations over into the presidential election year, traditionally a time when the confirmation process is slowed.[49] But whether one focuses on successful or unsuccessful presidential nominations to these courts, the underlying force of partisan politics clearly drives the process.

Gender and Race on Federal Courts

Considerations of race/ethnicity and gender are as much a part of judicial recruitment politics as are factors such as party, ideology, or professional merit. Indeed, these two variables are increasing in importance as women and racial/ethnic interest groups intensify their respective voices for a greater share of seats on our federal courts. Tables 6–2 and 6–3 reveal important differences in the preferences of recent presidents in this regard. Whereas President Carter broke all records up to that time in a successful effort to name more women as well as more racial minorities to the federal courts, President Reagan sharply reversed that policy, finding only seven blacks in all of his eight years in office worthy of elevation to the federal bench, representing but 1.9 percent of his federal constitutional court selections at the two lower levels. With the important exception of Sandra Day O'Connor to the Supreme Court, President Reagan's record of appointing women was also much less impressive than that of President Carter.

By the time President Bush began nominating federal judges, the number of women lawyers had increased significantly. Also, it became increasingly clear to Republicans, especially after the Clarence Thomas–Anita Hill fiasco, that there were strong political (electoral) reasons for finding more women for the federal bench. The result was that Bush's record on gender matched or exceeded that of President Carter (see Tables 6–4 and 6–5), although the Bush figures are tempered by the fact that there were many more eligible women lawyers in, say, 1990 than there were in 1978. The Bush record for African American appointees, however, is closer to that of the Reagan than of the Carter administration.

---

[48]"Senate Firmly Favors Carnes as New Appellate Judge," *Congressional Quarterly Weekly Report"* (Sept. 12, 1992): 2718–19.

[49]Goldman, "Bush's Judicial Legacy," 283–84. Even so, the Democratic-controlled Senate confirmed 66 Bush nominees in 1992, the year he sought reelection, whereas the Senate of the 104th Republican Congress confirmed only 17 of President Clinton's nominees in 1996. On confirmation delay generally, see Garland W. Allison, "Delay in Senate Confirmation of Federal Judicial Nominees," *Judicature* 80, No. 1 (July–Aug. 1996): 8–15.

For an excellent current analysis of the process of Senate conformations of judicial nominations, see Elliot E. Slotnick and Sheldon Goldman, "Congress and the Courts: A Case of Casting," in Herbert Weisberg and Samuel Patterson, eds., *Great Theater: the American Congress in Action* (Cambridge: Cambridge University Press, forthcoming, 1997). Judicial appointment prospects for the second Clinton term are discussed in Neil A. Lewis, "Clinton Has a Chance to Shape the Courts," *New York Times,* Feb. 9, 1997: 16.

Table 6–4   Race/Ethnic Federal Judicial Appointments by Administration, 1969–1996

	African Americans	Hispanic Americans	Asian Americans
Clinton (202) 1992–1996	38 (18.8%)	14 (6.9%)	3 (1.5%)
Bush (194) 1989–1992	11 (5.7%)	8 (4.1%)	1 (.5%)
Reagan (378) 1981–1988	7 (1.8%)	13 (3.4%)	2 (.5%)
Carter (258) 1977–1980	37 (14.3%)	16 (6.2%)	2 (.8%)
Ford (65) 1974–1976	3 (4.6%)	1 (1.5%)	2 (3.1%)
Nixon (227) 1969–1974	6 (2.7%)	2 (.9%)	1 (.4%)

Source: Alliance for Justice, Judicial Selection Project, *Annual Report, 1996* (Washington: Alliance for Justice, 1997): Table 3.

The overall result of twelve years of Republican control of the White House was an actual decline in the number of Blacks on the federal bench. Even with significant increases in judgeships, the number for *all* federal courts, including specialized and administrative tribunals dropped from 99 Black judges in 1986 to 73 in 1991, a 26 percent loss during a five-year period.[50] The liberal lobbying group Alliance for Justice marshaled figures depicting the record of the last five presidents on both race/ethnic appointees (Table 6–4 and 6–5) as well as gender (Tables 6–6 and 6–7). These data encompass Article III judges, including the Supreme Court. While the totals vary slightly from those of Professor Goldman (Tables 6–2 and 6–3), the latter tables enable the reader quickly to compare and contrast the "affirmative action" records of recent administrations.

THE CLINTON ADMINISTRATION, FIRST TERM

Thus far, discussion has centered on judicial appointments of recent presidents to federal district and appellate courts up through the Bush administration. But what direction has President Clinton taken as regards the variables we have been discussing? Data on Clinton's 202 federal judicial appointments (198 if one excludes Clinton appointees elevated from lower federal courts) are included in the foregoing tables. Two features of the Clinton selections stand out. First and perhaps foremost, he has "out Cartered" President Carter in his insistence on locating and appointing non-traditional federal judges, namely women and racial minorities. This trend was clear by mid-point in his first term and has continued throughout. As Professor Goldman put it in 1994,

---

[50]Joint Center for Political and Economic Studies and Judicial Council of the National Bar Association, *Elected and Appointed Black Judges in the United States, 1991* (Washington: Joint Center for Political and Economic Studies and the Judicial Council of the National Bar Association, 1991), 6.

Table 6–5 Minorities on the Federal Judiciary, 1976–1996

	1976 (534 seats)	1981 (686 seats)	1989 (752 seats)	1992 (837 seats)	1996 (837 seats)
African-Americans	18	49	46	43	72
Hispanic-Americans	5	19	31	35	36
Asian-Americans	3	4	5	6	5
Native-American	—	—	—	—	2

Source: Alliance for Justice, Judicial Selection Project, *Annual Report, 1996* (Washington: Alliance for Justice, 1997): Table 2.

The Clinton Administration is in the process of implementing a revolutionary change in the composition of the federal bench. More than three-fifths of all appointees through July 1, 1994, have been women and minorities. This pace of affirmative action judicial selection represents a sharp break from the past.[51]

Data found in the foregoing tables tell the story. Thus, nearly one-third of his appointments in 1992 through 1996 were women, the highest percentage ever reached by his predecessors being President Bush's 18.5 percent. Similarly, slightly over one-fourth of his selectees have been from the ranks of racial minorities, exceeding even that of President Carter.

Second, the Clinton Administration early determined that they would not seek to "out Reagan" President Reagan in his drive toward ideological purity on the federal bench. Thus, terms again and again used to describe Clinton nominees include "moderate," "cen-

Table 6–6 Gender Appointments to the Federal Bench by Administration, 1969–1996

	Women
Clinton (202) 1992–1996	63 (31.2%)
Bush (194) 1989–1992	36 (18.5%)
Reagan (378) 1981–1988	31 (8.2%)
Carter (258) 1977–1980	40 (15.5%)
Ford (65) 1974–1976	1 (1.5%)
Nixon (227) 1969–1974	1 (.4%)

Source: Alliance for Justice, Judicial Selection Project, *Annual Report, 1996* (Washington: Alliance for Justice, 1997): Table 3.

[51]Sheldon Goldman and Matthew D. Saronson, "Clinton's Nontraditional Judges: Creating a More Representative Bench," *Judicature* 78, No. 2 (Sept.–Oct. 1994): 68.

Table 6–7   Women on the Federal Judiciary, 1976–1996

Year	1976	1981	1989	1992	1996
Seats	534	686	754	837	837
Women	6 (1.1%)	45 (6.6%)	64 (8.5%)	90 (10.8%)	140 (16.7%)

Source: Alliance for Justice, Judicial Selection Project, early data supplied to author by George Kassoff, Director, Judicial Selection Project; Alliance for Justice, *Demographic Portrait of the Federal Judiciary, September 1, 1995* (Washington: Alliance for Justice, 1995); and Alliance for Justice, *Annual Report, 1996* (Washington: Alliance for Justice, 1997): Table 2.

trist," "mainstream" and the like. And this includes his two choices for the Supreme Court, discussed later.

Early in 1992 President Clinton, through Assistant Attorney General Eleanor D. Acheson, made it clear that intellectual ability, along with judicial temperament, were to be of prime importance in the selection process.[52] And the record to date, taken as a whole, tends to bear out this promise. The Clinton Administration has thus been able to achieve historic records in diversifying the federal courts without an apparent compromise of quality. As measured by ABA ratings, prior judicial experience, and education (the usual indicators of "quality"), the Clinton appointees measure up to, if they do not exceed, judges selected in prior administrations (see Tables 6–2 and 6–3). For example, the proportion of Clinton choices to district and appellate courts taken together who received the highest ABA rating is the largest since the ABA began rating federal judicial nominees. Other characteristics of Clinton's judicial appointees are set out in the foregoing tables.

THE SUPREME COURT

As noted, nominations to the Supreme Court are peculiarly the province of the president. This is not to say presidents are free to choose anyone they wish, for as with appointments to lower federal courts, there are traditions and informal constraints which limit any president in his or her choices. But within these parameters, the president, through his or her Supreme Court appointments, enjoys a unique opportunity to influence the course of judicial policy-making for the nation far beyond the term in office, and few chief executives have been unmindful or careless in their use of this power.

---

[52]Sheldon Goldman, "Judicial Selection Under Clinton: A Midterm Examination," *Judicature* 78, No. 6 (May–June, 1995): 278, 279.

On the Clinton administration's deemphasis of political ideology in the judicial selection process, see also Stephen Labaton, "President's Judicial Appointments are Diverse, but Well in the Mainstream," *New York Times* (Oct. 17, 1994): A-10. Not only has Clinton not used the so-called litmus test (usually, an antiabortion stance) alleged to have been the central criterion in the Reagan administration, but also in the selection of William Downes of Wyoming to sit on the federal district court, Clinton chose a vocal antiabortion rights lawyer. Professor Goldman is quoted as saying, "It is not possible to imagine that the Reagan or Bush Administrations would have selected someone who was as outspoken on the other side of the abortion issue" (Labaton, p. A-10). See also the follow-up piece by Neil A. Lewis, "In Selecting Federal Judges, Clinton Has Not Tried to Be Anti-Reagan," *New York Times* (Aug. 1, 1996): A-12.

In interesting recent research on President Clinton's lower federal court nominees, Ronald Stidham, Robert A. Carp, and Donald R. Songer find, not surprisingly, that the "moderate" judicial nominees President Clinton has selected have thus far turned in moderate decisions. See "The Voting Behavior of President Clinton's Judicial Nominees," *Judicature* 80, No. 1 (July–Aug. 1996): 16–20.

The Choices of Recent Presidents

From 1789 to the presidency of Ronald Reagan, 101 men had served on the Supreme Court. On July 7, 1981, President Ronald Reagan announced the name of the first woman nominee, Sandra Day O'Connor of the Arizona Court of Appeals, to replace Justice Potter Stewart who, on June 18, 1981, at the age of 66, announced his retirement. Following two days of hearings, the Senate Judiciary Committee, in a vote of 17–0 with one abstention, recommended that O'Connor's nomination be confirmed by the full Senate. On July 21, 1981, the Senate unanimously confirmed her nomination, and on July 25, 1981, Sandra Day O'Connor was sworn in as the first woman ever to serve on the Supreme Court.[53]

On average, a vacancy occurs on the Supreme Court about every two years. A president may therefore expect to make at least one appointment in a four-year term, hopefully two appointments. But as with the roll of the dice, not every player wins. President Franklin Roosevelt served his entire first term without the opportunity to select a member of the Court, a twist of fate often cited as one of the reasons for his inordinate difficulty with the Court. Nevertheless, he was ultimately able to appoint a total of 9 justices, more than any other president except Washington, who appointed 10. President Carter was likewise denied the opportunity to make an appointment to the Court, and in this he joins a short list of four presidents (Harrison, Taylor, and Andrew Johnson being the other three). As we have seen, however, President Carter's impact on the judiciary has been considerable because of his lower court appointments. President Nixon, in contrast to Carter, was unusually fortunate in being able to select a chief justice and three associate justices to the Supreme Court in but five and one-half years in office.

On June 17, 1986, Chief Justice Warren E. Burger handed President Reagan his second opportunity to nudge the Supreme Court in a conservative direction. On that date, the president announced the retirement of the chief justice and the selection of his replacement, Associate Justice William H. Rehnquist. Also announced was the choice of a young (age 50) archconservative Catholic jurist, Antonin Scalia, to replace Rehnquist.[54] True to its tradition, the Senate Judiciary Committee did not balk seriously on ideological grounds. After four days of hearings, the committee, on August 14, supported the Rehnquist nomination by a vote of 13–5, and on the same day unanimously recommended the confirmation of Antonin Scalia.[55]

Although subsequent action by the full Senate revealed little, if any, opposition to Judge Scalia (the confirmation vote on September 17 was 98–0), the case for Justice Rehnquist's nomination to the chief justiceship deteriorated in the three months of intense opposition to his confirmation. Indeed, although the final vote to confirm can be interpreted as supporting the foregoing generalizations guiding the politics of federal judicial selection, it can also be argued that the Rehnquist case served to modify these informal norms somewhat. As debate ensued, the line between ideological arguments and those supposedly based on merit became blurred, with a larger than expected number of senators (albeit all but two being Democrats) voicing opposition to the nomination on grounds of Rehn-

[53]See *New York Times* (July 22, and July 26, 1981): A-1. The history and politics of nominations to the Supreme Court are superbly described by Professor Henry J. Abraham in *Justices and Presidents: A Political History of Appointments to the Supreme Court,* 3rd. Edition (New York: Oxford University Press, 1992). This volume, covering all nominations up to but not including the Clarence Thomas case, is the standard work on the subject and is relied upon throughout this chapter.

[54]Full coverage may be found in the *New York Times* (June 18, 1986): 1, 11–14.

[55]Linda Greenhouse, "Senate Unit Backs Rehnquist, 13–5," *New York Times* (Aug. 15, 1986): 1. The Reagan nominations are authoritatively described in Abraham, *Justices and Presidents,* especially Ch. 12. See also Murphy, "Reagan's Judicial Strategy."

quist's alleged insensitivity to the rights of women and minorities as well as to matters of judicial ethics.

The ethics issue loomed larger in floor debate than in committee when more senators became convinced that Justice Rehnquist displayed poor ethical judgment in not disqualifying himself in the 1972 case of *Laird v. Tatum* (409 U.S. 824). The case involved a constitutional challenge to the Army's program of domestic surveillance of Viet Nam war protesters. Justice Department documents (first refused but later released by the Reagan Administration) indicated that Rehnquist, at the time a Nixon appointee in the Justice Department, played a significant role in formulating the policy in question. The plaintiff's request that Rehnquist disqualify himself on grounds of conflict of interest was rejected, after which he proceeded to cast the deciding vote to dismiss the case. Rehnquist's lack of candor in his Senate Committee testimony concerning this and other matters also became an issue. Senator Levin (D-Mich.) labeled his behavior "an example of cleverness, of obfuscation, and disingenuousness." On September 17, after a vote to close debate (forestalling a filibuster) of 68–31, the Senate voted 65–33 to confirm William H. Rehnquist as the sixteenth chief justice of the United States. But he assumed that position with the burden of more negative votes than any other chief justice in history.[56]

The last of the three Supreme Court vacancies during the Reagan years proved more difficult to fill. At the end of Rehnquist's first term as chief justice—on June 26, 1987—Justice Lewis F. Powell, Jr., like Rehnquist a Nixon nominee, announced his retirement. The departure of Justice Powell stirred great interest, for he was seen as a centrist and a crucial swing vote between the Court's liberal and conservative blocs. On July 1 of that year, President Reagan surprised no one by nominating the controversial Robert H. Bork.[57]

Bork had been a leading candidate for a seat on the Court at the time Scalia was chosen. Indeed, his name had appeared on lists of potential nominees as far back as the late 1960s, so popular was the ex–law professor in the conservative camp. He had been in the Nixon Justice Department, ultimately serving as Solicitor-General, and had taken the step that few others were willing to take in dismissing Watergate Special Prosecutor Archibald Cox in the famous "Saturday Night Massacre" of October 20, 1973.[58] In 1982 he was appointed by President Reagan to the U.S. Court of Appeals for the District of Columbia and was thus in a strategic position on the Supreme Court's "farm team."

The nomination set off a firestorm of opposition from liberals. The elections of 1986 had returned the Senate to Democratic control, and the Democrats, frustrated at the long string of successful Republican judicial nominees, were itching for a win. Senator Edward Kennedy led the attack. Within an hour of the announcement of the nomination, the Sena-

---

[56]However, this statement may mislead. Of the sixteen chief justices, confirmation votes were recorded in only seven cases: Oliver Ellsworth in 1796, 21–1; Roger B. Taney in 1836, 29–15; Morrison R. Waite in 1874, 63–0; Melville W. Fuller in 1888, 41–20; Charles E. Hughes in 1930, 52–26; Warren E. Burger in 1969, 74–3; and the 65–33 Rehnquist vote. Quick calculation reveals that Rehnquist was confirmed by approximately two-thirds of all Senate votes cast, the same proportion won by Taney, Fuller, and Hughes.

On the highlights of the Rehnquist confirmation struggle, see Linda Greenhouse's two *New York Times* items: "Senate Moves Toward Final Vote on Rehnquist To Be Chief Justice" (Sept. 18, 1986): A-1; and "Reporter's Notebook: Senators v. Rehnquist" (Sept. 19, 1986): A-24. For confirmation votes on all the justices, see the encyclopedic presentation of basic information on the Court in Congressional Quarterly, *Guide to the United States Supreme Court*, 2nd ed. (Washington: Congressional Quarterly, 1990), 995–98.

For an account of Rehnquist's role as Chief Justice after ten years in that position, see David J. Garrow, "The Rehnquist Reins," *New York Times Magazine* (Oct. 6, 1996): 64–71, 82, 85.

[57]See Gerald M. Boyd, "Bork Picked for High Court: Reagan Cites his 'Restraint'; Confirmation Fight Looms," *New York Times* (July 2, 1987): A-1.

[58]Kenneth B. Noble, "Bork Irked by Emphasis on His Role in Watergate," *New York Times* (July 2, 1987): A-8.

tor from Massachusetts set the tone of the anti-Bork crusade in a speech that has become famous in judicial confirmation history. Said Senator Kennedy in part,

> Robert Bork's America is a land in which women would be forced into back alley abortions, blacks would sit at segregated lunch counters, rogue police could break down citizens' doors in midnight raids, school children could not be taught about evolution, writers and artists could be censored at the whim of government, and the doors of the Federal courts would be shut on the fingers of millions of citizens for whom the judiciary is often the only protector of the individual rights that are at the heart of our democracy.[59]

The nomination was in trouble from the first. As a vocal conservative, Bork had written widely in scholarly journals on the sins of the Warren-Burger Court and had spoken in unusually harsh tones against many, if not most, contemporary approaches to constitutional interpretation.[60] For Bork, the only legitimate jurisprudence was that of "original intent" (see Chapters 1 and 2). More than this, the nominee's physical appearance and sometimes arrogant demeanor did not play well to TV audiences over the twelve days of committee hearings, which began on September 15, 1987.

To win confirmation would have required departure from the unwritten rule that nominees do not discuss substantive legal doctrine. Bork had to answer his critics on specific court decisions as well as general jurisprudential issues, providing the backdrop for a national debate on the work of the Court. He also sought to further his chances of winning confirmation by significantly modifying some of the more extreme views that he had frequently expressed in federal appellate decisions and scholarly articles, a move that came to be labeled "confirmation conversion."

In the end, his efforts and those of his supporters were not enough. On October 6 the Senate Judiciary Committee voted 9–5 against confirmation. Key votes were cast against confirmation by Senators Arlen Specter (R-Penn) and Howell Heflin (D-Ala). If Judge Bork could not win all of the Republican votes plus those of several Southern Democrats, his nomination was dead. These strong negative committee signals resulted in a 58–42 floor defeat for Bork on October 23, 1987. The vote was the largest margin by which any Supreme Court nominee has been rejected in our history. Fifty-two Democrats were joined by six Republicans to defeat the nomination; only two Democrats voted in favor of Judge Bork.[61]

In its length, intensity, and departure from the usual norms of Senate confirmation politics, the Bork fight made legal history. Not since the struggle over the confirmation of Louis Brandeis in 1916, or perhaps the New Deal court-packing episode in 1937, had the nation undergone so fundamental an assessment of the roles of the Supreme Court in our political and social system. The hearings were sufficiently lengthy that public opinion was injected into the fray, and it did not bode well for Judge Bork.[62] His stock seemed to de-

---

[59]*Congressional Record,* Vol. 113, No. 110 (July 1, 1987): S 9188. A useful narrative and analysis of the Bork nomination is Ethan Bronner, *Battle for Justice: How the Bork Nomination Shook America* (New York: W. W. Norton, 1989). See a pro-Bork view in Patrick B. McGuigan and Dawn M. Weyrich, *Ninth Justice: The Fight for Bork* (Washington: Free Congress Research and Educational Foundation, 1990).

[60]The entire issue of Vol. 9 of the *Cardozo Law Review* (1987) is given over to materials on the Bork fight, including a coverage of his judicial opinions and published articles.

[61]Linda Greenhouse, "Bork's Nomination Is Rejected, 58–42; Reagan 'Saddened,'" *New York Times* (Oct. 24, 1987): A-1. See also William Haltom and Patti Watson, "Sealing Judge Bork's Doom: The Role of the Usual Suspects," paper delivered at the Annual Meeting of the Western Political Science Association, Newport Beach, Calif., Mar. 22–24, 1990. This research finds that the change in party alignment in the Senate in the 1986 elections was the key factor in explaining the Bork vote.

[62]For the direction and role of public opinion in the Bork struggle, see Bronner, *Battle for Justice,* especially 151–52, 288–90, 301. See also Stuart Taylor, Jr., "Politics and the Bork Battle," *New York Times* (Sept. 28, 1987): A-1; and Kenneth B. Noble, "Bork Fever (Pro and Con) Intensifies as Senate Hearings Near," *New York Times* (Sept. 12, 1987): 6.

cline as the hearings proceeded, depressed not only by negative public opinion as to his extreme, if not radical, approach to constitutional interpretation but also by professional politico-legal incredulity over his departure from well-established principles of constitutional law. Worse, for some senators, was his seemingly unprincipled vacillation on key issues. Wrote Republican Senator Specter,

> On freedom of speech, I was surprised to find that Judge Bork . . . rejected Justice Oliver Wendell Holmes's "clear and present danger," Chief Justice Warren Burger's notion of constitutional protection for commercial speech and Justice . . . Rehnquist's . . . protecting a sexually explicit . . . movie from censorship.
> In Judge Bork's earliest views, only political speech was to be protected. He later modified that to include literature and art that involved political discussion. . . .
> Judge Bork's views on equal protection of the law also underwent a major change at the hearings. He committed himself to apply current case law after having long insisted that equal protection applied only to race and more recently, to ethnicity. His narrow position had put him at odds with Chief Justice Rehnquist and Justices Sandra Day O'Connor and Scalia, as well as 101 years of Supreme Court decisions that had applied equal protection to women, aliens, indigents, illegitimates and others.
> These significant shifts raised questions about Judge Bork's motives and the depth of his convictions.[63]

Six days after the Bork defeat, President Reagan picked one of Bork's colleagues on the U.S. Court of Appeals for the District of Columbia, Douglas H. Ginsburg, to fill the Powell vacancy. Almost immediately the nomination was awash not so much in partisan political controversy as in White House embarrassment due to Ginsburg's use of marijuana both as a student and later as a member of the faculty at Harvard Law School. An administration that had launched a major national campaign against the use of illegal drugs with the rallying cry "Just Say No" found it difficult to sustain the Supreme Court nomination of a man who preferred to say yes. The nomination stood nine days before it was withdrawn.[64] Finally, on November 10, 1987, the White House located a winner in Anthony M. Kennedy, a judge on the U.S. Court of Appeals for the Ninth Circuit in California. Straight, noncontroversial, Harvard-educated, a family man, Kennedy was a shoo-in, being confirmed by the Senate 97–0. On February 18, 1988, he was sworn in as the Court's 104th justice.[65]

In his four years in office, President George Bush was able to select two members of the Court. The first vacancy was created by the departure of the ailing Justice William J. Brennan, Jr., a Catholic Democrat nominated by President Eisenhower in 1956, who became a leading member of the Court's liberal bloc. Seeking to avoid successful attacks on his nominee on the basis of a controversial past record (the Bork "paper trail"), President Bush was able to locate a relatively unknown in the quiet New Hampshire bachelor, David H. Souter. The strategy of "The Stealth Nominee" succeeded. With little known (and virtually nothing controversial) concerning the nominee, opponents had little to shoot at, so that he was overwhelmingly confirmed by the Senate on October 2, 1990, as the 105th justice to serve on the Court.[66] However, the second vacancy led to a great deal more controversy.

At the end of the Court's October 1990 term—on June 27, 1991—the venerable Justice Thurgood Marshall, the first Black to have been appointed to the Court and the last justice

[63]Arlen Specter, "Why I Voted Against Bork," *New York Times* (Oct. 9, 1987): A-27.
[64]Steven V. Roberts, "Ginsburg Withdraws Name as Supreme Court Nominee, Citing Marijuana 'Clamor,'" *New York Times* (Nov. 8, 1987): A-1.
[65]Stuart Taylor, Jr., "Kennedy Sworn in as 104th Justice On High Court," *New York Times* (Feb. 19, 1988): A-8. For interesting background data on Kennedy, see Abraham, *Justices and Presidents*, 359–60.
[66]On the Souter nomination, see John M. Broder, "Souter: A Life Rooted in Law," *Los Angeles Times* (July 27, 1990): A-1; Richard L. Berke, "Senate Confirms Souter for Seat on Supreme Court," *New York Times*

selected by a Democratic president up to the first Clinton nomination, announced his retirement, effective upon the confirmation of his successor. Justice Marshall had been a leading champion of civil rights; indeed, he had spoken more vociferously for the civil and political rights of the downtrodden than perhaps any other justice in the Court's history. That he should be replaced by the nominee of a Republican president was a bit of irony not to the liking of Marshall's admirers.

President Bush, perhaps again wishing to avoid a nasty Senate battle, chose another Black, Judge Clarence Thomas, 43, again from the U.S. Court of Appeals for the District of Columbia. Thomas's politics, however, differed markedly from those of Marshall, particularly in areas such as affirmative action and related measures to achieve racial integration. Ironically, Thomas seemed opposed to the public policies of the 1950s through the 1970s that helped Blacks (including himself) to climb the ladder of success. The initial vote in the Senate Judiciary Committee on September 7, 1991, was 7–7, the nomination going to the floor with no recommendation one way or the other. Still, Senate confirmation seemed likely until the "leak" of sexual harassment charges against the nominee by Anita F. Hill, Professor of Law at the University of Oklahoma and former aide to Thomas at the Department of Education and later at the Equal Employment Opportunity Commission. The nation was then dragged through one of the most dramatic, emotionally painful spectacles in American judicial history.

The final outcome was something of a draw. Although severely damaged by the lurid details of Professor Hill's charges, the nominee won Senate confirmation on October 15 by a vote of 52–48, the closest confirmation vote since that of President Grover Cleveland's first appointee, Lucius Quintus Cincinnatus Lamar of Mississippi, who barely won his seat on the Court from an angry Northern Republican Senate in a 32–28 vote on January 16, 1888. Only two Republicans voted against Thomas, while eleven Democrats, mostly Southerners, did so.[67] The Bork and Thomas confirmation battles dramatically illustrate the high stakes involved in selecting justices for the Supreme Court, though they do not, as some have suggested, necessarily set new patterns of judicial selection politics.

President William Jefferson Clinton was unusually fortunate in being presented with a vacancy on the Supreme Court only two months into his first term of office. On March 19, 1993, as had been rumored for some time, Justice Byron R. White, the only remaining Democratic nominee on the Court, announced his retirement effective "at the time the Court next rises for its summer recess." This courtesy gave President Clinton several months to carefully choose a successor and shepherd the nominee through the Senate confirmation process prior to the Court's fall term. The slot was especially important for the Clinton ad-

---

(Oct. 3, 1990): A-1; Paul Reidinger, "Mr. Souter Goes to Washington," *American Bar Association Journal* 76, No. 12 (Dec. 1990): 48, 50–52; Abraham, *Justices and Presidents,* 366–369; and a useful overview of the entire process, "Senate Confirms Souter for High Court," *Congressional Quarterly Almanac,* 1990, 508–519.

[67]The Thomas nomination and subsequent hearings and the floor vote are described and analyzed in an excellent series of articles in the *New York Times* from July 2 to Oct. 16, 1991. See especially Maureen Doud, "Conservative Black Judge, Clarence Thomas, Is Named to Marshall's Court Seat," *New York Times* (July 2, 1991): A-1; and R. W. Apple, Jr., "Senate Confirms Thomas, 52–48, Ending Week of Bitter Battle," *New York Times* (Oct. 16, 1991): A-1. Also useful is a series of pieces in the *Congressional Quarterly Weekly Report* by Joan Biskupic, beginning July 6, 1991. See also CQ's summary article covering most major aspects of the Thomas fight, "Clarence Thomas Wins Senate Confirmation," *Congressional Quarterly Almanac,* 1991: 274–285. And a political analysis of the fight is found in L. Marvin Overby et. al., "Courting Constituents? An Analysis of the Senate Confirmation Vote on Justice Clarence Thomas," *American Political Science Review* 86, No. 4 (Dec. 1992): 997–1003.

Finally, a journalistic account of the Thomas story is Timothy M. Phelps and Helen Winternitz, *Capital Games: Clarence Thomas, Anita Hill, and the Story of a Supreme Court Nomination* (New York: Hyperion, 1992).

ministration, for it provided the only opportunity then on the horizon to replace a conservative voting member of the Court with a nominee having a more liberal cast. Although White had been nominated by his friend John F. Kennedy, his voting record on the Court had been something of a disappointment to Kennedy liberals. As his thirty-one years on the Court moved along, White appeared more and more on the side of the conservative Rehnquist-Scalia-Thomas faction on issues such as criminal procedures and the right to privacy, though at the same time he remained a staunch advocate of strong federal authority.[68]

On June 14, 1993, after a good deal of vacillation and the launching of trial balloons, President Clinton nominated Judge Ruth Bader Ginsburg as the 107th justice to serve on the Court.[69] The selection was greeted with near universal praise, even from the conservative camp. Ginsburg, who had herself argued cases before the Court, had become a noted national voice for women's rights. In 1980 she was selected by President Carter to serve on the U.S. Court of Appeals for the District of Columbia, and had become a centrist figure on that rather badly divided tribunal. At 60, Ginsburg had lived through—and indeed, fought through—the early gender rights struggle, herself having taken a job as a secretary because no firm would hire her just out of law school. On June 29 the Senate's Judiciary Committee voted unanimously for confirmation, and on August 3, 1993, the full Senate supported the nomination by a vote of 93–3.[70] Taking the Supreme Court's oath of office on August 10, 1993, Justice Ginsburg became only the second woman to serve on the Court and the first Jewish justice since Justice Fortas resigned in 1969.

On Wednesday, April 6, 1994, Justice Harry Blackmun, a Nixon appointee who had served on the Court twenty-four years, announced his retirement. At slightly over 85-and-a-half years of age by the time of the completion of his service, Justice Blackmun was the third oldest person ever to have served on the Court, behind Justice Oliver Wendell Holmes at 90 and Hugo Black at 85-and-a-half. Blackmun's retirement gave President Clinton the opportunity to make his second nomination, which eventually went to Judge Stephen G. Breyer, Chief Judge of the United States Court of Appeals for the First Circuit in Boston, a strong front-runner when Ruth Bader Ginsberg was chosen. As with his first Supreme Court selection, as well as most of his lower court choices, the President again opted for a moderate with strong professional credentials, who stood a good chance of being readily confirmed by the Senate. The confirmation hearings before the Senate Judiciary Committee were largely uneventful save for some conflict of interest allegation concerning Judge Breyer's rulings in certain pollution cases and some bad investments in Lloyds of London. On July 29, 1994, Judge Breyer was confirmed in a strong bipartisan Senate vote of 87–9, which followed unanimous approval of the nomination by the Senate Judiciary Committee. Taking his seat on August 3, 1994, Breyer became the 108th justice to serve on the Court.[71] All those nominated to the Supreme Court in this century are tabulated in Table 6–8.

---

[68]See Linda Greenhouse, "White Announces He'll Step Down from High Court," *New York Times* (Mar. 20, 1993): A-1.

[69]See the various background articles in *New York Times* (June 15, 1993): A-1, especially Richard Berke, "Clinton Names Ruth Ginsburg, Advocate for Women, to Court."

[70]Holly Idelson, "Ginsburg and Freeh Cruise Through Senate Panel," *Congressional Quarterly Weekly Report* (July 31, 1993): 2065; Linda Greenhouse, "Senate Easily Confirms Judge Ginsburg," *New York Times* (Mar. 20, 1993): A-1.

[71]As usual, the *New York Times* provided a reasonably complete coverage of the Blackmun-Breyer transition. See, e.g., Linda Greenhouse, "Justice Blackmun's Odyssey: From Moderate to Liberal," *New York Times* (Apr. 7, 1994): A-1; Gwen Ifill, "President Chooses Breyer, An Appeals Judge in Boston, for Blackmun's Court Seat," *New York Times* (May 14, 1994): A-1; Neil Lewis, "Taking Initiative, Nominee Defends Conduct as Judge," *New York Times* (July 13, 1994): A-1; and Linda Greenhouse, "Breyer Wins Confirmation to U.S. Supreme Court," *New York Times* (July 30, 1994): A-1.

The process of selecting Supreme Court justices is, in its major outlines, the same as that earlier described for choosing lower federal court judges. After the preliminary list is narrowed, the FBI runs a background check on the nominees, and the American Bar Association's Committee on the Federal Judiciary is given an opportunity to make its recommendations. The final selection is then announced, and the names are sent to the Senate, where the Senate Judiciary Committee holds hearings. After approval by the committee and a favorable vote by the full Senate, the appointee takes his or her seat on the Court. Given the higher stakes involved in Supreme Court nominations, and the considerably reduced power of individual senators, the president's preference constitutes by far the most important factor in the selection process. Yet, the considerations that weigh most heavily in the president's mind are anything but novel; they are quite familiar to the student of judicial politics. Political considerations, with the usual variables involved therein, head the list. Professional merit is also quite important. And other factors, as custom and tradition have come to dictate (or at least suggest), round out the list of relevant considerations.[72]

Politics, Partisan and Otherwise

Of the 108 justices who have served on the Court through the selection of Stephen G. Breyer, in only 13 instances (12 percent)—two of these being elevations from associate to chief justice—did a president cross party lines to make the selection. Doing so is sometimes considered "good politics" by lending credence to the president's "statesmanship"— his deference to the myth of nonpartisanship in judicial selections—and tends to defuse the charge that the president is "packing" the Court with party loyalists.[73] A closer look at these thirteen appointments, however, reveals that if political ideology (the "real" politics of the nominee) were considered, the correlation between a president's politics (policy preferences) and that of his nominee would be even higher. That is, when crossing party lines, presidents are quite careful to select lawyers whose public policy views are very close to their own, perhaps even closer than those of the available choices in the president's own party. This distinction between party label and the "real" politics was made in an unusually candid and widely cited letter from Republican president Theodore Roosevelt to Republican senator Henry Cabot Lodge in 1906. In discussing the possible candidacy of a Democrat, Horace Lurton, the president wrote,

> Nothing has been so strongly borne in on me concerning lawyers on the bench as that the nominal politics of the man has nothing to do with his actions on the bench. His real politics are all-important. In Lurton's case, Taft and Day, his two former associates, are very desirous of having him on. He is right on the Negro question; he is right on the power of the federal government; he is right on the Insular business; he is right about corporations, he is right about labor. On every question that would come before the bench, he has so far shown

---

[72]Abraham, in *Justices and Presidents,* has suggested four general criteria for this presidential decision: (1) objective merit, (2) personal friendship, (3) balancing representation, and (4) political and ideological compatibility (p. 5). For a more recent, in-depth analysis of the entire process of selecting Supreme Court justices, see George L. Watson and John A. Stookey, *Shaping America: The Politics of Supreme Court Appointments* (New York: HarperCollins, 1995). A close analysis of the president's decision making in this regard is contained in Ch. 3. See also an excellent recent work emphasizing the increased role of political interest groups in the confirmation process of Supreme Court nominees, by John Anthony Maltese, *The Selling of Supreme Court Nominees* (Baltimore: Johns Hopkins University Press, 1995).

[73]This phenomenon is discussed at length in Abraham, *Justices and Presidents,* 65–70. See also the thorough research on the social and political backgrounds of Supreme Court justices by John R. Schmidhauser, *Judges and Justices: The Federal Appellate Judiciary* (Boston: Little, Brown, 1979), especially 83–92.

Table 6–8 Supreme Court Nominations, 1900–1994

Name	Date of Birth	Nominated by	Date Nominated		Served Until
Oliver W. Holmes	3/8/1841	Roosevelt	12/2/1902		1/12/1932
William R. Day	4/17/1849	Roosevelt	2/19/1903		11/13/1922
William H. Moody	12/23/1853	Roosevelt	12/3/1906		11/20/1910
Horace H. Lurton	2/26/1844	Taft	12/13/1909		7/12/1914
Edward D. White[a]	11/3/1845	Taft	12/12/1910		5/19/1921
Charles E. Hughes	4/11/1862	Taft	4/25/1910		6/10/1916
Willis Van Devanter	4/17/1859	Taft	12/12/1910		6/2/1937
Joseph R. Lamar	10/14/1857	Taft	12/12/1910		1/2/1916
Mahlon Pitney	2/5/1858	Taft	2/19/1912		12/31/1922
James C. McReynolds	2/3/1862	Wilson	8/19/1914		1/31/1941
Louis D. Brandeis	11/13/1856	Wilson	1/28/1916		2/13/1939
John H. Clarke	9/18/1857	Wilson	7/14/1916		7/18/1922
William H. Taft	9/15/1857	Harding	6/30/1921		2/3/1930
George Sutherland	3/25/1862	Harding	9/5/1922		1/17/1938
Pierce Butler	3/17/1866	Harding	11/23/1922		11/16/1939
Edward T. Sanford	7/23/1865	Harding	1/24/1923		3/8/1930
Harlan F. Stone	10/11/1872	Coolidge	1/5/1925		4/22/1946
Charles E. Hughes[a]	4/11/1862	Hoover	2/3/1930		7/1/1941
John J. Parker	11/20/1885	Hoover	3/21/1930	(Rejected)	—
Owen J. Roberts	5/2/1875	Hoover	5/9/1930		7/31/1945
Benjamin N. Cardozo	5/24/1870	Hoover	2/15/1932		7/9/1938
Hugo L. Black	2/27/1886	Roosevelt	8/12/1937		9/17/1971
Stanley F. Reed	12/31/1884	Roosevelt	1/15/1938		2/26/1957
Felix Frankfurter	11/15/1882	Roosevelt	1/5/1939		8/28/1962
William O. Douglas	10/16/1898	Roosevelt	3/20/1939		11/12/1975
Frank Murphy	4/13/1890	Roosevelt	1/4/1940		7/19/1949
Harlan F. Stone[a]	10/11/1872	Roosevelt	6/12/1941		4/22/1946
James F. Byrnes	5/2/1879	Roosevelt	6/12/1941		10/3/1942
Robert H. Jackson	2/13/1892	Roosevelt	6/12/1941		10/9/1954
Wiley B. Rutledge	7/20/1894	Roosevelt	1/11/1943		9/10/1949
Harold H. Burton	6/22/1888	Truman	9/19/1945		10/13/1958
Fred M. Vinson	1/22/1890	Truman	6/6/1946		9/8/1953
Tom C. Clark	9/23/1899	Truman	8/2/1949		6/12/1967
Sherman Minton	10/20/1890	Truman	9/15/1949		10/15/1956

Table 6–8   (*Continued*)

Name	Date of Birth	Nominated by	Date Nominated		Served Until
Earl Warren	3/19/1891	Eisenhower	9/30/1953		6/23/1969
John M. Harlan	5/20/1899	Eisenhower	1/10/1955		9/23/1971
William J. Brennan, Jr.	4/25/1906	Eisenhower	1/14/1957		6/20/90
Charles E. Whittaker	2/22/1901	Eisenhower	3/2/1957		4/1/1962
Potter Stewart	1/23/1915	Eisenhower	1/17/1959		7/3/1981
Byron R. White	6/8/1917	Kennedy	3/30/1962		6/29/93
Arthur J. Goldberg	8/8/1908	Kennedy	8/29/1962		7/25/1965
Abe Fortas[b]	6/19/1910	Johnson	8/11/1965		5/14/1969
Thurgood Marshall	6/2/1908	Johnson	6/13/1967		10/2/91
Homer Thornberry	1/9/1909	Johnson	6/26/1968	(No action)	
Warren E. Burger	9/17/1907	Nixon	6/9/1969		6/17/1986
Clement Haynesworth, Jr.	10/30/1912	Nixon	5/21/1969	(Rejected)	
G. Harrold Carswell	12/22/1919	Nixon	1/19/1970	(Rejected)	
Harry A. Blackmun	11/12/1908	Nixon	4/14/1970		8/3/94
Lewis F. Powell, Jr.	9/19/1907	Nixon	10/21/1971		6/26/1987
William H. Rehnquist[a]	10/1/1924	Nixon	10/21/1971		
John Paul Stevens	4/20/1920	Ford	11/28/1975		
Sandra Day O'Conner	3/26/1930	Reagan	7/7/1981		
Antonin Scalia	3/11/1936	Reagan	6/17/1986		
William H. Rehnquist	10/1/1924	Reagan	6/17/1986		
Robert H. Bork	3/21/1927	Reagan	7/1/1987	(Rejected)	
Douglas H. Ginsburg	5/25/46	Reagan	10/29/1987	(Withdrawn)	
Anthony M. Kennedy	7/23/1936	Reagan	11/10/1987		
David H. Souter	9/17/1939	Bush	7/23/1990		
Clarence Thomas	6/23/1948	Bush	7/1/1991		
Ruth Bader Ginsburg	3/15/1933	Clinton	6/14/1993		
Stephen G. Breyer	8/15/1938	Clinton	5/13/1994		

[a]Indicates service as an associate justice of the Supreme Court prior to becoming chief justice.

[b]Fortas's nomination to the chief justiceship was withdrawn.

Source: Adapted from *Guide to the United States Supreme Court,* 2nd ed. Washington: Congressional Quarterly, 1990, 995–98, with updates.

himself to be in much closer touch with the policies in which you and I believe than even White because he has been right about corporations where White has been wrong.[74]

In reply, Senator Lodge wrote,

I am glad that Lurton holds all the opinions that you say he does and that you are so familiar with his views. I need hardly say that those are the very questions on which I am just as anxious as you that judges should hold what we consider sound opinions, but I do not see why Republicans cannot be found who hold those opinions as well as Democrats.[75]

As it turned out, Lurton did not get the appointment. Instead, it went to President Roosevelt's attorney general, a Republican, William Moody, who had been championed by Senator Lodge. Among other things, this incident hints at a somewhat stronger role for the Senate in such nominations than is usually credited. Lurton was, nonetheless, later selected for the Court by President William Howard Taft.

To be sure, presidents are sometimes disappointed in the performance of their selectees once they ascend the bench. President Theodore Roosevelt was not always happy with the decisions of Oliver Wendell Holmes, nor President Wilson with those of Justice McReynolds. Eisenhower said of his selection of Chief Justice Earl Warren, it was "the biggest damned-fool mistake I ever made.[76] And President Truman was not at all pleased with his appointment of Justice Tom Clark.[77] Of Clark, Truman was quoted as saying, "Tom Clark was my biggest mistake. No question about it." Probed, Truman explained,

That damn fool from Texas that I first made Attorney General and then put on the Supreme Court. . . . I don't know what got into me. He was no damn good as Attorney General, and on the Supreme Court . . . he's been even worse. He hasn't made one right decision that I can think of. . . .
It isn't so much that he's a *bad* man. It's just that he's such a dumb son-of-a-bitch.[78]

Angered by Justice Holmes's votes in antitrust cases, especially in *Northern Securities v. U.S.,* 193 U.S. 197 (1904), President Roosevelt said, "I could carve out of a banana a judge with more backbone than that."[79] In spite of such disappointments, the "real" politics in conjunction with party label remains the first principle of selection to the Supreme Court, and in most instances (the preceding being some of the exceptions), the performance of the nominee once on the bench is generally consistent with the president's political philosophy, at least in the short run.

Political considerations include a good deal more than party, whether defined by party label or political ideology. A president must be on guard against appointments that are likely to raise the ire of powerful political interest groups. The American Bar Association and kindred groups are obvious examples and will be discussed later. But there are many others as well. President Hoover's nomination of John J. Parker in 1930 ran into such strong opposition from labor unions, as well as from the NAACP on grounds of alleged racism, that these and similar groups, with the help of a few liberal Republicans, proved sufficient to defeat the nomination in the Senate in a very close vote, 39–41.[80] President Wilson experienced similar opposition in attempting to place Louis Brandeis on the Court in 1916. Not only was Mr. Brandeis a registered Massachusetts Republican and the first

[74]Quoted in Schmidhauser, *Judges and Justices,* 90.
[75]Quoted in Schmidhauser, *Judges and Justices,* 91.
[76]Bob Woodward and Scott Armstrong, *The Brethren* (New York: Simon & Schuster, 1979), 10.
[77]On presidential disappointments generally, see *Guide to the United States Supreme Court,* 686–87.
[78]See Merle Miller, *Plain Speaking* (New York: Berkeley, 1973), 225–26.
[79]Quoted in Abraham, *Justices and Presidents,* 69.
[80]Abraham, *Justices and Presidents,* 42–43.

member of the Jewish faith to be appointed to the Court, but also he was an attorney who had established a very strong record of social and political progressivism. This combination brought down the wrath of established legal and business interests, and it was only by skillful maneuvering on the part of the president and his political lieutenants that Brandeis was finally confirmed. Most presidents in similar situations would probably choose to avoid such a bitter struggle as was experienced in the Brandeis case.[81]

To partisan and group politics, we might add "personal politics" as the third ingredient of what we mean by political considerations in presidential appointments to the Supreme Court. There are several cases in which the personal ties of the nominees to the president emerge as the most significant factor in explaining the president's choice. We may include such personal considerations as political, because a president obviously does not select his purely personal friends for the bench. Rather, it is the close personal-political kinship that explains such nominations. Examples include President Lincoln's third appointment to the Court, his old friend from the Eighth Judicial Circuit of Illinois who was instrumental in obtaining for Lincoln his party's nomination for the presidency, Judge David Davis; Kennedy's choice of Byron R. White in 1961; Wilson's selection of Brandeis; and, most certainly, Lyndon Johnson's choice of Abe Fortas. This is not to say that in such cases the president did not have strong confidence in the appointee's professional ability (often, such nominees have turned out to be of the highest quality). It is only that in such instances, the personal factor loomed large in the final choice.

Finally, "political" most surely includes acceptability of the nominee to key senators and other important political figures—certainly those representing the home state of the nominee but also the chairperson and other members of the Senate Judiciary Committee. A president would normally need an unusually strong judicial candidate with solid outside support to hope to win against the determined opposition of home state political figures, prominent United States senators, and other relevant political leaders.

Professional Merit

From the Eisenhower presidency to the present, the American Bar Association has succeeded in persuading presidents to submit the names of potential nominees to their fifteen-member Committee on the Federal Judiciary for a preliminary evaluation. However, relations between presidential administrations and the ABA Committee have run hot and cold. Traditionally accused of overly conservative leanings in its recommendations, the committee in later decades found itself under sharp attack by conservatives themselves for pro-liberal tendencies. Thus, in the wake of criticism for approving President Nixon's unsuccessful nominations of Haynsworth and Carswell in 1969–1970 (see later, the committee changed its rating system for Supreme Court nominees from merely "qualified" or "not qualified" to a more refined "high standards of integrity, judicial temperament, and professional competence" (translate: "highly qualified"), "not opposed" (or simply "qualified"), and "not qualified." Further, beginning with the Blackmun nomination, the committee also intensified its investigation into the background of the nominees, for it was quite embarrassed to have negative aspects of Carswell's background revealed which its own brief investigation failed to unearth. Beginning with the Rehnquist and Scalia nominations ABA's rating categories of Supreme Court nominees became: "well-qualified," "qualified," and "not qualified."[82]

[81]See A. L. Todd, *Justice on Trial: The Case of Louis D. Brandeis* (New York: McGraw-Hill, 1964). For a useful, recent analysis of the role of interest groups in the politics of Supreme Court nominations, see Watson and Stookey, *Shaping America,* passim.

[82]See Abraham, *Justices and Presidents,* 34–37; and O'Brien, *Judicial Roulette,* Ch. 5.

Even with these changes, however, the ABA committee found itself under intense criticism in the Reagan administration, especially in the Bork evaluation. When ten members of the committee awarded the judge a "well qualified" rating, one "not opposed," and four "not qualified" (a further alteration in the categories), the action marked a degree of negativity not registered in the committee since its work became semi-formalized in the Eisenhower years.[83] Following their defeat in the Senate, Bork's supporters castigated the ABA for its partisan political role, helping to push along litigation challenging the committee's secret deliberations. In *Public Citizen v. Dept. of Justice,* 491 U.S. 440 (1989) the Supreme Court upheld the ABA's right to conduct its deliberations in secret. However, this ruling has not quieted the continuing storm over the role of the ABA committee, particularly in high-profile Supreme Court nominations.[84]

Given its secretive operations, the precise qualities that the ABA committee seeks have never been very clear. The committee's own publications speak in broad generalities of "integrity," "professional competence" (including intellectual capacity, judgment, and breadth of professional experience). An appellate nominee must have "an especially high degree of scholarship and academic talent and an unusual degree of overall excellence."[85] Considering the type of federal judges selected, though, the general preference seems to be a prestigious legal education, a high-quality (i.e., defendant) law practice, scholarly acumen, and judicial experience. Until 1980, the committee had a clear preference for nominees under 60 years of age, but that guideline has been dropped. Too, the traditional minimum of 15 years' legal experience has also been softened under pressure from the Senate, because it tended to discriminate against younger attorneys. Needless to say, ABA guidelines mention nothing about racial/gender/social factors. As indicated in Table 6–9, the American Bar Association seems to have been relatively successful in translating its standards into actual judicial characteristics present in the justices.

Some presidents (for example, Eisenhower after his appointment of Earl Warren to the chief justiceship) have insisted on prior judicial experience as a requisite to nomination, whereas others (FDR and Truman) placed much less emphasis on this factor. At the very least, such service gives the president an opportunity to scrutinize the judicial record of the nominee and thereby to be better able to predict judicial behavior on the high court.[86] But, of course, such service can also provide ammunition for the nominee's political opponents. For example, the nominations of John J. Parker, Clement Haynsworth, and G. Harrold Carswell were defeated by the Senate Judiciary Committee in part because of vulnerability on the basis of their past judicial records. And, of course, Judge Bork fell victim to a similar fate, though more on the basis of his off-the-bench writings and speeches than on his judicial opinions.

---

[83]Linda Greenhouse, "A.B.A. Rating of U.S. Judges Under Attack," *New York Times* (Dec. 27, 1987): A-1; and Marcia Coyle, "ABA Clout on Judges: Too Much?" *National Law Journal* (Apr. 17, 1989): 1. Actually, the ABA committee vote on Clarence Thomas was even more negative. Twelve of the committee gave Thomas a "qualified" rating, two said he was "not qualified," and one did not vote. That not a single member gave Thomas the highest rating of "well qualified" is unprecedented in the history of the ABA. See "Thomas: The Least Qualified Nominee So Far?" *National Law Journal* (Sept. 16, 1991): 5.

[84]For the continuing conflict over this matter, see Sheldon Goldman, "The Bush Imprint on the Judiciary: Carrying on a Tradition," *Judicature* 74, No. 6 (Apr.–May 1991), especially 294–98; Neil A. Lewis, "A.B.A. Walking Fine Line on Bench," *New York Times* (May 8, 1990: A-12; and Neil A. Lewis, "Senators Question Bar Association's Role in Selecting Judges," *New York Times* (May 22, 1996): A-11.

[85]American Bar Association, *The ABA Standing Committee on the Federal Judiciary,* 3–4.

[86]President Eisenhower said, "My thought was that this criterion [prior judicial experience] would insure that there would then be available to us a record of the decisions for which the prospective candidate had been responsible. These would provide an inkling of his philosophy." See Dwight D. Eisenhower, *The White House Years: Mandate for Change, 1953–1956* (New York: New American Library, 1965), 285.

Table 6–9   Qualifications of Supreme Court Justices

Quality of Law School Attended[a]	Percentage of Justices
Prestige	62
Nonprestige	38
Occupation at Time of Appointment[b]	
Federal Office Holder	20.2
Judge or Justice	46.8
Private Law Practice	16.5
Member of Congress	11.0
State Governor	2.7
Professor of Law	2.7
Prior Judicial Experience	
Federal	28
State	44
Total	72[c]

[a]Based on justices who attended law school and appointed since 1900. "Prestige" was judged to include Harvard, Yale, Stanford, Michigan, Columbia, Pennsylvania, and Northwestern. Interestingly, all eight nominees to the Court in the last 12 years (presidencies of Reagan and Bush) held prestige legal diplomas from only four law schools: Harvard, Yale, Stanford, and Chicago.

[b]As Abraham notes, many justices held more than one federal or state office before selection to the Court.

[c]Six justices (nearly 6 percent) had both federal and state judicial experience before their appointment to the Court.

Source: John R. Schmidhauser, *Judges and Justices: The Federal Appellate Judiciary* (Boston: Little, Brown, 1979), 72–79; Henry J. Abraham, *Justices and Presidents: A Political History of Appointments to the Supreme Court,* 3rd ed. (New York: Oxford University Press, 1992), 53–62; updated.

Whether prior judicial experience makes for "better" Supreme Court justices is quite another matter. Of the 101 justices who served on the Court up to the appointment of Justice O'Connor, only 22 had prior judicial experience that could be called substantial (10 or more years), whereas 42 had none at all. Among the latter, however, were some of the "greats" on the Court: Chief Justices Roger B. Taney and Earl Warren, Associate Justices Hugo Black, William O. Douglas, and Felix Frankfurter. Since work on the Court is as philosophic as it is narrowly legal, it is often argued that prior judicial experience should not be weighed so heavily in appointments. A classic statement in this vein was made by Justice Frankfurter, who argued that

Since the functions of the Supreme Court are what they are and demand the intellectual and moral qualities that they do, ... does it require an explicit statement that in choosing men for this task no artificial or irrelevant consideration should restrict choice?

The search should be made among those men ... who give the best promise of satisfying the intrinsic needs of the Court, ... no matter in what professional way they have manifested the needed qualities. . . . [The] correlation between prior judicial experience and fitness for the functions of the Supreme Court is zero.[87]

Yet, it is worth noting that of the eight nominees to the Court in the Reagan and Bush years (O'Connor, Rehnquist, Scalia, Bork, Ginsburg, Kennedy, Souter, and Thomas), as well as the Clinton choice, *all* had at least some judicial experience at the time of nomination. This fact suggests that aside from the matter of correlation with "greatness," prior judicial experience seems to be viewed by recent presidents as an important factor in selling their nominees to the Senate. Prior judicial experience or not, a strong majority of justices selected throughout history have been men (and two women) of public affairs with generally impressive academic backgrounds and considerable legal or governmental experience, who, if not the best available, were generally competent and brought credit to the Court.[88]

Other Factors

Tradition has, if not dictated, at least suggested the existence of a third set of criteria (in addition to political and professional considerations) for nomination to the Supreme Court—a group of factors that might be called *representational*. From era to era and from president to president, this has variously meant the representation of factors such as geography, religion, race, gender, national origin, and, it was once suggested, even "mediocrity." But these considerations must be seen as rough guidelines rather than as absolutes in the selection process. To be sure, geography has played an important role, as in President Lincoln's selection of Stephen J. Field from California, as well as President Nixon's attempts to place Southerners on the Court. But few presidents felt strongly obliged, as a first priority, to nominate a person from a particular section of the country.[89]

There has been much discussion of the "Catholic seat," the "Jewish seat," the "Black seat," the "woman's seat," and so forth. Chief Justice Roger B. Taney, appointed in 1835, was the first Roman Catholic to serve on the Court; Brandeis in 1916 was the first Jew; Thurgood Marshall (1967) was the first Black appointee; Sandra Day O'Connor (1981), the first woman; and Antonin Scalia (1986), the first Italian-American. Yet, there have been long periods without Roman Catholic or Jewish representation on the Court, and modern presidents (for example, Truman and Nixon) have insisted that considerations such as religion and race should not be of first importance in appointments. Thus, although balance as a general principle has certainly been important in past appointments, it is by no means a fixed rule.[90]

Overall, then, political, professional, and traditional representational considerations seem to constitute the chief factors that weigh in the mind of the president in making Supreme Court appointments. Although convenience suggests this tripartite decision, a

---

[87]Felix Frankfurter, "The Supreme Court in the Mirror of Justices," *University of Pennsylvania Law Review* 105, No. 6 (Apr. 1957): 795.

[88]Like presidents, Supreme Court justices are subjected to the rating game. See e.g., Albert P. Blaustein and Roy M. Merksy, "Rating Supreme Court Justices," *ABA Journal* 58, No. 2 (Nov. 1972): 1183–92. See also Abraham, *Justices and Presidents*, 9–11 and App. A.

Elsewhere, Abraham has argued that "merit" can, to some extent, be defined and that the quality of Supreme Court justices has been consistently high. See his "'A Bench Happily Filled': Some Historical Reflections on the Supreme Court Appointment Process," *Judicature* 66, No. 7 (Feb. 1983): 282–95.

[89]A brief history of the application of the geographic factor may be found in *Guide to the U.S. Supreme Court,* 791–93. See also a more recent discussion of this factor, reentitled "symbolic representation," in Thomas R. Marshall, "Symbolic versus Policy Representation on the U.S. Supreme Court," *Journal of Politics* 55, No. 1 (Feb. 1993): 140–50.

[90]See Abraham, *Justices and Presidents,* 63–65.

closer examination reveals that all of these factors are, at bottom, political. When the president ponders the significance of the ABA ratings, he or she is approaching a judgment about the political costs and benefits involved in accepting or rejecting such recommendations; when the president considers the possible significance of race or sex or geography, he or she must ultimately calculate the political advantage to self and party in honoring (or not honoring) such representational claims; and, most obviously, when making a choice on the basis of ideology, the president is angling for maximum policy impact, favorable to his or her overall political strategy. Hence, while we speak of the importance of representational or professional legal factors, we are ultimately talking about politics.

The Senate

Depending upon how one undertakes the count, there have been 145 nominations to the Supreme Court, including the selection of Stephen Breyer. Of these, 28 were either rejected outright by the Senate or were withdrawn or not acted upon.[91] Thus, the failure rate has not been high, just under 20 percent. There was nearly one in three failed nominations in the nineteenth century (actually, about 30 percent), whereas only eight nominations have ended in failure in the present century, or some 13 percent. Only four of these were outright Senate rejections (John J. Parker in 1930; the two Nixon nominees, Clement Haynsworth and G. Harrold Carswell in 1969 and 1970; and the Bork rejection in 1987), while four were withdrawn or no action was taken.[92]

These figures, though showing a failure rate much higher than that for lower federal courts nominations, nonetheless underscore the unwritten rule in federal judicial selection. That rule, noted earlier, is that the president's choices are to be shown considerable deference and can be expected to win Senate approval, barring serious issues of ethical or professional acceptability, unusually sharp ideological clashes, or lack of deference to Senatorial courtesy. Nominations to the Supreme Court in this century tend to support the generalization, although there have indeed been some notable exceptions.

One might cite as the first "problem" or exception in Supreme Court confirmation politics in this century the choice of John J. Parker by President Hoover in 1930. However, because the vote against confirmation was quite close, it is probably fair to say that the combined opposition of the labor unions and the NAACP would probably not have been sufficient to defeat the nomination without the few "anti-Hoover" senators, particularly Robert M. LaFollette of Wisconsin and George Norris of Nebraska. Hence, the Parker case could be seen as supportive of, rather than contradictory to, the preceding generalization.[93]

The monumental struggle surrounding the nomination of Louis Brandeis in 1916 can be seen as another case supporting the pro-president rule. Even with the staunch and persistent opposition of major bar and business interests, the Senate nonetheless confirmed Brandeis by a vote of 47–22. Additionally, when President Hoover appointed Charles Evans Hughes to the chief justiceship in early 1930, the bitter opposition of a large number of influential senators was not enough to prevent a strong confirmation vote of 52–26.

[91]See *Guide to the United States Supreme Court*, 652.
[92]On the politics of Senate confirmations, see Abraham, *Justices and Presidents*, 39–48; and John Massaro, *Supremely Political: The Role of Ideology and Presidential Management in Unsuccessful Supreme Court Nominations* (Albany: State University of New York Press, 1990). Massaro argues that the nominee's ideology, combined (to a lesser extent) with presidential mismanagement, can explain recent Senate defeats of Supreme Court nominees.
[93]See Abraham's account of this confirmation failure in his *Justices and Presidents*, 42–43.

What, then, befell President Nixon in his almost unprecedented failure to replace the discredited Abe Fortas first with Clement F. Haynsworth, Jr., then with G. Harrold Carswell?[94] Having just rejected the nomination of Abe Fortas to the chief justiceship on grounds of questionable ethical practices in his off-the-bench financial dealings, it was difficult for the Senate to set such considerations aside in the case of Haynsworth, whose insensitivity to conflict of interest matters while on the bench ultimately ensured his 55–45 defeat.[95] Though the nomination was clearly opposed by labor and minority groups, these forces would probably not have been sufficient to defeat him had it not been for the ethical issue.

In the case of Carswell, the best evidence suggests that in the face of the Haynsworth defeat, President Nixon nominated the ex-judge from Florida out of vengeance. He would show the Senate who was boss! He would push through the nomination no matter what![96] Few would deny that of the two, Haynsworth was the better choice, if not on ethical then clearly on professional grounds. Carswell's abject racism, even in the year 1969, might have been less than fatal[97]; but as the hearings proceeded, it became increasingly evident that the nominee was professionally and intellectually shallow, that his judicial record was singularly undistinguished, and that he was simply not up to Supreme Court caliber.[98] Even so, arguments of his opponents on this score might have been insufficient had not his *supporters* moved in to dispense all doubt. In one of the most widely quoted remarks in the annals of judicial politics, Senator Roman Hruska (R-Neb.) was reported as saying: "Even if he [Carswell] were mediocre, there are a lot of mediocre judges and people and lawyers. They are entitled to a little representation, aren't they, and a little chance? We can't have all Brandeises, and Frankfurters, and Cardozos and stuff like that there."[99] That was enough! The Senate, on April 9, 1970, voted 51–45 against confirmation. Following angry denunciations of the senators for their sectional prejudice and vicious assaults on his Southern nominees, the president moved to a Northerner, Harry A. Blackmun, a Minnesotan and friend of Chief Justice Burger. Blackmun was confirmed by the Senate on June 22, 1970, 94–0.

---

[94]Nixon's troubles were not quite unprecedented in that President Grover Cleveland suffered the same fate in 1894. See Joel B. Grossman and Stephen S. Wasby, "The Senate and Supreme Court Nominations: Some Reflections," *Duke University Law Review* (1972): 557–91.

[95]See "The Nomination Is Rejected," *Newsweek* (Dec. 1, 1969): 21–26. See also Joel B. Grossman and Stephen S. Wasby, "Haynsworth and Parker: History Does Live Again," *South Carolina Law Review* 23, No. 3 (June 1971): 345–59.

[96]At least this is the argument set forth by Abraham in *Justices and Presidents,* 15–19. See also the more lengthy study of the Carswell nomination by Richard Harris, *Decision* (New York: Dutton, 1971).

[97]See Harris, *Decision,* 15–16. In a speech in 1948, Carswell said:

I am a Southerner by ancestry, birth, training, inclination, belief and practice. I believe that segregation of the races is proper and the only practical and correct way of life in our states. . . . I yield to no man . . . in the firm, vigorous belief in the principle of white supremacy, and I shall always be so governed.

Carswell's later actions, as in his involvement in the conversion of a public golf course in Tallahassee to a private, all-white club, gave evidence of his continuing racism.

[98]In a widely quoted (and apparently effective) commentary, Louis Pollak, Dean of the Yale School of Law, said that Judge Carswell "presents more slender credentials than any nominee for the Supreme Court put forth in this century." Quoted in Grossman and Wasby, "Senate and Supreme Court Nominations," 585.

[99]See Harris, *Decision,* 110. It is interesting to note that although Hruska's mediocrity statement has become something of a joke, it was precisely this same argument which was used by supporters of Daniel Manion in his fight for confirmation in June and July of 1986. See, e.g., the remarks of Douglas McFadden regarding Manion in Paul Houston, "Manion Given a Bum Rap, Backers Say," *Los Angeles Times* (July 13, 1986): 1.

The "pro-president" rule in Senate response to Supreme Court nominations requires further comment in the light of President Reagan's unsuccessful nomination of Bork, as well as the near-defeat of President Bush's selectee, Clarence Thomas, both discussed before. Certainly Thomas's confirmation supports the rule, if any recent event can. Singularly undistinguished in his legal career, coming to the Senate with the weakest recommendation in the history of the American Bar Association, and in further consideration of a seriously besmirched record due to the accusations of Prof. Anita Hill, Thomas was nonetheless confirmed by a Democratically controlled Senate by a vote of 52–48, with 11 Democrats and 41 Republicans voting in the affirmative. Not since Carswell had a president chosen so weak a candidate for the high court. Thomas's confirmation clearly illustrates, among other things, the strength of the president's domination of the selection process and, paradoxically, is most reminiscent of the Brandeis struggle in that respect. But what of the Bork fiasco?

The "pro-president" rule, as with all generalizations about political outcomes, operates within certain constraints. Here, it is clear that President Reagan reached beyond the range of sociopolitical acceptability in his choice of Robert Bork. When the nominee was adjudged simply too extreme even for certain key Republicans, the game was up. And perhaps too little has been made of the fact that Judge Bork helped in his own defeat by an incredible disingenuous attempt to paint himself as something he was not. Ultimately, President Reagan had no difficulty in seating a justice of appropriate conservative coloration—Justice Anthony Kennedy—and this in the face of the president's lame-duck status and a Democratically controlled Senate. In sum, the four outright presidential defeats in this century—Parker, Haynsworth, Carswell, and Bork—represent but 7 percent of Supreme Court nominees who have faced Senatorial scrutiny since 1900,[100] and no one has argued that these presidents have been forced to accept unpalatable alternative choices. Thus, the record clearly reveals a presidentially dominated selection process for the Supreme Court, and even more so for the lower federal courts.

What, then, are the results of the Supreme Court selection process? A profile of the 108 Supreme Court justices up to 1994 may be gleaned from Table 6–10. Broadly speaking, the collective profile resembles that of lower court judges. John Schmidhauser gathered information on the socioeconomic backgrounds of 101 justices of the Supreme Court up to 1976 and analyzed that data by six historic eras: (1) 1789–1828, the gentry era; (2) 1829–1861, the Jacksonian era; (3) 1862–1888, the period of the rise of corporate America; (4) 1889–1919, an era of demand for social equality; (5) 1920–1932, a time of conservative resurgence; and (6) 1933–1976, the New Deal and its aftermath. Schmidhauser concluded that

Throughout American history there has been an overwhelming tendency for presidents to choose nominees for the Supreme Court from among the socially advantaged families. The typical Supreme Court justice has generally been white, Protestant (with a penchant for a high social status denomination), usually of ethnic stock originating in the British Isles, and born in comfortable circumstances in an urban or small-town environment. In the early history of the Court, he very likely was born in the aristocratic gentry class, while later he tended to come from the professionalized upper middle class. While nearly two-thirds of his fellows were selected from politically active families, a third of his fellows were chosen from families having a tradition of judicial service. In college and legal education, the average justice was afforded very advantageous opportunities for training and associations. His age at appointment has risen in each period from a median 47 years in

---

[100]The figure is 8 percent if we count the Abe Fortas case wherein the nomination was withdrawn in the face of a Senate filibuster.

Table 6–10 Characteristics of Supreme Court Justices

Social Club Membership	Percentage of Justices
National Upper Class	45
Local Elite	48
Religious Affiliation	
Protestant	88
Catholic	7
Jewish	5
Ethnicity	
Caucasian	98
Black	2
Hispanic	0
American Indian	0

Sources: John R. Schmidhauser, *Judges and Justices: The Federal Appellate Judiciary* (Boston: Little, Brown, 1979), 60–61; and Henry J. Abraham, *Justices and Presidents,* 3rd ed. (New York: Oxford University Press, 1992), 61–66.

the first to 51, 54, 55, and 58, with a decline to 54 in 1933–1976. Very few sons of families outside the upper or upper middle social economic classes have been able to acquire the particular type of education and the subsequent professional and especially political associations which appear to be unwritten prerequisites for appointment to the nation's highest tribunal.[101]

Clearly, the data paint a WASPish, elitist portrait, and the eight selectees since Schmidhauser's study have done little to change this overall picture, the Thomas nomination to the contrary notwithstanding. Socioeconomic status profiles of most political decision-making groups in American society have a similar appearance. Such findings give pause and make more understandable President Carter's and President Clinton's desire to open the ranks of the federal judiciary to groups heretofore excluded.

TENURE AND TURNOVER

As provided in Article III, Section 1 of the Constitution,

> The Judges, both of the supreme and inferior Courts, shall hold their Offices during good Behaviour, and shall, at stated Times, receive for their Services, a Compensation, which shall not be diminished during their continuance in Office.

---

[101]See Schmidhauser, *Judges and Justices,* 96.

Few policy-making positions in government are more secure than that of federal judges. They tend to achieve their positions midway in their professional careers and remain in their posts at their own pleasure. The average age for appointment to the federal trial bench in the six presidencies prior to President Clinton was 49.3, for the Courts of Appeals 51.5. Moving back in time to 1900, the average age at appointment of all lower federal court judges in this century has been 50.9. For district court judges alone, that figure is 50.2 years of age; for judges of the U.S. Courts of Appeals, 53.2 years old.[102] For the Supreme Court, the average age at appointment has been somewhat older, just under 56 for justices appointed from 1900 to the present.

The average length of service in the twentieth century for all Article III judges has been 13.9 years. For the district court judges alone, this figure is 14 years; for U.S. Courts of Appeals judges it is 13.3 years. The mean length of service for Supreme Court justices in this century is 14 years. At midterm, then, the average age of all lower court judges taken together is just under 58 years of age; for Supreme Court justices, midterm is about 70 years old. With the beginning of the Supreme Court's Fall 1995 term, the average age of the nine justices was a little over 61, a time when many citizens begin to consider retiring.

Given the view of the federal judgeships as the capstone of a person's legal or political career, along with the data indicating the rather advanced age at which appointment usually occurs, it is not surprising that our federal courts have suffered from the problem of superannuation—judges who, though long past their prime, have elected to remain on the bench. This has been a particular concern for the Supreme Court. Notable examples include Justice Robert Grier, who, in his mid-seventies, reached the point at which he could no longer perform his duties. In 1869, a group of his colleagues managed to persuade him to resign. Another example is Justice Stephen J. Field nominated by President Lincoln in 1863, who served on the Court for 34 years, and at the age of 80 found himself in severely failing health. Although he initially refused the suggestion of his colleagues that he resign, he eventually gave in. A more recent example is Justice William O. Douglas. Appointed by Franklin D. Roosevelt at the age of 40 (the youngest man appointed to the Court in this century), Justice Douglas had served on the Court nearly 36 years when, in January 1975, he suffered a stroke that left him severely impaired. Nonetheless, he continued on for nine more months. When he eventually retired in November 1975, he had established a new record for length of service, 36 years, 7 months, beating that set by Justice Field, who had served 34 years, 4 months.[103]

Congress was slow in legislating attractive retirement plans for federal judges. In 1869, it provided that any federal judge who reached 70 years of age, with at least 10 years of service, could resign on full salary. Nevertheless, power is not easily relinquished, and some judges continue to hang on to their positions. Oliver Wendell Holmes, Jr., having served on the Court 29 years, finally retired in 1932 at the age of nearly 90![104]

---

[102]Data on the tenure and ages at appointment of lower federal court judges were graciously provided by Prof. Gerald S. Gryski of Auburn University (letter to author Jan. 18, 1994). See also Gary Zuk, Gerald S. Gryski, and Deborah J. Barrow, "Partisan Transformation of the Federal Judiciary, 1969–1992," *American Politics Quarterly* 21, No. 1 (Jan. 1993): 439–57.

[103]Currently (Fall 1996) Justice Stevens, at 76, is the oldest justice on the Court. However, as noted earlier, Justice Blackmun (the last justice to retire from the Court, to be replaced by Justice Breyer) was over 85-1/2 when he relinquished his seat.

[104]The adult life of this remarkable man spans the period from the Civil War (he was a captain in the Union Army and was twice wounded) well into the first term of Franklin D. Roosevelt. Born March 8, 1841, he died three years after he left the Court, on March 6, 1935, two days before his 94th birthday. See Catherine Drinker Bowen, *Yankee from Olympus: Justice Holmes and His Family* (Boston: Little, Brown, 1944).

Some judges and justices have been known to remain on the bench for political reasons. Of late, Justices Brennan and Marshall were said to have preferred to be replaced by justices chosen by a Democratic president, although neither was successful in this strategy. In former times, Justice Nathan Clifford, the only Democrat left on the Court by 1880, endeavored to stay on until a Democratic president could name his successor. He did not make it. He died while on the bench at the age of 77, with 23 years of service. Chief Justice Taft, too, was determined to hang on as long as possible. In a widely quoted statement, he said,

> I am older and slower and less acute and more confused. However, as long as things continue as they are, and I am able to answer in my place, I must stay on the Court in order to prevent the Bolsheviki from getting control. . . . [The] only hope we have of keeping a consistent declaration of constitutional law is for us to live as long as we can . . . [The] truth is that Hoover is a Progressive just as Stone is, and just as Brandeis is and just as Holmes is.[105]

Actually, Chief Justice Taft wanted to avoid the appointment of his successor by Herbert Hoover. However, like Justice Clifford, he did not make it. Resigning in February 1930, he died one month later. His replacement, appointed by President Hoover, was Charles Evans Hughes. Justice Douglas's attempt to outlast the Republican administration of President Ford was likewise unsuccessful. It was ironic that President Ford was able to appoint Douglas's successor (John Paul Stevens), for it was Congressman Gerald Ford who had spearheaded an attempt to impeach Douglas. Other justices have remained on the Court for financial reasons. Justice Ward Hunt, for example, suffered a severe stroke seven years into his term, but remained on until he was eligible for pension.[106]

The departure of lower federal judges has also been associated with political considerations. Through extensive historical research, scholars have recently demonstrated that federal district and lower appellate judges's retirement decisions are heavily colored by political (party) as well as political-ideological factors, the usual game being attempts to time one's departure to ensure one's replacement by the "right" president.[107]

By 1932, the retirement options of Supreme Court justices had worsened. For all federal judges except Supreme Court justices, retirement rather than outright resignation was a possibility, entitling them to the full salary of their office, as well as any subsequent raises in that salary. Justices of the Supreme Court, however, could only resign, putting them at the mercy of Congress in its cost-cutting moods. For example, Oliver Wendell Holmes retired from the Court in 1932 on a salary of $10,000 per year, half his ordinary salary as Associate Justice. Such a system helps to explain why elderly justices of the New Deal period remained on the bench—to the utter frustration of President Roosevelt.

Although the FDR court-packing plan was not passed in Congress, a considerably liberalized retirement plan was, providing for retirement with full pay for Supreme Court Justices at age 70 who had 10 years of experience, or at age 65 with 15 years service. "Very quickly, Justice Willis Van Devanter announced his retirement, effective June 2, 1937. This

[105]See Henry F. Pringle, *The Life and Times of William Howard Taft,* Vol. 2 (New York: Farrar & Rinehart, 1939), 967.

[106]See *Guide to the United States Supreme Court,* 833.

[107]See the extensive research by Professors Deborah J. Barrow and Gary Zuk, e.g., "An Institutional Analysis of Turnover in the Lower Federal Courts, 1900–1987," *Journal of Politics* 51, No. 2 (May 1990): 457–76; and Zuk, Gryski, and Barrow, "Partisan Transformation of the Federal Judiciary," 457. A very useful follow-up of this line of inquiry is reported in James F. Spriggs, II, and Paul J. Wahlbeck, "Calling It Quits: Strategic Retirement on the Federal Courts of Appeals, 1893–1991," *Political Research Quarterly* 48, No. 3 (Sept. 1995): 573–97.

provided President Roosevelt his first Supreme Court vacancy, which he filled with the appointment of Hugo Black.[108]

Since 1937, federal judicial retirement options have been further sweetened. Currently, federal judges can retire under the "Rule of Eighty" (when the sum of their age and years of service reaches 80). Further, "senior status" may be taken; when the judges or justices opt for this category, salary increases continue (along with retaining their office and staff) provided that they assume at least 25 percent of the load of a full, active judge. Thus, a Supreme Court justice, for instance, may take senior status (as did Justices Powell and White), serve occasionally on lower federal courts, and continue a number of "perks" from their former full-service status. Despite these inducements, however, federal judges, especially justices of the Supreme Court, have shown themselves remarkably tenacious in holding on to their seats. Hence, in this century, only seven Supreme Court justices have departed for reasons other than age or ill-health.[109] As summed up by a prominent legal historian,

> After 1838 the average age at which members of the Supreme Court have been selected has been well over 50 years. Age and career status generally combined to reinforce the tendency of justices to view appointments as their final career advancement. Hence, there was little incentive to invoke the statutory options for retirement or resignation until health considerations made it imperative.[110]

As with the states, the federal system has limped along for some time with ineffective mechanisms for compulsory removal of judges. In fact, the federal judicial system still remains somewhat behind the states in this regard, for no unified federal disciplinary commission has ever been established. Despite the existence of judicial councils (which could serve as disciplinary bodies) within each of the appellate circuits, impeachment has remained the ultimate weapon for involuntary removal of federal judges throughout most of our history.

Up to 1986, the House of Representatives had voted bills of impeachment against only 10 federal judges, though 9 others resigned before formal charges could be brought. Of the 10, action was brought against a Supreme Court Justice only once (Samuel Chase in 1804), while on 8 occasions federal district judges, as well as an associate judge of the United States Commerce Court, have been impeached. The Senate convicted only 4 of these; Supreme Court Justice Samuel Chase and four of the district judges were acquitted. An examination of these 10 impeachment proceedings reveals a history of blatant political attacks on the courts. Actual malevolence in judicial office was much less in evidence than was judicial policy-making found to be repugnant to key members of Congress. Such has been the case with the periodic attempts or threats to impeach Supreme Court justices in recent decades, the two attempts to impeach Justice Douglas being perhaps the best examples.[111] On the other hand, the threatened impeachment of

---

[108]*Guide to the United States Supreme Court,* 657, 783.

[109]In The Twentieth Century Fund, *The Good Judge* (New York: Priority Press, 1989): 83, this number is reported as eight, but there is no listing. Prof. Abraham lists the seven as Chief Justice Hughes and Justices Clarke, Byrnes, Goldberg, Tom Clark, Fortas, and Stewart. Arguably, Chief Justice Burger might be added to this list. See Henry J. Abraham, *The Judicial Process,* 6th ed. (New York: Oxford University Press, 1993: 41–42.

[110]Kermit L. Hall, ed., *The Oxford Companion to the United States Supreme Court* (New York: Oxford University Press, 1992), 729. The importance of physical infirmity as a reason for Supreme Court retirements is underscored in research by Prof. Peverill Squire. See his "Explaining Retirement from the Supreme Court," a paper delivered at the Annual Meeting of the Western Political Science Association, Mar. 26–28, 1987.

[111]See *Guide to the United States Supreme Court,* 657–58. Douglas gives his own account in his autobiography, *The Court Years,* 355–77.

Justice Abe Fortas in 1969 for financial improprieties (or at the very least, indiscretions) which led to his resignation, though obviously political, seemed to have been guided by more tangible evidence.[112]

On June 3, 1986, Peter Rodino, Jr. (D-N.J.), chairman of the House Judiciary Committee, introduced articles of impeachment against Harry E. Claiborne, United States District Judge in Nevada. Judge Claiborne, a Carter appointee, was convicted of failing to report $106,000 income in 1978 and 1979, and on May 16, 1986, was sentenced to a two-year term in federal prison, the first sitting federal judge accorded this dishonor. Even so, he refused to resign his judicial seat (and relinquish his then $78,700 annual salary), maintaining that an impeachment trial in the Senate would afford him an opportunity to clear himself of the charges. The Judiciary Subcommittee on Courts, Civil Liberties, and the Administration of Justice voted unanimously on June 24 for impeachment, and the full committee voted likewise. The House kept the perfect record by also unanimously approving impeachment. The vote on July 22 was 406–0.[113]

Judge Claiborne enjoyed little support from either party, nor even from members of the Nevada congressional delegation, his behavior being viewed as scandalous and damaging to the integrity of the federal judiciary. His conviction thus seemed assured as deliberations opened before a 12-member special Senate committee on September 15, 1986.[114] After seven days of testimony, including two by Judge Claiborne himself, the Senate panel submitted its findings to the full body for final disposition, which came on October 9. The vote to convict was 87–10 and 90–7, respectively, on the first two articles of impeachment relating to the judge's criminal conviction on income tax evasion. On impeachment article 4, charging that Claiborne "betrayed the trust of the people of the United States," the vote was 89–8 for conviction. Impeachment article 3, simply charging Claiborne with being found guilty of these charges, did not pass. However, a two-thirds vote against Claiborne on any of the articles would have been sufficient for conviction and removal.[115]

This Senate action marked the first time in 50 years that a federal judge has been removed by impeachment. In April of 1936, Judge Halstead Ritter of the United States District Court for the Southern District of Florida was impeached by the House and convicted in the Senate, again for the offense, among others, of income tax evasion. The 1986 Senate action also made history in the use of a special committee. Previous impeachment proceedings were held only before the full Senate. Even this shortcut did not satisfy a number of senators who believe judicial impeachments are too cumbersome to be handled by the Senate.[116]

Three years following Judge Claiborne's forced removal from office, two more federal district judges were impeached. The first of these, Judge Alcee L. Hastings of the Southern District of Florida (a Carter appointee), was acquitted in Federal district court of conspiracy

---

[112]See *Congressional Quarterly Almanac, 1969* (Washington: Congressional Quarterly, 1969), 136–39. A lengthy study of the Fortas case is Robert A. Shogan, *A Question of Judgment* (Indianapolis: Bobbs-Merrill, 1972).

[113]See Philip Shenon, "Impeachment of U.S. Judge Passes House," *New York Times* (July 23, 1986): 1.

[114]See Linda Greenhouse, "Senate Preparing for Trial of Judge," *New York Times* (Oct. 5, 1986): A-41.

[115]Linda Greenhouse, "Senate Convicts U.S. Judge, Ousting Him from Office," *New York Times* (Oct. 10, 1986): A-1, 23. See also "Senate Finds Claiborne Guilty, Strips Him of Federal Judgeship," *Congressional Quarterly Weekly Report* 44, No. 41 (Oct. 11, 1986): 2569–70.

[116]See the two items by Linda Greenhouse on this point in the *New York Times:* "Senators Criticize Process for Impeaching Judges" (Oct. 11, 1986): A-8; and "After a Vote to Convict, Qualms in the Senate" (Oct. 12, 1986): E-6.

and obstruction of justice charges, alleging an attempt to obtain monetary payment in exchange for lighter sentences for two defendants in his court. The Senate nonetheless supported impeachment on October 20, 1989, primarily on the charge of conspiracy to obtain a bribe (69–26) as well as a number of other articles earlier voted by the House of Representatives.[117]

Only two weeks later, on November 3, the Senate repeated this action by convicting Judge Walter L. Nixon, Jr., on two counts of perjury and removing him from office. Judge Nixon, former Chief Judge of the Federal District Court for the Southern District of Mississippi, was named to the bench by President Johnson in 1968. The judge was convicted in 1986 in federal district court of lying to a federal grand jury and to Justice Department investigators in denying that he had intervened in a drug case to protect the son of a business associate. The judge was sentenced to five years in prison.[118] Judge Nixon was the seventh federal judge to be convicted in our history.

All three of these cases—those of Judges Claiborne, Hastings, and Nixon—were processed through the special twelve-member Senate committee established for that purpose, and all three judges complained of the unconstitutionality of the procedure. Judge Hastings won a reversal of his impeachment by U.S. District Judge Stanley Sporkin, who ruled that only the full Senate could impeach. Judge Nixon, on the other hand, lost his appeal before a special three-judge panel of the U.S. Court of Appeals for the District of Columbia, the court ruling that the judiciary was without power to review impeachment proceedings. The U.S. Supreme Court granted *certiorari* in the Nixon case, and on January 13, 1993, unanimously upheld the questioned Senate procedure (*Nixon v. U.S.*, 113 S.Ct. 732). The Court reasoned that the judiciary had no standing to review impeachments, since the Constitution gives the Senate the "sole power" in this area.[119] As an ironic finale to the Hastings affair, the former judge won a seat in the U.S. House of Representative from the 23rd District of Florida in the 1992 elections, and may now vote on the impeachments of future federal officials!

In the early 1990s, this historic flurry of impeachment proceedings was capped by the near-impeachment of two more federal judges. Judge Robert P. Aguilar of the Federal District Court of Northern California, another Carter appointee, was convicted on August 22, 1990, of informing a distant relative by marriage of a federal wiretap in early 1988 and of obstruction of justice by lying to federal agents about his role in the matter. Sentencing Aguilar to only six months in prison and assigning one thousand hours of community service, the presiding judge reasoned that Aguilar faced "long, humiliating, embarrassing and burdensome" proceedings involving disbarment and impeachment, justifying a departure from the ordinarily applicable federal sentencing guidelines. However, on June 24, 1996, after seven years, two trials, and three appeals, Judge Aguilar finally agreed to

[117]See Joan Biskupic, "Hastings Removed From Bench After Conviction by Senate," *Congressional Quarterly Weekly Report* (Oct. 21, 1989): 2800–02. The Claiborne, Hastings, and Nixon impeachments are covered in detail in an excellent study by Mary L. Volcansek, *Judicial Impeachment: None Called for Justice* (Urbana, Ill.: University of Illinois Press, 1993).

[118]Joan Biskupic, "Senate Convicts Judge Nixon, Removes Him From Bench," *Congressional Quarterly Weekly Report* (Nov. 4, 1989): 2955. Both the Hastings and the Nixon impeachments are discussed in some detail in Eleanore Bushnell, *Crimes, Follies and Misfortunes: The Federal Impeachment Trials* (Urbana: University of Illinois Press, 1992): 307–23.

[119]See Holly Idelson, "Senate Impeachment Powers Upheld by Justices," *Congressional Quarterly Weekly Report* (Jan. 16, 1993): 129–130. See also Linda Greenhouse, "Court Upholds a Shortcut Used to Impeach 2 Judges," *New York Times* (Jan. 14, 1993): A-15; and Stephen L. Wasby, "Legal Notes: Impeachment as a 'Political Question,'" *Justice System Journal* 16, No. 3 (1994): 113–116.

resign (with full pay of $133,600 annually) in return for the dropping of all federal charges.[120]

In the other case, Judge Robert F. Collins, appointed to the federal bench in New Orleans in 1978 by President Carter, was found guilty of three counts of bribery, conspiracy, and obstruction of justice in connection with accepting $100,000 from a convicted drug dealer in exchange for a lenient sentence. The judge was sentenced to six years and ten months in prison, which he began serving while continuing to enjoy his salary of $125,000 per year. On June 24, 1993, impeachment proceedings against Judge Collins were begun in the House, although prior to a House vote—on August 6, 1993—the judge submitted his resignation to President Clinton.[121]

The Supreme Court's *Nixon* decision, the first ever on the power of impeachment, has relieved the Senate of the burdensome chore of involving the entire body in such trials, as had been the practice prior to the Claiborne case. Still, impeachment remains a blunderbuss for dealing with much federal judicial misconduct (such as incompetence, infirmity, and minor ethical transgressions falling short of "Treason, Bribery, and other high Crimes and Misdemeanors" specified in the Constitution), and some senators have argued that a separate commission be established for such purposes.[122] Proposals to this end have been introduced in Congress. In the past, the judicial councils of each federal circuit might well have stepped into the disciplinary breech, but most choose not to involve themselves in this painful task. An exception was the action of the Judicial Council of the Tenth Circuit, which in 1966 relieved Judge Steven C. Chandler of his duties, though not his office and salary. In *Chandler v. Judicial Council of the Tenth Circuit,* 398 U.S. 74 (1970), the Supreme Court denied *certiorari,* thereby ostensibly upholding the legality of such disciplinary measures.[123]

After a number of attempts, Congress passed the Judicial Councils Reform and Judicial Conduct and Disability Act of 1980 (PL 96-458), which took effect October 1 of that year. The new legislation sought to fill the disciplinary sanction gap between impeachment, on the one hand, and mere informal pressure on the other, by restructuring the judicial councils of each circuit and empowering them to appoint investigatory committees to look into complaints of improper judicial conduct. While the act authorizes the councils to remove from office magistrates and bankruptcy judges, Article III judges may still be removed only by formal impeachment as provided for in the Constitution. Punishment short of impeachment may include a certification of disability, requesting voluntary retirement, private or public censure, or prohibiting further case assignment.[124] Data are lacking to provide a conclusive assessment of the Act, although it has clearly failed to deal with some of the more serious cases.[125] Meanwhile, Congress

---

[120]A brief overview of the Aguilar affair may be gleaned from Katherine Bishop, "Federal Judge Is Given Reduced Prison Sentence in Corruption Case," *New York Times* (Nov. 2, 1990): A-12; and Miranda Ewell, "Judge Aguilar Steps Down," *San Jose Mercury* (June 25, 1996): A-1.

[121]Frances Frank Marcus, "Federal Judge Is Found Guilty in Bribery Trail," *New York Times* (June 30, 1991): I-1; "U.S. Judge Is Given Prison Sentence," *New York Times* (Sept. 8, 1991): A-11; and "Impeachment Process Set for Convicted Judge," *Congressional Quarterly Weekly Report* (June 26, 1993): 1669.

[122]For a recent survey and analysis of the impeachment process at the national level, see Michael J. Gerhardt, *The Federal Impeachment Process: A Constitutional and Historical Analysis* (Princeton: Princeton University Press, 1996). See also the very useful work by Volcansek, *Judicial Impeachment.*

[123]See Robert R. Davis, Jr., "The Chandler Incident and Problems of Removal," *Stanford Law Review* 19, No. 1 (Feb. 1967): 448–67.

[124]See Stephen B. Burbank, "The Federal Judicial Discipline Act: Is Decentralized Self-regulation Working?" *Judicature* 67, No. 4 (Oct. 1983): 183–99, who finds a number of deficiencies in the act, particularly of a procedural nature.

[125]See Collins T. Fitzpatrick, "Misconduct and Disability of Federal Judges: The Unreported Informal Responses," *Judicature* 71, No. 5 (Feb.–Mar. 1988): 282–83.

continues to struggle with the continuing—and growing—problem of federal judicial discipline.

FURTHER READING

Abraham, Henry J. "'A Bench Happily Filled': Some Historical Reflections on the Supreme Court Appointment Process." *Judicature* 66, No. 7 (Feb. 1983): 282–95.

———. *Justices and Presidents: A Political History of Appointments to the Supreme Court,* 3rd ed. New York: Oxford University Press, 1992.

Berkson, Larry C., and Susan B. Carbon. *The United States Circuit Judge Nominating Commission: Its Members, Procedures and Candidates.* Chicago: American Judicature Society, 1980.

Bronner, Ethan. *Battle for Justice: How the Bork Nomination Shook America.* New York: W. W. Norton, 1989.

Chase, Harold W. *Federal Judges: The Appointing Process.* Minneapolis: University of Minnesota Press, 1972.

Goldman, Sheldon. *Picking Federal Judges: Lower Court Selection from Roosevelt to Reagan.* New Haven: Yale University Press, 1997.

Goldman, Sheldon. "Reagan's Judicial Legacy: Completing the Puzzle and Summing Up." *Judicature* 72, No. 6 (Apr.–May 1989): 318–330.

———. "Bush's Judicial Legacy: The Final Imprint." *Judicature* 76, No. 6 (Apr.–May, 1993): 282–97.

Grossman, Joel B. *Lawyers and Judges: The ABA and the Politics of Judicial Selection.* New York: Wiley, 1965.

Harris, Joseph P. *The Advice and Consent of the Senate.* Berkeley: University of California Press, 1955.

Harris, Richard. *Decision.* New York: Dutton, 1971.

Howard, J. Woodford, Jr. *Courts of Appeals in the Federal Judicial System.* Princeton: Princeton University Press, 1981, Ch. 4.

Jackson, Donald Dale. *Judges.* New York: Atheneum, 1974.

Murphy, Walter F. "Reagan's Judicial Strategy," in Larry Berman, *Looking Back on the Reagan Presidency.* Baltimore: Johns Hopkins University Press, 1990, 207–237.

O'Brien, David M. *Judicial Roulette: Report of the Twentieth Century Fund Task Force on Judicial Selection.* New York: Priority Press, 1988.

Schmidhauser, John R. *Judges and Justices: The Federal Appellate Judiciary.* Boston: Little, Brown, 1979.

Slotnick, Elliot E. "Federal Judicial Recruitment and Selection Research: A Review Essay." *Judicature* 71, No. 6 (Apr.–May 1988): 317–24.

Tribe, Lawrence H. *God Save This Honorable Court: How the Choice of Supreme Court Justices Shapes Our History.* New York: Random House, 1985.

Watson, George L. and John A. Stookey. *Shaping America: The Politics of Supreme Court Appointments.* New York: HarperCollins, 1995.

Zuk, Gary, Gerald S. Gryski, and Deborah J. Barrow. "Partisan Transformation of the Federal Judiciary, 1869–1992." *American Politics Quarterly* 21, No. 1 (Jan. 1993): 439–57.

7
The Politics of Legal Advice

The first thing we do, let's kill all the lawyers.
—Shakespeare,
King Henry VI, Act IV, Scene 2

But one of the lawyers answering, said to him, "Master, in saying these things, you insultest us also." But he said, "Woe to you lawyers also! Because you load men with oppressive burdens and you yourselves with one of your fingers do not touch the burdens."
—St. Luke, 11:45–46

I never overcame my dislike for the profession. . . . [Cases] wore on for years; nothing was ever finished. . . . [Corporations] were able to avoid responsibility for neglect by pleading . . . contributory negligence, the assumption of risk, or the negligence of a fellow employee. . . . It seemed incredible that a learned profession should countenance the absurdity of applying rules of by-gone days to modern industrial conditions.
—Fredrick C. Howe,
The Confessions of a Reformer

We have the heaviest concentration of lawyers on earth— . . . three times more than England, four times more than in Germany, twenty-one times more than in Japan. We have more litigation; but I am not sure we have more justice. No resources of talent and training in our society, not even medical care, are more wastefully or unfairly distributed than legal skills. Ninety percent of our lawyers serve ten percent of our people. We are over-lawyered, and under-represented.
—President Jimmy Carter,
Speech before the Los Angeles County Bar Association, May 4, 1978

One Million Lawyers and Other Disasters
—1985 Tom Paxton album title

Disapprobation of lawyers and the legal profession is timeless and universal.[1] From imperial Rome to the postindustrial United States, from Cicero to former president Jimmy Carter, commentary on the legal profession is replete with remonstrances against virtually every aspect of legal practice and against virtually everyone in any way identified with it.[2] The purpose here, however, is not to follow in the tradition of castigating lawyers, but rather to observe and better understand who they are and what they do from a distinctly political perspective.

THE ATTORNEY ROLE(S)

Scholars have traditionally studied the legal profession using three separate though related and overlapping conceptualizations: lawyers as lawyers, lawyers in other policy-making roles (for example, as legislators or governmental administrators), and lawyers in their quasi-legal, though still extraprofessional, social role. Social scientists and lawyers themselves have long been interested in following up de Tocqueville's celebrated observation on the political and social role of the legal profession in America,[3] focusing on lawyers in their nonlegal, or at least nontechnical legal roles—as legislators, for example,[4] or as governmental administrators.[5] The findings of such research are of obvious interest to the political scientist, for to the extent that lawyers play distinctive formal roles in community or national policy-making, they are, by definition, important subjects of study. An additional role that attorneys play is neither purely professional nor precisely extraprofessional, though it is perhaps more in the latter category—a function which has been said to exist

> in the penumbra of the professional role, so to speak. We may define it residually as those behavior expectations pertaining to the lawyer in relation to his community and society which are not those of every citizen and which are not part of the technical function of the lawyer.[6]

Lasswell and McDougal referred to this aspect of lawyering in 1943 when they wrote

> The lawyer is today, even when not himself a "maker" of policy, the one indispensable advisor of every policy-maker of our society—whether we speak of the head of a government department or agency, of the executive of a corporation or labor union, of the secre-

---

[1]See Lawrence Savell, "Why Are They Picking On Us?" *American Bar Association Journal* 78 (Nov. 1992): 72–75.

[2]See e.g., Richard W. Moll, *The Lure of the Law: Why People Become Lawyers, and What the Profession Does to Them* (New York: Penguin Books, 1990); David Kairys, ed., *The Politics of Law* (New York: Pantheon Books, 1990); Roy Grutman and Bill Thomas, *Lawyers and Thieves* (New York: Simon & Schuster, 1990); Gerry Spence, *With Justice for None* (New York: Pantheon Books, 1989); Duncan Kennedy, *Legal Education and the Reproduction of Heirarchy: A Polemic Against the System* (Cambridge, Mass.: Afar, 1983); Philip M. Stern, *Lawyers on Trial* (New York: Times Books, 1980); Jerome Frank, *Courts on Trial: Myth and Reality in American Justice* (New York: Atheneum, 1963).

[3]See Alexis de Tocqueville, *Democracy in America,* trans. Henry Reeve and Francis Bower (New York: Random House, 1981), Ch. 2

[4]See e.g., David R. Derge, "The Lawyer as Decision-maker in the American State Legislature," *Journal of Politics* 57, No. 2 (Aug. 1959): 408–33; Heinz Eulau and John D. Sprague, *Lawyers in Politics: A Study in Professional Convergence* (Indianapolis: Bobbs-Merrill, 1964); Paul L. Hain and James E. Peireson, "Lawyers and Politics Revisited: Structural Advantages of Lawyer-Politicians," *American Journal of Political Science* 19, No. 1 (Feb. 1975): 41–51.

[5]See e.g., Donald L. Horowitz, *The Jurocracy: Government Lawyers, Agency Programs and Judicial Decisions* (Lexington, Mass.: Heath, 1977); and Andrew C. Mayer, "The Lawyer in the Executive Branch of Government," *Law and Society Review* 4, No. 3 (Feb. 1970): 425–44.

[6]Walter F. Wardell and Arthur L. Wood, "The Extra-Professional Role of the Lawyer," *American Journal of Sociology* 61, No. 4 (Jan. 1956): 304.

tary of a trade or other private association, or even the humble independent enterpriser or professional man. As such an advisor the lawyer, when informing his policy-maker of what he can or cannot *legally* do, is, as policy-makers often complain, in an unassailably strategic position to influence if not create policy. It is a familiar story, too, of how frequently lawyers who begin as advisors on policy are transformed into makers of policy; "the law" is one of the few remaining avenues of "success" open to impecunious talent.[7]

So, too, were sociologists Vidich and Bensman referring to this "penumbra" role in their now classic study of the small town in America. In writing of the role of educated professionals in the community, these scholars note that

> In addition to the prestige which they are accorded by virtue of their being "educated," their overwhelming characteristic as a group lies in the influence which they have in mediating between the town and the larger society. They possess the knowledge and techniques necesssary for connecting the small town to the intricate organization of the mass bureaucratic society. . . . Thus, for example, the lawyer is counsel to political bodies as well as to free associations and other local organizations, in which capacity he gains an extensive and intimate knowledge of affairs of the town and thereby acquires a position of influence.[8]

However fruitful such research is for a general social and political view of the lawyer's role, it is the lawyer *qua* lawyer—the attorney in his or her professional roles—that is of prime interest to us here. Our approach to the study of the judiciary asks what forces and influences are at work in shaping the judicial decision and its impact on a larger society. As such, our first inquiry concerning the legal profession has to do with its immediate role in that process. If the judge is conceptualized as the essential "inside" decision maker in the judicial process, how are we to characterize the lawyer's role?

Contemporary political scientists have tended to emphasize two aspects of the attorney's roles that bear directly on judicial policy making. The first and most obvious of these is the lawyer's screening function. The judicial process is anything but self-activating; parties with disputes must be brought to court. Moreover, the process itself is complex, with a host of rules of substance and procedure with which only the attorney is familiar. In their capacity as experts in these matters, lawyers are given a monopoly in determining who has access to the judical system, at what price, under what conditions, and often to what ends. Lawyers thus exercise a profound influence on judicial policy-making by their critical initial decisions as to what individuals and groups may or may not utilize the judical process.[9] This gatekeeping function is most evident on the civil side of the law, but it is an equally useful conceptualization in criminal proceedings. The decisions made by the prosecutor in criminal matters, as well as those made by private attorneys in civil matters, together determine who enjoys (or is to suffer from) access to our judicial system. In both cases, it is the legal professional that turns the key that opens the gate to the judicial process itself.

A second aspect of the attorney role that bears even more directly on judicial policy outcomes is, of course, the development of legal ideas and devices in furtherance of client interests. The lawyer-craft in America has been characterized by creativity—even ingenu-

---

[7]Harold D. Lasswell and Myres McDougal, "Legal Education and Public Policy," *Yale Law Journal* 52, No. 2 (Mar. 1943): 208–09.

[8]Arthur J. Vidich and Joseph Bensman, *Small Town in Mass Society* (Garden City, N.Y.: Doubleday, 1960), 89.

[9]Herbert Jacob and Kenneth Vines have noted that "the bar acts as a gate-keeper to the court; it determines which groups shall have access to judicial proceedings. Moreover, by providing superior legal services to some, it enhances their chance of success." See their "The Role of the Judiciary in American State Politics," in Glendon Schubert, ed., *Judicial Decision Making* (New York: Free Press, 1963), 251.

ity—in devising instruments, doctrines, and approaches to serve new needs, whether of business, government, or the individual. The Civil War Constitutional Amendments, the quasi-independent U.S. Regulatory Commission, and the Constitution itself were, to a large extent, lawyer invented entities to aid in achieving certain governmental goals. At the same time, or more accurately, interspersed within these eras of lawyer creativity serving government, American lawyers were even more inventive in the service of private needs, the creation of the corporation, the trust receipt, the bill of exchange, and the development of the liberty of contract doctrine being prime examples. These are major historic creations on the order of what historian James Willard Hurst calls "social inventions."[10] But we need not take so broad a view to appreciate the direct policy-inducing role of the attorney *qua* attorney. In everyday public defender work, wherein the overburdened and often inexperienced attorney troops into court to plead for leniency or to defend the social causation theory of crime, he or she is engaging in a policy-inducing activity. Likewise, when a common divorce proceeding results in a grossly sexist child support arrangement or in the unexamined awarding of the custody of children to their mother—the lawyer again can be said to have made a significant contribution to the maintenance of community policy.

Although it is sometimes useful to separate these two lawyer roles—that of gatekeeping and that of policy-inducing—we must emphasize that in practice, they tend to merge. Except in limited arenas of lawyering, access tends to carry with it the policy-inducing factor. That is, one who is able to obtain quality legal services has, by definition, retained the policy-inducing skills accompanying that service. Conversely, one who enjoys little success in obtaining top-notch legal representation and advice also has little access to the creative skills of the legal profession in fashioning devices and doctrines to further client goals. The point is, access itself—the gatekeeping function—is the role unique to the attorney and, as well, the function most relevant to a political conceptualization of the legal profession. As Zemans and Rosenblum put it,

> As experts in and interpreters of law, lawyers . . . play a major role in the distribution of society's valuables, most particularly rights guaranteed by law. It is they who filter many of the public's demands on their government and determine when and under what circumstances public authority will be invoked; they are the primary gate keepers to the administration of justice. Their advice typically determines how economic exchanges are arranged and whether any sanctions will be pursued for unfilled obligations. Decisions to attempt to secure legal rights or fulfill legal obligations are most often dependent on the advice of counsel.[11]

In order to understand this gatekeeping function, we must first identify and explore the more prominent factors that help shape the critical decision of access. This, however, is not so easy. As social scientists have come to expect, seemingly simple phenomena are usually found to be conditioned by a host of forces. Here, those would include, but not be limited to, the history, economics, and politics of practice, as well as the development of professional ideology and its determinates. Political scientists wishing to explore this terrain more fully are thus led, almost inevitably, into the sociology if not the anthropology, of professions. It is perhaps useful to remind ourselves that lawyers, no more than judges, are anything but neutral role-players. To the task of lawyering, as to judging, is brought that familiar cargo of personal bias, professional constraints, and political and economic realities—a social philosophy, in other words—which significantly determines the alloca-

[10]James Willard Hurst, *The Growth of American Law: The Law Makers* (Boston: Little, Brown, 1950), 335–38.
[11]See Frances Kahn Zemans and Victor G. Rosenblum, *The Making of a Public Profession* (Chicago: American Bar Foundation, 1981), 2.

tion of advantages and disadvantages in the judicial process.[12] To these various influences on lawyering we now turn.

THE AMERICAN LEGAL PROFESSION: A PROFILE

In 1995, an estimated 900,000 people were licensed to practice law in the United States, a nationwide ratio of one lawyer for every 290 citizens (see Table 7–1). Although it is difficult to compare American lawyers with attorneys of other nations, partly because of different ways of defining attorney tasks, it is often said that with about one twentieth of the world's population, the United States has some two-thirds of the world's lawyers! That is almost certainly an exaggeration, often made for political purposes. No one knows how many lawyers there are in the world. Counting them would be a huge research undertaking, if it could be done at all. The most thoughtful statement in this regard is probably that of Prof. Marc Galanter of the University of Wisconsin Law School, who notes that American lawyers constitute somewhat less than one-third and "probably somewhere in the range of one-quarter of the world's lawyers."[13] Using the Galanter-Knight estimates, Table 7–2 presents rough estimates on lawyer-population ratios in various countries, including the United States, in the mid-1980s. These data suggest that while our ratio may be the lowest among the nations examined, some other countries come close, such as Belgium, West Germany before reunification, and Israel. When compared with the United States' proportion of the gross world product, or the world's expenditures on scientific research and development, for instance, the large numbers of American lawyers do not seem out of balance.[14]

As one might expect, attorneys in the United States, as elsewhere, tend to be concentrated in the most populous states and cities. Indeed, in the 1991 figures, just under a quarter of all American lawyers were licensed in but two states, California and New York. When one adds attorneys in the states of Texas, Illinois, Florida, and Pennsylvania, plus the District of Columbia, there are approximately half of the nation's licensed attorneys.

The concentration of attorneys in some cities is astounding. In Washington, D.C., for example, there is one licensed lawyer for every 15 people (1991)! In San Francisco, the estimated density of lawyers in 1955 was 1:58.[15]

---

[12]As earlier noted, lawyers and law schools continue to pretend this is not so—that theirs is a neutral, objective service-delivering system. But as Lasswell and McDougal remind us,

> None of us who deal with law, however defined, can escape *policy* when policy is defined as the making of important decisions which affect the distribution of values. Even those who still insist that policy is no proper concern for a law school tacitly advocate a policy, unconsciously assuming that the ultimate function of law is to maintain *existing* social institutions in a sort of timeless *status quo;* what they ask is that their policies be smuggled in, without insight or responsibility.

Lasswell and McDougal, "Legal Education and Public Policy," 207. This is, in part, the message of the Critical Legal Studies movement (see Ch. 2).

[13]Marc Galanter, "News From Nowhere: The Debased Debate on Civil Justice," *Denver University Law Review* 71, No. 1 (1993): 79. Prof. Dan Lev of the University of Washington, Seattle, reports that Iceland has the heaviest concentration of lawyers among nations he has studied, about 1:260, and Indonesia the lowest at about 1:161,000. See Ty Ahmad-Taylor, "Looking for a Lawyer? Dial Reykjavík (and forget Jakarta)," *New York Times* (Oct. 21, 1994): B-15.

[14]"News From Nowhere," 80.

[15]Basic data on lawyer demographics are taken from Barbara A. Curran, *The Lawyer Statistical Report* (Chicago: American Bar Foundation, 1985); Barbara A. Curran and Clara N. Carson, *Supplement to the Lawyer Statitstical Report: The U.S. Legal Profession in 1988* (Chicago: American Bar Foundation, 1991); and Barbara A. Curran and Clara N. Carson, *The Lawyer Statistical Report: The U.S. Legal Profession in the 1990s* (Chicago: American Bar Foundation, 1994). City lawyer densitiies are derived from population estimates and members of city bar associations, admittedly not the same as the total numbers of lawyers.

Table 7–1   National Lawyer-Population Ratios, Selected Years, 1951–1995

Year	Number of Lawyers	Lawyer-Population Ratio
1951	221,605	1:695
1954	241,514	1:672
1957	262,320	1:653
1960	285,933	1:627
1963	296,069	1:637
1966	316,856	1:621
1971	355,242	1:418
1980	542,205	1:403
1985	655,191	1:360
1988	723,189	1:340
1991	805,872	1:313
1995	896,172	1:290

Source: Bette H. Sikes, Clara N. Carson, and Patricia Gorai, *The 1971 Lawyer Statistical Report* (Chicago: ABF, 1972); Barbara A. Curran, *The Lawyer Statistical Report* (Chicago: ABF, 1985); and Barbara A. Curran, *The Lawyer Statistical Report* (Chicago: ABF, 1994). The 1995 figures are estimates.

Table 7–2   Estimated Lawyer-Population Ratios, Selected Countries, Mid-1980s

Country	Number of Lawyers	Year	Population	Ratio
Algeria	800	1983	21,790,000	1:27,237
Argentina	50,000	1983	29,431,000	1:588
Australia	22,320*	1985	15,345,000	1:687
Belgium	24,000	1984	9,872,000	1:411
Canada	42,710	1986	25,371,000	1:594
United Kingdom	55,028*,**	1985	56,423,000	1:1,025
West Germany	116,000	1985	60,950,000	1:525
India	247,373	1983	711,365,000	1:2,875
Ireland	2,500	1983	3,510,000	1:1,404
Israel	7,500	1993	4,146,000	1:552
Japan	100,000	1987	122,200,000	1:1,222
Netherlands	5,124	1986	14,940,000	1:2,915
Spain	34,234	1985	38,829,000	1:1,134
Switzerland	3,300	1983	6,430,000	1:1,948
United States	655,191	1985	235,868,000	1:360
USSR	207,000	1986	280,062,000	1:1,352

*Average of two figures reported for the same year.

**England, Wales, Scotland, and Northern Ireland.

Source: Marc Galanter and J. T. Knight, Appendix to "News from Nowhere: The Debased Debate on Civil Justice," *Denver University Law Review* 71, No. 1 (1993): 104–107. Population estimates from Arthur S. Banks, ed., *Political Handbook of the World* (Binghamton, New York: CSA Publications, designated years); and *World Almanac,* (New York: Press Publications Co., annual).

As shown in Table 7–1, the lawyer-to-population ratio in the United States remained fairly constant in the two decades of the 1950s and 1960s; at no time was it out of the range of 1:600 to 1:700. At the beginning of the 1970s, however, the large increases in the numbers of law students emerging from law schools began to be reflected in the rapidly changing ratios shown in Table 7–1.

The number of American lawyers increased nearly 130 percent over the quarter century from 1960 to 1985. These dramatic changes were not, however, limited to the United States. In the same period, the number of lawyers (barristers and solictors together) increased 147 percent in England, with a 253 percent increase in Canadian attorneys. The figure for West Germany was 156 percent.[16] These are astounding changes by anyone's definition, though neither the precise causes nor the long-term impact of these figures has yet to be fully assessed.

To be sure, not every lawyer is in private practice and available to the general client community. In 1991, only 73 percent (587,289) of American lawyers were private practitioners, though that is some 200,000 more than the approximately 68 percent so employed in 1980. This overall increase in the number of lawyers in private practice obviously creates a smaller pool of potential clients from which each of these attorneys can draw, creating the highly competitive atmosphere that now dominates private legal practice in the United States.

The rather dramatic increase in both the total number and the percent of licensed lawyers in private practice has been accompanied by another important shift in the distribution of American lawyer resources, namely that from solo to firm practice. In 1960, nearly two out of three private practitioners were in solo practice (64 percent), but by 1991, that figure had dropped to less than half (45 percent), at least 55 percent of private practitioners now being organized into partnerships or law firms (Table 7–3). Furthermore, both the number and the percentage of lawyers in small firms have decreased in favor of larger firm practice. Thus, in 1980, attorneys practicing in relatively small organizations of 2 to 20 lawyers represented nearly three-quarters of all firm practitioners, but by 1991, that figure had dropped to just a little over half. Concomitantly, the proportion of firm praciti oners working in firms of 101 or more lawyers, some 7 percent in 1980, jumped to nearly one-fourth by 1991.[17] To recap, what the last two or so decades have wrought in American legal practice has been

> (1) a decline in the practice of law on a solo basis; (2) an increase in the number of lawyers practicing in firm settings; (3) an increase not only in the number of firms but in the size of firms; and (4) an increase in the number of lawyers in firm practice who are employed as associates. [Thus] . . . the practice of law is shifting from the individual entrepreneurial, . . . model to organized groupings of lawyers in which the existence of hierarchial ordering of lawyers is increasingly made readily apparent.[18]

As indicated in Table 7–3, some 27 percent of American attorneys (218,583 lawyers) in 1991 were not in private practice, but rather worked, for the most part, either in private

---

[16]"News from Nowhere," 80.

[17]These data are taken from Curran and Carson, *The Lawyer Statistical Report: The Legal Profession in the 1990s:* 7–8. The *number* of large law firms (firms with over 101 lawyers), in both absolute terms as well as their proportion of all law firms, has also increased rapidly in recent years, moving from just under 7,000 in 1980 to almost 40,000 by 1991!

[18]Barbara A. Curran, "The Dynamics of Change in the Legal Profession and the Work of Lawyers," paper presented at the Conference of the National Association of Law Placement, May 7, 1986: 4–5. With the relatively recent growth of large firms in both number and size has come an increase in scholarly research on these changing organizations. See e.g., Robert L. Nelson, "Practice and Privilege: Social Change and the Structure of Large Law Firms," *American Bar Foundation Research Journal* 1 (Winter 1981): 97–140; and Marc Galanter and Thomas Palay, *Tournament of Lawyers: The Transformation of the Big Law Firm* (Chicago: University of Chicago Press, 1991).

Table 7–3   Employment of Lawyers, 1980 and 1991

Employment Setting	1980		1991		1980–1991
	Number	Percent	Number	Percent	Net Increase
Private practice	370,111	68.3	587,289	72.9	59%
Federal judicial department	2,611	0.5	3,119	0.4	19%
Other federal government	20,132	3.7	27,985	3.5	39%
State/local judicial department	16,549	3.1	18,417	2.3	11%
Other state/local government	30,358	5.6	38,242	4.7	26%
Private industry	54,626	10.1	71,022	8.8	30%
Private association	4,391	0.8	5,835	0.7	33%
Legal aid or public defender	8,239	1.5	8,816	1.1	7%
Education	6,606	1.2	8,177	1.0	24%
Retired or inactive	28,582	5.3	36,971	4.6	29%
Total	542,205	100.0	805,872	100.0	49%

Source: Barbara A. Curran and Clara N. Carson, *The Lawyer Statistical Report: The U.S. Legal Profession in the 1990s* (Chicago: American Bar Foundation, 1994), 7.

industry (nearly 9 percent of all attorneys) or for the government (12 percent). As shown, most government attorneys work at the state level, although over 30,000 were employed in some capacity for the federal government in 1991, an overall increase of nearly 37 percent since 1980. Except for the previously noted growth in the number of attorneys moving into private practice, federal attorney employment in nonjudicial settings represented the largest percentage increase in attorney work from 1980 to 1991.

Aside from the increase in the number of attorneys relative to population, the most dramatic changes in the lawyer statistics since the 1950s have related to age and gender, particularly the latter. With the unusually large numbers of young attorneys moving into the profession in the late 1960s and the 1970s, the median age of lawyers dropped from 46 in 1960 to 45 in 1971, and ultimately to 39 by 1980, the youngest in research history. Since then, however, the median age of the lawyer population began to rise as the large number of lawyers joining the profession entered their middle years. By 1991, the median age had crept back up to 41.[19]

Much more notable has been the change in gender distribution of the bar. Table 7–4 illustrates the most dramatic alteration in the gender composition of any profession in American history. The percentage of women lawyers hovered around 2.8 to 3.0 throughout the 1950s and 1960s but began to shoot up in the late 1970s and early 1980s. With the rapidly growing enrollment of women in law schools, now approaching 50 percent (see Table 7–5), the proportion of women in the bar has also grown rapidly. Table 7–4 contains projections of this figure at 27 percent by the turn of the century, but other observers have suggested that it may be closer to one-third by that time.

Reliable data on racial minorities in the lawyer population are more difficult to locate. With the push of affirmative action in the last two decades, we might expect to find a significant increase in the proportion of Black and Hispanic attorneys, (traditionally hovering in the range of 1.5 to 3 percent), but that does not appear to be the case. Estimates vary as to the precise percentages; but if the data from the Department of Labor are reliable, at

---

[19]*The Lawyer Statistical Report,* 1994, 4.

Table 7–4   Women Lawyers: Number and Percentage, Selected Years

Year	Number of Women Lawyers	Percent of Lawyer Population
1951	5,540	3
1960	7,434	3
1971	9,947	3
1980	44,185	8
1985	85,542	13
1988	116,421	16
1991	159,377	20
1995	207,738	23
1999	257,073	26
2000	269,068	27

Note: All statistics presented are as of the beginning of the year shown. Statistics for 1995, 1999, and 2000 are estimates.

Source: Barbara A. Curran and Clara N. Carson, *The Lawyer Statistical Report: The U.S. Legal Profession in the 1990s* (Chicago: American Bar Foundation, 1994), 4.

the beginning of 1994, 3.3 percent of the bar was Black, up from 2.6 percent in 1984, while the comparable reported figures for Hispanic lawyers were 3.1 percent, up from 1.7 percent a decade earlier.[20] An examination of law school enrollments touches on the roots of this rather unremarkable set of increases, at least as contrasted with the steady rise in the number and percentages of women lawyers.

These data, while providing an interesting and suggestive overview of the modern American legal profession, give little direct evidence bearing on the political issue of lawyer gatekeeping posed before. Lawyer-to-population ratios tell something about the roles of law and lawyers in our society but little about relative access—that is, which of our citizens enjoy access to legal advice with all the symbolic and material advantages implied therein. Likewise, data on age, race, and sex, while indirectly suggestive of access policies of the legal profession, provide little direct evidence as to who gets what, when, and how in judicial politics.

Actually, we can probably learn a good deal more about access from the American Bar Foundation lawyer statistics by focusing not on the changes but on what has remained unchanged, and ultimately, not on the data included, but on those excluded. For example, a focus on the dramatic increases in the number of women lawyers (and the considerably less dramatic increases in the percentages of black lawyers) may cause us to overlook the fact that the profession is still 80 percent male and about 97 percent non-Black—this in a nation that is approximately 51 percent female and 12 percent Black. Thus, the emphasis on demographics tells nothing about lawyer income (the economics of practice); or, except indirectly, about the stratification of the profession (the sociology of practice); and, of course, nothing

---

[20]See United States, Dept. of Labor, *Employment and Earnings* 32, No. 1 (Jan. 1985): 176; and United States, Dept. of Labor, *Employment and Earnings* 42, No. 1 (Jan. 1995): 176. These data vary somewhat from those reported in Ch. 6, illustrating the difficulty of locating reliable racial minority lawyer data. The American Bar Foundation, in its lawyer statistical reports, collects and reports age and gender, but not racial data.

directly about who has access to lawyers and to what ends (the politics of practice). As other writers have found, these facets of the legal profession can perhaps best be discovered through a developmental approach. We are, of course, not interested in the history of the profession for its own sake, but rather in the development of American lawyering and the influences along the way—influences that have shaped the modern American lawyer and significantly affected the decision relating to access to legal services.

THE LEGAL PROFESSION TO 1870

As noted in previous chapters, the antipathy of Americans toward lawyers is hardly a modern phenomenon; rather, it has been endemic in our political history. Professional pleaders were banned in many seventeenth-century colonies, the Fundamental Constitutions of the Carolinas of 1669 expressing a typical sentiment: it is "a base and vile thing to plead for money or reward."[21] Such attitudes carried over into the eighteenth century when lawyers were often blamed for the excesses of British colonial government, economic hardship, and even for general moral depravity. In late colonial North Carolina, lawyers were seen as "cursed hungry Caterpillars whose fees will eat out the very Bowels of our Common-wealth."[22] Riots against lawyers and judges marked the period.

Even so, the eighteenth century witnessed a significant transition from utopian-oriented colonial societies, which were almost lawyerless, to an increasingly prosperous, commercially oriented colonial America, wherein the necessary "evil" of an established legal profession was taking definite shape. As Friedman writes,

> as soon as a settled society posed problems for which lawyers had an answer or at least a skill, the lawyers appeared in force, and flourished despite animosity. Courts were in session; merchants were drawn into litigation; land documents had to be written, and the more skilled the better. So, men trained in law who came from England found a ready market for their services; so did laymen with a smattering of law; and the semi-professionals who had experience for sale.... Yet ... a competent, professional bar, ... existed in all major communities by 1750 despite oppositon and adversity.[23]

Problems attendant to a growing profession—training, certification, economic survival, for example—had to be addressed. With no system of formal legal education, the aspiring attorney either journeyed to England to train in the Inns of Court or, more frequently, apprenticed with a practicing lawyer in one of the colonies. Colonial governments began to establish standards for admission to practice; usually the judiciary was empowered to perform this function. Then, as now, the bar was anything but monolithic. Lawyers were rich as well as poor, retained by wealthy clients and also willing to take the lowliest clients for a small fee or at times no fee at all. Although some colonial bars (for instance, Rhode Island) sought to establish standard fee schedules,[24] control was loose and a great many ill-trained and often hungry lawyers were about to engender further public hostility.

---

[21]See Lawrence M. Friedman. *A History of American Law,* 2nd ed. (New York: Simon & Schuster, 1985), 94.
[22]Friedman, *History of American Law,* 96.
[23]Friedman, *History of American Law,* 96–97.
[24]Friedman reports that in 1745 a small group of Rhode Island lawyers signed a "compact" to ensure that no case be "pleaded at any Superior Court under a three pound fee," and that attorneys were not to sign "blank writs and disburse them about the colony, which practice ... would make the law cheap." According to Friedman, the Rhode Island attorneys agreed not to represent anyone who was suing an attorney for a fee unless a committee of three lawyers agreed that their fellow lawyer's fee was unreasonable. See Friedman, *History of American Law,* 100–101.

As John Adams noted in 1759, legal practice was "grasped in to the hands of deputy sheriffs, pettifoggers and even constables . . . [who] stirred up many unnecessary suits."[25]

The stratification of the American bar, even in the eighteenth century, is clearly seen in the contrast between the Adams complaint and the well-founded belief that lawyering could be the road to wealth and success. Whereas many lawyers were forced to struggle for a subsistence living, a good many were aristocrats—John Adams, Thomas Jefferson, James Wilson, to name a few. The influence in public affairs of such men is suggested by the fact that nearly half of the signers of the Declaration of Independence were lawyers, as were over half of the delegates to the Philadelphia Convention. With fits and starts, then, the eighteenth century established the outlines of the modern legal profession. Few major issues of modern-day bar politics were absent in the formative years, and all were part of bar politics of the day.[26]

Thus, despite negative public sentiment, the legal profession grew. Occasional attempts to make the profession a closed, elite guild were never successful. Qualifications for entry remained loose. Although a good many lawyers had college backgrounds, most did not, especially those in the West. With Blackstone's *Commentaries* in one hand and Kent's in the other, an ambitious young man could associate himself with a single practitioner or partnership, "read" the law in his spare time, and, within a very few years win admission to practice. That procedure was described by Jonathan Birch of Bloomington, Illinois, who testified to having met with his "examining board" in a hotel room. The lone examiner, an experienced and widely respected frontier lawyer named Abraham Lincoln, was partly undressed and taking a sponge bath as the examination proceeded:

> Motioning me to be seated, he began his interrogatories at once, without looking at me a second time to be sure of the identity of his caller. "How long have you been studying?" he asked. "Almost two years," was my response. "By this time, it seems to me," he said laughingly, "you ought to be able to determine whether you have in you the kind of stuff out of which a good lawyer can be made. What books have you read?" I told him, and he said it was more than he read before he was admitted to the bar. . . .
>
> As he continued his toilet, he entertained me with recollections—many of them characteristcally vivid and racy—of his early practice and the various incidents and adventures which attended his start in the profession. The whole proceeding was so unusual and queer, if not grotesque, that I was at a loss to determine whether I was really being examined at all or not. After he had dressed we went down stairs and over to the clerk's office in the courthouse, where he wrote a few lines on a sheet of paper, and, enclosing it in an envelope, directed me to report with it to Judge Logan, another member of the examining committee, at Springfield. The next day I went to Springfield, where I delivered the letter as directed. On reading it, Judge Logan smiled, and much to my surprise, gave me the required certificate without asking me a question beyond my age and residence, and the correct way of spelling my name. The note from Lincoln read:
>
> "My Dear Judge:—The bearer of this is a young man who thinks he can be a lawyer. Examine him, if you want to. I have done so, and am satisfied. He's a good deal smarter than he looks to be."[27]

The practice of law in the period 1800 to 1870 was closely related to the land. And since land was one of the more plentiful commodities, the services of an attorney were available even to Americans of relatively modest means. This was particularly true in the West, where problems with deeds and title searches were widespread. It was not uncom-

---

[25]Friedman, *History of American Law,* 101.

[26]In addition to Friedman, good sources for the history of the American bar include Hurst, *Growth of American Law,* Ch. 12 and 13; Charles Warren, *A History of the American Bar* (Boston: Little, Brown, 1911); and Auerbach, *Unequal Justice.*

[27]Quoted in Albert A. Woldman, *Lincoln Lawyer* (Boston: Houghton Mifflin, 1936), 153–54.

mon for land to become a means of payment of legal fees. Collections also constituted an important source of business for nineteenth-century lawyers.

Practice was largely courtroom oriented, as formal litigation was the chief means of exercising one's legal rights. Even the rather small, elite bar of the East was dominated by members who had won their spurs in courtroom encounters. Luther Martin, Daniel Webster, and Rufus Choate were examples. It was the same for a relatively obscure attorney such as Abraham Lincoln—the road to success was largely as a circuit-riding courtroom advocate.[28] Skill and eloquence in open court were means of advertising one's wares, and as one's community reputation grew, so did one's income and success as an attorney.

Legal services in this period were offered primarily through solo or partnership practice. Neither the institution of house counsel nor the dominance of the large prestigious firm was common until much later in the century. Attachment to one or even a few clients was rare. Rather, a lawyer's livelihood depended more on a large and diverse clientele attracted by the individual's general reputation in the community and enhanced by newspaper advertising and perhaps by involvement in politics.

Beginning in the last quarter of the ninetennth century and most visible in the first quarter of the present century, there occurred a series of changes of profound consequence for the practice of law in America. Although it is difficult to point to the precise causes, it is indisputable that after the Civil War—clearly after 1870—it grew increasingly obvious that the roles of the lawyer in American society underwent a metamorphosis. Historian, politician, social scientist, legal scholar, and practitioner alike have agreed with novelist John Dos Passos that the practice of law in America was transformed "from a profession to a business." The key factor in explaining the phenomenon appeared to be the growth of industrialization and urbanization following the Civil War. These forces, combined with immigration, shocked and transformed rural, agrarian, and Protestant America, and this included the practice of law. As corporate wealth increasingly skimmed the profession of its best and brightest, the quasi-independent professional man of decades gone by—the man who as often as not played the role of ombudsman in community affairs—was rapidly transformed into what Adolph Berle dubbed "an intellectual jobber and contractor in business matters." In his analysis of the legal profession for the *Encyclopaedia of the Social Sciences* in 1933, Adolph Berle wrote,

> The law firm became virtually an annex to some group of financial promoters, manipulators or industrialists; and such firms have dominated the organized profession, although they have contributed little of thought, less of philosophy and have nothing at all of responsibility or idealism. What they have contributed, however, is the creation of a legal framework for the new economic system, built largely around the modern corporation, the division of ownership of industrial property from control and the increasing concentration of economic power in the industrial east in the hands of a few individuals. . . .
>
> The complete commercialization of the American bar has stripped it of any social functions it might have performed for individuals without wealth. The great law office either does not care to or cannot profitably handle cases which, while of great importance to individuals, have only limited financial significance. The smaller offices and individual practitioners, especially if they are struggling for survival, will extract the maximum compensation from their clients, whether the service is worth it or not. Criminal cases are not infrequently prolonged for the sole purpose of procuring fees. One of the worst abuses has grown up in the administration of property left in trust: A lawyer who acts as attorney for the trustee or who has some other connection with the estate will often create litigation wherever possible, delaying the fulfillment of the trust and taking advantage of every technical obstacle in order to create work for himself, and ultimately dissipate the estate in fees.

---

[28]Hurst, *Growth of American Law,* 301–303.

Thus the importance and influence of the bar in American life has been distinctively modified by its changing standards. In the early history of the United States there was a tradition that lawyers were fit material for politics or statesmanship. They occupied a dominant ethical position analogous to that of clergymen and received a social recognition not given to the business classes. Their services in formation of the early state are exemplified by men like Chief Justice Marshall on the bench and Daniel Webster at the bar and in politics, who could and did mold the economic and political institutions of the country. With the rise of the industrial system and the tremendous drive for economic development occasioned by the opening up of the West leadership was shifted to the captains of industry and finance; and the influential leaders of the bar became adjunct to this group rather than an independent influence. Traditions of public service, such as are found in the medical profession, insensibly disappeared; the specialized learning of the lawyer was his private stock in trade to be exploited for his private benefit. This is roughly the position of the profession today.[29]

Berle further observed that the outlets for lawyers interested in public service all but dried up, leaving only scholarship or public office as means to that end.[30]

If this commentary on the legal profession in the mid-1930s seems a trifle harsh, witness the parade of distinguished writers whose analyses arrive at the same conclusion. In 1912, four years before his nomination to the Supreme Court, Louis Brandeis noted that

it is true that at the present time the lawyer does not hold that position with the people that he held seventy-five or even fifty years ago; but the reason is not lack of opportunity. It is this: Instead of holding a position of independence between the wealthy and the people, prepared to curb the excesses of either, able lawyers have, to a large extent, allowed themselves to become adjuncts of great corporations and have neglected their obligation to use their powers for the protection of the people. We hear much of the "corporation lawyers," and far too little of the "people's lawyer." The great opportunity of the American Bar is and will be to stand again as it did in the past, ready to protect also the interests of the people.[31]

Berle and Brandeis were but expanding on the observations of Lord Bryce, who as early as 1888 wrote,

Lawyers are now to a greater extent than formerly businessmen, a part of the great organized system of industrial and financial enterprise. They are less than formerly the students of a particular kind of learning, the practioners of a particular art. And they do not seem to be so much of a distinct professional class. . . .

But I am bound to add that some judicious American observers hold that the last thirty years have witnessed a certain decadence in the Bar of the great cities. They say that the growth of the enormously rich and powerful corporations willing to pay vast sums for questionable services has seduced the virtue of some counsel whose eminence makes their example important.[32]

---

[29]See A. A. Berle, Jr., "The Modern Legal Profession," *Encyclopaedia of the Social Sciences* 9 (1933), 341, 343–44. The Berle conclusions are essentially those of a recent writer, Anthony T. Kronman. See his *The Lost Lawyer: Failing Ideals of the Legal Profession* (Cambridge: Belknap Press of Harvard University Press, 1993). See also the same and similar issues addressed in Robert L. Nelson, David M. Trubek, and Rayman L. Solomon, *Lawyers' Ideals/Lawyers' Practices: Transformations in the American Legal Profession* (Ithaca: Cornell University Press, 1992). Even more recently, see Sol M. Linowitz's biting critique of the legal profession and legal education in his book, *The Betrayed Profession: Lawyering at the End of the Twentieth Century* (New York: Scribners, 1995).

[30]Berle, "Modern Legal Profession," 341.

[31]Louis Brandeis, "Business: A Profession," as quoted in Marks, *The Lawyer, The Public and Professional Responsibility*, 28–29.

[32]Lord Bryce, quoted in Marks, *The Lawyer, The Public and Professional Responsibility*, 28.

And, noted Albert M. Kales, distinguished Chicago lawyer and first research director of the American Judicature Society—himself hardly a radical in professional circles—the restraining influence of lawyers upon desirable social change is "notorious":

> It is the profession of client care-taking that chokes it down. The more important and able the lawyer, the more he is in touch with the most important business interests of the community, and the more clear it is that he cannot propose or advocate any reform of an extensive character which will not be unwelcome to some particular client's interest.[33]

Karl Llewellyn, writing in 1933 on the specialization of the bar, commented on the same transformation of the leading edge of the bar from a profession to a business,[34] as did no less a figure than Harlan Fiske Stone. Speaking at the dedicatory exercises of the new law school at the University of Michigan in 1934, Stone leveled a blistering attack on the legal profession, which echoed the foregoing critics:

> Steadily the best skill and capacity of the profession had been drawn into the exacting and highly specialized service of business and finance. At its best the changed system has brought to the command of the business world loyalty and a superb proficiency and technical skill. At its worst it has made the learned profession of an earlier day the obsequious servant of business, and tainted it with the morals and manners of the market place in its most anti-social manifestations. In any case we must conclude that it has given us a Bar whose leaders, like its rank and file, are on the whole less likely to be well rounded professional men than their predecessors, whose energy and talent for public service and for bringing the law into harmony with changed conditions have been largely absorbed in the advancement of the interests of clients.[35]

At the risk of beating a dead horse, we may update the Berle–Stone critique with that of Justice William J. Brennan who in 1967 quoted with approval Stone's complaints of thirty years before and added,

> The profession must . . . purge itself of the inbred precepts of another day, rethink its code of practice and reshape its internal mechanisms for meeting its public responsibilities. Else the dangerous cleavage between a public sector of the bar devoted to the developing issues of society and a private sector—the practicing bar—which ignores them, will only widen.[36]

Justice Brennan went on to note that the social responsibilities of the bar had been largely assumed by government lawyers, law professors, and young people who at that time were reorienting their thinking to service in the field of poverty law. He expressed grave doubt whether the profession, bifurcated really into two professions—public service and private practice—was in a position to meet its responsibilities.

Critiques of this nature could be quoted almost ad infinitum, the key point always being the same: that the new economic forces unleashed in the latter part of the nineteenth century had a profound effect on the aspect of lawyering that we are concerned with here—namely, access. Clearly, the public function of the bar both in affording access to legal services and in its broader service function has been sacrificed to the needs of business and the prestige associated with wealth. As observed by Theron G. Strong, a member of a Connecticut family of attorneys whose ancestors date back to the Revolution, the stature of the

---

[33]The Albert M. Kales critique can be found in Hurst, *Growth of American Law,* 372–73.
[34]K. N. Llewellyn, "The Bar Specializes: With What Results?", *Annals* 167 (May 1933): especially 177, 178, 179.
[35]Harlan Fiske Stone, "The Public Influence of the Bar," *Harvard Law Review* 48, No. 1 (Nov. 1934): 7.
[36]William J. Brennan, Jr., "The Responsibilities of the Legal Profession," in Arthur E. Sutherland, ed., *The Path of the Law From 1967* (Cambridge, Mass.: Harvard University Law School, Harvard University Press, 1968), 92.

American lawyer has been undermined by "the incursion of money making power." Argued Strong: "Many of the best-equipped lawyers of the present day are, to all intents and purposes, *owned* by the great corporate and individual interests they represent, and while enormous fees result they are dearly earned by the surrender of individual independence.[37]

Differences between the prebellum and postbellum practice of law amounted to differences originating not in the legal profession itself but rather in the economic and social character of American society. With the great concentrations of wealth required for and produced by corporate industrialization came the need for legal devices and doctrines to aid in the creation and use of that wealth. Lawyers were thus called upon to play a new role, to attach themselves to the great corporate machines of America as quasi-independent entities. As the trend continued, the corporate imperative gradually undermined any claim that the legal profession might have made earlier to professional independence. Indeed, the profession as a whole took on an ideological coloration similar to that of American capitalism. As historian Jerold Auerbach noted,

> The legal profession all too accurately mirrored American society; and it enjoyed anything but an independent existence. Every essential feature of professional organization and structure reflected prevailing national values: stratification along ethnic lines; recruitment patterns that rewarded corporate counseling with the highest income and status; availability of legal services according to income rather than need; and a skewed adversary process that distributed its benefits in proportion to the money and power of those who utilize it.[38]

Auerbach put his finger on the overriding feature of lawyering in modern America. It has been the preemption of the nation's legal talent by a relatively narrow set of wealthy economic and social interests, leading to a grossly inequitable availability of legal assistance, that has dominated the politics of legal advice in the late nineteenth and entire twentieth centuries. Every major facet of the profession—the politics of bar associations, legal education, professional and social stratification, legal aid, ethical issues—has been heavily influenced, if not determined, by this simple fact. At the same time, these factors feed back into the maintenance of this inequitable system of distribution of legal services. Let us examine this proposition through a brief exploration of three major aspects of the modern legal profession in America: recruitment and training, the politics of bar associations, and the distribution and nature of practice specialities. In each instance, take particular note of the forces and influence at work which shape the decisions that determine access to legal advice.

LEGAL EDUCATION IN AMERICA

Beyond marking a substantial change in the nature of legal practice, the latter portion of the nineteenth century also produced significant changes in the training of American lawyers. While the sometimes rarified air of a classroom might seem only tangentially connected to actual professional behavior, the link between legal education and elite legal practice has developed into an especially close, if at the same time a particularly deceptive, one. Indeed, the means by which American lawyers are trained are both the result of and a driving force behind the existing distribution of legal services.

As noted earlier, the young American nation went without a formal system of legal training through the first half of its history. Apprenticeship, with all its haphazardness,

---

[37]Theron G. Strong, *Landmarks of a Lawyer's Lifetime* (1914), as quoted in Auerbach, *Unequal Justice,* 33 (emphasis added).

[38]Auerbach, *Unequal Justice,* 163–64. See the various approaches to legal professionalism in the essays in *Lawyers' Ideals/Lawyers' Practices.*

was the almost universal system in use.[39] Some attorneys were adept as teachers, and it was out of these "teaching" law offices that the first formal schools sprang. One of the first such schools was established in Litchfield, Connecticut. Judge Tapping Reeve opened the school in 1794, and at its peak it boasted fifty students. Litchfield and other such proprietary schools, though influential in their time, declined in the 1820s and 1830s, partly because of the availability of adequate textbooks for study.[40] Also, established colleges were beginning to offer more regular instruction in law. By 1825, law professorships had been created at William and Mary, Columbia, Harvard, Yale, Pennsylvania, Virginia, and Maryland. Even so, until the 1870s, college-trained lawyers accounted for only a small fraction of the total number of private attorneys.

In these early beginnings of formal legal instruction, Harvard University was widely perceived as the most successful. Its first professor of law, Isaac Parker, was the former Chief Justice of Massachusetts, and Joseph Story an Associate Justice of the United States Supreme Court, filled the school's first endowed chair. Even during the pre–Civil War period, the Harvard law faculty proved to be prolific authors of treatises, and Harvard's now legendary law library grew to an impressive size as law became a separate academic discipline. Although the apprenticeship system continued to hold sway, Harvard demonstrated that formal, collegiate legal training was a workable concept.[41]

Despite reasonably promising beginnings, however, formal legal education did not expand rapidly; rather, between 1845 and 1870, it actually stagnated. Legal academics agreed on little, if anything, with respect to both the methods and the substance of legal education. While some institutions, such as Columbia University, adhered to the idea of a liberal education in politics, ethics, and law, offerings at other schools consisted of little more than one year of dogmatic lectures on narrow legal subjects. Standards were lax or nonexistent, and students were few, as the academic study of law began to decline almost before it truly got started.[42]

In 1870, the appointment of Christopher Columbus Langdell to be dean of the Harvard Law School, however, marked both the end of that decline and the beginning of modern American legal education. Langdell undertook a series of sweeping reforms that to this day remain the basic outlines of formal legal training. An undergraduate degree became first highly desirable and, after World War II, a prerequisite to law school admission. The course of study was extended, first to two and later to three years. Courses keyed to particular areas of legal practice were introduced, as were regular examinations. Moreover, Langdell instituted a profound shift in the methods of legal instruction.

Dean Langdell took the notion of a "science" of law seriously. He argued that each branch of law was founded upon a relatively few principles or doctrines that had evolved over several centuries. For Langdell, mastery of law was simply to obtain "a mastery of these [principles] and to be able to apply them with constant facility and certainty to the ever tangled skein of human affairs. . . ."[43] These doctrines, or principles, he thought, could be most effectively derived from the careful and studied reading of appellate judicial opinions. Directed by a learned professor through a classroom dialogue, dubbed "Socratic" in a rather poorly disguised attempt to impart the aura of intellectual legitimacy, a law student could be brought to realize the kernel of truth—the legal principle—contained within the words of each appellate decision. This method of public banter be-

---

[39]See Friedman, *History of American Law*, 97.

[40]On the Litchfield School, see Hurst, *Growth of American Law*, 258–60; and Warren, *History of the American Bar*, 357–61.

[41]See Friedman, *History of American Law*, 321–22.

[42]Friedman, *History of American Law*, 322.

[43]Friedman, *History of American Law*, 612.

tween instructor and student was perceived to be a radical departure from the more conventional lecture methods widely accepted in other academic disciplines.

Langdell's methodological revolution had no less profound an effect on law school faculties than it did on their students. Rather than drawing his faculty from the ranks of prominent practitioners, Langdell firmly believed his pure legal science required the devotion of full-time scholars, whose experience in the practice of law was almost entirely irrelevant to their role as law instructor. As historian James Willard Hurst noted, Langdell "inaugurated, as a new branch of the legal profession in the United States, the career of the scholar-teacher of law."[44]

Langdell's approach, in substance and especially in method, spread throughout formal legal education. From a languishing enterprise, legal education virtually exploded across the country. It had a methodology, it had a leader, and, by the late 1880s, it had an organized bar eager to support the formation of law schools that, through perceived intellectual rigor, would lend dignity and prestige to the legal profession. By 1910, more than half of the nation's law schools had "gone Harvard"and had adopted the Langdellian approach; ultimately every law school in the country followed suit.[45]

Although the Langdellian approach to legal instruction succeeded in providing law schools the aura of intellectual legitimacy that the profession was seeking, it also was, and remains, plagued with weaknesses. As noted in Chapter 2, chief among these is extreme narrowness of approach. Langdell, and those who have followed him, insisted upon a "science" of law in pure form, unfettered by the discordant strains of economic, political, or ethical considerations. Moreover, while Langdell purported to foster an empirically directed endeavor, he imposed unprecedented limitations on the range of evidence deemed worthy of study: judicially created law articulated in appellate decisions completely defined the parameters of formal legal education. These twin constrictions drew sharp lines between the study of law and the realities of life itself. Within Langdell's scheme, not even the full spectrum of legal materials was relevant; legislative, administrative, and lower court data were considered unnecessary, and more broadly cast social science materials were anathema. As historian Willard Hurst put it,

> The case method isolated the study of law from the living context of the society. The student of law needed to be aware of the pressure of politics, the strands of class, religious, racial and national attitudes woven into the values and patterns of behavior with which law dealt; he needed some appreciation of the balance of power within the community, the clash of interests, and the contriving of economic institutions, as all these influenced and were influenced by the effort to order the society under law. But of all this, so far as the law school was concerned, the student was made aware only incidentally—as he glimpsed the social context through recitals of fact and appraisal, of widely varying accuracy and imagination, in the reported opinions of appellate courts.[46]

Literally hundreds of commentators have echoed this basic criticism of modern legal education, even such conservative voices as Professor Lawrence Friedman:

> Langdell's proudest boast was that law was a science, and that his method was highly scientific. But his model of science was not experimental, or experiential; his model was Euclid's geometry, not physics or biology. Langdell considered law a pure, independent science; it was, he conceded, empirical; but the only date he allowed were reported cases. If law is at all the product of society, then Langdell's science of law was a geology without

[44]Hurst, *Growth of American Law,* 264.
[45]Friedman, *History of American Law,* 616.
[46]Hurst, *Growth of American Law,* 265–66.

rocks, an astronomy without stars. Lawyers and judges raised on the method, if they took their training at all seriously, came to speak of law mainly in terms of a dry, arid logic, divorced from society and life.[47]

As Professor Andrew Hacker explained:

[C]lasses allow for participation, at least of a sort. The professor brings to every lecture a list of perhaps a dozen students, who will be called on to state the facts of a case or some aspect of an argument. As no one knows when he or she will be called, the effect is one of suspense and dread. Law schools call this technique the "Socratic method," in part because no matter what answer a student gives the professor has heard it before and can show it to be wrong.[48]

In the face of these and similar criticisms, law school curricula have remained largely unchanged. True, the legal Realist movement of the 1930s brought about the limited use of social science and other "noncase" materials in some schools. Further, materials on administrative law and legislation became common if not typical, as did some coverage of issues related to what was labeled in the 1960s and early 1970s as "poverty law."[49] But for the most part, legal education remained, and remains, true to the Langdellian ideal, "revealing" the science of law through "Socratic" review of appellate decisions.[50]

As noted, Langdellian pseudoscience served the needs of an expanding profession by providing a useful symbol of academic prestige and respectability. Yet the pressure to fall

[47]Friedman, *History of American Law,* 617. See also Auerbach, *Unequal Justice,* 74–81; Eric E. Van Loon, "The Law School Response: How to Make Students Sharp by Making Them Narrow," in Bruce Wasserstein and Mark J. Green, eds., *With Justice For Some: An Indictment of the Law by Young Advocates* (Boston: Beacon Press, 1970), 334–52; John H. Schlegel, "Langdell's Legacy or The Case of The Empty Envelope," *Stanford Law Review* 36 (1984): 1517; and Richard D. Kahlenberg, *Broken Contract: A Memoir of Harvard Law School* (New York: Hill & Wang, 1992).

An entertaining colloquy on Dean Langdell's contributions is found in *Law and Social Inquiry* 20, No. 3 (Summer 1995), with essays running from "Hail Langdell" to "The Hell with Langdell."

[48]Andrew Hacker, "The Shame of Professional Schools," *Journal of Legal Education* 32 (1982): 278, 279.

[49]The impact of the war on poverty of the mid-1960s on legal education and legal services delivery is discussed in a wide range of books and articles. For an introduction, see Harry P. Stumpf, *Community Politics and Legal Services: The Other Side of the Law* (Beverly Hills, Calif.: Sage, 1975), especially 296–305.

[50]See Harry P. Stumpf et. al, "Whither Political Jurisprudence," *Western Political Quarterly* 36, No. 4 (Dec. 1983): 540, 541. Robert Stevens of Yale University wrote in 1970 that anyone who states that there have been no changes in legal education since 1870 is setting forth a "claim which is patently absurd." But in the next paragraph he notes that "there is considerable justification . . . in the indictment that the law schools are trapped in the structure of an earlier age." See Robert Stevens, "Aging Mistress: The Law School in America," *Change,* Jan.–Feb. 1970, 34–35. Lawrence Friedman has argued that aside from economics, social science approaches have made only marginal inroads into legal education. He writes,

To be sure, they have a foot, or at least a toe, in the door of some law schools. Prestigious law schools offer courses in sociology, history, or philosophy of law; or in psychology or anthropology of law. But everybody knows that these are elegant frills, like thick rugs in the dean's office; they have nothing to do with "real" legal education. A school can do without these frills, in a crunch. Indeed, being a frill is precisely what makes these courses valuable, even essential, to an elite law school. After all, *every* school has a course in torts; offering torts does not discriminate between elites and proletariat; a course in legal anthropology does.

Lawrence M. Friedman, "The Law and Society Movement," *Stanford Law Review* 38, No. 3 (Feb. 1986): 777.

A recent study of the development of American legal education tends to support the Friedman conclusions. In his work *Logic and Experience: The Origin of Modern American Legal Education* (New York: Oxford University Press, 1995), William P. LaPiana explains the failure of sociological jurisprudence to change law school curricula in terms of Roscoe Pound's extreme reluctance to accept the educational/pedagogical implications of his own legal philosophy. See especially Ch. 8.

in line behind the leading proponents of formalized legal instruction was countered by the increasing demand for legal education as a means of upward social mobility. While the spread of Langdellian law schools was rapid and wide-ranging, it was accompanied by a seemingly opposing trend toward part-time, so-called "night" law schools. These institutions replaced the move toward a study of "universal legal principles" with a focus on local legal practice as articulated by local practitioners. While the "leading" schools upped their admission and graduation standards, night schools tended to welcome any applicant and to award degrees based on minimal standards of performance. Moreover, while Harvard Law and its progeny tended to accept and train a WASPish social and economic elite, night schools became a ticket of admission to the bar for working-class members of ethnic immigrant minority groups.

Toward the end of the nineteenth century, the growth of night law schools actually overtook that of more conventional, "day" programs. In 1890, for example, 51 "day" programs existed in the United States, in contrast to just 10 "night" or "mixed" programs. By 1936, however, there were 86 full-time, conventional law schools and 107 part-time night schools. Although the latter eventually adopted many of the trappings of the Langdellian method—not particularly surprising given the intellectual legitimacy such trappings were understood to bestow—the night law schools created a relatively more accessible route into legal practice, intensifying the stratification of an already thoroughly stratified bar.[51]

This cleavage in legal education widened with the creation of the American Association of Law Schools (AALS) in 1900. Originally composed of thirty-five of the nation's most prestigious law schools, this organization assigned itself the task of upgrading law school standards. Many, if not most, of the night law schools, however, remained outside AALS, increasing the strife that already existed between traditional law instructors and administrators and those connected with part-time night programs. In addition, AALS symbolized the ever-growing division between legal practitioners and legal instructors, a professional disjunction that delayed the establishment of formal standards for admission to practice until well into the 1930s.

With its near-exclusive reliance on the case-by-case study of appellate decisions, modern American legal education parted company with its own history, which even in the days of apprenticeship involved a breadth of study and a concern for values characteristic of a classic liberal education. As Zemans and Rosenblum observed.

> with respect to socialization to the profession, this mode of instruction [the case method] was . . . quite distinct from the study of law grounded in philosophy, political economy, and social ethics. One could now enter the profession with neither the practical experience of apprenticeship nor the broad liberal education of the earlier university training in the law. Consistent with the nineteenth-century analytic jurisprudence of John Austin, which insisted on the separation of law from ethics, the study of law had now become technically divorced from concerns with social justice in both its theoretical formulations and its practical applications.[52]

---

[51]The clash between the advocates of day and night legal education, along with the intense social ramifications, is discussed in Auerbach, *Unequal Justice,* especially Ch. 4.

[52]Zemans and Rosenblum, *Making of a Public Profession,* 6. See also Kronman, *The Lost Lawyer,* especially Ch. 4 on legal education. Kronman's work is perhaps the most thoughtful analysis of the separation of law from concerns for social justice. But see also Linowitz, *The Betrayed Profession,* in which this distinguished lawyer and public servant argues for a near-complete reorientation of the American legal profession, beginning with more social science and humanities courses as part of legal education. See also Linda Greenhouse, "Linowitz's Call for Lawyers to Be People Again," *New York Times* (Apr. 22, 1988): A-23.

Given its insistence on a narrow, allegedly "scientific" approach based on the pretense of politically neutral intellectual objectivity, Langdellianism created an ethical vacuum into which the dominant business ethic of early twentieth century corporate capitalism rushed headlong. The standard law school curricula from 1900 to the present, the reformist glitches of the 1930s and the 1960s notwithstanding, evince the clear political and social orientation of Langdell's purportedly "neutral" undertaking. Professor Karl E. Klare's critique of contemporary law curricula suggests how little the passage of time has altered the original Langdellian adventure:

> The very structure of the law-school curriculum, then, is emblematic of the notion that the core of private property and private ordering arrangements constituitive of nineteenth-century capitalism is rational, structured, and central to the lawyering identity, and that to the extent that those arrangements need to be reconsidered, updated or refashioned, the appropriate mode of doing so is through public law reform via interstitial, ad hoc adjustments, that is, chiefly through regulation of the type championed during the New Deal. From this powerful set of symbolic messages law students learn that the only lawyer-like way to view the world is *moderately,* through the window of moderate conservatism or liberal reformism. They learn that the only lawyer-like way to think about social change is in terms of atomized, marginal, incremental reform through governmental regulation of private conduct, i.e., that the New Deal represents the outer boundary of human wisdom in the art of politics.[53]

Eric E. VanLoon, himself a 1971 graduate of Harvard Law School, made similar observations about contemporary law school offerings:

> Curricular offerings illustrate the orientation. In the first year, criminal and personal injury law, affecting great numbers of citizens, receive less thorough treatment than contracts or commercial property transactions; the course on legal procedure draws chiefly on business examples. The second-year law student is advised he is not a real lawyer without the three business-oriented courses known popularly as Making Money, Counting Money, and Keeping It From the Government (Corporations, Accounting, and Taxation). While these three are normally optional at Harvard, for example, 94 percent of the student body follows faculty urgings to elect them. Courses on estate planning abound, but few schools teach environmental planning; consumer law is only beginning to receive attention. . . .
> Law faculties also pride themselves on objective teaching of "how to think like a lawyer," imparting analytic skills and extolling rationality. Nonetheless, the courses impart an ethical bias toward business, for the business problems used to teach the lawyer's skills infiltrate the "value vacuum." Each day the student must play the role of corporate lawyer to be able to respond in class; he has no choice. The accompanying values transfer to him by osmosis. . . . Law school teaching is also characterized by a conceptual framework that filters out everything but "legal" reasons. When a recent Corporations class was asked to justify a company's giving a pension to a retiring employee, students strained to find a clever legal reason such that it could be deducted from profits to decrease taxes. Half the period passed before someone thought to answer that the employee deserved it, since he had no other means of support. As this anecdote illustrates, the lawyer comes to view his professional responsibilities as analogous with his client's interest.[54]

---

[53]Karl E. Klare, "The Law-School Curriculum in the 1980's: What's Left?" *Journal of Legal Education* 32 (1982): 336, 339.

[54]VanLoon, "Law School Response," 336–38. Yet another intriguing perspective on legal education is provided by Stephen C. Halpern,"On the Politics and Pathology of Legal Education," *Journal of Legal Education* 32 (1982): 383–94. See also Robert V. Stover, "Law School and Professional Responsibility: The Impact of Legal Education on Public Interest Practice," *Judicature* 66, No. 5 (Nov. 1982): 194–206.

236 I Part II Judicial Personnel

Taking a substantively similar tack, Dean Erwin Griswold stated in his convocation remarks marking the 150th anniversary of the founding of Harvard Law School that

> In exalting purely logical reasoning, sometimes almost of the chess or bridge game type, we are not giving sufficient weight to other elements in the situation which are equally relevant in any truly intellectual evaluation. . . . We stress logic as the ultimate objective, though we may be rather unaware that we are doing so. . . .
>   Much of the material that we teach is the stuff of business and finance—contracts, commercial law, taxation, creditors' rights—only recently has any interest in debtors' rights developed. Much of our best teaching has been in the property and business fields. Almost inevitably our students are led to feel that it is in these areas that the great work of the lawyer is to be found. By methods of teaching, by subtle and often unconscious innu- endo, we indicate to our students that their future success and happiness will be found in the traditional areas of the law. Of course that is where the teaching materials are most readily found. And it can be said, too, that as the method of providing legal services in this country has been organized in the past, that has been the way in which one was most likely to be able to make a living.[55]

If lawyers can be conceptualized as gatekeepers to the judicial process, with all the bene- fits of legality that the process can bestow, then legal education must be seen as the "gate- keeper" for the "gatekeepers." And as we have seen, this gatekeeping function of legal edu- cation has come to be almost totally monopolized by the nation's law schools.

That removal of legal training from the law office (and the certification process from Abe Lincoln's hotel room) to the law school classroom and the bar examiner's office brought vast improvement in the educational product can hardly be denied. But that we have witnessed the conversion of a quasi-liberally and ethically oriented educational process into one dominated by the business ethic is also true. And, as noted, the fruits have been an imbalance in availability of legal service in America that has reached scan- dalous proportions.

Nevertheless, as illustrated in Table 7–5, law schools continue to attract students in record numbers, the surge of women admissions leading the charge. During the thirty-year period 1963–1993, first-year enrollment in American law schools slightly more than dou- bled; but first-year *women* enrollments (not shown in the table) leaped nearly 22 times over, moving from only 877 in the fall of 1963 to 19,059 by the fall of 1993, reaching 19,462 by the fall of 1995.

As for racial minorities, while their *numbers* have increased over the years, their *per- centage* increases have been spotty, helping to explain the stagnation in the growth of cer- tain minorities discussed before. Thus, although Black attendance in law schools moved from 5,304 in the fall of 1977 to 9,779 by the beginning of the 1995 academic year, their *share* of total law school enrollments increased from about 4.5 percent to only 7.2 percent, a notable but hardly dramatic improvement. In examining Mexican-American enrollments alone, which account for a bit more than a third of all Hispanic-related categories tabulated by the American Bar Association, one finds their proportional progress has been slight in- deed, moving from 1.4 percent in the academic year 1978–1979 to only 1.8 percent in 1995–1996. It is true that overall minority enrollment in America's law schools grew to nearly 19 percent by the fall of 1995; however, the most dramatic gains were registered by

---

[55]Erwin N. Griswold, "Intellect and Spirit," in Sutherland, *Path of the Law from 1967,* 151. But for one (among several) exceptions to these characterizations of current law school curricula, see Joseph N. Boyce's piece on Northeastern University's Law School, "A Boston Law School Insists Students Get Real-World Training," *Wall Street Journal* (Dec. 21, 1995): A-1.

Hispanics other than Mexican-Americans and Puerto Ricans (this group increasing over fivefold in the period discussed) and Asian and Pacific Islanders, who improved their numbers by about the same figure in the period.[56]

The cause, or causes, for overall continued strong demand for law school admissions are a bit more elusive. Realization by the early 1960s of the role of law in social change no doubt caught the imagination of a good many young people, followed by the further catalyst of inordinately popular TV shows relating to law. The accompanying "rights revolution" added further fuel to the desire of college graduates to enter a profession in which they believed that they could "make a difference." Too, by the mid-1980s, the salaries of beginning firm associates, approaching $80,000 per year in the top firms, were also an important drawing card.[57] Finally, we must not forget the powerful force of the women's movement in the growth of the law student—and lawyer—pool. As pointed out by Richard Abel in 1989,

> During the five years following 1969, law school applications increased threefold, but women applicants increased *fourteen times.* [emphasis added]. . . .
>
> Between 1967 and 1983, the enrollment of women . . . increased 1,650 percent, from 4.5 to 37.7 percent of the total. . . . Indeed, because the absolute number of male law students has [had] not increased since 1973, *all* subsequent growth of law school enrollments is attributable to the entry of women.[58]

While the overall growth in law school enrollments since Abel wrote can no longer be totally explained by increases in women enrollees, women's percentage of total JD enrollments continues to climb, moving from only 20 percent in the fall of 1974 to 39 percent a decade later, and on to 44 percent by the last tablulation available, the fall enrollments of 1995.

Although legal education continues to be employed as a tool for social mobility, the socioeconomic background of those entering the legal profession remains middle to upper middle class. Somewhere between 60 and 70 percent of all law students come from professional, business-oriented, or managerial backgrounds as determined by parental occupations. As Professor Herbert Jacob observed,

> [M]ost fledgling lawyers come from relatively comfortable circumstances. Their families have had sufficient resources to provide seven years of post–high school education or at least do not need their children's help for the family's support. Very few lawyers are non-white even though law schools have made vigorous efforts to recruit non-white students in recent years. If a young lawyer has an interest in the poor, it is more likely to come from an intellectual concern rather than from personal experience with poverty. Although

---

[56]American Bar Association, Section of Legal Education and Admissions to the Bar, *A Review of Legal Education in the United States, Fall, 1994* (Chicago: American Bar Association, 1995): 67–70.

[57]Explaining the vast increases in law school enrollments since the early 1960s has not been easy. But see *The Making of a Public Profession,* Ch. 3; Richard H. Sander and E. Douglass Williams, "Why Are There So Many Lawyers? Perspectives on a Turbulent Market," *Law and Social Inquiry* 14, No. 3 (Summer 1989): 431–79; Moll, *The Lure of the Law;* and Harry P. Stumpf and John H. Culver, *The Politics of State Courts* (New York: Longman, 1992), 66–68.

Preliminary data on recent applications to law schools suggest that the glitter of a legal education may be dimming. Whereas about 94,000 applications were received in 1991 (an all-time high), only some 78,000 students applied for fall 1995 admission. Fewer law jobs, lower starting salaries, intensified lawyer-bashing, and even the passing of popular law-related TV programs are cited as possible causes. See Dirk Johnson, "More Scorn and Less Money Dim Law's Lure, *New York Times* (Sept. 22, 1995): A-1. However, more data are needed to determine whether this represents any more than a glitch in the continued high demand for a legal eduation.

[58]Richard L. Abel, *American Lawyers* (New York: Oxford University Press, 1989): 91.

Table 7-5   Enrollment in ABA-Approved Law Schools, Fall, 1963–1995

Year	Number of Schools	Total Enrollment[a]	First-Year Enrollment	Total JD Women	Blacks	Hispanics[b]	Total Minority[c]	JDs or LLBs Granted	Admitted to Bar
1963	135	49,552	20,776	1,739				9638	10,788
1964	135	54,265	22,753	2,056				10,491	12,023
1965	136	59,744	24,167	2,374				11,507	13,109
1966	135	62,556	24,077	2,520				13,115	14,644
1967	136	64,406	24,267	2,769				14,738	16,007
1968	138	62,779	23,652	3,554				16,077	17,764
1969	144	68,386	29,128	4,485				16,733	19,123
1970	146	82,041	34,289	6,682				17,183	17,922
1971	147	94,468	36,171	8,567				17,006	20,485
1972	149	101,707	35,131	11,878				22,342	25,086
1973	151	106,102	37,018	16,303				27,756	30,879
1974	157	110,713	38,074	21,283				28,729	30,707
1975	163	116,991	39,038	26,020				29,961	34,930
1976	163	117,451	39,996	29,343				32,597	35,741
1977	163	118,557	39,676	31,650	5,304	2,531	9,580	33,640	37,302
1978	167	121,606	40,479	35,775	5,350	2,788	9,952	33,317	39,068
1979	169	122,860	40,717	37,534	5,257	2,817	10,013	34,590	42,756

Year									
1980	171	125,397	42,296	40,834	5,505	3,014	10,575	35,059	41,997
1981	172	127,312	42,521	43,245	5,789	3,189	11,134	35,598	45,382
1982	172	127,828	42,034	45,539	5,852	3,406	11,611	34,846	42,905
1983	173	127,195	41,159	46,361	5,967	3,496	11,866	36,389	41,684
1984	174	125,698	40,747	46,897	5,955	3,507	11,917	36,687	42,630
1985	175	124,092	40,796	47,486	6,052	3,679	12,346	36,829	42,450
1986	175	123,277	40,195	47,920	5,894	3,865	12,550	36,121	40,247[d]
1987	175	123,198	41,055	48,920	6,028	4,074	13,250	35,478	39,918[d]
1988	174	125,870	42,860	50,932	6,321	4,342	14,295	35,701	46,528
1989	175	129,698	43,826	53,113	6,791	4,733	15,720	35,520	47,174
1990	175	132,433	44,104	54,097	7,432	5,038	17,330	36,385	43,286[d]
1991	176	135,157	44,050	55,110	8,149	5,541	19,410	38,800	54,577
1992	176	133,783	42,793	54,644	8,698	5,969	21,266	39,425	57,117
1993	176	133,339	43,644	55,134	9,156	6,312	22,799	40,213	49,135
1994	177	134,784	44,298	55,808	9,681	6,772	24,611	39,710	57,875
1995	178	135,518	43,676	56,923	9,779	6,970	25,554	39,191	NA

[a]Includes post-JD law students.

[b]Includes Mexican-Americans, Puerto Ricans, and "Other Hispanic Americans."

[c]In addition to Blacks and Hispanics, includes the two categories of "American Indian or Alaskan Native" and "Asian or Pacific Islander."

[d]Data are not complete; thus, figures are lower than for prior years.

Source: American Bar Association, Section on Legal Education and Admissions to the Bar, *Review of Legal Education in the United States, Fall, 1995* (Chicago: American Bar Association, 1994, 1995) (some footnotes and columns deleted).

he may have been exposed to analyses of poverty, racism, slums, or unemployment in college, he is not likely to have experienced these problems himself.[59]

Thus, there seems little reason to expect siginficant changes in the ideological orientation of law students and practicing lawyers from that already described, nor little hope for significantly increased access to the services that they control.

THE ORGANIZATION OF THE BAR

Organizing lawyers in the United States has been a long, uphill battle—one that is still in progress. Time was when lawyering was "one vast sprawling profession," with the few existing local organizations providing very little by way of cohesion or control.[60] Indeed, for most of the nineteenth century, no national organization of lawyers even existed, and state and local organizations were rare. Thus, training, admission, and internal discipline—three chief concerns within most professions—remained elusive subjects of control for the legal profession. The widespread movement of the bar toward business- and corporate-oriented practice, attendant increases in the wealth and prestige attached to being a lawyer, and the creation of a superficially academic methodology for the study of law, however, combined to encourage the formation of local, regional, and even national lawyer organizations. These facets of legal practice imbued attorneys with a level of social prestige to protect and nurture, along with an acceptable means of doing so. The gates would be closed to the hordes of would-be practitioners through academic and social qualifications, purifying the profession for its role as defender of American order and stability. As historian Jerold Auerbach noted,

> [w]hether corporate or country lawyers predominated [in bar politics] . . . the "best men" used bar associations as a lever of control over professional ethics, educational qualifications, and bar admission. Claiming the right to represent and to police the entire profession, they discriminated against an increasingly substantial number of urban practitioners from ethnic minority groups.[61]

On February 15, 1870, a group of New York lawyers, calling themselves "the decent part" of the profession, met to form the Association of the Bar of the City of New York. The movement to organize lawyers spread quickly. Attorneys in Chicago, Iowa, and seven other cities and states formed bar associations between 1870 and 1878. These early groups were largely social, but they were political entities as well, concerned with education, judicial selection and corruption, shysterism in the practice of law, and, of course, fees.

In like manner, in 1878, seventy-five genteel members of the "decent" bar met at Saratoga, New York, to form the American Bar Association in order to "advance the science of jurisprudence, promote the administration of justice, . . . uphold the honor of the profession, . . . and encourage cordial intercourse among the members of the American

---

[59]Herbert Jacob, *Urban Justice: Law and Order in American Cities* (Englewood Cliffs, N.J.: Prentice-Hall, 1973), 38. On the expectations and ideological-occupational orientations of current law students, see Linda F. Wightman, *Legal Education at the Close of the Twentieth Century* (Newton, Pa: Law School Admissions Council, 1995). See especially the section on employment aspirations, at 60–61.

[60]Friedman, *History of American Law,* 315. See also the very useful set of readings edited by Geoffrey C. Hazard, Jr., and Deborah L. Rhode, *The Legal Profession: Responsibility and Regulation,* 3rd ed. (Westbury, N.Y.: Foundation Press, 1994). Their coverage of the development of bar associations and techniques of regulation is especially relevant to the discussion here.

[61]Auerbach, *Unequal Justice,* 64.

bar."[62] The growth of this new organization was slow. By 1900, it was still little more than a social club of elite, primarily business lawyers. Beginning in the early twentieth century, however, the ABA gradually increased its membership while broadening the range of its activities and expanding its influence and control over critical areas of the profession. This expansion in no way altered the ABA's staunchly right-wing political posture, reflecting its entirely white, male, economically elite membership oriented toward corporate clients. From its beginning and throughout much of its history, the ABA actively excluded women and people of color from its ranks. When, in 1912, for example, three African American lawyers were unwittingly admitted to membership, it was agreed, after storms of controversy, that they should be permitted to remain, but that all future membership applications would disclose the applicant's race. Not until 1956 did the ABA rescind this policy of apartheid, although it remained hostile to minority lawyers well into the 1960s. While alternative national organizations—most notably the National Lawyers Guild,[63] founded in 1937 to combat the sexist and racist policies of the ABA—have been formed, such competing organizations have had difficulty in breaking the ABA's control of the profession.

The growth of state bar associations roughly paralleled that of the ABA. The major difference was that, in the 1920s, pushed by the American Judicature Society, states began to develop "integrated" bars (all attorneys wishing to practice in the state must join—a euphemism, actually, for a "closed shop"). North Dakota was the first state to integrate its bar in 1921, with several states following soon thereafter. As of 1992, 31 states had integrated their bars, with the remaining states having a voluntary, though usually quite active, bar association.[64] Since 1936, the ABA has sought to develop a federal relationship with state bars by including them in ABA membership.

Although the process of certifying would-be attorneys for practice was an early and continuing concern of the organized bar, that process remained largely in the hands of state legislatures. Local, state, and national bar associations thus sought to exert control over who was admitted to practice through law school standards. In 1921, for example, the American Bar Association adamantly supported requiring two years of undergraduate

---

[62]Friedman, *History of American Law,* 650. The celebrated constitutional scholar Edward S. Corwin, writing of the creation and early years of the American Bar Association, noted that "[t]he membership of the new organization comprised from the first the *haute nobleese* of the Bar." He continued in a paragraph worth quoting in its entirety:

> The association soon became a sort of juristic sewing circle for mutual education in the gospel of *laissez faire*. Addresses and papers presented at the annual meetings iterated and reiterated the tenets of the new creed: government was essentially of private origin; the police power of the State was intended merely to implement the common law of nuisance; the right to fix prices was no part of any system of free government; "in the progress of society, there is a natural tendency to freedom"; the trend of democracy is always away from regulation in the economic field; "the more advanced a nation becomes, the more the liberty of the individual will be developed," and so on. In brief, the guarantees which the Constitution affords private rights were intended to supply, above all other things, a legal and poltical sanction to the laws of political economy and to the process of evolution as forecast by Herbert Spencer. *The country was presented with a new, up-to-date version of natural law.*

Edward S. Corwin, *Liberty Against Government: The Rise, Flowering and Decline of a Famous Juridical Concept* (Baton Rouge: Louisiana State University Press, 1948), 137–38.

[63]See Ann Fagan Ginger and Eugene M. Tobin, *The National Lawyers Guild: From Roosevelt Through Reagan* (Philadelphia: Temple University Press, 1988), 136–59.

[64]In general, see Dayton McKean, *The Integrated Bar* (Boston: Houghton Mifflin, 1963); regarding integrated bar statistics, see The American Bar Association's *1991/92 Directory of Bar Associations* (Chicago: American Bar Association, 1992) at pages 367–81. An interesting analysis of the bar integration movement is Mark W. Granfors, Terence C. Halliday, and Michael J. Powell, "Organizations Between States and Markets: Explaining the Bar Unification Movement, 1915–1950," paper delivered at the American Sociological Association meeting, Atlanta, Aug. 28, 1988.

study and a three-year law degree as prerequisites for bar admission. Eventually, almost every state adopted these recommendations, and today only a handful will license an individual to practice law without a *juris doctorate* from an ABA-approved law school, and then only in extremely limited circumstances.

Indeed, as the American Bar Association gradually tightened control over standards of legal education (and indirectly, admission to practice), it became guildlike in its monopoly determination of such detailed educational matters as professors' salaries, paid leaves, teaching loads, student-faculty ratios, libraries, and so on. Until recently it was a cozy—one might say incestuous—arrangement: the ABA's Section of Legal Education and Admission to the Bar, the entity empowered to accredit law schools, was made up of about 90 percent law school faculty! Not surprisingly, one of the requirements for accreditation imposed by the committee was that all law schools must pay professors at levels comparable to all other ABA-approved law schools. Salary and similar data were shared among law schools, having the effect of "ratcheting up the salary data"—and salaries—leading to "inflated levels . . . having little to do with the quality of legal education," but much to do with the pecuniary advantage of law school professors. Similarly inflated standards were applied to libraries, teaching loads (no more than eight hours per week), and student-faculty ratios (twenty students to each faculty member).[65]

As has been the case since the creation of the ABA, the effect of such standards was to squeeze out proprietary schools, significantly increase the costs (tuition) of law school, thereby lending further class bias to legal education and the American legal profession. Law schools that could not meet the high costs created by the ABA standards could not compete with schools that were successful in prying funds from state legislatures or drawing from their enormous endowments.

In 1993 the Dean of the Massachusetts School of Law, Lawrence Velvel, filed suit against the ABA, claiming violation of the Sherman Antitrust Act. By mid-1995, the ABA rather quickly agreed to a settlement that included a reduction in the faculty domination of its accrediting committee, elimination of the ban on schools for profit, and deletion of faculty salaries as a criterion for accreditation. However, the long-term effects of these changes remain to be seen.[66]

Together with graduating from a recognized law school, most prospective attorneys must also pass a state-administered bar examination before being admitted to practice. In all but six states, that means completing a two-hundred-item, multiple choice, "Multi-State Bar Exam" covering six "core" legal topics, a one- or two-day battery of essay questions specific to a given state's laws and procedures, and a fifty-question, multiple-choice test called the "Multi-State Professional Responsibility Exam," focusing on issues of professional ethics.

As the legal profession's ultimate screening device, bar examinations have had a tendency to "feed back" into law school curricula, encouraging a narrow focus. Indeed, it is virtually a cardinal rule that law school classes covering "bar topics" are by far the most heavily subscribed by law students.

Beyond affecting law school curricula, bar examinations have also played a role in preserving the predominantly white, upper-middle class composition of the profession through their notorious cultural bias. Although a number of studies have been conducted, several articles published, and even a few lawsuits filed challenging this practice, little

---

[65]See Viveca Novak, "ABA Settles Law-School-Salary Charges," *Wall Street Journal* (June 28, 1995): B-5; and Steven A. Holmes, "Pact Overhauls Accreditation of Law Schools," *New York Times* (June 28, 1995): A-1.

[66]Novak, "ABA Settles," and Holmes, "Pact Overhauls."

about bar examinations has changed, and individuals from racial minorities and from working-class backgrounds continue to operate at a disadvantage.[67]

The efforts of the American Bar Association and that of state bars to influence admission to practice have met with considerably more success than have their attempts to establish an enforced standard of ethical behavior in the practice of law. For a considerable period following its founding, the ABA had little or nothing to say of a formal nature on the subject of ethics. In 1905, however, the organization was stunned by a sharply worded speech by Theodore Roosevelt, who castigated the new legal elite. Charged Roosevelt,

> Many of the most influential and most highly remunerated members of the bar in every centre of wealth make it their special task to work out bold and ingenious schemes by which their very wealthy clients, individual or corporate, can evade the laws which are made to regulate in the interest of the public the use of great wealth.[68]

Shortly thereafter the association appointed a committee to look into the development of a code of professional ethics, and after considerable debate, the new Canons of Ethics were adopted. The notorious ineffectiveness of the canons was due to several factors. First, they were grounded in a set of assumptions about the practice of law which were valid only for the pre-1870 era. In their emphasis on issues arising out of litigation, their strictures on advertising, ambulance chasing, and the like, the Canons of 1908, as revised in 1928, were essentially a throwback to the nineteenth century when a lawyer's reputation in the community was usually enough to enable him to earn a decent livelihood. At a time when the profession had grown increasingly heterogeneous and stratified, with a move of prestige practice to the urban financial and corporate centers of America, a set of ethical precepts was adopted that reflected a reverence for the small-town homogeneity of antibellum America. As such, the new canons contained a second shortcoming, an ill-concealed class bias. Though prompted by attacks on corporate practice, the canons were actually drawn up by ABA lawyers with a strong corporate slant. Thus, as Auerbach writes, they

> were easily adaptable to an equally homogeneous upper-class metropolitan constituency, where they served as a club against lawyers whose clients were excluded from that culture: especially the urban poor, new immigrants, and blue-collar workers. These lawyers confronted problems of client procedure which an established corporate practitioner did not experience.
>
> A cluster of canons pertaining to acquiring an interest in litigation, stirring litigation, and division of fees almost exclusively affected the activities of struggling metropolitan solo lawyers. They did not apply to the conduct of the firm members or securely established practitioners who formulated them.[69]

Finally, the canons strongly emphasized the interpersonal, contractual relationship of lawyer to lawyer and lawyer to client, while paying almost no attention to the social responsibility of the profession. Exhortations in the direction of the lawyers' obligation to the "law" or seeing that legal services were made available to all were notably lacking in the canons.[70]

---

[67]Regarding bar exam bias, see vol. 16. no. 3, of the *Thurgood Marshall Law Review* (1991), devoted to a symposium on this issue. See particularly Stephen P. Klein, "Disparities in Bar Exam Passing Rates Among Racial/Ethinic Groups: Their Size, Source, and Implications," *Thurgood Marshall Law Review*, 16, no. 3 (1991): 515. See also *The Legal Profession*, 538–42.

[68]Theordore Roosevelt, *Presidential Addresses and State Papers: May 10, 1905 to April 12, 1906* (New York: n.p., 1910), Ch. 4, 419–20.

[69]Auerbach, *Unequal Justice*, 42–43.

[70]Hurst, *Growth of American Law*, 328–33.

Realizing the woeful outdatedness of its ethical guidelines, the ABA finally undertook to revise the old canons in the 1960s, which led, in 1969, to the adoption of the new Code of Responsibility. However, the changes were largely superficial. High-sounding wording to the effect that legal services should be made available to all, for example, was undermined by a continued commitment to the concept of individual responsibility in such matters. As well, the bar's commitment to group legal services, and similar plans to provide lawyers to people of moderate means, went no further than the case law absolutely required. While the new code, in part, sounded modern, its emphasis, like that of the old canons, remained on economic interests rather than the professional responsibility of the American lawyer.

In 1983, the ABA adopted a set of Model Rules of Professional Conduct, intended to address and rectify some of the shortcomings identified with the Code. As of 1992, a majority of the states had adopted either the Model Rules, or a close approximation of them.[71]

The Distribution of Legal Services: The Unmet Need

Perhaps no aspect of American lawyer "ethics" has been criticized more than the relative lack of concern shown for promoting legal services for the poor. Indeed, research has shown that the needs of middle-class Americans have likewise been largely ignored by the legal profession.[72] The usually restrained analysis of Hurst is set aside in favor of rather sharp condemnation of the bar on this score:

> We have noted the tardy adoption and the limited and even superficial character of the canons of ethics which the organized bar finally sponsored.
> There was no clearer example of belated, narrow, and shallow treatment of the bar's "ethical" problems than in the manner of making legal services available to people of small means. Toward an issue which challenged the professed ideals of the profession and of American society the organized bar was inert, insensitive, unimaginative.[73]

The issues of unmet legal needs in the United States and of various attempts to solve the problem is a very large subject unto itself. But some of the highlights can be presented.[74] The legal aid movement in civil matters in the United States had its beginnings in

---

[71]Regarding the ABA *Model Rules* and the organized bar's influence and control over lawyer discipline, see Ch. 5 of Paul Wice, *Judges and Lawyers: The Human Side of Justice* (New York: HarperCollins, 1991). The process and politics of the adoption of ABA's *Model Rules* are discussed by Theodore Schneyer, "Professionalism as Politics: The Making of a Modern Legal Ethics Code," in *Lawyer's Ideals/Lawyers' Practices:* 95–143. Issues of legal ethics and the policing of the profession are intelligently discussed in a number of essays in the collection by Hazard and Rhode, *The Legal Profession.*

[72]See Douglas J. Besharov, ed., *Legal Services for the Poor* (Washington, D.C.: AEI Press, 1990); Barbara Curran, *The Legal Needs of the Public: The Final Report of a National Survey* (Chicago: American Bar Foundation, 1977); American Bar Association, Consortium on Legal Services and the Public, *Findings of the Comprehensive Legal Needs Study* (Chicago: American Bar Association, 1994); and Randal Samborn, "ABA Study: Legal Needs Not Met," *National Law Journal,* Feb. 14, 1994: 3.

[73]Hurst, *Growth of American Law,* 365.

[74]Research on legal services to the poor expanded rapidly in the mid-1960s, resulting in a very large bibliography. For starters, see Harry P. Stumpf, *Community Politics and Legal Services,* "Bibliographic Essay," 296–305. The description that follows in the text of the growth of legal aid in the United States draws heavily on this work. Civil legal aid has become the subject of extensive cross-national research since the 1960s. A highly informative survey of this work may be found in Richard L. Abel, "Law Without Politics: Legal Aid Under Advanced Capitalism," *UCLA Law Review* 32, No. 3 (Feb. 1985): 474–642. The picture of Legal services on the American scene is updated by Able, *American Lawyers, passim;* and Christopher E. Smith, *Courts and the Poor* (Chicago: Nelson-Hall, 1991). Particularly on the criminal side, see National Center for State Courts, *Indigent Defenders* (Williamsburg: National Center for State Courts, 1992). A brief update with useful sources is also found in *The Politics of State Courts:* 75–81. Finally, a very helpful series of essays is found in Hazard and Rhode, *The Legal Profession,* Part III.

New York City in 1876 with the German Legal Aid Society, created by laymen to aid indigent German immigrants. This private approach was duplicated in Chicago in the 1880s, and by 1910, legal aid offices had been established in eight additional cities.[75] In 1911, the National Legal Aid Association (now the National Legal Aid and Defenders Association, NLADA) was created to supersede two prior organizations, the National Alliance of Legal Societies and the National Association of Legal Aid Organizations. The NLADA provided a forum for the movement and established national standards for local program operations, although it had no supervisory powers.[76]

The movement grew slowly. By 1948, only 55 cities had offices with paid staff attorneys to serve the poor, and as late as 1964, NLADA statistics indicated that there were still 9 cities with a million or more population plus 15 slightly smaller communities with no civil legal aid at all.[77] Although most major cities could boast some form of civil legal aid, in middle-sized and smaller cities, small towns, and rural areas availability of such service was largely nonexistent. In 1964, the president of NLADA reported that 105 rural centers with over 100,000 population each were without organized legal aid at all, and although by 1967 there were 298 civil legal aid offices with paid attorneys and 90 with volunteer attorneys, 2,500 of the 3,100 counties in the United States remained unserved by any organized legal aid facility.[78] Despite geographic gaps, these data suggest that a majority of at least the urban poor had meaningful access to civil legal services, presumably approximating that available to paying clients. But a closer inspection of funding levels and criteria of service point to quite a different conclusion.

From the beginning, legal aid societies functioned on starvation budgets. Most of their funds were derived from private individual donations, bar associations, and community chests, the third being the most signficant component.[79] Staff attorneys were not only few in number, but poorly paid and recruited from the least competent sectors of the bar. In 1963, the 165 legal aid offices that reported costs of operations accounted for expenditures of $3,795,287, whereas 84 public defender (criminal) offices had gross receipts of $3,989,302, for a total of $7,784,589. This represented but .35 percent of all expenditures for legal services in the United States in 1963.[80] Even if we assume that legal aid and defender services were made available to all persons officially classified as being in poverty (though availability was far below this level), the annual per capita expenditure for legal services for the nonpoor was $14.50, whereas for the poor it was 23 cents.[81] Viewed differently, if the 34.5 million citizens in poverty had been provided with the services of an attorney at levels purchased by the remaining 152.7 million nonpoor, legal aid

[75]The history of the legal aid movement is detailed in Reginald Heber Smith, *Justice and the Poor* (New York: Carnegie Foundation for the Advancement of Teaching, 1919); and in Emery A. Brownell, *Legal Aid in the United States* (Rochester, N.Y.: Lawyers Cooperative, 1951).

[76]See, for example, NLADA, *Handbook of Standards* (Chicago: American Bar Center, 1965).

[77]See Lee Silverstein, "Thoughts on the Legal Aid Movement," *Social Services Review* 40, No. 2 (June 1966): 139.

[78]Lee Silverstein, "Eligibility for Free Legal Services in Civil Cases," *Journal of Urban Law* 44, No. 4 (Summer 1967): 555.

[79]In 1964, NLADA reported that 51.38 percent of civil legal aid costs came from community chests, 16.61 percent from bar associations and attorneys. See NLADA, *Summary of Conference Proceedings, 1965* (Chicago: NLADA, 1965), 85.

[80]Legal aid and defender figures are taken from NLADA, *Summary of Conference Proceedings, 1964* (Chicago: NLADA 1964), 29. According to the Department of Commerce, 1963 per capita expenditures for legal services were $2,218. In general, see Jerome E. Carlin and Jan Howard, "Legal Representation and Class Justice,"*UCLA Law Review* 12 (Jan. 1965): 381–437.

[81]This calculation is based on a poverty population of 34.5 million out of some 187.2 million people in 1963. See Herman P. Miller, "Changes in the Number and Composition of the Poor," in Margaret S. Gordon, ed., *Poverty in America* (San Francisco: Chandler, 1965): 84–5.

and defender offices would have cost $483 million, or more than 60 times actual expenditures in 1963.[82]

Leaving aside the debate over relative legal need at various levels of society and simply assuming that need is evenly divided throughout all income levels, the distribution of attorneys for the poor as contrasted to the nonpoor can be presented as follows. In 1970, there were 355,242 lawyers in the United States. With a population of 203,184,773, the ratio was 1 attorney for every 572 people. Attorneys with "directory listings" (that is, listed in the law directory and presumably in actual practice, either private or governmental) numbered 324,818, a ratio of 1 for every 622 persons. The poor, numbering some 25.5 million in 1970, or about 13 percent of the population, should presumably be served by a like percentage of practicing lawyers, or about 42,225. In fact, no more than 4,000–5,000 attorneys were then involved in serving the poor, [83] a ratio of about 1:5,000.[84]

Not only were programs, personnel, and funds for legal aid sparsely distributed, but bar and business pressures to avoid the loss of paying clients also kept these programs orthodox and limited. Financial eligibility standards were outright niggardly, as were subject matter guidelines. As with contemporary welfare standards, one had to be truly "deserving" to obtain assistance, and that determination usually involved a moral and ethical judgment of one class by another.[85]

In 1965, as part of President Johnson's War on Poverty, the Legal Services Program was created.[86] Intended as a new departure in legal services, it provided that

1. Neighborhood offices would be established within the poverty community itself, providing direct accessibility to the indigent client,
2. Programs would be structured and governed to ensure their independence from local business agencies, other political institutions, and private groups (including local bar associations) that might have opposing interests.
3. There would be "maximum feasible participation" of the poor in policy decisions in order to increase the responsiveness of the program to the needs of the indigent community.
4. Emphasis would be placed on aggressive creative advocacy in raising problems and pursuing issues that bear on the problems of the poor as a group.
5. Substantial increases in funding would ensure a genuine attempt to meet the civil legal needs of the poor.

---

[82]Of course these figures do not take into account the gratis legal services provided the poor by private attorneys. There are no reliable data by which we can accurately estimate the level and value of such service, but see Frederick R. Merrill, *Utilization of Legal Services by the Poor and the Private Practicing Bar,* Individual Report No. 2 (Chicago: American Bar Foundation, 1969); and Joel F. Handler et al., "Public Interest Activities Among Private Practice Lawyers." *American Bar Association Journal* 61 (Nov. 1975): 1388–94.

[83]This estimate includes some 2,000 employed by OEO Legal Services, another 2,000 public defenders, and 500 to 1,000 engaged in similar work such as in public interest law firms, pro bono work, the law communes, etc. See Nathan Hakman, "Political Trials in the Legal Order: A Political Scientist's Perspective," *Journal of Public Law* 21, No. 1 (1972): 73–126.

[84]One legal services attorney calculated in 1967 that if the poverty population (then 16.5 percent) were afforded legal representation at the level of persons with annual incomes in excess of $10,000, 137,000 or about 47 percent of all lawyers then in practice would have been required just to serve the poor! See Carol Ruth Silver, "Eminent Failure of Legal Services for the Poor: What and How to Limit Case Load," *Journal of Public Law* 46, No. 2 (1969): 218.

[85]See Joel F. Handler, *Reforming the Poor: Welfare Policy, Federalism and Morality* (New York: Basic Books, 1972); and Silverstein, "Eligibility for Free Legal Services in Civil Cases," 549–84.

[86]See Susan E. Lawrence, *The Poor in Court: The Legal Services Program and Supreme Court Decision Making* (Princeton, N. J.: Princeton University Press, 1990); and Stumpf, *Community Politics and Legal Services,* especially Ch. 4.

The social, political, legal, and economic ramifications of the Legal Services Program have been assessed elsewhere.[87] Suffice it to say that while the American Bar Association strongly supported the program, state and local bar associations, often in concert with community business and political interests, waged incessant attacks on it, accusing legal services attorneys of a wide array of improprieties.[88] In the 1960s and early 1970s, Ronald Reagan, then Governor of California, and Lewis K. Uhler, Reagan's state poverty program chief, leveled withering attacks on legal services programs and providers. A telling example is this quote from 1971:

> Why should we pay the salaries for a lot of guys to run around and look up rules so they can sue the state? The most a poor person is going to need a lawyer for is some divorce problem, some bankruptcy problems, some garnishment problems. What we've created in CRLA is an economic leverage equal to that existing in large corporations. Clearly that should not be.[89]

In his attempt to undermine the aggressive and highly successful California Rural Legal Assistance program (CRLA), Governor Reagan formally accused its lawyers and legal workers of fifty ethical and legal infractions. A committee of three state supreme court justices concluded Reagan's attack was "totally irresponsible and without foundation" and declared the work of California Rural Legal Assistance to be "competent, efficient, and exemplary." Governor Reagan was not dissuaded, however, and subsequently chose legal services for the poor as a chief target of his presidential administration's slash-and-burn policies regarding government-provided services.

The California story was repeated in varied form in many states. Providing legal services for the poor was an acceptable concept, so long as the services provided weren't sufficient to challenge established state and local economic interests. When legal services attorneys met with success in doing so—as CRLA did in California—the ax fell.

In 1974, Congress created the Legal Services Corporation in order to replace the Legal Services Program and to insulate legal services providers from further attacks. At present, the Corporation is overseen by an eleven-member board of directors responsible for making policy and funding decisions for more than three-hundred local and regional legal services programs across the nation. While the LSC has unquestionably succeeded in broadening access to civil legal representation, a 1975 speech by Roger Cramton, then LSC chairman, still rings true:

> The most generous estimates indicate that less than fifteen percent of the legal needs of the poor are being met today. . . . Less than 2,200 lawyers—only about one-half of one

[87]See Harry P. Stumpf, "Law and Poverty: A Political Perspective," *Wisconsin Law Review* No. 3 (1968): especially 697–98. An especially useful analysis of the program is Jack Katz, *Poor People's Lawyers in Transition* (New Brunswick, N. J.: Rutgers University Press, 1982). An insightful review of this book discussing major issues of the program and citing key items of the literature is by Stuart A. Scheingold, "The Dilemma of Legal Services," *Stanford Law Review* 36, No. 3 (Feb. 1984): 879–983.

[88]See Stumpf, *Community Politics and Legal Services,* especially Chs. 8 and 9; Earl Johnson, Jr., *Justice and Reform: The Formative Years of the OEO Legal Services Program* (New York: Russell Sage Foundation, 1974); and Ellen Jane Hollingsworth, "Ten Years of Legal Services for the Poor," in Robert H. Haveman, ed., *A Decade of Federal Anti-poverty Programs: Achievements, Failures and Lessons* (New York: Academic Press, 1977), 285–327.

[89]*Newsweek,* January 18, 1971, 19, as quoted in Stumpf, *Community Politics and Legal Services,* 291. The findings of the Reagan-Uhler criticisms of CRLA are contained in Robert B. Williamson, George R. Currie, and Robert B. Lee, "Report of the Office of Economic Opportunity Commission on California Rural Legal Assistance, Inc." (June 25, 1971): 83–88.

percent of the American Bar—are working full time to meet the legal needs of about one-sixth of the population.[90]

As with its predecessor, LSC's successes in the courtroom led to calls for its dissolution from established economic interests, championed by an old foe of legal assistance to the poor, President Ronald Reagan. Until the final year of his second presidential term, Reagan annually attempted to abolish the LSC outright, coming closest to doing so in 1981, when Congress slashed the LSC budget by one-quarter.[91] Moreover both Reagan and his successor, George Bush, insisted on appointing individuals to the LSC board who had declared their intention to dismantle the program. Although staunch congressional supporters kept both presidents from achieving their ultimate goal, LSC funding, when adusted for inflation, remained substantially below its pre-Reagan/Bush level.[92]

The saga of civil legal services seems never-ending, continuing to follow the familiar pattern outlined just above. As heavily pressed, low-paid poverty lawyers throughout the country attempt to help the poor with their legal problems, local, state and national political pressures have, if anything, increased to eliminate or emasculate the program. Although the first two years of the Clinton administration promised some relief from incessant threats to wipe out the program, the election of the Republican Congress in 1994 meant a return to the barricades to defend the Legal Services Corporation from the distinct possibility of total annihilation.

By 1994, some $415 million dollars annually were going out to some 320 programs (about 1,200 separate legal services offices) throughout the nation. Also funded were a number of support centers such as the Center on Social Welfare Policy, and the National Housing Law Project, where research is undertaken and national strategies are planned for attacking the widespread legal problems of the poor. Of some 1.7 million cases handled in 1994, 33 percent were family matters such as divorce, spousal abuse, child support, and child custody; 16 percent involved legal problems related to welfare and other government benefits, such as veterans' claims; and 11 percent were consumer issues. The remaining cases related to education, employment, health care, and individual rights.[93]

Especially galling to many Republicans have been court victories led by poverty lawyers against illegal attempts to reduce welfare benefits in such states as California, Wisconsin, Minnesota, and New Jersey.[94] The Christian Coalition also became incensed over the number of divorces handled for poor people, claiming that the program was subsidizing the breakup of families.[95] Hence, ordinary, day-to-day casework as well as the court "successes" of the program became reasons for congressional limitations on program funds and activities.

---

[90]As quoted in Richard Abel, "The Legal Profession, Course Syllabus," UCLA School of Law (Spring 1977), mimeo, 7. A somewhat more complete picture of ratios of lawyers to the poverty population may be found in Roger C. Cramton, "Promise and Reality in Legal Services," *Cornell Law Quarterly* 61, No. 4 (June 1976): 670–80.

[91]See Besharov, *Legal Services for the Poor,* xiii.

[92]Historical materials on the dispute over legal services funding can be found in Gerald M. Caplan, "Understanding the Controversy Over the Legal Services Corporation," *New York Law School Law Review* 28, No. 3 (1983): 583–91, and in Anthony Champagne, "Legal Services: A Program in Need of Assistance," in Anthony Champagne and Edward J. Harpham, eds., *The Attack on the Welfare State* (Prospect Heights, Ill.: Waveland Press, 1984), 131–48. Data regarding LSC funding is available in Congressional Quarterly's annual *Congressional Quarterly Almanac.* For general information regarding the provision of legal services to the poor and the operation of LSC-funded legal services providers, see monthly issues of *The Clearinghouse Review,* published by the National Clearinghouse for Legal Services, Inc.

[93]Robert Pear, "As Welfare Overhaul Looms, Legal Aid for Poor Dwindles," *New York Times* (Sept. 5, 1995): A-1; and Peter T. Kilborn, "Hard Times for Legal Aid, and Getting Harder," *New York Times* (Oct. 7, 1995): A-6.

[94]David Savage, "Budget Ax Hangs Heavily Over Legal Aid Services for the Poor," *Los Angeles Times* (Feb. 15, 1995): A-5.

[95]Savage, "Budget Ax"; and Kilborn, "Hard Times."

For example, when poverty law attorneys began to win federal court decisions challenging the manner in which poor (usually Black and Hispanic) legislative districts were malapportioned to reduce their voting strength, Bush administration national program officials directed that such suits be discontinued.[96] Similarly, some 2,000 New Hampshire state prison inmates made the mistake of winning a federal court action in 1977 in which the judge likened prison conditions to a "medieval dungeon." In the action it was found that "[P]risoners, including a known epileptic and an inmate who had just attempted suicide, were stripped naked and left in the dark in unheated isolation cells for weeks at a time."[97] Following a consent decree, The New Hampsire Legal Assistance program was appointed to monitor compliance. But when a program attorney filed a motion in 1993 claiming continuing mistreatment of mentally ill prisoners, the program came under severe attack in Congress. In early 1995, both the House and the Senate passed bills prohibiting the poverty lawyers from representing prisoners and reducing the program's budget by 25 percent. In fact, the legislation as adopted bans *all* Legal Services Corporation programs from class actions against *all* government agencies. New Hampshire Legal Assistance attorneys sent out a nationwide plea for private attorneys to step in to represent the prisoners, but there were no takers. Anticipating passage of the crippling legislation, program lawyers noted that "[prison inmates are] a very unpopular, powerless constituency."[98]

Emerging from the notorious federal budget fight between President Clinton and the Republican Congress was the Omnibus Budget Act of 1996, signed into law on April 26, 1996. Legal Services, though surviving—barely—was cut 30 percent, from $400 million in 1995 to $278 million in 1996.[99] Additionally, Congress was successful in imposing further limits on program activities. Class action suits, by which program attorneys were able to address problems common to the poor as a group, were eliminated entirely. Also, prison inmates may no longer be represented, LSP attorneys may not lobby on any issue, nor may they engage in litigation to reform federal or state welfare systems. Short of eliminating the program entirely, it is difficult to imagine legislation more destructive to program effectiveness.

For fiscal 1997, Republicans in Congress were angling for a further 50 percent decrease in funds for the Legal Services Corporation. But as election day 1996 approached, such extreme budgetary measures were not playing well with the electorate. Hence, 1997 LSP funds were actually increased by $5 million over the previous year, though the crippling limits on program activities were retained.[100]

---

[96]Robert Pear, "Poor Given Right to Legal Aid to Fight Redistricting Plans," *New York Times* (July 3, 1990): A-1. Program attorneys won a federal court ruling that overturned this restrictive policy on legal services activities.

[97]Nina Bernstein, "As Trial Nears, 2,000 Inmates Face a Cutoff of Legal Help," *New York Times* (Nov. 25, 1995): A-9.

[98]Bernstein, "As Trial Nears." Mark Kessler, in "Legal Mobilization for Social Reform: Power and Politics of Agenda Setting," *Law and Society Review* 24, No. 1 (1990): 121–43, nicely illustrates the tools employed by local politicians to undermine the efforts of Legal Services Corporation attorneys.

[99]See Robert Pear, "Spending Drops 10 Percent As Clinton Signs Budget Bill," *New York Times* (April 27, 1996): A-1; and a more detailed account by William Booth, "Killing the Lawyers," *Washington Post National Weekly Edition* (June 10–16, 1996): 32.

[100]"Legal Services on the Ropes," *New York Times Editorial* (July 16, 1996): A-16; and Booth, "Killing the Lawyers;" and Jerry Gray, "Senate Approves A Big Budget Bill, Beating Deadline," *New York Times* (Oct. 1, 1996): A-1, 14. See also Henry Weinstein, "Great Society's Legal Aid for Poor Targeted by Budget Ax," *Los Angeles Times* (Dec. 29, 1995): A-1. For the impact of program cuts on the California Rural Legal Assistance Program, see Mark Thompson, "CLRA Is Hindered by New Limits on Suits," *Los Angeles Daily Journal* (July 16, 1996): 1.

On December 26, 1996, Justice Beverley Cohn, a state trial judge in Manhattan, held that Congressional restrictions on legal services class actions suits were unconstitutional. See Don Van Natta Jr., "New York Lawyer Cleared to File Class Suits for Poor," *New York Times,* Dec. 27, 1996: A-11.

The plight of civil legal services since the inception of federal funding in 1965 provides an unusually clear illustration of the importance of the attorney's political role. The reader might wonder why a program of such modest (indeed, grossly inadequate) proportions and with such limited reach could so enrage the conservative political community. It is precisely because the availability of legal assistance, or sometimes even the suggestion of it, carries the potential for redistributing social goods, posing a perceived threat to those who have long enjoyed the sociopolitical advantage of legal representation. The poor have so long gone without the benefits of a lawyer's assistance that when one introduces this new factor into the political equation, established interests are shocked, the social equilibrium is threatened, and the countervailing power of dominant political interests comes into play. The point is best made by a Yvette McGee and her mother, Fraiser McGee, who, following a letter from a legal services attorney to the landlord, were happy finally to see a huge hole in the side of their apartment repaired:

> Business people don't hear [you]. . . . They talk to you like you are dumb. The legal aid lawyer comes in and tells [the landlord], "that's not the way it's supposed to be." When you have a lawyer, they talk to you like you are a person.[101]

Repairing the McGee's "big picture-frame-size hole in the wall to the outside" is hardly a major change in "who gets, what, when, and how" in American society. But in incremental fashion, such legal action can slowly improve the lot of the poor, or the other way around, can require significant expenditures by landlords to keep properties in good repair. More than the reallocation of material benefits, such legal action changes, if ever so slightly, the power relationship of the "haves" and "have-nots" in our society, which, even if symbolically, suggests significant social change. Such changes are perceived by established interests to be a threat to their social position, as indeed they are. Legal representation, even if inadequate, only periodic, and addressing seemingly minute matters, has sociopolitical potential far out of proportion to its immediate material significance. Legality is a political resource, and those with it, or even those who can appear to possess it, have a distinct political advantage.[102]

Since the United States Supreme Court decisions in *Gideon v. Wainwright*[103] and *Argersinger v. Hamlin,*[104] legal representation for those accused of crimes has been a right rather than merely a privilege. In attempting to meet the obligation of provididng lawyers to indigent defendants, each state has established a public defender program based on salaried, full-time public defenders, or appointed private attorneys who are paid by the state on a case-by-case basis, or some combination thereof. Irrespective of the system chosen, the quality of representation provided by public defenders is widely perceived to be inferior to that the wealthy can afford to purchase from private criminal defense attorneys.[105] Almost from the outset, public defender offices have been grossly underfunded, with a consequent negative impact on virtually every facet of the representation that they can provide—the time available for interaction between lawyer and client, for example, and the investigative resources that can be committed to a given case. Given the relatively

---

[101]"Hard Times."

[102]This analysis is extended in Stumpf, *Community Politics and Legal Services,* especially Chs. 8 and 9. See also Harry P. Stumpf, "The Failure of Legal Services, or Let Them Clean Out Cellars," paper presented at the Conference on the Delivery and Distribution of Legal Services, State University of New York at Buffalo Law School, Oct. 11, 12, 1973. Smith, in *Courts and the Poor,* explains the plight of legal services more in terms of America's commitment to a socioeconomic policy of inequality, pp. 141–43.

[103]372 U.S. 335 (1963).

[104]407 U.S. 25 (1972).

[105]See Lisa J. McIntyre, *The Public Defender: The Practice of Law in the Shadows of Repute* (Chicago: University of Chicago Press, 1987), particularly Ch. 4, "Institutionalized Accommodations: The Stigma of Ineptitude.

low level of prestige attached to criminal defense work, it is certainly no surprise that representing indigent defendants would carry even less social luster. Still, as the National Center for State Courts reports from a recent survey of public defender offices, despite insufficient funding and relatively low social prestige,

> there are few statistically significant differences in conviction rates, charge reduction rates, incarceration rates, and the lengths of prison sentences in cases represented by different types of criminal defense attorneys (public defenders, contract attorneys, assigned counsel, and privately retained counsel). Moreover, where the type of attorney does have an effect on these rates, the impact is very weak and not always in a more favorable direction toward the defendants represented by privately retained counsel.[106]

Even so, indigent defendants who are on the criminal as well as the civil side constitute a rather unpopular constituency, resulting in little or no political support for the maintenance of public defender systems beyond bare minimums.[107]

The 1970s brought several changes in the contours of legal practice that seemed to portend improvements in the availability of legal services to low- and moderate-income individuals. Given the difficulties experienced in attempting actually to provide legal services to the poor, most observers agreed that mechanisms for decreasing the cost of existing private legal representation were crucial to broadening access. One such mechanism has been the creation of prepaid legal services plans, intended to function something like health insurance by covering legal costs for plan members who pay periodic premiums. Although presently operating in most states, these plans have not had a major impact on access, largely because of their relatively high cost and limited applicability.[108]

Of greater significance in the legal profession itself, if not exactly in access to its services, has been the expanding use of legal paraprofessionals. Typically handling research and preliminary drafting tasks without actually providing legal representation or advice, paralegals have become common personnel both in large, commercial law firms and in the offices of small firms and solo practitioners. Although paralegals unquestionably lower the actual cost of accomplishing certain legal tasks, it is unclear whether that lower cost translates into more accessible representation, or instead, simply makes the representation of existing clients more profitable.[109]

Along with calls for decreasing the cost of obtaining private legal representation, there has also been relatively widespread support for "delegalizing" certain types of disputes and encouraging the use of nonlitigation dispute-resolution methods. In most metropolitan areas, for example, arbitration and mediation services can be easily located to facil-

---

[106]National Center for State Courts, *Indigent Defenders: Getting the Job Done and Done Well* (Williamsburg, Va: National Center for State Courts, 1992); 103–104. However, there is a body of literature which disputes this finding. See, e.g., Smith, *Courts and the Poor,* Ch. 2; Stumpf and Culver, *The Politics of State Courts,* 75–77; Peter Applebome, "Study Faults Atlanta's System of Defending Poor," *New York Times* (Nov. 30, 1990): B-3; David Margolick, "Texas Death Row Is Growing, but Fewer Lawyers Will Help," *New York Times* (Dec. 31, 1993): B-13; Ronald Smothers, "Court-Appointed Defense Offers the Poor a Lawyer, But the Cost May Be High," *New York Times* (Feb. 14, 1994): A-10; and Jane Fritsch, "A Program of Lawyers for New York's Poorest Grows Without Monitors," *New York Times* (May 23, 1994): B-12.

[107]See generally, Paul C. Drecksel, "The Crisis in Indigent Criminal Defense," *Arkansas Law Review* 44 (1991): 363, describing the nationwide lack of funding for the provision of competent defense counsel to indigent people. Basic data on indigent defense systems may be found in United States, Dept. of Justice, Bureau of Justice Statistics, *Indigent Defense* (Washington: Bureau of Justice Statistics, NCJ-158909, 1996).

[108]See Abel, *American Lawyers,* 136–37, indicating that the lack of success of prepaid legal services plans is in part due to bar hostility.

[109]With respect to the growing use of paralegals and its potential results, see Abel, *American Lawyers,* 197–99.

itate the resolution of civil disputes without the involvement of courts and often without attorneys. These "alternative dispute resolution," or "ADR," mechanisms, which are generally suggested to be both far less costly and more efficient than formal litigation, have gained a broad following, particularly for the resolution of domestic disputes.[110]

Although primarily of historical interest, for decades state and local bar organizations enforced minimum fee schedules that effectively undermined the possibility of price competition and maintained legal fees at artificially high levels. In 1975, however, the United States Supreme Court concluded that such fee schedules violated federal antitrust laws and prohibited their enforcement.[111]

Certainly as important as any other factor in the death of attorney price-fixing has been the development of legal advertising. While a blanket prohibition on advertising legal services was maintained by state bar associations throughout most of this century, those prohibitions were successfully challenged in 1977 as violative of First Amendment protections.[112] What followed was a significant increase in lawyer advertising, particularly among solo pracititioners and small firms, that remains a topic of heated discussion, both inside and outside the profession.[113]

Despite the *Bates* decision, state bar associations have continued throwing roadblocks in the path of really effective, widespread lawyer advertising. Typical was a ruling by the Florida Supreme Court, at the behest of the Florida bar, requiring attorneys in the state to wait thirty days before contacting accident victims via direct mail. Although overturned by lower federal courts as clearly contrary to *Bates,* Justice O'Connor, speaking for a sharply divided (5–4) Court, upheld the Florida rule, reasoning that the restricition was useful in

> protecting injured Floridians from invasive conduct by lawyers and in preventing the erosion of confidence in the profession that such repeated invasions have engendered.[114]

Speaking for himself and Justices Stevens, Souter, and Ginsburg, Justice Kennedy strongly disagreed, calling the decision "censorship pure and simple."

One of the immediate results of expanded opportunities for lawyer advertising was the development of "legal clinics," such as Hyatt Legal Services, Inc., and The Law Offices of Jacoby & Meyers. Based on a franchise-like concept, these "clinics" typically attempt to

---

[110]See generally Stephen P. Doyle and Roger S. Haydock, *Without the Punches: Settling Disputes Without Litigation* (Minneapolis, Minn.: Equilaw, Inc., 1991) (a handbook of ADR mechanisms); Linda R. Singer, *Settling Disputes: Conflict Resolution in Business, Families, and the Legal System* (Boulder, Colo: Westview Press, 1990); Erika S. Fine, ed., *Containing Legal Costs: ADR Strategies for Corporations, Law Firms and Government* (St. Paul, Minn.: Butterworth Legal Publishers, 1988).

[111]Minimum fee schedules were prohibited by the Court in *Goldfarb v. Virginia State Bar Association,* 421 U.S. 773 (1975).

[112]See *Bates v. State Bar of Arizona,* 433 U.S. 350 (1977).

[113]See, e.g., American Bar Associaton Commission on Advertising, *Report on the Survey on the Image of Lawyers in Advertising* (Chicago: American Bar Association, 1990); see also the Commission's *Yellow Pages Lawyer Advertising: An Analysis of Effective Elements* (Chicago: American Bar Association, 1992), indicating that the average size of law firms presently advertising in the Yellow Pages is 3.5 lawyers.

[114]Linda Greenhouse, "High Court Backs Florida Restriction on Solicitation of Accident Victims by Lawyers," *New York Times* (June 22, 1995): A-14. See also Linda Greenhouse, "At the Bar: In the Longtime War Over Lawyer Advertising, the Latest Shot Leaves as Many Wounds as Ever," *New York Times* (June 23, 1995): B-11. This piece includes major excerpts from the decision *Florida Bar v. Went For It, Inc.,* 63 *Law Week* 4644 (1995). These two pieces, together with the O'Connor opinion itself, review the *Bates* as well as the post-*Bates* rulings on the lawyer advertising issue.

For general background on the subject, see Hazard and Rhode, *The Legal Profession,* 377–410, and accompanying bibiliography. See also Lauren Bowen, "Advertising and the Legal Profession," *Justice System Journal* 18, No. 1 (1995): 43–54.

lower the cost of their services by standardizing as many procedures as possible. Although initially perceived as a potentially successful mechanism for broadening access to legal services for those of low to moderate incomes, these so-called "clinics" now are almost nonexistent. One suggested explanation for this trend is that medium- to large-sized law firms adopted, and in many cases perfected, cost-cutting procedures—standardized forms, routinized operations, pool word-processing, and extensive use of paralegals, to name a few—that were pioneered by legal "clinics," decreasing the clinics' ability to significantly undermine standard fee structures.[115]

The precise impact of these newer trends in legal service delivery is still unknown. Although their long-term effect could be quite significant, access to legal services remains, by the mid-1990s, not a great deal different from what it was in 1970. The cost of the product is still beyond the reach of most individual Americans, and the intelligent selection of an attorney for most of us is still next to impossible. Meanwhile, the bulk of the service supply in both quality and quantity remains reserved for business and other established collectivities, this while the number of attorneys relative to population increases dramatically each year. That we are overlawyered and underrepresented, as asserted by President Carter, seems more a truism than a debatable statement.[116]

PROFESSIONAL STRATIFICATION

Perhaps no two characteristics are so central to the legal profession as are stratification and hierarchy. Likewise, nothing—including legal education and the organizational history of the bar—more clearly illustrates the co-optation of the profession by entrenched, elite interests. In 1975, for example, the range of incomes reported by attorneys in Chicago was vast. The median income for attorneys in private practice was $34,118, with those holding shareholder or partner positions averaging $47,778. For attorneys in other-than-private practice, median income was much lower—about $25,405. At the top of that group were appellate judges, who earned about $36,500. Next came law school instructors and government attorneys, with public defenders and legal aid attorneys falling substantially farther back at around $18,197.

By 1995, the incomes of American lawyers had of course increased, with the disparity between the top and the bottom income categories, if anything, widening. Currently, it is not uncommon for senior partners of the largest law firms to enjoy gross income in excess of $1 million. Salaried general counsel for major corporations could earn even more, often in excess of $3 million per year. Beginning associates of the largest firms might well earn annual salaries in the range of $70,000 to $80,000. On the other hand, attorneys working as public defenders or legal service attorneys might often make as little as $25,000 to $30,000 per year.[117]

These figures represent only a brief glimpse of the professional stratification and hierarchy that has come to characterize the American legal profession. As described by Richard Abel,

---

[115]See American Bar Association, Standing Committee on the Delivery of Legal Services, *Report on the Survey of Legal Clinics & Advertising Law Firms* (Chicago: American Bar Association, 1990) (concluding that advertising "legal clinics" have no significant impact on improving access to justice).

[116]See Abel, *American Lawyers,* passim. And Richard L. Abel, "Yes, There's a Glut of Lawyers . . . but Only for the Wealthy," *Los Angeles Times* (Dec. 26, 1989): B-7.

[117]See "What Lawyers Earn," *National Law Journal* (May 30, 1994), (Supplement). This source lists the salary of the general counsel of Merrill Lynch at $3,850,000, whereas a public defender in Boston in 1994 suffered a beginning annual salary of $28,600!

in few . . . professions do some members earn fifty times more than others or some subcategories (such as Supreme Court justices) bask in popular adulation while others (such as criminal defense, personal injury, and divorce lawyers) are ranked [in public opinion polls] with garbage collectors. And there is virtually no movement between the hemispheres.[118]

The concept of "hemispheres" of the legal profession was introduced by Professors Heinz and Laumann in their classic study of Chicago lawyers in the late 1970s, although the basic finding of the bifurcation of the bar dates back to much earlier sociological research.[119] The fundamental idea is that there are at least two rather distinct legal professions, separated by a number of dominant characteristics, beginning with the choice of law schools.

As previously discussed, there exists a well-recognized pecking order among law schools. Although there is plenty of room for debate as to the underlying substantive content of law school prestige-rankings, there is little doubt that the law school one attends has a powerful credentialing effect on one's subsequent legal career. Currently, *U.S. News and World Report* carries one of the most widely discussed law school rankings. In 1995, the top twenty-five law schools, listed in order of declining prestige, were Yale, Harvard, Stanford, Chicago, Columbia, New York University, Virginia, Duke, California-Berkeley, Michigan, Northwestern, Pennsylvania, Georgetown, Cornell, Southern California, Vanderbilt, Texas, Minnesota, Iowa, Illinois, Washington and Lee, George Washington, Wisconsin, UCLA, and Emory.[120] The link between attending one of these law schools and moving into a high prestige legal career, demonstrated by Professors Zemans and Rosenblum and confirmed by the Heinz and Laumann study, remains strong. Graduates of top law schools much more frequently wind up with high-paying, high-prestige positions, while those from less prestigious schools generally fill the lower ranks of the professional practice ladder. Tables 7–6 and 7–7 illustrates these critical relationships.

A more recent analysis makes the same point in nonquantified terms. In his widely read polemic against contemporary legal education, Professor Duncan Kennedy, a well-published Critical Legal Studies scholar (see Chapter 2) argues that law schools essentially shape and prepare their students both to participate in and actively to perpetuate the hierarchies and stratification inherent to the legal profession. Kennedy suggests that the relentless ranking of both law students and law schools makes it seem more natural that the profession itself should be rigidly stratified. The hierarchical structure within and between schools—fiercely defended by law school administrators and instructors on meritocratic grounds—is then carried out the law school door and into conventional law practice by young lawyers. What develops is essentially a symbiotic relationship in which conventional law firms depend on law schools to indoctrinate their students with an acceptance

[118]Able, *American Lawyers,* 236–237.

[119]John P. Heinz and Edward O. Laumann, *Chicago Lawyers: The Social Structure of the Bar* (New York: Russell Sage Foundation, 1982). Early studies demonstrating the "two bar" thesis include Jack Ladinski, "Careers of Lawyers, Law Practice and Legal Institutions," *American Sociological Review* 28, No. 1 (Feb. 1963): 47–54; and Richard A. Watson and Rondal G. Downing, *The Politics of Bench and Bar* (New York: Wiley, 1969). Subsequent research (e.g., Abel's *American Lawyers*) suggests that in addition to legal education and income, practice speciality, practice setting, political party affiliation, race, and stands on central issues of the politics of the legal profession—these and other factors vary significantly with whether one is in the "Defendant" or "Plaintiff" hemisphere of practice.

[120]*U.S. News and World Report* (Mar. 20, 1995): 84. The 1992 rankings were slightly different. The 25 top schools at that time, in descending order, were Yale, Harvard, Stanford, Chicago, Columbia, Michigan, New York University, Virginia, Duke, Pennsylvania, Georgetown, California-Berkeley, Northwestern, Cornell, Texas, Vanderbilt, UCLA, Southern California, California-Hastings, Notre Dame, Minnesota, Boston College, Washington-Seattle, George Washington, and Iowa. *U.S. News and World Report* (Mar. 23, 1992): 70.

For a study of the empirical basis of such ratings, see Scott Van Alstyne, "Ranking the Law Schools: The Reality of Illusion," *American Bar Foundation Research Journal* 1982, No. 3 (Summer 1982): 649–84.

Table 7–6   Distribution of High-Prestige Law School Graduates Among Areas of Practice

Practice	Percentage	N
Solo practice	22.1	86
Small firm (2–8)	34.0	141
Medium firm (9–49)	46.7	90
Large firm (50 or more)	72.8	81
Government lawyer	29.6	54
Business legal staff	35.6	59
Other	26.3	19
		530

Note: X^2 = 56:58; p <0.001.

Source: Frances Kahn Zemans and Victor G. Rosenblum, *The Making of a Public Profession* (Chicago: American Bar Foundation, 1981), 99.

of, and even a passion for, stratification in return for the financial and other forms of support (e.g., endowed professorships, and library wings) that those firms can provide.[121]

The degree to which lawyers are stratified is somewhat less in small-town and rural America, where there is generally less emphasis on legal specialization.[122] Even in smaller communities, however, the delivery of legal services to the poor—the government assistance recipient, the unemployed person, the immigrant for whom English is a second language—remains outrageously at variance with even the most rudimentary interpretation of "equal justice under law," as legal services attorneys discovered in the mid-1960s and early 1970s, and continue to find today.[123]

Thus, legal services in America are organized largely for service to American business, the top talent being found in the large firms and devoted to corporate practice, the lesser talent in medium to small firms serving lesser business interests, whereas the small firm and solo practitioner and government lawyer are left to serve "small people"—that is, individuals who deal with government as individuals: the middle-class citizen with a legal problem in the nature of a will, divorce, or real estate transaction; or the poor person with a landlord or credit problem. Solo and small-firm lawyers are occasionally able to capture some of the more lucrative business practices, but large-firm attorneys handle virtually none of the low prestige work. As Zemans and Rosenblum put it,

> It is not so much, as Ladinsky says in "Careers of Lawyers," that solo practitioners do the dirty work of the bar but rather, as Smigel points out in *The Wall Street Lawyer,* that members of large firms do virtually none of it. No large-firm lawyers in our sample of Chicago lawyers list any of the following as their predominant specialty: criminal law, family law, poverty law, creditor-debtor law. To the extent that graduation from certain law schools predicts large-firm practice, it also eliminates the possibility of concentrating one's time in work rated low in prestige by the bar.[124]

---

[121]Kennedy, *Legal Education and the Reproduction of Hierarchy:* 45–72.

[122]See Donald D. Landon, *Country Lawyers: The Impact of Context on Professional Practice* (New York: Praeger, 1990). Also see Michael J. Kelly, *Lives of Lawyers: Journeys in the Organization of Practice* (Ann Arbor: University of Michigan Press, 1994), which presents studies of two large corporate firms and a small urban firm, concluding that there is no one "legal profession," but many, requiring a pluralist perspective.

[123]See, e.g., Joel F. Handler, *The Lawyer and His Community* (Madison: University of Wisconsin Press, 1967); and Stumpf, *Community Politics and Legal Services,* Chs. 3, 6, and 7.

[124]Zemans and Rosenblum, *Making of a Public Profession,* 107–108.

Table 7–7 Distribution of Law School Graduates Among High- and Low-Prestige Areas of Practice

Law School	Prestige of Specialty (by percentage)		
	High	Low	N
Harvard	61.5	7.7	26
Michigan	52.0	12.0	25
Chicago	44.0	10.0	50
Northwestern	42.1	21.1	57
Illinois	34.4	21.9	32
Loyola	26.7	26.7	30
IIT-Chicago Kent	13.9	38.9	36
DePaul	31.9	31.9	94
John Marshall	32.0	40.0	50

Note: X^2 = 37.10; p <0.005.

Source: Frances Kahn Zemans and Victor G. Rosenblum, *The Making of a Public Profession* (Chicago: American Bar Foundation, 1981), 105 (footnotes deleted).

In a 1975 study of a large (N = 777) sample of Chicago lawyers, Laumann and Heinz were able to document this prestige ranking of practice specialties as attorneys view themselves. A subsample of the Chicago attorneys was asked to rate a list of specialites on a five-point scale from outstanding to poor. The refined prestige score for each of the specialties is contained in Table 7–8.[125]

As mentioned by Abel before, once in a practice specialty, the attorney has a very strong tendency to remain there throughout his or her career. Both the legal profession and the client community are thus locked into a semipermanent relationship dubbed the "hemispheres of practice." Although the American business community and other established organizations can usually pay the price of access to the best of legal advice, the middle- and lower-class individual client is ill-served. As Herbert Jacob indicates,

> A large portion of the population sees the courts and law as principally a concern of business. Many attorneys view the law as principally concerned with property and the propertied. Except for divorce actions, automobile accidents, and the administration of estates, the ordinary man has few occasions under present circumstances to contemplate legal action. The organization of the bar insures that the common man remains a secondary client of the law.[126]

Given this, it is little wonder that the ordinary citizen views the legal profession with such disdain. From the emergence of the modern lawyer in 1870 to the present, the American bar may be characterized by abject elitism, racism, sexism, and a general abdication of its social responsibilities in favor of economic gain. If, in deference to the bar, we can say that these characteristics are little more than reflections of the society at large over the past century, the problem remains of a profession, by definition, dedicated to equal access to

---

[125]See Laumann and Heinz, "Specialization and Prestige in the Legal Profession," 166–67.
[126]Jacob, *Urban Justice,* 51.

Table 7–8   Prestige Scores of Legal Specialties

Legal Specialty	Prestige Score[a]
1. Securities	68
2. Tax	67
3. Antitrust (Defendants)	65
4. Patents	61
5. Antitrust (Plaintiffs)	60
6. Banking	59
7. Public Utilities	59
8. General Corporate	59
9. Probate	58
10. Municipal	56
11. Admiralty	55
12. Civil Litigation	54
13. Labor (Management)	53
14. Real Estate	51
15. Commercial	49
16. Labor (Unions)	49
17. Environmental (Defendants)	49
18. Personal Injury (Defendants)	48
19. Environmental (Plaintiffs)	47
20. Civil Rights/Liberties	46
21. Criminal (Prosecution)	44
22. General Family (Paying)	42
23. Criminal (Defense)	41
24. Consumer (Creditor)	40
25. Personal Injury (Plaintiffs)	38
26. Consumer (Debtor)	38
27. Condemnations	37
28. Landlord-Tenant	37
29. Divorce	35
30. General Family (Poverty)	34
Total Sample	50

[a]A random subsample (N = 224) of the total sample of Chicago lawyers was asked the following question: "On the following specialty list would you please indicate the general prestige of each specialty within the legal profession at large." The respondents rated each specialty on a five-point scale, from "outstanding" to "poor." We then computed the mean rating for each specialty. To facilitate comparing the prestige ratings, we calculated a standard score for each specialty by determining the grand mean of the 30 specialty means and dividing by the standard deviation. To eliminate decimal points and negative numbers, we multiplied the standard score by 100 and added 50 to the result. Thus, "50" represents the average mean prestige rating, with 10 points being the standard deviation. To illustrate: "Securities," the most highly regarded specialty, is 1.8 standard deviations above the average mean prestige rating, while "General Family (Poverty)," with its score of 34, is 1.6 standard deviations below the average mean.

Source: John P. Heinz and Edward O. Laumann, *Chicago Lawyers* (Chicago: Russell Sage Foundation and American Bar Foundation, 1982), 91 (as revised).

the judicial process making the availability of its services dependent upon social and economic class. Such a condition both reflects and reinforces not equality but inequality.[127]

It remains difficult to disagree with Karl Llewellyn who over fifty years ago stated,

> It is clear that the activity of most skillful lawyers will be upon the side of the Haves and not upon the side of the Have-nots. . . . The best talent of the bar will always muster to keep Ins in and to man the barricade against the Outs. . . . [Yet] not law or lawyers, but society, gives fighting advantage to the propertied, puts the screws on in favor of the Ins.[128]

FURTHER READING

Abel, Richard L. *American Lawyers.* New York: Oxford University Press, 1989.

Auerbach, Jerold S. *Unequal Justice: Lawyers and Social Change in Modern America.* New York: Oxford University Press, 1976.

Countryman, Vern, Ted Finman, and Theordore J. Schneyer. *The Lawyer in Modern Society.* 2nd ed. Boston: Little, Brown, 1976.

Curran, Barbara A. *The Lawyer Statistical Report: A Statistical Profile of the U.S. Legal Profession in the 1980s.* Chicago: American Bar Foundation, 1985.

Curran, Barbara A., and Clara N. Carson. *The Lawyer Statistical Report: The U.S. Legal Profession in the 1990s.* Chicago: American Bar Foundation, 1994.

Galanter, Marc, and Thomas Palay, *Tournament of Lawyers: The Transformation of the Big Law Firm.* Chicago: University of Chicago Press, 1991.

Hazard, Geoffrey C., Jr., and Deborah L. Rhode, *The Legal Profession: Responsibility and Regulation.* 3rd ed. Wesbury, N.Y.: Foundation Press, 1994.

Heinz, John P., and Edward O. Laumann. *Chicago Lawyers: The Social Structure of the Bar.* New York: Russell Sage Foundation and the American Bar Foundation, 1982.

Katz, Jack. *Poor People's Lawyers in Transition.* New Brunswick, N.J.: Rutgers University Press, 1982.

Kronman, Anthony T., *The Lost Lawyer: Failing Ideals of the Legal Profession.* Cambridge, Mass.: The Belknap Press of Harvard University Press, 1993.

LaPiana, William P. *Logic and Experience: The Origins of Modern American Legal Education.* New York: Oxford University Press, 1994.

Linowitz, Sol M. *The Betrayed Profession: Lawyering at the End of the Twentieth Century.* New York: Scribners, 1995.

McIntyre, Lisa J. *The Public Defender: The Practice of Law in the Shadows of Repute.* Chicago: University of Chicago Press, 1987

Stevens, Robert B. *Law School: Legal Education in America from the 1850s to the 1980s.* Chapel Hill: University of North Carolina Press, 1983.

Zemans, Francis K., and Victor G. Rosenblum, *The Making of a Public Profession.* Chicago: American Bar Foundation, 1981.

---

[127]See Auerbach, *Unequal Justice,* 10. See also Derek C. Bok, "A Flawed System, Part I," *New York State Bar Journal* 55, No. 6 (Oct. 1983): 8–16. For a revealing report on gender discrimination in the current American legal profession, see American Bar Association, Commission on Women in the Profession, *Unfinished Business: Overcoming the Sisyphus Factor* (Chicago: ABA, 1995).

[128]Karl N. Llewellyn, *The Bramble Bush: On Our Law and Its Study,* 3rd ed. (Dobbs Ferry, N.Y.: Oceana, 1960), 144–45.

PART III
THE JUDICIAL PROCESS

8

The Civil Judicial Process

The prophesies of what the courts will do in fact, and nothing more pretentious, are what I mean by the law.

—Oliver Wendell Holmes, Jr.,
"The Path of the Law"

The principal institution of the law in action is not trial; it is settlement out of court.
—H. Laurence Ross,
Settled out of Court

In this and the following three chapters we examine the judicial process in the formal sense. Chapters 8 and 9 will explore the workings of trial courts, civil and criminal respectively, while Chapters 10 and 11 take up the appellate process, concluding with a description of the inner workings of our most celebrated of tribunals, the United States Supreme Court. The foregoing examination of our ideas about courts (Chapters 1 and 2), judicial structure (Chapters 3 and 4), along with our discussion of key judicial personnel (Chapters 5, 6, and 7) bear directly on the process of selecting and deciding cases, and ultimately on the substance of the judical decision. But now we move into the "black box" itself to gain some understanding of the more immediate forces and influences that shape judicial outcomes.

In the 1950s, following the tenets of political jurisprudence, professional students of the judicial process came to the realization that the judicial decision is hardly more final than other political determinations. Rather, it is most realistically viewed, in the words of Jack Peltason, as "but one phase in the never-ending group conflict, a single facet of the [continuing] political process."[1] Such conceptualizations encouraged a spate of research on the aftermath of court decisions, providing us with a considerable body of systematic

---

[1]Jack W. Peltason, *Federal Courts in the Political Process* (New York: Doubleday, 1955), 64.

knowledge concerning attempts at reversal of decisions, patterns of compliance and opposition, and so on (often termed "impact research," see Chapter 12).

If, as these research excursions demonstrate, the policy process is indeed a seamless web of discretion and action, it was only a matter of time before it occurred to political jurisprudents that "impact" can work two ways.[2] That is, not only ought we explore the series of events following judicial decisions but also the events that precede entry into the judicial forum. Thus, if the line between judicial decisions and their implementation becomes blurred in the rush of political activity and counteractivity following a decision (and if indeed a court's decision itself might well be determined in part by anticipation of such postdecisional events), then it seems to follow that one might look for the same or a similar sort of blurring of lines between formal adjudication and informal bargaining that precedes and often supplants adjudication itself. Further, the anticipation of what a court would do in the event of formal adjudication would weigh heavily in informal preadjudication negotiations. Hence, the shift represented in this chapter from prelitigation processes to the stage of formal adjudication—is, on closer examination, one of gradual shading rather than a sharp break, and the more we examine formal adjudication, the more we find an admixture of adjudication, mediation, and arbitration, with no clear boundaries separating these processes. This was a point made by Martin Shapiro in his book *Courts:*

> The bulk of conflict resolution through legal channels occurs by negotiation between the parties and their attorneys under the compulsion of eventual court proceedings should negotiations fail. To dismiss the vast bulk of conflict resolutions by law in modern societies as somehow extra-judicial would both direct the student of courts away from the central phenomenon and lead to fundamental distortions of reality. For previously announced judicial rules and anticipation by the disputants of the costs and benefits of eventually going to trial are key parameters in such negotiations. They are not free bargaining based solely on the wills and immediate resources of the parties, but legalized bargaining under the shadow supervision of an available court. Such negotiation is not purely mediatory, because the bargain struck may depend in part on the "legal" strength of the parties, that is, predictions of how each would fare in court. Yet such negotiations aim at, and in most instances achieve, a solution sufficiently satisfactory to both parties to avoid litigation. Failed negotiations may end up in court, where their judicial resolution sets the parameters for further negotiations. Thus, the principle arena of modern legalized dispute settlement intimately intermixes elements of mediation and dichotomous solution, consent and judicial imposition.[3]

A closely related argument for paying greater attention to the prelitigation phase of judicial politics was the simple fact that judicial outcomes, the dependent variable we have been attempting to explain for so long, are obviously influenced by judicial input. Indeed, we discovered that we really knew very little about the factors that determine the flow of disputes into the judicial arena. What and how judges are selected, the policy biases of court structure, the role of the legal profession—these and other preadjudicative forces all help us understand judicial policy outcomes. But until recently, relatively less attention had been given to the factor of case flow. Who uses courts? (And who does

---

[2]This is a point made by Marc Galanter in "Justice in Many Rooms: Courts, Private Ordering, and Indigenous Law," *Journal of Legal Pluralism* 19 (1981): 1–47. This chapter is heavily indebted to the pioneering work of Professor Galanter and to that of the Civil Litigation Research Project, jointly of the University of Wisconsin and the University of Southern California. A valuable source in reference to that project is *Law and Society Review,* Special Issue on Dispute Processing and Civil Litigation, Vol. 15, Nos. 3–4 (1980–1981).

[3]Martin Shapiro, *Courts: A Comparative and Political Analysis* (Chicago: University of Chicago Press, 1981), 10–11.

not?) What kinds of cases get into court? (And what cases do not?) In short, what explains litigation flow?

What researchers over the past two decades or so have learned about preadjudicative activities in American courts is probably less impressive than what we have yet to learn. The scholarly forays thus far have clearly revealed the significance of informal dispute resolution in the overall roles of courts in our society and have thus served to broaden considerably our conception of the judicial process. Hence, to discuss the process at work in either civil or criminal trial courts in the United States, one must begin not with courts themselves, but with the set of activities and processes that helps us to understand how cases do, or do not, reach courts.

GRIEVANCES TO DISPUTES: THE TRANSFORMATION PROCESS

All civil disputes—those between and among private parties, be they individuals, groups, or organizations—might be said to begin with a grievance, defined as "an individual's belief that he or she (or a group or organization) is entitled to a resource which someone else may grant or deny."[4] We have all felt grievances from time to time—perceived injustices in the process of commercial transactions; grievances against employers, or perhaps between employees; personal or neighborhood feuds of various types; differences arising out of family discord—these and other "trouble spots" in life are the source of almost daily grievances of various degrees of intensity, duration, and severity. In the vast majority of cases, however, no action is taken.

We quickly, almost subconsciously, undertake a calculation in the nature of a cost-benefit analysis: Is the cost in dollars, time, and effort worth the probable benefit to be derived from moving the grievance into the stage of a formal or informal claim against the perceived source of the grievance? In other words, is it worth filing a formal grievance with the union against one's employer? Is it worth the trouble of going into small claims court (if one is available) to seek judgment against a "friend" who bilked you out of $400? Is it worth taking action against the appliance dealer whose $130 three-month-old food processor goes on the blink? Is it worth it to file suit against your neighbor because his dog bit your child? Sometimes it is, but usually it is not. A quick calculation suggests that the various costs, tangible and intangible, would not be worth the probable payoff.

A "grievance calculation" might look something like this. Bob owes Alan $250. Alan calls a law firm asking for assistance in collecting the money from Bob. Alan is told the lawyer's hourly fee is $125. The lawyer suggests that Alan pursue the matter himself in small claims court. Subsequently, Alan learns that he must take time off work to file the claim himself, supply the court with appropriate documentation, pay a $20 filing fee to the court and an $18 service fee to the sheriff. Then Alan must wait until Bob is served and a date is set for the hearing. He must then take off work again to present his case to the judge, a very anxiety-filled moment for most people. Assuming Alan is granted a judgment against Bob, he is still in the same practical situation as before: he has "won" his case, but Bob still owes the $250. Unless Bob voluntarily pays Alan, Alan must pursue the matter further, requiring more of his own time and money!

---

[4]Richard E. Miller and Austin Sarat, "Grievances, Claims, and Disputes: Accessing the Adversary Culture," *Law and Society Review* 15, Nos. 3–4 (1980–1981): 527. On the transformation process, see also William L. Felstiner, Richard L. Abel, and Austin Sarat, "The Emergence and Transformation of Disputes: Naming, Blaming, Claiming . . ." *Law and Society Review* 15, Nos. 3–4 (1980–1981): 631–54. Much of the discussion herein draws on these two articles.

Anticipating just such an outcome, the grievant more often than not simply takes his or her lumps. "Lumping it" has its costs, too—frustration, the harboring of resentment—which may be later visited on innocent parties (the cat or dog) or which may explode in other unexpected ways.[5] Still, it is easy to picture ourselves lumping a great many grievances rather than pursuing the probably fruitless course of escalating a relatively petty matter into a major conflict. Usually we chalk it up to the aches and pains of daily living. The overall social cost of lumping many of life's grievances is unknown but is perhaps very high.

In the event a person chooses to move to the stage of initiating a *claim,* that claim may be accepted, rejected, or partially accepted. If, in response to an individual's complaint that his or her automobile is not functioning properly, the dealer agrees and solves the problem, the matter may well end there. If, however, such claim is met with a partial or total rejection (the response that the problem was half the fault of the buyer or was entirely the buyer's fault), the person has moved from *claim* to *dispute.* A dispute, then, exists when a claim is either wholly or partially rejected.[6] Further, a "civil legal dispute" arises when claims are made that could be subject to judicial determination.

However, what has come to be called "the disputing process" is not, as the previous discussion might suggest, a closed system. At any point along the way from grievance to formal litigation, parties may (and usually do) opt out. Formal litigation carries high costs (and risks), and there are many means a disputant can employ to gain some level of satisfaction short of going to court. Lumping it, as we have noted, is an early course of action. Though it is not without cost, such cost may be somewhat reduced by the process of rationalization, a line of thinking we have all experienced: "Well, I'm happy I'm not the kind of person who has to act that way; if I behaved as he has, I would certainly make restitution; he'll get his some day; the chickens come home to roost for everyone," and so on. These are thoughts rather than actions, verbal or otherwise, and are part of the internal process involved with *acceptance,* the essence of lumping it.

At a somewhat higher level of escalation a person may select a course of action amounting to withdrawal, again usually combined with a rationalizing process and/or a measure of self-help ("What ever happened to that case you had against the company?" "Well, I told so and so what I thought of her, and that fixed her; I got transferred to another department, and I like my job a lot better now."). Notice that no mention is made of the actual claim. It has in fact, been dropped in favor of an alternative solution. As discussed in the dispute-processing literature, "exiting" may be seen as a form of self-help. According to Galanter, the grievant, perhaps seeing the low probability of successfully pursuing her claim, decides upon

> withdrawal from a situation or relationship by moving, resigning, severing relations, finding new partners, etc. This is of course a very common expedient in many kinds of trouble. Like "lumping it," it is an alternative to invocation of any kind of remedy system—although its presence as a sanction may be important to the working of other remedies. The use of "exit" options depends on the availability of alternative opportunities or partners (and information about them), the costs of withdrawal, transfer, relocation, development of new relationships, the pull of loyalty to previous arrangements—and on the availability and costs of other remedies.[7]

---

[5]See Miller and Sarat, "Grievances, Claims and Disputes": 539; and Felstiner, Abel, and Sarat, "The Emergence and Transformation of Disputes": 639. See also Dan Coates and Steven Penrod, "Social Psychology and the Emergence of Disputes," *Law and Society Review* 15, Nos. 3–4 (1980–1981): 655–80.

[6]Miller and Sarat, "Grievances, Claims, and Disputes": 527.

[7]Marc Galanter, "Why the 'Haves' Come Out Ahead: Speculations on the Limits of Legal Change," *Law and Society Review* 9, No. 1 (Fall 1974): 125–26.

Exiting can, of course, be exercised as an option at any point on the escalation scale at which the disputant feels the costs, psychic or otherwise, are outweighing the benefits. In fact, lumping it and exiting are in all probability the chief means by which grievances are handled. Few of us have experienced what we would regard as "pure justice" in all areas of our lives. But rather than persist in causes we feel are just, we either acquiesce early on or exit at a later point in the unsuccessful pursuit of a claim. In some cases, of course, our claims may have been accepted or won in litigation, whereas in other cases self-help can take the form of violent or quasi-violent forms of dispute resolution. Yet another avenue in pursuing grievances is neither exiting nor formal complaint-lodging, but "voicing"—verbally attempting to change practices and policies of an individual or organization. The effectiveness of this technique, however, is likely to correlate with the possibility of using other sanctions.[8]

The point of this discussion is not to map thoroughly the disputing process; our present knowledge is woefully insufficient for that task. Rather, our purpose is to suggest the many avenues of grievance, claim, and dispute resolution (or, if you wish, nonresolution) that are available to the grievant, the overall point being that out of perhaps thousands of grievances and hundreds of claims, only a relative handful of potentially actionable matters end up in the judicial arena.

An initial empirical investigation of this process provides us with somewhat more tangible evidence supporting these conclusions. As part of a much larger study of civil litigation,[9] a telephone survey was made in January 1980 of approximately one thousand randomly selected households in each of five federal judicial districts: South Carolina, Eastern Pennsylvania, Eastern Wisconsin, New Mexico, and Central California.[10] Respondents were asked whether they had experienced any of a lengthy list of problems in the past three years and, if so, how the problem was handled. Inquiry was also made as to whether the problem involved more than $1,000, that being the threshold for the project's definition of the middle-range disputes which were its focus. Although a much more complete picture of the disputing process could have been obtained had the study included all disputes, not just those involving $1,000 or more, the data nonetheless provided a rough picture of dispute processing, at least at the upper end of the "funnel."

Some 40 percent of the households reported having had at least one middle-range grievance, while about 20 percent reported having two or more. The most common type reported were those involving landlord-tenant relations (17.1 percent of the households reported this type of problem). Second in frequency were general tort complaints, 15.6 percent. Table 8–1 provides a snapshot of the pattern of grievances reported in order of frequency, as well as the proportion of grievances that were transformed into claims.

The focus of the study was on grievances that presumably would be worth fighting for ($1,000 or more in 1980), but the willingness of these middle-range grievants to do something about their problem nevertheless seems quite high, as shown in Table 8–1. For example, 94.6 percent of those who reported having a debt grievance said they actually filed a claim, whereas 87.3 percent of consumer grievants escalated their grievance into a claim. An exception seems to be in the area of discrimination, where only 29.4 percent of

[8]Galanter, "Why the 'Haves' Come Out Ahead": 111–12.

[9]Reference is made here to the Civil Litigation Research Project mentioned in note 2. A useful overview of the project is contained in David M. Trubek, "Studying Courts in Context," *Law and Society Review* 15, Nos. 3–4 (1980–1981): 485–501.

[10]For a discussion of the methodology of this particular phase of the Civil Litigation Research Project, see Miller and Sarat, "Grievances, Claims, and Disputes": 533–35.

Table 8–1   Grievances and Claims over $1,000, Civil Litigation Research Project

Problem	Percentage of Households	
	Grievances	Claims
Tort		
Auto accident, work injury, other injury to or damage to property of a household member	15.6	85.7
Consumer		
Problem with a major purchase, medical or other services, home builder or home improvement contract	8.9	87.3
Debt		
Problem collecting money from employer, debtor, or insurance company, disagreement with a creditor or other problems paying debts or problems with a mortgage	6.7	94.6
Discrimination		
Employment problems, problems in schooling or education, buying or renting housing, etc.	14.0	29.4
Property[a]		
Problems over what was permissible to build, boundary lines, someone else using the property, or other problems with ownership or use (excluding problems with business or rental property)	7.2	79.9
Government		
Problems of collecting social security, veterans or welfare benefits, or tax refunds, obtaining services or benefits from local government. Problems with any organization which claimed household owed money	9.1	84.9
Post-Divorce[a]		
Property divisions, alimony and child support, visitation or custody	10.9	87.9
Landlord[a]		
Problems over rent, eviction, condition of property, or other problems with a landlord	17.1	87.2

[a]These are percentages of households "at risk"—that is, households that qualified under the category.

Source: Richard E. Miller and Austin Sarat, "Grievances, Claims, and Disputes: Assessing the Adversary Culture," *Law and Society Review* 15, Nos. 3–4 (1980–1981): 537, 566.

grievances became claims, probably because remedial forums for filing claims in this area are less available and less accessible.[11]

The telephone interviewers asked about resistance to claims (which, by definition, constitute disputes), use of lawyers, actual court filings, and so on. Figure 8–1 presents data depicting the general pattern of grievance transformation, whereas Figure 8–2 presents the transformation pattern of three specific types of grievances.

Overall, the chances of a claim becoming a dispute were almost as great as those of a grievance becoming a claim. Some 63 percent of claims were met with partial or total rejection, thereby becoming disputes. With the exception of torts and property matters, there was not a great deal of variation among types of claims as to their propensity to become disputes: 73 percent of discrimination claims, 82 percent of landlord claims, and 87 percent of postdivorce claims moved into the arena of disputes. Tort claims were least likely to be contested, probably because of the routinization of settlement processed by insurance companies and the like.[12]

The inverted funnels or pyramids used by Miller and Sarat and depicted in Figures 8–1 and 8–2 point to one of the most important findings for purposes of the present discussion, namely the low incidence of the use of lawyers in processing middle-range disputes in the United States. Lawyers were used in slightly less than one-fourth of all disputes, though the incidence of lawyer use was much higher in post-divorce disputes (77 percent) and tort matters (58 percent). This incidence is probably due to the way the legal system frames these disputes: post-divorce processing normally requires in-court activity, and tort action usually involves contingent fees.[13]

Only about 10 percent of all disputes (and 5 percent of grievances) end up as court filings (Figure 8–1), though there was considerable variation by type of grievance, post-divorce problems being the most likely to become matters for formal judicial attention, again probably because of the law. This is not to say that courts and lawyers are irrelevant to the settlement of grievances in our society, for as Galanter, Mnookin, and others have emphasized, most of dispute processing takes place under the shadow of possible court action should negotiation fail.[14] Further, as we shall see later, even the small percentage of issues that reach court are mostly dealt with in a process of further bargaining. Thus, the work of our civil judicial system is largely a process of informal bargaining with final adjudication being a last resort. Again, as Shapiro has noted,

> This dynamic interaction between settlement and [formal adjudication] . . . is the real center of the judicial process. This is the true meaning of Holmes' definition of law as prediction of court behavior. Thus, paradoxically, [students of] . . . the judicial process should

---

[11]Miller and Sarat, "Grievances, Claims, and Disputes": 540. The entire pattern of grievances and claims found in the research by the Civil Litigation Research Project, as well as the low level of transformation of discrimination grievances, is consistent with other research on the dispute-processing funnel. For an extensive follow-up of the findings on discrimination grievances in the CLRP, see the excellent work by Kristin Bumiller, *The Civil Rights Society: The Social Construction of Victims* (Baltimore: Johns Hopkins University Press, 1988). A more recent "mini–case study" of the difficulty in filing discrimination claims is Joseph F. Sullivan, "Getting Action on a Racial Bias Complaint, A Worker Finds, Is No Easy Task," *New York Times* (May 3, 1995): A-11. A much more detailed and insighful case study of the civil judical process at work in a major discrimination filing is Thomas A. Dawson, "Women in Law Enforcement: *Fanchon Blake v. City of Los Angeles,* Ph.D. Dissertation, Claremont Graduate School, 1984. Ms. Blake has written an extensive account of her own case—and life—which is soon to be published.

[12]In general, see H. Laurence Ross, *Settled out of Court: The Social Process of Insurance Claims Adjustment* (New York: Aldine, 1980).

[13]Miller and Sarat, "Grievances, Claims, and Disputes": 543.

[14]See Galanter, "Why the 'Haves' Come Out Ahead"; and Robert H. Mnookin and Lewis Kornhauser, "Bargaining in the Shadow of the Law: The Case of Divorce," *Yale Law Journal* 88, No. 5 (Apr. 1979): 950–97.

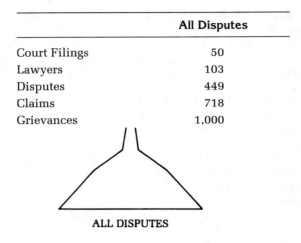

	All Disputes
Court Filings	50
Lawyers	103
Disputes	449
Claims	718
Grievances	1,000

ALL DISPUTES

Figure 8–1   Dispute Pyramid: All Disputes, Civil Litigation Research Project (SOURCE: Richard E. Miller and Austin Sarat, "Grievances, Claims, and Disputes: Assessing the Adversary Culture," *Law and Society Review* 15, Nos. 3–4 (1980–1981): 544.)

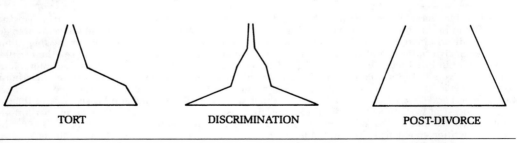

	Tort	Discrimination	Post-Divorce
Court Filings	38	8	451
Lawyers	116	29	588
Disputes	201	216	765
Claims	857	294	879
Grievances	1,000	1,000	1,000

TORT   DISCRIMINATION   POST-DIVORCE

Figure 8–2   Dispute Pyramids: Three Specific Problems (SOURCE: Richard E. Miller and Austin Sarat, "Grievances, Claims, and Disputes: Assessing the Adversary Culture," *Law and Society Review* 15, Nos. 3–4 (1980–1981): 544.)

[be more concerned with] what goes on outside the court room than inside, or at least should focus heavily on how judicial outcomes affect the bargaining position of perspective litigants as well as what happens to actual litigants.[15]

This contemporary emphasis on the importance of the preadjudicative phase of the work of our courts has led some scholars to see the main flow of legal traffic not in the *centripetal* movement of issues *into* courts, but rather the *centrifugal* flow of legal signals *out* into the bargaining arena. Galanter has most clearly articulated this view of the judical process:

> The principle contribution of courts to dispute resolutions is providing a background of norms and procedures against which negotiations and regulation in both private and governmental settings take place. This contribution includes . . . communication to prospective litigants of what might transpire if one of them sought a judicial resolution. This includes the rules that govern adjudication of disputes, possible remedies, and some estimates of the difficulty, certainty, and costs of securing particular outcomes.[16]

In the following sections, this process will be more fully illustrated in a discussion of the bargaining phase of issues that have officially reached the courts.

What factors help us to understand why some grievances are ultimately transformed into issues of formal litigation when others are not? A quick review of the foregoing discussion will suggest the complexity of the process. Literally thousands of variables no doubt account for dispute processing outcomes, and no contemporary scholar pretends to possess sufficient knowledge to explain the process fully. However, the extant literature suggests the following foci as critical in understanding transformation.

Parties

Obviously, the immediate parties to a potential dispute are central in determining why transformation does or does not take place. Factors of personality as modified by experience are of prime importance. As noted,

> Personality variables that may affect transformations include risk preferences, contentiousness, and feelings about personal efficacy, privacy, independence, and attachment to justice (rule-mindedness). Both experience and personality are in turn related to social structure variables: class, ethnicity, gender, and age.[17]

Substance of Grievance

As a previous section makes clear, the subject matter of the dispute is also a critical variable in the escalation of grievances. This is precisely because external factors (attitudes, availability of forums, and external assistance) serve to encourage the transformation of certain types of claims while discouraging others. The structure, procedures, and environments surrounding dispute processing mechanisms inevitably serve to suppress certain grievances and promote others.

External Factors

Aside from personal variables particular to the parties and the substance of the dispute itself, a host of external factors round out our rough typology for understanding the transformation process. Among the more frequently mentioned external factors are (1) relationship

---

[15]Personal letter to author from Martin Shapiro, Feb. 13, 1978.
[16]Galanter, "Justice in Many Rooms": 6.
[17]Felstiner, Sarat, and Abel, "Emergence and Transformation of Disputes": 640.

of the parties (social or occupational context in which they have come together, their relative status, and so forth);[18] (2) the structure, jurisdiction, availability, and accessibility of dispute processing forums (a major hypothesis in the dispute processing literature is that lumping it is so common because forums are not available, or if existent, are not realistically accessible for potential claimants)[19]; (3) the role of key representatives (for instance, lawyers, counselors)[20]; (4) the prevailing social attitudes about disputing (Galanter cites examples of societies both much more and much less disputatious than our own)[21]; and (5) extant legal norms (Do legal rules as currently understood afford a remedy for an individual's grievance, or must new legal ground be broken to pursue a claim successfully?)[22]

Admittedly, other factors also account for grievance transformation, but the ones listed here should suffice to suggest the dimensions of the process. Since most researchers agree that exiting or lumping it occur most frequently in the early stages of the process, we are most in need of research as to why experiences tend not to be perceived as injurious, and why grievances tend not to become claims.[23] It is for this reason that the University of Wisconsin–University of Southern California Civil Litigation Research Project, valuable though it is, tends to focus on the wrong end of the funnel, so to speak. In all probability it is in that vast array of grievances involving less than $1,000 that we need to search for factors explaining attrition.

THE LITIGIOUS SOCIETY?

The very high incidence of what has been dubbed "grievance apathy" (the disinclination to pursue grievances) would seem to suggest that Americans are by no means as disputatious as recent writings would suggest.[24] A widespread belief presently exists that we have become a "super-litigious" society—a people rushing about filing claims, disputing and litigating at the drop of a hat.

We have been struck with the disease of "hyperlexis," notes one observer,[25] wherein we can hardly "tolerate more than five minutes of frustration without submitting to the temptation to sue."[26] Everyone sues everyone, so the charge goes: mothers sue for the right to breast-feed in public; a child sues his/her parents for being improperly reared; "unfair"

[18]Felstiner, Sarat, and Abel, "Emergence and Transformation of Disputes": 640. See also Joel B. Grossman et al., "Dimensions of Institutional Participation: Who Uses the Courts and How?" *Journal of Politics* 44, No. 1 (Feb. 1982): 88.

[19]See, e.g., Miller and Sarat, "Grievances, Claims, and Disputes": 563; and Laura Nader, ed., *No Access to Law: Alternatives to the American Judicial System* (New York: Academic Press, 1980), especially Ch. 1.

[20]As widely noted in the dispute processing literature, the role of lawyers in the preadjudicative process is underresearched. See Miller and Sarat, "Grievances, Claims, and Disputes": 542–43; Felstiner, Abel, and Sarat, "Emergence and Transformation of Disputes": 645–47; and Galanter, "Why the 'Haves' Come Out Ahead": 114–19. But see Austin Sarat and William L. Felstiner, "Law and Strategy in the Divorce Lawyer's Office," *Law and Society Review* 20, No. 1 (1986): 93–134.
A major addition to our knowledge of the lawyers' bargaining role in civil litigation is Herbert M. Kritzer's, *The Justice Broker: Lawyers and Ordinary Litigation* (New York: Oxford University Press, 1990). Kritzer's work is based on, though a significant extension of, data from the CLRP.

[21]Galanter, "Why the 'Haves' Come Out Ahead": 104–107.

[22]Galanter, "Why the 'Haves' Come Out Ahead": 123–24.

[23]Felstiner, Abel, and Sarat, "Emergence and Transformation of Disputes": 633.

[24]Felstiner, Abel, and Sarat, "Emergence and Transformation of Disputes": 636.

[25]See Bayless Manning, "Hyperlexis: Our National Disease," *Northwestern University Law Review* 71, No. 6 (Jan.–Feb., 1977): 767–82. Much of the ensuing discussion draws on Harry P. Stumpf and John H. Culver, *The Politics of State Courts* (New York: Longman, 1992): Ch. 5.

[26]Jerold S. Auerbach, "A Plague of Lawyers," *Harpers* 253, No. 1517 (Oct. 1976): 42.

referee-calls in a football game become the subject of litigation; and a woman who spills hot coffee on herself wins a suit against McDonald's![27] Punitive damage awards have become outrageous, and malcontents are clogging our courts with frivolous, petty grievances.

At first blush, this assessment seems well grounded in empirical evidence. We have more lawyers per person, we are often told, than any other country in the world (see Ch. 7), and we read almost daily of lawsuits filed over issues that in former decades, or in other societies, would scarcely be actionable.[28]

Former Chief Justice Warren Burger, for instance, joined, if he did not help to initiate, the chorus of condemnation of our nation's "litigation explosion" when in 1977 he commented on the "inherently litigious nature of Americans" and deplored the notion that litigation "is the cure-all for every problem that besets us."[29] And former Vice President Dan Quayle, himself a lawyer, spoke for the Council on Competitiveness which he chaired in the Bush administration, in calling our civil justice system "a self-inflicted competitive disadvantage." Decrying their count of "eighteen million" lawsuits filed in America every year, the Council set forth a fifty-point plan for improving the civil justice system—a scheme that would tilt the balance in our civil procedures away from the individual plaintiff in favor of corporate defendants.[30] Many of these proposals found their way into legislation, introduced into the post-1994 Republican Congress in the name of "tort reform."[31] In short, the American public has been treated to a constant drumbeat along these lines for some thirty years.

The problem with this view of America's litigation pattern is that, like "up," assertiveness or litigiousness is a relative term, and no agreed-upon baseline exists to measure such a variable. The debate often proceeds on the basis of civil court filings per capita, comparing contemporary American caseload data either with those of other nations or with earlier periods of our own history.

Comparative-filing data—that is, data from other systems—present a mixed picture but give little support to the "hyperlexis" hypothesis. In some roughly comparable systems such as Germany or Sweden, available figures indeed suggest lower civil filings rates than in the United States, but similar data also indicate that Americans are about in the same litigation range as England, Denmark, and New Zealand.[32]

---

[27]An interesting reinterpretation of the widely discussed coffee spill case in Albuquerque, New Mexico, is contained in *Consumer Reports* 60, No. 5 (May 1995): 312.

[28]A useful early work on this issue is Jethro K. Lieberman, *The Litigious Society* (New York: Basic Books, 1981), especially Ch. 1. See also Marc Galanter, "Reading the Landscape of Disputes: What We Know and Don't Know (and Think We Know) About Our Allegedly Contentious and Litigious Society," *UCLA Law Review* 31, No. 1 (1983): 4–71; Marc Galanter, "The Day After the Litigation Explosion," *Maryland Law Review* 46, No. 1 (Fall 1986): 3–39; and Michael J. Saks, "Do We Really Know Anything About the Behavior of the Tort Litigation System—and Why Not?" *University of Pennsylvania Law Review* 140, No. 4 (Apr. 1992): 1147–1293.

[29]Warren E. Burger, "Remarks at the American Bar Association Minor Dispute Resolution Conference," May 27, 1977, as cited in Galanter, "Reading the Landscape of Disputes": 8, 10.

[30]Proposals of the Council on Competitiveness are discussed in Deborah R. Hensler, "Taking Aim at the American Legal System: The Council on Competitiveness's Agenda for Legal Reform," *Judicature* 75, No. 5 (Feb.–Mar., 1992): 244–50. See also in the same issue the response by Gregory Brian Butler and Brian David Miller, "Fiddling While Rome Burns: A Response to Dr. Hensler": 251–54. Also see David Margolick, "Bar Group Renews Feud with Quayle," *New York Times* (Feb. 3, 1992): A-12.

[31]See, e.g., Stephen Labaton, "G. O. P. Preparing Bill to Overhaul Negligence Law," *New York Times* (Feb. 19, 1995): A-1; Neil A. Lewis, "Vast Overhaul of Tort System Fails in Senate," *New York Times* (May 5, 1995): A-1; and Neil A. Lewis, "Push for Limits on Lawsuits Seems to Have Lost Its Way," *New York Times* (Sept. 11, 1995): A-1.

[32]Galanter, "Reading the Landscape of Disputes": 55. An overview of comparative litigation rates, which again fails to support the American "hyperlexis" claim, is Erhard Blankenburg, "A Flood of Litigation? Legal Cultures and Litigation Flows Before European Courts in Historical and Comparative Perspective," *Justice System Journal* 16, No. 1 (1992): 101–110.

Critics often look to Japan as having the prototype system of dispute processing. With few lawyers, fewer judges, and a lower litigation rate, Japan is said to be a model to which we should aspire. However, scholars who have taken a closer look at the data come away with a much more cautious set of conclusions. Two points in particular are relevant.

First, it appears that recent Japanese regimes have adopted a deliberately constrictive set of policies designed to close formal avenues of disputing in favor of conciliation and other quasi-private and wholly private dispute resolution modes. This process reflects a "concern on the part of the governing elite that litigation was destructive of a hierarchial social order based on personal relationships." Thus, although the Japanese use courts less frequently than Americans, there is every indication that this fact is in part the result of artifically imposed restrictions on their ability to sue, rather than being a reliable measure of disputatiousness.[33]

Secondly, as indicated in Chapter 7, the frequently cited contrast between the numbers of Japanese and of American lawyers (to the extent that such figures are indicative of levels of litigiousness) is also misleading. Ten to twelve thousand Japanese lawyers—the usual figures cited—is the number of *bengoshi,* who are in-court attorneys similar to the English barrister. But Japan has a number of other personnel who perform tasks similar to those of American lawyers, such as in-house legal advisers and administrative scriveners, whose work would in some degree be similar to that of American attorneys. Data that were presented in the Galanter-Knight survey and that were discussed in Chapter 7 suggest that Japanese lawyers as defined in the American sense probably number in the range of 95,000 to 100,000, figures which, per capita, place Japan in the low-middle to middle range of comparative lawyer-population ratios.[34] Too, stringent limitations on the numbers of Japanese law graduates admitted to practice artificially understate the otherwise qualified *bengoshi.* Actually, Japan graduates more law students than does the United States, but whereas some three-quarters of American law graduates pass the bar exam, the comparable rate in Japan is said to be around 2 percent.[35]

As for other systems, an Australian scholar, Jeffrey FitzGerald, replicated the survey by the Civil Litigation Research Project (CLRP) in the state of Victoria, Australia, in 1981–1982. He found that his countryfolk were, on average, slightly more willing both to perceive a problem as a grievance (12.8 percent as opposed to CLRP's 11.8 percent) and to pursue it to a claim (77 percent versus America's 70 percent). Although there was a somewhat greater tendency on the part of Americans to take their claims to court, that finding, according to FitzGerald, "amounts to only 10.7 percent of disputants. . . ."[36] At the least, then, the Australian data, in contrast to the U.S. findings, lend little support to the notion that Americans have litigation fever. Indeed, if we are litigation-crazy, so are the Australians, for the central conclusion of the FitzGerald research is the striking similarity between the American and Australian transformation processes.

Perhaps more to the point in the litigation debate would be data comparing present civil litigation (filing) rates with those from earlier periods in American history. It is to the state courts that one would first look for relevant data in this regard, inasmuch as they process over 98 percent of all litigation in the United States. But again, to the extent that

[33]See John O. Haley, "The Myth of the Reluctant Litigant," *Journal of Japanese Studies* 4, No. 2 (Summer 1978): 359. However, see a critique of the Haley analysis in David T. Johnson's Review Essay: "Authority Without Power: Haley on Japan's Law and Politics," *Law and Society Review* 27, No. 3 (1993): 619–45.
[34]Marc Galanter and J. T. Knight, Appendix to "News from Nowhere: The Debased Debate on Civil Justice," *Denver University Law Review* 71, No. 1 (1993): 104–107.
[35]Marc Galanter, "Beyond the Litigation Panic," in Walter Olson, ed., *New Directions in Liability Law* (New York: The Academy of Political Science, 1988), 28
[36]Jeffrey FitzGerald, "Grievances, Disputes and Outcomes: A Comparison of Australia and the United States," *Law in Context* 1 (1983): 35.

court records reveal reliable data, researchers report little or no support for the claims of a current litigation explosion. In his study of the St. Louis courts from 1820 to 1970, Prof. Wayne McIntosh found that the civil litigation rate (cases filed per capita) in 1970 was *only about half* of what it had been in the early part of the nineteenth century. Moreover, although the research revealed a steady rise in case filings in these courts since 1900, McIntosh reports that "the litigation rate has remained fairly stable during the last six decades."[37] Authors of a similar longitudinal study of trial court litigation in two Bay Area counties in California from 1890 to 1970 report similar findings, namely the absence of a precipitous rise in litigation rates since the turn of the century. In some instances, this study reported an apparent decline during the period under study in the rate at which citizens sue each other in state trial court.[38]

Data from the more distant past are difficult to obtain and are certainly open to varying interpretations. But what figures we do have suggest anything but a reluctance on the part of our colonial forebears to go to law. Historical research reported by Marc Galanter, for instance, reveals that in Accomack County, Virginia, litigation rates in the year 1639 were *more than four times* those of any county in contemporary America, while studies of litigation rates in Essex County, Massachusetts, from the mid-seventeenth century reveal similarly high levels of litigation.[39]

We turn, then, to more current data, for it is sometimes argued that America's litigiousness is a relatively recent phenomonon, swooping down on us especially hard in the 1970s and 1980s. But to repeat the by-now tiresome conclusion, this argument again is not supported by the available data. National Center for State Courts statisticians compiled state court civil case filing figures from courts of both general and special jurisdiction for 1978 and again for 1981 and 1984. The results, as related to the issue of litigiousness, are best summarized by Marc Galanter of the University of Wisconsin Law School:

> The litigation explosion view would lead us to expect this [1978–1984] to be a period of steeply rising caseloads. But the NCSC data . . . portrays nothing that resembles the assumed explosion. Filings of civil cases surged faster than population from 1978 to 1981, but from 1981 to 1984 . . . per capita rates of filing actually declined. . . . Filings in small claims courts . . . also fell. Tort filings rose steadily, but over the six year period they grew by 9% while population grew by 8%.[40]

Since the mid 1980s, civil case filing data from state courts continue to confound those who spread the alarm of a litigation crisis and the need for tort reform. One might reasonably examine tort filings in this regard, for they are at the heart of the debate over America's alleged litigiousness. Torts include any civil wrong, but most prominently, according to the National Center for State Courts, "suits against doctors for malpractice, against manufacturers [or other businesses] for dangerous products, and against motorists involved in accidents."[41] Far from indicating a surge in such filings, the data give us a rela-

---

[37]Wayne McIntosh, "150 Years of Litigation and Dispute Settlement: A Court Tale," *Law and Society Review* 15, Nos. 3–4 (1980–1981): 828, Fig. 1.

[38]Lawrence M. Friedman and Robert V. Percival, "A Tale of Two Courts: Litigation in Alameda and San Benito Counties," *Law and Society Review* 10, No. 1 (Fall 1975): 292.

[39]Galanter, "Reading the Landscape of Disputes": 41.

[40]Galanter, "The Day After the Litigation Explosion": 6.

[41]Brian J. Ostrom and Neal B. Kauder, *Examining the Work of State Courts, 1993* (Williamsburg, Va.: National Center for State Courts, 1995), 19. See also a very useful discussion of the tort debate, including a presentation of the most recent NCSC research findings, in "Special Issue: A Dialogue on Tort Litigation in the States: The Williamsburg Report," *State Court Journal* 18, No. 2 (Fall 1994). For a useful summary of recent research on torts, see "Torts: Understanding the Patterns in the Courts," *The Justice System Journal* 16, No. 2 (1993): 1–172.

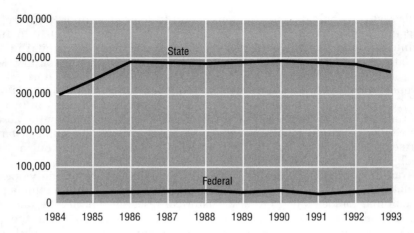

Figure 8–3 Tort Filings in State and Federal Courts, 1984–1993 (SOURCE: United States, Dept. of Justice, Bureau of Justice Statistics, *Tort Cases in Large Counties* (Washington: Bureau of Justice Statistics, April 1995), 2. Included are data from 22 states.)

tively flat profile in state courts of general jurisdiction from 1986 to 1993. Thus, in a sampling of such data in 23 states, the National Center for State Courts found that such filings moved from 386,954 in 1986 to only 389,381 in 1991, an increase less than the population growth in those states![42] And since 1991, reports NCSC, state tort filings in these same courts actually declined by about 6 percent, meaning the per capita rate of such filings dropped even further.[43] Figure 8–3, depicting tort filings over the last ten years in both federal trial courts and in state general trial courts, summarizes the relevant findings.

This limited coverage does not, of course address all the complexities of this raging national debate. Securities disputes, punitive damage awards, the pace of civil judicial procedures, the workings of civil juries, and a number of other subissues are also entangled in the controversy.[44] Too, federal trial court filing data, though a small percentage of the total civil litigation picture, have thus far not been introduced into the discussion (see later). But enough has been said to raise questions as to the presence of a litigation explosion.

The point of our discussion is not that as Americans, we can boast of an ideal civil judicial process free of abuse or overloading. Rather, we are merely saying that the loud assertions of an American litigation mania, heard throughout the land for several decades now, with an intensification in the 104th Congress, does not appear to be supported by the bulk of evidence. Indeed, if anything, the available data, from the early Civil Litiga-

---

[42]National Center for State Courts, *State Court Caseload Statistics: Annual Report, 1991* (Williamsburg, Va.: National Center for State Courts, 1993), Chart 1–14.

[43]Ostrom and Kauder, "Examining the Work:" viii.

[44]On civil jury competence, see the entire issue of *Law and Contemporary Problems* 52, No. 4 (Autumn 1989). More generally, see Robert E. Litan, ed., *Verdict: Assessing the Civil Jury System* (Washington: The Brookings Institution, 1993).

There is a large literature on punitive damage awards, much of it cited in the excellent piece by Stephen Daniels and Joanne Martin, "Myth and Reality in Punitive Damages," *Minnesota Law Review* 75, No. 1 (Oct. 1990): 1–64.

tion Research Project to the more recent research on tort filings, suggest that we as a people may have the opposite problem, namely a surprising reluctance to go to law with our problems.

The composite picture painted by the bulk of research findings is of a relatively passive American people, who live with wrongs, hurts, and injustices, petty or otherwise, because they feel nothing much can be done. The cost of this passivity can be high, too. As suggested by anthropologist Laura Nader,

> We have a mass phenomenon in which large segments of the population, reflective of all socioeconomic groups, are exposed to low-profile, undramatic, petty exploitation which is ruinous to the quality of democratic life. Despite our GNP, access to purveyors of justice is more readily available in some underdeveloped parts of the world than it is in this country.[45]

With so little supporting empirical evidence, then, why do we continue to hear the cry for civil justice (largely tort) reform? If political jurisprudence, the fundamental orientation of this text, means anything, it should be clear by now that claims of legal reformers are likely to have raw political roots, which are embedded in the ongoing, overriding process of the allocation and reallocation of advantages and disadvantages. As seen in foregoing chapters, this situation is true of the continuing struggle over methods of selecting judges, the structuring and restructuring of judicial bodies, and most clearly in the controversy over legal services.

As with governing elites in Japan, American elites, confronted with unaccustomed legal challenges, are largely responsible for the cry of alarm over current patterns of civil litigation, along with the now widespread movement toward informal modes of settling disputes.[46] Businesses facing product liability suits, physicians and hospitals being brought to account for their mistakes, securities and insurance companies being sued for bilking their clients, and, dare we say, college professors called to task for irresponsible behavior—such are some of America's elites who have sounded the alarm. As Galanter has observed,

> The kind of litigation that once dominated the system—lawsuits to enforce market relations—has given way to tort, civil rights, and public-law cases that "correct" the market. It is litigation aimed "upwards"—by outsiders, clients, and dependents *against authorities and managers of established institutions*—that excites most of the reproach of this litigious society.[47]

In short, the same political struggle taking place over legal services to the poor is in progress over so-called "tort reform," and for the same reasons. Established interests unaccustomed to being called to account for their behavior (or even the mild threat of accountability, as we saw in the legal services struggle) are mounting massive attempts to retain their privileged positions. It is the familiar game of "who gets what, when, and how" ever bubbling within the cauldron of American judicial politics. And as is so frequently the case in judicial politics, as in other politics, "Reform" is the subterfuge, the euphemism,

---

[45]Nader, *No Access to Law:* xix. Another angle on the litigation explosion debate is provided by Robert A. Kagan. See his interesting essay, "The Political Construction of American Adversarial Legalism," in Austin Ranney, ed., *Courts and the Political Process: Jack W. Peltason's Contributions to Political Science* (Berkeley, Calif.: Institute of Governmental Studies Press, 1996), 19–39.

[46]Richard L. Abel, ed., *The Politics of Informal Justice,* 2 vols. (New York: Academic Press, 1982), I: Ch. 10.

[47]Galanter, "Beyond the Litigation Panic," 30.

for this campaign, in the words of Deborah Hensler, "to change the current balance between individual plaintiffs and corporate defendants, in favor of the latter."[48]

FORMAL AND INFORMAL DISPUTE PROCESSING

As noted earlier, recent research on prelitigation activity has heightened our awareness of the tremendous breadth of the process itself and the numerous avenues open to the parties for the resolution (or nonresolution) of disputes. Of major significance for our study of courts is not only the realization that courts engage extensively in informal dispute processing but also that the judiciary is merely one among many forums available for the resolution of disputes. An early foray into this subject by Sarat and Grossman provides a useful typology of such forums. These scholars suggest that we think of mechanisms of conflict resolution in terms of two variables: level of formality of procedures used; and degree of "publicness"—that is, the relationship of a given procedure to the formal coercive power of government. Thus, we can conceive of various means of dispute processing in terms of four ideal types: private-informal, private-formal, public-informal, and public-formal.[49]

Private-informal mechanisms are those in which a third party attempts dispute settlement at the behest of the disputants themselves. Usually working at the most informal level, mediators are often selected because of their prestige or power within a social, religious, or occupational grouping, or perhaps because they have been preselected by the organization itself to play that role. Priests, ministers, credit counselors, peer group committees, or perhaps the patriarch or matriarch of a family are prime examples of third party mediators in the private-informal setting. Procedural rules are minimal in such forums, and sanctions are strictly nongovernmental. Private-informal mechanisms can be found everywhere, but they appear to be more characteristic of primitive societies. However, even in more well-developed countries, such as Japan or Korea, we can find widespread use of this method of dispute adjusting. In fact, these societies and others seem to prefer

---

[48]Hensler, "Taking Aim": 250. A useful discussion of the symbols and euphemisms employed in this debate, with special reference to jury competence, but with much broader applicability, may be found in Stephen Daniels, "The Question of Jury Competence and the Politics of Civil Justice Reform: Symbols, Rhetoric, and Agenda-Building," *Law and Contemporary Problems* 52, No. 4 (Autumn 1989): 269–310.

Researchers and commentators have noted that the mass of business litigation is seldom criticized. See, e.g., Ross E. Cheit, "Corporate Ambulance Chasers: The Charmed Life of Business Litigation," *Studies in Law, Politics, and Society,* Vol. 11 (1991), 119–140; Amy Stevens, "Corporate Clients, Some Lawyers Differ on Litigation Reform," *Wall Street Journal* (March 17, 1995): B-10; and Richard B. Schmitt, "Why Businesses Sometimes Like Punitive Awards," *Wall Street Journal* (Dec. 11, 1995): B-1.

In a study of an Illinois county where there were some ten times more contract (mostly business) filings than personal injury cases, a researcher wrote,

> One might expect that concerns about litigiousness . . . would focus on . . . [businesses]. Yet, I heard no complaints about contract plaintiffs being "greedy" or "sue happy" or "looking for the easy buck." Such criticisms were reserved exclusively for injured persons who made the relatively rare decision to press their claims in court.

David M. Engel, "The Oven Bird's Song: Insiders, Outsiders, and Personal Injuries in An American Community," *Law and Society Review* 18, No. 4 (1984): 575.

Additional evidence supporting the "Have versus Have-Not" explanation for the continued misperception of the realities of American civil litigation is provided by David Neubauer and Stephen S. Meinhold, "Too Quick to Sue? Public Perceptions of the Litigation Explosion," *Justice System Journal* 16, No. 3 (1994): 1–14.

[49]Austin Sarat and Joel B. Grossman, "Courts and Conflict Resolution: Problems in the Mobilization of Adjudication," *American Political Science Review* 69, No. 4 (Dec. 1975): 1200–17.

the use of private-informal processes in contrast to public or semipublic resolution of disputes. In the case of Japan, Kawashima writes,

> When people are socially organized in small groups and when subordination of individual desires in favor of group agreement is idealized, the group's stability and the security of individual members are threatened by attempts to regulate conduct by universalistic standards. The impact is greater when such an effort is reinforced by an organized political power [as argued earlier]. Furthermore, the litigious process, in which both parties seek to justify their position by objective standards, and the emergence of a judicial decision based thereon tend to convert situational interests into firmly consolidated and independent ones. Because of the resulting disorganization of traditional social groups, resort to litigation has been condemned as morally wrong, subversive, and rebellious.

At this point Kawashima enters a footnote that speaks of a Japanese farmer near Tokyo whose whole family has been ostracized by all the villagers because his deceased father had sued another farmer in a dispute about the boundaries of his farm.[50]

A second dispute processing mode suggested by Sarat and Grossman is the private-formal device, whereby professional ethics committees, ecclesiastical courts, labor arbitration panels, college student disciplinary boards, and similar organizations act as the mediators. Still private, these forums differ from the first category in their adherence to more standardized procedures, often quasi-judicial in nature. Such mechanisms usually depend for their effectiveness on peer (labor, professional, ethnic, or perhaps religious) group sanctions. Compliance is still voluntary, as in the first mode of dispute resolution, although sanctions such as removal from the group (for example, loss of license to practice or dismissal from school) have a quasi-legal impact of significant magnitude.[51] The use of such mechanisms tends to be characteristic of parties who have continuing relations with one another.

Public-informal mechanisms are those involving formal decision makers acting in an informal manner to resolve disputes at an early stage and to forestall the need for the use of formal mechanisms. On reflection, the prevalence of such dispute processing mechanisms will be apparent to the reader. The police attempting to "cool off" the parties in a family quarrel, plea bargaining in criminal cases, the pretrial conference in civil matters, the city fire inspector negotiating with the building owner over code violations—these are examples of the broad array of actors in this dispute settlement category. The chief characteristic of this mechanism is its emphasis on bargaining within close proximity to—indeed, as we have said, under the shadow of—formal, public forums. Such processes usually represent the last step prior to formal litigation and are, in fact, quasi-public in nature. Although procedures tend to be informal, usually characterized by the push and pull of bargaining, the use of these forums over time has tended to shape at least some of them into semi-institutionalized processes.

Public-formal means of settling disputes are, of course, the most familiar and most visible of our four types and are best exemplified by the judicial establishment itself. Courts represent the full flowering of formality of procedure and "publicness" among dispute processing mechanisms. More than other mechanisms—sometimes much more—

---

[50]Takeyoshi Kawashima, "Dispute Resolution in Contemporary Japan," in Arthur Taylor VonMehren, ed., *Law in Japan: The Legal Order in a Changing Society* (Cambridge: Harvard University Press, 1963), 44–45.

[51]In fact, some have argued that present college disciplinary boards have run amuck, replacing formal adjudicative processes. See, e.g., Scott Gottlieb, "A Mockery of Justice on Campus," *Wall Street Journal* (Sept. 27, 1993): A-22. Other items on the same theme include a two-article series by Nina Bernstein: "With Colleges Holding Court, Discretion View with Fairness," *New York Times* (May 5, 1996): A-1; and "Behind Some Fraternity Walls, Brothers in Crime," *New York Times* (May 6, 1996): A-1.

courts have institutional imperatives of their own that tend to shape the type of cases they take and the decisions they reach. Oriented somewhat less to the needs of parties and more to their own institutional concerns, as well as to the interests of the state itself, courts are more likely than other disputing mechanisms to be concerned with the impact of their rulings on other policy-making institutions, as well as on the larger political and social system. Their formality of procedures invites a larger role for attorneys and other representatives than in the other forums. In fact, attorneys play a significant role in determining what disputes reach courts and how such cases are decided, so that, as we made clear in Chapter 7, courts can hardly be understood apart from the role of the bar.

As we have seen, the flow of grievances into the disputing process, formal or informal, is a function of a cost-benefit calculation, which tends to dictate that as costs, tangible and intangible, rise, the flow of cases falls. Generally, the more formal and public the disputing forum, the higher the cost, hence the rapidly diminishing flow of issues into the system as we approach formal adjudication itself. Far from being center stage in the settlement of disputes, court processes are but the proverbial tip of the iceberg, there being a vast array of informal or quasi-formal avenues available for processing disputes both prior to and subsequent to court action. Let us now cross that invisible line between informal and formal processes to consider the flow of civil disputes into courts themselves.

THE FLOW OF CIVIL LITIGATION

We know only slightly more about the flow of disputes into the judicial arena than we do about the key variables explaining the informal disputing process. As noted in Chapter 3, the lion's share of court filings are to be found at the state level, and, unfortunately, it is there that we encounter the greatest difficulty in presenting reliable statistics.[52] The largest number of disputes, of course, pass from informal arenas into formal judicial cognizance at the lowest level of state trial courts, those of limited jurisdiction, and it is precisely at that level that we have the least reliable data. Many of these courts are not courts of record at all; others keep records but are lax in gathering and reporting caseload data to central collecting agencies within the state; and of course, we have the perennial problem of the definition of a "case." Records of state trial courts of general jurisdiction (Chapter 3) afford us somewhat more reliable if less voluminous data on civil case flow; yet even there, the figures are subject to the vagaries of state reporting systems. Federal court case flow data are the most reliable, but as with all data, there are problems of interpretation in the light of the socioeconomic issues we want to discuss.

With these caveats in mind, what are the chief characteristics of civil case flow in the United States? The answer, of course, will vary with the type of court in question. The characteristics of cases filed in, let us say, small claims court may be expected to differ significantly from cases filed in the lowest of our federal trial courts, the federal district courts. Also, the flow of civil litigation is a function of the nature of parties and the subject matter of the dispute. We can hardly discuss the process of dispute resolution in probate matters, for example, as though it were the same as the process in automobile accident cases or an-

---

[52]See U.S. Law Enforcement Assistance Administration, *State Court Caseload Statistics: The State of the Art* (Washington: GPO, 1978). Problems in gathering and analyzing state caseload data are also discussed in National Center for State Courts, *State Court Caseload Statistics, Annual Report, 1984* (Williamsburg, Va.: National Center for State Courts, 1986), 3–7.

A more recent piece that clearly explains the difficulty of gathering reliable statistics on caseflow—a problem also discussed in Chapter 3—is by Margaret A. Jacobs, "Reliable Data About Lawsuits Are Very Scarce," *Wall Street Journal* (June 9, 1995): B-1.

Table 8–2   Civil Case Filings in General Jurisdiction Courts in 29 States, 1993

Case Type	Total	Percent
Total Number	5,929,537	100
Domestic relations	2,448,150	41
Small claims	732,977	12
Contracts	639,783	11
Estates	606,722	10
Torts	572,041	10
Real property rights	439,947	7
Civil appeals	93,339	2
Mental health	90,608	2
Other	305, 970	5

Source: United States, Dept. of Justice, Bureau of Justice Statistics, *Tort Cases in Large Counties* (Washington: Bureau of Justice Statistics, NCJ-153177, Apr. 1995), 2.

titrust actions.[53] Civil adjudication in the United States is, thus, a mixed bag of petty matters, middle-range disputes, and litigation involving major money claims, if not major policy issues. A civil case may take as long as ten years to resolve and may involve hundreds of millions of dollars, as in the case of the Penzoil-Texaco suit in the Texas courts, or it may take three minutes of court time in a controversy involving 40 dollars. Perhaps the best approach to describing the civil judicial process is, first, to survey the broad sweep of cases flowing into the three major categories of courts (state courts of limited jurisdiction, state courts of general jurisdiction, and federal district courts), then to explore in somewhat greater depth the process involved in adjudicating the chief types of civil claims filed.

Table 3–1 (Chapter 3) provides the best and latest available estimate of the *total volume* of civil trial court filings at the state level, while comparable current data on federal civil trial court filings may be found in Chapter 4. As shown, an estimated 19 million civil cases were filed in state courts of both limited and general jurisdiction in 1994, whereas only about 236,000 were filed in federal district courts that year (recall that the federal judicial year ends on September 30). The 19 million state filings include approximately 4.7 million domestic relations case filings, the civil category showing the largest increases over the last ten years.[54] These state civil filings, including domestic relations, are divided approximately evenly between state courts of general jurisdiction and those of limited jurisdiction, with a slight edge toward the latter. Using data from 29 state courts of general jurisdiction that have roughly comparable reporting definitions, Table 8–2 depicts the major types of civil cases filed in the states and the percentages of each type.

Setting aside domestic relations cases (which grew 65 percent from 1984 to 1994), Figure 8–4 depicts the trends in filings in state courts of *general jurisdiction* for the remaining eight categories of civil cases. As shown, small claims continue to represent the largest single category of cases. This situation is even more true in state courts of limited jurisdiction,

---

[53]A research report that emphasizes the uniqueness of populations and subpopulations of civil cases is Marc Galanter, "The Life and Times of the Big Six; or, The Federal Courts Since the Good Old Days," *Wisconsin Law Review* 88, No. 6 (1988): 921–54.

[54]These data are taken from Brian J. Ostrom and Neal B. Kauder, *Examining the Work of State Courts, 1994: A National Perspective from the Court Statistics Project* (Williamsburg, Va: National Center for State Courts, 1996), 10.

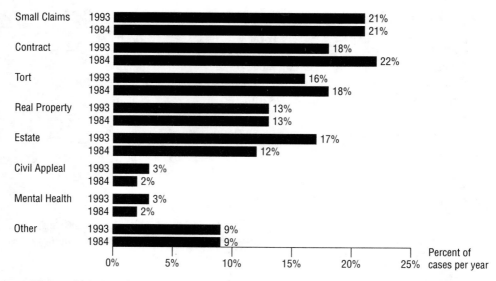

Figure 8–4   Civil Cases in State General Jurisdiction Courts in 23 States, 1984 versus 1993 (SOURCE: Brian J. Ostrom and Neal B. Kauder, *Examining the Work of State Courts, 1993* (Williamsburg, Va.: National Center for State Courts, 1995), 11.)

where they account for approximately one-third of all cases in those lower courts (small claims litigation is discussed more fully later). Both contract and tort filings are down over the past decade, whereas filings in the areas of estates, civil appeals, and mental health now account for a slightly larger share of the total than they did ten years ago.

The rapid growth in domestic relations case filings in state general trial courts in the last ten years is accounted for primarily by the rather startling increase in domestic violence cases (up 83 percent just from 1989 to 1994), support-custody cases (up 35 percent from 1988 to 1994), and paternity (up 31 percent in the same period). While divorce itself still accounts for the largest single category of domestic relations cases—about 39 percent in these courts—support/custody matters are now the second largest category at 18 percent, with domestic violence filings now comprising some 16 percent of the filings, according to the 1994 NCSC data.[55]

Although total tort filings are down somewhat, especially since 1991, at 10 percent of all state trial court civil filings, they still occupy center stage in the ongoing national debate over the alleged litigation explosion (see earlier discussion). In an intensive study of tort cases in state courts of general jurisdiction in 1992—the closest we have to a comprehensive national study—it was found that auto accident cases comprised by far the largest category at 60 percent.[56] These were followed in frequency by premises liability issues at 17 percent, in which the plaintiffs alleged harm from poorly maintained or dangerous property. No other type of tort case reached even 5 percent of total tort filings in these courts. Thus, medical malpractice filings, which will be covered in more detail, represented 4.9 percent of all torts, according to the study, whereas product liability cases, also

---

[55]Ostrom and Kauder, *Examining the Work of State Courts 1994*, 39–40.

[56]United States, Dept. of Justice, Bureau of Justice Statistics, *Tort Cases in Large Counties* (Washington: Bureau of Justice Statistics, Apr. 1995), 2–3.

Table 8–3   Civil Case Types in Limited Jurisdiction
Courts, 1994

Case Type	Percent of Caseload
Small claims	32
Real property	31
Contract	6
Tort	4
Domestic relations	3
Estate/Mental health	2
Other	22

Source: National Center for State Courts, *Examining the Work of State Courts, 1994* (Williamsburg, Va: National Center for State Courts, 1996, 23.

close to the heart of the controversy over "tort reform," accounted for only 3.4 percent of total tort filings. The remaining case types rounding out the tort profile in state courts of general jurisdiction were intentional injury (such as vandalism and intentional personal injury) at 2.9 percent; nonmedical malpractice, 1.8 percent; toxic substance (primarily asbestos cases in this particular sampling), 1.6 percent; unknown tort issues, 1.2 percent; slander/libel, 0.8 percent; and other negligence matters, 5.9 percent.

Finally, although domestic relations cases, as shown, have come more and more to dominate the dockets of state trial courts of general jurisdiction, the opposite is true of issues involving controversies between and among businesses and between individuals and businesses over terms of contracts. Whereas such cases accounted for some 65 percent of the dockets of these courts around the turn of the century, their proportion in 1976–1977 was only about 30 percent, dropping to barely 11 percent in the current era.[57]

Although we can be less confident of the reliability of available data on civil cases in state courts of limited jurisdiction, we do have a rough idea of their caseloads. First, as explained in Chapter 3, these courts are indeed the workhorses of the entire American judicial system, processing some 75 percent of all state cases. By leaving aside traffic and local ordinance matters, which represent the lion's share (some 70 percent) of case filings in these courts, we find that their remaining current annual civil caseload of some 9.4 million filings (1994) comprises the categories presented in Table 8–3. These data were gleaned from a survey conducted by the National Center for State Courts of these courts in thirteen states which reported relatively complete, comparable data.

Typical of a civil case in these courts would be a small claims matter—most likely a dispute over the rental of property (nonreturn of an apartment damage deposit, perhaps), minor property boundary issues, damage dispute between neighbors, a mixture of family quarrels, collection of bad checks, evictions, and a few estate matters. Such is the hodgepodge of case types addressed by judges in these courts day in and day out (see further discussion in Chapter 3 and the small claims case study that follows).

Both civil and criminal proceedings in our nation's limited jurisdiction courts may be characterized as "quick and dirty." In civil cases, it is not uncommon for one of the par-

[57]Ostrom and Kauder, *Examining the Work of State Courts, 1993:* 26.

ties to be absent, resulting in a large number of default judgments. Prelitigation mediation or conciliation is the rule, and disputes that do reach the trial stage are likely to be processed perfunctorily. Moreover, the appeal rate from these courts is so low as to render them virtual courts of last resort for millions of litigants annually.[58]

Data on civil caseflow in our federal courts are both more reliable and more easily interpreted, although as previously emphasized, federal courts together account for only some 2 percent of all litigation in the nation in a given year. In the year ending September 30, 1993, 229,850 civil cases were filed in our federal trial courts, representing 83 percent of all filings in these courts. The comparable 1994 figures are 236,391, or 84 percent of total filings. Of course these figures do not include the large flow of bankruptcy and federal magistrate work—types of cases which at the state level would likely be handled by courts of limited jurisdiction. The most comparable figure to this federal civil filings total would be civil filings in state courts of general jurisdiction, which, as noted before, numbered about 9 million in 1994. By this measure, federal trial court civil filings again represent only some 2 percent of similar case filings in state courts. However, we must recognize that in some senses litigation at these two levels of courts is not comparable in that federal cases are likely to involve more complex matters, in both tangible and intangible terms, than is so at the state level. But whatever the comparability, our picture of American civil litigation is hardly complete until we add data on federal court caseloads.

The growth in federal trial court civil filings is presented in Chapter 4, Table 4–2. Over the two decades 1970 to 1990, these filings grew from 87,323 to 217,879, a two-and-a-half-fold increase, while America's population grew only 22 percent in that period. Too, the growth in the number of federal judges was insufficient to keep pace with the burgeoning civil caseload in that era, the cases-per-judge figure increasing from 218 in 1970 to 379 in 1990. However, both the per-judge figure and the rate of growth of federal civil cases have abated in recent years. Over the five-year period 1990 to 1994, for example, total civil trial filings grew by only about 7 percent, while the per-judge load dropped from 381 to 364.[59]

Table 8–4 presents a longitudinal profile of civil filings in federal district courts. The top categories in the table represent what has been called "The Big Six" inasmuch as these cases over most of the period covered make up some 75 to 80 percent of all federal civil filings and serve the further purpose of pointing up the areas of greatest controversy in the debate over America's litigiousness.[60] In ordering the categories by percentage of total cases filed in 1960, one can quickly determine which types of litigation increased or decreased the most over this 35-year period. Also, the last column of the table points up the case types responsible for the largest percentage of the total growth from 1960 to 1994.

While absolute numbers of cases filed tell us much about the nature of civil litigation, it should be recalled that our judicial process at both trial and appellate levels is one of informal, pre-court bargaining. Indeed, this could be said to be the overriding fact that emerges in all studies of the actual processing of disputes in American courts, and it is certainly demonstrated in a closer look at the flow of civil cases at the federal district level.

---

[58]Descriptions of the work of these courts may be found in American Judicature Society, *Courts of Limited Jurisdiction: A National Survey* (Chicago: American Judicature Society, 1975); Council on the Role of Courts, *The Role of Courts in American Society* (St. Paul: West Publishing Co., 1984), especially 35–38; and Doris M. Provine, *Judging Credentials: Non-Lawyer Judges and the Politics of Professionalism* (Chicago: University of Chicago Press, 1986). See also the discussion of small claims processes that follows.

[59]United States, Administrative Office of the U.S. Courts, *Judicial Business of the United States, 1994* (Washington: Administrative Office of the U.S. Courts, n.d.), 7. To remind the reader, these statistical reports are published under different and sometimes confusing titles. Usually they may be found under the title *Report of the Proceedings of the Judicial Conference of the United States,* which includes *Activities of the Administrative Office of the United States Courts* and *Judicial Business of the United States.* The 1993 report, however, is entitled *United States Courts: Selected Reports.*

[60]See Marc Galanter, "The Life and Times of the Big Six": 924.

Table 8–4   Civil Case Filings in Federal District Courts, 1960, 1986, and 1994

Case Type	1960 (%)	1986 (%)	1994 (%)	% of Net Increase
Total minus local[a]	51,063	254,249	236,149	
Torts	19,586 (38.4)	41,979 (16.5)	47,595 (20.2)	15.1
Other contracts[b]	13,248 (26.0)	47,443 (18.7)	28,893 (12.2)	8.5
Recovery[b]	2,251 (4.4)	40,824 (16.1)	2,329 (.99)	.04
Prisoner petitions	2,177 (4.3)	33,758 (13.3)	57,928 (24.5)	30.1
Social security	537 (1.1)	14,407 (5.7)	10,927 (4.6)	5.6
Civil rights	280 (.5)	20,128 (7.9)	32,622 (13.8)	17.5
Other				
Forfeiture and penalty	2,371 (4.6)	3,480 (1.4)	3,285 (1.4)	.49
Real property	2,304 (4.5)	10,642 (4.2)	7,553 (3.2)	2.8
Labor law	1,900 (3.7)	12,839 (5.0)	15,662 (6.6)	7.4
Tax suits	1,545 (3.0)	2,722 (1.1)	2,183 (.92)	.34
Intellectual property	1,545 (2.9)	5,681 (2.2)	6,902 (2.9)	2.9
Bankruptcy	308 (.6)	4,561 (1.8)	5,497 (2.3)	2.8
Securities, commodities, exchanges	267 (.5)	3,059 (1.2)	1,810 (.77)	.83
Other suits[c]	2,822 (5.5)	12,726 (5.0)	12,963 (5.5)	5.5

[a]A declining portion of federal cases (e.g., 14% in 1960, .10% in 1994) are under local jurisdiction, hence not included in this table. Table C-2 of the *Annual Reports* details these cases.

[b]Recovery of overpayments, etc., together with contracts, make up the statistical category labeled *contracts* in the *Annual Reports*.

[c]The "other" category includes principally other miscellaneous (unspecified in the federal reports) types of suits, along with suits on such subjects as the environment, antitrust, banking, commercial (ICC rates, etc.), deportations, RICO, Freedom of Information Act, the constitutionality of state statutes, state reapportionment suits, etc.

Source: United States, Administrative Office of the U.S. Courts, *Judicial Business of the United States Courts, 1960, 1986, 1994* (Washington: Administrative Office of the U.S. Courts, n.d.), Table C-2A; and Marc Galanter, "The Life and Times of the Big Six; or, The Federal Courts Since the Good Old Days," *Wisconsin Law Review* 1988, No. 6 (1988): Table I, 925.

The number of cases that were actually tried (jury plus nonjury) was only 12,570 in 1985, or 4.7 percent of all cases terminated. By 1994 the respective figures were 7,910 and 3.5 percent.[61] Over time, the proportion of federal civil cases tried has decreased; it was 10.8 percent in 1969. What one might term the "federal district court case flow pyramid for 1985 and 1994" is depicted in Table 8–5. Thus, as with state courts, the proportion of cases actually going to trial is but a small fraction of total cases terminated. For all courts over time, that figure is usually in the range of 5 to 15 percent. By 1994 we dropped well below this minimal figure for civil case processing in federal district courts.[62]

---

[61]*Judicial Business of the United States Courts, 1994*, Table C-4. The data show 2.0 percent jury trials, 1.5 percent nonjury.

[62]For 1993, in a sampling of trial courts of general jurisdiction in 27 states, the National Center for State Courts reported the civil trial rate at 7.6 percent, with 6.4 percent being bench trials, 1.2 percent jury trials. See Ostrom and Kauder, *Examining the Work of State Courts, 1993*, 14.

Table 8–5 Federal Civil Case Terminations, 1985–1994

Disposition	Number of Cases and Percentage	
	1985	1994
Cases tried	12,570 (4.7)	7,910 (3.5)
Jury	6,278 (2.4)	4,450 (2.0)
Nonjury	6,292 (2.4)	3,460 (1.5)
Settled during or after pretrial hearing	31,103 (11.6)	20,947 (9.2)
Settled before pretrial hearing	95,507 (35.5)	159,277 (69.9)
Settled or withdrawn prior to court action	129,429 (48.2)	39,789 (17.5)
TERMINATED	268,609 (100.1)	227,923 (100.0)

Source: United States, Administrative Office of the U.S. Courts, *Judicial Business of the United States Courts, 1985, 1994* (Washington: Administrative Office of the U.S. Courts, n.d), Table C-4.

Current federal district court caseflow data indicate that the civil disputes most likely to go to trial are those involving personal injuries, civil rights matters, and issues under the Fair Labor Standards Act, all having trial dispositions in the range of 6 to 9 percent. Least likely to be resolved by trial were suits involving social security questions, contract actions, and bankruptcy, all running around 1 percent or less of all civil dispositions in 1994. Prisoner petitions, too, had an extremely low trial rate.[63]

As made clear in the foregoing discussion of the "tort reform" debate, the lineaments of which need not be reiterated here, the significance one attaches to these (sometimes dramatic) changes in the federal trial court caseflow depends in large part on one's perspective, if not one's political ideology. Observers not comfortable with this level of increased judicial activity might well decry some of these trends as a dangerous move toward "government by judiciary."[64] Certainly such observer-participants as the late Chief Justice Warren E. Burger viewed these data in this light when he observed that

> Since 1942 civil case filings in the Federal District Courts have multiplied more than six times. . . . [Such filings have] increased seven times faster than the population. . . . We live up to the statement that we are the most litigious people in the world.
>
> There has been another very significant change in the work of the courts, and that is a change in the content of cases, presenting issues far more novel and complex than in the past. Part of the reason is that in the past fifteen years Congress has enacted approximately 100 statutes creating new causes of action and enlarging federal jurisdiction.[65]

Implicit (and at times quite explicit) in such statements, of course, is the notion that courts, supposedly Hamilton's "least dangerous" branch of government, are becoming both the most dangerous and the most assertive, with the desired balance among our three great branches of government being dangerously tilted in the direction of an "imperial judiciary."[66]

---

[63] *Judicial Business of the United States Courts, 1994*, Table C-4.

[64] Raoul Berger, *Government by Judiciary* (Cambridge, Mass.: Harvard University Press, 1977).

[65] Remarks by Chief Justice Warren E. Burger at the Arthur T. Vanderbilt dinner, New York City, Nov. 18, 1982.

[66] Nathan Glazer, "Toward an Imperial Judiciary," *Public Interest* 41 (Fall 1975): 104–23. A more recent series of essays in this vein is "Symposium: The End of Democracy," *First Things,* No. 67 (Nov. 1996): 18–42; and "The End of Democracy: A Discussion Continued," *First Things,* No. 69 (Jan. 1997): 19–28.

A contrary view, however, has it that such increases in the number as well as novelty of civil filings reflects a welcome shift in public policy. Recognition of the precarious position of the individual vis-à-vis both government and private organizations, increasingly evident in our postindustrial society, is long overdue. Increased judicial involvement in a wide variety of citizens' complaints is but a minor ripple resulting from more intense legislative and even more widespread societal concerns that the quality of American life as expressed or implied in the Bill of Rights is being severely undermined. Examples abound, all giving rise to federal civil litigation: environmental quality, prison conditions, employee safety conditions, defendants' rights, discrimination on the basis of sex or race, and many more. According to this view, the flow of federal civil litigation is only beginning to correspond to widespread grievances heretofore not heard in our troubled society. So, at bottom, a person's interpretation of civil litigation statistics depends in no small part on his or her answer to that age-old issue of the proper role of government in our lives and, more especially, the proper role of the judiciary in public policy-making.[67]

CIVIL JUSTICE: TWO CASE STUDIES

Although caseflow data provide the basis for a useful overview of the civil justice system, they afford little insight into the details of the process itself. The student has a right to ask such questions as these: What is a typical civil case? How is it handled, in court and out? Who are the parties? What happens to them? Such questions can perhaps best be answered through the presentation of snapshots, so to speak, of some of the more characteristic civil actions. In the following sections, we have selected two types of civil cases that together represent a significant slice of the civil judicial process in America. In each, it is important to note the factors inhibiting or encouraging court use, types of parties, the chief characteristics of the proceedings, and of course, outcomes.

Small Claims Court: Poor Man's Justice

As previously discussed, the National Center for State Courts estimates that small claims actions vie with domestic relations cases for the largest single category of civil actions in state trial courts. At 12 percent of all civil cases in general jurisdiction courts (21 percent of all filings if one sets aside domestic relations cases) and some 32 percent of cases in state courts of limited jurisdiction, there were roughly 4.3 million small claims cases processed by state courts in 1993 (the domestic relations estimate is 4.5 million).[68] When one adds to these small claims filings the large number of cases in state courts of limited

---

[67]For an elaboration of this interpretation, see Galanter, "The Life and Times of the Big Six," data from which constitute part of Table 8–4. Galanter concludes that

> The patterns we have observed [in federal civil filings] cast considerable doubt on the notion that increasing case loads in the federal district courts can be explained in terms of a heightened propensity of Americans to seek legal remedies and engage in litigious combat. (p. 951)

[68]In other reports, the National Center for State Courts reported higher proportions of small claims than indicated in the 1993 data: ". . . 40 percent of all civil case filings in state limited jurisdiction courts and 27 percent of all civil case filings in general jurisdiction courts." These figures may be computed on total trial court civil filings after deleting domestic relations cases. See John A. Goerdt, "The People's Court: A Summary of Findings and Policy Implications from a Study of 12 Urban Small Claims Courts," *State Court Journal* 17, Nos. 3 and 4 (Summer/Fall 1993): 38.

jurisdiction, not technically small claims matters but which are processed in a manner quite similar to small claims, we can conclude that small claims in the broader sense make up a clear majority of all state civil filings.[69]

For as long as we have had courts, Americans have exhibited an ambivalent attitude toward small claims cases. At times we have perceived them as troublesome issues involving petty, private disputes of no major relevance to the legal system as a whole, while at other times we have seen them as deep-felt grievances of the "common person," the processing of which might well be taken as a barometer of the health of our entire sociolegal system.[70] Throughout American history reformers have intermittently sought to simplify the judicial process in order to realize that age-old dream of "everyone his or her own lawyer"—to create a simple and speedy dispute-resolution process that is understandable and workable by ordinary citizens. The last major wave in this regard prior to our own generation was in the Progressive Movement of 1890–1930.

As part of this Progressive agenda, legal reforms brought into being civil legal aid societies as well as small claims and/or conciliation courts. The expense, delay, complexity, inaccessibility, and injustices of the regular courts were all to be ameliorated, if not entirely eliminated, through the creation of small claims courts, to which the average citizen could turn for easy and inexpensive resolution of grievances. The specific characteristics of this "new" approach were to be simplified procedures, lower (or no) cost, little or no attorney participation, few appeals, an enhanced role for court clerks to guide inexperienced litigants, an expanded role for judges to draw out the key elements of the case, fully qualified and fully paid judges, and, where possible, the use of mediation and/or conciliation.[71] Clearly, the focus of reform was *procedural,* to the end that ordinary citizens could benefit from enhanced access to an easy, workable mode of dispute processing. With such a procedural focus, small claims could be, and were, grafted onto existing courts, there being no need in most jurisdictions for the creation of separate tribunals.

By 1940, at least 19 states had created statewide small claims courts of varying structures and jurisdictions, and by 1972, a survey of these courts and procedures revealed that only 9 states were without some form of small claims processing.[72] In one sense, then, the small claims movement had succeeded, such a reform being an ongoing part of the judicial system in virtually every state and city. But there were flaws in their conceptualization—flaws that eventually led to the perversion of their alleged function.

First, the assumption had always been that in the "courts for the poor," the claims filed would be relatively simple and honest, coming from that most noble of all characters in American folklore, "the working-class poor." In practice, these courts were therefore created with a built-in bias for the plaintiff, the claims initially being assumed to be valid. Second, although ordinary judicial proceedings were to be "informalized," the small claims model retained the basic, though watered-down, adversarial process. And inas-

[69]NCSC reports that two-thirds of civil filings in limited jurisdiction courts are either small claims or real property cases, many of the latter of which are processed as if they were small claims. Ostrom and Kauder, *Examining the Work of State Courts,* 11.

[70]A useful history of the small claims idea is Eric H. Steele, "The Historical Context of Small Claims Courts," *American Bar Foundation Research Journal* 1981, No. 2 (Spring 1981): especially 293–337.

Parts of the discussion here on small claims matters, as well as the subsequent section on medical malpractice, rely on Harry P. Stumpf and John C. Culver, *The Politics of State Courts* (New York: Longman 1992): 6.

[71]Steele, "The Historical Context of Small Claims Courts": 330–35.

[72]A very useful review of small claims court research is Barbara Yngvesson and Patricia Hennessey, "Small Claims, Complex Disputes: A Review of the Small Claims Literature," *Law and Society Review* 9, No. 2 (Winter 1975): 218–74.

much as this model contains the assumption of the equality of litigants (ensured through the kindly interposition of the judge), there was an implicit assumption of the sociopolitical neutrality of the parties in litigation—that is, the absence of the possibility of any net social gain by one party over the other. As later researchers noted, this faulty conceptualization meant that "the court bore within it the seeds of its gradual transformation," or, depending on one's viewpoint, one might say "destruction."[73]

Few judicial procedures have been so widely studied as small claims processes. Moreover, many of these studies have involved empirical field research, giving us rich data that are useful in understanding the realities of small claims processes. The first point usually made by researchers is that far from serving the needs of the "honest poor," the ideal litigant assumed by progressive reformers, these courts have become, to a great extent, forums for the business community to collect debts with ease and economy from the working poor.[74]

For example, an early study undertaken by the Consumer's Union of 107 randomly selected complaints filed with the Hartford, Connecticut small claims court found *one* case involving auto damage, *one* consumer complaint, *one* complaint against a business establishment, *one* tax matter, *one* malicious damage claim, and *103* debt collection cases! These debt cases included twenty-six doctors' bills (plus a large number of hospital bills), eleven corporation bills, twenty department store bills, and fifteen gas company bills.[75] Similarly, in a latter review of research on 14 separate small claims courts throughout the nation, in only 2 of these tribunals did nonbusiness claimants make up more than 42 percent of the plaintiffs, whereas individuals appeared as defendants in over three-fourths of the contests in all but two of these courts.[76] An update of these findings was presented in the latest survey by the National Center for State Courts in 1990. Here it was reported that in a sampling of 12 urban jurisdictions, businesses filed 64 percent of the claims, a vast majority of these (91 percent) being debt collection cases.[77] Other studies repeat these findings, almost ad nauseam.[78]

An excellent empirical study of small claims courts in two counties in Ohio concluded that

> It is clear that the courts of both counties are currently dominated by business plaintiffs who use the small claims court as an economical means of collection from individuals who are their prime targets.

---

[73]Yngvesson and Hennessey, "Small Claims, Complex Disputes": 227.

[74]Yngvesson and Hennessey, "Small Claims, Complex Disputes": 235.

[75]National Institute for Consumer Justice, *Staff Studies on Small Claims Courts* (Boston: National Institute for Consumer Justice): App. B, 452.

[76]Yngvesson and Hennessey, "Small Claims, Complex Disputes": 236.

[77]Goerdt, "The People's Court": 1–2. But for a rather different view of the small claims process—and outcomes—see Neil Vidmar, "The Small Claims Court: A Reconceptualization of Disputes and an Empirical Investigation," *Law and Society Review* 18, No. 4 (1984): 515–50.

[78]Nearly all the earliest studies surveyed in this article, as well as more recent studies, report this finding. See, e.g., the excellent study of Ohio's small claims court: Robert J. Hollingsworth, William B. Feldman, and David C. Clark, "The Ohio Small Claims Court: An Empirical Study," *University of Cincinnati Law Review* 42, No. 3 (1973): 479, 480. In a more recent, detailed study of Iowa's small claims court, it was reported that 62 percent of the plaintiffs in their sample were businesses, 22 percent landlords, 2 percent government entities, and only 14 percent individuals. See Suzanne E. Elwell with Christopher D. Carlson, "The Iowa Small Claims Court: An Empirical Analysis," *Iowa Law Review* 75, Nos. 1–2 (Jan. 1990): 443–538, especially 483–85.

The study by Arthur Best et. al., "Peace, Wealth, Happiness, and Small Claim Courts: A Case Study," *Fordham Urban Law Journal,* 21, No. 2 (Winter 1994): 343–79, of Colorado's small claims court, appears to be an exception, but the actual identity of plaintiffs is not clearly stated. Moreover, Colorado's small claims statute bans the use of the court by collection agencies and limits repeated use of the court, compliance with which is also not clear from the study.

Adding to the discomfiture of the individual defendant is the fact that among business plaintiffs in Hamilton County, 75 percent of proprietorships and virtually all corporations were represented by counsel at the trial. Representation by itself does not assure success but the fact that over 65 percent of all plaintiffs were represented belies the image of the court as a forum where plaintiffs of average means can obtain justice without incurring the expense of legal representation. . . .

The most frequently occurring claims were for nonpayment for goods, services, and the combination of the two, again illustrating the collection-agency nature of the court. Together they accounted for over 64 percent of the claims in Hamilton County and 88 percent of the claims in Claremont County.[79]

A closely related finding from small claims research is the pattern of repeated use of these courts by the business community. A 1972 study in Cambridge, Massachusetts, for example, found that the principal and recurrent plaintiffs in the small claims forum in that community were the New England Telephone Company, Macy Furniture Company, and a local hospital. In other cities, plaintiffs with high levels of repeated use of small claims processes included the county, the local utility company, and, quite frequently, collection agencies representing hospitals and physicians.[80]

Individuals do initiate claims in these courts, usually in cases of property damage involving auto accidents, attempting to obtain refunds for rent deposits, alleged damages of clothing by dry cleaning establishments, and the like. But the individual plaintiff is at a disadvantage on a number of counts, most of which are nicely summarized in Galanter's concepts of "one shotters," as opposed to "repeat players."[81] Businesses, even small businesses—not to mention utility companies, banks, universities, department stores, hospitals, and so forth—are apt to have been in court a number of times. They are familiar with the process and have built up expertise in pressing their claims (even without the use of an attorney, although they are usually represented). They often enjoy cozy informal relations with the judges and other court personnel, and in all, they posses the legal, political, and financial resources to push a claim to victory. They are what Galanter terms the "haves" in litigation. Individual plaintiffs, on the other hand, tend to be the "have nots," lacking all of these advantages. Thus, in the previously mentioned Ohio study, 95 percent of the defendants in one county were appearing in court for the first time; and in the other Ohio county, every single one of the individuals were "one shotters"![82] Under these circumstances, the individual defendant often does not even bother to show up in court, thereby giving the victory to the (usually business) plaintiff by default. Such default judgments are common in small claims court, often running to 60 to 70 percent of the cases, with an average of 52.4 percent among nine small claims courts studied.[83]

The individual small claims litigant, whether plaintiff or defendant, seems to be squeezed out of the small-claims game on other grounds. One researcher described some of the practical aspects of small claims litigation for the individual:

It [the court] is downtown, it is expensive to get to, . . . it requires hours of waiting, it may require coming back three or four times before a $15 or $20 claim can be heard, its procedures are difficult to understand and most important of all the experience is simply an unpleasant one.[84]

[79]Hollingsworth et. al., "The Ohio Small Claims Court": 479, 480.
[80]Yngvesson and Hennessey, "Small Claims, Complex Disputes": 236–40.
[81]See Marc Galanter, "Why the 'Haves' Come Out Ahead."
[82]Hollingsworth et. al., "The Ohio Small Claims Court": 466.
[83]Yngvesson and Hennessey, "Small Claims, Complex Disputes": 244–45, Table 6. In the Iowa study 66 percent of court judgments were by default. See Elwell with Carlson, "The Iowa Small Claims Court": 505–06.
[84]National Institute for Consumer Justice, *Staff Studies*, 17.

Some excerpts from researchers' notes of a study of the Boston Small Claims Court illustrates some of the problems:

1. A college graduate, an engineer, age twenty-seven, experienced the following:

   > Mr. M. was hit in his car by an MBTA bus. He prepared his case and went to court without a lawyer. His case was almost defaulted because no one was there from the MBTA. However, another lawyer, who sometimes works for the MBTA heard the MBTA's name mentioned and asked the hearing be extended for a week. Thus, the plaintiff lost two days of work. He furthermore lost the case.

2. A retired truck driver, age eighty-four, who did not finish grammar school experienced the following:

   > Plaintiff was suing a union to collect on thirteen weeks' benefits ($70) for medical expenses afforded by his membership paid to the union. When he showed the judge his records of membership and medical forms, the plaintiff was told he was an embarrassment and to get out of court—(the implication of this statement according to the plaintiff, was that $70 was a trifling sum to be suing for). The judge then politely listened to the union's representative who claimed the plaintiff was specifically exempted from collecting under the old by-law. The plaintiff was so angered by the judge's treatment of him that he wrote to the Chief Judge of Boston Municipal Court to report the first judge's conduct. Thus far, he has not received a response to this letter. The plaintiff feels that if small claims courts are going to be administered [by] such "fish-monger judges," then they ought to be abolished.

3. An engineer aid, age fifty-six, a high school graduate, experienced the following:

   > When Mr. F. and the law student (his counsel) arrived in court on the appointed day they were told in an abrupt and off-handed manner by a clerk that there had been no service on the complaint. Neither Mr. F. nor the law student knew what "no service" meant and the court employee, who seemed to think that they really ought to know, was unpleasant. Mr. F. is upset because he lost a full day's pay and he thinks he should have been notified when the letter was undeliverable and told what to do at that time.[85]

Probably because of low cost and simplified procedures, a larger percentage of small claims cases actually reaches trial than in most other courts. Among 11 separate small claims studies that gathered data on this point, an average of 53.4 percent of the claims actually went to trial, the remainder being dismissed at the request of the plaintiff or otherwise settled before trial.[86] As in other courts, the filing of a claim is often sufficient to induce the defendant to come to terms in private negotiations. In fact, this is the deliberate strategy frequently employed by businesses in order to coerce the customer, tenant, or medical patient into settlement. Usually represented by an attorney, such business plaintiffs are often successful in these tactics. In the Ohio study, attorneys reported that they commonly called defendants before trial in an attempt to settle. As an executive of a dry-cleaning business in Boston stated, "Small Claims Court is efficient in scaring people into paying debts."[87]

An important part of the small claims procedure is the mediation and conciliation process prior to, or even part of, the "trial." Court clerks, pretrial mediators or arbitrators, or often the judge will lean on the parties in an attempt to settle the matter. Thus, the most

---

[85]National Institute for Consumer Justice, *Staff Studies:* 389.

[86]Yngvesson and Hennessey, "Small Claims, Complex Disputes": 244–45, Table 6. Small claims trials are discussed in some detail in Elwell with Carlson, "The Iowa Small Claims Court": 494–505.

[87]National Institute for Consumer Justice, *Staff Studies,* 391.

important function these courts often play is as "conversation pits" for bringing the parties together under the threat of uncertain and possibly unfavorable adjudicatory consequences should such pretrial talks fail.[88] A common scene in small claims court will find the judge speaking to the parties a few moments, then suggesting that they go outside in the hall and settle the matter, after which they return to court and inform the judge of the nature of the settlement.

The "trial" itself in small claims court is likely to be less time-consuming than the preliminaries. Quite frequently, the judge's ruling is merely an approval of the previously agreed-upon settlement. An observer of 200 cases in Los Angeles Small Claims Court noted that, even in contested cases, the average trial took only 8.9 minutes, with a range of 1 minute to 21 minutes.[89] Typically, the parties are each given a brief opportunity to present their arguments, the judge may ask a question or two, and that is it! The shortage of time, often leading to cutting the litigants short, is reported as a common occurrence in small claims courts. In fact, one observer noted that even some of the plaintiffs, who are typically better prepared and more familiar with their claim than are the defendants, complained that they "felt that they had been 'pushed through' a maze of legal boxes by unfeeling and disinterested court personnel, and consequently, that they were given little time to explain their cases."[90]

Although the plaintiffs, whether they be corporations, proprietorships, or individuals, are the overwhelming winners in small claims court (in separate courts in six states, plaintiffs won at least 85 percent of the cases), collection is another matter. Few, if any, of the small claims courts have institutionalized collection procedures, meaning that the "victorious" plaintiff must rely on yet other processes to realize actual payment of an award. Overall, small claims studies indicate that at least 25 percent of successful plaintiffs were unable to collect anything at all. For the two Ohio courts studied, this figure was 60 percent. Again, the corporate and proprietorship plaintiffs fared much better than did individual plaintiffs, the former collecting at least partial payment, in the Ohio study, in 68 percent of the cases.[91] Frustrations with small claims courts on the collection issue were angrily recorded by "successful" individual plaintiffs in the Boston Small Claims Court:

---

[88]National Institute for Consumer Justice, *Staff Studies:* see "Settlement," 156–63. Mediatory services of a somewhat more formal nature are becoming more common in small claims courts. See, e.g., Roselle L. Wissler, "Mediation and Adjudication in the Small Claims Court: The Effects of Process and Case Characteristics," *Law and Society Review,* 29, No. 2 (May 1995): 323–58; and J. Peder Zane, "Tell It to the Judge . . . but Only If You Really Feel You Must," *New York Times* (July 16, 1995): F-8. Eighty-five percent of the claims in New York City, it is said, are settled through mediation or arbitration, never reaching a judge except for final approval.

[89]As reported in Yngvesson and Hennessey, "Small Claims, Complex Disputes": 252, n. 27. In the Iowa study, perhaps because the settings are a bit more rural, trial time was a little longer: 38 percent of the plaintiffs and 22 percent of the defendants reported trial time of 15 minutes or less, while half-hour trials were reported by 32 percent of plaintiffs and 26 percent of defendants. See Elwell with Carlson, "The Iowa Small Claims Court": 498.

[90]Yngvesson and Hennessey, "Small Claims, Complex Disputes": 252. An almost identical finding is reported from the Iowa study. In questioning litigants, the researchers said, "It is clear from the comments made that some of these individuals were quite distressed by being rushed through the trial and by the seeming unwillingness of the judge to listen to them." Elwell with Carlson, "The Iowa Small Claims Court": 498, n. 391.

[91]See Hollingsworth et. al., "Ohio Small Claims Court": 483. This misunderstanding about the power of these courts to force compliance was touched on in five case studies by William M. O'Barr and John M. Conley, "Lay Expectations of the Civil Justice System," *Law and Society Review* 22, No. 1 (Feb. 1988): 137–61. In the study of the Colorado small claims court, it was found that successful plaintiffs ". . . collected only 31% of the amounts awarded; 55% of the plaintiffs collected no part of their judgments." Best, et. al., "Peace, Wealth, Happiness": 365.

1. A teacher, age twenty-nine, college graduate said that:

> She would never go to small claims court again because of the inefficient collection procedure. She had won her case against a towing company driver, who had damaged her car, but because the driver quit the company and the company changed its name and address, she was unable to collect. Mrs. H. said that it was an extremely frustrating procedure.

2. A forty-year-old college graduate, a manufacturer's representative, experienced the following:

> Six years ago Mr. S. took action against a corporation, and received a judgment. He was never able to collect his money because the corporation "escaped payment, refused to pay, they're in a special position." Mr. S. tried to collect in person, and when that failed he hired a constable who told him that it would take twenty-one years to get the money.
>
> Mr. S. thinks that if a person goes to the trouble to bring the case to small claims court and wins, it should be the court's responsibility to penalize the defendant if he doesn't pay. He thinks it is unfair to let corporations bring their attorneys into the courtroom, who use one delaying tactic after another to discourage lay plaintiffs. After sitting in the courtroom for some time watching retained corporation lawyers use legal tricks, he began to wonder if anything ever got tried.[92]

Such are the realities of "civil justice" in small claims courts. Quite similar conditions characterize other, more specialized limited jurisdiction courts and proceedings, such as housing courts,[93] mental commitment proceedings,[94] and other courts dealing with minor civil claims.[95] A low level of adversariness, lax procedural standards, and an almost "do-it-yourself" atmosphere in which the party with the greater resources—characteristic of Galanter's "repeat player"—is strongly favored.

Medical Malpractice: Obstetrics and Gynecology Cases

Our second case study of the civil judicial process is in the general area of torts, that almost indefinable category of civil actions which, in the broadest sense, encompasses virtually all civil wrongs other than breach of contract. From the early part of the twentieth century, American tort law has been dominated by automobile accident cases. As already noted, these, together with other personal injury disputes, property damage, and wrongful death issues, make up the bulk of tort litigation, now accounting for about 14 percent of all civil cases in state general trial courts. Approximately one million tort actions were filed in all state courts in 1993, with another 43,000 filings in federal district courts. On the basis of a nationwide study of such litigation in seventy-five of the largest (most populous) counties for 1992 in state courts of general jurisdiction (tribunals that process some 96 percent of all tort actions), the breakdown of specific types of tort cases is presented in Table 8–6.

---

[92]National Institute for Consumer Justice, *Staff Studies,* 390–91.

[93]See, for example, an excellent study by Mark H. Lazerson, "In the Halls of Justice, The Only Justice Is in the Halls," in Richard L. Abel, ed., *The Politics of Informal Justice,* Vol. 1, *The American Experience* (New York: Academic Press, 1982), 119–63.

[94]See, e.g., Thomas J. Scheff, "Social Conditions for Rationality: How Urban and Rural Courts Deal with the Mentally Ill," *American Behavioral Scientist* 7, No. 7 (Mar. 1964): 21–24.

[95]In general, see Jerome E. Carlin, "Courts and the Poor," Paper prepared for delivery at the 1966 annual meeting of the American Political Science Association, New York City, Sept. 6–10.

A very good example of the repetition of the small claims process is the "eviction court" in Los Angeles. See Bob Baker, "Crowded Courtrooms Serve as Battleground for L. A.'s Eviction Wars," *Los Angeles Times* (June 11, 1989): Metro 1.

Table 8–6   Types of Tort Cases in State Courts of General Jurisdiction, 1992

Type of Case	Percent of Total
Auto accident	60.1
Premises liability[a]	17.3
Product liability[b]	3.4
Intentional injury[c]	2.9
Malpractice	
Medical[d]	4.9
Nonmedical[e]	1.8
Slander/libel[f]	.8
Toxic substance[g]	1.6
Unknown tort	1.2
Other negligence	5.9

[a]Injury caused by the dangerous condition of property.
[b]Injury or damage caused by defective products.
[c]Vandalism or other personal injury.
[d]By doctor, dentist, or other medical practitioner.
[e]Engineers or architects.
[f]Injury to reputation.
[g]Injury caused by toxic substances, here primarily asbestos.
Source: U.S. Dept. of Justice, Bureau of Justice Statistics, *Tort Cases in Large Counties* (Washington: Bureau of Justice Statistics, Apr. 1995): Table 1, and p. 6.

With medical malpractice cases at only some 5 percent of all state court tort actions (and less than 4 percent of federal tort filings), this particular grievance does not weigh heavily in the overall statistical picture of tort cases. Yet, these cases are at the very heart of the raging national debate over tort reform. Partially for that reason, medical malpractice has been the subject of intense research in recent years—research of an unusually high quality. It is for these reasons that we have selected this subject for our second case study.

For some three decades now, a cry of alarm has been heard from the medical community, bolstered by a chorus of conservative political voices, over the malpractice "crisis."[96] Malpractice is often seen as the most serious issue facing medical practitioners. A particularly sharp cry has been heard from specialists in the area of obstetrics and gynecology (ob-gyn), the emphasis of this case study. Thus, in his address to the Central Association of Ob-

[96]See, e.g., Frank A. Sloan et. al., *Suing for Medical Malpractice* (Chicago: University of Chicago Press, 1993), Editorial, "Beyond Tort Reform," *Journal of the American Medical Association* 257, No. 6 (Feb. 13, 1987): 827–28; Neil Vidmar, *Medical Malpractice and the American Jury: Confronting Myths About Jury Incompetence, Deep Pockets, and Outrageous Damage Awards* (Ann Arbor: University of Michigan Press, 1995): Sec. I; Michael J. Saks, "Malpractice Misconceptions and Other Lessons About the Litigation System," *Justice System Journal* 16, No. 2 (1993): 7–8; and Hensler, "Taking Aim at the American Legal System." The literature of the malpractice debate is also reviewed in Paul C. Weiler et. al., *A Measure of Malpractice: Medical Injury, Malpractice Litigation, and Patient Compensation* (Cambridge: Harvard University Press, 1993), Ch. 2

stetricians and Gynecologists in Detroit in 1984, Dr. Kenneth J. Vander Kolk rhetorically asked his medical colleagues, "Will the unlimited classes of graduating lawyers increase the number involved in unbridled, insensitive, inconsiderate, and unethical litigation?" He went on to complain that it is the physicians who "are the logical scapegoats and are an easy prey for the hustling attorney who initiates a lawsuit."[97] Thus, once again, it is the evils of the legal profession and the legal system, rather than the incompetence of the medical practitioner[98] or the greed of insurance companies[99] that are at fault for the alleged crisis. Juries decide cases irrationally, it is charged, giving excessively large awards to undeserving patients.[100] Advanced but imperfect medical techniques, rather than physician error, are said to be the cause of much medical malpractice litigation. Driven by such beliefs, pressures mount to bring about reform in our entire tort system.

Such are the claims, but what are the facts? Are aggrieved medical patients quick to name, blame, claim, and push for unconscionably high jury awards? Has litigation run wild in this area? Or does the transformation process from grievance, or potential grievance, to disputing, and on to the filing of a civil claim, more closely resemble the now familiar patterns just described? An insightful and, as it turns out, quite representative study of ob-gyn cases going to jury trial from 1981 to 1985 in 46 counties in 11 states was undertaken by Stephen Daniels and Lori Andrews. Data from this research, originally presented in an ABF (American Bar Foundation) working paper, forms the basis of most of what follows.

To understand the processing of disputes in this area, as in any other, it is necessary—or certainly highly desirable—to begin with a baseline of the universe of at-risk cases; here, that would mean an estimate of just how much malpractice there is. For all other areas of tort research, what might be called the "injury base" has never been determined.[101] Much recent research on medical malpractice, however, has been successful in establishing this base.

---

[97]Kenneth J. Vander Kolk, "Is That All There Is?" *American Journal of Obstetrics and Gynecology* 152, No. 2 (May 15, 1985): 140, 142. The Vander Kolk speech was used as a starting point for a study of jury awards in ob-gyn cases. See Stephen Daniels and Lori Andrews, "The Shadow of the Law: Jury Decisions in Obstetrics and Gynecology Cases," in Victoria P. Rostow and Roger J. Bulger, eds., *Medical Professional Liability and the Delivery of Obstetrical Care: An Interdisciplinary Review,* Vol. II (Washington: National Academy Press, 1989): 161–62.

[98]Numerous studies have documented the high, if not shocking, incidence of medical negligence, most of which goes uncontested. Notes one writer:

> This research has found rates of negligent injury ranging from 1 of every 46 hospital discharges . . . to 1 of every 127 . . . to 1 in 100. . . . In the most recent study, more than half of the "adverse events" . . . resulted in minor transient disability, 9 percent resulted in disability of greater than 6 months, and 14 percent resulted in death. About 2,500 cases of permanent total disability resulted from medical injury in New York [state] hospitals in 1984. About 27 percent of all the injuries were judged to be the result of medical negligence.

Saks, "Malpractice Misconceptions": 9–10.

See also the disturbing data presented in Sam Howe Verhovek, "Whispered Factor in Rising Cost of Care: Medical Incompetence," *New York Times* (April 9, 1994): A-1; and Joseph T. Hallian and Susan M. Headden, "A Case of Neglect: Medical Malpractice in Indiana," *Indiana Star* (June 24, 1990): A-1.

[99]For the role of the insurance industry in the "tort crisis," see Sylvia Law and Steven Polan, *Pain and Profit: The Politics of Malpractice* (New York: Harper Row, 1978), especially Ch. 9; and Ralph Nader, "The Assault on Injured Victims' Rights," *Denver University Law Review* 64, No. 4 (1988): 625–39. The insurance industry's attack on civil juries is also discussed in Daniels, "The Question of Jury Competence": passim.

[100]A significant portion of medical malpractice research has been devoted to jury behavior. See especially Vidmar, *Medical Malpractice and the American Jury,* in which a considerable body of research is reviewed and new data presented from a North Carolina study.

[101]See Saks, "Malpractice Misconceptions": 9.

For example, using data supplied by the ABF study of ob-gyn cases by Daniels and Andrews, it was suggested that as many as 1 in 20 medical decisions may be made erroneously, with some studies placing the figure much higher, perhaps as many as 1 in 4. Using the more conservative 5 percent estimate and drawing data from the state of Texas as an example, with 295,000 live births in that state in 1983, there would presumably be some 14,750 ob-gyn medical errors. Daniels and Andrews have suggested that no more than 10 percent of such aggrieved patients may be expected to file a claim, probably fewer. For ob-gyn cases in Texas in that year, then, a 10 percent ratio would have been expected to produce some 1,475 civil filings for malpractice. In fact, however, there were only 219 claims filed in all ob-gyn cases in the state that year, or only about 1.5 percent of possible suits! Even if researchers have overestimated the incidence of medical error by 100 percent (giving us a ratio of 1:40 rather than 1:20), one could still predict nearly 750 malpractice suits filed in Texas in 1983, whereas less than a third of even that reduced estimate were actually filed.[102]

Using these estimates, then, ob-gyn cases may be represented by a pyramid with extremely flat sides, the ratio of actual court filings to possible claims being about 1 for every 150 possible medical errors. Such a ratio, or even half this many claims, can hardly be said to reflect litigation mania on the part of aggrieved patients. Rather, what we find is a relatively timid patient population hesitant to perceive a grievance; and, if a patient does perceive a grievance, that patient will likely be reluctant to resort to litigation, formal or informal, to assuage his or her loss. Citing similar findings in malpractice claims in Wisconsin, researchers Daniels and Andrews conclude that "[M]ost patients who are injured by medical error will not pursue a claim. . . . The most common responses to patient dissatisfaction were to 'lump it' (do nothing) or simply to change doctors."[103]

Stated differently, the transformation process here, which is quite similar to that seen in other areas of civil law, negates claims of extreme litigiousness. In fact, a comparison of the grievance-to-court claim pyramid in tort cases in general with that just described for ob-gyn cases suggests that these medical grievants are less than half as likely to go to court as are tort victims in general.

Other research undertaken since the ob-gyn study tends to support these general conclusions. Perhaps the most widely cited recent study of medical malpractice is the so-called *Harvard Medical Malpractice Study,* released in 1990 and published in a series of books and articles since then.[104] From a sample of 31,000 medical patients hospitalized in New York state in 1984, physicians and other researchers developed the inverse dispute pyramid depicted in Figure 8–5. Other studies in North Carolina, Florida, and California report similar transformation profiles.[105]

Returning to the ob-gyn data, what happens when these cases reach court? From our general knowledge of the civil litigation process, we might expect most of these cases to be settled out of court, with very few going to trial. And indeed, this is the outcome. Estimates of the percentage of filings of ob-gyn cases settled before trial run from 70 to 90 percent, about the same proportion as in other areas of both civil and criminal law. To what extent does the plaintiff win in these cases? Again, estimates vary with the particular study and jurisdiction, but in general less than half result in some payment to the patient. A study by the National Association of Insurance Commissioners in 1980 found that only 46 percent

---

[102]Daniels and Andrews, "Jury Decisions in Obstetric and Gynecology Cases": 166–67.

[103]Daniels and Andrews, "Jury Decisions in Obstetric and Gynecology Cases": 166.

[104]See, e.g., Weiler, *A Measure of Malpractice.* The Harvard Study's findings are also reviewed in Saks, "Malpractice Misconceptions," and in a number of newspaper items, such as Jane E. Brody, "Personal Health," *New York Times* (Apr. 26, 1990): B-7; and John J. Goldman, "4% Got Disabling Injury in N.Y. Hospitals, Study Finds," *Los Angeles Times* (Mar. 1, 1990): A-1.

[105]Again, the best brief review of these studies is Saks, "Malpractice Misconceptions."

Of every 10,000 hospital patients:

- 9,630 will experience no adverse events.
- 370 of these will suffer adverse events, but
- 270 will be without negligence. Of the
- 100 negligent adverse events, in
- 98 no claims for compensation will be made. Of the
- 2 claims made, only
- 1 will receive any compensation.

Figure 8–5   Medical Negligence and Resulting Litigation (SOURCE: *Patients, Doctors, and Lawyers: Medical Injury, Malpractice Litigation, and Patient Compensation in New York: The Report of the Harvard Medical Practice Study to the State of New York* (Boston: Harvard School of Public Health, 1990), passim. This chart is drawn from the Harvard study data as presented in Michael J. Saks, "Malpractice Misconceptions and Other Lessons About the Litigation System," *Justice System Journal* 16, No. 2 (1993): Table 1, p. 9.)

of insurance claims in malpractice cases generally resulted in any payment to the claimant, whereas from the Texas data unearthed by Daniels and Andrews, only 20 percent of the ob-gyn claims resulted in a payment.[106]

The percentage of cases going to jury trial, then, is quite small, usually well under 10 percent. However, as we have learned, jury verdicts can cast a long shadow over the contours of future bargaining, so it is useful to examine briefly jury outcomes in this area.

The ob-gyn study tabulated the particulars of 24,625 civil jury verdicts in 46 trial court jurisdictions in 11 states in the years 1981–1985. Of these, 7.7 percent (1,885) were medical malpractice cases, and of this group 364 cases were identified as ob-gyn cases (19.3 percent of malpractice cases and 1.5 percent of all civil jury cases).

If one defines success as the award of at least one dollar by the jury, one finds that the patients filing these cases and going to jury trials did not fare well. The success rate of plaintiffs in general malpractice was 32.4 percent; in obstetrics and gynecology cases it was slightly higher, at 36.8 percent. This rate may be contrasted with the success rate of civil jury outcomes in general, which was 57 percent.[107] Thus, contrary to the nationwide outcry over the malpractice "crisis," juries are not overly anxious to find for the medical patient in these cases.

Daniels and Andrews dug into their data to answer at least two further questions: First, was there evidence of irrational jury verdicts, or did the jury decisions bear a logical relationship to the type and severity of the injury inflicted by the medical practitioners? Second, were these medical errors associated with, if not caused by, the newer, untested technologies, as alleged by many physicians, or were they more closely correlated with old and well-established procedures inappropriately applied? Measuring the severity of injury (from death to emotional injury only) on a four-point scale, these researchers found that the jury was somewhat more likely to find for the plaintiff if the injury were more severe. And again contrary to claims of the medical profession, juries tended to react more harshly against defendants when the injury was associated with the older, more well-established technologies.

[106]Daniels and Andrews, "The Shadow of the Law": 166.
[107]Stephen Daniels and Joanne Martin, "Jury Verdicts and the 'Crisis' in Civil Justice: Some Findings from an Empirical Study," *Justice System Journal* 11, No. 3 (1986): 332.

One particularly poignant example illustrating both of these points was the use of oxytocin (usual trade name: *Pitocin*) to induce labor. The dangers of this well-known drug had been widely publicized in physicians' reference works and journals for several decades. Of the 16 jury trials involving the alleged misuse of oxytocin (when the drug was contraindicated by the medical literature), the plaintiff was successful in 14 (87.5 percent).[108] This rate may be contrasted with a 45 percent success rate for all labor and delivery jury trials in the sample and the 37 percent success rate for all ob-gyn cases. Of these 16 cases, *all* led to permanent injury or death. As the ABF researchers conclude, "In the oxytocin cases . . . juries appear to have responded in no uncertain terms to the misuse of an old, established technology whose limitations and contraindications were well known and widely disseminated."[109]

Do the data support the claim that monetary jury awards in medical malpractice, and particularly ob-gyn cases, have become excessive? This, of course, is similar to the question of whether the glass of water is half empty or half full. But weighed against the background of the average or, more precisely, the median jury award in these nearly 26,000 cases, how did the medical awards compare? The median jury award in all of these civil cases was only $25,000 (1985), whereas in ob-gyn cases it was much higher, $390,000. However, in view of the seriousness of these cases, nearly 60 percent involving a permanent injury or death and in view of the tendency of juries to award the higher settlements to the more severely injured, this figure might not seem inordinately high.

In conclusion, researchers have found that patients are still highly reluctant to bring legal action against their physicians and hospitals, even when medical error seems apparent. And when they do sue, the physician usually wins the case. In the few but significant cases decided by juries, capricious or random decision making does not appear to be the rule. Rather, there is a relationship between the severity of injury (as well as the type of medical procedure) and jury awards. In the relatively infrequent cases in which the plaintiff wins, the amount of jury awards, especially in ob-gyn cases, are high but perhaps reasonable in relation to the seriousness of the injury. Thus, as with the cry of hyperlexis in general, little if any empirical evidence from medical malpractice cases thus far discovered can be said to support charges of a litigation explosion. Rather, it seems more likely that as Galanter remarked, it is the case of entrenched elites complaining because they are being forced to the bar of public accountability, even though the level of accountability as measured by suits filed and compensation awarded seems not unreasonably high.

Because so few medical patients ever resort to legal action, and because only about half of those who do receive any compensation at all, the Harvard Study concluded that "there are about sixteen times as many patients who suffer an injury from [medical] negligence as there are persons who receive compensation through the tort system."[110] That medical malpractice is but a microcosm of tort litigation generally as regards compensation

---

[108]Daniels and Andrews, "The Shadow of the Law": 190.

[109]Daniels and Andrews, "The Shadow of the Law": 191.

[110]*Patients, Doctors, and Lawyers: Medical Injury, Malpractice Litigation, and Patient Compensation in New York: The Report of the Harvard Medical Practice Study to the State of New York.* (Boston: Harvard School of Public Health, 1990): Ch. 7, 7–1.

The claim that the poor and uninsured file a disproportionate share of medical malpractice claims, perhaps with a view to gaining a "fast buck," is also refuted by empirical evidence drawn from the Harvard Study. In fact, the reverse is true, with poor patients bringing claims only about 10 percent to 20 percent as often as middle- and upper-middle-class patients. See Douglas P. Shuit, "Poor Unlikely to Sue for Malpractice, Study Finds," *Los Angeles Times* (Oct. 13, 1993): B-8. The complete data are reported in H. R. Burstin et. al., "Do the Poor Sue More? A Case Control Study of Malpractice Claims and Socioeconomic Status," *Journal of the American Medical Association* 270, No. 14 (Oct. 13, 1993): 1697–1710.

was underscored in a Rand Corporation study published in 1991.[111] Drawing from that study, Michael Saks reasoned that

> [I]n a given year Americans suffered *$175.9 billion* in direct losses . . . from nonfatal accidents of all kinds. Awards and settlements resulted in compensation of only $7.7 billion, a little more than *4 percent* of the total. The victims themselves and the public treasury . . . wind up bearing most of the burden, not those responsible for the injuries. As an injury compensation system, the tort system thus approaches non-existence[112] (emphasis added).

CONCLUSIONS

Several additional areas of civil law could be explored, from complex tort actions to the highly focused administrative process in probate court. But the central point would remain the same, and it is nowhere better stated than by H. Laurence Ross in his classic study of automobile accident litigation:

> This is a book about law, though it seldom mentions court rooms, judges, pleadings and motions, or even juries and verdicts. This book is concerned with the law in action, with the legal system as it operates for the ordinary citizen on a day-to-day basis. *The principal institution of the law in action is not trial; it is settlement out of court.*[113]

The emphasis in contemporary social science approaches to judicial studies on pretrial bargaining should not blind us to the continuing role of formal litigation. Courts, of course, still conduct trials, and court holdings still constitute rules of conduct having significant effects on the political-legal system. However, the Pound-Llewellian "Law in Action" view suggests that day-to-day judicial outcomes are the *direct* result of informal, often do-it-yourself bargaining (as seen in small claims, divorce actions, and medical malpractice cases), and only *indirectly* the result of formal judicial action. This is as true in and around small claims court as it is in major actions in federal district courts. The basic figures tell much of the story. Going to trial are only about 10 percent of divorce filings, no more than 20 percent of all cases in general jurisdiction trial courts, and less than 5 percent even in federal district courts, with the proportion there in a steady decline. As Galanter writes,

> The impact of courts on disputes is to an important extent accomplished by the dissemination of information. Courts produce not only decisions, but messages. Their product is

---

[111]See Deborah Hensler et. al., *Compensation for Accidental Injuries in the United States* (Santa Monica, Calif.: Rand Corporation, 1991).

[112]Michael J. Saks, "Malpractice Roulette," *New York Times* (July 3, 1993): A-11. Despite the small percentage of medical injury for which compensation is ever awarded, medical practitioners continue to push for a reduction in levels of litigation, often via public relations campaigns designed to place the most favorable light on medical "accidents." Thus, in his address to the Central Association of Obstetricians and Gynecologists, Dr. Kenneth J. Vander Kolk, while labeling lawyers ". . . insensitive, inconsiderate, and unethical . . . ," pushed strenuously for the use of euphemisms in ob-gyn cases:

> . . . [L]et us drop the word "malpractice," which literally means bad practice, and use the words "professional liability." We must make every attempt to substitute the term "neurologically deficient" in place of "brain-damaged child," which generates those megabucks settlements from misinformed juries."

Vander Kolk, "Is That All There Is?" 140, 142.

[113]Ross, *Settled Out of Court,* 3 (emphasis added).

double: what they do and what they say about what they do. Messages about both are mediated through various channels to different audiences. These messages are resources which parties and others use in envisioning, devising, pursuing, negotiating and vindicating claims (and in avoiding, defending and defeating them).

. . . Law is more capacious as a system of cultural and symbolic meanings than as a set of operative controls. It affects us primarily through communication of symbols—by providing threats, promises, models, persuasion, legitimacy, stigma, etc.[114]

For too long we have tended to ignore or understate the many-faceted civil judicial process, instead focusing inordinate attention on the attractions of criminal law. Relatively recent research such as the Civil Litigation Research Project, empirical studies of divorce proceedings,[115] the boom in tort studies, and a host of other research forays have brought new excitement to the study of civil law, focusing attention on the entire "landscape of disputing," terrain that heretofore has been under-appreciated by students of the American judiciary.[116] Although we have long understood the importance of pretrial bargaining in criminal cases, it is only recently that we are beginning to explore the world of private and semiprivate dispute processing and settlement in the millions of civil legal disputes that dominate the American judicial process. Research findings presented here should help alert readers to this important and fast-developing field of scholarship.

FURTHER READING

Blakenburg, Erhard. "A Flood of Litigation? Legal Cultures and Litigation Flows Before European Courts in Historical Perspective." *Justice System Journal* 16, No. 1 (1992): 101–10.

Daniels, Stephen, and Joanne Martin. "Myth and Reality in Punitive Damages. *Minnesota Law Review* 75, No. 1 (Oct. 1990): 1–64.

Elwell, Suzanne E., with Christopher D. Carlson. "The Iowa Small Claims Court: An Empirical Analysis." *Iowa Law Review* 75, Nos. 1–2 (January 1990): 433–538.

Galanter, Marc. "Justice in Many Rooms: Courts, Private Ordering, and Indigenous Law." *Journal of Legal Pluralism* 19 (1981): 1–47.

---

[114]Galanter, "Justice in Many Rooms": 13.

[115]The first edition of this text presented a case study of divorce proceedings. There, much of the commentary relied on the seminal article by Mnookin and Kornhauser, "Bargaining in the Shadow of the Law: The Case of Divorce," and on Ralph C. Cavanaugh and Deborah L. Rhode, "The Unauthorized Practice of Law and Pro Se Divorce: An Empirical Analysis," *Yale Law Journal* 86, No. 1 (Nov. 1976): 126–27. For subsequent research, see Sarat and Felstiner, "Law and Strategy in the Divorce Lawyer's Office"; Herbert Jacob, *The Silent Revolution: The Transformation of Divorce Law in the United States* (Chicago: University of Chicago Press, 1988); Herbert Jacob, "The Elusive Shadow of the Law," *Law and Society Review* 26, No. 3 (1992): 565–90; and Craig A. McEwen, Lynn Mather, and Richard J. Mainman, "Lawyers, Mediation and the Management of Divorce Practice," *Law and Society Review* 28, No. 1 (1994): 149–87.

[116]Such highly focused empirical research has now made possible some excellent, more broadbrush works on the civil judicial process, such as Kritzer's *The Justice Broker*; and Wayne V. McIntosh, *The Appeal of Civil Law: A Political-Economic Analysis of Litigation* (Urbana: University of Illinois Press, 1990).

The plea here for a broadening of political scientists' traditional concerns (often limited to, or at least heavily focused on, constitutional law) is made more fully, and with specific reference to the "litigation explosion" and the expansion of research on tort law, by Stephen L. Wasby in his recent piece, "What Public Law Scholars Should Know: More than Constitutional Law," *Law and Courts: Newsletter of the Law and Courts Section of the American Political Science Association* 5, No. 1 (Spring 1995): 6–7. Of course, the same point is made in a different way by Martin Shapiro in his survey of research in the subfield, "Public Law and Judicial Politics," in Ada W. Finifter, *Political Science: The State of the Discipline, II* (Washington: American Political Science Association, 1993), especially his concluding argument on 376–77.

——. "Reading the Landscape of Disputes: What We Know (and Think We Know) About Our Allegedly Contentious and Litigious Society." *UCLA Law Review* 31, No. 1 (Oct. 1983): 5–71.

——. "News from Nowhere: The Debased Debate on Civil Justice." *Denver University Law Review* 71, No. 1 (1993): 77–113.

——. "Why the 'Haves' Come Out Ahead: Speculations on the Limits of Legal Change." *Law and Society Review* 9, No. 1 (Fall 1974): 95–160.

Harvard Medical Malpractice Study. *Patients, Doctors, and Lawyers: Medical Injury, Malpractice Litigation, and Patient Compensation in New York.* Boston: Harvard School of Public Health, 1990.

Kritzer, Herbert M. *The Justice Broker: Lawyers and Ordinary Litigation.* New York: Oxford University Press, 1990.

Law and Society Review. Special Issue on Dispute Processing and Civil Litigation 15, Nos. 3–4 (1980–1981).

McIntosh, Wayne V. *The Appeal of Civil Law: A Political-Economic Analysis of Litigation.* Urbana: University of Illinois Press, 1990.

Mnookin, Robert H., and Lewis Kornhauser. "Bargaining in the Shadow of the Law: The Case of Divorce." *Yale Law Journal* 88, No. 5 (Apr. 1979): 950–97.

Nader, Laura, ed. *No Access to Law: Alternatives to the American Judicial System.* New York: Academic Press, 1980.

Ostrom, Brian J., and Neal B. Kauder. *Examining the Work of State Courts, 1993.* Williamsburg, Va.: National Center for State Courts, 1995.

Ross, H. Laurence. *Settled Out of Court: The Social Process of Insurance Claims Adjustments.* New York: Aldine, 1980.

Saks, Michael J. "Do We Really Know Anything About the Behavior of the Tort Litigation System—And Why Not?" *University of Pennsylvania Law Review* 140, No. 4 (April 1992): 1147–1291.

——. "Malpractice Misconceptions and Other Lessons About the Litigation System." *Justice System Journal* 16, No. 2 (1993): 7–19.

Sarat, Austin, and Joel B. Grossman. "Courts and Conflict Resolution: Problems in the Mobilization of Adjudication." *American Political Science Review* 69, No. 4 (Dec. 1975): 1200–17.

Sloan, Frank A. et. al. *Suing for Medical Malpractice.* Chicago: University of Chicago Press, 1993.

Vidmar, Neil. *Medical Malpractice and the American Jury: Confronting Myths about Jury Incompetence, Deep Pockets, and Outrageous Damage Awards.* Ann Arbor: University of Michigan Press, 1995.

Weiler, Paul C., et. al. *A Measure of Malpractice: Medical Injury, Malpractice Litigation, and Patient Compensation.* Cambridge: Harvard University Press, 1993.

9

The Judicial Process in Criminal Cases

All the significant participants in the court's social structure are bound into an organized system of complicity. Patterned, covert, informal breaches and invasions of "due process" are accepted as routine—they are institutionalized—but are nevertheless denied to exist.

—Abraham Blumberg,
Criminal Justice

The public has been led to believe that the purpose of the judicial system is to search for truth. That's not so. The purpose of the judicial system is to get convictions.

—Jerry Paul,
"We Won Because I Could Buy the Things to Win"

Even more than on the civil side, the process and outcomes of our criminal judicial system have become matters of intense and widespread public concern, resulting in the politicization of criminal legal issues far beyond that of any other aspect of the judicial process. Indeed, "law and order," "crime in the streets," and similar symbolic manifestations of the "crime problem" have spilled over into academe, where criminal justice has become the subject of a veritable explosion of research and teaching. Matters relating to police behavior, training, and socialization; the multifaceted prosecutorial role; the function and effectiveness of defense attorneys; issues involving the jury system, the insanity plea, juvenile justice, sentencing, the impact of imprisonment—these and many other aspects of the criminal justice system have become the focus of increased sociolegal research (much of it federally funded), leading to the development of a quasi-separate, if not fully detached, discipline of criminal justice studies in and around the traditional disciplines of law, political science, and sociology.[1]

---

[1]See, for example, Lloyd E. Ohlin and Frank J. Remington, eds., *Discretion in Criminal Justice* (Albany, New York: State University of New York Press, 1993), 301–302, describing the establishment of undergrad-

Given this dramatic escalation in research, it is now all but impossible to cover the salient aspects of the criminal justice process in a single chapter. For example, what was once but a handful of empirical studies on police behavior has now grown to hundreds, if not thousands, of research forays.[2] The same can be said for most other topics of the judicial process in criminal cases. However, as with the civil justice process, we can focus on a relatively narrow set of questions, leaving ancillary issues for consideration by specialists in the field.

What we have learned thus far about the civil judicial system gives some guidance as to which questions must be addressed. First, it is important to make explicit the linkages between the subsystem (here, the criminal judicial process) and the larger legal, political, and social system. We now have enough knowledge about courts to conceptualize them as subunits of the larger political system, but it is important, particularly concerning the criminal judicial process, to note the precise ways in which system and subsystem interact. This is because, as we noted earlier, the criminal judicial process, perhaps more than any other part of the American judicial system, is sensitive to the push and pull of forces outside itself, so that a person simply cannot understand the ways we adjudicate criminal cases without giving attention to these linkages. Second, our orientation suggests that we will need to emphasize the "is's" rather than the "oughts" of the process, or as Pound would have it, the "law in action" as opposed to "law in the books." Hence, we will be calling up the Llewellyn concept of law as "what officials do . . . about disputes" rather than what formal descriptions of the process indicate officials should do. Lastly, as we did in the previous chapter on the civil judicial process, we will describe the forces and influences at work in explaining outcomes. That is, what factors help us to explain the movement of cases through the process? These three points of departure should suffice to help us thread our way through the maze which has become the modern American criminal judicial process.

THE POLITICS OF CRIMINAL LAW

That criminal laws even exist reflects the desire, and perhaps the need, felt by discrete social groups for a mechanism by which to exercise and maintain control over individual group members. Certainly, criminal law does not stand alone as a means to that end: religion and other "moral" codes, customs and traditions, schools, families, even the civil legal system all play some part in the maintenance of social order. However, criminal law is somehow

---

uate and graduate level programs devoted to the study of criminal justice. Particularly with respect to political science, one may contrast the extremely sketchy coverage of criminal law issues in Henry J. Abraham's first edition of his monumental work, *The Judicial Process* (New York: Oxford University Press, 1962), with entire texts such as George F. Cole's *The American System of Criminal Justice,* 6th ed. (Belmont, Calif.: Wadsworth Publishing Co., 1995); David W. Neubauer's *America's Courts & the Criminal Justice System,* 4th ed. (Belmont, Calif.: Wadsworth Publishing Co., 1992); Samuel Walker's *Sense and Nonsense About Crime: A Policy Guide* (Pacific Grove, Calif.: Brooks/Cole Publishing Co., 1985); and Stuart Nagel, Erika Fairchild, and Anthony Champagne, eds., *The Political Science of Criminal Justice* (Springfield, Ill.: Charles C. Thomas, 1983), which suggest the explosion of recent interest in the area.

[2]For a recent example, see Ellen Scrivner, "Police Brutality," in Mark Costanzo and Stuart Oskamp, eds., *Violence and the Law* (Thousand Oaks, Calif.: Sage Publications, 1994), 181–202; and Jerome H. Skolnick and James J. Fyfe, *Above the Law: Police and the Excessive Use of Force* (New York: Free Press, 1993). But also see Mark Blumberg, "Police Use of Excessive Force: Exploring Various Control Mechanisms," in Albert R. Roberts, ed., *Critical Issues in Crime and Justice,* (Thousand Oaks, Calif.: Sage Publications, 1994), 111, suggesting that most studies of police behavior are confined to a single, local department and significantly dated.

unique, perhaps, as the British legal theorist Nicola Lacey suggests, owing to the fact that it is understood to embody urgently needed collective responses to threatened or actual serious violations of society's basic, shared interests.[3] The central role of criminal law, then, has historically been both to discourage and to punish what is perceived to be seriously deviant conduct through first the threat of, and subsequently, the imposition of, various sanctions.

These fundamental notions clearly suggest the essentially political nature of criminal law and the processes by which society administers it. Although all but the hard-core anarchist will acknowledge the necessity of some form of imposed social control—a system of "criminal" law for our purposes—disagreement inevitably emerges both as to what behavior is appropriately labeled "criminal" and as to what should be done with those members of society who engage in it.

This battle is in many ways one of semantics. The behavior of certain group members is threatening or uncomfortable because other members of the group define it as such. From this perspective, "criminal" conduct is simply behavior to which we attach such a label. Thus, at any given time, the corpus of criminal law is a statement of public policy—a fundamentally *political* statement—regarding what is and what is not taboo.

Furthermore, those doing the "labeling" are typically the same individuals or groups who dominate the allocation of social resources. Thus, while "crime" may at first blush appear as a constant in society, an idea grounded in the notion of first principles that exist a priori, it is far more likely a matter of transient public policy, susceptible to significant change over time.

An obvious example of this definitional, and inherently political, phenomenon is society's response to homicide, generally understood to be the taking of a human life. Indeed, what "crime" one actually commits, if any, in killing another human being is bound up in whatever social and political norms hold sway at the time. Such acts as the execution of a death sentence by state officials, actively assisting in euthanasia, driving a motor vehicle into a pedestrian, fatally shooting a police officer, and fatally shooting a soldier from a force that the government labels "hostile"—all at least can involve killing human beings in one way or another; yet each action subjects the actor to differing levels of criminal sanction.

Clearly, then, social attitudes reflecting particular norms and values strongly influence the criminal law as it is written, as it is interpreted, and as it is enforced. The result seems to be that the sanction applied to a given action depends almost entirely upon what individual or group wields power and authority at the time that the action occurs. This is public policy—which is to say, politics—at work.

There simply is no escaping the fact that criminal law, even more clearly than civil law, reflects and responds to the political and social climate of any given period. While society certainly has a stake in the outcome of most civil disputes, as their resolutions generally extend beyond the parties themselves, criminal law is perceived to affect the immediate safety and security of virtually everyone, giving rise to more direct and intense public concern.

Thus, it is not surprising to find that particular crimes are both defined and dealt with differently at different times. Likewise, "crimes" themselves emerge and disappear from era to era, generally reflecting the policy preferences of those in power. For instance, the sale and use of alcoholic beverages in the United States was once defined as criminal conduct, largely because of the rise of politically powerful interest groups that viewed alcohol consumption as immoral. Today, there exists a different alignment of political forces, so that the widespread use, and even abuse, of alcoholic beverages is permitted.

---

[3]Nicola Lacey, *State Punishment: Political Principles and Community Values* (London: Routledge, 1988), 100–105.

Similarly, what is now regarded as a matter of privacy—attending a church, for example, or the use of contraceptives—was in times past proscribed as criminal conduct.

Linkages between the dominant sociopolitical characteristics of a particular period and the means and ends of criminal justice extend beyond initial definitions of "outlawed" behavior. Police, for example, generally act in accord with the attitudes of those in power, with the result that people of color and people living in poverty are treated more harshly than are members of the economic elite.[4]

Similarly, prosecutors are typically chosen by those who dominate a given social and political structure, and thus tend to act in accord with the prevailing values and interests of that structure. Much the same can be said of judges. As employees of the state, judges can certainly be expected to support and uphold those general sociopolitical mandates that reflect society's dominant values. All of this adds up to a criminal justice system closely linked to the political realities of the era in which it exists.

Examples of this circumstance abound. As community pressures favoring enforcement of alcohol-related traffic laws wax and wane, for instance, the treatment of offenders within the criminal justice system generally follows suit.[5] Along the same line, police, prosecutors, and judges all tend to join forces when city government periodically declares that prostitution must be brought to a halt. Furthermore, tough "law and order" talk from the executive and legislative branches typically results in longer jail or prison sentences and more frequent death sentences. Finally, any concerns regarding the conditions found in so-called "correctional" facilities are filtered through the political process, thus assuring that prisons reflect dominant attitudes toward race, class, and gender.[6]

From first to last, then, the criminal justice system is itself a political structure affirmatively charged with allocating significant resources and benefits, including individual liberty. As such, the system can be fully understood only through a thorough appreciation of the external forces that guide and shape its functioning. At the same time, because the criminal justice system is staffed throughout its ranks by professional and quasi-professional personnel seeking to implement agendas of their own—as the chief prosecutor who decides to deal more harshly with juvenile offenders or the judge who disdains uniform sentencing guidelines—an examination of the system's internal workings is also necessary.[7]

[4]Differential police treatment of individuals based upon race and perceived socioeconomic class is well documented. In general, see Skolnick and Fyfe, *Above the Law,* in which the authors discuss the brutal beating of Rodney King, an African American citizen, by Los Angeles police officers.

[5]See James B. Jacobs, *Drunk Driving: An American Dilemma* (Chicago: University of Chicago Press, 1989); and H. Laurence Ross, *Deterring the Drinking Driver: Legal Policy and Social Control* (Lexington, Mass.: Heath, 1982). For perspectives on recent attempts to generate federal government responses to drunk driving, see transcripts of the hearings chaired by New York Representative Charles Schumer on the subject, Congress, House of Representatives, Committee on the Judiciary, *Allowing Formula Grants to Be Used to Prosecute Persons Driving While Intoxicated: Hearing Before the Subcommittee on Crime and Criminal Justice of the Committee on the Judiciary,* 103rd Cong., 1st Sess., July 1, 1993. On the more general topic of the influence that local and state political values have on criminal sentencing decisions, see Martin A. Levin, *Urban Politics and the Criminal Courts* (Chicago: University of Chicago Press, 1977).

[6]See, for example, Nicole Hahn Rafter, *Partial Justice: Women, Prisons, and Social Control,* 2d. ed. (New Brunswick, N.J.: Transaction Publishers, 1990), which addresses the origin and development of prisons for women in the United States; see also Ch. 6 of Coramae Richey Mann, *Unequal Justice: A Question of Color* (Bloomington, Ind.: Indiana University Press, 1993), 220–54, entitled "Warehousing Minorities: Corrections."

[7]On the critical role of "insiders" in the criminal justice process, see Abraham S. Blumberg, "The Practice of Law as a Confidence Game: Organizational Co-option of a Profession," *Law and Society Review* 1, No. 2 (June 1967): 15–39; Abraham S. Blumberg, *Criminal Justice: Issues and Ironies,* 2nd ed. (New York: New Viewpoints, 1979); and the concept of "work group" developed in James Eisenstein and Herbert Jacob, *Felony Justice: An Organizational Analysis of Criminal Courts* (Boston: Little, Brown, 1977), Ch. 2.

CONCEPTUALIZING THE CRIMINAL JUSTICE PROCESS

In Chapter 8, we contrasted the formal, adversarial processes ascribed to the civil justice system with the rather informal, cooperative arrangements that appear to drive the actual day-to-day functioning of civil courts. This same distinction is very clearly drawn within the scholarship focused on the criminal justice system. Indeed, two models tend to dominate most discussion of criminal court operations: the *adversarial* or *due process* model, and the *crime control* model.[8]

The adversarial or due process model is the traditional, and some might say "ideal," vision of criminal court systems. It begins with the assumption that an individual accused of criminal conduct must be treated as innocent until proven otherwise, either by voluntary admission or by other evidence establishing guilt beyond a reasonable doubt. Characterized by skepticism regarding the exercise of authority, the due process model emphasizes eliminating mistakes and preventing official misconduct, even when doing so significantly hinders the efficiency with which the criminal justice system operates. As Professor Herbert Packer suggests, the due process model greatly resembles a manufacturing operation that devotes a significant effort to quality control, accepting decreases in output as the cost of error-free production.

Also critical to the due process model is the proposition that the criminal justice system itself is the appropriate forum for addressing and correcting that system's own errors and abuses. "The constable has blundered—the accused shall go free," indeed encapsulates a core due process value. Only by penalizing police and prosecutors who overstep the bounds of their authority through barring illegally seized evidence or reversing erroneously obtained convictions, can individual rights against illegitimate and intrusive government practices be protected. While the societal costs of doing so may be high—as measured in time, money, and the possibility that some individuals who are factually guilty will escape criminal sanction—they are adequately offset by the greater good achieved by protecting the appearance, as well as the reality, of "justice."

In contrast, the administrative or crime control model begins with quite different assumptions. Rather than seeing the criminal judicial process as a mechanism for effecting justice through the discovery of truth, the crime control model takes as its point of departure the perceived threat of crime and the need for institutions to deal with that threat. Criminal courts, which are such institutions, stand ready to process cases to the end that criminal activity will be suppressed.

The assumption at the outset is that the accused is guilty. The police do not go about rounding up innocent people. Those appearing on the criminal docket must, therefore, be guilty of something, and the task of the judicial process is to determine the nature of the offense as well as the appropriate punishment.

Beginning with these assumptions, the criminal justice process becomes not adversarial but administrative in nature, emphasizing the core value of efficiency. Rather than judging the process on the basis of fairness, the primary concern becomes how many cases can be processed per unit of time and money expended in doing so. Since formal trials, with prerequisite pretrial proceedings, are plodding and time-consuming exercises, the administrative model demands a system characterized by informal fact-finding, co-

---

[8]In general see Herbert L. Packer, *The Limits of the Criminal Sanction* (Stanford, Calif.: Stanford University Press, 1968); Malcolm M. Feeley, *The Process Is the Punishment: Handling Cases in Lower Criminal Courts* (New York: Russell Sage Foundation, 1979); Cole, *Criminal Justice,* 34–37; and Samuel Walker, *Taming the System: The Control of Discretion in Criminal Justice 1950–1990* (New York: Oxford University Press, 1993), 5–6.

operation, and compromise, which combine to form what has become known as "plea bargaining."

Plea bargaining involves a number of values, assumptions, and practices at odds with the due process model. Beginning with a presumption of guilt rather than of innocence, and driven by the necessity of processing maximum numbers of cases in a minimum amount of time, all elements of the system are bent on the attainment of either a guilty plea or the dismissal of charges—far more frequently, the former.

As the immediate goal, a guilty plea is sought through informal mediation and bargaining aimed at forging an acceptable compromise. Sharing the common value of efficiency, key parties involved in a particular criminal case—the prosecutor, defense counsel, the defendant, often the judge, and increasingly, the alleged victim—join in a cooperative effort to persuade the defendant to plead guilty in return for what typically become rather nebulous rewards. High bail (which results in the defendant's inability to obtain pretrial release), multiple and exaggerated charges, subtle hints aimed at the defendant's friends or family, and outright threats of heavy fines and long periods of incarceration are all tactics employed to press the accused toward an admission of guilt, thereby advancing the efficient disposition of the criminal docket. The uneven nature of this "contest," along with the predictability of its outcomes, has become a notable feature of the crime control model.

By replacing fairness with efficiency and a presumption of innocence with a presumption of guilt, the crime control model takes the adversarial process and reshapes it into a systematic means of achieving dispositions, characterized by cooperation and accommodation. Universality and formality are replaced as central tenets by a focus on individual circumstances and by informal procedures that turn, to a high degree, on prosecutorial and police discretion. The due process principle of an open and public process is set aside in favor of particularized and generally covert bargaining; the presumption of evenly matched parties to a dispute is supplanted by a decidedly paternalistic view of the defendant as the "ward" of the system, and the unpredictability of trial outcomes is replaced by a more-or-less certain result.

All of these crime control model characteristics are strikingly similar to the reality of civil litigation discussed previously in Chapter 8. In both instances, informal administrative procedure aimed at efficiently disposing of docketed cases has become the rule. However, both the civil and the criminal justice systems also maintain the adversarial ideal as something of a "last resort," available for use where nothing else succeeds in accomplishing a resolution.

Scholars of the criminal justice system seem to agree that, while neither of these models is a completely accurate guide to reality, the administrative conception comes closer to describing the actual day-to-day activities of criminal courts. For example, Professor George Cole suggests that

> [u]nlike the values expressed in the Due Process Model, in which decisions are made in the courtroom as a result of adversarial conflict, the reality of criminal justice in America is more compatible to the Crime Control Model, in which guilt is administratively determined early in the process and cases are disposed of through negotiation.[9]

Likewise, Professor David Neubauer observes that

> [t]he formal adversarial model is present only to a limited degree. Few cases ever go to trial; most defendants either plead guilty or have their cases dismissed before trial. The adversary model assumes conflict, but judges, prosecutors, and defense attorneys cooperate on a number of matters, whereas the main goal of the adversary model is to discover

---

[9]Cole, *The American System of Criminal Justice,* 36.

truth and decide guilt, a great deal of the court's attention is directed toward determining the appropriate penalty.[10]

These comments notwithstanding, few scholars of criminal law would deny that due process values continue to play an important role in actual court proceedings. Fairness can be a value in administrative as well as in adversarial procedure, just as cooperation between prosecutors and defense attorneys need not necessarily do violence to a just outcome for both society and the accused. In the main, however, most contemporary scholarship suggests that, to the extent that due process values continue to play a role within the criminal justice system, those values have been effectively subordinated to the administrative concerns inherent in the crime control model.[11]

CRIME IN AMERICA

As with the process in civil cases, it will be useful to begin our discussion of the criminal justice system by reaching back to the beginnings of criminal activity. This is not to say that we need to delve deeply into the causes of crime, for in the main we do not have answers to that perennial question. But we must develop an appreciation of the nature, variety, and extent of crime in our society in order to gain some perspective on the role that the judiciary plays in processing criminal cases.

If our knowledge of civil disputing is incomplete, we are probably only slightly better off when it comes to measuring crime. As with civil disputes, there is no way to determine accurately the actual amount of crime in our society, since a large percentage of incidents that might be labeled criminal are never reported. Further, even the incidents that are reported can be interpreted by police officers in such a way as to significantly alter the statistics. Victimization studies (sample surveys to determine crime rates by interviewing victims) are undoubtedly superior to crime reports and usually indicate two to three times the amount of crime reported and tabulated in the FBI's Uniform Crime Reports. However, exaggerated responses and sampling error present serious problems of distortion—not to mention the difficulty of pinpointing a victim for a good many crimes (for example, insurance fraud or public corruption).[12]

---

[10]Neubauer, *America's Courts,* 23.

[11]On this point, see John F. Decker, *Revolution to the Right: Criminal Procedure Jurisprudence During the Burger-Rehnquist Court Era* (New York: Garland Publishing, Inc., 1992), particularly Ch. 6. Professor Sam Walker cautions, however, that much has changed in the criminal justice system since Packer formulated the crime control/due process dichotomy in the late 1960s, and that much more is now understood regarding the actual functioning of that system, which tends to feather the edges of Packer's sharply drawn distinction. See Walker, *Taming the System,* 5.

[12]A useful discussion of the disparities among various collections of crime statistics appears in James P. Levine, Michael C. Musheno, and Dennis Palumbo, *Criminal Justice: A Public Policy Approach* (New York: Harcourt Brace Jovanovich, 1980), 492–529 ("Measuring Crime and Other Criminal Justice Concepts"). For statistics generated by the FBI, see Federal Bureau of Investigation, *Crime in the United States* (the "Uniform Crime Reports") (Washington, D.C.: U.S. Department of Justice, Annual); with respect to statistics derived from crime surveys, see Robert G. Lehnen and Wesley G. Skogan, eds., *The National Crime Survey: Working Papers* (Washington, D.C.: U.S. Department of Justice, 1981), and Marianne W. Zawitz et al., *Highlights From 20 Years of Surveying Crime Victims: The National Crime Victimization Survey, 1973–1992,* NCJ-144525 (Washington, D.C.: U.S. Department of Justice, Oct. 1993), 31–38. The U.S. Department of Justice publishes a compendium of crime statistics in its annual *Sourcebook of Criminal Justice Statistics.* Finally, a brief but useful overview of crime statistics appears in U.S. Department of Justice, Bureau of Justice Statistics, *Report to the Nation on Crime and Justice: The Data,* 2nd ed., NCJ-105506 (Washington, D.C.: U.S. Department of Justice, Aug. 1988).

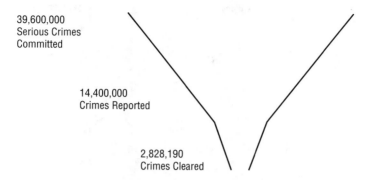

39,600,000
Serious Crimes
Committed

14,400,000
Crimes Reported

2,828,190
Crimes Cleared

Figure 9–1   Serious Crime Flow, 1995 (SOURCE: U.S. Department of Justice, Bureau of Justice Statistics, *National Crime Victimization Survey: Criminal Victimization, Preliminary 1995* (Washington, D.C.: U.S. Department of Justice, September 1996); and U.S. Department of Justice, Bureau of Justice Statistics, *Sourcebook of Criminal Justice Statistics, 1994:* 408, Table 4.24.)

With these caveats in mind, it is nonetheless useful to portray the overall flow of serious crime as a funnel, with a very large, even indeterminate, number of crimes actually committed at the top and far smaller numbers of crimes reported to and processed by authorities at the bottom. Figure 9–1, which represents such a funnel for 1995, reflects a ratio of approximately three to one between crimes committed and crimes reported, a ratio that has been consistent over the past two decades.

Figure 9–1 is based on data from the U.S. Department of Justice "National Crime Victimization Survey" and on the FBI's "Uniform Crime Reports." The National Crime Victimization Survey is conducted annually by the Justice Department's Bureau of Justice Statistics. In 1995, the BJS reports surveying about 100,000 people at least twelve years of age as to crimes of which they may have been a victim during the six months preceding the survey. As Figure 9–1 indicates, the 1995 survey indicated that approximately 39,600,000 serious violent and property crimes were committed in 1995, down from 42,360,000 in 1994 and 43,547,400 in 1993.

In contrast, the FBI's Uniform Crime Reports (UCR) are based upon the reports of law enforcement agencies across the nation. The UCR tabulates what the FBI labels "index crimes"—homicide, rape, robbery, aggravated assault, burglary, theft, and arson. For 1995, the FBI recorded approximately 14,400,000 index crimes that were reported to law enforcement agencies, also down from the 15,190,000 reported in 1994. The "crimes cleared" at the base of Figure 9–1 represents those cases in which law enforcement officials know of an alleged crime, have identified a suspect, and have effected an arrest.

Although based on sometimes questionable police reporting practices, Figure 9–1 does provide a rough idea of the contrast between crimes supposedly committed and those that become known to police. Given that something less than one in three crimes committed is reported and that about 20 percent of those reported are subsequently "cleared," we can then estimate that only about one crime in fifteen is likely to find its way into the criminal justice system.

Table 9–1 represents the percentage of those crimes believed committed that were actually reported to law enforcement officials from 1986 to 1995. In general, the data presented suggest that the likelihood a particular crime will be reported is largely a function of its severity. For instance, crimes of personal larceny in which the perpetrator did not di-

Table 9–1 Percentage of Crimes Reported to the Police, 1986–1995

	1986(%)	1987(%)	1988(%)	1989(%)	1990(%)	1991(%)	1992(%)	1993(%)	1994(%)	1995(%)
Personal Crimes										
Crimes of violence	50	48	48	45	48	49	50	42	42	43
Rape	48	52	45	51	54	59	52	35	31	32
Robbery	58	55	57	51	50	55	51	56	55	57
Assault	48	46	46	43	47	47	49	40	40	42
Theft crimes										
Larceny with contact	38	36	35	30	37	38	31	26*	27**	27**
Larceny without contact	28	27	27	29	28	28	30	26*	27**	27**
Motor vehicle theft	73	75	73	76	75	74	75	78	78	75
Household larceny	28	27	26	28	27	28	26	26	—	
Household burglary	52	52	51	50	51	50	54	49	51	54

*As of 1994, "Personal Larceny Without Contact" and "Household Larceny" are computed together.

**All thefts excluding motor vehicle thefts computed together.

Source: United States Department of Justice, Bureau of Justice Statistics, *Criminal Victimization 1991*, (Washington, D.C.: U.S. Department of Justice, Oct. 1992) (NCJ-136947); *Criminal Victimization 1992* (Washington, D.C.: U.S. Department of Justice, Mar. 1994) (NCJ-145125); *Criminal Victimization 1993* (Washington, D.C.: U.S. Department of Justice, May 1995) (NCJ-151658); *Criminal Victimization 1994* (Washington, D.C.: U.S. Department of Justice, Apr. 1996); *Criminal Victimization, Preliminary 1995* (Washington, D.C.: U.S. Department of Justice, Sept. 1996).

rectly contact the victim are reported to police at a rate of less than 25 percent. In contrast, over 50 percent of all aggravated assaults—those involving injury to the victim and the use of a weapon—are reported.

Many other factors in addition to seriousness affect the reporting of criminal conduct. Obviously the "it isn't worth the hassle—nothing can be done" type of thinking is important. So is the embarrassment attendant to public exposure of oneself as a "victim," as in cases of rape. Furthermore, police involvement in people's private affairs is often unwelcome, especially for those whose lifestyle may suggest other questionable activities or for those victimized by close friends or family members.[13] In any case, the gap between crimes occurring and those reported is tremendous, possibly even greater than the data presently available indicate.

The second major statistical break in the crime funnel (Figure 9–1) is between crimes reported and crimes cleared. In any recent year, only about 20 percent of all FBI index crimes reported to law enforcement are cleared by an arrest. The factors explaining this situation have to do with the exercise of police discretion in making arrests, which will be discussed later.[14]

Is crime increasing or decreasing? To answer that question, we must again emphasize the political context of the criminal judicial process. It should come as no surprise that criminal justice statistics are themselves subject to manipulation for political purposes.

Scholars have described the tendency of law enforcement officials to underreport crime when it is in their interest to do so, as, for example, to demonstrate the effectiveness of anticrime programs. Conversely, law enforcement officials tend to exaggerate the level of criminal activity when they seek to gain support for increased public expenditures.[15]

Moreover, the accuracy of crime rates, such as those reported by the FBI in its Uniform Crime Reports, is also a function of the methods of data collection used. The inauguration of sophisticated data processing techniques also can be linked to apparent increases in crime reporting, even when the incidence of crime remains constant. Finally, as previously noted, reported increases in crime may, in part, result from changes in public attitudes. A portion of the purported "crime explosion" is likely attributable to increases in public pressure on law enforcement to apprehend more criminals. "More crime" may therefore actually mean simply enhanced and more effective law enforcement. These are but some of the reasons why it is difficult to answer the seemingly simple question, "Is crime on the rise?"

According to FBI statistics compiled through the Uniform Crime Reporting Program, there has been a dramatic increase in the total number of crimes committed in the United States over the past three decades, even taking into account the small decreases that the Bureau reported in both violent and property crimes between 1994 and 1995. The tally of FBI

---

[13]For other correlates of crime reporting, see Bureau of Justice Statistics, *Criminal Victimization in the United States, 1994* (Washington, D.C.: U.S. Department of Justice, 1995); Wesley Skogan, "Dimensions of the Dark Figures of Unreported Crime," *Crime and Delinquency* 23, No. 1 (Jan. 1977), 41–50; *Sourcebook 1992*, 256–57, Table 3.13; *Sourcebook 1993*, 254–55, Table 3.8; *Sourcebook 1994*, 246, Table 3.34 (estimated percent distribution of reason for not reporting personal and household victimizations to police).

[14]See Skolnick, *Justice Without Trial*, 263–64, as to the almost complete unreliability of crime "clearance rates" as measures of law enforcement effectiveness.

[15]See the discussion of the history of crime statistics reported in Harold E. Pepinsky and Paul Jesilow, *Myths That Cause Crime* (Cabin John, Maryland: Seven Locks Press, 1984), 21–34; and David Seidman and Michael Couzens, "Getting the Crime Rate Down: Political Pressures and Crime Reporting," *Law & Society Review* 8, No. 3 (Spring 1974): 457–93.

See also Fox Butterfield, "Survey Finds That Crimes Cost $450 Billion a Year," *New York Times* (24 April 1996), 8 (A), reporting the statement of United States Representative Charles Schumer of New York that a U.S. Department of Justice survey concluding that crime costs Americans $450 billion each year "shows that while most people think a $1 billion anti-crime program is a large number, it's really just a drop in the bucket."

index crimes suggests that 3,384,200 serious crimes against persons and property, or approximately 1,887.2 such crimes per 100,000 inhabitants, were committed in the United States in 1960. That number then swelled to 3,984.5 per 100,000 in 1970 and again to 5,482.9 per 100,000—a total of 14,141,000 index crimes, in 1993. Such numbers are obviously more than sufficient to fuel a massive national "war on crime" backed by enormous expenditures at the local, state, and federal levels.[16]

It is interesting to compare the FBI figures on serious crimes reported to police, which are derived from law enforcement agencies, with data drawn from the National Crime Victimization Survey, which reflects information obtained from self-reported victims of criminal activity. For example, the FBI reports that violent crimes increased 52 percent between 1973 and 1990.[17] In sharp contrast, the National Crime Victimization Survey suggests violent crime increased approximately 11 percent during the same period.[18] Even recognizing differences in methodology, such a wide difference in statistics is worth noting.

Similarly, the FBI Uniform Crime Reports reflect a 40 percent increase in total index crimes committed during the 1973 to 1991 period.[19] Conversely, the National Crime Victimization Survey indicates total crime victimization *decreased* by 3.7 percent during the same period.[20]

More recently, the Department of Justice reported that, while the National Crime Victimization Survey indicates rape, robbery, and aggravated assault together decreased by a rather substantial 17.1 percent between 1994 and 1995, the FBI Uniform Crime Reports suggest a drop in these crimes of only 4 percent. Likewise, the NCVS reports thefts were *down* 3.7 percent from 1994 to 1995; the UCR, however, concludes theft was *up* a percentage point.

What can we conclude from these data? Overall, there is little doubt that reported crime has been on the increase in most categories in recent decades, though probably not by the rates claimed by the FBI. Assuming the National Crime Survey to be the more accurate of the two sets of data (and acknowledging that some scholars find the FBI Uniform Crime Reports to be virtually useless for purposes of social science research), we can conclude that the rise in criminal victimization from 1973 to 1991 has been modest, with a definite and rather dramatic drop in both the level and rate in almost all categories in the early and mid-1980s and a moderate decrease in the mid-90s. Thus, while we can take little comfort in the overall level and incidence of crime in America, we also cannot conclude that criminal activity is growing by leaps and bounds, as some of the FBI data would suggest.

Adopting a historical perspective, it seems appropriate to question whether crime in the United States is indeed exploding, as we are constantly warned that it is, when compared with the crime rate of a hundred years ago. Although there exists no reliable century-old data for purposes of such a comparison, some historians do suggest that violent crime probably peaked in the United States during the 1870s and that present levels of criminal activity pale when measured against those common to that era.[21]

---

[16]See *Sourcebook 1994*, 305–306, Table 3.94.

[17]FBI, *Crime in the United States, 1991*, 58, Table 1. For purposes of its Uniform Crime Reports, the FBI defines "violent crime" as the offenses of murder, forcible rape, robbery, and aggravated assault.

[18]Bureau of Justice Statistics, *Criminal Victimization in the United States, 1990*, 2, Table 1. The Bureau of Justice Statistics defines "violent crime" as the offenses of rape, robbery, and assault.

[19]FBI, *Crime in the United States, 1991*, 58, Table 1.

[20]Bureau of Justice Statistics, *Criminal Victimization in the United States 1990*, 2, Table 1.

[21]See Pepinsky and Jesilow, *Myths*, 21–24.

It may be that, as a society, we have simply become more aware that "crime" exists and more concerned with potential responses than were previous generations. Furthermore, we cannot overlook the impact of an exploding population, such that even stable rates of criminal conduct mean significant increases in the raw numbers of crimes committed.[22]

Whatever the facts, what we know about comparative crime rates does not lend unqualified support to the rhetoric of crisis that is so much a part of contemporary political debate. Indeed, President Taft was sounding the crime alert in 1905 with nearly the same strident pitch as did Ronald Reagan, George Bush, and Bill Clinton in more recent campaign years.

Still, there is no denying that crime, often rated as among the most pressing problems our society must address, has become a focus of both public and private life in the United States. Although crime rates do appear to have stabilized, and in some instances have decreased, over the past three decades, they have done so at a very high level when compared with the crime reported in other wealthy, industrial, and post-industrial nations.

Thus, as Prof. Samuel Walker suggests, "even if we achieved a genuine 30 or 40 percent reduction in serious crime, a feat no one realistically promises, our cities would still be unacceptably unsafe by international standards."[23] The bottom line is that crime and crime control policy will remain near the top of our political agenda, as well as at the fore of campaign rhetoric, irrespective of shifts in crime statistics.

While available data simply do not permit a clear conclusion regarding how much crime is actually occurring in contemporary society and how crime rates today compare with those from much earlier periods, we can at least suggest that responses to crime are fundamentally local in nature. The court caseflow data presented in Chapter 3 and in Chapter 4, together with statistical information on criminal justice system expenditures, indicate that criminal justice is state- and community-funded and organized to an extent well beyond what most citizens would expect.

For example, only about 19 percent of the 1994 federal district court docket consisted of criminal case filings.[24] In contrast, state general trial court dockets were flooded with 13,481,778 cases, or about 40 percent of these court's cases, excluding traffic and local ordinance filings. This gave state courts a per-judge load of 417 criminal cases as opposed to only 74 for federal trial judges.[25] For each criminal filing at federal trial level in 1994, there were nearly 300 in state general trial courts.

In order to deal with large criminal dockets, states, counties, and cities employ veritable armies of criminal justice personnel. For instance, as Table 9–2 illustrates, in fiscal year 1992 the federal government paid for only about 16 percent of the nation's various forms of police protection, while state and local governments together carried the burden for approximately 84 percent of all police costs. Likewise, about 79 percent of prosecution expenses and of the cost of providing criminal defense services to indigent defendants and 92 percent of all corrections costs were borne by state and local government.[26] Thus, while many governmental tasks may have been centralized within our federal system, responding to crime remains very much a state and local function.

---

[22]See Jay A. Sigler, *Understanding Criminal Law* (Boston, Mass.: Little, Brown, 1981), 9, regarding the link between large youth populations and increases in crime.

[23]Samuel Walker, *Sense and Nonsense About Crime*, 3.

[24]See Administrative Office of the U.S. Courts, *Judicial Business of the U.S. Courts, 1994* (Abbrev.) (Washington: Administrative Office of the U.S. Courts, n.d.), 7–9.

[25]See Brian J. Ostrom and Neal B. Kauder, *Examining the Work of State Courts, 1994* (Williamsburg, Va.: National Center for State Courts, 1996), 20–21.

[26]*Sourcebook 1994*, 5, Table 1.5.

Table 9–2   Percentage of Criminal Justice Employment Expenditures by Level of Government, 1992

Level of Government	Police Protection	Judicial and Legal	Corrections	Total Justice System
Federal	16.2	21.0	7.7	14.4
State governments	12.0	31.2	59.6	32.3
Local governments	71.8	47.7	32.7	53.3

Source: United States, Dept. of Justice, Bureau of Justice Statistics, *Sourcebook of Criminal Justice Statistics, 1994*, 5, Table 1.5.

JUSTICE WITHOUT TRIAL: THE DECISION TO ARREST

Just as civil justice should be understood as a largely preadjudicative process that relies heavily upon bargaining, criminal justice likewise occurs by and large in the pretrial arenas of police and prosecutorial discretion. Indeed, the vast majority of all criminal prosecutions are disposed of at early and relatively informal stages in the process.

Although the casual observer's view of police work tends to emphasize the law enforcement function—that is, the application of sanctions to alleged illegal conduct, typically via arrest—studies of actual police responses to dispatch calls suggest that this function, while primary, represents perhaps only 10 percent of official police activity.[27] A second primary police function, representing some 30 percent of police activity in one study, is "order maintenance," or police undertaking to control events that threaten or may threaten public safety. This function might involve controlling crowds at public events, warning overzealous partiers to restrain themselves, interceding in domestic disputes, and other similar activities.[28]

Police also have two secondary functions of significant community concern: information gathering and service duties. Together, these two functions may represent as much as 60 percent of all police responses to requests for assistance. Information gathering, which probably accounts for 20 to 25 percent of all police work, includes such activities as completing report forms, asking questions at the scene of a crime or disturbance of some sort, and investigating alleged criminal activity. Service-related duties involve a very wide range of activities, constituting as much as 35 or 40 percent of all official police conduct. Providing assistance to firefighters, making public presentations, participating in animal control, and providing aid to injured persons are all activities that fall under the "service-related" heading.

Since the law enforcement function, particularly the act of arrest, triggers the whole criminal justice process, it is this aspect of police work that is of primary concern here. As scholars have so often noted, no other public official exercises such awesome power over her or his fellow citizens as does the police officer effecting an arrest. For example, Professor Blumberg has noted that

> [i]n a simple situation involving a defendant of modest means, arrest may cause a loss of job, a period of detention, the indignities of being fingerprinted and photographed, immeasurable psychological pain, at least several court appearances, and the expenditure of hundreds, even thousands, of dollars for bail bond and a lawyer. Arrest can be a powerful weapon—indeed, a form of summary punishment.

---

[27]See James Q. Wilson's research as reported in Bureau of Justice Statistics, *Report to the Nation*, 47.
[28]Bureau of Justice Statistics, *Report to the Nation*, 47.

Figure 9–2   Crimes Cleared by Arrest, 1993 (SOURCE: U.S. Department of Justice, Bureau of Justice Statistics, *Sourcebook of Criminal Justice Statistics, 1994,* 408 (Table 4.23).)

        . . . The crux of the matter is that the police perform more important judicial functions in many ways than do judges; and that critical variable is the source of anxiety, resentment, confrontation, and violence that invariably occur between the police and other groups in society.[29]

Even more striking is the fact that the modern police department stands out as one of few organizational structures in which maximum discretion rests not with the supervisory personnel at the top of the organization, but rather with those at the bottom of the ladder— the cops on the beat. The notorious lack of both external and internal control over individual police officers[30] and the low public visibility typical of most police work combine to enhance the discretion available to law enforcement agencies in general.

As noted in Figure 9–1, only about 20 percent of the crimes reported to police and indexed by the FBI in a given year are subsequently "cleared" by the arrest of at least one suspect. That number alone suggests that an enormous amount of discretion is exercised by law enforcement officials.

One factor that may help explain how police wield this discretion is the severity of the offense involved. As one might expect, available data indicate that the more serious the crime, the more likely an arrest will be made. For example, as indicated in Figure 9–2, 66 percent of the murders reported to police in 1993 were cleared by the arrest of at least one suspect. In contrast, only 14 percent of the motor vehicle thefts reported to police during

---

[29]Abraham S. Blumberg, *Criminal Justice: Issues and Ironies,* 2d ed. (New York: New Viewpoints, 1979), 54.
[30]See generally Skolnick and Fyfe, *Above the Law;* and Walker, *Taming the System,* Ch. 2, "Police Discretion," 21–53.

the same year ended with an arrest.[31] Such wide variations in crime clearance rates are usually attributed to a combination of three factors: (1) criminals perpetrating more violent crimes are more likely to be confronted by their victims; (2) witnesses are more likely to make themselves known and available to police in connection with violent crimes; and (3) violent crimes are more likely to become the focus of intense investigation, increasing the likelihood of an arrest.

Another perhaps obvious factor that may help explain why arrest rates differ among offenses is the degree to which a crime itself is visible. In a nutshell, a crime committed in broad daylight is less likely to be ignored and to require an intense investigatory effort than is one that has been concealed in some way. Clearly, this factor is one of many that are related to the exercise of police discretion and that can also be linked to the fact that impoverished people—who tend to lead far more "public" lives than those who are affluent—are more frequently the subject of arrest than are individuals with greater economic resources at their disposal.

In addition to characteristics attributable to the offense itself, another factor that seems important in the exercise of police discretion is the relationship between the alleged perpetrator and the reporting victim. In domestic violence incidents, complaints between business associates, barroom brawls, and the like, police often assume the role of "peacemaker" rather than that of law enforcement official in the strictest sense. In such situations, police may have a difficult time determining precisely whom to arrest, and formal sanctions may be perceived as inappropriate.[32]

In contrast, where the alleged perpetrator of a crime and the alleged victim are not known to one another, an arrest may be more likely in the absence of other significant factors than would be the case were victim and perpetrator acquainted.[33]

The incidence of arrest also varies widely as a result of the relationship between the police and the parties to the alleged offense. It is common knowledge that the more deferential and respectful the suspect, the less likely that individual will be subjected to arrest. Likewise, the apparent age, race, and socioeconomic class of a suspect plays into police decision making with respect to arrest.[34] To state the obvious, a young male of African descent who resides in a poverty-stricken neighborhood is far more likely to be detained, questioned, and arrested by police than is a white college student.

Similarly, the characteristics and behavior of the complainant affect arrest decisions. As one might expect, police are more likely to pursue the complaint of a "respectable" citi-

---

[31]It is interesting to note that, of all the crimes measured as part of the Bureau of Justice Statistics' National Crime Victimization Survey, motor vehicle theft is the crime most likely to be reported to police. Based on preliminary data compiled for the 1996 survey, it appears that about 90.3 percent of all completed motor vehicle thefts were reported to police during 1995. This is consistent with the 92 percent reporting rate for completed motor vehicle theft reported for the 20-year period 1972 to 1992. See U.S. Department of Justice, Bureau of Justice Statistics, *Criminal Victimization, Preliminary 1995* (Washington, D.C.: U.S. Department of Justice, Sept. 1996); and United States Department of Justice, Bureau of Justice Statistics, *Highlights From 20 Years of Surveying Crime Victims: The National Crime Victimization Survey, 1973–92*, (Washington, D.C.: U.S. Department of Justice, Oct. 1993) (NCJ-144525), 14.

[32]Particularly with respect to the issue of domestic violence, it is important to note recent efforts to displace police discretion and the phenomenon of "arrest avoidance" through the implementation of mandatory arrest policies. For a thorough discussion of this trend and its implications, see Walker, *Taming the System*, 33; see also Cole, *The American System of Criminal Justice*, 154–59.

[33]See Herbert Jacob, *Urban Justice: Law and Order in American Cities* (Englewood Cliffs, N.J.: Prentice-Hall, 1973), 28; Walker, *Taming the System*, 34. But see U.S. Department of Justice, Bureau of Justice Statistics, *Highlights From 20 Years of Surveying Crime Victims*, 32, suggesting that victim-perpetrator relationship has no bearing on police exercise of discretion.

[34]On the importance of race as a factor in the operation of police discretion, see Skolnick, *Justice Without Trial*, 77–87; and Walker, *Taming the System*, 21–24, 31–32.

zen from a wealthy neighborhood than that of a street dweller. Professor Skolnick's participant observations of police behavior during the 1960s are equally relevant today:

> In ghetto communities where people do not have the housing facilities that they have in middle-class communities, such activities as drinking and gambling often take place in public or semi-public areas. For instance, when I was working with the vice squad, we raided a Friday night poker game in a hotel in the ghetto. We received a tip from an informant, a warrant was duly drawn out, and five white police plus one white professor pretending to be a policeman, kicked in a hotel room door and discovered six black men, most of whom were gainfully employed, playing poker. From all I could gather these men were doing nothing other than what I and some of my professional colleagues may do with some regularity—play Friday night poker. But they were subject to the indignity of having the door of their rented room kicked in, of being searched, of being transported to police headquarters and booked, and finally of being prosecuted and found guilty. This sort of demeaning experience need never have taken place if there were not laws on the books which attempted to enforce conventional morality. In fact, these laws tend to enforce conventional morality among the poor, while allowing the rich to go along relatively freely in their own vices, harmless or otherwise.[35]

Well-known criminal defense attorney Jerry Paul offered a similar account of the double standard created by police discretion regarding the enforcement of gambling laws:

> It's poor people who go to jail because poor people cannot get justice in this judicial system. My first week of practicing law, I went over to court to watch a trial, and I saw four poor people get severe sentences for gambling. Then I went to a bar association meeting, and they're all sitting around with slot machines.[36]

The political views of suspects can of course profoundly influence the likelihood of their arrest, as F. K. Heussenstamm found in a widely cited study of police relations with members of the Black Panthers during the late 1960s. Fifteen California State college students (five white, five black, five Chicano; three males and two females of each race) were asked to place Black Panther bumper stickers on their cars. The cars were of various types, from low riders to well-kept, new sedans. Although none of the cars had a moving traffic violation within twelve months of the study and all drove safely during its pendency, the fifteen students received a total of 33 traffic citations in seventeen days! Not one student finished the study without receiving a ticket.[37]

A final factor that may influence the decision to arrest is the policy stance of a particular police department. James Q. Wilson, a noted scholar of criminal justice systems, has identified three styles of police discretion: the watchman style, the legalistic approach, and the service stance. A city police force assuming the "watchman style" is not likely to make arrests absent a significant threat to public order and safety. In this "style" of police work, the mere fact that an act is illegal or that it produces a citizen complaint is not sufficient cause for detaining suspects.

In contrast, a police force that adopts a "legalistic" approach will typically enforce the law, no matter what. Such a stance is likely to emerge from city reform movements dedicated in part to reducing police discretion.

Something of a midpoint between the rigid legalistic approach and the more casual watchman style is what Wilson calls the "service stance." Here, police perceive their role to comprise a healthy dose of public relations: the job of a cop is to handle citizen com-

---

[35]Jerome H. Skolnick, *the Police and the Urban Ghetto* (Chicago: American Bar Foundation, 1968), 27.
[36]Jerry Paul, "'We Won Because I Could Buy the Things to Win,'" *National Observer* (Nov. 15, 1975): 4.
[37]F. K. Heussenstamm, "Bumper Stickers and the Cops," *Transaction* 8 (1971): 32–33.

plaints and in doing so, to maintain and enhance positive feelings within the community. Keep the citizens satisfied, this style suggests, and all will be well.

Although these different policing styles may come and go within a particular jurisdiction, Wilson found the watchman style to be most prevalent in small cities where city politics were not the subject of a dedicated reform movements. "Reformed" cities adopting a legalistic approach included Oakland, California, and Highland Park, Illinois, at the time of Wilson's research. Brighton, a midsize city in Massachusetts, exemplified Wilson's service mode.[38]

Professor Wilson's point that various police styles or policies help determine arrest rates probably ought to be expanded to include other policy influences on police behavior. New departures in judicial policy, state legislative enactments, and shifts in public mood with respect to a given crime issue can also be cited as having an important impact upon the arrest decision. For example, driving-while-intoxicated arrests have been on the rise throughout the nation for many years, not so much owing to a shift in policing styles or to particular legislative enactments as to a distinct and overt public outcry against drunk driving.

In sum, since only a few cases enter the criminal justice system without initial police action, the decision to arrest is clearly of tremendous importance. An individual taken into police custody finds herself or himself tangled in a bureaucratic web from which, in most cases, there is no escape without some penalty. As hosts of scholars have pointed out, the initial stages of the criminal justice process—police contact and arrest, booking, fingerprinting, and perhaps time in jail prior to trial—are significant forms of sanction in and of themselves.

Meanwhile, criminal acts that the police overlook, ignore, or never learn have occurred—the overwhelming majority of crimes we believe are actually committed—are generally forgotten forever. The cop riding in a patrol car or walking a neighborhood beat is thus law enforcement officer, prosecutor, judge, and jury in many, many instances. Table 9–3 summarizes the arrest decisions made by police throughout the nation during 1993.

PROSECUTORIAL DISCRETION AND PLEA BARGAINING: THE HEART OF THE PROCESS

The fate of a suspect in custody rests almost entirely in the hands of a prosecutor. Unlike the practice in the United Kingdom and in some former Commonwealth countries, where prosecution is perceived as a quasi-private matter similar to our law of personal injury, American criminal jurisprudence is based upon the notion that crime, and therefore criminal prosecution, is a public issue to be addressed by public servants.

If the power and discretion of the typical police officer are remarkable, those of an American prosecutor border on awesome. Within their respective jurisdictions, County, District, and United States Attorneys initially decide whether to charge a suspect with one or more crimes. Precisely what charges to file, whether to seek a grand jury indictment or to proceed with a criminal complaint or information, what bail amount to request of the court or whether to oppose bail altogether, what, if any, plea agreement to offer up front, and what sentence to threaten—each of these decisions falls within the prosecutor's extremely broad discretion.

Partisan politics typically play an important role in the selection of public prosecutors. The chief prosecutor of a city, a county, or a state judicial district is usually elected to

---

[38]James Q. Wilson, *Varieties of Police Behavior* (Cambridge, Mass.: Harvard University Press, 1968).

Table 9–3   Estimated Police Arrests by Offense Charged, 1993

Offense Charged	Number of Arrests
Total	14,036,300
Murder and nonnegligent manslaughter	23,400
Forcible rape	38,420
Robbery	173,620
Aggravated assault	518,670
Burglary	402,700
Larceny-Theft	1,476,300
Motor vehicle theft	195,900
Arson	19,400
Violent crime	754,110
Property crime	2,094,300
Total crime index	2,848,400
Other assault	1,144,900
Forgery and counterfeiting	106,900
Fraud	410,700
Embezzlement	12,900
Stolen property; buying, receiving, possessing	158,100
Vandalism	313,000
Weapons, carrying or possessing	262,300
Prostitution	97,800
Sex offenses (except forcible rape and prostitution)	104,100
Drug abuse violations	1,126,300
Gambling	17,300
Offenses against family and children	109,100
Driving under the influence	1,524,800
Liquor laws	518,500
Drunkeness	726,600
Disorderly conduct	727,000
Vagrancy	28,200
All other offenses (except traffic)	3,518,700
Suspicion	14,100
Curfew and loitering laws	100,200
Runaways	180,500

Source: United States Department of Justice, Bureau of Justice Statistics, *Sourcebook of Criminal Justice Statistics, 1994,* Table 4.1, p. 374.

a multiple-year term after running for office in a partisan election on a party platform espousing a "get tough on crime" message.[39] At the federal level, the President appoints a United States Attorney for each federal judicial district to serve under the United States Attorney General and to oversee federal prosecutions, a position considered among the most important patronage plums. City, County, District, and United States Attorneys are

---

[39]"Prosecutors virtually own the politically potent symbols of 'law and order' politics. Judges cannot openly play this game, and defense attorneys, tainted in the public view by the people they represent, are politically disqualified." Roy B. Flemming, Peter F. Nardulli, and James Eisenstein, *The Craft of Justice: Politics and Work in Criminal Court Communities* (Philadelphia: University of Pennsylvania Press, 1992), 23 (footnote omitted). In every state except Connecticut and New Jersey, prosecutors are elected to office, typically for a term of four years. See Cole, *The American System of Criminal Justice,* 269. Also very useful is Stuart Diamond's "Prosecutorial Discretion: Worthy of Defense?" *New York Times* (July 22, 1988): A–21.

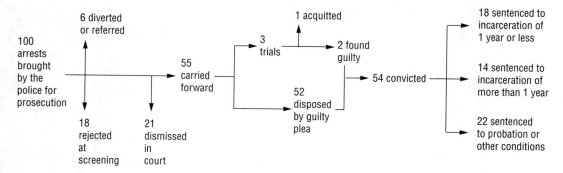

Figure 9-3 Typical Outcome of 100 Felony Arrests Brought by the Police for Prosecution (SOURCE: Barbara Boland, Paul Mahanna, and Ronald Sones, *The Prosecution of Felony Arrests, 1988* (Washington, D.C.: U.S. Department of Justice, Bureau of Justice Statistics, Feb. 1992) (NCJ-130914): Figure 1, p. 3.)

then responsible for appointing attorneys to their staffs, usually referred to as "deputies" or "assistants," who handle the day-to-day business of carrying out prosecutions in the nation's courts. Becoming a prosecutor has long been considered an excellent first step for young attorneys with political ambitions of their own.[40]

Prosecutorial Discretion: The Early Stages

The first decision a prosecutor must immediately make follows the arrest of a suspect: should charges be filed and, if so, what charges? Typically there is also the matter of bail: Is this a case in which the prosecutor wants to argue for a high cash bail he knows the defendant can't make, or is this a defendant whom the prosecutor can afford to "go easy" on?

Figure 9-3 depicts the typical outcomes for every 100 adult felony arrests made in a major metropolitan jurisdiction based upon data collected by the U.S. Department of Justice. The figure indicates that approximately 45 of every 100 such arrests do not result in a conviction, with some 18 being screened out at the outset by a prosecutor and another 21 being dismissed at the suspect's first court appearance. Often a lack of sufficient evidence to prove criminal conduct beyond a reasonable doubt leads to a case being rejected at this early stage. Witness problems—witnesses who cannot be located or who do not wish to participate—may lead to the same result.

Official policies may also result in a large number of cases being "dumped" from the system early on. A particular prosecutor's office may, for example, have determined that certain charges simply are not appropriate for prosecution; such charges might include loitering, public urination, or possession of very small amounts of marijuana.

Similarly insubstantial charges can also be dealt with through "diversion" programs, in which suspects with no prior criminal history are usually offered the opportunity to enter some form of treatment or to participate in community service activities in return for having their cases dismissed.

---

[40]See Joseph Schlesinger, *Ambition and Politics: Political Careers in the United States* (Chicago: Rand-McNally, 1966), 72–73; see also Joan E. Jacoby, *The American Prosecutor: A Search for Identity* (Lexington, Mass.: Heath, 1980).

Table 9–4   Disposition of Cases Involving Felony Charges in Five Major U.S. Metropolitan Jurisdictions, 1988

Jurisdiction	Number of Felony Arrests	Diversions	Rejection or Dismissal	Guilty Plea	Trial Conviction	Trial Acquittal
Manhattan, New York	38,601	117	16,841	20,669	679	295
Portland, Oregon	10,281	581	4,392	4,283	893	132
San Diego, California	30,234	2,951	9,421	17,285	476	101
Seattle, Washington	9,368	401	2,889	5,356	613	109
Washington, D.C.	15,283	278	6,626	7,465	637	277

Source: Barbara Boland, Paul Mahanna, and Ronald Sones, *The Prosecution of Felony Arrests, 1988* (Washington, D.C.: U.S. Department of Justice, Bureau of Justice Statistics, Feb. 1992) (NCJ-130914), Table 1, pp. 20–23.

At times, prosecutors will essentially be forced to dismiss one or more charges for which a suspect has been arrested because of "due process" problems. These may come in the form of police searches and seizures conducted without an appropriate warrant, coerced or uncounseled confessions, or detention based upon something less than probable cause to believe the suspect has committed a criminal offense. Table 9–4 presents data collected by the U.S. Bureau of Justice Statistics with respect to criminal case disposition in five major jurisdictions.

To assist in reaching a decision regarding whether to go forward and on what charges, a prosecutor may employ, and in some jurisdictions must employ, a preliminary hearing, a grand jury, or both. A preliminary hearing is held before a judge without a jury and is typically limited in scope to determining whether probable cause exists to believe that the accused actually committed each of the offenses with which she or he is charged. The probable cause standard if far easier for a prosecutor to satisfy than is that of proof beyond a reasonable doubt, the standard of proof that must be satisfied in order to obtain a conviction at trial. Furthermore, the prosecution is assisted by relaxed rules of evidence that often permit the introduction of otherwise inadmissible hearsay.[41]

Preliminary hearings can vary from proceedings of mere minutes to multiday minitrials where a defendant is charged with a large number of serious offenses. The prosecutor will usually call one or more police officers to testify as to their investigation of the alleged crime; sometimes the victim or other eyewitnesses will testify as well. At the close of the evidence, the court renders its determination as to the existence or absence of probable cause. The defendant is then "bound over" for trial on those charges for which the court concludes that probable cause exists. Defense attorneys sometimes advise their clients to waive a preliminary hearing where a plea bargain has already been negotiated or where a prosecutor threatens to withdraw a potentially desirable plea agreement if the defendant refuses to waive the hearing.

---

[41]For example, see Rule 5 (a) (4) (II) of the Colorado Rules of Criminal Procedure, which provides that "[t]he judge presiding at the preliminary hearing may temper the rules of evidence in the exercise of sound judicial discretion."

At least as often, however, defense counsel will favor going forward with a "prelim," as the hearing itself provides an opportunity to observe how at least some of the prosecution's witnesses will perform on the stand and to pin those witnesses to a particular version of their testimony. For example, a police officer who testifies to one version of the facts at a preliminary hearing and then to another version at trial can be effectively cross-examined regarding the disparities in his or her stories.[42]

Rather than—or, at times, in addition to—a preliminary hearing, the prosecutor may turn to a grand jury in search of obtaining an indictment. The grand jury is a remnant of English common law. In those states that still employ one, a grand jury consists of between six and twenty-three citizens who typically serve for three months. During that time, the jurors meet periodically to consider evidence presented by a prosecutor.

Following the prosecutor's presentation, the jurors vote whether to return a "true bill," instructing the prosecutor that probable cause exists to issue an indictment formally charging an individual with one or more crimes, or a "no true bill," indicating that the evidence of criminal conduct is too weak to warrant proceeding.

Although grand juries theoretically exist to protect the accused from being frivolously charged, they are almost universally regarded as tools of prosecutors. Working in near total secrecy, these citizen bodies usually hear only one version of events—that carefully presented by a prosecutor—and are likely to be heavily influenced by the prosecutor's legal advice and analysis. For these reasons, the grand jury may ironically become an instrument of political oppression, directly contravening its original purpose of standing between the citizen and the state to guard against irresponsible prosecution.[43]

Having been arrested for allegedly committing a serious misdemeanor or a felony, an individual is typically taken into police custody and held in a police lockup, a county jail, or a federal detention facility. On any given day, more than half the adults being held in jails (not state or federal prisons) are awaiting trial or some other disposition of their cases.[44]

Usually within a day or two, a determination is made as to whether a suspect in custody is eligible for release on bail. "Bail" is simply a guarantee—a promise that the accused will appear for scheduled court proceedings, secured by something of value, such as cash or property. If the accused does indeed make all of the scheduled court appearances, the security is released; if not, the court is entitled to keep it.

Whether every citizen has a "right" to bail is not directly addressed in the federal Constitution. The only mention of bail appears in the Eighth Amendment's declaration that "excessive bail shall not be required." Until recently, however, the federal government and most states recognized a statutory right to pretrial bail in all but certain capital (i.e., murder) cases, making it possible for the U.S. Supreme Court to avoid defining the scope of the constitutional bail provision.[45] The language of these statutes notwithstanding, the

---

[42]With respect to criminal defense counsels' approaches to preliminary hearings, and particularly to waiving those hearings, see Flemming et al., *The Craft of Justice*, 164–68.

[43]On the issue of grand jury abuse and reform, see Leroy Clark, *The Grand Jury: The Use and Abuse of Political Power* (New York: Quadrangle Books, 1975); and Richard E. Gerstein and Laurie O. Robinson, "Remedy for the Grand Jury: Retain But Reform," *American Bar Association Journal*, 46 (1978): 337–40. A review of grand jury problems is found in Deborah Day Emerson, *Grand Jury Reform: A Review of Key Issues* (Washington, D.C.: U.S. Department of Justice, National Institute of Justice, Jan. 1983).

[44]According to the Bureau of Justice Statistics, an estimated 541,913 persons were being held in or supervised by local jails on June 30, 1995. Of that number, only about 44 percent had been convicted of the current charge or charges pending against them. See U.S. Department of Justice, Bureau of Justice Statistics, *Prison and Jail Inmates, 1995* (Washington, D.C.: U.S. Department of Justice, Sept. 1996) (NCJ-161132), 1, 17.

[45]On the history of bail, see Caleb Foote's essay "Bail" in Leonard W. Levy, Kenneth L. Karst, and Dennis J. Mahoney, eds., *Criminal Justice and the Supreme Court: Selections from the Encyclopedia of the American Constitution* (New York: MacMillan, 1990), 108–12.

"right to bail" has never existed as an actual right to pretrial *release,* but only to a timely and impartial *determination* of the amount and type of security required to guarantee subsequent court appearances.

Where the accused is suspected of a relatively minor offense, bail will likely be set immediately after booking by the arresting officer, by an assistant district or county attorney, or by a bail commissioner. Typically, a bail "schedule," which establishes particular bail amounts for particular charges, will be consulted. The amount set forth in the schedule may be discounted by the presence of factors that seem to suggest that the accused will appear for court dates—a brief or nonexistent criminal history, some form of employment, and family in the local area, for instance.

Where the charged offense is more serious, bail is set by a judge, who will on occasion hear arguments from the prosecution and from defense counsel (if counsel has been retained or appointed) as to the appropriate bail amount. In making bail determinations, judges tend to rely quite heavily upon the accused's criminal history, as well as upon the nature of the charged offense or offenses. Other factors, such as the accused's tie to the community, record of employment, and substantiated or suspected alcohol or substance abuse, may also weigh into bail decisions. As one would probably assume, the prosecutor is the dominant figure in the court's bail decision, while defense counsel is typically marginalized. In some jurisdictions, a judge may also be required to factor in the concerns of the alleged victim, who is permitted to appear and address the court during bail hearings.

In determining whether an individual may be released from custody while awaiting trial and under what circumstances, a court has several options. First, it may simply require the accused to promise to appear at subsequent hearings, releasing the accused on his or her "own recognizance." This most lenient of pretrial release arrangements is usually considered appropriate where the charges pending are relatively minor and where the accused has both a clean criminal record and substantial ties to the community.

Alternatively, the court may set bail in some amount but require only that the accused promise to pay that amount should she or he fail to appear for a subsequent court date. Because the accused is not required to actually post any money or property as security for the promise, this arrangement is known as "unsecured" bail.[46]

Often a court will attach conditions to the accused's release that he or she must satisfy in order to avoid being returned to custody. The particular conditions can include alcohol and drug testing, counseling, no contact with either the alleged victim or the witnesses, and maintenance of employment. "Conditional release" can occur in the context of either secured or unsecured bail.

Once a court determines that some bail amount is appropriate, the accused is usually faced with four options for gaining actual release. First, the accused can simply pay the bail amount in full to the court, obtaining the funds to do so from personal resources, or from family or friends. Posting cash bail in this fashion is typically well beyond the capacity of a criminal defendant.

In addition to those awaiting trial, defendants who have been convicted but not sentenced or whose cases are pending before an appellate court may also be entitled to release on bail. This section, however, deals exclusively with pretrial release.

[46]The Justice Department reports that, as of February 1994, "[t]he most common type of pretrial release for Federal felony defendants was unsecured bond, used in half of all releases." In sharp contrast, only 8 percent of those released from pretrial confinement by state courts were granted unsecured bail. U.S. Department of Justice, Bureau of Justice Statistics, *Pretrial Release of Federal Felony Defendants* (Washington, D.C.: U.S. Department of Justice, Feb. 1994) (NCJ-145322), 1, 11.

Second, the accused may use property of some sort—usually an interest in real estate, such as a family home—to secure release. Courts often require that the value of the property pledged must amount to at least double the accused's bail.

Third, and most likely, the accused can seek the services of a bail bonding agent. Often referred to simply as a "bondsperson," a bail bonding agent is a private businessperson to whom the government essentially subcontracts the job of determining which individuals are good bail risks, along with the task of tracking down those who fail to appear after being released pending trial.[47]

On the basis of a brief interview with the accused, as well as on whatever reputation the individual has in the local community, a bonding agent will determine whether that person is a reasonable risk. If so, the agent secures a nonrefundable fee—usually 10 to 15 percent of the bail amount—in return for agreeing to post the accused's bail. The agent then pays approximately 10 percent of that fee to an insurance carrier, which posts a bond for the full amount of the accused's bail with the court. If the accused fails to appear and the bonding agent cannot locate her or him, the court may declare the bond forfeited and require the insurance company to pay the full amount posted. A bonding agent who has more than a few bonds "go bad" usually doesn't last long in the bail business.

Among the numerous complaints leveled against the bail bonding industry is that the fee paid by an accused is entirely nonrefundable. Even if the accused makes every court appearance and is acquitted at trial, he or she is still out the substantial amount paid the bonding agent to secure pretrial release. Along the same line, most bail bonding agreements permit the agent to return the accused to the custody of the court at any time without refunding the entire fee. The agent is then no longer responsible for the accused's court appearances, and the accused is back in custody without the money already paid to the bonding agent.

Bonding agents also generally hold extraordinary authority to locate, apprehend, and return an accused who "jumps bond" and fails to appear. Bondspersons are often permitted to require that an accused waive extradition as part of the bonding agreement, authorizing the agent to retrieve the accused from across state lines without formal law enforcement or judicial intervention. Such "retrievals" are obviously prone to no small amount of physical violence, as a bondsperson will frequently secure the assistance of a paid bounty hunter to track the accused down before the bond is forfeited.

During the 1960s, significant legislative efforts were undertaken at both state and federal levels to reform existing bail systems, in large part as a result of concerns about the private bail bonding industry and its wide-ranging, highly discretionary authority. One such reform was the creation of "court deposit" bail, which can provide a fourth option for obtaining pretrial release. Rather than paying a bondsperson a nonrefundable fee, an accused is permitted to deposit 10 percent of the bail amount directly into the court registry. If the individual appears as required, the deposit is returned, minus a small amount retained to cover administrative costs. Court deposit bail was adopted for the federal courts and for the District of Columbia in the Federal Bail Reform Act of 1966. This legislation also created a presumption in favor of releasing individuals on their own recognizance, adopted "conditional release" as an alternative to cash bail, and emphasized that individuals should be released pending trial under the least restrictive circumstances available to assure their subsequent appearances. By 1970, more than a dozen states followed suit and adopted similar reforms.[48]

[47]See Neubauer, *America's Courts and the Criminal Justice System,* 236.
[48]See Andy Hall, with Elizabeth Gaynes, D. Alan Henry, and Walter F. Smith, *Pretrial Release Program Options* (Washington, D.C.: U.S. Department of Justice, National Institute of Justice, June 1984), vii, 5.

Bail reform, founded primarily upon the argument that cash bail systems discriminate against low-income and impoverished people, was so successful that it spurred a backlash in the form of "preventive detention" policies. First included in the District of Columbia Court Reform and Criminal Procedure Act of 1970, and now on the books in over half the states, preventive detention systems permit, and often mandate, that judges consider "community safety" and the likelihood that an accused will commit further crimes as part of the formal bail determination process. When a court finds that an individual may pose a risk to the public if released, the court is authorized to deny bail altogether, irrespective of whether there is any reason whatsoever to believe the accused will fail to appear.[49]

Federal courts were authorized to begin formally using preventive detention by the Crime Control Act of 1984. We use the term "formally" to recognize the fact that preventive detention has been part of the prosecutorial process for about as long as that process has lasted. In the past, judges would simply set cash bail at a level clearly beyond what a particular defendant could achieve, thereby assuring that the defendant remained in custody until his or her case was disposed of and sentence was imposed. As Professor Sam Walker points out, "Preventive detention laws simply provided legal justification for traditional practices. These laws have the virtue of making public a covert decision-making process."[50]

Although courts and prosecutors no doubt still impose high cash bail as a means of effecting de facto "preventive detention" without adhering to a complicated and time-consuming statutory mechanism, recent statistics suggest that the use of formal preventive detention is increasing, at least in the federal courts.[51] Nevertheless, the percentage of criminal defendants actually detained prior to trial appears to have increased little, if at all, as a result of preventive detention. Perhaps more importantly, formal preventive detention mechanisms have had no significant affect on the percentage of defendants rearrested for committing crimes while free on bail. Therefore, to the extent that the goal of preventive detention is a reduction in crime, it has been a failure.[52]

Assuming an individual either cannot make bail or is determined to be ineligible for bail pursuant to a preventive detention statute, the ramifications for that person of being held in pretrial custody may well be far-reaching and extreme. That person will likely lose his or her job and may be unable to keep up with day-to-day financial obligations. Without a source of income, it is difficult to hire an attorney, but the services of a public defender are generally available only to those who are indigent. It is also almost impossible to assist in the preparation of one's own defense—through locating witnesses, obtaining important records, and the like—while in custody. Thus, it comes as no surprise that a defendant in custody is far more likely to be convicted than one released on bond, if only because of the pressure exerted on that individual to plead guilty and "just get it over with."

Moreover, as Professor Neubauer has suggested, the impact of pretrial detention can easily extend even beyond conviction:

> Detained defendants have a greater likelihood of being sentenced to prison for longer terms than those who posted bond. Often pretrial detention has stripped defendants of attributes that might contribute to a lighter sentence. If they had a job, they have lost it.

---

[49]Hall et al., *Pretrial Release Options,* viii. More than half the states and the District of Columbia have passed one or more "preventive detention" measures into law. These provisions range from the exclusion of particular offenses from automatic bail eligibility to mandated pretrial detention on the finding that an individual may pose a threat to public safety if released. See U.S. Department of Justice, Bureau of Justice Statistics, *Report to the Nation on Crime,* 77; and Cole, *The American System of Criminal Justice,* 342–44.

[50]Walker, *Taming the System,* 75.

[51]See Bureau of Justice Statistics, *Pretrial Release of Federal Felony Defendants,* 10.

[52]Walker, *Sense and Nonsense About Crime,* 47–53; Walker, *Taming the System,* 77–80; Cole, *The American System of Criminal Justice,* 343–44, suggesting justifications for preventive detention.

Their family lives have been disrupted, thereby making them poorer probation risks. Moreover, those who have been detained present a very different physical appearance in court. Dressed in jail garb, with a pallid complexion caused by confinement, detained defendants are less able to project a favorable image. Finally, the special status of detained defendants is underscored by the fact that they are brought to court in handcuffs by sheriff's deputies who maintain a watchful vigilance, another cue that society has already labeled these people as dangerous.[53]

The discussion thus far leads to the conclusion that prosecutorial discretion, while important, is limited in important ways. For example, it is not unknown for the police virtually to dominate the charging process in a particular city, leaving prosecutorial discretion to operate at later stages of the process. In other jurisdictions, the complainant plays a relatively large role in determining whether and what charges are to be pursued; with little pressure from the victim, the case may be dropped. In still other jurisdictions, the court has substantial input into the charging process. Such variations make meaningful generalizations difficult, if not impossible.[54]

Regardless of local variations, it is most useful to conceptualize the prosecutorial role as a pattern of interaction among several key figures—the police officer, the prosecuting and defense attorneys, the judge, the victim, and the accused. This "work group," as Eisenstein and Jacob have labeled it, is the entity that actually processes cases through the criminal justice system.[55]

The Work Group and Plea Bargaining

The key actors in the work group of most courts are the judge, the prosecuting attorney, and defense counsel. Each has a specialized role, engages in a variety of tasks, and employs different work techniques.[56] But all three share some common goals that tend to meld them together into a fairly cohesive unit.

To the outsider, it may seem that the prosecutor and the defense attorney would necessarily be in an adversarial relationship, with the prosecutor pushing for conviction and sentencing on the most serious applicable charges and with the defense attorney pushing just as hard for acquittal. However, a set of shared perspectives and common goals belie this assumption.

Researchers Eisenstein and Jacob posited four shared goals that help draw the courtroom work group together. These goals are set forth in Table 9–5. Note that the goals of "doing justice" and "maintaining group cohesion" are characterized as "expressive" to reflect their primarily symbolic role in work group functioning. Conversely, "disposing of caseload" and "reducing uncertainty" are both "instrumental," in that each has much to do with accomplishing the day-to-day work of the group.

Eisenstein and Jacob hypothesized that each of these goals could be either "externally rooted," responding to pressures from outside the courthouse—such as those exerted by the media, the police, or the public in general—or "internally noted," imposed by the work group environment itself and necessary to the organizational integrity of the group.

---

[53]Neubauer, *America's Courts and the Criminal Justice System*, 240.

[54]James Eisenstein and Herbert Jacob, *Felony Justice: An Organizational Analysis of Criminal Courts* (Lanham, Md.: University Press of America, 1991), Ch. 2.

[55]Eisenstein and Jacob, *Felony Justice*, Ch. 2; see also James Eisenstein, Roy B. Flemming, and Peter F. Nardulli, *The Contours of Justice: Communities and Their Courts* (Boston: Little, Brown & Company, 1988), 19–39.

[56]Regarding the "craft" of each of these three actors, see Flemming et al., *The Craft of Justice*.

Table 9-5   Goals of Courtroom Work Groups

	Origins of Goal	
Function of Goal	External	Internal
Expressive	Doing justice	Maintaining group cohesion
Instrumental	Disposing of caseload	Reducing uncertainty

Source: James Eisenstein and Herbert Jacob, *Felony Justice: An Organizational Analysis of Criminal Courts* (Lanham, Md.: University Press of America, 1991), 25.

Immediately apparent from Eisenstein and Jacob's construction is that even though criminal courts have a genuine need to *appear* to be "doing justice," they are internally oriented toward efficiently disposing of the cases on their dockets in a manner that produces few surprises and makes for a cohesive, predictable work environment. Since an acceptable level of group cohesion contributes to these ends, it is a "real," rather than merely symbolic, goal pursued not for its own sake, but to grease the internal workings of the system.

It is out of this matrix of interacting roles and shared aims that the much-discussed practice of plea bargaining emerges. Indeed, "bargained justice" is a perfectly natural, if not logical, method of conflict resolution in the criminal courts, given the courts' combination of roles, methods, and goals.

Of the two chief methods of resolving conflict—fighting and talking—talking appears by far the better choice, as it is more likely to achieve the twin goals of efficient processing of cases and reduction of uncertainty. By contrast, trials—"fighting" for the work group—are grossly inefficient from almost every perspective. They are ragged, uncertain, nasty affairs that demand the use of scarce resources (time, money, and professional talent), while tearing at the cohesiveness of the group. Negotiated settlements, on the other hand, permit a high level of efficiency and of certainty, maximum group cohesion, and the *appearance* of doing justice. Whether the accused agrees with the process is not necessarily determinative; indeed, he or she may well be more like a pawn in the game than a principal player.[57]

A glance back at Figure 9-3 will reveal the significant role of the guilty plea in the latter stages of the criminal case-processing funnel. Of a hypothetical 1,500 crimes committed, perhaps 500 (one-third the total) are reported to the police, resulting in 100 arrests (20 percent of the total crimes committed). Of these 100 cases, a little less than half are screened out by the time that formal charges are filed. Of the 55 cases remaining in the system following the defendant's first court appearance, 52 are disposed of through guilty pleas, leaving only 3 of the original 100 cases that go forward to trial. This result comports with the majority of contemporary criminal justice research, which suggests that on average, some 90 percent of all convictions are obtained through guilty pleas. The data presented in Table 9-6 support this conclusion and suggest that guilty-plea rates vary but little with changes in population.

In simple terms, plea bargaining is a process by which the accused agrees to plead guilty in return for either explicitly or impliedly favorable treatment from the state. Indeed, the process is not entirely unlike the purchase of an automobile.

---

[57]For an early and entertaining description of the bargaining process, see Abraham S. Blumberg, "The Practice of Law as a Confidence Game: Organizational Co-Option of a Profession," *Law and Society Review*, 1, No. 2 (June 1967): 15–39; see also Cole, *The American System of Criminal Justice*: 346–59.

The dealer (prosecutor) explains the superiority of the product (the state's position), points to the full sticker price (the maximum possible sentencing outcome), and suggests—if not threatens—that as the likely outcome. In response, the buyer (defense counsel) identifies the obvious flaws and imperfections in the product (lack of probable cause for arrest, an ill-gotten confession, no credible eyewitnesses, and so forth), and mentions the invoice price (the least punitive sentence short of outright acquittal) as the more reasonable figure.

A period of bargaining ensues, with the seller suggesting that she or he has offered an enormous discount (dropping more serious charges, making sentencing concessions) and with the buyer recognizing that he or she is getting the deal for a little more than wholesale (probation with conditions on a misdemeanor rather than a felony). The deal is struck, and the case resolved.

From the outset, both prosecutor and defense counsel are aware that, much as in civil disputing, few criminal cases go to trial. Furthermore, it is rare indeed that every charge threatened in the early going could actually be proven beyond a reasonable doubt. Rather, the vast majority of cases are disposed of through this system of barter and exchange.

In some instances, plea bargaining can take place informally— between a prosecutor and a defense attorney walking down the hall between courtrooms, for instance. In others, it is extremely formal, occurring at a time and place established by court order.

Although primarily a matter for the prosecuting and defense attorneys to hash out, a plea agreement also inevitably involves the court. Generally the process takes place with only indirect participation from a particular judge until a proposed disposition is achieved. The negotiations, however, always have the judge's policies as a backdrop; that is, both prosecutor and defense counsel know what kind of deal the judge will permit and which concessions the judge will reject. In many instances, judges will set time limits for negotiating a plea agreement; for example, if the case is not resolved at least 30 days prior to trial, it goes forward unless the defendant is willing to plead guilty to all of the charges with no concessions from the state. In other jurisdictions, a plea agreement is acceptable even after trial commences.

Typically, plea bargaining is also bounded by the office policies of the prosecutor. Because of a number of factors that can include public disposition toward and media attention regarding a particular crime issue, chief prosecutors generally establish the parameters within which their deputies may "deal" their cases. Such policies can place some cases off-limits to plea bargaining altogether and can set limits with respect to sentence concessions on others.

By contrast, defense attorneys rarely enter the plea negotiation process with policy limitations. As Flemming, Nardulli, and Eisenstein conclude,

> public defender offices typically are loosely structured, are non-hierarchically administered, and develop few policies. Chief public defenders shun bureaucracy. Unlike their peers in the prosecutor's office, they feel that defense work is a matter of professionalism that cannot and should not be reduced to following policy guidelines.[58]

While rigid guidelines may not influence the way in which a defense attorney approaches plea negotiations, the needs and desires of the defendant most certainly do. Having a vested interest in moving cases along, criminal defense attorneys are usually anxious to sell their clients on reasonable deals. At the same time, private defense counsel must earn, and collect, a fee from the accused. Thus, a defense attorney is often placed between a rock and a

---

[58]Flemming et al., *The Craft of Justice,* 157 (footnote omitted).

hard place, with a clearly desirable offer from the state on the one hand and the accused's need to feel that the lawyer is zealously defending him or her on the other.

In general, however, the accused stands to benefit from plea bargaining for many of the same reasons that the other members of the courtroom work group do. As one might expect, then, each party endeavors to expend his or her bargaining chips to maximize the likelihood of obtaining those benefits.

For the prosecutor, plea bargaining is a way to obtain convictions without lengthy and uncertain trials. This process, of course, looks good to the public, to which chief prosecutors must typically turn for election. Prosecutors may also at times exploit the plea bargaining process to reel in bigger fish. Particularly in federal prosecutions, it is common for a prosecutor to offer a reduced charge in return for information regarding other alleged criminals.

Defense counsel is likewise in a position to reap the benefits of plea bargaining. He or she has an obvious interest in avoiding trial: because they are time-consuming to prepare and to conduct, trials simply do not permit the high turnover rate necessary to maintaining either a public defender's office or a private legal practice. Although in a relatively weak position as compared with that of the prosecutor, defense counsel does hold significant bargaining chips. The defense counsel can, for example, use delaying tactics in the hope that an important witness will become unavailable or that the complainant will lose interest. By contrast, the defense attorney can also employ the defendant's right to a speedy trial in order to force the case along such that the state does not have sufficient time to orchestrate complicated, unavailable, and perhaps nonexistent evidence.

In general, however, defense counsel gains the most from going along with the system, working out deals with prosecutors and functioning as a good team player. Defense attorneys certainly understand that future clients can be hurt by overly recalcitrant tactics. Neither prosecutors nor judges are likely to forget a defense attorney who refuses to play ball. In other words, the organizational imperative underlying the courtroom work group co-opts defense counsel into a cooperative stance.[59]

The defendant, while often in the dark about the nuances of the plea bargaining process itself, clearly has something to gain by participating in that process: a reduction in the number or in the severity of charges, less jail time or none at all, lower cost than that necessary for preparation of a full-blown trial, and the emotional relief that comes from simply "getting it over with." Furthermore, going to trial can deepen the problems of the accused, permitting the full details of various transgressions to become known and to influence the court that subsequently passes sentence. Thus, defendants usually find it desirable to plead guilty in accord with the prosecutor's offer of a more certain and potentially less harsh result.

Despite being the weakest player in the courtroom work group, the defendant does hold certain bargaining strengths of his or her own, primarily in the form of constitutional rights that, if exercised, substantially slow the process. That these are potentially powerful factors helps explain the forces brought to bear upon the defendant by other work group participants in an effort to persuade him or her to plead guilty.

Finally, the court has a vested interest in plea bargaining. Processing a maximum number of cases is almost always to a judge's advantage. Trials take up valuable time and consume other resources that could be devoted to clearing cases from the docket. Although in many jurisdictions an individual judge can influence the plea bargaining process only indirectly, that influence may significantly affect case outcomes. Either formally or infor-

---

[59]See Blumberg, "The Practice of Law as a Confidence Game." Professor Walker identifies a similar "go along to get along" phenomenon with respect to prosecutors. See Walker, *Taming the System,* 87–88.

mally, most judges make known to all who practice in their courts their policies regarding plea agreements. It is not at all unusual, for example, to find that some judges in a given jurisdiction will accept most any deal that the prosecutor is willing to offer, while others in the same courthouse make a thorough enquiry into the circumstances of each case and reject plea agreements that do not satisfy their own criteria. In such instances, the prosecutor and defense attorney find themselves working together to "sell" a plea to the court.

Even in those jurisdictions where court policies prohibit formal judicial intervention in plea negotiations, a judge may exercise many, often subtle, bargaining tools. An experienced judge knows where old skeletons of past bar and bench politics are hidden and can subtly remind attorneys on both sides of this fact. A judge can also directly or indirectly threaten harsh sentences and can make clear to an attorney that an intransigent attitude will be remembered when next that attorney appears.[60]

In sum, the bureaucratic imperative tends to co-opt all criminal court participants into what has been called an "agent-mediator role," to the end that the work is accomplished, the structure survives, and careers are enhanced and preserved. But who loses in this process? Why, with all its apparent advantages, is plea bargaining so controversial?

Without proceeding through the whole of what has now become a classic debate, it will be useful to outline two major criticisms of this practice. First, many argue that a covert, behind-the-scenes process of this sort violates fundamental notions of fairness inherent to the concept of "due process." This argument grows primarily, although by no means exclusively, out of concern for the rights and protections afforded the accused. The presumption of guilt that seems endemic to the process as well as the use of various forms of influence to manipulate the defendant toward the desired result—the guilty plea—are perceived as antithetical to the notion of adversarial justice that theoretically protects individuals against illegitimate prosecution and punishment.

On the other side, generally characterized as the political right side of the fence, plea bargaining is criticized for leading to unconscionably light sentences for serious criminal offenders. The argument is frequently made that in its focus on efficiency, the largely administrative plea bargaining process allows too many charges to be reduced or dropped, thereby permitting hundreds of defendants to escape "justice." This alleged leniency is criticized most harshly by police, who often voice the opinion that defendants should as a matter of course be tried on every charge originally pressed.

Ironically, these two classic lines of criticism have resulted in bringing elements of the political left and right together. Judicial politics, like other politics, can make for strange bedfellows. Thus, civil libertarians concerned with protecting the rights of criminal defendants have joined with right-wing law-and-order types concerned with closing procedural loopholes and lengthening sentences to condemn plea bargaining.

In response, some jurisdictions have attempted to severely limit, or even eliminate, plea bargaining. The Attorney General of Alaska formally banned plea bargaining in the summer of 1975. The following year, the State of Michigan statutorily prohibited sentence bargaining for gun-related offenses.[61] In 1982, California voters took up the matter of plea bargaining limitation in a ballot initiative advertised to be a "Victims' Bill of Rights."[62]

Despite being almost entirely subsumed by calls to "get tough on crime" through plea bargaining bans, there are arguments posited in favor of the process, voiced primarily

---

[60]For anecdotes regarding judicial intervention in the plea bargaining process, including a four-part description of the "styles" such intervention can adopt, see Flemming et al., *The Craft of Justice,* 112–132.

[61]Walker discusses both of these responses to the perceived leniency of plea bargaining; see Walker, *Taming the System,* 94–100.

[62]Candace McCoy analyzes California's "Proposition 8," including its purported "ban" on plea bargaining, as a reflection of right wing, law-and-order political strategy in her *Politics and Plea Bargaining: Victims' Rights in California* (Philadelphia: University of Pennsylvania Press, 1993).

by those involved in the criminal justice system. Most often such arguments proceed along pragmatic lines: all institutions manufacture efficient means for getting the work done; the adversarial model has proven unworkable in the "real world" of the courthouse; bargained justice *can* and *does* reflect the guarantees of due process and fundamental fairness in most cases; and, above and beyond all else, the system would drown almost immediately if every case went to trial.[63] Defenders of plea bargaining also point out that doubts about the guilt or innocence of a given defendant are handled at the earliest stages of the case-screening process. Thus, the cases that remain in the system, and that are subject to disposition through a plea agreement, are based upon evidence suggesting the defendant's factual guilt of some crime. Lengthy, expensive, and uncertain trials in such circumstances are simply unnecessary. Rather, the plea bargaining process offers an adequate, and even a desirable, administrative substitute.

Contrary to popular belief, plea bargaining has been around a long time. Milton Heumann discovered that between 1880 and 1910, the rate of bargained guilty pleas in the State of Connecticut was around 90 percent—the same rate as reported in courts in contemporary decades across the nation.[64] Thus, although few data are available to indicate the actual patterns of criminal case disposition prior to the industrial revolution, we know that at least since that time, plea bargaining has been common. We could therefore argue that bargained criminal justice occurring within an administrative model is merely part of a widespread shift from the ideal of deliberative democracy to the more "realistic" and workable model of administrative decision making characterized by the creation and growth of bureaucratic institutions—a shift that has clearly been experienced in both the legislative and the executive branches of government.

Leaving aside the question of whether such ideal deliberative institutions ever actually existed, we know that, as government moved from a more passive to a more active player within organized society, the classic legislative process contemplated by the founders broke down and was replaced by an administrative state with a vast array of specialized agencies and bureaus. It is certainly reasonable to assume that similar forces brought about "bargained justice" as a workable process capable of efficiently and effectively responding to the realities of twentieth century criminal adjudication.[65]

TRIALS

It would be a mistake to describe the criminal justice system wholly in terms of pretrial negotiations. Trials, though infrequent, *do* occur, requiring substantial commitments of time and resources from each member of the courtroom work group.

---

[63]See Professor Walker's discussions of the "myth" of case pressure as an essentially unfounded justification for plea bargaining in Walker, *Taming the System,* 95–99, and in Walker, *Sense and Nonsense About Crime,* 125–130.

More recent research by Thomas Church suggests that the persistence of plea bargaining may be due simply to the belief among lawyers and judges that it is a fair way to dispose of cases. See Thomas W. Church, "Plea Bargaining and Local Legal Culture," in Lee Epstein, ed., *Contemplating Courts* (Washington: Congressional Quarterly Press, 1995), 132–154.

[64]Milton Heumann, *Plea Bargaining: The Experiences of Prosecutors, Judges and Defense Attorneys* (Chicago: University of Chicago Press, 1978), 28–32; other discussions of the history of the plea bargaining process may be found in *Law and Society Review* 13, No. 2 (Winter 1979).

[65]See Dwight Waldo, *The Administrative State* (New York: Ronald Press, 1948). An alternative view of the history and current impact of plea bargaining is provided by Malcolm Feeley. See his "Plea Bargaining and the Structure of the Criminal Process," and the commentary on that piece, in *Justice System Journal* 7, No. 3 (Winter 1982): 338–60. Feeley's central thesis is that plea bargaining is not necessarily a nonadversarial process but rather may have enhanced the competitiveness of the criminal justice process.

Before describing the trial process, however, it seems relevant to ask why any particular case goes to trial. How does the bargaining process break down such that a case requires the most formal means of resolution?

As previously noted, the probability that a given case will go to trial is directly related to the seriousness of the offense or offenses involved. Charges such as rape and murder are much more likely to be tried than are property or drug crimes. An informal calculus at work here runs roughly as follows: in general, with crimes carrying long prison sentences, or even capital punishment, trial is likely because the slim chance of acquittal is worth the effort. Such crimes also typically fall into that category of offenses a prosecutor is unlikely to "deal down" significantly—as from a felony to a misdemeanor—offering the defendant little incentive to avoid the risk of trial.

Along the same line, where the chances of acquittal are relatively high, such as where the victim is the only witness and cannot clearly identify the accused, the probability of trial, absent an extremely favorable plea bargain, increases. Conversely, where property crimes are at issue, the prosecution generally has strong, often physical, evidence (fingerprints or a security system videotape, for example), making both acquittal and trial itself much less likely.

A criminal trial may take place with or without a jury. In the latter circumstance, a judge sits as the finder of fact and determines whether the prosecutor has proved the case beyond a reasonable doubt. Petty offenses (e.g., shoplifting) and many juvenile matters are typically tried, if at all, to a judge rather than to a jury, primarily in order to conserve judicial resources.

In most instances, a defendant accused of a misdemeanor or a felony may waive the right to trial by jury and request a bench trial, although in many jurisdictions the prosecutor must agree to such a waiver and is therefore empowered to force a jury trial. Defendants charged with sexual assault, and particularly those accused of sexually assaulting a child, are often counseled to request a trial to the court on the assumption that a judge is better able to view objectively the evidence presented and to set aside sympathy for the victim.

The constitutional right to trial by a jury has never been absolute. However, the United States Supreme Court has gradually extended that right so that today, all adult defendants in both state and federal courts have the right to demand a jury trial if the offense with which they are charged could result in punishment of more than six months' incarceration.[66]

At the same time, the old common law structure of "twelve good men and true" reaching a unanimous verdict has given way to six-, seven-, and eight-person juries. The Supreme Court has concluded that juries of as few as six persons are acceptable in noncapital cases[67] and has held that nonunanimous, majority verdicts are sufficient for a conviction when the jury has more than six members.[68] While all states continue to require unanimous verdicts from twelve-person juries in order to convict in death penalty cases, almost half the states now permit juries of less than twelve in misdemeanor cases, and a handful allow such juries to try felonies.

Jury trials typically include the following steps: (1) jury selection; (2) opening statements; (3) presentation of testimony and exhibits during the prosecution's case in chief; (4)

---

[66]*Duncan v. Louisiana,* 391 U.S. 145 (1968) (concluding that the Sixth Amendment right to trial by jury in federal cases is incorporated into the Fourteenth Amendment right of due process and therefore applicable to the States).

[67]*Williams v. Florida,* 399 U.S. 78 (1970).

[68]*Burch v. Louisiana,* 441 U.S. 130 (1979) (holding that conviction by a nonunanimous vote of a six-member jury contravenes the Sixth Amendment guarantee of trial by jury).

presentation of testimony and exhibits on behalf of the defendant, although the defendant, who is presumed innocent, need not put on a case at all; (5) rebuttal testimony and exhibits; (6) closing arguments; (7) instructions to the jury from the court; and (8) the jury's verdict.

Out of all of these steps, jury selection has grown to be one of the most controversial. In the typical case, a pool of potential jurors is created, usually via jury duty summons that command individuals to appear at the local courthouse for jury duty. The pool is winnowed down until a given jury is finally selected.

Voter registration lists are usually the means by which names are obtained for the jury pool, injecting an obvious bias into the process from the outset. Large segments of the population, such as the poor and racial minorities, are generally underrepresented by this selection procedure. Moreover, physicians, teachers, lawyers, and other professionals are frequently excused from jury duty, further undermining the likelihood that any particular jury will reflect the composition of the community. Although some jurisdictions have replaced or supplemented voter registration lists with drivers license lists, juries on the whole continue to represent only a small segment of society.[69]

As an added measure of fairness, both prosecution and defense attorneys are permitted to participate in the jury selection process. During *voir dire,* attorneys may challenge individual jurors, requesting that the court not seat them for service on a given jury. These challenges take two forms: challenges "for cause" and "peremptory challenges."

Challenges for cause must reflect some reason that a particular juror likely could not fairly and objectively consider the evidence presented. Such a challenge might be based on the fact that the juror knows the alleged victim or has a close relative who is a police officer. Each for-cause challenge must be presented to and ruled upon by the court.

In contrast, peremptory challenges can be based on guesses or hunches. Each side is allowed a certain number of such challenges—six or eight are not unusual, although many more are sometimes allowed in murder trials—and the exercise of each challenge is final. Peremptory challenges allow each side to work toward a jury that will favor its position, or at least will not be stacked against it.[70] In the past, peremptory challenges could be used for any purpose whatsoever. However, recent decisions from the U.S. Supreme Court have prohibited using peremptories to strike a juror solely on the basis of that individual's race or sex.[71]

---

[69]Conducting research on juries and jury verdicts has been a favorite pastime of lawyers and social scientists. The early, classic study focusing more on jury decision making than on jury selection is Harry Kalven, Jr., and Hans Zeisel, *The American Jury* (Boston: Little, Brown, 1966). A more recent review of jury research is Rita James Simon, ed., *The Jury System in America: A Critical Overview* (Beverly Hills, Calif.: Sage, 1975). On the issue of jury selection, see Jon M. VanDyke, *Jury Selection Procedures* (Cambridge, Mass.: Ballinger, 1977). See also Barbara F. Reskin and Christy A. Visher, "The Impacts of Evidence and Extra-Legal Factors in Jurors' Decisions," *Law and Society Review* 20, No. 3 (1986): 423–38, and James P. Levine, *Juries and Politics* (Pacific Grove, Calif.: Brooks/Cole Publishing Co., 1992).

[70]James Levine recites the following passage regarding the use of peremptory challenges from a handbook prepared for assistant district attorneys in Dallas, Texas:

> WHAT TO LOOK FOR IN A JUROR: 1. You are not looking for a fair juror, but rather a strong, biased and sometimes hypocritical individual who believes that defendants are different from them in kind, rather than degree.

Levine, *Juries and Politics,* 51.

[71]See *Batson v. Kentucky,* 476 U.S. 79 (1986) (holding that peremptory challenges may not be used to strike those of the defendant's race or ethnic group from the jury on the grounds of their race or ethnicity); and *J. E. B. v. Alabama ex rel. T. B.,* 114 S. Ct. 1419, 1430 (1994) (". . . the Equal Protection Clause prohibits discrimination in jury selection on the basis of gender, or on the assumption that an individual will be biased in a particular case for no reason other than the fact that the person happens to be a woman or happens to be a man.").

The selection of jurors is considered so crucial that an entire industry has developed to assist trial lawyers with the task. Professional legal publications such as *The National Law Journal* and *The American Bar Association Journal* frequently contain advertisements from jury selection experts such as the following:

> "[Our jury expert] helped us select the jury in *California v. Powell,* the Rodney King case," said Michael Stone, counsel for Officer Lawrence Powell. "Many trial lawyers feel they can select appropriate jurors without the help of a professional. In *Powell* we weren't willing to gamble. [Our expert] worked with us for a full month selecting the jury. The defense lawyers still performed their individual analysis, but we combined our efforts with [our expert's] to produce the best predictions possible. We succeeded in impaneling the right jury.[72]

Once a sufficient number of jurors has been selected and sworn by the court, the trial commences with opening statements delivered to the jury by the prosecution and, if desired, by the defense. In these opening remarks, each side typically attempts to outline its case, making "friends" with the jury and setting the stage for its trial strategy.

The prosecution then presents its case in chief, introducing the testimony of witnesses and various exhibits calculated to prove the defendant's guilt. This presentation must be accomplished in accord with state and, when applicable, federal, rules of criminal procedure and rules of evidence, which can be complex and need not be detailed here. Suffice to say that many trials turn on the admissibility of challenged evidence, a decision that belongs to the judge.

At the conclusion of the prosecution's case, the defense will typically move the court to dismiss the case on the ground that the prosecutor has failed to present evidence sufficient to permit the defendant's conviction beyond a reasonable doubt. This motion, called a "motion for judgment of acquittal" or a "motion for a directed verdict," is usually denied, and the trial then proceeds.

Recall that the prosecution bears the burden of proving its case and that the defendant is constitutionally protected against being forced to testify. Indeed, the court instructs the jury that it cannot consider the defendant's decision *not* to testify as evidence of guilt and carefully questions the defendant regarding that decision. It is not at all unusual for a defendant to decline to testify owing to the damage that may be done by the prosecution during cross-examination.

Even when the decision is made that the defendant will not take the stand, defense counsel must still prepare a strategy to undermine the prosecution's case. This can usually be accomplished by casting doubt on the prosecution's witnesses and other evidence through effective cross-examination and, sometimes, through rebuttal testimony. Alternatively, the defense can mount its own case, affirmatively defending against the prosecution's charges—for instance, with an alibi or a claim of self-defense.

Both the prosecution and the defense have the opportunity to discredit the evidence presented by the other in the rebuttal phase of the trial, which precedes closing arguments. During closing, sometimes referred to as "summation," each side is permitted to argue its theory as to why the facts in evidence indicate that the defendant either is or is not guilty beyond a reasonable doubt.

Following closing arguments, the court instructs the jury as to what it must find in order to convict the defendant. Each side has the opportunity to argue for particular instructions; and, given the importance of the instructions in guiding the jury's delibera-

---

[72]Quoted from an advertisement for Litigation Sciences, Inc., in *The National Law Journal* (Monday, Feb. 22, 1993): S5. The defendant, Officer Lawrence Powell, was acquitted in the trial to which the advertisement makes reference. He was, however, subsequently convicted on essentially the same facts by a federal jury.

tions, the arguments presented can be substantial. Jury instructions typically include a definition of proof beyond a reasonable doubt, an explanation that the burden of proof lies entirely with the prosecution, definitions of each element of the particular offenses at issue, and directions regarding certain evidentiary rulings that the court may have made during the trial.

Having been instructed, the jury retires to the jury room to begin its deliberations. The processes and outcomes of jury deliberations have been the focus of both sociological research and jurisprudential critiques for a long time. Space does not permit a discussion of them all here. However, in general, juries seem to favor conviction, the percentages varying with different screening policies and plea bargaining practices across jurisdictions. In a study of felony verdicts in 13 U.S. cities of varying sizes, the conviction rate ranged from 96 percent down to 64 percent, with an average of about 73 percent of all cases tried resulting in a conviction.[73]

Research suggests that jury deliberations are likely subject to the effects of social status, with white males—particularly those with relatively extensive education—tending to dominate discussions. Moreover, researchers have also determined that juries tend to be only slightly more lenient than judges are in most instances. In about three-fourths of all jury trials, the ultimate decision ends up being the same as it would have been if the case had been tried before a judge sitting alone.[74] It appears that most judge-jury disagreement regarding verdicts grows out of the phenomenon of "jury nullification," in which jurors reach a verdict on extralegal grounds, essentially modifying the law as stated in order to suit community norms. Although instances of perceived and of known jury nullification garner tremendous immediate attention, they are almost certainly extraordinary and rare.[75]

As earlier noted, trials, especially jury trials, should not be assessed merely in terms of their frequency. It is undeniably true that the vast majority—upwards of 90 percent in most jurisdictions—of criminal cases are bargained to a resolution well short of trial. Indeed, if there is one lesson the media circus surrounding the double-murder prosecution of O. J. Simpson taught, it is that the existing system of criminal justice functions primarily as an administrative process. The fact that "the Simpson matter," which featured every possible component of a felony prosecution played out in extraordinary detail, was the focus of such widespread attention and public amazement clearly indicates how rarely the criminal justice system is actually pushed to its outer limits.

Nevertheless, trials, and particularly jury trials—like the judicial rulings in civil cases discussed in Chapter 8—play an important "feedback" role in shaping the far more common process of plea bargaining. From the police precinct to the final stages of the disposition, the central issue remains the same in each criminal prosecution: What would a jury do? That "prediction," as Justice Holmes would have it, is the very essence of criminal law and serves as the guiding force in all pretrial decision making.

SENTENCING

Case disposition, whether with or without trial, concludes with sentencing. If the first stage of that process—arrest—is fraught with controversy, this final event is even more contentious.

---

[73]See Bureau of Justice Statistics, *Report to the Nation,* 65; see also "Jurors Prefer Lawyers Who Are Well-Prepared—And Not Arrogant," *The National Law Journal* (Monday, February 22, 1993): S10, which reports results of a recent juror survey, including a decided preference for prosecutors over defense attorneys.

[74]As reported in Kalven and Zeisel, *The American Jury.*

[75]See the discussion of jury nullification presented in Ch. 6 of Levine, *Juries and Politics,* 100–117.

Spurred on by both print and broadcast media, the typical citizen cannot help but notice the apparent disparity and inequity in criminal sentences among states, among different crimes, and among particular classes of defendants. One sees the wealthy or politically privileged defendant convicted of a serious offense yet "getting off" with a seemingly light sentence, while others who lack wealth or status are shipped away to prison and even to the death chamber. Concurrently, the political right is prone to publicly identify violent or repeat offenders sentenced to less-than-maximum punishments and to call for more "tough-on crime" policies and jurists.

Against this background, it may come as a surprise that U.S. courts impose the longest prison terms on the most people of any country in the Western world, explaining in part the fact that it has by far the highest rate of incarceration of any present-day, nontotalitarian state. Moreover, our imprisonment rate is shooting skyward, both relatively and absolutely.

According to U.S. government statistics, approximately 1,585,400 persons were incarcerated in the United States in 1995, a rate of about 1 person in every 167 U.S. residents. As of June 30, 1995, there were approximately 507,044 people being held in city and county jails across the nation, with another 34,869 being supervised by jail authorities on programs such as home detention, electronic monitoring, and work release. There were 1,026,882 people in the custody of state prisons, and 100,250 were incarcerated in federal correctional facilities, an increase of 6.8 percent in the total number of prisoners since 1994.[76]

By way of comparison, in 1983, approximately 430,000 persons were being held in prisons and jails, a rate of about 177 prisoners per 100,000 people in the general population. This number reflected a 70 percent increase over 1974, when there were some 230,000 people serving prison or jail sentences.[77]

At least one reason for the enormous increase in prison populations is the increase in drug offenders serving time in both state and federal facilities. Between 1980 and 1993, the percentage of those serving sentences for drug offenses in state prisons increased from 8 percent to 26 percent of total state prison populations. During the same period, the number of federal prisoners doing time for drug-related convictions jumped from 25 percent to 60 percent of all federal prisoners.

As stated previously, the increasingly large numbers of people incarcerated across the nation in no way mirror the racial and socioeconomic composition of the general population. Indeed, in the period between 1983 and 1993, "the proportion of inmates in state and Federal prisons who were Black rose to 50.8 percent from 46.5 percent, while the proportion of prisoners of Hispanic descent almost doubled to 14.3 percent from 7.7 percent.[78]

Likewise, American jail populations reflect a racial composition vastly different from that of the general population. As of the summer of 1995, a majority of local jail inmates were African American or Hispanic, while 40.1 percent were white. Approximately 90 percent of all jail inmates were male.

It has been argued that, adding the 1.5 million or so people presently in jail or in prison to the approximately 3.5 million more on probation or parole, and assuming a continuation of current sentencing trends,

---

[76]See U.S. Department of Justice, Bureau of Justice Statistics, *Prison and Jail Inmates, 1995* (Washington, D.C.: U.S. Department of Justice, September 1996) (NCJ-161132), 1. See also Fox Butterfield, "More in U.S. Are in Prisons Report Says: Number of Inmates at the End of 1994 Has Tripled Since 1980," *New York Times* (August 10, 1995): A–7.

[77]See U.S. Department of Justice, Bureau of Justice Statistics, *Prisoners at Mid-Year 1983,* (Washington, D.C.: U.S. Department of Justice, 1983) (NCJ-91034).

[78]Butterfield, "More in U.S. Are in Prisons," U.S. Department of Justice, Bureau of Justice Statistics, *Prison and Jail Inmates, 1995,* 16–17.

the number of Americans behind bars or on probation or parole will soon approach the 6 million students enrolled full-time in four-year colleges and universities nationwide; within a decade the number of people behind bars will exceed the entire New York City population, currently about 7.3 million.[79]

Clearly, irrespective of political rhetoric to the contrary, there is no shortage of people being punished through incarceration across the country. A brief overview of sentencing patterns and practices will help us assess the role of the judiciary in this apparent "incarceration frenzy."

At base, sentencing is so extremely controversial because our society is deeply divided as to the *purpose* of criminal sanctions. Not only are groups within the United States at war with one another over this issue at any particular moment in history, but opinion shifts over time, as is evident in contemporary American society.

There are essentially four significantly different perspectives from which to view criminal punishment and to discern its primary purpose:

1. *Rehabilitation.*   This is the "treatment" approach, based on the notion that criminals are somehow misguided, perhaps even ill, and susceptible to resocialization via careful intervention. This approach was dominant in America for several decades prior to the 1980s, when corrections policies then turned sharply and rapidly away from it.

2. *Retribution.*   The "eye-for-an-eye" perspective, this approach assumes that the offender *deserves* punishment in a measure roughly proportional to the seriousness of the crime. Inherent in the retributive perspective is the belief that offenders are responsible for their actions, have committed wrongs of their own volition, and are justifiably required to pay a debt to society. In a nutshell, the appropriate "pound of flesh" must be exacted. This approach is marked primarily by a desire for vengeance and is gaining in acceptance among both theoreticians and policy makers.

3. *Incapacitation.*   This approach looks to prevent crime more effectively by locking up more proven criminals for longer periods of time. This approach would support the chemical castration of sex offenders, heavy fines for white collar criminals, and long prison terms for all. Like the Retribution approach, adherents of Incapacitation as the primary goal for criminal punishment are becoming more numerous and more vocal.

4. *Deterrence.*   From this perspective, punishment should be calculated to have the maximum impact on society by discouraging others from becoming offenders themselves. Moreover, the sanction should also be imposed so as to discourage the particular offender from ever again breaking the law. The resurgence of the prison chain gang among Southern jurisdictions and the institution of "boot camps" that give a taste of prison life to young criminals exemplify the widespread acceptance of deterrence as a valid goal for criminal sanctions.

Obviously, these four perspectives are interrelated; a person need not subscribe to one to the total exclusion of the others, though only a moment's reflection will reveal that the goals of each approach tend to conflict with one another. Since we are anything but clear as to what causes crime, however, it seems reasonable to expect that we would likewise be uncertain as to its cure.

Each of us at times becomes convinced that one or another of these approaches to punishment will solve the crime problem. However, research on criminal sanctions has failed to provide us with the answers we have long sought. While as a society, we seem to

---

[79]Butterfield, "More in U.S. Are in Prisons."

have rebelled against the rehabilitative approach, finding that it has little effect upon criminal recidivism, our move toward more punitive measures carries with it no promise for actual reductions in crime.[80]

Although a "tougher" approach may have some psychic satisfaction for a society frustrated by increases in criminal conduct, there is little evidence to suggest that the severity of the potential punishment in and of itself leads to a decrease in criminal behavior. Indeed, if we have learned anything about deterrence, it is that the *certainty* of punishment is far more important in deterring aberrant conduct than is its nature or severity. Yet, consistent, equitable, and certain punishment meted out in like fashion to all similarly situated offenders is extremely difficult to bring about.[81]

In a practical sense, sentencing can take many forms. Incarceration in a county jail for short-term punishment or the state penitentiary as a much more severe sanction are certainly common occurrences in the criminal justice system. Probation, however, with no significant jail time attached as a condition,[82] is the far more likely sanction in most criminal matters. Then, too, judges may impose fines, order restitution, or, in rare instances, sentence an offender to death. Informal punishment, present at virtually every stage of the criminal justice process, must also be recognized as a powerful sanction.[83]

As most judges will attest, arriving at a sentencing decision can be the most lonely and difficult of tasks. It is here that judicial discretion can have its most dramatic effect. In most jurisdictions, a typical, nonviolent felony conviction can result in a sentence ranging from probation with no jail time to a lengthy prison stay. As in all previous steps of the criminal justice process, we wish to concentrate on the factors that help us understand how this decision is reached.

At the outset we should recall that only about 10 percent of all prosecutions actually end in a trial; the vast majority are plea bargained. And in the process of bargaining toward a plea agreement, the potential sentence is of course a critical element. As noted earlier, the judge may well play an important, albeit indirect, role in establishing the sentencing component of the deal that the defendant eventually accepts. Furthermore, that deal is almost certain to include a sentence guarantee that falls significantly below the maximum that could potentially be imposed.

Likewise, in a case that goes to trial and ends in a conviction, the court plays a significant—and this time a very direct—part in the determination of the defendant's sentence. While judicial discretion at every other stage of the criminal justice process may be indirect and somewhat "kept under wraps," at the sentencing stage, the discretion of an individual judge to mete out justice to an individual defendant for decades served as the very cornerstone of what was perceived to be appropriate sentencing policy.[84] Increasingly,

---

[80]There is an enormous literature on modes of punishment as related to crime. See, e.g., Norval Morris and Michael Tonry, *Between Prison and Probation: Intermediate Punishments in a Rational Sentencing System* (New York: Oxford University Press, 1990); Marvin E. Frankel, *Criminal Sentences: Law Without Order,* (New York: Hill & Wang, 1972); Eric Q. Wright, *The Politics of Punishment* (New York: Harper & Row, 1973); Karl Menninger, *The Crime of Punishment* (New York: Viking Press, 1968); and Twentieth Century Fund Task Force on Sentencing, *Fair and Certain Punishment,* (New York: McGraw-Hill, 1976).

[81]See H. Laurence Ross and Gary D. LaFree, "Deterrents in Criminology and Social Policy," paper presented at the National Academy of Sciences Symposium on Knowledge in Social and Behavioral Sciences: Discoveries and Trends Over Fifty Years, Washington, D.C., November 1983, and the sources cited therein.

[82]While not widely recognized outside the criminal justice system itself, in almost every instance in which probation is an acceptable sanction, a period of incarceration can also be imposed as a condition of that probation. It is thus not at all unusual to see an offender with a brief criminal record sentenced to probation for a period of years, as well as incarceration in the county jail for a period of weeks or months.

[83]See Cole, *The American System of Criminal Justice,* 440–57, on the forms of punishment.

[84]Walker, *Taming the System,* 113.

however, a given court's latitude in fashioning a particular sentence is being limited by restrictive legislation. Indeed, driven by discontent over what has been perceived as uncontrolled sentencing discretion, almost every state, along with the federal government, has enacted major changes in sentencing policies since the mid-1970s.

Prior to this period of sweeping reform, incarceration as a criminal sanction in the United States was characterized by the *indeterminate* sentence. Consistent with the rehabilitative model that held sway in corrections theory, though certainly not in corrections practice, throughout much of the twentieth century, indeterminate sentencing assumed that punishment needed to be highly individualized. Thus, the nature and length of incarceration depended entirely upon the individual convict's response to the sanction imposed. Typically, that determination was left in the hands of corrections officials and parole boards.[85]

Perhaps the pinnacle of indeterminate sentencing policy in this country was the practice in the State of California of making all sentences of imprisonment entirely indeterminate. The State Adult Authority was empowered to determine the length of time each individual who was sentenced to a term of imprisonment actually served.

Such open-ended discretion in sentencing was strongly criticized in publications such as the American Friends Service Committee's 1971 publication *Struggle for Justice*[86] and Frankel's 1972 *Criminal Sentences: Law Without Order*.[87] These and similar publications influenced California's policy-makers to adopt that state's Determinate Sentencing Law in 1976, which mandated that sentencing judges select a specific term of years from an express set of options and eliminated the authority of the parole board to determine actual release dates.[88]

The reforms enacted since the mid-1970s have, similar to California's, attempted to restrict judicial discretion in imposing incarceration to restrict parole board discretion in determining the actual length of incarceration, or sometimes both. Together, they can be thought of as moves toward "structured" sentencing policies.

In most instances, structured sentencing reform has emphasized the implementation of *determinate* sentences—sentences that reflect a fixed term of imprisonment that can generally be reduced by "good time" and by "earned time" awarded administratively by correctional officials for appropriate behavior and participation in prison work programs. Some states, as well as the federal government, have also turned to *mandatory minimum* sentencing structures in which a minimum term is specified by statute for particular offenses or for committing an offense under specific circumstances.

Sentencing guidelines have garnered wide support among criminal justice theorists in recent years. Such guidelines typically require that a court sentence an offender within a predetermined, "presumptive" range based on the offense committed and on the defendant's criminal history, or to provide a written justification for imposing a more severe or a more lenient sentence.

As of 1996, twenty states reported having implemented determinate sentencing, and sixteen indicated the adoption of sentencing guidelines in one form or another. All fifty

---

[85]On the history of indeterminate sentencing, see Tamasak Wicharaya, *Simple Theory, Hard Reality: The Impact of Sentencing Reforms on Courts, Prisons, and Crime* (Albany, New York: State University of New York Press, 1995), 27–40.

[86]American Friends Service Committee, *Struggle for Justice: A Report on Crime and Punishment in America* (New York: Hill & Wang, 1971).

[87]Marvin E. Frankel, *Criminal Sentences.*

[88]See Jonathan D. Casper, David Brereton, and David Neal, *The Implementation of the California Determinate Sentencing Law* (Washington, D.C.: U.S. Department of Justice, National Institute of Justice, Office of Research Programs, May 1982).

338 | Part III The Judicial Process

states and the District of Columbia have implemented some form of mandatory minimum sentencing policy.[89] Table 9–6 reflects the current sentencing policies in each of the states and the District of Columbia, while Table 9–7 illustrates the general categories of offenses for which each state has adopted mandatory minimum sentencing.

Beginning with the Sentencing Reform Act of 1984 [90] the federal government also undertook the creation and implementation of sentencing guidelines. The Act mandated the formation of the United States Sentencing Commission, an independent agency located within the judicial branch. At present, the Commission is composed of seven voting and two nonvoting members.

The Commission was responsible for drafting the original Federal Sentencing Guidelines, which were reviewed and adopted by Congress in 1987. It also retains continuing authority to amend the Guidelines, with congressional approval, on an annual basis.[91]

In order to "rationalize the federal sentencing process,"[92] the Sentencing Commission is statutorily directed to develop sentencing guidelines "that will further the basic purposes of criminal punishment: deterrence, incapacitation, just punishment, and rehabilitation."[93] The Commission is to accomplish this task by creating systems of offense categories and of offender characteristics.[94]

> An offense behavior category might consist, for example, of "bank robbery/committed with a gun/$2500 taken." An offender characteristic category might be "offender with one prior conviction not resulting in imprisonment." The Commission is required to prescribe guideline ranges that specify an appropriate sentence for each class of convicted persons determined by coordinating the offense behavior categories with the offender characteristic categories.[95]

As in most state systems, compliance with the Federal Sentencing Guidelines is mandated by statute.[96] Should a sentencing court determine that justice demands a sentence either more harsh or more lenient than is permitted by the Guidelines, the court must state on the record the specific reasons underlying the sentence it imposes. Such a sentence is then subject to being modified or rejected altogether on appeal.[97]

Although touted by their proponents as a means toward a more just and workable system of punishment, the Federal Sentencing Guidelines and the Sentencing Commission itself were harshly criticized almost as soon as they were created. As U.S. Senior Circuit Judge Donald P. Lay recently observed,

> The [U.S. Sentencing] Commission, dignified by the important role delegated to it, appears to feel largely immune from criticism. I sense that this attitude emanates in part from the Commissioners' misguided reading of their alleged statutory mandate to impose a rigid and harsh sentencing structure without regard to the human cost. Although they

---

[89]Bureau of Justice Assistance, *National Assessment of Structured Sentencing* (Washington, D.C.: U.S. Department of Justice, Office of Justice Programs, Bureau of Justice Assistance, February 1996) (NCJ-153853), 19.

[90]28 U.S.C. § 994, et seq.

[91]For example, on May 1, 1995, the Commission promulgated 27 amendments to the Guidelines. See 60 Fed. Reg. 25,074 (1995). Congress rejected 2, with the remaining 25 becoming effective Nov. 1, 1995.

[92]United States Sentencing Commission, *Guidelines Manual* (Washington, D.C.: U.S. Sentencing Commission, 1995): 1.

[93]*Guidelines Manual.* See also 28 U.S.C. § 991 (b) (1) (a) (citing 18 U.S.C. § 3553 (a) (2) (A)–(D) (purposes of criminal sentencing)).

[94]28 U.S.C. § 994.

[95]U.S. Sentencing Commission, *Guidelines Manual,* 1.

[96]18 U.S.C. § 3553 (b) (application of guidelines in imposing sentence).

[97]18 U.S.C. § 3553 (b), (c); 18 U.S.C. § 3742 (a), (b).

Table 9–6   Sentencing Policies in the United States, 1994

State	Determinate Sentencing	Indeterminate Sentencing	Sentencing Guidelines	Mandatory Minimum Prison Sentencing*
Alabama	◆(P)§	◆		◆
Alaska	◆(P)	◆		◆
Arizona	◆			◆
Arkansas	◆		◆	◆
California	◆			◆
Colorado	◆(P)			◆
Connecticut	◆(P)			◆
Delaware			◆	◆
District of Columbia		◆		◆
Florida			◆	◆
Georgia		◆		◆
Hawaii		◆		◆
Idaho	◆(P)			◆
Illinois	◆			◆
Indiana	◆			◆
Iowa		◆(P)		◆
Kansas			◆	◆
Kentucky		◆		◆
Louisiana	◆		◆	◆
Maine	◆			◆
Maryland			◆	◆
Massachusetts		◆		◆
Michigan		◆	◆	◆
Minnesota	◆		◆	◆
Mississippi	◆(P)			◆
Missouri	◆(P)			◆
Montana		◆		◆
Nebraska		◆		◆
Nevada		◆		◆
New Hampshire		◆(P)		◆
New Jersey		◆		◆
New Mexico	◆(P)			◆
New York		◆(P)		◆
North Carolina		◆(P)	◆§§	◆
North Dakota		◆		◆

(*continued*)

Table 9–6 *(Continued)*

State	Determinate Sentencing	Indeterminate Sentencing	Sentencing Guidelines	Mandatory Minimum Prison Sentencing*
Ohio	◆	◆		◆
Oklahoma		◆		◆
Oregon			◆	◆
Pennsylvania		◆(P)	◆	◆
Rhode Island		◆		◆
South Carolina		◆		◆
South Dakota		◆		◆
Tennessee	◆		◆	◆
Texas		◆(P)		◆
Utah		◆	◆	◆
Vermont		◆		◆
Virginia			◆	◆
Washington	◆		◆	◆
West Virginia	◆	◆		◆
Wisconsin		◆(P)	◆	◆
Wyoming		◆		◆
Totals	20	29	16	51

*Although all States reported having mandatory sentencing, this term has a very broad definition and varies State by State.

§(P), partially determinate.

§§North Carolina's guidelines took effect in October 1994.

Source: Bureau of Justice Assistance, *National Assessment of Structured Sentencing* (Washington, D.C.: U.S. Department of Justice, Office of Justice Programs, Bureau of Justice Assistance, Feb. 1996) (NCJ 153853), 20–21, Table 3–1.

may not intend to do so, some of the Commissioners display little empathy or compassion for offenders as people. They convey the totalitarian mindset reminiscent of a bygone era. As Professor [Daniel J.] Freed notes, the Commission has rejected constructive criticism from the bench, preferring instead "to show how tough an administrative agency can be in the face of consumer opposition, even when the consumers are Article III judges."[98]

In commenting specifically on the Commission's role, Judge Lay continues,

[t]here is little evidence that the Commission will act on its own to make the guidelines more flexible or imprisonment policies less severe. Although the Commission may be an agency of the federal judiciary, it seems to lack supervision from any branch of government, and it reflects the Department of Justice's severe sentencing philosophy. The drug hysteria that has swept across the country has led recent [Commission] Administrators to endorse the concept of longer sentences and broader incarceration. As the Commission

---

[98]Donald P. Lay, "Rethinking the Guidelines: A Call for Cooperation," *Yale Law Journal* 101, No. 8 (June 1992): 1755–56 (quoting Daniel J. Freed, "Federal Sentencing in the Wake of Guidelines: Unacceptable Limits on the Discretion of Sentencers," *Yale Law Journal* 101, No. 8 (June 1992): 1681, 1720). Judge Lay served as Chief Judge of the U.S. Court of Appeals for the Eighth Circuit from 1980 to 1992.

Table 9–7   Mandatory Minimum Incarceration Sentencing Policies in the United States by Category of Offense, 1994

State	Mandatory Minimum Offense*					
	Repeat/ Habitual	Drunk Driving	Drugs	Possession of Weapons	Sex Offenses	Other
Alabama	◆	◆	◆	◆		
Alaska	◆		◆	◆		◆
Arizona	◆	◆	◆	◆	◆	
Arkansas	◆		◆	◆		
California	◆		◆	◆	◆	◆
Colorado	◆	◆	◆	◆	◆	◆
Connecticut		◆	◆	◆	◆	
Delaware	◆		◆	◆		
District of Columbia			◆	◆		◆
Florida	◆		◆	◆		
Georgia	◆	◆	◆	◆	◆	
Hawaii	◆			◆		◆
Idaho	◆	◆	◆	◆	◆	
Illinois	◆	◆	◆	◆	◆	◆
Indiana	◆		◆	◆		
Iowa	◆		◆	◆		
Kansas		◆				
Kentucky	◆	◆		◆	◆	
Louisiana	◆			◆		
Maine		◆				
Maryland	◆		◆	◆		
Massachusetts		◆	◆	◆		
Michigan	◆	◆	◆	◆		
Minnesota	◆		◆	◆		
Mississippi	◆		◆	◆		
Missouri	◆		◆	◆		
Montana	◆	◆	◆	◆		
Nebraska	◆	◆			◆	
Nevada	◆		◆	◆		
New Hampshire	◆	◆		◆	◆	
New Jersey	◆	◆	◆	◆	◆	
New Mexico	◆	◆		◆		
New York	◆					

(continued)

Table 9–7 (*Continued*)

State	Repeat/ Habitual	Drunk Driving	Drugs	Possession of Weapons	Sex Offenses	Other
North Carolina	◆	◆	◆		◆	
North Dakota		◆	◆	◆		
Ohio	◆	◆		◆		
Oklahoma	◆			◆		
Oregon		◆				
Pennsylvania	◆	◆	◆	◆	◆	◆
Rhode Island	◆	◆	◆	◆	◆	◆
South Carolina	◆		◆	◆		
South Dakota			◆	◆		
Tennessee		◆				
Texas	◆	◆		◆		
Utah	◆				◆	
Vermont	◆			◆		
Virginia		◆		◆		◆
Washington	◆				◆	◆
West Virginia	◆		◆	◆		
Wisconsin	◆	◆	◆	◆	◆	◆
Wyoming	◆					

*Not all offenses, especially drunk driving, are felonies.

Source: Bureau of Justice Assistance, *National Assessment of Structured Sentencing* (Washington, D.C.: U.S. Department of Justice, Office of Justice Programs, Bureau of Justice Assistance, Feb. 1996) (NCJ 153853), 24–25, Table 3–3.

members display an increasingly defiant attitude toward judicial input, the courts of appeals and district courts may begin to interpret the Commission's guidelines as inconsistent with Congressional intent.[99]

Judge Lay's comments bring into sharp focus the tremendous concern that determinate sentencing—and particularly rigid sentencing guidelines—raise for the judiciary. In addition, with the implementation of guidelines, prosecutors, the defense bar, and those involved in corrections all now "find themselves torn between allegiance to rigid rules and an urge to do justice in individual cases."[100]

It should be noted that while the concepts of "parole" and of prison "good time" have been widely and resoundingly criticized, 48 states maintain some sort of one or both of these practices, irrespective of structured sentencing policies. At present, only Hawaii, Pennsylvania, and Utah report permitting no good time to be awarded in their state correctional systems; and only Maine and the federal government have gone so far as to com-

---

[99]Lay, "Rethinking the Guidelines": 1762. Regarding judicial conclusions that the Commission has overstepped its statutory authority, see, e.g., *United States v. Galloway,* 943 F.2d 897 (8th Cir. 1991).
[100]Freed, "Federal Sentencing": 1684.

pletely abolish parole boards and all forms of postrelease offender supervision. In a number of jurisdictions, California, Delaware, Illinois, and Oregon among them, "parole" has been replaced in name by some modified version of postrelease supervision.[101]

The sentencing judge almost always has the assistance of a *presentence investigation report* to rely upon in fashioning punishment. Typically prepared by a probation officer and based upon a single interview with the convicted defendant, these reports contain personal and prior criminal data, such as employment experience, family history, the circumstances surrounding the offense, and previous run-ins with the criminal justice system. Presentence investigations often reflect the particular social or political leanings of the officer preparing them and generally carry tremendous weight with the court in determining the appropriate sentence. Carter and Wilkins report that, at least during the late 1960s, judges followed the sentencing recommendation included in the presentence investigation report 96 percent of the time.[102]

What, then, are the factors that emerge as most significant in the exercise of judicial discretion in sentencing? Research has suggested that the two most important factors in the decision between prison and probation are the nature of the offense for which the defendant is to be sentenced and the record of the defendant's prior offenses. In addition, other background data such as whether the defendant is married or single, whether addicted to drugs or alcohol, and whether employed, all typically weigh in on the sentencing decision.

Public opinion also unquestionably plays a role in sentencing decisions. It is difficult to imagine, for instance, that a judge could completely ignore the hue and cry over alcohol-related traffic offenses or the widespread concern regarding illegal drugs. Sentencing can also vary considerably from state to state, and even between cities or counties in the same state, owing to differing community sociolegal norms.[103]

Finally, we cannot overlook the philosophies of individual judges. Those with rehabilitative viewpoints are more likely to seriously consider probation or short jail terms than those concerned primarily with deterrence or retribution. However, judicial attitudes on sentencing have been found to be anything but unidimensional, with individual judges' philosophies being at best an imperfect predictor of sentencing outcomes.[104]

A rather widespread notion is that criminal sentencing varies considerably according to the key traits of the offender, such as race, sex, or socioeconomic status. A good deal of research has been undertaken on this issue, and while some studies do report sentencing discrimination along these lines, most fail to identify systematic biases. The one notable exception that must be mentioned is that, with respect to the imposition of capital punishment, a solid body of evidence has been collected suggesting that both the race of the victim and the race of the defendant affect whether the death penalty will be imposed.[105] In

[101]Bureau of Justice Assistance, *National Assessment of Structured Sentencing,* 26.

[102]Robert M. Carter and Leslie T. Wilkins, "Some Factors in Sentencing Policy," *Journal of Criminal Law, Criminology, and Police Science* 58 (1967): 503–14, as reported in Walker, *Taming the System,* 118.

[103]See, e.g., Martin A. Levin, "Urban Politics and Judicial Behavior," in Sheldon Goldman and Austin Sarat, eds., *American Court Systems: Readings in Judicial Process and Behavior* (San Francisco: Freeman, 1978), 338–47.

[104]Although research has been somewhat sparse on the relationship between sentencing and judges' attitudes, two frequently cited works are John Hogarth, *Sentencing as a Human Process* (Toronto: University of Toronto Press, 1971); and Anthony Partridge and William B. Eldridge, *The Second Circuit Sentencing Study: A Report to the Judges of the Second Circuit* (Washington, D.C.: Federal Judicial Center, Aug. 1974).

[105]See, e.g., the arguments presented in support of the petitioner in *McClesky v. Kemp,* 478 U.S. 1019 (1987), particularly those included in Justice Thurgood Marshall's dissent. McClesky unsuccessfully relied upon studies clearly demonstrating that, in the State of Georgia, an individual who killed a white person was more likely to receive a death sentence than one who killed a Black person, particularly where the accused was Black. See the discussion of this case presented in Cole, *The American System of Criminal Justice,* 453–54.

general, however, it appears that race and socioeconomic status have more to do with whether an individual becomes mired in the criminal justice system at all than with what sentence will eventually be imposed.

Take social class, for example. Although it is clear that poverty or the lack thereof may make a difference—poor people are more frequently imprisoned and for longer terms than wealthy people—we must question whether this phenomenon is the product of intentional discrimination against the poor by the judiciary, or whether it is more likely the result of longer criminal histories and more serious offenses that together create exposure to stiffer sentencing. There is no clear answer to these questions; however, most research points to the latter conclusion as correct.[106]

This is not to say that the perception of serious sentencing disparities is ill-founded. We have already noted the important differences in sentencing among various states and in different regions of the nation—Southern courts and those in rural areas tend to sentence more harshly—as well as among judges with varying perspectives on the underlying purposes of criminal sanctions. Moreover, upper-class defendants and prominent public officials are often treated with great deference when they become the focus of a prosecution. Such disparity might be justified by the argument that the punishment should fit not only the crime but also the criminal. Thus, the stigma of a criminal conviction alone may be as onerous for a nonviolent offender from society's upper echelons as is a prison term for a habitual criminal.

Whatever one's view on the issue, it is likely that disparate sentencing will be all but impossible to eliminate as long as we remain divided on basic issues of crime and punishment and as long as our criminal courts reflect those deep-seated divisions.

FURTHER READING

Blumberg, Abraham S. "The Practice of Law as a Confidence Game: Origanizational Co-Option of a Profession. *Law and Society Review* 1, No. 2 (June 1967): 15–39.

Cole, George F. *The American System of Criminal Justice,* 6th ed. Belmont, Calif.: Wadsworth Publishing Co., 1995.

Eisenstein, James, Roy B. Flemming, and Peter F. Nardulli. *The Contours of Justice: Communities and their Courts.* Boston: Little, Brown, 1988.

Eisenstein, James, and Herbert Jacob. *Felony Justice: An Organizational Analysis of Criminal Courts.* Lanham, Md.: University Press of America, 1991.

Feeley, Malcolm M. *The Process Is the Punishment: Handling Cases in Lower Criminal Courts.* New York: Russell Sage, 1979.

Flemming, Roy B., Peter F. Nardulli, and James Eisenstein, *The Craft of Justice: Politics and Work in Criminal Court Communities.* Philadelphia: University of Pennsylvania Press, 1992.

Heumann, Milton. *Plea Bargaining: The Experience of Prosecutors, Judges and Defense Attorneys.* Chicago: University of Chicago Press, 1978.

Levin, Martin A. *Urban Politics and the Criminal Courts.* Chicago: University of Chicago Press, 1977.

Levine, James P. *Juries and Politics.* Pacific Grove, Calif.: Brooks/Cole, 1992.

---

[106]For a useful overview of the issue of discrimination and sentencing, see Casia Spohn, John Gruhl, and Susan Welch, "The Effect of Race on Sentencing: A Re-examination of an Unsettled Question," *Law and Society Review* 16, No. 1 (1980–1981): 71–88. These researchers present data that demonstrate a clear pattern of racial discrimination in sentencing.

Neubauer, David W. *America's Courts and the Criminal Justice System,* 4th ed. Belmont, Calif.: Wadsworth Publishing Co., 1995.

Skolnick, Jerome H. and James J. Fyfe. *Above the Law: Police and the Excessive Use of Force.* New York: The Free Press, 1993.

United States, Dept. of Justice, Bureau of Justice Statistics. *Report to the Nation on Crime and Justice: The Data,* 2nd ed. NCJ. 1055506. Washington, D.C.: Dept. of Justice, 1988.

———. *Sourcebook of Criminal Justice Statistics.* Washington: Dept. of Justice, annual.

Walker, Samuel. *Sense and Nonsense About Crime: A Policy Guide,* 2nd ed. Pacific Grove, Calif.: Brooks/Cole, 1989.

———. *Taming the System: The Control of Discretion in Criminal Justice, 1950–1990:* New York: Oxford University Press, 1993.

Zawitz, Marianne W., et al. *Highlights from 20 Years of Surveying Crime Victims: The National Crime Victimization Survey, 1973–1992.* NCJ. 144525. Washington: Dept. of Justice, 1993.

10

The State Appellate Process

[There is an] emerging societal consensus that state supreme courts should not be passive, reactive bodies . . . but that these courts should be policy-makers and . . . legal innovators.
—Robert Kagan et al.,
"The Evolution of State Supreme Courts"

APPEALS: FUNCTION AND PROCESS

Appeals lie at the very core of the American system of adjudication and, as we have noted, constitute the focus of most scholarly research, university teaching, and public debate about courts. Indeed, so enamored are we with appellate courts, especially the United States Supreme Court, that a leading scholar-judge of the Realist school, Jerome Frank admonished us against acceptance of the "upper court myth" which "creates and perpetuates the illusory notion that upper courts can offset all the failings of the trial judges, [and] the public puts too much reliance on, and gives too many kudos to, upper-court judges."[1]

Although the Realist school of jurisprudence has helped to redirect our attention to the significance of trial courts, this is not to deny the important role of the appellate process in adjudication. To say that we have overstressed appellate courts is not to suggest that they are unimportant. Martin Shapiro, in an insightful commentary on appeals, discusses several perspectives from which we may view the appellate function.

The first, and perhaps the most obvious function of appeal, is legitimation—to lend to the adjudicative process the appearance if not the reality of justice. Appeal provides the loser at trial with the face-saving "out" of asserting his or her "right" to try again in an-

---

[1]See Jerome Frank, *Courts on Trial: Myth and Reality in American Jurisprudence* (Princeton: Princeton University Press, 1950), 223. See also Frank's earlier work, *Law and the Modern Mind* (New York: Coward-McCann, 1930).

other court at a higher level. In this sense, appeal not only provides the loser with an important cathartic alternative, but also it helps to guard against arbitrary or capricious actions on the part of trial courts. Viewed in this way—from the perspective of the loser at trial—appeal is of obvious importance in the overall adjudicative process. As Shapiro notes,

> The purpose of a trial is to effect a termination of conflict. But too abrupt a termination may be counterproductive of true conflict resolution. Appeal, whether actually exercised, threatened, or only held in reserve, avoids adding insult to injury. The loser can leave the courtroom with his head held high talking of appeal and then accept his loss, slowly, privately, and passively by failing to make an appeal.[2]

Appeal can also be seen from a "lateral" perspective in that appellate courts serve the important function of supervising trial courts in order to ensure the uniformity of rule application at the lower level.[3] If we were to undertake a content analysis of the literature on the American appellate process, we would find the bulk of coverage devoted to this perspective. The "substantive errors" of lower trial courts have formed the basis of a number of legal treatises in which attention is focused on the contrast between trial court error and appellate court enlightenment.

Finally (and from the point of view of the political scientist, most significantly), appeal can be seen as a useful mechanism that aids the central regime in its task of governance. A closer look at the institution of intermediate appellate courts (universally present at the federal level and increasingly popular in the states) makes it clear that the appellate court functions of individual catharsis and of correcting trial court error can be, and are, adequately performed at this intermediate level. Why then do we need state supreme courts at all? From a historical perspective, one answer is that judicial appeal has been used as a device for the central government to engender loyalty to itself—in other words, as something of a patronage tool to bring the citizens and the regime closer together. Thus, the personnel of trial courts and even of intermediate appellate courts, may be seen as low-level bureaucrats who lack the sympathetic understanding of courts of last resort. The latter, by awarding final favors of relief from oppressive, erroneous lower court rulings, serve as benevolent instruments for fostering fealty to the central regime. For purposes of regime maintenance, as Shapiro points out, this function may well be more important in the long run than correcting lower court error.

Similarly, appeal can also be seen as a means of integrating diverse sections of the empire. The use of the English Privy Council as an ultimate font of appellate justice in the British Empire is an example that comes readily to mind. An even more familiar example may be found in the role of the United States Supreme Court in the American federal system. Anyone who has studied the gradual centralization of power in our federal system cannot fail to appreciate the role of the Supreme Court in this historic process. In almost countless decisions from the early rulings of the John Marshall Court (for example, *McCulloch v. Maryland,* 4 Wheaton, 316 [1819]; *Gibbons v. Ogden,* 9 Wheaton 1 [1824]; or *Shapiro v. Thompson,* 394 U.S. 618 [1969]), the Supreme Court has tended to side with the national government in federal-state conflicts of power, thereby serving to integrate the fifty states under the all-encompassing umbrella of national authority.[4]

---

[2]Martin Shapiro, *Courts: A Comparative and Political Perspective* (Chicago: University of Chicago Press, 1981), 49. A more extensive discussion of appeals can be found in Martin Shapiro, "Appeal," *Law and Society Review* 14, No. 3 (Spring 1980): 629–61.

[3]The term "lateral" is Shapiro's. See his "Appeal," 629.

[4]See, e.g., John Schmidhauser, *The Supreme Court as Arbiter in Federal-State Relations, 1787–1957* (Chapel Hill: University of North Carolina Press, 1958).

A final aspect of appeal as a political or regime-maintenance mechanism can be seen in its command or policy-enunciating function. This is the most familiar interpretation of the appellate court decision in American jurisprudence and has given rise not only to inordinate attention to appellate court decision making, but also to considerable research on the impact of, or compliance with, those appellate court edicts. The central question in such research has been whether or not lower courts, other governmental agencies, or private entities do, in fact, alter their behavior in accordance with upper court holdings.[5]

The appellate decision as political directive, rule, or command is a clear and obvious example of the political role of the appellate process, but what we might call the justice-distributing or cathartic, as well as the error-correcting, the political integrative, and the fealty-inducing, aspects of appeal must not be overlooked in our understanding of the appellate function. Much more than lower courts, appellate courts are nearer to, if not at the very center of, the exercise of ultimate power within the regime. Indeed, no set of rulers can tolerate for long a significant departure of judicial rule making from the regime's central policy thrust. On the contrary, symbolic aspects of the exercise of appellate judicial power are ordinarily put to good use in the overall task of governing. Thus, it is at the appellate level that we find the clearest expression of the political role (or, as we have shown, roles) of adjudication.

The actual process of appellate court decision making, including those procedures by which cases are accepted for review, varies from court to court, but in general it is sufficiently different from trial court procedures to warrant general comment. Neither witnesses, nor jurors, nor the litigants themselves are ordinarily present in appellate courts, for these individuals have to do with fact-finding. Appellate courts are more likely to focus on legal issues rather than determinations of fact. For instance, a trial court in a criminal case may face the task of determining whether the accused did, in fact, commit the burglary or did shoot the victim, while an appellate court, if it deals with the case at all, will be called upon to address those legal issues appealed to it, such as whether or not the evidence presented at trial is admissible, whether or not press coverage prevented a fair trial, or perhaps whether or not the accused was represented by competent counsel. These examples point to two features of appellate courts that set them apart somewhat from trial courts. Not only are they less likely to deal with factual issues, but the legal issues in question are often of a procedural nature.

In place of the jury or the single judge making decisions in trial courts, appellate courts are collegial bodies in which decisions are rendered by panels of judges. Relying only upon the evidence present in the record of the case briefs of counsel, the appellate court typically juxtaposes the established facts contained in the record with the existing rule of law to arrive at a decision. Oral arguments are sometimes heard, but even so, appellate courts normally address issues in a relatively scholarly fashion, usually devoid of the passion and drama of trial courts. *Amicus curiae* (friend of the court) briefs from interested parties are sometimes allowed. Legal research undertaken by clerks of the judges will typically ground the appellate opinion. Appellate decisions are announced formally, sometimes orally, but typically in writing as well, accompanied by a reasoned statement justifying the ruling. While procedures vary from court to court, the decisional stages outlined for the United States Supreme Court are common (with some variation) in state appellate courts.

---

[5]See Shapiro, "Appeal," 643; and the sources cited in Chapter 11 of this text. Shapiro's coverage of the appellate function is more extensive than this threefold classification.

As we have come to expect, the funneling effect of the adjudication process continues as we move from trial to appellate courts. For a number of reasons, relatively few cases are appealed, leaving appellate courts with a nonrepresentative sample of issues to address and, of course, rendering trial courts the court of last resort for the vast majority of cases. Beyond these general comments, an understanding of appellate processes is best obtained by focusing on particular courts. We begin with state appellate courts, then move to a discussion of the workings of the United States Courts of Appeals, ending with a more extended coverage of the United States Supreme Court. For all of these courts, we will focus on the same general set of questions: What factors explain access to appellate courts? What is the level and nature of case flow? What are the chief characteristics of the appellate decisional process? What are the key factors explaining decisional outcomes? Our present knowledge does not permit precise answers to all of these questions, but they can serve, nonetheless, as general guidelines for our discussion.

STATE INTERMEDIATE APPELLATE COURTS

Although all states have established appellate courts of last resort (COLRs)—usually termed state supreme courts, only fairly recently have intermediate appellate courts (IACs), become popular in the states. As of 1994, 38 states had created these courts, with some additional state legislatures on the verge of enacting enabling legislature creating such bodies. The chief reason for the creation of these courts has been to relieve the ever-increasing workload of the states' supreme courts, to the end that the highest court may concentrate on the more important legal issues, thereby becoming a more articulate voice in state judicial policy-making.[6] In some respects, the move has been successful, while in others, the establishment of these courts has created as many problems as it has solved.

The establishment of intermediate appellate courts usually has measurably reduced the caseload of that state's supreme court, which as anticipated, has freed it to concentrate on broad policy-making.[7] Sometimes, there are unanticipated consequences. The intermediate appellate tribunal in these states assumes an excessive caseload itself; the state appeal process is opened to new claims, and total state appellate caseload again becomes unmanageable.

Leaving caseload aside for the moment, let us address the prior question of appellate rates. From the vast number of trial dispositions, how many cases are appealed at the state level? The answer is, we do not know, or at least we do not know with any comfortable degree of certainty. Most state courts' statistics are gathered at the filing stage, which does not tell us how many cases are settled out of court and how many reach the formal stage of ap-

---

[6]State intermediate appellate courts are discussed in a number of publications, although much is still unknown regarding their operations. See, e.g., Joy A. Chapper and Roger A. Hanson, *Intermediate Appellate Courts: Improving Case Processing* (Williamsburg, Va.: National Center for State Courts, 1990); Marlin O. Osthus, *State Intermediate Appellate Courts* (Chicago: American Judicature Society, 1980), revised by Thomas B. Marvell and Mae Kuykendall, "Appellate Courts: Facts and Figures," *State Court Journal*, 4, No. 2 (Spring 1980): 9–14, 33–37; and Edmund B. Spaeth, Jr., "Achieving a Just Legal System: The Role of Intermediate Appellate Courts," *The Annals*, 462 (July 1982): 48–58. Research reports on these tribunals often appear in *Judicature* and *State Court Journal*. Much of the discussion herein draws on data from National Center for State Courts, *State Court Caseload Statistics: Annual Report, 1990, 1993, 1994* (Williamsburg, Va.: National Center for State Courts, 1992, 1994, 1996) (hereinafter referred to as *State Court Caseload Statistics*); and Harry P. Stumpf and John H. Culver, *The Politics of State Courts* (New York: Longman, 1992): Ch. 7.

[7]In general, see Robert A. Kagan, Bliss Cartwright, Lawrence M. Friedman, and Stanton Wheeler, "The Evolution of State Supreme Courts," *Michigan Law Review* 76, No. 6 (May 1978): 961–1005.

pellate court decision. Also, available data do not indicate the origin of appellate filings. Hence, without case tracking data (the actual tracking of cases through the entire process), we cannot be certain where state supreme court cases began or whether or not we might be counting cases twice.[8] Hence, the available data must be viewed as highly tentative.

It is possible to gain an approximate picture of the appellate funnel through the device of "appellate ratio" (defined as the ratio of cases disposed of in limited and general jurisdiction courts, to total state appellate filings in intermediate appellate courts, as well as state courts of last resort). Table 10–1 presents such data for the 19 states that reported complete data sets for relevant courts for the calendar year 1994.

The data in Table 10–1 document, if not dramatize, what we have noted earlier—namely, the very small percentage of state trial court cases appealed. At least as measured by dispositions in 19 states, an average of only 1 case of 493 disposed of by trial courts will find its way into state appellate tribunals, though as shown, the ratio can vary widely from state to state.

Partly because of the inclusion of dispositions of courts of limited jurisdiction in Table 10–1 (including masses of traffic cases, for instance), these ratios may be misleading as to the percentage of realistically appealable state trial court determinations that are actually appealed. Considering only civil and criminal dispositions (omitting domestic relations, and limited jurisdiction juvenile cases on the grounds that few such dispositions are appealed) in 15 selected state trial courts of general jurisdiction, again as related to filings in all levels of appellate courts in those states, we find what we've called the "appellate ratio" ranging from 1:67 to 1:7, with an average of 1:30, or about 3.3 percent.[9]

Although there is a dearth of empirical research on the point, scholars have nonetheless set forth several possible explanations for why cases are appealed.[10] At the outset it must be recalled that with some exceptions, the vast majority of state trial court determinations are not appealable at all because they were bargained, out-of-court settlements. Thus, as suggested in our earlier coverage of the civil and criminal judicial process, only about 8 to 10 percent of filings in each category are usually processed by trial courts in such a way that the decisions are appealable. The actual trial rate (percentage of case dispositions in trial courts of general jurisdiction by jury and nonjury trials combined) in 1993 was 7.2 percent for criminal cases and 7.6 percent for civil cases.[11] Further, it is clear that courts themselves, by the content and manner of their decision making, emit signals encouraging or discouraging appeals. Lengthy delays in disposing of appeals, narrowing legal doctrine on substantive points of law, and similar judicial actions can significantly affect the propensity to appeal.

---

[8]On the general problems of state caseload statistics, see Marvell and Kuykendall, "Appellate Courts," and the sources cited therein.

[9]The states are Alaska, California, Hawaii, Indiana, Kansas, Michigan, Missouri, New Jersey, New Mexico, Ohio, Oklahoma, Pennsylvania, Texas, Virginia, and Vermont, selected on the basis of their inclusion in civil and criminal disposition tables in Brian J. Ostrom and Neal B. Kauder, *Examining the Work of State Courts, 1993* (Williamsburg, Va.: National Center for State Courts, 1995), 14, 41, 55.

Henry A. Glick, in his text *Courts, Politics and Justice,* 3rd. ed. (New York: McGraw-Hill, 1993) reports "2 percent or less" of general trial court verdicts are appealed in Kansas and Florida (p. 274), although he cites neither source nor year. G. Alan Tarr, in *Judicial Process and Judicial Policy-Making* (St. Paul: West Publishing Co., 1994): 167, notes that less than 10 percent of trial court decisions are appealed, although his notes make clear that this figure is derived from comparing trial court filings, not *dispositions,* with appellate court filings.

[10]On the lack of research on the decision to appeal, see Susan E. Lawrence, "Appealing: Who and What," *Law, Courts and Judicial Process Newsletter, American Political Science Association* 6, No. 3 (Spring 1989): 52–57.

[11]Ostrom and Kauder, *Examining the Work of State Courts,* 14, 41.

Table 10–1   Appellate Ratio in Nineteen States, 1994

State	Trial Court Dispositions	Appellate Filings	Appellate Ratio
Alaska	125,996	1,090	1:116
Arizona	1,777,496	4,885	1:364
California	9,894,412	28,171	1:351
Delaware*	355,336	488	1:728
Florida	3,784,451	20,951	1:181
Hawaii	656,330	943	1:696
Indiana**	1,325,276	3,051	1:434
Kansas	883,332	2,656	1:333
Kentucky	715,891	4,225	1:169
Michigan	3,256,197	13,910	1:234
New Jersey	6,969,438	10,511	1:663
North Carolina	2,386,903	2,410	1:990
Ohio	2,305,852	13,801	1:167
South Carolina	1,753,778	954	1:1838
Vermont	58,336	657	1:89
Virginia	3,579,868	4,892	1:732
Washington	1,705,674	5,157	1:331
Wisconsin	1,356,423	4,503	1:301
Wyoming	221,898	335	1:662

*State has no IAC.

**State has multiple appellate courts.

Source: National Center for State Courts, *State Court Caseload Statistics, 1994* (Williamsburg, Va.: National Center for State Courts, 1996), Tables 2, 8. States in the table are those having their grand total of trial court dispositions and appellate filings tabulated in tables.

Moreover, Baum has suggested three other factors that help to explain the decision to appeal: the cost of the procedure, the degree of satisfaction with the trial court decision, and the calculation of one's chance of success on appeal. First, in civil cases, it is usually only the relatively prosperous litigant, most commonly Galanter's "Repeat Players," who can afford the several thousand dollars usually required for appellate expenditures.[12] Trial transcripts, filing fees, briefs arguing points of law raised at trial—all of these are quite costly, discouraging large numbers of otherwise meritorious appeals. The reverse of this outcome is revealed in the high number of criminal appeals, encouraged by rulings in federal courts that indigents have a right to counsel and free trial transcripts, at least on their first appeal.[13]

---

[12]Stanton Wheeler, Bliss Cartwright, Robert A. Kagan, and Lawrence M. Friedman, "Do the 'Haves' Come Out Ahead? Winning and Losing in State Supreme Courts, 1870–1970," *Law and Society Review* 21 (1987): 403–45.

[13]See *Griffin v. Illinois,* 351 U.S. 12 (1956).

Second, and rather obviously, those most dissatisfied with their trial outcome are most likely to appeal. For example, Davies found that jury trial convictions constituted over 70 percent of all criminal appeals to California's First District Intermediate Appellate Court in the late 1970s, such convictions being appealed at the rate of 46.5 percent. This figure may be contrasted to the less than 1 percent of guilty plea convictions being appealed.[14] The two factors most prominent in explaining this difference are the imposition of jail terms (obviously leading to a rather high level of dissatisfaction) and the law itself, which with a few exceptions, prevents appeals of guilty pleas.

Finally, the potential appellant must calculate the probability of success. Even if money is no object in a case in which the outcome is extremely unsatisfactory to the loser, no appeal may be forthcoming if the chances of success are seen as dismal. In some types of cases the advice of appellate attorneys may be crucial. They are likely to be highly knowledgeable in predicting appellate outcomes. Of course, an appeal may be brought as a bargaining tool—to persuade the opposition to settle out of court on terms more favorable than the trial court's award.

Except in a small percentage of cases in which state law provides for automatic appeal, one of the parties usually initiates the action. Since it is the (sometimes unwritten) rule that all litigants have the opportunity of appellate review, at least at the first level, the first appeal brought is almost always granted. Normally a verbatim record of the trial transcript is required, along with several copies of a written brief covering the issues of fact and law, setting forth arguments about why the decision of the lower court should be reversed. State law usually provides a time deadline by which appeals must be filed. Afterward, the opposing party is given a limited time to file a response.

Despite the low incidence of appeal of state trial court determinations, the absolute numbers of state appellate court filings continue to rise. State appellate court filing data are usually separated into mandatory and discretionary appeals, the former being appeals which, by state law, appellate courts are required to hear. These are by far the most numerous. In 1994, there were 263,693 total filings in state appellate courts, 189, 553 (72%) of these being mandatory appeals. As noted, the vast majority of state appeals are handled by state intermediate appellate courts (IACs), their portion now running about 70 percent of the total state appellate load. Not unexpectedly, their mandatory load is also quite high. For every discretionary appeal accepted by state IACs, there are nearly eight appeals they must take. IAC mandatory appeals rose an average of almost 5 percent from 1984 to 1994, while discretionary appeals, the bulk of COLR filings, increased about 4 percent per year over the same period.[15]

The extent to which IACs have become the draft animals of state appellate review is suggested by the astounding fact, reported by Thomas Marvell, that as measured either by case filings, decisions on the merits, or increases in numbers of judgeships, some 98 percent of overall state appellate growth from 1974 to 1984 occurred in intermediate appellate courts![16] Although allowances must be made for different methods of reporting as well as for how opinions are reached (whether by the entire court or by panels of judges) in the various states, the excessive workloads of these intermediate appellate tribunals, however measured, have become one of the major problems in the smooth functioning of the process of state appellate review. Thus, it has come to pass that caseloads reflect both the *raison d'etre* as well as portend the *modus operandi* of IACs, the problem becoming the focus of the bulk of commentary and research on these courts.

Scholars have cataloged at least seven techniques, some quasi-experimental, others

---

[14]Thomas Y. Davies, "Affirmed: A Study of Criminal Appeals and Decision-Making Norms in a California Court of Appeals," *American Bar Foundation Research Journal* No. 3 (Summer 1982): 558–59.

[15]These data are found in Ostrom and Kauder, *Examining the Work of State Courts 1994,* 71–75.

[16]Thomas B. Marvell, "State Appellate Responses to Caseload Growth," *Judicature* 72, No. 5 (Feb.–Mar., 1989): 285.

rather well-established, that state judges and legislatures have developed to address the general issue of state appellate overload. The first technique is the establishment of IACs in the first instances, just discussed, while the second is the simple device of increasing the number of judges where the load is most heavily felt, usually at the IAC level. Thus, the number of IAC judges increased 73 percent in the decade 1974 to 1984, and the growth continues unabated. By 1993, 860 judges served on these courts, up some 20 percent since 1986. These judges traditionally work in panels of three, a third and quite significant time-saving technique, although some states use somewhat larger panels. This arrangement, of course, permits a reduction in the number of arguments heard for the court as a whole, as well as fewer briefs to be read per judge, and also less work in preparing and reading drafts of opinions. The panel system, also used in the U.S. Courts of Appeals as well as some state supreme courts, is often cited as one of the reasons for the low incidence of dissent on these courts. With this smaller group of decision makers, dissent is by definition a one-person game. In explaining this phenomenon for federal appellate courts, Richardson and Vines remarked,

> Since there are only three judges to a panel . . . the objective probability of dissent is much less than on a court with nine [or 5 or 7] judges. Furthermore, a judge, when he dissents, always dissents alone. The intrinsic loneliness of dissent . . . may well act as a deterrent. . . .[17]

These considerations, combined with the general press of time, make dissents a luxury usually bypassed by judges of these courts. As one California judge confessed, "I hate to say this, but just the workload alone may encourage one judge to agree with the others, because otherwise he or she would have to write a dissenting opinion."[18]

Abbreviated practices relating to oral argument, the handling of opinions, and summary judgments are three further devices used on state IACs (as well as some state supreme courts) to help handle large caseloads. Since the drafting, circulation, and preparation of opinions for publication constitute the most time-consuming steps in the work of appellate judges, it is in these areas that IACs can gain the most ground in keeping up with their caseloads. Deciding cases with no opinion is practiced in at least some cases by about half of all state appellate courts. Even more common is the practice of not publishing opinions, one observer concluding that unpublished opinions take about half the time of fully published ones.[19] Wold and Caldeira report that the California Court of Appeals published only 15.7 percent of its opinions in 1977.[20] At present, well over half of the decisions issued by state IACs nationwide are unpublished, and the practice is definitely growing—in California and elsewhere.

Oral argument, too, seems to be passing from the scene in a growing number of state appellate courts. In 1984, only 30 percent of cases heard before state IACs were accompanied by oral argument, and over the past 20 years the time limit for oral argument has been reduced by nearly half. When one adds the growth in the practice of summary judgment—a procedure permitting decisions quite early in the appeals process, even before the filing of case records or briefs—one can hardly avoid the conclusion that American state appel-

---

[17]Richard J. Richardson and Kenneth N. Vines, *The Politics of Federal Court: Lower Courts in the United States* (Boston: Little, Brown, 1970), 138–39.

[18]Greg A. Caldeira and John T. Wold, "Routine Decision-making in Five California Courts of Appeal," paper presented at the meeting of the Western Political Science Association, Los Angeles, March 16–18, 1978: 18. Also see an earlier piece reporting this phenomenon: Robert J. Sickels, "Research Note. The Illusion of Judicial Consensus: Zoning Decisions on the Maryland Court of Appeals," *American Political Science Review* 59, No.1 (Mar. 1965): 100–104; and Philip L. Dubois, "The Illusion of Judicial Consensus Revisited: Partisan Conflict on an Intermediate State Appellate Court," *American Journal of Political Science* 32, No. 4 (Nov. 1988): 946–67.

[19]Marvell, "State Appellate Responses": 287–88.

[20]Wold and Calderia, "Routine Decision-making": 15.

late procedure may well have been curtailed to the point of seriously endangering its value from the point of view of error correcting, aside from the important function of developing new law. This conclusion is buttressed by the incidence of the seventh technique frequently employed by state IACs as well as a growing number of supreme courts—the use of law clerks and screening personnel in the form of staff attorneys.

Law clerks, of course, are used in all appellate courts in the land, and staff attorneys, too, are becoming increasingly common. But it is the pace of growth, combined with the significantly enhanced role of these additional court personnel, that is causing increased concern among a number of observers. The most frequent criticism is that our appellate courts, state IACs being perhaps the best (or worst) examples, are becoming little more than faceless (or judgeless) bureaucracies, with these various shortcuts to genuine appellate adjudication increasingly devaluing the supervisory role of legal appeal. A particularly telling study pointing to this conclusion is that of Thomas Davies in his research on California's Intermediate Appellate Court for the First Appellate District, sitting in San Francisco.

California's IAC was created in 1905 and now addresses nearly 80 percent of all appellate filings in the state. Its caseload in 1977 was about 11,000 filings per year, the work at that time being divided among 51 appellate judges throughout the state. This number, of course, helped to provide that state's supreme court with the freedom to pick and choose its own cases, resulting in a high-discretion, low-caseload supreme court, which moved to first rank as perhaps the most creative policy-making state judicial body in the nation. At the same time, California's IAC has shouldered an immense caseload in that state of 30 plus million population. In 1988 it handled nearly 18,000 filings among 88 judges, or about 204 per judge; and it issued over 8,600 signed opinions, the largest output of any appellate court in the nation, probably in the world![21]

Early in its history this court, especially its First District, moved to abbreviated procedures in processing its cases. Shortened opinions, the panel approach, a reduction in the number of written opinions, an increasing use of clerks, and a central staff of attorneys to screen cases became the principal means to handle its ballooning caseload. But as Davies studied the work of this court, he found something of a Gresham's Law at work.[22] That is, these shortcuts to full appellate review were not applied to all cases equally. Rather, as one might expect from extant organizational theory, this court distributed its scarce resources in a manner appropriate to its central concerns of political survival and the enhancement of values shared by its most significant political constituents.

Thus, with the criminal bar having low status, with criminal defendants having little or no political influence, and with criminal cases affording little opportunity for creative lawmaking leading to the enhancement of the careers of IAC judges, criminal appeals are given short shrift as contrasted to civil cases.[23] Lawyers involved in civil litigation, especially those representing corporate interests, enjoy much higher prestige in the practicing bar. Such attorneys are more likely to be active participants in the politics of their communities and in the local bar, and being highly paid counsel, they have a much greater interest in the development of full and complete court processes as a demonstration to their clients of the results of their often expensive handiwork.[24] Moreover, in part because of the

---

[21]By 1994 filings had shot up to 21,386 for California's Intermediate Appellate Court, which, still divided among 88 judges, produced 243 filings per judge. In that year this court issued 12,090 signed opinions, or 137 per judge, while the state Supreme Court's 7 justices issued a total of only 99 opinions. See *State Court Caseload Statistics, 1990, 1994,* Tables 2, 6.

[22]Thomas Y. Davies, "Gresham's Law Revisited: Expedited Processing Techniques and the Allocation of Appellate Resources," *Justice System Journal* 6, No. 3 (Fall 1981): 372–404.

[23]See Ch. 7, Table 7–8; and John P. Heinz and Edward O. Laumann, *Chicago Lawyers: The Social Structure of the Bar* (New York: Russell Sage and ABF, 1982), 166–67.

[24]Davies, "Gresham's Law Revisited": 379.

greater resources usually invested in the civil appeal, the briefs are more likely to contain interesting, even novel, legal claims more attractive to appellate judges.

For these and other reasons, the organizational imperative of this IAC led to a highly disproportionate amount of resources expended on civil as opposed to criminal appeals. Research findings indicate a rather remarkable bias, even in the planning stages of court operations. Thus, when California's Administrative Office of the Courts undertook to estimate the resources required to process various types of cases, civil appeals were assigned a weight of 20, criminal appeals only 10. Similarly, civil writ petitions were given a weight of 2 units, habeas corpus petitions 1 unit.

Criminal appeals much more frequently led to nonpublished or, if published, brief, opinions (civil opinions were, in fact, three times more likely to be published). Furthermore, criminal appeals were two and one-half times as likely to be processed by the attorney staff serving the court as opposed to receiving the full attention of the judges. Even among civil cases, Davies found that the more prestigious (commercial/corporate money claims and the like) were over three times as likely to receive full judicial attention as were lower status civil appeals such as divorce or personal injury cases.[25] Thus, in the business of allocating scarce resources to the important issues of legal appeal, all parties are not equal, with the criminal cases, theoretically involving the most significant issues for society as a whole, receiving only minimal attention. As Davies concludes, the danger is that

> . . . expedited processes might divert the Court of Appeal's attention away from criminal appeals to such an extent as virtually to preclude meaningful appellate supervision over the quality of criminal justice proceedings. What supervision is possible when staff attorneys write two-thirds of the court's criminal opinions with the expectation that they are dealing with only "routine" or "frivolous" cases?[26]

Although the findings from one court do not conclusively demonstrate a serious decline in the quality of state appellate review, such case studies, along with ancillary commentary suggest that this may be happening in a number of jurisdictions.[27] Given the continued, and increasing, pressure of caseloads on these courts, we probably cannot avoid a

---

[25]Davies, "Gresham's Law Revisited": 396.

[26]Davies, "Gresham's Law Revisited": 399.

[27]Commentary tending to support Davies's conclusions is found in Wold and Calderia, "Perceptions of 'Routine' Decision-Making"; Paul D. Carrington, "Ceremony and Realism: Demise of Appellate Procedure," *American Bar Association Journal* 66, (July 1980): 860–62; and Wade H. McCree, "Bureaucratic Justice: An Early Warning," *University of Pennsylvania Law Review* 129, No. 4 (Apr. 1981): 777–97.

For an extension of the debate over the "bureacratization" of appellate review, see the study of Michigan's intermediate appellate court: "Mary Lou Stow and Harold J. Spaeth, Centralized Research Staff: Is There a Monster in the Closet?" *Judicature* 75, No. 4 (Dec.–Jan. 1992): 216–21, followed by a series of responding letters and a further article by David J. Brown, "Facing the Monster in the Judicial Closet: Rebutting the Presumption of Sloth," all in *Judicature* 75, No. 6 (Apr.–May, 1992): 288–93. The central argument of these latter pieces is that many—indeed, most—of the appeals filed in state intermediate appellate courts are frivolous and easily labeled as such by court staff, thus precluding the need for "hands-on" attention by judges themselves. In this regard, see John T. Wold and Greg A. Caldeira, "Going Through the Motions: The Monotony of Appellate Court Decision-Making," *Judicature* 62, No. 2 (Aug. 1978): 58–65, and Caldeira and Wold, "Routine Decision-Making." A widely cited passage from the latter piece reads,

> I take most of the criminal stuff just to get it out of the way, because I was in that as a trial judge and as a trial lawyer. . . . Once in a while I cheat a little bit to get an interesting case out of there, but generally I try to give the more interesting cases to the other judges who have more time to devote to them. *My job here is to get rid of the garbage, because I get rid of the garbage faster than anyone else.* . . . I am reminded of a Municipal Court Judge . . . who was newly appointed and went to see the senior judge and said, "What do you do?" "Very simple," he responded. "Every morning you come here and you take your pitchfork, I take my pitchfork. There's a big pile of manure and we pitch it all out and when we're through we go home. And tomorrow there's going to be another pile of manure." . . . Somebody's got to do it (p. 8).

deterioration of meaningful review of state trial court decision making, a development that also appears rather well advanced at the federal level.

THE EVOLUTION OF STATE SUPREME COURTS

As Shapiro's conceptualization of the appellate process makes clear, the function of what he terms "hierarchical political management" at the state level falls largely to state courts of last resort, hereinafter "state supreme courts." Notes Shapiro,

> The extension of judicial services outward and downward is a device for wedding the countryside to the regime . . . for keeping the strings of legitimacy tied directly between the ruled and the person of the ruler or the highest institutions of government. . . . The ability to reach down occasionally into the most particular affairs of the countryside provides an important means of reminding the rank and file that the rulers are everywhere, that no one may . . . hide from [the] central authority. . . . Thus, appellate institutions are more fundamentally related to the political purposes of central regimes than to the doing of individual justice. That this is true is evidenced by the nearly universal existence of appellate mechanisms in politically developed societies. . . .[28]

Appellate courts carry out this function largely through policy-making, with state supreme courts leading the way. True, their role in this regard has been eclipsed of late by the relatively recent surge of federal judicial power. But it should be recalled that state courts antedate federal courts, and at one time state supreme court justices represented the finest legal minds of the nation and were accorded the respect now customarily reserved for justices of the U.S. Supreme Court. Chancellor James Kent of New York, Lemuel Shaw and Joseph Story of Massachusetts, John Gibson of Pennsylvania, and George Wythe and Spencer Roane of Virginia were among the leading judges and legal scholars of their day who graced the state appellate bench at the beginning of nationhood.[29] Although the conversion of the colonies to states occurred at a time of rising state legislative dominance, state courts soon made good their claim to a leading role in state policy-making.

The enunciation of the doctrine of judicial review by Chief Justice John Marshall in *Marbury v. Madison* in 1803 (1 Cranch 137) was warmly embraced by many state appellate judges, who used the doctrine to enhance their own stature against the growing power of the state legislature. But even before Marshall's celebrated edict, state courts had held void legislative enactments in a number of instances. Although there was understandable judicial reluctance to use this power to excess (it was not unknown for state legislatures to impeach judges for the "crime" of invoking judicial review), the doctrine came to be employed as a powerful symbol, enchancing the image of state supreme courts as apolitical agencies with the solemn duty of upholding the great principle of constitutionalism in the workings of state government.[30]

The conception of judicial review in this early period was what legal historian Kermit Hall called "departmental," the power being used primarily as a protective measure against legislative and executive encroachments on the province of the judicial department. Thus, although legislative supremacy was generally honored, state supreme courts tended to focus on issues of separation of powers in which judicial territory was being

---

[28]Shapiro, *Courts,* 52.

[29]Lawrence M. Friedman, *A History of American Law,* 2nd ed. (New York: Simon and Schuster, 1985), 134–38.

[30]Charles Grove Haines, *The American Doctrine of Judicial Supremacy,* 2nd ed. (Berkeley: University of California Press, 1932).

threatened.[31] However circumspect state courts were in this period of legislative dominance, they nonetheless were quite willing to assert their traditional role as creative interpreters of the common law. As legislative supremacy began to wane in the mid-nineteenth
century, state supreme court justices "embraced common law decision-making with im-
passioned enthusiasm, and judge-made law began to fill the law reports."[32] In pointing to
this second, more expansionist era of state judicial activism in the interpretation of the
common law, one commentator noted:

> Two facts are basic. The first is that, in the complex system of government we adopted,
> most questions of private law were left to the states. The national government had almost
> no part in establishing or developing the law of property, contracts, wills, personal injury,
> or damages. The second is that within the states it was often the courts rather than the leg-
> islatures that actually formulated such law.[33]

One example of such common law development by state courts in the mid-
nineteenth century was set forth by Benjamin Cardozo in his classic work, *The Growth of
the Law*. There, he discusses the progressive demise of the old doctrine of "privity"
through decisions rendered by the New York Court of Appeals in the 1850s. Literally, privity means a connection or bond between two parties in a transaction. In our early industrial period it had come to mean that unless there was a contractual relationship between a
manufacturer and a customer, say, the latter had no claim to damages from faulty merchan-
dise. This interpretation created virtual immunity for commercial interests from suits for
damages suffered by purchasers of their products, a doctrine befitting the laissez-faire,
caveat emptor thinking of nineteenth- and early twentieth-century America.

Through a series of decisions beginning with *Thomas v. ·Winchester* (6 N.Y. 397) in
1852, the New York Court of Appeals gradually expanded the categories of defective products for which American manufacturers could be found liable. Later, other state appellate
courts broadened the newer doctrines; in Connecticut, for example, in 1961 that state's
highest court held that by marketing products in sealed containers, the manufacturer implicitly warrants the item to be suitable and safe for its intended and advertised use.[34] The
growth of the law in such a fashion often escapes our attention, thereby leading the student
of American law to ignore the important legal pioneering undertaken by state appellate
courts.[35]

Thus, throughout much of the nineteenth century, state supreme courts were probably a good deal more creative in the use of their own powers than were the federal courts,
many launching out to fashion bold, new legal doctrine. With the unwillingness of state
legislatures to address the needs of a growing America, especially in the last half of that
century, state courts stepped into the breach through their common law decisions, trans-
forming whole areas of law, such as the law of property, contracts, and negligence, and in
doing so laying the groundwork for the industrial revolution.[36]

---

[31]Charles H. Sheldon, "Judicial Review and the Supreme Court of Washington, 1890–1986," *Publius* 17,
No. 1 (Winter 1987): 72.

[32]Sheldon, "Judicial Review": 74.

[33]Victor G. Rosenblum, "Courts and Judges: Power and Politics," in James F. Fesler, ed., *The 50 States
and Their Local Governments* (New York: Knopf, 1967), 406.

[34]Rosenblum, "Courts and Judges": 407.

[35]An excellent essay in this regard is Lawrence Baum and Bradley C. Canon, "State Supreme Courts as
Activists: New Doctrines in the Law of Torts," in Mary Cornelia Porter and G. Alan Tarr, eds., *State
Supreme Courts: Policy-Makers in the Federal System* (Westport, Conn.: Greenwood Press, 1982), 83–108.

[36]G. Alan Tarr and Cornelia A. Porter, *State Supreme Courts in State and Nation* (New Haven: Yale University Press, 1988), 51.

Roughly around the turn of the century, state legislatures began to reassert themselves, leading to a more restrained period of state judicial policy-making. As one commentator put it, quoting Roscoe Pound,

> The ". . . cautious eking out of the traditional law" by interstitial law-making lost favor in ". . . an impatient age accustomed to instant communication, super-rapid transportation and government activities of the first moment. . . ."[37]

Other developments, too, augured for a reduced role for state appellate courts. The expansion of federal court jurisdiction through various congressional acts in the 1875–1925 period raised the specter of competition from federal courts.[38] Moreover, the nation was moving to a more formalistic model of jurisprudence and judicial decision making, a view that depreciated the social creativity of common law decisions and replaced it with the deception of mechanical jurisprudence—the notion that judges decided cases strictly in accordance with *the law* as written.[39] The ever-increasing pace of social and economic change as we moved into the twentieth century continued to leave state courts in a noncompetitive position, with legislatures and their offshoots, boards, agencies, and commissions, at both the national and state level taking center stage in policy-making.

As this is being written there is considerable evidence that state appellate courts are in a fourth era of their history, with greater attention now being given to developments in state constitutional law as the leading edge of national judicial policy-making.[40] As with previous shifts in the fortunes of state judicial power, there is probably no single explanation for this important development. The current national trend toward decentralization of political power throughout our federal system, as seen in the administrations of Ronald Reagan and George Bush, is usually cited as a leading factor, although the historic swings of the pendulum of American federalism make this anything but a novel development.

An important, indeed crucial, aspect of this general trend has been the propensity of the Burger-Rehnquist Supreme Courts to move away from the major policy thrusts characteristic of the Warren Court. In its increasing deference to lower (especially state) courts, the Supreme Court is literally inviting an increased activism in state judicial policy-making, and in many instances state supreme courts have displayed their willingness, if not at times their eagerness, to move into the vacuum.[41] These developments will be more fully discussed later as part of our assessment of a newly emerging state appellate judiciary. But it should be clear from this brief overview that despite the ebb and flow of state power, state appellate courts remain major players in the overall growth of American law.

One further factor may be suggested as a reason for the renaissance of state judicial power in the late twentieth century—the evolution of state supreme courts, as a group, from rather passive, inefficient agencies of government to more modern adjudicative bodies rem-

---

[37]Francis R. Aumann, *The Changing American Legal System: Some Selected Phases* (Columbus: Ohio State University Press, 1940), 215.

[38]These developments are discussed in Chapter 4. See also Paul M. Bator et. al., *Hart and Wechsler's The Federal Courts and the Federal System,* 3rd. ed. (Westbury, N.Y.: The Foundation Press, 1988), Ch. 1.

[39]Sheldon, "Judicial Review": 75, 78.

[40]The literature on what has come to be called "The New Judicial Federalism" is vast. The discussion here, and in the last section of this chapter, relies in part on the coverage in Stumpf and Culver, *The Politics of State Courts:* Ch. 7; and on Stanley H. Friedelbaum, ed., *Human Rights in the States: New Directions in Constitutional Policy-Making* (Westport, Conn.: Greenwood Press, 1988); Peter J. Galie, "The Other Supreme Courts: Judicial Activitism Among State Supreme Courts," *Syracuse Law Review,* 33, No. 3 (Summer 1982): 731–93; Tarr and Porter, *State Supreme Courts;* and "New Developments in State Constitutional Law," *Publius* 17, No. 1 (Winter 1987): 1–12; and "Symposium, Part I: New Directions in State Constitutional Law," *Perspectives on Political Science* 22, No. 3 (Summer 1993): 101–23.

[41]Tarr and Porter, "New Developments in State Constitutional Law."

iniscent of the U.S. Supreme Court. By the 1980s, state supreme courts thus found themselves in a much better position to assume leadership roles in state and national policy-making.

During the late 1970s, Robert A. Kagan, Bliss Cartwright, Lawrence M. Friedman, and Stanton Wheeler conducted a major comparative study of sixteen state supreme courts, producing a body of data that remains probably the best existing foundation for limited generalizations in this regard.[42] The Kagan study sampled approximately 6,000 state supreme court decisions across a 100-year period of time (from 1870 through 1970) for such variable factors as type of parties, procedural history, legal issues, nature of opinion, and court structure from which particular decisions arose. One of its most important conclusions suggests a virtually inextricable link between the various facets of state supreme court performance and the seemingly endless struggle to relieve these courts of high-volume, mandatory caseloads. In a particularly incisive summary statement, Kagan et. al. noted that

> By arranging and rearranging our information on fluctuating supreme court caseloads, and comparing it with other quantitative measures of court performance, such as dissent rates, length of opinions, and types of issues decided, we discerned a rough pattern of evolution: as a state's population grew, its supreme court's caseload (measured by published opinions) usually grew along with it, sometimes quite dramatically. The increase in caseload naturally evoked efforts to reorganize the judiciary to relieve the pressure on the court. Eventually, states with heavy caseloads introduced structural reforms, principally intermediate appellate courts, and increased the supreme court's control over its docket. These changes, moreover, seemed to affect the court's legal role, for they coincided with changes in the type of case heard, the way courts make decisions, and the results of cases.[43]

This last conclusion is supported in the work of Professors G. Alan Tarr and Mary Cornelia Aldis Porter.[44] From a detailed comparative analysis of the Alabama, Ohio, and New Jersey supreme courts, Tarr and Porter likewise conclude that efforts to lighten the caseloads of these tribunals tend to substantively affect their performance. Particularly where a state intermediate appellate court is created, and concomitantly the state supreme court's mandatory jurisdiction is reduced or eliminated, the justices of the high court begin to perceive themselves more clearly as articulators of important state policy and to act on that perception.

> Discretionary review at the highest level . . . transforms the nature of the judicial process. The high court is no longer merely reacting to disputes brought to it by adversaries; it is selecting those disputes in which it chooses to participate. Almost surely this has affected the self-perception of the judges of the high courts, who tend to view themselves primarily as policy-makers and secondarily as conflict-resolvers, thus reversing the traditional

[42]Reports of this research (NSF grant no. GS-348-13) may be found in a variety of sources. See Robert A. Kagan, Bliss Cartwright, Lawrence M. Friedman, and Stanton Wheeler, "The Business of State Supreme Courts, 1870–1970," *Stanford Law Review* 30, No. 1 (Nov. 1977): 121–56; and the same authors' "Evolution of State Supreme Courts." See also "Court Reversal: The Supervisory Role of State Supreme Courts," *Yale Law Journal* 87, No. 6 (May 1978): 1191–1218; and Bliss Cartwright, "Afterword: Disputes and Reported Cases," *Law and Society Review* 9, No. 2 (Winter 1975): 369–84. The 16 state supreme courts studied were Alabama, California, Idaho, Illinois, Kansas, Maine, Michigan, Minnesota, Nevada, New Jersey, North Carolina, Oregon, Rhode Island, South Dakota, Tennessee, and West Virginia.

For a critique of this research, see Stephen Daniels, "A Tangled Tale: Studying State Supreme Courts," *Law and Society Review* 22, No. 5 (1988): 833–63, along with "Comment on Daniels," by Lawrence Baum, 865–68.

[43]Kagan et al., "Evolution of State Supreme Courts": 962.

[44]Tarr and Porter, *State Supreme Courts.*

relationship between those dual functions and taking leave of a fundamental assumption of the Common Law. In sum . . . [t]he architecture of the system tells the judges of the top court to be creative. . . .[45]

Tarr and Porter go on to suggest that although the creation of an intermediate court of appeals is a necessary prerequisite to a given state supreme court's playing a substantial policy-making role, other state legislative and regulatory actions—encouraging, discouraging, or even eliminating particular causes of action, for instance, or tightening appellate procedures so as to make access more limited—also significantly affect supreme court performance.[46] In short, it appears that the generalized effort to relieve state supreme courts of overly burdensome caseloads has also encouraged these courts, in varying degrees, to move beyond the role of mere legal error correction to that of active participation in the development of state governmental policy.

It is important to emphasize that not all states have followed this trend, and it is not possible to conclude that the reforms instituted in this century, particularly those enacted during the 1960s and 1970s, constitute permanent solutions to the problem of expanding appellate caseloads. What can be said is that presently, something of a "model" state supreme court has developed, closely resembling the United States Supreme Court in that it can control its caseload through the exercise of its discretionary jurisdiction and through its use of alternatives to full-blown, en banc opinions. As Robert Kagan and his associates wrote, these developments pointed to

> . . . an emerging societal consensus that state supreme courts should not be passive, reactive bodies, which simply applied "the law" to correct "errors" or miscarriages of justice, in individual cases, but that these courts should be policy-makers and, at least in some cases, legal innovators.[47]

DECISION MAKING ON STATE SUPREME COURTS

Some indication of the winnowing process of state supreme courts is suggested by the data in Table 10–2, incomplete though they are. In the 23 states with full sets of figures, the table presents the number of petitions—mandatory and discretionary combined—filed with these COLRs for 1994, the number of filings granted (determined in accord with state law), and the number of full published opinions (some additional opinions may be written in abbreviated form and/or not published). Relying only on these 23 states as a sample, full signed opinions represent an average of only 12.7 percent of filings and 39 percent of petitions granted. The figures in the last column may be compared with an average of around 100 full-dress opinions being issued by the United States Supreme Court in recent terms. Using a somewhat different sample, the National Center for State Courts reports that state courts of last resort granted approximately 11 percent of discretionary petitions filed in 1994, though that figure varied from a high of 29 percent (Massachusetts) to a low of 1.4 percent (California) among 22 courts sampled that year.[48]

There are four basic ways state COLRs dispose of cases: full written and published opinions, averaging in the overall NCSC statistics about 100 per court per year, very close

---

[45]Paul D. Carrington, Daniel J. Meador, and Maurice Rosenberg, *Justice on Appeal* (St. Paul, Minnesota: West, 1976), 150, as quoted in Tarr and Porter, *State Supreme Courts,* 49.

[46]Tarr and Porter, *State Supreme Courts,* 50–54.

[47]Kagan et. al., "The Evolution of State Supreme Courts": 983.

[48]Ostrom and Kauder, *Examining the Work of State Courts,* 1994, 79.

Table 10–2   Dispositions in State Courts of Last Resort, 1994

State	Petitions Filed	Petitions Granted	Full Published Opinions
Alaska	668	507	145
California	6,785	124	99
Georgia	1,954	791	401
Illinois	3,121	1,356	138
Indiana**	896	264	147
Kansas	859	369	210
Louisiana	3,171	660	150
Massachusetts	807	322	234
Michigan	3,188	122	108
Minnesota	982	347	156
Mississippi*	1,073	1,023	236
Montana*	744	639	368
Nevada*	1,256	1,256	164
North Carolina	620	240	126
Oregon	1,002	315	94
South Carolina	493	493	503
South Dakota*	408	356	196
Tennessee**	1,142	394	254
Texas**	1,407	174	146
Vermont*	657	634	108
Virginia	2,240	408	168
West Virginia*	2,442	679	275
Wyoming*	335	335	167

*State has no IAC.

**State has multiple appellate courts.

Source: National Center for State Courts, *State Court Caseload Statistics, 1994* (Williamsburg, Va.: National Center for State Courts, 1996), Tables 2, 6. States included are those reporting complete sets of data reported for 1994.

to recent U.S. Supreme Court output; memorandum (abbreviated, often unpublished) decisions, which can number higher than full opinions in some states; denial of review, the most frequently used method of disposition; and dismissals or transfers. Dismissals may occur because the parties have settled the matter, the case has been dropped by one of the parties, or one side did not comply with proper procedures. Most transfers are cases received by the court of last resort but delegated to the lower appellate court—particularly commonly in Hawaii, Iowa, North Dakota, South Carolina and Utah.[49] Table 10–3 provides data on dispositions in twenty-six courts of last resort in 1993.

[49]Ostrom and Kauder, *Examining the Work of State Courts, 1993*, 64–65.

Table 10–3   Manner of Case Disposition in 26 Courts of Last Resort, 1993

State	Full Published Opinions	Memorandum Decisions	Denial of Petition	Other Disposition	Total
Alabama	745	200	707	382	2,034
Arizona	69	2	1,255	9	1,335
Arkansas	347	75	227	84	733
California	102	0	3,814	1,912	5,828
Colorado	150	43	885	73	1,151
Connecticut	189[a]	21	157	32	399
Florida	428	1,503	n/a	n/a	1,931
Georgia	344	199	956	397	1,896
Hawaii	60	107	55	525	747
Illinois	88[b]	1,181	1,440	0	2,709
Iowa	306	162	230	1,341	2,039
Kansas	183	25	487	112	807
Kentucky	104	173	617	140	1,034
Louisiana	120	94	2,158	612	2,984
Michigan	90	182	2,201	43	2,516
Minnesota	120	115	540	84	859
New Mexico	67	58	360	70	555
New York	298[c]	0	3,668	506	4,472
North Dakota	255	n/a	n/a	127	382
Oregon	128[b]	42[a]	797	120	1,087
Pennsylvania	188	0	2,015	430	2,633
South Carolina	206	366	304	1,362	2,238
Tennessee	222[d]	153	660	n/a	1,035
Texas	229	n/a	917	495	1,641
Utah	139	0	134	445	718
Washington	134	1	809	245	1,189

[a]Includes some per curiam opinions; Oregon's dispositions are all published.

[b]Includes some opinions that are consolidated.

[c]Includes all dispositions of appeals on the merits, including per curiam and memorandum opinions.

[d]Of the 222, the number of published opinions is unknown.

Source: Brian J. Ostrom and Neal B. Kauder, *Examining the Work of State Courts, 1993* (Williamsburg, Va.: National Center for State Courts, 1995), 64.

Less is known about the internal operating procedures of state appellate courts than of federal appellate court procedures. For what could be called "full dress treatment" by state supreme courts, oral argument is usually scheduled, followed by a discussion and vote of the justices in conference, either in person or by phone. Although oral argument has been somewhat reduced in these courts over the past several years, some seven out of ten cases considered on the merits are still accompanied by this important procedure.[50]

---

[50]Marvell, "State Appellate Responses": 290.

Following (though sometimes preceding) the conference discussion and vote, the task of drafting the court's opinion is assigned to one of the justices. In a few states the chief justice has the prerogative of assigning the opinion, but much more commonly it is determined by lot or by rotation.[51] The drafting, circulating, and bargaining involved at this stage can be important in determining the outcome of the case.

Justices unable to agree fully with the emergent majority opinion are at liberty to draft and submit a concurring or dissenting opinion. Although very common on the U.S. Supreme Court, such open disagreement is relatively rare on state supreme courts. For example, in a study of six such courts in 1975 (Arizona, California, Kentucky, Michigan, Nebraska, and Rhode Island), an average of about 72 percent of their *en banc* (full court) decisions were unanimous, that is, without either concurring or dissenting opinions. Dissent alone occurred in an average of only about 17 percent of the opinions.[52] This frequency of dissent would be closer to 10 percent were it not for three rather high-profile, "lighthouse" supreme courts in this sample (California, Michigan, and New Jersey), which are close to the Kagan profile of high-discretion, low-caseload courts—tribunals usually registering dissent rates higher than the national average. State supreme courts frequently report dissent rates below 10 percent, with only about a dozen or so courts above 25 percent.[53] As already noted, however, rates of dissent appear to be rising.

Following the behavioral research movement focused on the United States Supreme Court, a number of scholars have turned their attention to the dynamics of state supreme court decision making. These research efforts have typically aimed at identifying factors in three general areas presumed to relate to appellate court decision making: (1) socioeconomic backgrounds of individual judges and courts; (2) attitudinal or ideological factors; and (3) individual and collective conceptions of the judicial role.

Studies related to socioeconomic background have tended to reveal at least some correlation between this factor and judicial voting behavior. An older study completed by Stuart Nagel, for example, indicated that political party affiliation, which typically reflects socioeconomic background, correlated, though only mildly, with the voting behaviors of individual state supreme court judges.[54] Similarly, a study in the early 1960s of the Michigan Supreme Court revealed a measurable relationship between political party affiliation and voting behavior of the judges on that court.[55] Political scientists Goldman and Sarat have cautioned, however, that over time the impact of political party affiliation may tend to wash out as a decision making factor.[56]

While affiliation with a particular political party may not strongly affect the actual decisions that an individual judge makes, Tarr and Porter point out that the simple fact

---

[51]Melinda Gann Hall, "Opinion Assignment Procedures and Conference Practices in State Supreme Courts," *Judicature* 73, No. 4 (Dec.–Jan. 1990): 209–14.

[52]Susan P. Fino, *The Role of State Supreme Courts in the New Judicial Federalism* (Westport, Conn: Greenwood Press, 1987), 72.

[53]Glick, *Courts, Politics and Justice,* 284–85. For factors associated with dissents, see Henry R. Glick and George W. Pruet, Jr., "Dissent in State Supreme Courts: Patterns and Correlates of Conflict," in Sheldon Goldman and Charles M. Lamb, eds., *Judicical Conflict and Consensus: Behavioral Studies of State American Appellate Courts* (Lexington: University of Kentucky Press, 1986), 199–214.

[54]See Stuart Nagle, "Political Party Affiliation and Judges' Decisions," *American Political Science Review* 61, No. 4 (Dec. 1961): 843–50.

[55]S. Sidney Ulmer, "The Political Party Variable in the Michigan Supreme Court," *Journal of Public Law* 11 (1962): 352–62; but see also Malcolm M. Feeley, "Research Note: Another Look at the 'Party Variable' in Judical Decision-Making," *Polity* 4, No. 1 (Autumn 1971): 91–104. Feeley argues that intervening variables other than political party of the judges could explain equally well the variance in the voting behavior reported.

[56]Sheldon Goldman and Austin Sarat, *American Court Systems: Readings in Judicial Process and Behavior* (San Francisco: Freeman, 1978), 373–74.

that state supreme court judges are typically selected from the ranks of established party leadership limits the parameters within which their decisions will fall. In short, few political renegades find their way onto state high courts, assuring that appellate decisions will reflect the prevailing political norms of a given state.[57]

Studies regarding judicial role perception have been less conclusive with respect to the impact this factor may have an decision making behavior. "Role perception" in this context refers to an individual judge's understanding of her or his proper or acceptable range of behaviors within the perceived institutional norms of the office. Early studies regarding the relationship between this variable and state supreme court judicial voting behavior were undertaken by Kenneth Vines and Henry Glick,[58] and separately by John Wold.[59] Vines and Glick asked supreme court justices in Louisiana, Pennsylvania, New Jersey, and Massachusetts to assess the difference between the idea of "policy-making" on the one hand and that of "adjudication" or "legal interpretation" on the other. Each justice was further asked to indicate which position she or he believed was proper for an appellate judge to take. A majority of the justices questioned, approximately 54 percent, chose the traditional "legal interpretation" role as that with which they felt most comfortable. In contrast, the "policy-making" role was selected by only 23 percent of the justices. A third category of judges adopted a middle position, identified by Vines and Glick as "pragmatic," indicating that the proper judicial role required a combination of policy-making and interpretation.[60]

Glick and Vines found little difference, however, in the decisional behavior of those justices who identified with the "policy-making" role and those who identified with the "adjudication-interpretation" role. Wold, too, found relatively high intracourt cohesion with respect to judicial role, despite variations between individual justices. Commenting on these findings, Tarr and Porter state that "whatever the patterns of activism or restraint, intervention or deference, the main point is that courts do develop consistent patterns, reflecting coherent judgements about the circumstances under which judicial involvement in policy-making is appropriate."[61] They suggest that the most important factor underlying this phenomenon is the impact of each state's legal culture, "that is, the norms and expectations that govern the legal processes in the state and guide the behavior of participants in the process. For the judge, this legal culture is communicated and reinforced through legal training, experience in legal practice, and interactions with other participants in the legal process."[62] In short, state supreme court justices are lawyers whose understanding of the judicial role is unquestionably influenced—even shaped—by the legal environment in which they have trained and practiced.

Studies focusing on the relationship between the political ideologies of appellate judges and the decisions that those judges make have also proven fruitful, even though serious limitations attend this type of research. One such limitation is the necessity that measurable voting variances exist in order to produce research results; one must be able to identify both the way a particular judge votes in a given case and the reasons for which that vote is cast in order to meaningfully link voting behavior with apparent ideology. While the historically high rate at which justices of the United States Supreme Court write detailed dissenting

---

[57]Tarr and Porter, *State Supreme Courts in State and Nation,* 55–57.

[58]Henry R. Glick and Kenneth N. Vines, *State Court Systems* (Englewood Cliffs, N.J.: Prentice-Hall, 1973).

[59]John T. Wold, "Political Orientations, Social Backgrounds, and Role Perceptions of State Supreme Court Judges," *Western Political Quarterly* 27 (1974): 239–41.

[60]Glick and Vines, *State Court Systems,* 62.

[61]Tarr and Porter, *State Supreme Courts in State and Nation,* 59.

[62]Tarr and Porter, *State Supreme Courts in State and Nation,* 58.

opinions provides sufficient data for this type of study, the substantially lower rate of dissent on most state supreme courts has to date offered researchers little to work with.

Nevertheless, as Tarr and Porter suggest, political ideology can be effectively linked with the policy orientations of particular courts, if not with each vote of an individual judge. Where a single party dominates state government, as occurred in Southern states during the 1950s and 1960s, party elites—from whose ranks state judges are drawn—tend to protect state policy against perceived external attacks. Similarly, where state political parties are highly competitive, state supreme court justices will almost always be selected because of their partisan activity and can be expected to carry the ideological orientations that grounded their activism with them to the state's high bench. Further,

> the sorts of cases that state supreme courts decide may render the justices' partisan and ideological attachments particularly important. [T]he detail and specificity of state constitutions, the absence of limitations on justiciability, and (in some states) the duty to render advisory opinions all serve to involve state supreme courts in day-to-day governmental operations, where divisions along party lines are common. Other issues addressed by state supreme courts may also furnish opportunities for judges' partisan views to come to the fore. When a state supreme court rules on a workers' compensation case, for example, its decision depends largely on how sympathetically it views workers' claims. Similarly, the absence of a legal text to interpret in common law cases may tempt justices to advance their personal conceptions of proper policy.[63]

A somewhat different way of viewing extant research on state appellate court decision making has been suggested by Paul Brace and Melinda Gann Hall.[64] They divide foci of past research into studies emphasizing (1) case characteristics, which is to say, the traditional stare decisis model; (2) policy preference studies, or the attitudinal or behavioral approach;[65] (3) studies focusing on state environmental variables such as socioeconomic and political characteristics of states (e.g., urbanization, levels of state expenditures, partisan competition); and (4) institutional arrangements (other than judicial role conceptions, discussed before), including such variables as the presence of intermediate appellate courts, methods of selecting judges, ways opinions assignments are made, and so on. These scholars set forth an interactive, integrated model of decision making in which variables in all four categories are weighed. Their conclusion is,

> . . . [I]n a fully specified model of judicial choice, case characteristics, personal attributes, environmental context, and institutional features all exert a statistically discernible effect on judicial voting. . . . Any comprehensive explanation of judicial behavior must incorporate all of these types of variables. . . .
>
> Moreover, institutional arrangements not only exert an independent influence on individual judicial behavior but they also serve to condition the effects of other categories of variables.[66]

[63]Tarr and Porter, *State Supreme Courts in State and Nation,* 57.

[64]Paul Brace and Melinda Gann Hall, "Studying Courts Comparatively: The View from the States," *Political Research Quarterly* 48, No. 1 (March 1995): 5–29.

[65]For the contemporary lineaments of this approach, see Harold J. Spaeth, "The Attitudinal Model," in Lee Epstein, *Contemplating Courts* (Washington: Congressional Quarterly Press, 1995), 296–314. Spaeth sharply contrasts this approach to the traditional legal model. For an expanded coverage, see Jeffrey A. Segal and Harold J. Spaeth, *The Supreme Court and the Attitudinal Model* (Cambridge, England: Cambridge University Press, 1993), along with a debate on the claims of this model: "Symposium: The Supreme Court and the Attitudinal Model," *Law and Courts Newsletter of the Law and Courts Section of the American Political Science Association* 4, No. 1 (Spring 1994), 3–12.

[66]Brace and Hall, "Studying Courts Comparatively": 24–25. These authors set out a brief but useful review of past research on state appellate court decision-making.

In addition to the clusters of influences just noted, we must not forget that state supreme courts operate within the broader context of the American system of federalism. The most obvious dimension of our federal system in this regard is the relationship between state supreme courts and national courts, most notably the United States Supreme Court. This is typically labeled "vertical federalism," reflecting the constitutional principle that federal law is superior to conflicting state law and the well-established doctrine that all courts—state and federal—are obliged to abide by U.S. Supreme Court interpretations of federal law. Given this hierarchical relationship, decisions rendered by the United States Supreme Court necessarily define the legal parameters within which state supreme courts must operate and often tend to influence the positions adopted by these courts with respect to particular legal issues.[67]

Equally important is the relationship among various state supreme courts, usually termed "horizontal federalism." While not obligated to do so, state supreme courts often look to the courts of other states for guidance in resolving common law, statutory, and occasionally even constitutional issues. The most important reason underlying this tendency may well be the generally positive regard in which adherence to precedent is held at all levels of the American judiciary.[68] As Martin Shapiro has suggested,

> [u]nder the rules of the game, the lawyer-communicator has the highest chance of winning if he can show a court that his client must prevail if the court keeps doing exactly what it has been doing; the next highest chance if he can persuade the court that it should do exactly what some other court has been doing.[69]

Thus, particularly where a given court is addressing an issue for the first time, it may well be influenced by the treatment given that issue by the supreme court of a sister state.[70]

Finally, the fact that a state supreme court must function alongside two co-equal branches of a given state's government clearly carries a potential impact on court decision-making. As Baum states,

> These other institutions [the legislature and the executive] hold considerable power over the courts, and this power helps them to influence judicial action. The other institutions in state government also provide alternative forums for those who seek to shape public policy. Interest groups that fail to secure what they want from other institutions may bring their demands to the courts. Similarly, those who are unhappy with court decisions may "appeal" to the legislature, the executive branch, or the voters.[71]

In conclusion, it should be clear that the decision-making behaviors of state supreme court justices are complex and dynamic, making generalizations difficult. There is no "typ-

---

[67]Tarr and Porter provide a lengthy explanation of vertical federalism and its impact on state supreme court decision making. See *State Supreme Courts in State and Nation,* 1–27. See also, Lawrence Baum, "Supreme Courts in the Policy Process," in Carl E. Van Horn, ed., *The State of the States,* 3rd ed. (Washington: Congressional Quarterly Press, 1996), 143–60. The Baum essay in the 1989 edition of this book is also worthwhile. Another item which clearly sets forth these concepts is Shirley S. Abrahamson and Diane S. Gutmann, "The New Federalism: State Constitutions and State Courts," *Judicature* 71, No. 2 (Aug.–Sept. 1987): 88–99. This essay is reprinted in Elliot E. Slotnick, ed., *Judicial Politics: Readings from Judicature* (Chicago: American Judicature Society and Nelson-Hall Publishers, 1992), 575–98.

[68]Tarr and Porter, *State Supreme Courts in State and Nation,* 27–28.

[69]Martin A. Shapiro, "Toward a Theory of Stare Decisis," *Journal of Legal Studies* 1 (1972): 131.

[70]Generally, see Gregory A. Caldeira, "The Transmission of Legal Precedent: A Study of State Supreme Courts," *American Political Science Review* 79, No. 1 (March 1985): 178–93, where the author identifies several factors influencing the decision of one state supreme court to rely on one or more decisions of sister state high courts, including geographical proximity, perceived judicial professionalism, apparent social complexity, prestige, and similarities in political culture. See also Baum and Canon, "State Supreme Courts as Activists."

[71]Baum, "State Supreme Courts": 104.

ical" state supreme court, and thus attempts to understand the work of these courts must always account for their substantial differences. It does appear reasonable to conclude, however, that state supreme courts in general will continue to play an increasingly significant and visible role in the formulation of state policy, particularly in view of the emergence of the "New Judicial Federalism," discussed in the next section.

STATE SUPREME COURTS: THE EMERGENCE OF THE "NEW" JUDICIAL FEDERALISM

If one doubts the reemergence of state supreme courts as major policy-making institutions in our political-legal system, one has only to consider the events surrounding the California Supreme Court. In perhaps the most intense, celebrated, and expensive judicial "election" in American history, three members of that court were, as one activist put it, "slam dunked out of business," giving then Governor George Deukmejian an opportunity to replace them with justices more sympathetic to a conservative, "law and order" orientation. Although retention elections under merit selection plans usually produce little voter interest, this referendum was probably the hottest issue in the 1986 California elections.[72] In excess of $6 million was spent in the campaign to defeat these three justices—Chief Justice Rose Elizabeth Bird and Justices Cruz Reynoso and Joseph Grodin—and some $2 million dollars were expended on behalf of these justices in their unsuccessful fight for retention.

By all accounts, the record of these "liberal" justices in death penalty cases was the prime issue in the campaign. In 56 cases in which the California Supreme Court was asked to review death penalties imposed by California trial courts, the justices overturned the sentence in 95 percent of the cases. Chief Justice Bird became the lightening rod of the whole campaign, in part because of her record of voting to overturn death penalty cases *100 percent* of the time. With the replacement of these justices by those having a greater willingness to please the voters, the sustaining of death penalty sentences rose dramatically, 58 of 83 such sentences being upheld between 1986 and 1989.

Although there may not be a frequent replay of these dramatic events in other states,[73] the California election graphically demonstrates the intense interest of voters, interest groups (including bar associations), political parties, and of course other politicians in the outcome of state appellate court decisions, all of which underscore the political character of the work of these tribunals. Indeed, by 1990, in California and elsewhere, political candidates considered it political suicide to run for office without announcing that they stood foursquare behind capital punishment.

---

[72]These events in the mid-eighties in California are detailed in John H. Culver and John T. Wold, "Rose Bird and the Politics of Judicial Accountability in California" and "The Defeat of the California Judges: The Campaign, The Electorate, and the Issue of Judicial Accountability," *Judicature* 70, No. 2 (Aug.–Sept. 1986); and No. 6 (April–May 1987): 81–89 and 348–355.

[73]But recalling the material presented in Chapter 5 and pursuing the current press reports provide some evidence to suggest that the politics of state appellate court decision-making is intensifying in several other states. See, e.g., Donald W. Jackson and James W. Riddlesperger, Jr., "Money and Politics in Judicial Elections: The 1988 election of the Chief Justice of the Texas Supreme Court," *Judicature* 74, No. 4 (Dec.–Jan. 1991): 184–89.

That the post–Rose Bird California Supreme Court is not completely driven by the "tough on crime" sentiment in that state is underscored by its June 1996 decision seriously undermining California's harsh "three strikes" law. The court held that state judges had the right to set aside a defendant's prior convictions if the justices thought a mandatory prison sentence was excessive. See Carey Goldberg, "California Judges Ease 3-Strike Law," *New York Times* (June 21, 1996): A-1.

As suggested, the historic swing in our federal system of government signaled by the Reagan presidency portends a significantly enhanced role for state supreme courts. With the increased modernization of these tribunals at the apex of state adjudicatory systems, we now find ourselves in an exciting new era of state appellate court activism. Indeed, whereas only two or three decades ago, American constitutional law was viewed as almost exclusively the province of the federal courts, it is now impossible to understand the leading edge of American legal doctrine without serious attention to developments in state constitutional law.

To highlight the renaissance of state constitutional law, it is helpful to take a quick look backward to an earlier, more familiar, era of judicial policy-making. Since the early 1950s, an entire generation of scholars, teachers, and commentators have become accustomed to stating American constitutional law almost entirely in terms of the evolution of federal, especially Supreme Court, doctrine. An examination of current scholarly texts and treatises on the subject will quickly reveal the almost total exclusion of state constitutional law.[74] This bypassing of state court activity grew out of the dramatic judicial activism of the Warren Court, particularly in the civil liberties field. Although the "nationalization" of the federal Bill of Rights began in the 1920s with decisions such as *Meyer v. Nebraska* (262 U.S. 390, 1923) and, more pointedly, *Gitlow v. New York* (268 U.S. 652, 1925), the Warren Court decisions in the 1960s greatly accelerated this important constitutional development, causing observer and practitioner alike to look to the U.S. Supreme Court for the protection and enhancement of basic rights.[75]

Decisions applying the Bill of Rights to the states in the areas of right to counsel, protection against unreasonable searches and seizures (the exclusionary rule), prohibition against cruel and unusual punishment, the right to trial by jury, and so on virtually transformed American criminal law from a two-level system of national (federal) versus state criminal law to a set of standards universally applied to all courts and police activities in the nation. When one adds the startling Warren Court doctrines in the areas of racial segregation, separation of church and state (e.g., prayer in public schools), legislative reapportionment, and a newly created national right of privacy, it is easy to understand why American constitutional law came to be defined as national or federal in nature, state supreme courts being brought into the picture largely as examples of evasion of federal legal doctrine.[76]

Beginning in the early 1970s, however, the thrust of liberal judicial activism began to wane under the more conservative orientation of the Burger Court. Although the somewhat realigned Court did not engage in outright reversal of important Warren Court decisions, the broadening of civil rights slowed considerably, and the Burger Court justices began to chip away at a number of Warren Court doctrines.[77] More important for our discussion, the Burger and Rehnquist Courts have shown signs of actually inviting a larger role for state

---

[74]Lawrence M. Friedman, "State Constitutions in Historical Perspective," *Annals* 495 (1988): 34; and Peter J. Galie, "Teaching About Civil Liberties: The Missing Dimension," in *Perspectives on Political Science* 22, No. 3 (Summer 1993): 116–123.

[75]For readers unfamiliar with the meaning of the "nationalization" of the Bill of Rights, see any standard treatment of American constitutional law such as Alpheus T. Mason and Donald Grier Stephenson, Jr., *American Constitutional Law,* 11th ed. (Englewood Cliffs, N.J.: Prentice Hall, 1996), especially Ch. 9.

[76]See, e.g., Charles A. Johnson and Bradley C. Canon, *Judicial Policies: Implementation and Impact* (Washington: Congressional Quarterly Press, 1984. A more pointed reference is Walter F. Murphy's early piece, "Lower Court Checks on Supreme Court Power," *American Political Science Review* 53, No. 3 (Sept. 1959): 1017–31. See also Galie, "Teaching Civil Liberties": 116.

[77]Vincent Blasi, ed., *The Burger Court: The Constitutional Revolution That Wasn't* (New Haven: Yale University Press, 1983).

appellate courts, either by refusing to hear cases (thereby allowing state courts to make these final determinations) or by setting forth doctrine rather clearly intended to encourage a larger role for state supreme courts.[78]

In 1972, for example, Justice Lewis Powell wrote for the Supreme Court in the watershed case of *San Antonio Independent School District v. Rodriquez* (411 U.S. 1). The Court was faced with the question of whether or not wide disparities in state funding of public schools between richer and poorer school districts violated the equal protection clause of the U.S. Constitution. Earlier, in August 1971, the California Supreme Court had made national headlines in its decision in *Serrano v. Priest* (5 Cal. 3rd 584), by holding that the state's school-funding formula violated the equal protection clause of both the state and federal constitutions. And about the same time, a three-judge federal district court in Texas had ruled that the gross inequalities in the funding of education between the wealthier and poorer school districts in that state stood in violation of the federal equal protection clause (*Rodriguez v. San Antonio Independent School District,* 337 F. Supp. 280 (W.Dst.) Texas, 1971).

Although Justice Powell declined to declare either education to be either a fundamental right or poverty to be a "suspect classification," he was not content simply with reversing the federal district court decision in Texas. Rather, in a wide-ranging essay on American education and American federalism, he shunned "judicial intrusion into otherwise legitimate state activities," denounced a too long and heavy reliance by states on local property taxes for the funding of education, and in general encouraged innovative and creative policy-making at the state level to handle the problem.[79] Few who read the decision could doubt the strong encouragement it gave for state action, and a number of states responded positively.

As seen, the California Supreme Court, as it often did, led the nation in using its own state constitution's equal protection clause to reorder public school financing in that state. Under the influence of "horizontal federalism" a number of other states followed suit. In New Jersey, for example, the supreme court held, in *Robinson v. Cahill* (62 N.J. 473, 1973), that the state's constitutional provision requiring the legislature to provide a "thorough and efficient system of free public schools" mandated at abandonment of public school financing strictly on the basis of property taxes. The court subsequently forced the state legislature to adopt an income tax law to help bring about a more equitable distribution of school funds.[80] Since then, more than a dozen additional states have moved in a similar direction, either by state supreme court decision or by legislative enactment or both.[81]

---

[78]Widely mentioned as a catalyst for increased state court policy-making are the remarks of Justice William J. Brennan, Jr. See, e.g., "State Constitutions and the Protection of Individual Rights," *Harvard Law Review* 90, No. 3 (Jan. 1977): 489–504, and Brennan's "The Bill of Rights and the States: The Revival of State Constitutions as Guardians of Individual Rights," *New York University Law Review* 61, No. 4 (Oct. 1986): 535–53. These and related issues are discussed by Judith S. Kaye, "State Courts at the Dawn of a New Century: Common Law Courts Reading Statutes and Constitutions," *New York University Law Review* 70, No. 1 (Apr. 1995): 1–35; and by Robert C. Post, "Justice Brennan and Federalism," *Constitutional Commentary* 7, No. 2 (Summer 1990): 227–38.

Two useful press items briefly summarizing some of these developments are Robert Pear, "State Courts Move Beyond U.S. Bench in Rights Rulings," *New York Times* (May 4, 1986): A-1; and David G. Savage, "High Court Puts Its Faith in 'Laboratory of the States'," *Los Angeles Times* (July 1, 1990): A-1.

[79]Stanley H. Friedelbaum, "Reactive Responses: The Complementary Role of Federal and State Courts," *Publius* 17, No. 1 (Winter 1987): 39–42.

[80]For an overview of these developments in the early years, see Richard Lehne, *The Quest for Justice: The Politics of School Finance Reform* (New York: Longman, 1978).

[81]A useful update in the form of a brief case study of this policy area is contained in Tarr, *Judicial Process and Judical Policy-Making,* 369–380.

In another key decision of the U.S. Supreme Court, the invitation to state judicial creativity was stated more explicitly. In *Robins v. Pruneyard Shopping Center* (592 P. 2d 341, 1979), the California Supreme Court (Justice Frank Newman) held that in spite of U.S. Supreme Court rulings to the contrary, private shopping centers, under California's constitution, could not ban student appearances on the premises to circulate political petitions. In an earlier decision, *Lloyd Corp. v. Tanner* (407 U.S. 551) in 1972, the U.S. Supreme Court had ruled that private shopping centers were not required to permit such free speech.

Although many observers expected the Burger Court to reverse California's *Pruneyard* ruling, the exact opposite occurred. In a unanimous decision written by Justice Rehnquist, the High Court emphasized the doctrine of independent state grounds in upholding, "the State's asserted interest in promoting more expansive rights of free speech than conferred by the Federal Constitution" (*Pruneyard Shopping Center v. Robins,* 447 U.S. 74, 85, 1980). As one scholar noted,

> If there is any unifying element that permeates the opinions in *Pruneyard* [several justices wrote concurrent opinions] it is adherence to the principle of state-created rights independently derived.... Justice Rehnquist's sweeping pose ... def[ies] any meaningful rationale except for this dedication to a "new" judicial federalism.... [The Court's unanimity] was grounded upon the untapped and largely untried resources of the state courts.[82]

If there remains any doubt about the leanings of the U.S. Supreme Court on this matter, we may refer to the remarks of Associate Justice William Brennan, who in a speech at Harvard Law School argued that the "dimunition of federal scrutiny and protection [of civil rights] mandates the assumption of a more responsible state court role."[83] He added that he was certain that the Court's recent retreat on civil rights "should be interpreted as a plain invitation to state courts to step into the breach." And step into the breach they did!

Before surveying more recent state court policy developments, it might be well to describe briefly the tools available to state appellate courts to enter into their new policy activism. Although the doctrine of supremacy of federal law significantly limits the range of policy-making available to these courts, there is nothing preventing states from either breaking new ground in state constitutional law or extending rights and liberties beyond those minimally guaranteed under the national Constitution as interpreted by the U.S. Supreme Court. The constitutions of the fifty states are rich in detail and novel provisions, affording state appellate court judges fertile soil for the nurturing of unique if not exotic legal doctrine. For example, seventeen state constitutions contain "little ERAs"; ten embody specific provisions protecting the right to privacy; and a number of others provide, in varying language, for the protection of the environment.[84] As long as state constitutional doctrine does not minimize federal guarantees and/or where the state courts explicitly stake out their decisions on "bona fide separate, adequate, and independent [state] grounds . . ." (*Michigan v. Long,* 463 U.S. 1041, 1983), state court rulings may be presumed to be valid.[85]

Additionally, state judges enjoy several advantages of flexibility usually denied their federal colleagues. First, states are the recipients of inherent, plenary power rather than

[82]Stanley H. Friedelbaum, "Reactive Responses:" 38. In 1994 New Jersey's supreme court, in a closely divided 4–3 decision, handed down a similar ruling, and in doing so, cited holdings in six other state supreme courts which, since 1979, had allowed citizens to " . . . engage in certain types of expressive conduct in privately owned malls." See Joseph F. Sullivan, "Court Protects Speech in Malls," *New York Times* (Dec. 21, 1994): A-1. The case was *New Jersey Coalition Against War in the Middle East v. J. M. B. Realty Corp,* 650 A 2d 757 (N. J. 1994).

[83]William J. Brennan, Jr., "Remarks of William J. Brennan, Jr., 100th Anniversary Dinner," *Harvard Law Review* (April 11, 1987).

[84]G. Alan Tarr and Cornelia A. Porter, "State Constitutions and State Constitutional Law," *Publius* 17, No. 1 (Winter 1987): 4.

[85]Abrahamson and Gutmann, "The New Federalism": 96–99.

specific, delegated powers. In these circumstances, state courts are not required to search for constitutional provisions *supporting* state policies; rather, they have only to satisfy themselves that there are no specific federal or state constitutional provisions *prohibiting* the action in question.[86]

Second, Article III of the Constitution expressly limits federal courts to hearing "cases and controversies." In cases such as *Hayburn's Case,* 2 U.S. (2 Dallas) 409 (1792), and *De Funis v. Odegaard,* 416 U.S. 312 (1974), the U.S. Supreme Court has interpreted this passage restrictively, prohibiting federal courts from rendering advisory opinions where no live dispute between identified parties exists.

In contrast, at least 10 state specifically permit their courts to issue advisory opinions. In Massachusetts, for example, "the advisory opinion is used regularly and in connection with matters of major constitutional significance."[87]

Another difference between the exercise of state and federal judicial power lies in the Fourteenth Amendment. As a basis for the application of federal constitutional standards to state law, this amendment is specifically limited to *state action:* "No *state* may make or enforce any law which shall abridge the. . . ." Although federal court rulings have sometimes circumvented this language, the doctrine of state action unquestionably limits the ability of federal courts to scrutinize the private activities of citizens within the states. The Supreme Court's *Pruneyard* ruling, discussed before, is only one example of this limitation in operation. But whatever constraints this amendment places on federal courts, it operates on state judicial policy-making not at all, leading to a much broader range of activity subject to state judicial cognizance.

Finally, considerations of federalism per se can often interfere with federal judicial policy-making, whereas by definition state courts have no such restriction. The holding of the U.S. Supreme Court in the landmark case of *San Antonio Independent School District v. Rodriguez* (411 U.S. 1, 1973), discussed more fully before, is a prime example. The fact that we have a federal system of government, with powers divided between the two levels, means in law as well as in practice that federal courts are reluctant to play a hands-on role in many state and local policy disputes. State supreme courts, on the other hand, have been known to mention specifically this absence of federalism's restraints in moving ahead with important policy pronouncements.[88] Clearly, additional factors work to the advantage of state courts in fashioning public policy in helping to determine the policy agenda for other state agencies. But this discussion should suffice to suggest the broad legal base that these courts enjoy as they launch into the current era of increased judicial activism.

At the same time, one can easily overstate the contemporary activism of state supreme courts. To the extent that their opportunities for creative policy-making lay in the reliance on their own state constitutions rather than hewing to federal constitutional interpretations, recent research has revealed that this decisional approach is not frequently adopted by these tribunals. Thus, in a broad-gauged study measuring state court activism in the area of criminal procedures only, Barry Latzer reports that the "New Judicial Federalism" is hardly a wholly liberal legal movement.[89] Rather, he cites several reasons, such as the constraints of vertical and horizontal federalism, limitations imposed by other so-

[86]Peter J. Galie, "Why Does He Write It Twice? The Role of State Supreme Courts in State Political Systems," paper presented at the meeting of the American Political Science Association, Aug. 29–Sept. 1, 1984: 3.

[87]Galie, "Why Does He Write It Twice?": 4. Another view of *Hayburn's Case* is set forth by Maeva Marcus and Robert Teir, "Hayburn's Case: A Misinterpretation of Precedent," *Wisconsin Law Review* 1988, No. 4: 527–46.

[88]Galie, "Why Does He Write It Twice": 6–7.

[89]Barry Latzer, "The Hidden Conservatism of the State Court Revolution," *Judicature* Vol. 74, No. 4 (Dec.–Jan., 1991): 190–197.

ciopolitical forces within the state, not to mention the supremacy clause, to explain the rather conservative, compliant stance of most state courts of last resort in most instances. The rejection, on state grounds, of conservative U.S. Supreme Court holdings is, Latzer, admits, ". . . a major development deserving all the attention it has received."[90] But if states are seen as political laboratories in this context, one must report all data gathered therein.

Research by Emmert and Traut sets forth somewhat complementary findings. In a study of instances of judicial review in all fifty state supreme courts for 1981 through 1985, they found that a strong majority of decisions were based on both state and federal constitutional grounds, rather than on the former alone, though when based on state constitutions alone, as heralded in the New Judicial Federalism, there was a much greater likelihood of these tribunals declaring state law unconstitutional.

There are other considerations arguing for a more restrained view of the New Judicial Federalism. James Gardner, for instance, sets forth a thesis holding that "state constitutional law today is a vast wasteland of confusing, conflicting, and essentially unintelligible pronouncements."[91] The underlying cause for this, he maintains, is the lack of a coherent discourse on state constitutional law—a language," that is, "in which it is possible for participants in the legal system to make intelligible claims about the meaning of state constitutions." And in turn, the absence of such a discourse, according to Gardner, is occasioned by the lack of a consistent theory of state constitutions.[92]

There are, of course, opposing views. Donald Lutz, for instance, has argued that

> [S]tate constitutions together contain and embody a coherent political theory which is, in important respects, at variance with Federalist theory which underlies the United States constitution. . . . American constitutional history is the story of a competitive interaction between Federalist political theory and the Whig theory informing the state constitutions.[93]

Whatever the appropriate caveats attendant to the development of the New Judicial Federalism, it remains true that creative state court decisions, carving out new and expanded rights for state (American) citizens, continue to be forthcoming, even if by only a

---

[90]Latzer, "The Hidden Conservatism": 190. See also, by the same author, "Four Half-Truths about State Constitutional Law," *Temple Law Review* 65, No. 4 (Winter 1992): 1123–52.

Reaching similar conclusions about the conservatism of state appellate courts are analyses by Michael Esler, "State Supreme Court Commitment to State Law," *Judicature* 78, No. 1 (July–August 1994): 25–32; and Baum, "State Supreme Courts": 104–27.

[91]See James A Gardner, "The Failed Discourse of State Constitutionalism," *Michigan Law Review* 90, No. 4 (Feb. 1992): 763.

[92]Gardner's more complete introductory statement on this point is

> . . . [T]he failure of state constitutionalism is that a state constitution reflects the fundamental values, and ultimately the character, of the people of the state. . . . [But this] . . . is not a good description of actual state constitutions; it embraces theoretical inconsistencies that undermine its value as a framework for a coherent discourse; and it takes an obsolete and potentially dangerous view of the texture and focus of American national identity." Gardner, "The Failed Discourse": 764.

[93]Donald S. Lutz, "From Covenant to Constitution in American Political Thought," *Publius* 10, No. 4 (Fall 1980): 101–33. This same line of argument is pursued, and this passage quoted by Robert F. Williams in "State Constitutionalism: Completing the Interdisciplinary Study of Constitutional Law and Political Theory," *Perspectives on Political Science* 22, No. 3 (Summer 1993): 110.

There is also a series of direct responses to the Gardner thesis. Most of these are cited in Judith S. Kaye, "State Courts at the Dawn of a New Century: Common Law Courts Reading Statutes and Constitutions," *New York University Law Review* 70, No. 1 (April 1995): 12, n. 60. In particular, see Ronald L. Nelson's response to Gardner's notions in "Welcome to the 'Last Frontier,'" Professor Gardner: Alaska's Independent Approach to State Constitutional Interpretation," *Alaska Law Review* XII, No. 1 (June 1995): 1–41; and Nelson's "Alaska's New Judicial Federalism: Antecedents—History, Culture, and Jurisprudence," paper delivered at the Annual Meeting of the Western Political Science Association, San Francisco, Mar. 14–16, 1996.

small minority of these courts. Indeed, it is not too much to say that the field of state constitutional law is currently characterized by a richness and variety unknown since the rather aggressive development of the common law in the late nineteenth century.[94] Although it is impossible to cover this entire terrain in this brief discussion, we may begin by noting that in the field of civil liberties alone, scholars have catalogued over six-hundred instances in which state courts of last resort have interpreted their own constitutions as providing rights broader than those contained in U.S. Supreme Court rulings. A few examples will illustrate these new departures in state judicial policy making.

In addition to the school-funding revolution noted earlier, freedom of speech and press, as in the *Pruneyard* case, has been a subject of considerable activity. One of the most notable departures of state supreme courts has been in the area of public access to judicial proceedings. In *Gannett v. DePasquale* (443 U.S. 368) in 1979, the U.S. Supreme Court upheld the exclusion of the press from a pretrial court hearing. Although the Court later seemed to retreat from that position, *DePasquale* caused considerable concern in the states, not to mention in the press. In North Dakota, for example, the supreme court there interpreted the state constitution to the contrary, that is, as guaranteeing public and press access to virtually all judicial proceedings. Similar rulings came from the Oregon and West Virginia supreme courts. In other states, restrictions on press access to court sessions have been severely curtailed, the overall impact being a more liberal view of the freedom of the press in such matters relative to the doctrine set forth in *DePasquale*.[95]

Since California's *Pruneyard* ruling, other state appellate courts have been careful to stake out independent state positions on the right of free speech on private property. Although few states have followed the California lead in toto, some state supreme courts (e.g., New Jersey, Pennsylvania, and Washington) have upheld petition drives or the distribution of leaflets on private property, in seeming contradiction to federal court interpretations of the First Amendment.[96]

In part because the U.S. Supreme Court has been unable to develop uniform, clear-cut guidelines on what types of expression (e.g., alleged obscenity) are protected by the First Amendment, state supreme courts are developing their own approaches, often taking into

---

See also the essays contained in Ellis Katz and G. Alan Tarr, eds., *Federalism and Rights* (Lanham, Md: Rowman and Littlefield, 1996), especially Dorothy Toth Beasley's "Federalism and the Protection of Individual Rights: The American State Constitutional Perspective," 101–21; and Talbot D'Alemberte, "Rights and Federalism: An Agenda to Advance the Vision of Justice Brennan," 123–38. In "Waiting for Godot? The New Judicial Federalism, 1987–1992: Reality or Hoax?" Paul A. Kramer entered this debate by examining state judicial review cases over a five-year period. See paper delivered at the Annual Meeting of the American Political Science Association, San Francisco, Aug. 29–Sept. 1, 1996.

[94]Not unexpectedly, there has been a concomitant growth, if not an explosion, in primary and secondary materials on state constitutional law. In addition to the sources cited above and below, see, Robert F. Williams, *State Constitutional Law: Cases and Materials,* 2nd ed. (Charlottsville, Va.: Michie Co., 1993; and National Association of Attorneys General, *State Constitutional Law Bulletin* (Washington: National Association of Attorneys General).

Much relevant material is cited and discussed by Robert F. Williams in "State Constitutionalism": 112; and Galie, "Teaching Civil Liberties": 121. Also useful is the symposium "Emerging Issues in State Constitutional Law," *Temple Law Review* 65, No. 4 (Winter 1992), which includes items on both constitutional theory as well as doctrinal developments such as ERAs, privacy, education, etc.; and Kaye, "State Courts at the Dawn of a New Century:" especially 11–18. Worthwhile press items also occasionally appear, such as Joseph F. Sullivan, "New Jersey Court Seen as Leader in the Expansion of Individual Rights," *New York Times* (July 8, 1990): A-11; and Stephen Wermiel, "State Supreme Courts are Feeling Their Oats About Civil Liberties," *Wall Street Journal* (June 5, 1988): A-1.

[95]See G. Alan Tarr, "Civil Liberties Under State Constitutions," *The Political Science Teacher* 1, No. 4 (Fall 1988): 8.

[96]Sue Davis and Taunya L. Banks, "State Constitutions, Freedom of Expression, and Search and Seizure," *Publius,* 17, No. 1 (Winter 1987): 13–31; and Tarr, "Civil Liberties Under State Constitutions": 9.

consideration the political culture and history of their state. Thus, in a rather remarkable opinion striking down the conviction of an adult bookstore owner in 1987, the Oregon Supreme Court rejected the strictures of the federal doctrine in holdings such as *Miller v. California* (413 U.S. 15, 1973), reasoning that the Oregon constitution was written by "rugged and robust individuals" who did not look kindly on "governmental imposition of some people's views of morality on the free expression of others." The court then held that "In this state any person can write, print, read, say, show or sell anything to a consenting adult even though that expression may be generally or universally considered 'obscene.' "[97]

Indeed, Oregon's Supreme Court, under the leadership of Justice Hans Linde, has become a national beacon in the development of a body of state constitutional law on freedom of expression.[98] However, a number of other states have also been quite active in the field, prime examples being New York, California, and New Jersey.

Criminal procedure issues have also provided a fruitful arena for state judicial policy-making in this era of the new judicial federalism. In the area of search and seizure, particularly the application and interpretation of the exclusionary rule, the states have often been at some variance with federal judicial doctrine. A number of state supreme courts had instituted the exclusionary rule well before the U.S. Supreme Court did so in 1961 in *Mapp v. Ohio* (367 U.S. 643). And when the Supreme Court, in *U. S. v. Leon* (468 U.S. 897, 1984) and *Maryland v. Garrison* (480 U.S. 79, 1987), began to chew away at the requirements of that rule (that evidence illegally seized in violation of the Fourth Amendment may not be admitted in court), a number of state courts refused to go along. Again on independent state grounds of their own constitutions, states such as New Jersey, New York, Michigan, Mississippi, and Massachusetts struck out in other directions, generally hewing to a fairly strict exclusion of tainted evidence.[99] Additionally, the supreme courts of Washington and Oregon have given advance notice that their states' exclusionary rules rest on independent state ground, should the U.S. Supreme Court further water down this right.[100]

In a similar vein, as the current Supreme Court shows signs of moving away from the requirements of *Miranda v. Arizona* (384 U.S. 436, 1966)—holding that criminal suspects must be warned of their rights, including the right to remain silent and to have the assistance of an attorney—a number of states have not been willing to follow that lead, preferring a closer observance of these rights. The California and Hawaii supreme courts are but two examples.[101]

In a wide-ranging set of other civil liberties issues, state supreme courts are making new law at a surprising rate. The right to privacy, issues of gender discrimination, further issues having to do with search and seizure, variations of federal rights in jury trials, right to counsel, state aid to religion, and so on—these and other areas suggest the spread of current policy-making by state supreme courts.[102] But it is not only in the field of civil rights that state supreme courts are breaking new ground. Property and economic rights are also being reexamined by these tribunals.

---

[97]732 P. 2d 9 (Ore. 1987).

[98]G. Alan Tarr, "State Constitutionalism and 'First Amendment' Rights," in Stanley H. Friedelbaum, ed., *Human Rights in the States:* 46, n. 74.

[99]Stanley Mosk, "The Emerging Agenda in State Constitutional Rights Law," *Annals* 496, (Mar. 1988): 60–61.

[100]Tarr, "Civil Liberties Under State Constitutions," 9. See also more recent rulings discussed in Kaye, "State Courts at the Dawn of a New Century," 11–18.

[101]Mosk, "The Emerging Agenda": 58.

[102]See, e.g., Davis and Banks, "State Constitutions"; Friedelbaum, *Human Rights in the States*"; Mosk, "The Emerging Agenda"; Kaye, "State Courts at the Dawn of a New Century."

Whereas students of constitutional law are familiar with the abandonment of the substantive due process doctrine of liberty of contract in federal courts, state courts, under long-established interpretations of state constitutions, continue to use such concepts as due process and equal protection to judge the reasonableness of public incursions into private property rights. After a detailed study of such adjudication at the same level, Galie concluded;

> State supreme courts continue to . . . grant greater protection to economic rights than would be forthcoming from the federal judiciary. All but three states have refused to follow the lead of the U.S. Supreme Court in its rejection of substantive due process and equal protection in the area of economic regulation. There is no doubt about the continued solicitude for economic rights on the part of state supreme courts; there are doubts about the justification for such activism.[103]

At the same time, supreme courts in other states are developing new doctrines to move public policy in an opposite direction, so to speak. In New Jersey, for example, the state's highest court held in 1975, and again in 1983, that municipalities must provide their fair share of low-cost housing. These widely heralded rulings, dubbed *Mt. Laurel I and II,*[104] were based on the doctrine of "regional general welfare"—that states may be required to use their powers to promote the general welfare, particularly in economically deprived areas. This was probably the most far-reaching judicial decision on exclusionary zoning in the nation.[105] The impact of these rulings on the state's economic and political system was profound. Said one observer, the court "irrevocably changed the name of the political game in New Jersey."[106] The main result of these decisions, as it was in a number of other state supreme court policy forays, was to create a policy agenda item for the state legislature:

> Of lasting benefit [of Mt. Laurel] is the conversation that it set off. What the court did was to force upon the legislature consideration of an issue that the legislature did not want to think about and would not have done anything about but for the litigation. The problem was brought into the sunlight by litigation.[107]

Land use cases in general have helped to change the face of cities and towns in a number of states. State courts are increasingly showing their willingness to limit private land development in the interest of the community as a whole. An example recently cited was the Fairfax County (Virginia) Board of Supervisors, which replated a housing development from 40,000 to 8,000 homes on the basis of earlier Virginia Supreme Court holdings indicating support for such action. Faced with voter initiatives and doctrines, such as regional general welfare and/or environmental protection clauses in state constitutions, private land developers are being forced to curtail their activities in favor of long-dormant environmental concerns. Thus, joined either by the grassroots sentiments of citizens or by the legislature or both, state supreme courts are increasing their relevance across a broad terrain of state and local policy-making.

This discussion is hardly intended as a definitive statement on the subject. As this book is going to press, policy tendencies in every facet of the field are undergoing constant change, not only in response to the normally expected evolution of judicial doctrine in the narrow

---

[103]Peter J. Galie, "Social Services and Egalitarian Activism," in Friedelbaum, ed., *Human Rights in the States:* 81–82.

[104]See *Southern Burlington County NAACP v. Township of Mt. Laurel,* 336 A. 2d 713, N. J. 1975; and 456 A. 2d 390, N. J. 1983.

[105]Galie, "Social Services and Egalitarian Activism": 109.

[106]Elder Witt, "State Supreme Courts: Tilting the Balance Toward Change," *Governing* 1 (1988): 33.

[107]Witt, "State Supreme Courts": 35.

[108]Kaye, "State Courts at the Dawn of a New Century,": 14.

legal sense but also molded by what one writer termed the whirlwind of new age politics,"[108] where all the expected pressures of state politics, partisan and otherwise, are being brought to bear on judicial outcomes.[109] But as one observer has noted, "[t]he realm of state constitutional law is a beehive of activity," with state supreme courts for the first time in over fifty years beginning to experiment in policy areas previously thought to be exclusive federal domain. "Truly," as Justice William Brennan has said, "state courts have responded with marvelous enthusiasm to many not-so-subtle invitations to fill the constitutional gaps left by the decisions of the Supreme Court."[110] As the U.S. Supreme Court continues to move in the direction of a lower level of policy creativity, it may be expected that state supreme courts will increasingly, "define the quality of life" in American states and communities.[111]

CONCLUSION

With the heavy measure of appellate judicial policy-making taking place in the states, combined with the swing toward decentralization within the American federal system, a whole new (or actually, renewed) chapter in the study of the American judiciary is opening up for scholar and practitioner alike. Not only may American constitutional doctrine (the substance of the law) no longer be stated purely in terms of the work of federal courts, but also important new lessons having to do with the process or politics of our judicial system are being written at the state level. Surely the case has been made that in our teaching and research, state courts can no longer be ignored as stepchildren of our judicial system. And nowhere is the evidence supporting this proposition more convincing than in the current work of state appellate tribunals.

On the order of a sobering reminder is the recent note by Robert Williams that for twenty years, from 1929 to 1949, the *American Political Science Review,* the central organ for the discipline of political science, published an annual survey of developments in state constitutional law.[112] Today, by way of contrast, it is difficult to find a major constitutional law casebook used in political science classes devoting more than a minuscule portion of its coverage, if any at all, to this burgeoning field.[113]

FURTHER READING

Baum, Lawrence. "Supreme Courts in the Policy Process," in Carl E. Van Horn, ed. *The State of the States.* 3rd ed. Washington: Congressional Quarterly Press, 1996, 143–60.

---

[109]Examples abound. See, e.g., Culver and Wold, "Rose Bird and the Politics of Judicial Accountability"; and a recent editorial, "The Governor's Attack on the Judges," where the *New York Times* takes New York Governor George Pataki to task for attacking the state's highest court's ruling setting forth a strict interpretation of the exclusionary rule. *New York Times* (February 3, 1996): A-14. The governor introduced legislation to strip the court of the right to make decisions on unlawfully seized evidence under the state constitution.

[110]Brennan, "Remarks at the 100th Anniversary Dinner, *Harvard Law Review* (April 11, 1987).

[111]Witt, "State Supreme Courts": 30.

[112]Williams, "Constitutional Law and Political Theory": 113, n. 14.

[113]Political science–constitutional law textbooks are discussed in this context by Galie, "Teaching Civil Liberties," especially 117–120. It should be noted that casebooks written for the law schools, as well as law school curriculum generally, are equally bereft of state constitutional law coverage. At the same time, course materials for political science written in the judicial process or politics tradition are recently beginning to include significant amounts of state appellate court materials. See especially Tarr, *Judicial Process and Judicial Policymaking;* and Stumpf and Culver, *The Politics of State Courts.*

Brace, Paul, and Melinda Gann Hall. "Studying Courts Comparatively: The View from the American States." *Political Research Quarterly* 48, No. 1 (Mar. 1995): 5–29.

Brennan, William J., Jr. "The Bill of Rights and the States: The Revival of State Constitutions as Guardians of Individual Rights." *New York University Law Review* 61, No. 4 (Oct. 1986): 535–53.

Chapper, Joy A., and Roger A. Hanson. *Intermediate Appellate Courts: Improving Case Processing.* Williamsburg, Va.: National Center for State Courts, 1990.

Davies, Thomas Y. "Gresham's Law Revisited: Expedited Processing Techniques and the Allocation of Appellate Resources." *Justice Systems Journal* 6, No. 3 (Fall 1981): 372–404.

Davis, Sue. "Rehnquist and State Courts: Federalism Revisited." *Western Political Quarterly* 45, No. 3 (Sept. 1992): 773–82.

"Emerging Issues in State Constitutional Law: (Symposium). *Temple Law Review* 65, No. 4 (Winter 1992).

Friedelbaum, Stanley H., ed. *Human Rights in the States: New Directions in Constitutional Policymaking.* Westport, Conn.: Greenwood Press, 1988.

Kagan, Robert A., et. al. "The Evolution of State Supreme Courts." *Michigan Law Review* 76, No. 6 (May 1978): 961–1005.

Kaye, Judith S. "State Courts at the Dawn of a New Century: Common Law Courts Reading Statutes and Constitutions." *New York University Law Review* 70, No. 1 (April 1995): 1–35.

"New Developments in State Constitutional Law" (Symposium). *Publius* 17, No. 1 (Winter 1987).

Ostrom, Brian J., and Neal B. Kauder. *Examining the Work of State Courts, 1993, 1994.* Williamsburg, Va.: National Center for State Courts, 1995, 1996.

Porter, Mary Cornelia, and G. Alan Tarr, eds. *State Supreme Courts: Policy-Makers in the Federal System.* Westport, Conn.: Greenwood Press, 1982.

"State Constitutions in a Federal System" (Symposium). *Annuals* 496 (March 1988).

Stumpf, Harry P., and John C. Culver. *The Politics of State Courts.* New York: Longman, 1992.

"Symposium, Part I: New Directions in State Constitutional Law." *Perspectives on Political Science* 22, No. 3 (Summer 1993).

Tarr, G. Alan, and Cornelia Aldis Porter. *State Supreme Courts in State and Nation.* New Haven: Yale University Press, 1988.

Williams, Robert F. *State Constitutional Law: Cases and Materials.* 2nd ed. Williamsburg, Va.: Michie Co., 1993.

11
Federal Appeals

Assembly lines are becoming the mode for error correction in large classes of litigation. . . .
Judges . . . [are] becoming administrators running "human machines."
—J. Woodford Howard, Jr.
Courts of Appeals in the Federal Judicial System

[J]udges . . . are influenced in their judging by personal predilections, by their commitments to
ethical norms, and by their understanding of the realities of political life. But at the same time
it must never be forgotten that the freedom of a judge is limited by the institutional ethos and
by the traditions of his calling. A judicial decision is an amalgam of personal judgment and
institutional control.

Walter F. Murphy and C. Herman Pritchett
Courts, Judges and Politics

THE UNITED STATES COURTS OF APPEALS

Sometimes called the forgotten courts, the often mislabeled "circuit courts of appeals"
have usually been portrayed in teaching and research as the ugly step-child of the
United States Supreme Court. Yet, recent research forays into the functioning of the
federal judiciary at this level suggest that a great deal can be learned about American
judicial politics from a closer examination of these tribunals. Our coverage of the structure, jurisdiction, and history of these courts in Chapter 4 might be reviewed as a useful backdrop for the more focused discussion here of the decisional aspects of their
operations.

As with state intermediate appellate courts, United States Courts of Appeals were
created as, and continue to serve the function of, a screening device, enabling the Supreme
Court to concentrate on pressing policy issues. As such, they have little control over their
own dockets (caseload). This does not mean that decisions of our federal intermediate appellate courts have no broad policy implications. As a few seemingly ordinary trial court

determinations are transformed into questions raising important policy issues at the appellate level, Courts of Appeals decisions not infrequently make law in important ways. Too, the significance of these tribunals is enhanced by virtue of their being courts of last resort in the overwhelming majority of federal cases.

Two separate studies focusing on the flow of litigation in a sample of three circuits have estimated that review of U.S. Courts of Appeals decisions is sought in some 20 percent of their dispositions.[1] However, with the Supreme Court accepting fewer and fewer cases, especially relative to the growing numbers of appellate court determinations, on average only about one-half of one percent of these decisions is even reviewed by the Supreme Court, let alone reversed! "The result," noted one study, "is in 99.5 percent of all appeals court cases the circuit decision is left undisturbed by the Supreme Court."[2]

What has developed, in fact if not in law, is a division of labor between these intermediate federal tribunals and the Supreme Court. Increasingly, while the Supreme Court focuses on broad policy concerns with an emphasis on issues of constitutional law, the so-called circuit courts, in the words of a leading scholar of their work, ". . . concentrate on statutory construction, administrative review, and error correction in masses of routine adjudication."[3] And with a majority of Supreme Court justices now bent on a policy of decentralization of judicial (and other political) power, the decisions of these regional federal tribunals are taking on ever increasing importance.[4]

Appellate Caseload: Origin and Substance

As reported in Chapter 4, the workload of the judges of the United States Courts of Appeals is expanding at a rapid rate. From 11,662 cases in the year ending June 30, 1970, their load nearly doubled in the next ten years, rising to 23,200 filings by 1980. In the year ending June 30, 1985, 33,360 cases were filed in the twelve regional United States Courts of Appeals, nearly a 44 percent increase over the 1980 figure. In spite of an increase in authorized judgeships in 1978 (from 97 to 132), these sharp increases in caseloads resulted in a per panel load of 527 in 1980, up from 361 in 1970. Likewise, though the number of federal appellate judges was increased to 156 in 1984, caseload data in the year ending June

---

[1]The best general study of the United States Courts of Appeals is J. Woodford Howard, Jr., *Courts of Appeals in the Federal Judicial System: A Study of the Second, Fifth, and District of Columbia Circuits* (Princeton: Princeton University Press, 1981). Useful follow-up research on the caseflow in these courts is reported in Sue Davis and Donald R. Songer, "The Changing Role of the United States Courts of Appeals: The Flow of Litigation Revisited," *Justice System Journal* 13, No. 3 (1988–1989): 323–40. Both of these studies (Howard at 57 and Davis/Songer at 335) cite the appeal rate in the range of 20 percent.

Using data drawn from the 1967–1970 period, Howard found that some 1.9 percent of all appeals court decisions were actually reviewed by the Supreme Court, but only about two-thirds of these rulings were reversed. Howard, 57–59. But, report Davis and Songer, "the proportion of circuit decisions reviewed by the Supreme Court has dropped dramatically from the already low rates reported in Howard's earlier study," p. 335.

[2]Davis and Songer, 335.

[3]Howard, *Courts of Appeals,* 76. A revealing study comparing the English Court of Appeal with the U.S. Courts of Appeals is Burton Atkins, "Interventions and Power in Judicial Hierarchies: Appellate Courts in England and the United States," *Law and Society Review* 24, No. 1 (1990): 71–103.

[4]A reorientation of the American federal system, moving it back to an alignment more fitting of precivil war America, is suggested in the recent Supreme Court rulings of *U.S. v. Lopez,* 63 LW 4343 (1995) and *Seminole Tribe v. Florida,* 64 LW 4167, March 26, 1996. An earlier work pointing up this conservative realignment of American political power with particular reference to the jurisprudence of Chief Justice William Rehnquist is Sue Davis's *Justice Rehnquist and the Constitution* (Princeton: Princeton University Press, 1989), especially Part Four.

Table 11–1 U.S. Courts of Appeals, Appeals Filed, Terminated, and Pending, Fiscal Years 1990 –1994

| Year | Authorized Judgeships | Filed | | Terminated | Pending |
		Number	Cases per Panel		
1990	156	40,858	786	38,790	32,299
1991	167	43,027	768	41,640	33,428
1992	167	47,013	840	44,373	35,799
1993	167	50,224	902	47,790	38,156
1994	167	48,322	868	49,184	37,294
1995	167	50,072	899	49,805	37,536

Source: U.S. Administrative Office of the U.S. Courts, *Judicial Business of the United States Courts, 1994, 1995* (Washington: Administrative Office of the U.S. Courts, n.d.), Table 1.

30, 1985, indicate a further increase in the per panel load to 642, nearly four times the 1960 figure of 172.[5]

By 1990, with the same number of authorized judgeships and an increase in filings to 40,858 annually, the per panel load increased to 786, the latter figure moving up to an historic high of 902 in the year ending September 30, 1993. But by 1994, these courts enjoyed a slight lightening of their work, the first decline since 1978. These data for fiscal years 1990 through 1995 are presented in Table 11–1.[6]

The great majority of cases heard at this level originate in appeals from the federal district courts. Such appeals accounted for almost 88.5 percent of the United States appellate court caseload in the year ending September 30, 1995. Using these 1995 data, the ratio of appeals taken from United States district courts to the number of cases terminated at the federal trial level was 1:5; in other words, roughly 20 percent of federal court terminations find their way into the filing figures reported for the United States Courts of Appeals. However, caseload data from the late 1960s indicate that about 32 percent of *contested* federal district court judgments were appealed.[7]

The second major source of cases on the dockets of the United States Courts of Appeals is the administrative appeal. Federal appellate courts receive appeals from a wide variety of federal administrative agencies, currently (1995) accounting for about 6.5 percent of the appellate workload. In 1995, appeals from rulings of the Immigration and Nationalization Ser-

---

[5]As explained in previous chapters (see especially Chapter 2, note 6), data on federal court caseloads are taken from U.S. Administrative Office of the U.S. Courts, *Judicial Business of the United States* (Washington: Administrative Office of the U.S. Courts, n.d.). These particular data come from these reports as indicated by the year.

Recall that structural changes in the United States Courts of Appeals in 1984, discussed in Chapter 4, along with changes in fiscal year reporting patterns, make 1980–1985 comparisons difficult.

Factors tending to explain the increase in caseload for these courts are widely discussed in the literature. A brief but useful discussion is Thomas J. Meskill, "Caseload Growth: Struggling to Keep Pace," *Brooklyn Law Review* 57, No. 2 (1991): 299–305. Meskill focuses on the work of the Second Circuit, but many of his remarks are applicable to all circuits.

[6]*Judicial Business, 1995* (Abbrev.), 19–20. These figures exclude the small number of filings handled by the U.S. Court of Appeals for the Federal Circuit.

[7]See Howard, *Courts of Appeals,* 34. As suggested in our earlier discussion of state appellate rates, estimating the appeal rate presents several methodological problems. For federal appeals, these problems are discussed by Howard in *Courts of Appeals,* Ch. 2 and 3 and App. 1 (300–303) and 3.

vice weighed in as the largest single category of administrative law cases to be handled by the U.S. Courts of Appeals, but cases coming from the National Labor Relations Board, the Federal Energy Regulatory Commission, and the U.S. Tax Court were also numerous. As shown in the annual statistics of these courts, subject matter varies widely from circuit to circuit. Thus, because most federal regulatory agencies are headquartered in Washington, D.C., approximately half of the appeals heard by the U.S. Court of Appeals for the D.C. Circuit touch on administrative law. Similarly, with banking and financial entities centered in New York City, the Court of Appeals for the Second Circuit addresses large numbers of banking issues. Not surprisingly, the rate of appeal from administrative agencies also varies widely, but overall it is quite low, reportedly in the range of 1–3 percent.[8]

The remaining 5 percent of appeals heard by these tribunals consists primarily of bankruptcy cases (about 3.5 percent). The final 1.5 percent are original proceedings such as writs of mandamus and prohibition.

Following the pattern of nationwide shifts in the types of issues adjudicated, dockets of our United States Courts of Appeals reveal marked changes over time. A study of matters appealed to the Second, Fifth, and Ninth circuits from 1895 to 1975 indicates a strong upward trend in criminal appeals, from an average (for the three circuits) of 4 percent of the caseload in the 1895–1910 period to more than 29 percent in the 1960–1975 era. Conversely, real property issues declined from an average among the circuits of about 15 percent around the turn of the century to no more than 1 percent in the 1960–1975 period.[9] The proportion of business issues, such as contract and business organization cases, also declined over the period of study, though less drastically than did real property cases. Public law issues as represented in patent, trademark, and tax cases also declined. In their place were increases in issues having to do with governmental regulation of the economy (for instance labor and business regulation), which together grew from almost zero in the early era to around 20 percent of the cases decided by these courts by 1975. Overall, the substantive workload of United States Courts of Appeals reflects the familiar pattern noted earlier in state supreme courts—namely, a drop in private economic disputes and a sharp rise in issues involving governmental activity. As the role of government in our lives has increased over the last eighty years, there has been a concomitant rise in government-related litigation.

Comparing terminations (cases processed) by United States Courts of Appeals in fiscal years 1984 with those in 1994, one finds that overall, appellate judges in the 12 circuits processed well over twice as many matters (49, 184 versus 22,829) in 1994. As to subject matter, administrative appeals dropped from an average of 11 to 7 percent of total terminations, whereas all civil actions, though still dominant in the overall caseloads, dropped slightly, moving from 68.7 to 65.2 percent of terminations. Criminal appeals, although projected in earlier studies to grow rapidly, moved from 17.6 percent of all cases processed in 1984 to only 23.8 percent in 1994.[10] Of course these figures mask very wide variations in subject matter among the circuits. For example, criminal appeal terminations accounted for only 14 percent of cases handled in the D.C. Circuit in 1994, but 32 percent in the Eleventh Circuit.

Although a right of appeal in federal cases formally exists, informal barriers severely limit the "real" opportunity of appeal. Among these, psychological and material costs

[8]See Martin Shapiro, *The Supreme Court and Administrative Agencies* (New York: Free Press, 1968), 95, 262.

[9]These data are taken from Lawrence Baum, Sheldon Goldman, and Austin Sarat, "The Evolution of Litigation in the Federal Courts of Appeals, 1875–1975," *Law and Society Review* 16, No. 2 (1981–1982), 291–309. Data on criminal and real property caseloads may be found on 295 and 297, respectively.

[10]Data for 1994 are found in *Judicial Business of the United States Courts, 1994*, Table B–1. Some 1984 date are taken from Davis and Songer, "The Changing Role of the United States Courts of Appeals": 326–28.

loom large.[11] Court fees per se are relatively small, but attorney fees, as well as the costs of transcribing the trial court record, may run into many thousands of dollars. Also, the certainty of outcome is delayed: many litigants must wait perhaps a year or more for the appellate decision. Even the losing party in the trial court may prefer to forgo the anguish of an uncertain appeal in favor of the lower psychological cost involved in accepting the ruling of the trial court. These considerations help to explain the relatively low incidence of appeal, even when the right exists.

Researchers who have studied the appellate process have discovered a number of reasons for appeal aside from the intrinsic merit of the case. Richardson and Vines have suggested five types of appeal:

1. *Ritualistic appeals* An adverse decision in a civil rights suit or a products liability class action, for two examples, may be appealed in order to:
   a. Shift responsibility for an adverse outcome to the appellate tribunal and ensure the client that all possible steps were taken, and
   b. permit potentially "friendly" judges the opportunity to state a position that may, in the future, garner a court majority.[12]
2. *Frivolous appeals* While often associated with prisoner suits, truly frivolous appeals are not so common as sometimes supposed, as they can result in court-imposed sanctions against the appealing party and against that party's attorney.
3. *Bureaucratic appeals* As we saw, about 10 percent of federal appellate court caseloads in recent years originate in federal administrative agencies, such as the Interstate Commerce Commission, the tax court, and so on. While reversal of an agency or commission ruling is relatively rare, it is important symbolically—or if one prefers, in the name of due process of law—to maintain the institution of judicial review of administrative determinations. Further, in the small percentage of appeals that are brought, there lurk policy issues of potential importance for all of society. Thus, bureaucratic appeals are far more significant than their numbers might suggest.[13]
4. *Consensual appeals* This type of appeal, called by Richardson and Vines the "bread and butter" issues of appellate dockets, represents the constant "beating at the door"—the set of policy issues that certain interests are constantly seeking to change. Income tax issues and governmental regulations of certain business activities are examples. These are called "consensual" appeals because a substantial consensus exists among the judges as to the policy that does and should apply. Yet, these are policies about which individuals and groups entertain a seemingly unfounded hope of changing.
5. *Nonconsensual appeals* These are the major issues in politics. They represent policies about which there is considerable disagreement in society and for which a real potential for change exists—that is, a potential for new directions in judicial policy. Issues having to do with separation of church and state, reapportionment, civil rights of the accused, abortion, and so forth—these are issues that bring about landmark policy-making judicial decisions.[14]

Screening and Other Shortcuts at the Federal Appellate Level

With an ever-rising number of cases on appeal, it is not surprising that judges of the United States Courts of Appeals, like (and indeed preceding) their state appellate court colleagues have devised several mechanisms for dealing with an otherwise unmanageable workload.

---

[11]See Herbert Jacob, *Justice in America: Courts, Lawyers and the Judicial Process,* 4th ed. (Boston: Little, Brown, 1984), 232.

[12]See Richard J. Richardson and Kenneth N. Vines, *The Politics of Federal Courts* (Boston: Little, Brown, 1970), 118.

[13]For an excellent discussion of the impact of judicial review on administrative rulings, see Shapiro, *The Supreme Court and Administrative Agencies,* especially 95–103.

[14]For a fuller explanation of these categories, see Richardson and Vines, *Politics of Federal Courts,* 118–19.

It is convenient to discuss these various case-management techniques in pyramidal fashion—that is, by describing the funneling process at work in the federal appellate caseflow from raw material (total number of matters presented on appeal) down to the full-dress written opinion. Using case data reported for the fiscal year ending September 30, 1995, for the twelve regional courts of appeals, we begin with the total number of new filings, 50,072. This figure consists of 49,184 cases originally commenced that year plus 888 cases reinstituted from older filings for which procedural defaults had been corrected. The first reduction in the pyramid comes in the category of cases terminated, that is, disposed of. Usually, this is less than the number filed. In 1995, these courts terminated 49,805 cases.[15]

Matters of a similar nature are often consolidated into a single appeal, thereby reducing the judges' workload. Consolidations totaled 3,177 cases in 1995, lowering the number of cases terminated by some 6 percent, to 46,628.

By far the most significant initial reduction in the number of matters processed in a given year by these tribunals occurs in the practice of procedural terminations. Totaling 18,856 in 1995, these cases were disposed of in abbreviated fashion on technical grounds or because of supposed lack of merit. This category represented 38 percent of all cases terminated in 1995, though 40 percent of cases terminated *after consolidation*. These dispositions usually run at about this proportion—somewhat over a third of filings.[16] Of these, 12,039, or a little over two-thirds of procedural terminations, were processed by staff attorneys attached to these courts; the remainder are reported as terminations by the judges, usually in very brief, perfunctory actions.

Many of these cases were settled informally; others were dropped by the appellant or were dismissed for want of jurisdiction. Once again, this points up the importance of out-of-court bargaining processes in understanding the work of our judicial system. As noted earlier, appeals are often filed less to obtain a ruling than for the purpose of delaying judgment or inducing settlement. In fact, some circuits (and often state appellate courts) now encourage prehearing conferences, to expedite out-of-court resolution of appeals.[17]

The remaining 27,772 cases processed by lower federal appellate courts in 1995 were terminated on the merits, the vast majority of these being heard by three-judge panels. However, of the total number of decisions on the merits, oral argument was heard in only 11,080 cases, or 40 percent of cases terminated on the merits (down from 57 percent in fiscal 1985), the remainder being decided in more abbreviated fashion, often after preliminary screening and recommendations by the Courts' attorneys.

Following the hearing, the three-judge panels may issue a brief per curiam (for the court) opinion, a brief memorandum, or even an oral order, further reducing the workload by reducing the number of full written opinions issued. Oral argument is typically followed by a conference during which the judges vote and one of them is assigned to write an opinion. In all, the percentage of full written, signed, and published opinions has significantly dropped over the years, in 1995 accounting for only 6,118, or 22 percent of cases

---

[15]*Judicial Business of the U.S. Courts, 1995,* Table B–1.

[16]The figure was 37 percent of the initial caseload in fiscal 1985, though 43 percent of cases terminated after consolidation. For fiscal 1993, the respective figures were again 37 percent of all filings, 42 percent of terminations after consolidation.

[17]Howard, *Courts of Appeals in the Federal Judicial System,* 38. A more detailed statistical picture of these procedural terminations is found in *Judicial Business, 1995* (Abbrev.), Table B–5A.

The reader should be aware that aggregate data for all circuits tend to mask wide differences in screening practices among the circuits. Diverse approaches to screening and shortcut methods of case disposition among the circuits are discussed in John B. Oakley and Robert S. Thompson, "Screening, Delegation, and the Values of Appeal: An Appraisal of the Ninth Circuit's Screening Docket During the Browning Years," in Arthur D. Hellman, ed., *Restructuring Justice: The Innovations of the Ninth Circuit and the Future of Federal Courts* (Ithaca, N.Y.: Cornell University Press, 1990), 97–137. Differences among the circuits are covered at 106–109.

Table 11–2   Case Disposition in Twelve Regional United States Courts of Appeals, Fiscal Year 1995

Disposition	Number
Written, signed, published opinions	6,118
Published opinions	6,689
Oral hearings	11,080
Terminated on merits	27,772
Terminated after consolidation	46,628
Terminated	49,805
Cases commenced (filings)	50,072

Source: United States, Administrative Office of the U.S. Courts, *Judicial Business of the United States, 1995* (Abbrev.) (Washington: Administrative Office of the U.S. Courts, n.d.), Tables S–3, B–1.

disposed of on the merits (and only 12 percent of total terminations). Oral opinions, along with written but unsigned, and written and unsigned without comment, are the three other types of decisions handed down by these courts.[18] It is through these shortcuts that these courts are able to handle the large mandatory caseloads each year. The winnowing process just described is presented in pyramidal, abbreviated form in Table 11–2.[19]

A final device for reducing workloads in the United States Courts of Appeals is to recruit assistance from their own senior (semiretired) judges, from district judges in the circuit, or from judges from outside the circuit. Research on this practice in the 1960s and 1970s revealed that about half of the three-judge panels used in that period included at least one "outside" judge. In some circuits as many as 70 percent of the panels had at least one "designated" judge in service.[20] In fiscal 1995, the Administrative Office of the U.S. Courts reported a total of 84,335 "participations" (three-judge panels) in all twelve geographic circuits. Of these, some 78 percent were those in which regular, resident, active circuit judges only sat on these panels; about 14 percent were panels that included resident senior judges; and in about 7.2 percent, visiting judges from outside the circuit participated.[21]

Circuit Court Decision Making

Decision making by three-judge panels has a number of political (that is, policy-influencing) ramifications. First, it enhances the potential power of the circuit's presiding judge, who can, through the selection of panel members, influence the outcome of cases. The selection of the chief judge is automatic: he or she is the judge with the longest contin-

---

[18]Categories of dispositions (decisions) on the merits issued by the U.S. Courts of Appeals are set out in *Judicial Business, 1995* (Abbrev.), Table S–3. A more detailed examination of unpublished opinions is by Lauren K. Robel, "The Myth of the Disposable Opinion: Unpublished Opinions and Government Litigants in the United States Courts of Appeals," *Michigan Law Review* 87, Nos. 4–6 (April 1989): 940–62. See also the earlier piece by Daniel N. Hoffman, "Nonpublication of Federal Appellate Court Opinions," *Justice System Journal* 6, No. 3 (Fall 1981): 405–34.

[19]Shortcuts used in the Second Circuit are covered in Meskill, "Caseload Growth": 301–05. Approaches employed in the mammoth Ninth Circuit are explained in various essays contained in Heller, *Restructuring Justice.* For some time, Congress has considered restructuring the Ninth Circuit.

[20]See Stephen L. Wasby, "Extra Judges in 'The Court Nobody Knows': Some Aspects of Decision-Making in the United States Courts of Appeals," paper delivered at the American Political Science Association Meeting, Washington, D.C., Aug. 31–Sept. 3, 1979.

[21]*Judicial Business, 1995* (Abbrev.), Table S–2.

uous service on the circuit and who is under 70 years of age. This requirement is the replication of the seniority system that operates within congressional committees. The chief judge's power to select members of the three-judge panels, plus the authority to call other senior judges into service, gives the senior judge at least potential influence over the outcome of decisions in the circuit. In many circuits, the panel rotation system and panel selection are random, decreasing or eliminating the role of the chief judge.[22] But the "stacking" of panels to achieve desired results is not unknown. For example, Judge Ben Cameron of the Fifth Circuit claimed that Chief Judge Elbert Tuttle weighed the panels of that circuit in favor of Black civil liberties claims in the 1960s. And Chief Judge John Minor Wisdom of the same circuit was often said to have used the same ploy.[23]

Second, three-judge-panel decision making means that the work of a given court is sometimes less predictable than in a court with a constant panel of judges, such as the Supreme Court. Thus, for example, while there may be a preponderance of conservative judges in a given circuit, there is no guarantee that an appellant will not draw a panel dominated by liberal judges. This process in turn suggests a good deal of intracircuit conflict. The "majority" in the circuit may shift in each three-judge panel, thereby producing inconsistent decisions. In 1993, for example, odd or unexpected results emerged in two of the D.C. Circuit's decisions, one striking down the Pentagon's ban on gays in the military, the other voiding governmental regulations of indecency in broadcasting. By chance, both of these prominent issues were addressed by a panel selected at random but consisting of Abner Mikva, Patricia Wald, and Harry Edwards, all liberal Carter appointees, even though a majority of the judges (8 of 11) were Republican appointees.[24]

Finally, the operation of three-judge panels, as discussed in the previous chapter, has a notable impact on dissent rates, which average roughly 5 to 8 percent, according to various studies, though the rate varies widely with type of case, type of decision, and circuit.[25] Such figures are much lower than the United States Supreme Court and many high profile state supreme courts, partially because dissent is a lonely business among three judges and is thereby somewhat discouraged. But also, dissent only increases the workload of the appellate judge who may already be inundated with court work.[26]

On very rare occasions, en banc (full circuit) decision making is undertaken, as mentioned earlier. In the year ending September 30, 1995, of the 27,772 cases terminated on

---

[22]For a more detailed discussion of panel assignments, see Howard, *Courts of Appeals in the Federal Judicial System,* 232–47.

[23]Howard, *Courts of Appeals in the Federal Judicial System,* 239–40; Richard and Vines, *The Politics of Federal Courts,* 140; Howard Ball, *The Federal Judicial System,* 2nd ed. (Englewood Cliffs, N.J.: 1987), 251.

[24]See Richard B. Schmitt, "Appeals Court Rulings Reflect Makeup," *Wall Street Journal* (Dec. 6, 1993): B–5. See also Richardson and Vines, *The Politics of Federal Courts,* 121–24.

[25]For detailed research on dissent on U.S. Courts of Appeals, see Sheldon Goldman, "Conflict on the U.S. Courts of Appeals, 1965–1971: A Quantitative Analysis," *University of Cincinnati Law Review* 42, No. 4 (1973): 635–58; Donald R. Songer, "Factors Affecting Variation in Rates of Dissent in the U.S. Courts of Appeals," in Sheldon Goldman and Charles M. Lamb, *Judicial Conflict and Consensus: Behavioral Studies of American Appellate Courts* (Lexington, Ky.: University of Kentucky Press, 1986); 117–38; and in the same volume Justin J. Green, "Parameters of Dissensus on Shifting Small Groups," 139–53, along with prior research cited in these sources.

Factors most significantly associated with higher dissent rates seem to be the difficulty/complexity of the legal issue involved, the political (ideological) diversity present on the panels, the extent to which the court is urban in coloration, whether the panel is reversing the court below, and whether the panel is overturning a precedent. See Songer, "Factors Affecting Variation in Rates of Dissent": 135.

[26]See Richardson and Vines, *The Politics of Federal Courts,* 122–24; and Howard, *Courts of Appeals in the Federal Judicial System,* 193. There is little doubt that these low dissent rates understate the real level of conflict on these courts. Summarizing research on that point is Green, "Parameters of Dissensus on Shifting Small Groups."

the merits, only 77, or .27 percent were en banc dispositions.[27] To conserve court resources, en banc proceedings are discouraged. With issues of unusual importance and/or when there is serious disagreement among panels, the full complement of a circuit's judges is called into service to address the matter collectively. There is a real question whether these full-circuit gatherings resolve or worsen conflict, for bringing disagreeing judges face to face may increase rather than reduce tensions. On occasion, when there is a need for intracourt agreement, as, for example, in disciplinary cases (see Chapter 4) or when the court wishes to present a united front to the Supreme Court, the en banc device can be useful.[28]

In the 1980s there was evidence that conservative Reagan appointees on these courts had taken to using en banc proceedings to reverse liberal three-judge panel decisions not to their liking. Judge Frank Easterbrook, a conservative in the mold of Robert Bork and a 1985 Reagan appointee to the Seventh Circuit in Chicago, defended this practice as a "stabilizing process that makes sure the majority's voice is heard." Other judges called these en banc groupings "truth squads" or "thought police."[29]

A classic issue in the theory of appellate court decision making, one touched upon in Chapter 2, is the extent to which these bodies should, do, and can effectively engage in policy-making. A very large body of literature has grown out of this issue, which will be taken up again in the concluding chapter. For now, it is relevant to inquire about the attitudes of fedeal appellate judges on this matter. Unlike an apparent majority of state supreme court judges who are not willing to embrace openly a law-making or political role,[30] almost all judges of the United States Courts of Appeals questioned in Howard's mid-1970 study agreed that policy-making was inherent in their role—that it was all but unavoidable. A typical response cited by Howard was the following:

> If you mean by innovation radical departures from existing law, my feeling is to sit tight. But I mean that in a limited way. Practically every sitting judge has a case in which to some extent we're plowing new ground. That's why the term "activist" is so difficult; it covers such a wide spectrum of degrees. Any court doing its job has to be an activist court. We have to face up to change and the necessities of life. We have to cut and trim the law to meet them, and we do it every time we sit. If you're thinking of revolutionary changes like *Brown v. Board of Education,* that's different. I'd leave that to the Supreme Court. On our court, some judges feel that we should advise the Justices, . . . but they have had little success.[31]

The preceding was in response to the following question:

> Some people think circuit judges should be legal innovators, thus illuminating issues for the Supreme Court; others argue that circuit judges should merely apply the law, leaving legal innovations to legislatures and the Supreme Court. What do you think?[32]

[27]En Banc dispositions numbered 85, or .76 percent, of appeals terminated after oral hearing in 1994. See *Judicial Business, 1994* (Abbrev.), Table S–1.

[28]Howard, *Courts of Appeals in the Federal Judicial System,* 215–19. See also "En Banc Review in Federal Circuit Courts: A Reassessment," *Michigan Law Review* 72, No. 8 (Aug. 1974): 1637–55; and Daniel Egger, "Court of Appeals Review of Agency Action: The Problem of En Banc Ties," *Yale Law Journal* 100, No. 2 (Nov. 1990): 471–89.

[29]See Stephen Wermiel, "Full-Court Review of Panel Rulings Becomes a Tool Often Used by Reagan Judges Aiming to Mold Law," *Wall Street Journal* (Mar. 22, 1988): A–64. But see a somewhat different view in Christopher E. Smith, "Polarization and Change in the Federal Courts: *En Banc* decisions in the U.S. Courts of Appeals," *Judicature* 74, No. 3 (Oct.–Nov. 1990): 133–37, where it is argued that Reagan appointees per se are not more conservative than other Republican judges.

[30]See, e.g., Henry R. Glick, *Supreme Courts in State Politics* (New York: Basic Books, 1971), passim.

[31]Howard, *Courts of Appeals in the Federal Judicial System,* 160, n.a.

[32]Howard, *Courts of Appeals in the Federal Judicial System,* 160, n.a.

Aside from the consensus that, within limitations circuit judges are inevitably policy-makers, the responses of the judges to this question tend to place them in one of three broad categories, which have been labeled *innovators, interpreters,* and *realists. Innovators* were the few judges who saw their task as making law whenever the opportunity arose, thereby testing new ideas and approaches for final Supreme Court consideration. *Interpreters,* also a small group of judges at the opposite end of the continuum, held that modern trends toward judicial legislation (activism) were dangerous—judges should interpret the law and not much more. *Realists*—about two-thirds of the judges questioned— were in the middle; they were willing to give more leeway to judicial creativity than the *interpreters,* but somewhat less than the *innovators.* This middle group of judges could be labeled as pragmatists; they could see the necessity at times of judicial innovation, though they were equally aware of the pitfalls of excessive judicial activism.[33]

As to the outcome of this role conception in actual cases, the record of the United States Courts of Appeals over time abundantly demonstrates its significance in fashioning policy. As the Supreme Court continues to struggle with its burgeoning caseload, our circuit courts have not been shy in using their power to nudge the Supreme Court here and there, to help bring some consistency to the law applied by federal district courts, and often to insist on maintaining of the status quo in certain areas (this insistence can also be seen as policy-making). Although the incidence of reversal of federal district court and administrative agency holdings seems rather low (10.4 percent of cases terminated on the merits in 1994), such figures probably do not reveal the significant supervisory force of the United States Courts of Appeals, for rulings at the lower level can be selected for review and at least partial reversal.[34]

As with other appellate courts discussed herein, a great deal of research attention has been given over to determining the variables explaining substantive decision making on the U.S. Courts of Appeals. The results of this research do not vary significantly from findings relating to other courts. In a recent summary piece written by Segal, Songer, and Cameron, three familiar models of appellate decision making (the legal or traditional model, the attitudinal model, and a combination of the two, the hierarchial model) were empirically tested, using search and seizure decisions of the U.S. Courts of Appeals from 1961 to 1990.[35] Not surprisingly, these scholars report that while both the legal (stare decisis) and the attitudinal (ideological) explanations of decision making on these courts account for significant levels of decisional variance, the latter is the more powerful predictor, though combining the two (the hierarchial model) gives us the best overall explanation of decision making. Put differently, judges on these courts use both "the law" in the sense of relevant doctrine emanating from the Supreme Court *together with* their own political attitudes about correct judicial policy to guide their voting.[36]

Outside political-environmental-regional (contextual) factors play a role as well. Decision making on the U.S. Courts of Appeals has been studied with particular reference to whether there are regional variations in their decisions. One study in this vein, focusing on judicial decisions in environmental law in both federal district and appellate courts, clearly demonstrated the regional pull at both levels, though it was found to be especially strong in the trial courts. Even when holding constant such variables as type of litigating

---

[33]Howard, *Courts of Appeals in the Federal Judicial System,* 38–47.

[34]Howard, *Courts of Appeals in the Federal Judicial System:* 38–39; Richardson and Vines, *The Politics of Federal Courts,* 131. See also *Judicial Business of the United States Courts, 1994,* Table B–5.

[35]Jeffrey A. Segal, Donald R. Songer, and Charles M. Cameron, "Decision Making on the U.S. Courts of Appeals," in Lee Epstein, ed., *Contemplating Courts* (Washington: Congressional Quarterly Press, 1995), 227–45.

[36]Segal, Songer, and Cameron, "Decision Making," 242–43.

party, presidential appointments to these courts, and subject matter of case, regional influences were demonstrably at work in helping to explain decisional outcomes.[37] Such quantitative research underscores the content of interviews of these judges conducted by Prof. J. Woodford Howard in the 1970s. While many federal appellate judges eschewed notions of regionalism in describing their work, several embraced the idea of their courts as regional counterweights to national power. Noted Howard,

> . . . working in regional centers tempered the judges' conceptions of themselves as instruments of national power. . . . As intermediates, Courts of Appeals may synthesize "cultures"—local and national, legal and political—in deciding federal appeals.[38]

Stepping back a few paces, one finds that clusters of variables tending to explain decision making on U.S. Courts of Appeals are similar to those at work in other courts studied, especially at the appellate level. These are the attitudes/values of the individual judge; the extant legal rule; and environmental/sociopolitical variables, both from within and without, which impinge on the judges in their day-to-day work.

Overall, perhaps the most significant development in the work of U.S. Courts of Appeals in the late twentieth century is their move in the direction of their state counterparts—that is, becoming bureaucratic entities almost devoid of the personal judicial gatekeeping function one might imagine they perform. As Howard remarks in his detailed study of the Second, Fifth, and D. C. circuits,

> As law making takes precedence over the goals of uniformity and justice between the parties, so assembly lines are becoming the mode for error correction in large classes of litigation. All circuits in one way or another mass-produce decisions and ration judicial time. Is justice rationed in the bargain?
> . . . In the 5th circuit [before the split into two circuits], 95 percent of summary decisions were made "round-robin style," by mail or phone. One-fourth received no explanation at all. Little wonder lawyers complained that the tribunal was no longer "a real court. . . . It is a judicial bureaucratic institution." Judge-time was not only being rationed, but others were doing the rationing. What began as judicial gate keeping to rationalize caseloads was becoming a staff operation under the nominal supervision of judges already complaining about excessive administrative burdens. Judges, as Brandeis had warned, were becoming administrators running "human machines." Eroded in the process was a basic norm of personal accountability; judges should do their own work.[39]

Moreover, screening procedures in the United States Courts of Appeals have been shown to reflect the same apparent biases in favor of certain business or civil cases and against criminal appeals as that found in state appellate courts. Again using data from the Fifth Circuit in the mid-1970s, Howard reports that most private civil cases, as well as tax issues, were given oral hearings, whereas prisoner petitions without counsel and social security and direct criminal appeals were screened (often by staff counsel) and treated in a summary fashion. Rhetorically, Howard asks, "Who is to say what is junk litigation? Why were petitioners with counsel much more likely to be heard than those without?"[40]

Judges in many circuits are torn between quality and quantity. Nonjudge screening is being increasingly substituted for direct judicial decision making. Whether the loss of something we call "justice," especially in the area of criminal appeals, is only apparent or

---

[37]Lettie McSpadden Wenner and Lee E. Dutter, "Contextual Influences on Court Outcomes," *Western Political Quarterly* 41, No. 1 (March 1988): 115–34.

[38]Howard, *Courts of Appeals in the Federal Judicial System*, 147–48. This view was also suggested by Richardson and Vines, *The Politics of Federal Courts*, 173–74.

[39]Howard, *Courts of Appeals in the Federal Judicial System*, 277, 179.

[40]Howard, *Courts of Appeals in the Federal Judicial System*, 279–80.

substantial is not clear. But as with so many other areas of our judicial system, appellate processes cry out for more research attention.[41]

THE UNITED STATES SUPREME COURT

Alternately labeled "the most dazzling jewel in the judicial crown of the United States," and "nine black beetles in the Temple of Karnak,"[42] our national Supreme Court is at once the most studied, the most revered, as well as the most vilified of American judicial bodies. Its nine members, Justice Holmes once remarked, work in a quiet atmosphere, but "the quiet is the eye of a storm."[43] Functioning less as a court in the generic sense and more as a continuous constitutional convention or council of elders, our Supreme Court has become the arena for debate and at least tentative resolution of many of the great issues in American history and politics. We have but to turn to decisions such as *Gibbons v. Ogden,* 9 Wheat. 1 (1824), the great Steamboat Monopoly case; *McCulloch v. Maryland,* 4 Wheat. 316 (1819), on the extent and nature of congressional power (if not the nature of the constitution itself); *Dred Scott v. Sandford,* 19 How. 393 (1857), the decision that came close to destroying judicial power in America; or *Roe v. Wade,* 410 U.S. 113 (1973), on the constitutionality of abortion—these and countless other rulings attest to the Court's centrality as a vantage point from which to view the history and politics of the nation. And surely a review of such decisions confirms, better than any other aspect of our legal system, Tocqueville's statement that "Scarcely any political question arises in the United States which is not resolved, sooner or later, into a judicial question.[44]

Our commitment to a balanced coverage of American judicial politics precludes a detailed description of the warp and woof of Supreme Court decision making.[45] But we do want to explore the factors that influence the two broad areas of the Supreme Court's work—namely, its screening process, or put another way, deciding what to decide; and its decision making on the merits. Coverage of these topics will be preceded by a brief de-

[41]Not infrequently, sitting appellate judges respond to (or sometimes support) these charges of court bureaucratization. See, e.g., Gilbert S. Merritt (Chief Judge, Sixth Circuit), "The Decision Making Process in Federal Courts of Appeals," *Ohio State Law Journal* 51, No. 5 (1990): 1385–97; and in a somewhat different vein see Meskill (Chief Judge, Second Circuit), "Caseload Growth." And again, essays describing work on the Ninth Circuit may be found in Hellman, *Restructuring Justice.*

Another useful essay in this regard is Judge Alvin Rubin, "Bureaucratization of the Federal Courts: The Tension Between Justice and Efficiency," in Mark W. Cannon and David M. O'Brien, *Views from the Bench: The Judiciary and Constitutional Politics* (Chatham, N.J.: Chatham House Publishers, 1985), 64–70. Finally, see essays contained in Cynthia Harrison and Russell R. Wheeler, eds., *The Federal Appellate Judiciary in the Twenty-first Century* (Washington: Federal Judicial Center, 1989).

[42]Henry J. Abraham, *The Judicial Process,* 6th ed. (New York: Oxford University Press, 1993), 170; and Mary Ann Harrell and Burnett Anderson, *Equal Justice Under Law: The Supreme Court in American Life,* rev. ed. (Washington: Supreme Court Historical Society, 1988), 126.

[43]Harrell and Anderson, *Equal Justice Under Law,* 7.

[44]Alexis de Tocqueville, *Democracy in America,* ed. Richard D. Heffner, (New York: New American Library, 1956), 126.

[45]For more extended treatments of the subject from a political perspective see, in alphabetical order, Lawrence Baum, *The Supreme Court,* 5th ed. (Washington: Congressional Quarterly Press, 1995); Phillip Cooper and Howard Ball, *The United States Supreme Court: From the Inside Out* (Upper Saddle River, N.J.: Prentice-Hall, 1996); David M. O'Brien, *Storm Center: The Supreme Court in American Politics,* 4th ed. (New York: W. W. Norton, 1996); and Stephen L. Wasby, *The Supreme Court in the Federal Judicial System,* 4th ed. (Chicago: Nelson-Hall Publishers, 1993). Abraham's *The Judicial Process* also contains an extensive treatment of the Court and its procedures. The best brief history of the Court with an emphasis on its decisions remains Robert G. McCloskey, *The American Supreme Court,* 2nd ed., revised by Sanford Levinson (Chicago: University of Chicago Press, 1994).

scription of the setting or framework within which Supreme Court decision making occurs. The more general jurisdictional and structural features of the Supreme Court were discussed in Chapter 4.

The Setting

The United States Supreme Court sits in regular annual sessions of about 36 weeks each, from the first Monday in October until late June. On very rare occasions the justices will meet in special session, such as their meeting of July 6, 1972, to consider the controversy (more accurately, to consider whether to consider the controversy) over the seating of delegates to the Democratic National Convention.[46] Since 1935, the Court has convened in its "marble palace," a temple-like structure across the street from and west of the Capitol and just north of the main Library of Congress building in Washington, D.C.[47] The motto "Equal Justice Under Law" is carved high in the marble above the eight Corinthian columns on the façade of the building. Entering the huge bronze doors, one walks through the majestic Great Hall to the small courtroom itself, which is encircled by maroon velvet drapes and dominated by a high wooden bench. Here, in their black robes, the nine justices sit in their custom-fitted, high-back black chairs in order of seniority, the chief justice in the center, the senior associate justice at his right, the next senior associate on his left, and so on in alternate fashion.

A visit to the Supreme Court can be a memorable experience, for it is here that America's reverence for law finds its clearest expression. But it is here, too, that the chasm between legal myth and reality, which exposes the widespread ignorance of the workings of the Court, is also most in evidence. "Where does the victim sit?" asked one visitor. "There isn't any victim," answered a guard. "Oh," exclaimed the woman, "this is a murder case."[48] Other citizens call the Court's public information office to ask about obtaining a marriage license or to request an "audience" with a justice.[49] Writes one observer,

> A visit to the Supreme Court is a combination of the august and the asinine. The courtroom itself, with its 24 marble columns and 44-foot-high ceiling is an inspiring place that seems to make even high school students sit up straight. But then there are the "I've been to the Supreme Court" plastic tote bags on sale at the souvenir stand, and the "double jeopardy sandwich" in the cafeteria.[50]

The Court handles its work in sittings of approximately two consecutive weeks out of each month and "recesses" for about the same period. During the two weeks the Court sits,

---

[46]See the near-exhaustive description of the history, politics, and procedures of the Supreme Court in *Guide to the United States Supreme Court,* 2nd ed. (Washington: Congressional Quarterly, 1990). Special sessions of the Court are discussed on 736–37.

Two more recent volumes containing detailed information on the history, procedures, personalities and decisions of the Supreme Court are Kermit L. Hall, ed., *The Oxford Companion to the Supreme Court of the United States* (New York: Oxford University Press, 1992); and Lee Epstein et. al., *The Supreme Court Compendium: Data, Decisions and Developments,* 2nd ed. (Washington: Congressional Quarterly Press, 1996). The latter work presents its wealth of data mostly in tabular or quantitative form.

[47]Architecturally, the Court's building was patterned after the Temple of Diana in ancient Greece. This and other pithy details of the Court, its building, its justices, and its procedures are revealed in Abraham, *The Judicial Process:* 170–244. Even more detail on the Court can be found in *Guide to the United States Supreme Court,* 777–81. Finally, for the reader who has not visited the Court, a high-quality, colorfully illustrated essay on its history, the building, and the justices may be found in Harrell and Anderson, *Equal Justice Under Law.*

[48]Linda Greenhouse, "Supreme Court in Law: No Murders, No Marriages" *New York Times* (Sept. 16, 1980), 16.

[49]Greenhouse, "Supreme Court in Law": 16.

[50]Greenhouse, "Supreme Court in Law": 16.

it usually hears oral arguments the first three (sometimes four) days of the week. In addition to oral arguments, these sessions may include the announcement of formal decisions, oral notice of actions on petitions, and the like. During the two weeks of "recess," the justices devote most of their time to their individual work—the writing of opinions, responses to others' opinions, digesting memos on cases and petitions that are pending, and so on.[51]

Friday is conference day. Recently, conferences have also been scheduled on Wednesday afternoon during the weeks the Court is sitting, at which time votes are taken on cases argued the previous Monday.[52] The Friday conferences are day-long affairs covering cases argued Tuesday and Wednesday in addition to action on the flow of petitions for *certiorari* and appeals reaching the Court during the term. (The justices normally meet a week before the opening of the Court's regular October session to dispose of petitions for *certiorari* and appeals filed over the summer recess.) Conferences are held in the rather small but impressive room adjoining the chief justice's office. Conference proceedings are strictly confidential, though many justices have taken notes and left them for future research. The chief justice leads off the discussion of issues to be addressed in conference, affording him or her an opportunity to influence the outcome. The other justices then comment in descending order of seniority. The opinions that the justices express are tentative and may be changed at a later point.

In cases that receive full-dress treatment (the presentation of formal briefs, oral argument, and the submission of full opinions), the chief justice, following the conference vote, assigns the writing of the opinion, provided he or she is in the majority; if not, the senior associate justice in the majority either drafts the opinion or makes the assignment.[53] Drafts of the opinion are then circulated to other members of the Court each of whom may add comments and criticisms. In the course of circulating opinions, votes may change in a bargaining and negotiation process, which may result in a final opinion quite different from that suggested by the initial discussion and vote in conference.[54] Concurring and dissenting opinions are the work of the individual justices, although these too are circulated for comment and criticism since they are part and parcel of the bargaining process.

The final stage in the Supreme Court's decisional process is the actual announcement of decisions. For denials of *certiorari* or refusal to grant appeal, such "opinions" come quickly and briefly, scattered throughout the term. For full written opinions, there has been a tendency, as in legislative bodies, for the decisions to pile up, many being announced at or near the end of the term in June or even early July. Time was when full written opinions, even lengthy ones, were read verbatim. The ever-increasing time constraints under which the justices work, however, have led to the announcement of decisions via short statements which summarize the facts, issues, and essential holding of the case. The manner in which decisions are announced tends to vary with the justices. The Court has also shifted from Mondays as the only day on which decisions are announced to a more flexible schedule, spreading decision announcements throughout the week. This shift has

[51]See Baum, *The Supreme Court,* 20–21.
[52]*Guide to the United States Supreme Court,* 736–37, 742–43.
[53]Chief Justice Burger was alleged to have developed the practice of withholding his vote in conference to determine how the other justices would vote, after which he cast his vote with the majority in order to enhance his role in the assignment of opinions. See Bob Woodward and Scott Armstrong, *The Brethren* (New York: Simon & Schuster, 1979), 65 and passim. For a different view of the former chief justice's opinion assignments, see Harold J. Spaeth, "Distributive Justice: Majority Opinion Assignments in the Burger Court;" *Judicature* 67, No. 6 (Dec.–Jan. 1984): 299–304.
[54]See the extended bargaining that preceded the Court's decision in, for example, *Furman v. Georgia,* 408 U.S. 238 (1972), the leading death sentence case, discussed in Woodward and Armstrong, *The Brethren,* 205–20.

assisted the media in reporting Court decisions. Decision days, as with oral arguments, can become spectator affairs, accompanied by great emotion, particularly, of course, when the issues are of widespread interest.[55]

Access and Caseflow

The mechanics of Supreme Court decision making are not without significance, but our orientation emphasizes the flow of cases and the more direct factors that influence the flow. In this section, we focus on the screening of cases—or, how the justices decide what to decide.

To begin, it is useful to summarize the traditional gatekeeping tactics used by the Supreme Court (and to some extent other courts) in filtering cases to be heard. These rules of access are vague and not invariably applied, nor are they immune to bending and shaping in accordance with the policy proclivities of an individual justice at any given time. But they do constitute a set of early barriers that are very much a part of the screening process.

First, and most obviously, issues must meet jurisdictional requirements, as outlined in Chapter 4. For example, state cases raising no question of federal law will not be reviewed. A jurisdictional dispute of continuing interest has involved the power of federal courts to entertain suits against states in the face of the Eleventh Amendment which would appear to prohibit such actions. Suits against state and local *officials* (as opposed to the state itself) have often been allowed, usually when they allege improper official conduct.[56]

A major reinterpretation of the Eleventh Amendment came in early 1996 in the case of *Seminole Tribe v. Florida,* 64 LW 4167, in which the conservative wing of the present Court (Rehnquist, O'Connor, Kennedy, Scalia, and Thomas) held that congressional legislation under the commerce clause (which includes most federal regulatory law) is unenforceable against states in federal court under a rediscovered conception of state sovereignty. The dissenters (Justices Stevens, Souter, Ginsburg, and Breyer) termed the decision a "sharp break with the past," the significance of which "cannot be overstated." Under this ruling, environmental legislation, along with federal copyright, antitrust, and bankruptcy laws, for example, could be violated by the states with impunity, there being no judicial recourse available.[57] Clarification of the ruling will undoubtedly come in future decisions.

Bearing a closer relationship to the work of the Court itself are the various norms often discussed under the label "standing to sue."[58] That is, even though the jurisdictional hurdle may have been cleared, the Court may nonetheless refuse to accept a case because of other gatekeeping rules. One of these relates to "standing," defined by Pritchett as requiring: "(1) that the interest is peculiarly personal and not one shared with all other citizens generally; and (2) that the interest being defended is a legally protected interest, or right, which is immediately threatened by government action."[59] An example of the first requirement would

---

[55]On the release of opinions, see Wasby, *The Supreme Court,* 233–35; and O'Brien, *Storm Center,* 340–42.

[56]See *Osborn v. Bank of the U.S.,* 9 Wheat. 738 (1824). A more extended discussion of the historic meaning of the 11th Amendment is found in Jack W. Peltason, *Corwin and Peltason's Understanding the Constitution,* 12th ed. (San Diego: Harcourt Brace Jovanovich, 1991), 307–10. The law of access generally is discussed in C. Herman Pritchett, *Constitutional Law of the Federal System* (Englewood Cliffs, N.J.: Prentice-Hall, 1984), Ch. 7.

[57]See Linda Greenhouse, "Justices Curb Federal Power to Subject States to Lawsuits," *New York Times* (Mar. 28, 1996): A–1; and Nina Bernstein, "An Accountability Issue," *New York Times* (Apr. 1, 1996): A–1.

[58]See Alpheus T. Mason and Donald Grier Stephenson, Jr., *American Constitutional Law,* 10th ed. (Englewood Cliffs, N.J.: Prentice-Hall, 1993), 28–29.

[59]Pritchett, *Constitutional Law,* 159.

be taxpayers' suits against government funding of certain programs. The Court has generally held that a taxpayer's interest in an issue, per se, is insufficient for standing to sue; some more substantial direct injury must be alleged.[60] The second point is illustrated in the Court's holding in *Alabama Power Company v. Ickes,* 302 U.S. 464 (1938). Here, the Court denied standing to sue to the Alabama Power Company in its claim that the Public Works Administration of the New Deal Era was engaging in unfair competition in helping local power companies in Alabama to build an electric generating plant which would be in competition with the established private firm. The Court held that since there was no legal right to be free from competition, Alabama Power had no standing to sue.

Another rule is that the Court will not entertain a suit unless it involves a real case or controversy—in other words, a "live" dispute. For example, in *DeFunis v. Odegaard,* 416 U.S. 312 (1974), the Court held moot the claim of a University of Washington law student that he had been unconstitutionally denied admission to law school due to the university's preferred admission program for minorities. Since he had been admitted pending the outcome of the case and was about to graduate, the Court could see no live controversy to address.

Other rules restricting access include the ban on advisory opinions, the rule of finality, and the political question doctrine. When President Washington wished to have the Court's advice on the proper interpretation of certain treaties, the Court on August 18, 1793, politely declined to become involved, citing the impropriety of "extra-judicially deciding the questions alluded to."[61]

The doctrine of finality, which follows English judicial practice, declares that judges will not entertain cases that by law are the responsibility of other branches or divisions of government to decide. Thus, in the classic *Hayburn's* case in 1792 (2 Dall. 409), the Court refused to enforce aspects of the pension act for Revolutionary War veterans because the statute left the power of final determination of eligibility to the Secretary of War. In 1948, the Court reemphasized this doctrine in *Chicago and Southern Airlines v. Waterman Steamship Company* (333 U.S. 103) by rejecting the claim that following judicial review of Civil Aeronautics Board rulings, the president could in turn ignore the Court's determinations.

The Supreme Court's application of the political question doctrine illustrates the malleability of technical rules of access. Used by the Court at various times throughout its history—for example, the issue of what is a republican form of government, *Luther v. Borden,* 7 How. 1 (1849); or whether or not a state has ratified a proposed amendment to the Constitution, *Coleman v. Miller,* 307 U.S. 433 (1939)—the doctrine has been roughly defined as stating that courts will not address issues that are patently political or the resolution of which has been left to the political branches of government. But not many years after the Court was perceived to label the issue of legislative apportionment a political question (*Colegrove v. Green,* 328 U.S. 549 [1946]), it turned around and, in effect, reversed itself in *Baker v. Carr,* 369 U.S. 186 (1962), thereby launching the judiciary into a "political thicket" that resulted in a massive reapportionment of state legislatures in the 1960s. The Court's uneven application of the political question doctrine in these two cases, and the absence of a logical, self-contained category of political questions has led political scientists to conclude that the doctrine is tautological: "Political questions are those which judges choose not to decide, and a question becomes political by the judge's refusal to de-

---

[60]The leading case is *Frothingham v. Mellon,* 262 U.S. 477 (1923). But also see *Flast v. Cohen,* 292 U.S. 83 (1968).

[61]President Washington's request, via Secretary of State Thomas Jefferson, for an advisory opinion as well as the Court's reply are reprinted in Walter F. Murphy and C. Herman Pritchett, eds., *Courts, Judges and Politics: An Introduction to the Judicial Process* (New York: Random House, 1961), 248–49.

Table 11-3   Supreme Court Workload, 1935-1995

October Term	New Filings	Carried Over from Previous Term	Total Cases on Docket	Cases Disposed Of	Carried Over to Next Term
1935	983	109	1,092	990	102
1945	1,316	144	1,460	1,292	168
1955	1,644	205	1,849	1,630	219
1965	2,774	482	3,256	2,665	591
1975	3,939	822	4,761	3,904	857
1985	4,413	745	5,158	4,376	782
1995	6,597	968	7,565	6,649	916

Source: Federal Judicial Center, *Report of the Study Group on the Caseload of the Supreme Court* (The Freund Report) (Washington, D.C.: United States Courts Administrative Office, 1972), Table I and II, supplemented by *U.S. Law Week* data for the 1975, 1985, and 1995 terms.

cide it."[62] Though hardly a complete cataloging of access doctrines, this discussion should serve to illustrate the Supreme Court's self-denying rules.

Casual observation had led many to conclude that the Burger Court, bent on a more "restraint-oriented" jurisprudence, was more restrictive in its access decisions than was the Warren Court. But empirical research suggests otherwise. An article published in 1985 concluded that although the Burger Court exhibited a greater proclivity for examining and debating issues of standing and the like, it did not "exhibit a tendency to be more restrictive than the Warren Court in granting access to the Supreme Court."[63] However, we may not conclude from this finding that access doctrine issues are policy neutral. On the contrary, although the justices' votes on access are difficult to explain fully, we know that substantive policy preferences, along with attitudes concerning caseloads and jurisprudential concerns about the proper role of the Court, are prime factors.[64] As for the Rehnquist Court, problems of access have been handled less through the interpretation of the foregoing doctrines than through the simple method of denial of *certiorari*. This phenomenon was discussed at some length in Chapter 4.[65]

Although technical screening criteria have a large (though probably indeterminate) impact on reducing the number and kinds of cases brought to the Court, the pool of requests for review of lower court rulings has grown immensely in recent decades. As detailed in Chapter 4, during the October 1995 term (1995–1996), the Court received 6,597 such requests. With 968 carried over on the docket from previous terms, the total number of cases on the docket

---

[62]See Jack W. Peltason, *Federal Courts in the Political Process* (New York: Random House, 1955), 10. In addition, see Philippa Strum, *The Supreme Court and "Political Questions": A Study in Judicial Evasion* (University, University of Alabama Press, 1974). A useful review of the political question doctrine is Robert F. Nagel, "Political Law, Legalistic Politics: A Recent History of the Political Question Doctrine," *University of Chicago Law Review* 56, No. 2 (Spring 1989): 643–69. A particularly useful discussion of "threshold issues" is contained in O'Brien, *Storm Center*, 196–213.

[63]William A. Taggart and Matthew R. DeZee, "A Note on Substantive Access Doctrines in the U.S. Supreme Court: A Comparative Analysis of the Warren and Burger Courts," *Western Political Quarterly* 8, No. 1 (Mar. 1985): 89. Both O'Brien (*Storm Center,* 201) and Wasby (*The Supreme Court,* 167) maintain that the Burger Court loosened some rules of standing but tightened others.

[64]See Wasby, *The Supreme Court,* 167.

[65]However, see *Lujan v. Defenders of Wildlife,* 504 U.S. 555 (1992), in which the Court (Justice Scalia) denied standing in two important environmental cases, on grounds that no immediate injury was involved, an unusually narrow view of standing compared with previous norms.

for the term was 7,565.[66] Comparable figures from 1935 forward are listed in Table 11–3. The result is that in sixty years, the workload of the Supreme Court, at least as measured by total cases docketed, has increased about seven fold! The Court's staff has grown somewhat over this period, but the number of justices has remained the same, resulting in the crisis of volume discussed earlier (Chapter 4).

Of the relatively small number of cases given full dress treatment (92 cases addressed in only 75 conventional full written and published opinions in the fall term, 1995), approximately 70 to 80 percent are normally requests for review from lower federal (in large part appellate) courts, most of the remainder being from state supreme courts. In the fall 1994 Term, for example, 81 percent of the full written opinions were in disputes arising in lower federal courts, with only 16 percent coming from state courts. Only two cases were decisions on matters in the Court's original jurisdiction.[67] In the past, filings tended to be about evenly divided between paid cases and those filed in forma pauperis, although by the 1990s, cases in the latter category have shot up to at least twice the number of paid cases, reflecting increased filings from federal and state prisoners. Using data gathered by the editors of the *Harvard Law Review,* Table 11–4 provides a statistical overview of the Court's disposition of cases over the six terms, 1990–1995.

The substance of Supreme Court cases has changed along with docket size. Perhaps the most important change has been that the Court has become a constitutional court, whereas in the last century and the first few decades of the present century, private law issues dominated the dockets. Thus, civil rights and liberties cases, accounting for only about 10 percent of the docket in the decade of 1933–1942, represented over half of the filings in the 1978–1987 era. Criminal procedure issues have constituted a growing portion of such cases, moving from only about 5 percent of the Court's decisions in the 1933–1942 period to nearly 23 percent by 1978–1987. Even so, economic issues, especially those involving securities and environmental regulation, still represent a significant portion of the Court's work. Issues of federalism too, while declining in number over the long term, remain important, especially with the Rehnquist court.[68]

Thus, while the Court has developed a degree of specialization along the lines mentioned, this should not imply a narrow range of issues before the Court. On the contrary, the spectrum of controversies addressed in recent years is staggering, ranging from antitrust actions involving hundreds of millions of dollars to seemingly petty individual claims over the food served in prisons. These disputes have involved questions such as the following:

- Whether making animal sacrifices are protected by the freedom of religion provision of the First Amendment?
- Whether Congress may require states to adhere to certain guidelines in disposing of nuclear waste?
- Whether federal law permits employers to reduce or withdraw health insurance coverage for AIDS-related ailments?
- What is the extent and nature of state-enacted limits on the right of abortion?

---

[66]These data are taken from the annual statistical profile published in *LAW WEEK.* See 65 LW3100 of Aug. 6, 1996. These figures may vary slightly from those published annually in *Harvard Law Review* and presented in Table 4–10.

[67]See "The Supreme Court, 1994 Term: IV, The Statistics," *Harvard Law Review* 109, No. 1 (Nov. 1995): Table III.

[68]See Baum, *The Supreme Court,* 192–197, for a useful discussion of the substance of the Court's agenda over time. These quantitative data were drawn from Richard Pacelle, *The Transformation of the Supreme Court's Agenda from the New Deal to the Reagan Administration* (Boulder, Colo.: Westview Press, 1991), as presented in Baum, *The Supreme Court,* 196. See also Pacelle's "The Dynamics and Determinants of Agenda Change in the Rehnquist Court," in Epstein, *Contemplating Courts,* 251–74, in which the author explores the Rehnquist Court's move away from civil liberties cases and what this might portend for the Court as an institution.

Table 11–4 Final Disposition of Cases on the United States Supreme Court, 1990–1995

October Term:	1990	1991	1992	1993	1994	1995
Original Docket	3	1	1	1	2	5
Appellate Docket	1986	2069	2087	2058	2151	2099
On Merits	184	155	167	111	135	154
Review Granted	114	103	83	78	83	92
(Percent Granted)	(5.7)	(5.0)	(4.0)	(3.8)	(3.9)	(4.4)
Summarily Decided	81	52	84	34	52	62
Appeals and Petitions for Review Denied, Dismissed, or Withdrawn	1802	1914	1920	1947	2016	1945
Miscellaneous Docket	3,423	3,755	4,248	4,617	4,979	4,507
On Merits	54	39	39	51	24	68
Review Granted	27	17	14	21	10	13
(Percent Granted)	(0.8)	(0.5)	(0.3)	(0.5)	(0.5)	(0.3)
Summarily Decided	28	22	25	30	14	55
Appeals and Petitions for Review Denied, Dismissed, or Withdrawn	3,369	3,716	4,209	4,566	4,955	4,439
TOTAL	5,412	5,825	6,336	6,676	7,132	6,616
Remaining	904	945	909	1111	964	954

Method of Disposition

October Term:	1990	1991	1992	1993	1994	1995
By Written Opinion	129	127	119	96	95	92
Number of Opinions	120	114	114	87	86	79*
By Per Curiam or Memorandum Decision	112	68	107	67	65	114
By Denial, Dismissal, or Withdrawal of Appeals or Petitions for Review	5,171	5,630	6,110	6,513	6,971	6,384

Disposition of Cases Reviewed on Writ of Certiorari

October Term:	1990	1991	1992	1993	1994	1995
Percentage Reversed	62.7	62.0	52.8	42.6	61.6	56.0
Percentage Vacated	5.6	6.5	10.4	8.5	5.8	11.9
Percentage Affirmed	31.7	31.5	36.8	48.9	32.6	32.1

*Includes four lengthy *per curiam* decisions

Source: "The Supreme Court, 1994 Term, IV: The Statistics," *Harvard Law Review,* 109, No. 1 (Nov. 1995): Table I; and "The Supreme Court, 1995 Term," *Harvard Law Review,* 110, No. 1 (Nov. 1996): "The Statistics:" Tables I and II. (Footnotes omitted)

- Whether, under habeas corpus, a federal court has jurisdiction to hear a state prisoner's argument that he is not guilty?
- Whether a state's higher education system must produce positive results of actual racial integration, or whether a bonafide open-door policy will suffice?
- What rights does the U.S. government have to kidnap foreigners?
- May a city ban "hate crimes" in the form of cross-burning on a neighbor's lawn?
- What constitutes the "principal place of business" for the purpose of home office deductions for federal income tax?
- Whether having to suffer secondhand smoke from a fellow prisoner constitutes "cruel and unusual punishment" in violation of the 8th Amendment?
- May a state fine a federal agency for violation of state antipollution laws?
- May the federal government be sued over allegedly illegal procedures in administering the amnesty law?[69]

DECIDING WHAT TO DECIDE: THE *CERTIORARI* PROCESS

Since 1970, cases arriving at the Court have been placed on one of two dockets, the Appellate Docket and the Original Docket. Since the latter is reserved for the extremely small number of cases in the Court's original jurisdiction (for example, 0.14 percent of the total cases on the docket in the October 1995 term of the Court—11 out of 7,565 cases on the docket), all cases for all practical purposes are filed on the Appellate Docket, or simply "the docket." Upon arrival at the Court, the cases are examined by the clerk and are assigned a number that indicates, among other things, the time of arrival as well as whether the filing is in forma pauperis (unpaid cases, usually without the required number of copies of the petition).

From Chapter 4, recall that, leaving aside the seldom-used writ of certification, there are fundamentally two methods by which cases reach the Supreme Court: petitions for *certiorari* and appeals. But since the latter was all but eliminated by the 1988 legislation (appeals now number only about a dozen per term),[70] the overwhelming majority of cases on the Court's docket each term—approximately 99.7 percent—arrive there by *writ of certiorari*. The law clerks of the justices undertake the initial screening of both appeals and *certiorari* (*cert* for short) petitions. In recent years a "cert pool" has been formed consisting of the clerks of eight of the nine justices. Justice Stevens does not participate. He has said that his clerks select a small percentage of petitions for his review, but he does not "ever look at over eighty percent of the cases that are filed."[71] The very large body of initial requests for

---

[69]These examples were drawn from the *New York Times* coverage of the work of the Supreme Court over the period 1980–1993.

[70]Baum, *The Supreme Court,* 109.

[71]Remarks by Justice John Paul Stevens, Annual Banquet of the American Judicature Society, Fairmont Hotel, San Francisco, California, August 6, 1982, 5. The full paragraph from Justice Stevens's speech on the subject of the screening of *certiorari* petitions reads as follows:

Reviewing approximately 100 certiorari petitions each week and deciding which to grant and which to deny is important work. But it is less important work than studying and actually deciding the merits of cases that have already been accepted for review and writing opinions explaining those decisions. Because there simply is not enough time available to do the more important work with the care it requires and also to read all the certiorari petitions that are filed, I have found it necessary to delegate a great deal of responsibility in the review of certiorari petitions to my law clerks. They examine them all and select a small minority that they believe I should read myself. As a result, I do not even look at the papers in over 80 percent of the cases that are filed. I cannot describe the practice of any of my colleagues, but when I compare the quality of their collective efforts at managing the certiorari docket with the high quality of their work on argued cases, I readily conclude that they also must be treating the processing of certiorari petitions as a form of second-class work. My observation of that process during the past seven Terms has convinced me that the Court does a poor job of exercising its discretionary power over certiorari petitions. Because we are too busy to give the certiorari docket the attention it deserves, we grant many more cases than we should, thereby making our management problem even more unmanageable.

review are also screened by the clerks of the chief justice, who prepare a "Discuss List" for conference use which initially includes only those cases that the chief justice's clerks consider of prime importance. Although other justices may add to this list simply by request, they usually do not do so, the result being that about two-thirds or more of all requests for review coming to the Court are rejected out of hand, without discussion or vote![72]

This does not necessarily mean that this large body of petitions for review are not considered by one or more of the justices, but there seems to be increasing evidence that this important prescreening process is largely dominated by clerks. That the exercise of such discretion can have important policy consequences is illustrated by a memo written by a white, male clerk of Justice Burton in 1947. (The clerks of the justices have been predominantly white and male.) The case involved a Michigan law that banned female barkeeps. The clerk wrote,

> Next it is argued that the statute arbitrarily and unreasonably discriminates between male and female bartenders. The statute in its terms does prohibit all women from being barkeeps. It does this despite the fact that women may lawfully get a license to own and operate a place selling liquor at retail. I don't see anything unreasonable here.[73]

Even with seven or eight out of ten petitions for review being rejected at the prescreening stage, the Discuss List in a given Court term may still include 1,000 to 1,500 cases which are brought to the Friday conference for consideration.

From this initial screening, the justices can move in three possible directions: they may (1) deny review or *certiorari* completely; (2) grant the case a full hearing, inviting the submission of briefs and the scheduling of oral arguments, presumably leading to a full written opinion; or (3) decide the case in summary fashion, usually resulting in a brief per curiam opinion based on the papers at hand.[74] In recent years, some 75 to 80 percent of the cases on the Discuss List were rejected by the Court in conference, resulting in perhaps 150–200 cases selected for decisions on the merits. Of these, somewhat over half are given full-dress treatment by the Court (written opinions, tabulated in Table 11–4), the remainder being handled in summary fashion (designated "Per Curium or Memorandum Decision" in Table 11–4). We have already noted in Chapter IV the declining number and percentage of cases the Court selects for decision "On the Merits." Table 11–5 graphically illustrates this development over ten terms of the Court—1986 to 1995.

Tables 11–4 and 11–5 together depict the radical funneling process at work on the United States Supreme Court. On average, only 103 cases were decided by full written

[72]See Doris Marie Provine, *Case Selection on the United States Supreme Court* (Chicago: University of Chicago Press, 1980), 28–29. A Study of the history and composition of the "Discuss List" is Gregory A. Caldeira and John R. Wright, "The Discuss List: Agenda Building in the Supreme Court," *Law and Society Review* 24, No. 3 (1990): 807–33. The Discuss List is also described in a broader empirical study of the Court's case selection process: H. W. Perry, Jr., *Deciding to Decide: Agenda Setting in the United States Supreme Court* (Cambridge: Harvard University Press, 1991). Caldeira and Wright fix the proportion of cases disposed of in a given term that appear on the discuss list at about 20–30 percent.

[73]Provine, *Case Selection,* 24. Provine goes on to note: "Burton must have agreed with his clerk. He voted against taking the case up on the merits, but four of his colleagues disagreed and granted review. On the merits, a majority of the Court, with somewhat more hesitation than Burton's clerk found the Michigan statute unconstitutional." Perry, in *Deciding to Decide,* maintains that previous studies have tended to understate the role of clerks in the decisional process. See Ch. 3 and p. 121.

[74]Wasby, in *The Supreme Court in the Federal Judicial System,* has a good discussion of the various categories of disposition used by the justices, along with the case selection process generally, at 203–19.

As earlier mentioned as endemic to the appellate process, the selection of cases for review on the merits is not the same as determining the particular issue or issues in the case that the appellate tribunal will address. Issue transformation, as it is sometimes called, is usefully discussed by Kevin T. McGuire and Barbara Palmer in "Issue Fluidity on the Supreme Court," *American Political Science Review* 89, No. 3 (September 1995): 691–702.

Table 11–5   The Supreme Court Docket and Case Selection, 1986–1995

Rehnquist Court Terms	Total Cases on the Docket	Number of Cases Granted and Decided	Percentage
1986	5,123	175	3.4
1987	5,268	167	3.1
1988	5,657	164	2.8
1989	5,746	146	2.5
1990	6,316	125	1.9
1991	6,770	127	1.8
1992	7,245	116	1.6
1993	7,786	90	1.1
1994	8,100	94	1.1
1995	7,565	92	1.2

Source: David O'Brien, *Supreme Court Watch, 1995* (New York: W. W. Norton, 1996), 12; 65 LW 3100, Aug. 6, 1996.

opinion in the last five terms of the court, 1991–1995, representing some 2 percent of all cases disposed of over this period. In the Fall Term 1995, only 92 cases, or a mere 1.4 percent of cases acted upon, and only 1.2 percent of all cases on the docket that term, received the full treatment usually associated with the work of the Supreme Court! With the justices enveloping sometimes two or three cases into one written opinion, a mere 75 full conventional written opinions (plus four lengthy per curiam opinions) were issued for the 1995–1996 term, the lowest figure since the 1953–1954 term of the Warren Court. It is certainly open to question whether the Court can maintain its role as formulator of the nation's major legal doctrine via such a small percentage of issues addressed. Yet, one's view of this decline in the decisional output of the Supreme Court inevitably turns on one's conception of the proper role(s) of the judicial establishment in our polity.

Debate has ensued for some time over the significance of denial of *certiorari*. Some justices have long maintained that no conclusions are to be inferred as to the state of the law, only that for a variety of reasons four votes were not found to grant the writ. To some observers, however, the debate seems largely academic, since for all practical purposes the lower court ruling in such actions is left to stand as a statement of the law.[75]

An issue more central to our concerns relates to the factors influencing the granting or denying of review, especially votes on *certiorari* petitions. Since the Court seldom provides clear reasons for its screening actions, the whole process is shrouded in a good deal of mystery. Rule 10, revised in 1990, is intended to guide the Court in these matters, but its imprecise language leads to widely varying interpretations. The rule reads,

1. A review on writ of certiorari is not a matter of right, but of judicial discretion, and will be granted only when there are special and important reasons therefor. The following, while neither controlling nor fully measuring the Court's discretion, indicate the character of reasons that will be considered.

(a) When a United States court of appeals has rendered a decision in conflict with the decision of another United States court of appeals on the same matter; or has de-

[75]Again, Wasby, *The Supreme Court in the Federal Judicial System,* at 215–18, has a useful discussion of the significance of denial of *certiorari.*

cided a federal question in a way in conflict with a state court of last resort; or has so far departed from the accepted and usual course of judicial proceedings, or so far sanctioned such a departure by a lower court, as to call for an exercise of this Court's power of supervision.

(b) When a state court of last resort has decided a federal question in a way in conflict with the decision of another state court of last resort or of a United States court of appeals.

(c) When a state court or a United States court of appeals has decided an important question of federal law which has not been, but should be, settled by this Court, or has decided a federal question in a way that conflicts with applicable decisions of this Court.

A number of scholars—and often the justices themselves—have attempted to shed light on the *certiorari* process, but no completely satisfactory explanation has been forthcoming. In arguing against the creation of a new National Court of Appeals, Chief Justice Warren noted that

> The standards by which the Justices decide to grant or deny review are highly personalized and necessarily discretionary. Those standards cannot be captured in any rule or guideline that would be meaningful to an outside group of judges. As Mr. Justice Harlan used to say, "Frequently the question whether a case is certworthy is more a matter of 'feel' than of precisely ascertainable rules." In short, the *certiorari* "feel" of the nine Justices cannot be transmitted to others by any formal or informal judicial osmosis.[76]

Chief Justice Vinson was probably correct (and a little more helpful) when he observed that

> The function of the Supreme Court is . . . to resolve conflicts of opinion on federal questions that have arisen among lower courts, to pass upon questions of wide import under the Constitution, laws, and treaties of the United States, and to exercise supervisory power over lower federal courts. . . . The . . . Court must continue to decide only those cases which present questions whose resolution will have immediate importance far beyond the particular facts and parties involved.[77]

Political scientists have developed a "cue theory" to attempt to explain the *certiorari* behavior of the justices. Tanenhaus and his associates found that the nature of the parties in the case as well as the subject matter are cues that relate to the granting of *certiorari*. For example, there seems to be a positive correlation between the federal government as the party seeking review (seemingly the most powerful predictor), or a civil liberties claim, and the probability that the justices will grant *certiorari*.[78] Also, dissension among lower court judges portends the granting of *certiorari*. Cue theory has been widely debated among scholars; some subsequent research has supported the Tanenhaus findings,[79] whereas other scholars have tended to minimize the importance of these cues.[80] Whatever

---

[76]"Retired Chief Justice Warren Attacks, Chief Justice Burger Defends Freund Study Groups' Composition and Proposal," *American Bar Association Journal* 59 (July 1973): 728.

[77]Chief Justice Vinson's remarks are contained in Walter F. Murphy and C. Herman Pritchett, eds., *Courts, Judges, and Politics: An Introduction to the Judicial Process* (New York: Random House, 1961), 55. This author is indebted to Stephen Wasby, *Supreme Court in the Federal Judicial System*, 160, for the references to the remarks of Chief Justice Warren and Justice Vinson.

[78]See Joseph Tanenhaus, Marvin Schick, Matthew Muraskin, and Daniel Rosen, "The Supreme Court's Certiorari Jurisdiction: Cue Theory," in Glendon Schubert, ed., *Judicial Decision-Making* (New York: Free Press of Glencoe, 1963), 111–32. A discussion of cue theory can be found in Provine, *Case Selection*, 77–83.

[79]See Virginia Armstrong and Charles A. Johnson, "Certiorari Decisions by the Warren and Burger Courts: Is Cue Theory Time Bound?" *Polity* 15, No. 1 (Fall 1982): 141–50.

[80]See Provine, *Case Selection*, 77–83.

such research reveals, it is certain that the Court's view of the broad significance of this issue, as colored by the policy preferences of the individual justices, will remain dominant factors in the Supreme Court's screening decisions.

For cases to be decided on their merits, the justices may opt for summary disposition. This alternative may be chosen for one or more of several reasons. In some instances, an issue has already been rather fully aired by the Court and little more than an exclamation mark needs to be added. In *Alexander v. Holmes County Board of Education,* 396 U.S. 19 (1969), for example, the justices in a brief, curt per curiam decision held that the old formula of "all deliberate speed" was at an end in the racial integration of public schools.[81] In other instances, the Court may attempt to cover a large number of cases with one quick ruling, as in the area of taxation where several lower courts have set forth contradictory rulings. Some members of the conservative side of the Burger court, for instance, took to using summary per curiam decisions to overturn liberal judicial doctrine (e.g., *Florida v. Meyers,* 460 U.S. 380) (1984). Such tactics have sometimes met with biting dissents by more liberal justices, resulting in per curiam decisions that read more like full-blown formal opinions. Since the Court has indicated that summary holdings are not to be taken as settled law in the same way that full written opinions are, the use of this strategy appears to be just that—strategic—indicating that, for one reason or another, a majority of the Court wished to deal with an issue without having to face it squarely with full oral argument and a formal, negotiated opinion.[82]

Formal Decision Making

In cases neither rejected outright nor handled summarily, the justices, in conference, agree to invite the submission of briefs and schedule oral argument. Most of these decisions to move to plenary consideration are made early in the term, many during the first week before the formal opening of the Court's October term. Actions on request for review from the previous spring also often result in the scheduling of oral argument the following fall and winter.

Forty copies of the briefs are required to be filed in a prescribed format well in advance of the time that oral argument is heard. The Court may also permit the filing of amicus curiae (friend of the court) briefs by interested parties—perhaps various state attorneys-general, the AFL–CIO, the American Civil Liberties Union, and the like. Over fifty such briefs were submitted in the case of *University of California v. Bakke,* 438 U.S. 265 (1978), involving the constitutionality of racial quotas for admission to medical school. The significance of such outside briefs in influencing the Court's decision making is not completely clear.[83] But the amicus curiae practice does give the justices the benefit of a very wide spectrum of views on critical politicolegal issues, helping to satisfy the goal (or as some would say, give the appearance) of pluralistic policy-making.

In a study of the role of interest groups in adjudication generally, Lee Epstein found that in its October 1987 term, 1,600 interest groups participated in the filing of some 460 amicus briefs before the Court. Such briefs were filed in the processing of 80 percent of

---

[81]In general, see C. Herman Pritchett, *Constitutional Civil Liberties* (Englewood Cliffs, N.J.: Prentice-Hall, 1984), 264–68.

[82]See Wasby, *Supreme Court in the Federal Judicial System,* 206–08.

[83]Research on the impact of amicus briefs in substantive decision making is briefly reviewed by Donald R. Songer and Reginald S. Sheehan in "Interest Group Success in the Courts: Amicus Participation in the Supreme Court," *Political Research Quarterly* 46, No. 2 (June 1993): 339–54. In matched pairs of Supreme Court decisions in odd numbered years from 1967 to 1987, Songer and Sheehan found no significant difference in the outcome of full dress opinions whether the case was or was not accompanied by amicus briefs. Nor did the number of such briefs increase the likelihood of success for litigants.

cases decided with full opinions that term. Not unexpectedly, government itself, represented by the Department of Justice or state attorneys-general accounted for the largest single category of "group" representation before the court. Among private interests, however, commercial groups such as chambers of commerce and large corporations such as Delta Airlines together accounted for more than all other categories of interests combined. Nevertheless, legal groups such as the national and state bar association, labor unions, and educational groups (e.g., the National Education Association) also filed significant numbers of briefs.[84]

Amicus curiae briefs may also be filed at the *certiorari* stage of litigation before the Supreme Court and have been shown to be a significant factor in explaining the *certiorari* decision. In a study of such interest-group participation before the Court in the fall 1982 term, Caldeira and Wright found that

> When a case involves real conflict or when the federal government is petitioner, the addition of just one amicus curiae brief in support of certiorari increases the likelihood of plenary review by 40–50%. Without question, then, interested parties can have a significant and positive impact on the Court's agenda by participating as amicus curiae prior to the Court's decision on certiorari or jurisdiction.[85]

In times past, oral argument before the Court was something of a spectator event, lasting several days. Now, a half hour is usually allotted to each side. Rather than a monologue by counsel, oral argument is much more a dialogue among attorneys and justices, with the former spending a large portion of their time answering questions of the justices. As with most issues, the question of whether oral argument is a determining factor in the ultimate outcome of cases before the Court is a matter on which the justices seem to disagree. Justice Brennan, for instance, has said that on many occasions his judgment turned on the give and take of oral argument.[86] But Chief Justice Warren took the view that oral argument is "not highly persuasive."[87] Basically, oral arguments provide the justices with information usually not found in the briefs. It affords the decision makers an opportunity to explore the implications of alternative courses of action with individuals who are extremely well informed on the issues at hand. Thinking out loud, sometimes with the use of rhetorical questions, is often an important element of the oral argument sessions of the Court.[88]

Following oral argument, the justices take up the case in conference, making an initial determination of the alignment of votes and assigning the drafting of an opinion, along

[84]See Lee Epstein, "Courts and Interest Groups," in John B. Gates and Charles A. Johnson, *The American Courts: A Critical Assessment* (Washington: Congressional Quarterly Press, 1991), 350–56.

[85]Gregory A. Caldeira and John R. Wright, "Organized Interests and Agenda Setting in the U.S. Supreme Court," *American Political Science Review* 82, No. 4 (Dec. 1988): 1122.

[86]Wasby, *Supreme Court in the Federal Judicial System,* 229; see also William J. Brennan, Jr., "How the Supreme Court Comes to Arrive at Decisions," *New York Times,* Western edition (Oct. 12, 1963): 7.

[87]See Abraham, *The Judicial Process,* 191.

[88]See Stephen L. Wasby, Anthony A. D'Amato, and Rosemary Metrailer, "The Functions of Oral Argument in the Supreme Court," *Quarterly Journal of Speech* 62, No. 4 (Dec. 1976): 410–22. See also Justice John M. Harlan, Jr., "The Role of Oral Argument," in Canon and O'Brien, eds., *Views from the Bench:* 87–90.

In May 1996, Chief Justice William Rehnquist undertook to instruct attorneys on how to argue a case before the Court. See Linda Greenhouse, "Chief Justice Offers Advice to Lawyers: Be Prepared," *New York Times* (May 18, 1996): A–7.

A clear example of the dialogue (perhaps "multi-log" is a better word) that takes place in oral argument may be seen in the colloquy of the justices and attorneys in *Schenck v. Pro-Choice Network,* No. 95–1065, argued Oct. 16, 1996. See Linda Greenhouse, "Court Hears Challenge to Anti-Abortion Curb," *New York Times* (Oct. 17, 1996): A–8.

with the other decisional steps previously discussed. Our chief concern here is with the factors that help to explain the votes of the justices.

Since at least the 1950s, a significant portion of political science-public law research effort has been expended in attempts to explain the decisional behavior of appellate judges, especially rulings of the Supreme Court. Socioeconomic background variables, conceptions of the judicial role, values and attitudes on public policy matters—these and related variables have been intensely studied, using a wide variety of sometimes sophisticated (often quantitative) research methods.[89] Weak correlations have sometimes been reported that, on closer examination, do not seem to explain very much.[90] Studies of attitudes and values, sometimes through bloc analyses of voting patterns and the like, have been seen by some scholars as documenting the obvious. Yet, empirical data systemically gathered that demonstrate bloc voting on the Court, or that point up the importance of the justices' values in their decision making, can add significantly to our knowledge of the subject, so that research from the behavioral wing of the discipline has taken its place alongside more traditional work in contemporary explanations of judicial decision making.

Explaining judicial policy-making is frustrated by the same fundamental problem involved in attempts to explain any other public decision behavior—namely, the complexity of the process. No one is so wise as to be able to specify all the factors at work in policy choices. The range of possible influences is almost infinite, from the personal idiosyncrasies of the decision maker to broad philosophical, historical, or political influences that are extremely difficult to isolate and measure. One of the shortcomings of some past empirical research has been that it has focused on too narrow or specific a set of variables (such as political party affiliation or other background factors) to explain such a highly complex, subtle process as human decision making. The difficulty with some socioeconomic background research has been described as follows:

> It is inaccurate to assert that someone behaves in a certain way because that person is black, female, Catholic, Democrat, old, Harvard educated, in solo law practice, and so forth. Rather, what is essentially being argued is that the fact that one has certain attributes means that one will have certain socializing experiences that have stimulated the development of certain attitudes and values or even conceptions of the judicial role. But in reality each of

---

Oral arguments before the Court are not published, per se, but some oral recordings have been converted to print and published by political scientist Peter H. Irons. See his *May It Please the Court: The Most Significant Oral Arguments Made Before the Supreme Court Since 1955* (New York: The New Press, (W.W. Norton), 1993). Several of the justices were displeased when this book appeared. The controversy concerning this issue, along with the details of oral argument before the Court, are discussed in O'Brien, *Storm Center,* 150–51 and passim.

[89]Good examples of this so-called "behavioral research" (see Ch. 1) are Glendon A. Schubert, *Judicial Decision-Making;* and by the same author, *The Judicial Mind Revisited* (New York: Oxford University Press, 1974).

The contemporary "buzz word" for this genre of research is the "attitudinal model." See David W. Rohde and Harold J. Spaeth, *Supreme Court Decision-Making* (San Francisco: W. H. Freeman, 1966); Harold J. Spaeth, *Supreme Court Policy-Making: Explanation and Prediction* (San Francisco: W. H. Freeman, 1979); and the more recent work by Segal and Spaeth, *The Supreme Court and the Attitudinal Model* (Cambridge: Cambridge University Press, 1993). The latter work became the subject of an interesting debate. See "Symposium: The Supreme Court and the Attitudinal Model," *Law and Courts,* Newsletter of the Law and Courts Section of the American Political Science Association 4, No. 1 (Spring 1994): 3–12. The debate is carried over into the Spring 1996 issue of *Law and Courts,* at 3–14, especially the Spaeth contribution: "Different Strokes for Different Folks: A Reply to Professor Shapiro:" 11–12.

Other examples of behavioral (attitudinal) research are included in Goldman and Lamb, *Judicial Conflict and Consensus.*

[90]A brief but useful critique of background studies may be found in Sheldon Goldman and Austin Sarat, eds., *American Court Systems: Readings in Judicial Process and Behavior* (San Francisco: W. H. Freeman, 1978), 372–74.

the background or attribute variables tested using aggregates of judges is too crude to be associated with the same or similar experiences; hence each of the variables is not easily linked to just one set of attitudes and values.[91]

Yet, if we move back to broader or more general explanations, we may be able to say something useful about decision making on collegial courts. Three areas within which decision making on the Supreme Court can be profitably discussed are (1) traditional legal variables, (2) the policy preferences of the justices, and (3) the political, both strategic and tactical, environment within which judicial decision making takes place.

Before conceptualizing judicial decision making as mere unencumbered policy-making by political actors, it is well to remember that courts are legal (as well as political) bodies, and judges are not completely free to select their own preferred interpretations of a statute or constitutional provision. The existing law on the subject—the understanding of relevant legal authorities, precedent, and the like—significantly constrains the choices that judges (or, for that matter, any other human decision makers) can make. This is not to say that stare decisis dictates a given policy choice in every case, but it narrows the range of alternatives. In one of the most celebrated essays in sociological jurisprudence, Associate Justice Benjamin Cardozo remarked that

> In a system so highly developed as our own, precedents have so covered the ground that they fix the point of departure from which the labor of the judge begins. Almost invariably, his first step is to examine and compare them. If they are plain and to the point, there may be need of nothing more. *Stare decisis* is at least the everyday working rule of our law.[92]

If factors other than precedent did not enter into the decision making of courts of last resort, the process would be little more than the mechanical one described by Justice Roberts in *U.S. v. Butler* (Chapter 1). But clearly, other considerations press for ascendancy in appellate adjudication, among which the policy preferences of the justices, as molded and shaped by a lifetime of experience, emerge as highly important. If precedents clearly dictated the path to be followed, it is not likely that the case would be before the Supreme Court in the first place. Where precedents clash, where the law cries out for clarification or, if you will, growth, one finds the bulk of issues presented to the Supreme Court. Predictability, the sureness and security of the law, is a comfortable mindset learned in law school, but the reality of judicial decision making as a creative, expansive process is often not realized, even by the practicing attorney, until he or she is faced with the agonizing choices almost daily presented to justices of the Supreme Court. In making these choices, they inevitably rely on what Oliver Wendell Holmes called "the prevalent moral and political theories, intuitions of public policy, avowed or unconscious, even the prejudices which judges share with their fellow men."[93] Or as all presidents know but few have acknowledged so baldly as did Theodore Roosevelt in his annual message to Congress in 1908, quite simply, "The decisions of the courts on economic and social questions depend upon their economic and social philosophy."[94]

In his autobiography *The Court Years,* Justice Douglas tells the story of an interchange between Chief Justice Hughes and Justice Reed in conference. Having a difficult time decid-

---

[91]Goldman and Sarat, *American Court Systems,* 374. The proposition that judicial decisions are predictable, the notion at the heart of attitudinal studies as well as the behavioral movement in political science generally (see Ch. 1) is challenged in a useful essay by Lawrence Baum. See "On the Unpredictability of the Supreme Court," *P. S.: Political Science and Politics,* XXV, No. 4 (Dec. 1992): 683–88.

[92]See Margaret E. Hall, ed., *Selected Writings of Benjamin Nathan Cardozo* (New York: Fallon, 1947), 112.

[93]Oliver W. Holmes, *The Common Law* (Boston: Little, Brown, 1881), 1.

[94]This passage from Theodore Roosevelt may be found in Murphy and Pritchett, *Courts, Judges, and Politics,* 19.

ing which way to go on a close vote, Justice Reed finally told the chief justice, "I am inclined to reverse [the lower court]," whereupon Hughes replied, with a twinkle in his eye, "Brother Reed, I will enter you in the docket as voting to reverse. For my experience is that if a justice inclines a certain way, he has the facilities and resourcefulness to marshal the reasons to back his inclination."[95] Thus, it is not too wide of the mark to view the written opinions of the Court as "the reconstituted logic by which the justices justify themselves."[96]

Indeed, writing of his own conversion from Positivism to Realism, Justice Douglas said,

> I had thought of the law in terms of Moses—principles chiseled in granite. I knew judges had predilections. I knew that their moods as well as their minds were ingredients of their decisions. But I had never been willing to admit to myself that the "gut" reaction of a judge at the level of constitutional adjudications, dealing with the vagaries of due process, freedom of speech, and the like, was the main ingredient of his decision. The admission of it destroyed in my mind some of the reverence for the immutable principles. But they were supplied by Constitutions written by people in conventions, not by judges. Judges are, after all, not creative figures; they represent ideological schools of thought that are highly competitive. No judge at the level I speak of was neutral.[97]

Another way of demonstrating the dominance of personal-political values in the decisional equation is through some of the behavioral research discussed previously. To use but one example, Harold Spaeth has demonstrated that the positions which justices took on both the Warren and Burger Courts with respect to but three identifiable values—freedom, equality, and New Deal economics—together account for some 85 percent of the Court's decisions. Using the technique of cumulative scaling and drawing data from the votes of eighteen justices, Spaeth found that Justice Douglas ranked the highest in scale score on all three values, followed in order by Justices Warren, Fortas, Goldberg, Brennan, and Marshall.[98] These justices he labeled *liberal.* Moving to the bottom of the scale, we find, in ascending order, Justices Rehnquist, Harlan, Burger, Whittaker, Powell, and Blackmun, all of whom cast votes indicating a relatively low commitment (all in the minus column in terms of scale score) to these three values.[99] They were labeled *conservative.* The justices in the middle rankings were labeled *moderate,* or in the case of Justice Clark, a *New Dealer.* Hence, whether measured by what they do (vote) or what they say, the value or policy preferences of the justices clearly emerge as strong if not overriding factors in explaining the choices they make on the Court. As Spaeth remarks,

> These eighteen individuals respond neither to alien nor to inscrutable influences. Their decisions are not dictated by whim, nor by the side of the bed they got up on. The Justices are not motivated by veniality or personal aggrandizement. They respond rather to values that are an integral part of our heritage, that touch Americans generally, and that have a fundamental impact upon the character of American life. If we must entrust our fate to others, we could do a lot worse.[100]

---

[95]William O. Douglas, *The Court Years: 1939–1975* (New York: Random House, 1980), 8.

[96]This is from William Haltom in a remark at the American Political Science Association meeting in 1982, quoted in Stephen L. Wasby, *The Supreme Court in the Federal Judicial System,* 2nd ed. (New York: Holt, Rinehart and Winston, 1984), 207.

[97]Douglas, *The Court Years,* 8. Research demonstrating this proposition in the case of Chief Justice William Rehnquist's almost unswerving commitment to conservative policy outcomes is found in Sue Davis, *Justice Rehnquist and the Constitution;* and by the same author "Rehnquist and State Courts: Federalism Revisited," *Western Political Quarterly* 45, No. 3 (Sept. 1992): 773–82.

[98]Spaeth, *Supreme Court Policy-Making,* 135.

[99]Scaling procedures are discussed in Spaeth, *Supreme Court Policy-Making,* 118–27.

[100]Spaeth, *Supreme Court Policy-Making,* 137.

Another value often studied in conjunction with Supreme Court decision making is conception of judicial role, the view held by a justice on the proper policy role (or roles) of the Court in our system of government. The scale usually associated with this value runs from *judicial activism* on the one side to *judicial restraint* on the other, although role values can extend to other decisional behavior, such as one's views on the propriety of dissent, overturning congressional statutes, and the like. The difficulty with role analysis is that, on closer examination, it appears to mask raw policy preferences. Certainly this view is supported by the history of the debate since the 1930s over the Court's proper role. Thus, in the 1930s, political liberals in control of the executive and legislative branches were highly critical of an activist Supreme Court, arguing that the judiciary should defer to the "political" branches of the government. Yet in the 1960s and 1970s, these same liberals were applauding an activist Court that was pressing to complete the New Deal program in areas such as civil and political rights (racial desegregation, legislative reapportionment, a sharper separation of church and state, and so forth), while the conservatives were, ironically, calling for judicial self-restraint. We now seem to have come full circle, with conservatives once again dominating the judiciary, or tending in that direction, while liberals raise questions about the policy activism of an increasingly conservative Court. In observing this classic debate on activism versus self-restraint, it is difficult to avoid the conclusion that it depends on whose ox is gored, with raw policy preferences rather than conceptions of the judicial role being the real issue. Thus, both liberals and conservatives are perfectly willing to support an activist judiciary when their respective policy preferences are being embodied into judge-made law.[101]

Neither precedent, nor the values of the justices, nor the two combined have ever been shown to explain all Supreme Court decision making. It is well to recall that the Court is a human institution existing in time and place and, hence, subject to a host of other influences, both external and internal, which also shape the choices the justices make. As for internal pressure, both political science scholarship and political journalism have demonstrated that the bargaining within the Court can sometimes explain the votes cast.[102] Thus, there are instances in which voting can be seen neither as a reflection of political values nor in response to the pull of precedent, but rather as a tactic to accomplish other ends within the group, or as a by-product of group interaction. Collegiality, the need for the respect of one's colleagues, loyalty (or opposition) to certain blocs on the Court, the intellectual power of a colleague's argument, the attractiveness (or unattractiveness) of personality—these and similar factors growing out of group life on the Court can sometimes play a crucial role in determining outcomes. For example, Earl Warren's leadership is often cited as an explanation of the unanimous decision in *Brown v. Board of Education;* Chief Justice John Marshall's pervasive influence on the Court of his day is a similar example. Irascible personalities such as those attributed to Justices McReynolds and Frankfurter undoubtedly served to reduce their influence on the Court and on the voting of their brethren. The widespread bargaining and negotiation attendant to the circulation of draft

---

[101]In general, see Stephen C. Halpern and Charles M. Lamb, eds., *Supreme Court Activism and Restraint* (Lexington, Mass.: Heath, 1983), especially the essay by Harold J. Spaeth and Stuart H. Teger, "Activism and Restraint: A Cloak for the Justices' Policy Preferences," 277–301.

It requires no more than casual observation to see the contrast on the current Court between the promise of "judicial restraint" with which Reagan and Bush justices were selected and their aggressive activism in translating their policy preferences into law. Using the 1994–1995 term as an example, see Linda Greenhouse, "Farewell to the Old Order of the Court: The Right Goes Activist and the Center Is a Void," *New York Times* (July 2, 1995): Sec. 4–1.

[102]The best scholarly treatment of this process is Walter F. Murphy's *Elements of Judicial Strategy* (Chicago: University of Chicago Press, 1964). On the same point, an interesting work of questionable scholarship is Woodward and Armstrong's *The Brethren,* passim.

opinions suggest the "fluidity of judicial choice" and, hence, the importance of internal pressures in fully understanding the justices' voting behavior.[103]

It is almost impossible to enumerate the many external environmental factors that at times can influence Supreme Court decision making. The McCarthyism of the 1950s, the Vietnam war protests and accompanying social pressures of the 1960s and early 1970s, or the law-and-order wave of sentiment of the latter half of the 1970s—such forces undoubtedly affect at least some decisional outcomes. Congressional pressures, executive policies, and professional legal criticism are other factors that can influence the justices. That the judiciary does not exist in a vacuum, that it is open to a considerable extent to what Dooley called "the 'eliction returns" is a core notion of political jurisprudence. Most of these factors are discussed in the next chapter as ways of checking or limiting judicial power, but they also may be included here as ways of understanding judicial decisional outcomes.

In sum, it is probably a mistake to focus on any single set of forces as dominant in the decision making of courts of last resort in common law systems. While policy preferences do indeed loom large in the equation, factors in the larger political environment can and do press in to significantly modify or constrain such raw value choices. Indeed, seemingly trivial considerations of personality or perhaps matters of strategy attendant to group life on the Court can also be important factors. The norms and traditions of the legal profession have also been cited at times, as important in explaining judicial choices. As Murphy and Pritchett conclude, any understanding of the way in which the American judicial system actually operates

> must take fully into account the fact that judges . . . are influenced in their judging by personal predilections, by their commitments to ethical norms, and by their understanding of the realities of political life. But at the same time it must never be forgotten that the freedom of a judge is limited by the institutional ethos and by the traditions of his calling. A judicial decision is an amalgam of personal judgment and institutional control.[104]

Given the extremely small percentage of requests for review ultimately granted by the Supreme Court, we might guess that the incidence of reversals of lower court rulings might be rather high, for it does not seem to make much sense to use the Court's limited resources to sustain existing legal rules. Generally, this is so. Over the past three decades the reversal rate of cases granted *certiorari* and decided in full-dress opinions has been in the range of 60 to 70 percent. If one adds cases decided in summary fashion, the long-term reversal rate is often higher. Not atypically, as shown in Table 11–4, in its fall 1994 term the Court reversed lower court holdings in nearly 62 percent of the cases brought via *certiorari*. Hence, the justices clearly use their limited time to overturn lower court rulings and set new policy in wide-ranging areas of public life.

Although perhaps overstudied relative to other judicial bodies, the United States Supreme Court is nonetheless the standard-bearer of judicial policy-making within the federal and, to a considerable extent, state judicial systems. Its procedures, policy outputs, and even personalities tend to set the tone for the American judicial process as a whole. Its decisions have often been the windows through which one may view the clash of issues of the era, and its work reveals in a particularly clear fashion the interdisciplinary character of law in society. Having examined the major inputs into judicial policy-making—philosophical,

---

[103]See J. Woodford Howard, Jr., "On the Fluidity of Judicial Choice," *American Political Science Review* 62, No. 1 (Mar. 1968): 43–56.

[104]Murphy and Pritchett, *Courts, Judges and Politics,* 10. More recent research that draws essentially the same conclusion though based on quantitative analysis is Tracey E. George and Lee Epstein, "On the Nature of Supreme Court Decision Making," *American Political Science Review* 86, No. 2 (June 1992): 323–37.

historical, political, structural, and the like—we now turn to the impact of judicial decision making on the larger political and social system.

FURTHER READING

Baum, Lawrence. *The Supreme Court.* 5th Ed. Washington, D.C.: Congressional Quarterly, 1995.

Baum, Lawrence, Sheldon Goldman, and Austin Sarat. "The Evolution of Litigation in the Federal Courts of Appeals, 1875–1975." *Law and Society Review* 16, No. 2 (1981–1982): 291–309.

Congressional Quarterly, *Guide to the U.S. Supreme Court.* 2nd Ed. Washington, D.C.: Congressional Quarterly, 1990.

Davis, Sue. *Justice Rehnquist and the Constitution.* Princeton: Princeton University Press, 1989.

Epstein, Lee. "Courts and Interest Groups," in John B. Gates and Charles A. Johnson, *The American Courts: A Critical Assessment.* Washington, D.C.: Congressional Quarterly, 1991: 335–71.

Epstein, Lee, et al. *The Supreme Court Compendium: Data, Decisions and Developments.* 2nd ed. Washington, D.C.: Congressional Quarterly, 1996.

Goldman, Sheldon, and Charles M. Lamb, eds. *Judicial Conflict and Consensus: Behavioral Studies of American Appellate Courts.* Lexington, Ky.: University of Kentucky Press, 1986.

Hellman, Arthur D., ed. *Restructuring Justice: The Innovations of the Ninth Circuit and the Future of The Federal Courts.* Ithaca, N.Y.: Cornell University Press, 1990.

Howard, J. Woodford, Jr. *Courts of Appeals in the Federal Judicial System: A Study of the Second, Fifth, and District of Columbia Circuits.* Princeton: Princeton University Press, 1981.

Murphy, Walter F. *Elements of Judicial Strategy.* Chicago: University of Chicago Press, 1964.

O'Brien, David M. *Storm Center: The Supreme Court in American Politics.* 4th Ed. New York: W. W. Norton, 1996.

Perry, H. W., Jr., *Deciding What to Decide: Agenda Setting in the United States Supreme Court.* Cambridge, Mass.: Harvard University Press, 1991.

Provine, Doris Marie. *Case Selection in the United States Supreme Court.* Chicago: University of Chicago Press, 1980.

Segal, Jeffrey A., Donald R. Songer, and Charles M. Cameron, "Decision Making on the U.S. Courts of Appeals," in Lee Epstein, ed., *Contemplating Courts.* Washington: Congressional Quarterly, 1995: 227–50.

Segal, Jeffrey A., and Harold J. Spaeth. *The Supreme Court and the Attitudinal Model.* Cambridge: Cambridge University Press, 1993.

Spaeth, Harold J. *Supreme Court Policy-Making: Explanation and Prediction.* San Francisco: W. H. Freeman, 1979.

Wasby, Stephen L. *The Supreme Court in the Federal Judicial System.* 4th Ed. Chicago: Nelson-Hall, 1993.

PART IV
COURTS AND SOCIETY

12

Judicial Policies

Compliance, Implementation, and Impact

There are many contexts in which the latitude of those charged with carrying out a policy is so substantial that studies of policy implementation should be turned on their heads. In these cases, policy is effectively "made" by the people who implement it.

—Michael Lipsky,
"Standing the Study of Public Policy Implementation on Its Head"

A judicial decision is but one phase in the never-ending group conflict, a single facet of the political process.

—Jack W. Peltason
Federal Courts in the Political Process

IMPACT RESEARCH: THE STATE OF THE ART

To complete our survey of American judicial policy-making, we need to examine the final stage of the process—namely, policy implementation and impact. In Chapter 2, the importance of this last step was made clear. There, the policy process was seen as a seamless web with implementation every bit as important as the initial policy decision, it being difficult at times to distinguish between the two. "Policy is made as it is administered and administered as it is being made," notes Anderson.[1] And since policy, as we have defined it, has more to do with what actually happens (law in action) than with what seems to have been intended (law on the books), we really have not completed our study of the politics of courts until we begin to understand the impact of their decisions on the larger sociopolitical system.

Research on the impact of court decisions increased dramatically in the earliest years of the ascendancy of political jurisprudence. In *Federal Courts in the Political Process*, published in 1955, Jack Peltason entitled his last chapter, "After the Lawsuit Is Over."

---

[1]James E. Anderson, *Public Policy-Making* (New York: Praeger, 1975), 98.

There he noted that a "judicial decision is but one phase in the never-ending group conflict, a single facet of the political process,"[2] and he documented this observation with numerous random bits of data on the responses of Congress, lower courts, and interest groups to Supreme Court decisions. At that early juncture, there were few research data on which Peltason and other writers could rely for general descriptions of judicial impact. Research questions far outnumbered reliable answers.

The decades since have given rise to an impressive barrage of studies aimed at closing this gap in our knowledge. However, the current literature still falls far short of providing reliable, across-the-board findings as to the impact of judicial decision making on public policy.[3]

Several shortcomings have characterized impact research. First, as we might expect from the prevalence of the "upper-court myth," most work has focused on the impact of United States Supreme Court decisions. This is not, of course, an inappropriate subject of study, for that Court is the most prominent judicial policy-making body in the whole of American government. At the same time, because the Supreme Court is unique, we might at least expect that the implementation and the impact of its decisions would differ somewhat in both substance and degree from that of state trial court decisions.[4] With few exceptions, however, the impact of the latter not only has been given short shrift in the literature but also has been almost entirely ignored.[5]

Likewise, we know little about the impact of decisions rendered by federal trial courts, by federal courts of appeals, and by state intermediate appellate and supreme courts. Since trial court decisions can be appealed, there is perhaps more reason for impact research on the decisions of appellate courts. Nevertheless, the low rate of appeal we noted earlier suggests that impact studies of trial court decisions would be worthwhile.

Second, the substantive focus of most impact studies has been surprisingly narrow. Bradley Canon notes that the bulk of research has concentrated on but five policy areas: racial desegregation, criminal justice issues, prayer in public schools, First Amendment obscenity cases, and abortion. Perhaps this orientation exists because these are highly visible, controversial judicial policies which have tended to attract the attention of the nation. This rather journalistic orientation to impact research has meant that we have tended to ignore everyday impact patterns, which, in turn, has probably distorted our overall view of the politics of impact.

Related to this imbalance of substantive concerns have been conceptual problems in impact studies. For example, being enamored of compliance-noncompliance, particularly the latter, we have delighted in pointing up where court decisions are not obeyed and by whom. The early compliance studies were exciting, perhaps because many of us were in

---

[2]Jack W. Peltason, *Federal Courts in the Political Process* (Garden City, N.Y.: Doubleday, 1955), 64. One of the best early studies of resistance to and implementation of a Supreme Court decision was also by Peltason. See his *Fifty-Eight Lonely Men: Southern Federal Judges and School Desegregation* (New York: Harcourt, Brace and World, 1961).

[3]See Bradley C. Canon, "Studying the Impact of Judicial Decisions: A Period of Stagnation and Prospects for the Future," paper presented at the annual meeting of the American Political Science Association, Denver, Sept. 2–5, 1982.

[4]Canon, "Studying the Impact." This and the following points concerning the shortcomings of impact research were drawn from the Canon paper. This paper was a forerunner of more extended treatments of impact/compliance/implementation research in Charles A. Johnson and Bradley C. Canon, *Judicial Policies: Implementation and Impact* (Washington, D.C.: Congressional Quarterly, 1984) (second edition forthcoming, 1998); and Bradley C. Canon, "Courts and Policy: Compliance, Implementation, and Impact" in John B. Gates and Charles A. Johnson, *The American Courts: A Critical Assessment* (Washington, D.C.: Congressional Quarterly Press, 1991), 435–66. The Johnson and Canon book is the most comprehensive treatment of the subject.

[5]But see Kenneth M. Dolbeare, *Trial Courts and Urban Politics* (New York: Wiley, 1967).

early withdrawal from the static, mechanistic model of judicial decision making wherein "the case" was the near-exclusive focus of study. Such an orientation seemed to involve an unspoken assumption that judicial decisions, at least those of the Supreme Court, were final. Period. Empirical studies reporting that (mostly liberal) judicial edicts were meeting with (mostly conservative) resistance opened up new and fertile areas for research, and follow-up studies continued the compliance orientation.[6]

The problem with the concept of compliance is not only that it is difficult to operationalize (with often unclear judicial policies, how can one say what behavior constitutes noncompliance?), but also that compliance is only part of impact. Thus, it is possible to conceive of judicial policies meeting with a high level of compliance but having relatively little impact. The Supreme Court's decisions on legislative reapportionment in the 1960s have been said to have followed that pattern. The long-standing campaign to persuade the courts to render justiciable the issue of legislative apportionment was not for the ultimate purpose of reapportioning legislatures per se (although that was an interim goal), but rather to reorient rurally dominated legislatures to a policy posture more favorable to urban interests.

That the hoped-for policy shift never occurred (or at least did not occur to the extent expected) is said to have been due to intervening variables not anticipated by reapportionment reformers. For instance, urban needs, such as greater state expenditures on city schools, streets, and so forth, could not be met simply by significant increases in urban representation in state legislatures. The general level of state wealth is probably a better predictor of such expenditures. Also, state legislative delegations from urban areas failed to vote as a bloc for urban (often liberal) interests. In fact, the net effect of reapportionment, along with other changes characterizing the era, was sometimes to enhance conservative and rural political power. This effect was due in part to the conservative orientation of suburban state legislators.[7]

Later, researchers called for a move from compliance to implementation as a more useful orienting concept.[8] Implementation involves a richer focus, including various types of responses to judicial decisions. Moreover, such an orientation joins judicial impact studies with implementation research in the broader field of public policy studies, thereby helping to alleviate the intellectual semiisolation that had theretofore characterized judi-

---

[6]Three of the early studies (in addition to the Peltason work cited in n. 2) were Gordon Patrick, "The Impact of a Court Decision: Aftermath of the McCollum Case," *Journal of Public Law* 6 (Fall 1957): 455–63; Frank J. Sorauf, "*Zorach v. Clauson:* The Impact of a Supreme Court Decision," *American Political Science Review* 53, No. 3 (Sept. 1959): 777–91; and Walter F. Murphy, "Lower Court Checks on Supreme Court Power," *American Political Science Review* 53, No. 3 (Sept. 1959): 1017–31. Glendon A. Schubert summarized much of the early impact literature in his *Constitutional Politics* (New York: Holt, Rinehart & Winston, 1960): 256–65. A much broader survey and analysis of impact research through the 1960s was Stephen L. Wasby, *The Impact of the United States Supreme Court: Some Perspectives* (Homewood, Ill.: Dorsey Press, 1970). Coinciding with the Wasby book was a useful reader by Theodore L. Becker and Malcolm M. Feeley, eds., *The Impact of Supreme Court Decisions: Empirical Studies,* 2nd ed. (New York: Oxford University Press, 1973). Another edited work of the period that focused on compliance per se was Samuel Krislov et al., *Compliance and the Law: An Interdisciplinary Approach* (Beverly Hills, Calif.: Sage, 1977). To repeat, the most complete overview of this entire body of research is the Johnson and Canon volume, *Judicial Policies,* slated for its second edition in 1998.

[7]In addition to the five topics listed by Canon, the impact of judicial decisions in the area of legislative reapportionment became a popular subject of study. See David C. Saffell, "Reapportionment and Public Policy: State Legislators' Perspectives," in Bernard Grofman et al., ed., *Representation and Redistricting Issues* (Lexington, Mass.: Heath, 1982), 203–19. See also Michael A. Maggiotto et al., "The Impact of Reapportionment on Public Policy: The Case of Florida, 1960–1980," *American Politics Quarterly* 13, No. 1 (Jan. 1985): 101–21.

Another policy area in which compliance and impact are said to have been quite different relates to the required *Miranda* warnings. See, e.g., Johnson and Canon, *Judicial Policies,* 119–24, and the sources cited therein.

[8]See, e.g., Lawrence Baum, "Implementation of Judicial Decisions: An Organizational Perspective," *American Politics Quarterly* 4, No. 1 (Jan. 1976): 86–114.

cial impact research.[9] Just as a focus on compliance-noncompliance with the "original intent of the framers" would not be a very productive way of understanding the Supreme Court's interpretation of the Constitution, so the compliance framework is far too narrow to include the rich diversity of possible responses to judicial policies.

A fourth shortcoming of contemporary impact studies relates to the time frame of most research. Our emphasis on compliance has tended to encourage short-term impact research to the near exclusion of long-term or longitudinal studies. Implementation or impact is almost by definition a lengthy process and calls for research over a period of time. Virtually all studies of the impact of *Miranda v. Arizona*, 384 U.S. 436 (1966), for instance, were undertaken shortly after the decision was handed down; few if any scholars have studied the long-term and possibly unanticipated consequences of this judicial policy. Short-term measures of impact may very well prove to be inaccurate over time and this may, indeed, be the key problem with much of the research we have undertaken on the impact of the legislative reapportionment edicts.[10]

Finally, our impact studies have tended to focus on the responses of agencies charged with implementing judicial decisions (such as police departments, school boards, lower courts) or on the other branches of government (Congress, the White House), rather than on the ultimate consumers of decisions (such as suspects arrested, school children and their parents, pregnant women facing abortion decisions). Again, the former focus is not altogether inappropriate. Clearly, to study judicial policy implementation is to study the response of implementing agencies and the like. But some may argue that the best measure of impact is an assessment of change in attitudes and behavior of consuming populations, and not much of this type of research has been undertaken.[11]

This brief critique of impact studies should not lead us to conclude that the "after the lawsuit is over" research movement of the 1960s and 1970s has been fruitless. Rather, it is set forth to suggest the limits within which we can describe and assess judicial impact. If our studies reveal a pattern (or perhaps nonpattern) of more or less haphazardly chosen substantive topics oriented to the compliance or other types of responses of implementing agencies, largely in response to Supreme Court decisions, then such must be the rough parameters of our discussion. Within these limits, what can be said about the impact of judicial policies in America?

It is well to remember that the American policy process is characterized by a high degree of diffusion of power. The judiciary shares power with the legislative and executive branches of government, not to mention regulatory agencies, political interest groups, and so on. Furthermore, the diffusion is multiplied by our system of federalism, which leaves a degree of semiindependent power to the states and communities. For these reasons, we can expect that the first set of responses to judicial decisions would be from, or at least through, these competing power centers, making them logical foci for our discussion of judicial policy impact. We will therefore begin with the judiciary's coequal branches of government, the legislative and executive, moving then down and out, so to speak, to lower courts, then to nonjudicial governmental agencies. Finally, we will conclude with a summary of judicial impact on political interest groups, so-called consumer groups, the media, and the public.

Where appropriate, the coverage will proceed within an implementation framework, asking not merely whether judicial policy met with compliance or opposition (although that will be included) but, more generally, what spectrum of responses from these target popula-

---

[9]See, e.g., George C. Edwards III, *Implementing Public Policy* (Washington, D.C.: Congressional Quarterly, 1980).

[10]This general point is made in Canon, "Studying the Impact," 21–23.

[11]Canon, "Studying the Impact," 21.

tions and other relevant power centers have been reported. By compliance, we mean simply whether or not the judicial policy (decision) has been obeyed. Implementation may be defined as the array of responses (or nonresponses) to judicial policy by officials, citizens, or groups charged with carrying such policy into effect, or who possess power to determine such judicial policy effectuation. Impact is broader yet, including, as suggested, all effects of judicial policy as evidenced in the attitudes or behavior of all populations, targeted or not. Of course, our coverage will be limited by the available data.

To the extent that impact includes the broad legal, political, and social consequences of judicial policies in American society *writ large* (and most definitions are at least this inclusive), the concept involves the ultimate issues this text addresses and will be taken up in the concluding chapter. This points up the conceptual difficulty with "impact"—namely its breadth. Actually, most of our research on the impact of judicial policies since the 1940s has been mislabeled; compliance and implementation studies are what we have actually produced, even though the term "impact" continues in use.

Throughout the discussion we will attempt to move beyond mere description to explain, even if tentatively, the patterns we are reporting—in short, what factors can be identified as explaining outcomes. Judicial implementation research has not been notably successful in nailing down precise explanatory variables, but suggestive explanations will be set forth where possible.

One final introductory point: almost of necessity the compliance-noncompliance issue will loom large in the discussion, suggesting widespread opposition to judicial policies. To reiterate the point made earlier, this is because research has tended to focus on compliance and noncompliance with highly controversial judicial policies of broad implications for society—judicial decisions which, almost by definition, are likely to evoke at least spotty if not widespread resistance. This is an important part of implementation, but tends to obscure the more typical day-in, day-out response pattern characterized by high levels of compliance. As noted,

> In the usual kind of civil litigation, compliance with the decision is routine, at least after all appeals have been exhausted. When a judge determines ownership of property, settles a tax claim, awards compensation, or forbids construction of a dam, the loser typically, if reluctantly, obeys without the court's having to use its coercive power to punish for contempt. If the court's verdict in a criminal case is not guilty, police release the defendant immediately. When the verdict is guilty, and there is no reversal on appeal, judicial personnel, police, and prison officials act together or separately to collect the fine or incarcerate the defendant.[12]

Hence, a balanced view of judicial implementation and impact, as with most other areas of American judicial politics, requires that we make appropriate allowances for the distortion produced by the highly selective—often faddish—research foci characterizing our work.

LEGISLATIVE RESPONSES

Congress and the Supreme Court

As perhaps the most open and accessible of policy-making agencies, Congress and state legislatures tend to be central focal points for responding to judicial policies. The founding fathers created a number of important links between Congress and the Supreme Court,

---

[12]Walter F. Murphy and C. Herman Pritchett, eds., *Courts, Judges, and Politics: An Introduction to the Judicial Process,* 4th ed. (New York: Random House, 1986), 320.

links which have become ready-made tools for congressional reaction to judicial policy making. The same is true of legislative-judicial relations in the states, although as usual, we know a good deal less about that subject.

Relations between Congress and the Court have been the subject of considerable research attention, particularly since the great Court-Congress-president clash of New Deal days. Historians have documented the frequent Court-Congress crises wherein members of Congress, angry with Supreme Court decisions, have hauled out their arsenal of weapons to strike back at the Court.[13] Political analyses of the relationship have included, at times, highly quantitative techniques designed to move us beyond description to explanation.[14] Finally, journalists have had their say as well in adding to the literature on the subject.[15]

At the outset, we should note that congressional responses are determined in part by the nature of the Supreme Court ruling in question. Supreme Court decisions interpreting federal statutes can be reversed, so to speak, by rewriting the statute. Constitutional rulings, however, are not as easily changed, and should Congress be highly dissatisfied with such decisions, other than mere statutory responses may be called for. Further, Supreme Court decisions can treat general policy matters, as most do, or they may focus on the internal powers and procedures of Congress itself (for example, powers of congressional investigating committees as in *Watkins v. U.S.*, 354 U.S. 178 [1957]).

As for congressional reaction, it may fall into four broad categories: Congress may not respond at all, it may respond positively, it may respond in a more or less negative vein to the decision (though lacking hostile overtones against the Court itself), or there may be a largely hostile response. Research has tended to focus on the last category, although by all accounts the most common response of Congress is to do nothing. Many, if not most, Supreme Court rulings are relatively narrow and noncontroversial, evoking no really significant congressional reaction. Legislation responding to Court decisions (or to a pattern of judicial decision making), as with legislation on most other subjects, is difficult to pass. Even with sizable sectors of Congress expressing concern with Supreme Court rulings, legislation is usually stymied by, among other forces, equally sizable numbers of legislators who oppose the bills in question, resulting in little noteworthy congressional reaction. Much more common are Supreme Court rulings that evoke no congressional response at all, even of a mixed variety, though perhaps there may be scattered individual congressional responses. Thus, in a study of Supreme Court statutory rulings in the area of antitrust and labor relations from 1950 to 1972, in only 12 percent of the cases did Congress even attempt to respond legislatively to the Court, and laws were passed in response to only 9 out of 222 rulings (about 4 percent).[16] Hence, in approximately nine out of ten Court

---

[13]See, e.g., C. Herman Pritchett, *Congress Versus the Supreme Court, 1957–60* (Minneapolis: University of Minnesota Press, 1961); Walter F. Murphy, *Congress and the Court* (Chicago: University of Chicago Press, 1962); and Stuart S. Nagel, "Court-Curbing Periods in American History," *Vanderbilt Law Review* 18, No. 3 (June 1965): 925–44.

[14]See John R. Schmidhauser and Larry L. Berg, *The Supreme Court and Congress: Conflict and Interaction, 1945–1968* (New York: Free Press, 1972); Harry P. Stumpf, "Congressional Response to Supreme Court Rulings: The Interaction of Law and Politics," *Journal of Public Law* 14, No. 2 (1966): 377–95; Beth Henshen, "Statutory Interpretations of the Supreme Court: Congressional Responses," *American Politics Quarterly* 11, No. 4 (Oct. 1983): 441–58; Richard A. Paschal, "The Continuing Colloquy: Congress and the Finality of the Supreme Court," *The Journal of Law and Politics* VIII, No. 1 (Fall 1991): 143–226 (and the many sources cited therein); and Joseph Ignagi and James Meernik, "Explaining Congressional Attempts to Reverse Supreme Court Decisions," *Political Research Quarterly* 47, No. 2 (June 1994): 353–71.

[15]See, e.g., Joseph W. Alsop and Turner Catledge, *The One-Hundred-Sixty-Eight Days* (Garden City, N.Y.: Doubleday, 1938).

[16]See Henshen, "Statutory Interpretations," 445. Using a different definition of "congressional response," Ignagni and Meernik found that in a sample of instances of possible response from 1954 to 1990, 71 percent resulted in no response from Congress. Ignagni and Meernik, "Explaining Congressional Attempts": 364.

decisions in policy areas in which we might expect congressional response, Congress did nothing.

The second category of response is positive in tone: Congress welcomes a ruling and responds in a laudatory, compliant fashion. Such responses may range from quietly adjusting to the ruling—obeying the "new law," in other words—to legislators publicly praising the decision. Again, we have a good deal less documentation of this type of response, but it is nonetheless important in understanding Court-Congress relations. The response of Congress to the celebrated Supreme Court decision of *Gideon v. Wainwright*, 372 U.S. 335 (1963), is a case in point. In holding that indigent defendants in felony cases are to have legal representation, the Court significantly altered criminal trial procedures. The main congressional response seemed to be the passage of legislation establishing federal public defender systems, thereby implementing the ruling. This is not to imply that all members of Congress applauded this decision, nor is the federal public defender plan necessarily the ideal implementation mechanism, but congressional reaction to the *Gideon* decision was largely positive.[17]

Such responses suggest the cooperative aspect of Court-Congress relations, and it is in this mood that the category of antidecision responses is to be understood—antidecision though not anti-Court response within the working framework of ongoing legislative-judicial relations. Court and Congress, after all, live in the same town (indeed, on the same block); philosophical positions expressed in Court rulings are widely represented in Congress; many members of Congress are attorneys and, as such, adhere to the professional norm that Court decisions ought to be obeyed; and at bottom, both branches are attempting to achieve the same broad goal—namely, fashioning public policy that effectively deals with society's problems. When the Court hands down a decision, particularly a statutory ruling, which may be at variance with the common understanding of the law, key members of Congress and representatives of relevant interest groups, or both, may be moved to press for changes in the statute to return the law to its supposed original state, or to fashion an interpretation more to their liking. Such congressional responses are usually labeled statutory "reversals" or "modifications," and indeed they are, but they need not be seen as necessarily hostile. In fact, it is not uncommon for the Court, in effect, to invite Congress to "correct" the ruling if it sees fit. Numerous examples illustrate this important statutory reversal process.

Tax law is common ground for such legislative-judicial interaction.[18] In 1960, for example, the Supreme Court ruled that an Indiana sewer (clay) pipe firm must compute its depletion allowance on the value of the mined, raw material rather than on the much larger figure of sales of finished sewer pipe (*U.S. v. Cannelton Sewer Pipe Company*, 364 U.S. 76 [1960]). The industry's pleas to Congress were soon heeded, and by the fall of 1961, Public Law 87-312 provided that for years prior to 1960, the old rule would apply. Although not actually reversing the doctrine of the Court, the law altered the effect of the decision and granted significant tax relief to the industry.[19]

Antitrust law and labor-management relations are two other areas in which statutory reversals have been rather common. Both the Sherman Anti-Trust Act as well as the National Labor Relations Act are statements of broad, major congressional policy providing few details to guide judicial interpretation. These situations are ready-made for judicial "misinterpretation," which, in turn, invites congressional "correction." An example of a

---

[17]Johnson and Canon, *Judicial Policies,* 155.

[18]"Congressional Reversal of Supreme Court Decisions, 1945–1957," *Harvard Law Review* 71, No. 7 (May 1958): 1324–37. See also the tax reversals reported by Justice Douglas in Russell Porter, "Douglas Says High Court Won't Take a Back Seat," *New York Times* (November 9, 1958): 44.

[19]Harry P. Stumpf, "The Congressional Reversal of Supreme Court Decisions, 1957–1961." Ph.D. dissertation, Northwestern University, 1964: 29.

"reversal" in the latter category began with the Court's 1957 decision in *Guss v. Utah Labor Relations Board,* 353 U.S. 1. In that case, the Court created what came to be known as the no-man's land of labor law. From the time it was created, the National Labor Relations Board (NLRB) had refused to take jurisdiction of certain kinds of labor disputes, in particular those involving an interstate business having less than a minimum annual dollar volume. In theory, state labor agencies were to handle labor relations in those smaller industries. However, the *Guss* decision voided this tacit agreement, holding that the National Labor Relations Act had "preempted" the field of labor relations in interstate commerce, preventing states from regulating in the area. This no-man's land was closed by Section 701 of the Labor-Management Reporting and Disclosure Act of 1959 (the Landrum-Griffin Act) by empowering state labor boards to handle labor relations in the vacuum created by the *Guss* ruling. In fact, the Landrum-Griffin Act reversed or modified the effect of Court rulings in two additional areas: secondary boycotts (*NLRB v. International Rice Milling Co.,* 341 U.S. 665 [1951]); and "hot cargo" agreements (*Local 1976 v. NLRB,* 357 U.S. 93 [1958]).[20]

Policy-making in the antitrust field has bounced back and forth between Congress and the Supreme Court almost since the passage of the Sherman Act of 1890. In the Henshen study, six of the nine bills passed to reverse or modify Court decisions were in the antitrust field. One such reversal involved the Supreme Court's determination in 1958 that "dual rate" or preferred customer shipping rates set by steamship conferences violated the ban on discriminatory rate practices of the Shipping Act of 1916 (*Federal Maritime Board v. Isbrandtsen,* 356 U.S. 481 [1958]). Shipping conferences lobbied Congress intensely to be permitted to reintroduce their dual-rate system to discourage nonconference competition. After a stopgap measure passed in May of 1958, Congress permanently reversed the *Isbrandtsen* ruling in the Bonner Act by moving to legalize dual-rate schemes. President Kennedy signed the bill on October 3, 1961 (Public Law 87-346).[21]

Later, Congress responded to the Court's holding in *NLRB v. Bildisco and Bildisco,* 465 U.S. 513 (1984)—that a company may use the bankruptcy laws to abrogate its collective bargaining contract—by closing that significant gap in labor-management policy (Public Law 98-353).[22] And in a different policy area, when the Court held in June 1981 that state courts could not require the spousal sharing of military retirement pay in the case of divorce (*McCarty v. McCarty,* 453 U.S. 210), Congress adopted an amendment to the fiscal 1983 defense authorization bill that in effect reversed this ruling.[23] In *McCarty,* as has been true in other cases, the Court invited, if not urged, Congress to act. Wrote Justice Blackmun for the majority,

> We recognize that the plight of an ex-spouse of a retired service member is often a serious one. . . . Congress may well decide . . . that more protection should be afforded a former spouse. . . . This decision, however, is for Congress alone.[24]

These specific examples should suffice to make the point: Although congressional reversal of the Court's statutory rulings is neither easy nor pro forma, it is, nevertheless, a recurring dimension of Court-Congress relations and is best viewed as nonhostile. Indeed, it is sometimes welcomed by the justices of the Supreme Court. Thus, Justice Sherman Minton once protested in a letter to Felix Frankfurter that he thought the "liberal press"

---

[20]Stumpf, "Congressional Reversal": 88–96.

[21]Stumpf, "Congressional Reversal": 73–78. See also John P. Gorman, "Shipping Conferences and the Bonner Act, 1961," *Journal of Business Law* (1962): 24–30.

[22]See "Law/Judiciary," *Congressional Quarterly Almanac, 1984* (Washington, D.C.: Congressional Quarterly, 1985): 25–26.

[23]See *Congressional Quarterly Almanac,* 1982 (Washington D.C.: Comgressional Quarterly, 1983): 100.

[24]*McCarty v. McCarty,* 453 U.S. 210, 236 (1981).

overplayed these attempted reversals. He concluded, "I was never conscious . . . while I was there that the Court felt there was an attack on it when Congress laid down a policy reversing or nullifying the Court's decision in a non-constitutional case."[25]

Anti-Court or otherwise hostile congressional reaction to Supreme Court decisions has been more thoroughly documented, and properly so, for these situations enable the student of judicial politics to estimate the relative power of these two branches in national policy-making. Congressional responses of this genre differ from the three foregoing categories in several important respects. First, they are more likely to be responses to constitutional rather than to statutory rulings, although as we shall see, there are exceptions. Second, hostile reaction of this type is often a response to a series or pattern of rulings rather than just one decision (again, with exceptions). Third, such legislative response tends to come in waves or crises; hostility tends to build over time to a point where something of a showdown occurs between the branches of government. And fourth, congressional response in this category usually involves a wider spectrum of participants than is the case in the other categories. Political parties are more likely to take stands on the issues in dispute, and presidential candidates may even treat them as worthy of campaign attention. In short, the matters become salient national political issues. Finally, the legislative response we are pointing to here may be distinguished from other types of reaction by the content of the bills actually introduced in Congress.

In general, anti-Court legislation can be defined as any congressional bill or other action having as its purpose or effect, either expressed or implied, alteration in the structure or functioning of the Supreme Court as an institution within the context of legislative-judicial conflict. This differs from a simple reversal bill, which may be defined as proposed congressional legislation, the intent or effect of which is to modify the legal result or impact, or perceived result or impact, of a specific Supreme Court decision.[26] In summary, anti-Court legislation is hostile action usually aimed at the judicial institution itself, whereas decision-reversal reaction most often focuses on the decision only. There are exceptions to these generalizations, as noted later, but negative or hostile congressional reaction can generally be described in these terms.

Scholars have identified nine separate historical periods of relatively intense anti-Court congressional behavior, beginning with the 1801–1804 crisis over the Republican Congress's negative reaction to the Federalist Party's Court-packing plan (leading to the ruling in *Marbury v. Madison*), through the 1955–1959 conflict—largely over national security issues—to more recent hostilities concerning abortion, prayer in public schools, and criminal procedures.[27] In these crisis periods, a wide variety of measures has been employed by Congress in attempts to punish the Court or to turn it around and force it into compliance with the congressional (allegedly national) will.

The Court-packing plan of New Deal days is perhaps the best-known example. In addition to increasing (or decreasing) the number of justices on the Court, at least nine other

---

[25]David N. Atkinson, "Justice Sherman Minton and Behavior Patterns Inside the Supreme Court," *Northwestern University Law Review* 69, No. 5 (Nov.–Dec. 1974): 733. Two more recent studies of congressional reversals of Supreme Court statutory rulings are Michael E. Solimine and James L. Walker, "The Next Word: Congressional Response to Supreme Court Statutory Decisions," *Temple Law Review* 54, No. 2 (Summer 1992): 425–58; and William N. Eskridge, Jr., "Overriding Supreme Court Statutory Interpretation Decisions," *Yale Law Journal* 101, No. 2 (Nov. 1991): 331–417.

[26]These definitions are from Stumpf, "Congressional Response": 382.

[27]A particularly useful description and analysis of anti-Court congressional response is Gerald N. Rosenberg, "Judicial Independence and the Reality of Political Power," paper delivered at the annual meeting of the American Political Science Association, New Orleans, August 29–September 1, 1985. In particular, see Table 1: 19.

tactics have been identified as having been either used or threatened by Congress over the years. They range from the relatively petty device of cutting the Court's budget, or refusing to increase the salaries of the justices, to the impeachment or attempted impeachment of one or more of the justices. Refusing to confirm appointees to the Court, proposals for changing the method of selecting and removing justices (for instance, requiring prior judicial service for appointment to the Court), requiring extraordinary majorities for the Court to hold acts of Congress unconstitutional, providing for an appeal of cases beyond the Supreme Court, stripping the Court of the power of judicial review itself, amending the Constitution to reverse Supreme Court decisions, and withdrawing the appellate jurisdiction of the Court in certain areas—these measures have all been attempted in Congress at one time or another to curb the Court.[28]

Constitutional Amendments Eleven, Fourteen, Sixteen, and Twenty-six were, of course, adopted to overturn specific Supreme Court decisions: the Eleventh to overturn *Chisholm v. Georgia,* 2 Dall. 419 (1793), by increasing the states' immunity to lawsuits; the first sentence of the first section of the Fourteenth to reverse *Dred Scott v. Sandford,* 19 How. 393 (1857), by awarding citizenship to blacks; the Sixteenth to reverse *Pollock v. Farmers' Loan and Trust Co.,* 158 U.S. 601 (1895), by permitting a federal income tax; and the Twenty-sixth to avoid the Court's holding in *Oregon v. Mitchell,* 400 U.S. 112 (1970), by permitting Congress to lower the voting age to eighteen in all elections, federal as well as state. In periods of Court-Congress conflict, hostile congressional response has quite frequently included proposals of this kind to amend the Constitution in order to reverse the Court. Although ostensively antidecision only, such responses have almost always been strongly anti-Court in their intent and context. Congressional response to legislative reapportionment rulings, school desegregation (especially busing to achieve desegregation), the decisions barring Bible-reading and prayers in public schools, and abortion are recent examples. In the year and a half following the initial prayer decision (*Engel v. Vitale,* 370 U.S. 421 [1962]), 146 proposals for constitutional amendments reversing the Court on this subject were introduced in Congress.[29] However, the amendment process is fraught with difficulty, making many of these attempts only symbolic of congressional displeasure.

Another approach to strike at the Court has involved various strategies to alter the Court's personnel or the manner in which the justices are selected. At least four techniques have been used in this regard, the most well known being what has come to be termed packing or unpacking the Court. As noted in Chapter 4, the size of the Supreme Court has changed seven times in its history, the last being in 1869 when Congress increased the number of justices from seven to nine. Some have suggested that, in general, when Congress has reduced the number of justices (from six to five in 1801 and from ten to seven in 1865), it did so to curtail the president's influence by denying him appointments to the Court, whereas the increases in Court size (five to six in 1802, six to seven in 1807, seven to nine in 1837, nine to ten in 1863, and seven to nine in 1869) were for philosophical reasons, to move the Court in a decisional direction desired by Congress.[30] Denying the president nominations however, is an attempt to promote or deter certain judicial policies thought by Congress to be important. Hence, all changes in Court personnel have been essentially "philosophical"—that is, policy motivated.

Court packing was a nineteenth-century phenomenon. The only serious attempt along these lines in the twentieth century has been President Roosevelt's proposal, submitted to Congress in early 1937, to increase the number of justices to a maximum of

---

[28]Rosenberg, "Judicial Independence: 7–10. See also Paschal, "The Continuing Colloquy."
[29]See Stumpf, "Congressional Response": 379.
[30]*Guide to the United States Supreme Court,* 2nd ed. (Washington, D.C.: Congressional Quarterly, 1990), 661.

15.[31] Reaction to that plan was so unfavorable as to suggest that the passage of time had reduced this tactic to the category of unacceptability—in violation of the rules of the game, so to speak—forcing Congress to other modes of retaliation to achieve its ends.

Rejection of nominees to the Court, as in the case of John J. Parker in 1930 or the Robert Bork rejection, or even significant Senate opposition to a nominee can be a message that Congress is dissatisfied with certain tendencies in judicial decision making or that it does not wish "dangerous" (that is, ideologically unacceptable) justices or judges on the federal bench. As discussed in Chapter 6, threats of nonconfirmation are more frequent than actual rejection of nominees, but along with more subtle uses of its confirming power (such as ex parte Congressional influences on the president's choices) can be effective congressional inputs in the personnel—hence, policy—selection process.[32] For example, much of the acrimony in the Senate hearings on the promotion of Justice Rehnquist to the chief justiceship was actually congressional reaction to the nominee's judicial behavior. And the hairbreadth vote in the Manion case (Chapter 6) can be read as a warning that Congress did not look favorably on racist or perhaps other archconservative judicial policies.

Impeachment as a means of attacking the Court through its personnel, an approach favored by President Jefferson, was effectively blunted by the failure to convict Justice Samuel Chase in 1805. Even so, impeachment is occasionally threatened by Court critics in Congress, and in the case of Justice Abe Fortas undoubtedly led to his resignation in 1969. Talk of impeaching Justice William O. Douglas, however (first in 1953, then in 1970), led to nothing and was probably motivated less by improper conduct than by partisan political considerations.[33]

A final congressional tactic to alter judicial decision making through the Court's personnel has been the frequent push to require specific qualifications for nomination to the Court, typically prior judicial experience. Since statutory requirements along these lines are at least arguably unconstitutional, constitutional amendments to this end have frequently been proposed. However, no bill on this subject has ever been approved by both houses of Congress.[34]

In some ways the most potent tool in the anti-Court congressional arsenal is the power to alter the Court's appellate jurisdiction. Employed in the immediate post–Civil War period to forestall a probable invalidation of the Reconstruction Acts, the tactic was acceded to by the Court itself in *Ex Parte McCardle*, 7 Wall. 506 (1869), thereby establishing an important precedent in Court-Congress relations. Many have argued that, as with Court packing, this power has slipped from the hands of Congress through lack of use.[35]

---

[31]Leonard Baker, *Back to Back: The Duel Between FDR and the Supreme Court* (New York: Macmillan, 1967).

[32]See *Guide to the United States Supreme Court,* 651–54.

[33]*Guide to the United States Supreme Court,* 654–59.

[34]*Guide to the United States Supreme Court,* 651. See also Rosenberg, "Judicial Independence:" 8–10.

[35]See Pritchett, *Congress Versus the Supreme Court,* 121–23. The issue of congressional power (and wisdom) in withdrawing the appellate jurisdiction of federal courts is discussed in a number of articles in *Judicature* 64, No. 4 (Oct. 1981), passim. See also Gerald Gunther, "Congressional Power to Curtail Federal Court Jurisdiction: An Opinionated Guide to the On-Going Debate," *Stanford Law Review* 36, No. 4 (April 1984): 895–922. For a somewhat different view of the Court's appellate jurisdiction, see Paschal, "The Continuing Colloquy:" 177–79, and the sources cited therein.

Of course we are talking here of punitive Congressional actions in an "anti-Court" mood. On numerous occasions, the most recent being the 1988 Act for the Improvement of the Administration of Justice, which removed most of the obligatory appeals to the Court, Congress has altered (usually narrowed) the Court's obligatory jurisdiction. And in Chapter 4 we discussed *Felker v. Turpin,* 64 LW 4677 (1996), in which a unanimous Court held that the Anti-Terrorism and Effective Death Penalty Act of 1996 did not deny the Supreme Court appellate jurisdiction in the area of habeas corpus. See Linda Greenhouse, "Justices, With Rare Speed, Agree to Review New Law on Appeals," *New York Times* (May 4, 1996): A-1, 8; and 65 LW 3144–45, Aug. 27, 1996.

In 1958, the Senate came within one vote of passing the infamous Jenner bill, which would have withdrawn the Court's appellate jurisdiction in five substantive areas corresponding to several highly controversial national security decisions of the mid-1950s.[36] Although this vote, along with other threats in this vein in the 1970s and 1980s, might be taken as good evidence that this imposing congressional power is very much alive, the prevalent view of scholars appears to be that argued by C. Herman Pritchett:

> The clause in the Constitution giving Congress control over the Court's appellate jurisdiction has in effect now been repealed by the passage of time and by the recognition that exercise of such power would be in the truest sense subversive of the American tradition of an independent judiciary. The language of Article III section 2, sounded reasonable in 1787, just as did choosing a President by indirect election. Then the Supreme Court was only a few words in an unadopted document. Today it is preeminently the most respected judicial body in the world. For a hundred and fifty years it has been recognized as having the authority to pass on the constitutionality of acts of Congress. It symbolizes the rule of law in a world which has seen too much of executive dictatorship and legislative irresponsibility. Under these conditions Congress can no longer claim with good conscience the authority granted by Article III section 2, and every time proposals to exercise such authority are rejected, as the Jenner and Butler proposals were rejected by Congress and public opinion, the Court's control over its appellate jurisdiction is correspondingly strengthened.[37]

Events since 1958 seem to have supported the Pritchett thesis. Although numerous proposals to strip the Court of its appellate jurisdiction in various subject areas have been made in Congress since that time, none have become law. In the late summer of 1985, Senator Jesse Helmes (R–N.C.) once again failed to persuade the Senate to adopt his bill (S-47), which would have prohibited federal courts from hearing cases on prayers in public schools. Even Senator Barry Goldwater (R-Ariz.) opposed the measure, inquiring,

> Did he [Jesse Helmes] really write this bill? Is this really his? I am a little surprised that the senator from North Carolina decided to outlaw the Supreme Court from our life. . . . I just wanted to say to my friend from North Carolina, I am really kind of surprised that he would write this bill. If I wrote it, I would have been ashamed of it.[38]

Perhaps Pritchett is correct when he argues that Congress's power to withdraw the Court's appellate jurisdiction has been permanently neutralized. Attempts to provide for appeals beyond the Supreme Court, requiring extraordinary majorities for certain kinds of decisions, or abolishing judicial review itself, all seem to fall into the category just noted—often threatened but never passed. And it is probable that such tactics exceed the bounds of acceptability in the ongoing legislative—judicial struggle.

Finally, congressional dissatisfaction with decisions of the Supreme Court has not infrequently led to attempts to punish the justices through the congressional power of the purse. Though petty, a number of measures of this type have been enacted, or by omission rather than commission, Congress has sent signals to the Court through the pocketbook of the justices. In 1964, for example, Congress increased the salaries of the federal judges by $7,000, though for Supreme Court justices the increase was only $4,500. The legislators made it clear that the slight was intended as a slap at the Court for some of its decisions of that period, most notably the reapportionment and prayer rulings.[39] Similarly, Congress

[36]Pritchett, *Congress Versus the Supreme Court*, 31–40.
[37]Pritchett, *Congress Versus the Supreme Court*, 122–23.
[38]"Senate Rejects Bill to Permit School Prayer," *Congressional Quarterly Weekly Report* 43, No. 37 (Sept. 14, 1985): 1842.
[39]See *Guide to the United States Supreme Court*, 659.

has refused to enhance the physical security of the justices by providing them with limousine service, one Southern senator suggesting busing instead. "Couldn't we get a bus to bus the judges? I learned about busing from reading the *Swann case.*"[40]

Occasionally, anti-Court congressional responses occur as exceptions to the preceding generalizations pertaining to the process. At times, for example, statutory rulings will evoke congressional hostility on the order of a landmark constitutional decision. Such was the case in the response of Congress to *Yates v. U.S.,* 354 U.S. 298 (1957). In *Yates,* the Warren Court reversed the conviction of fourteen communist leaders and, in doing so, emasculated the 1940 Smith Act. The holding was based on several grounds, one being a rather narrow definition of the term "organize" in the Act. The statute made it a crime to organize any group or assembly of persons for the purpose of advocating the violent overthrow of any government in the United States. If "organize" means to establish or bring into existence, then the communist leaders were illegally convicted in lower court, because the three-year federal statute of limitations had expired. If "organize" is defined as a continuing activity, however, the convictions could be upheld.[41] The Court opted for the first interpretation, which infuriated a Congress already aroused to a fever pitch of hostility over the "pro-Red" rulings of the Warren Court. After several attempts, Congress redefined "organize" in the act to include the recruitment of new members, forming new units, and so forth, thereby statutorily reversing that portion of the *Yates* ruling. Though on its face a simple statutory reversal, this legislative response was strongly anti-Court, for it was actually a reaction to a series of decisions to which Congress was hostile, and it occurred in the heat of a notable Court-Congress crisis.

Similarly, as the Burger and particularly the Rehnquist Courts moved to a more conservative posture, they began rewriting America's civil rights law, less through constitutional than statutory means. As they did so, tension mounted between the Court and the then more-liberal Congress. A major struggle extending over the 1988–1991 period developed over a number of statutory rulings that had the effect of narrowing the rights of citizens, largely in the area of employment discrimination. In July 1990 Congress passed the Civil Rights Act of 1990, which was designed to overturn six separate Supreme Court rulings that had considerably increased the difficulty of proving job discrimination and of collecting monetary damages for racial discrimination.[42] President Bush vetoed the bill, and the Senate, on October 24, 1990, failed by one vote in overriding the veto.[43] However, the Civil Rights Act of 1991 prevailed by reinstating a more liberal meaning to various civil rights statutes in order to counter restrictive, conservative interpretations in *ten* separate Court rulings.[44] Hence,

---

[40]Johnson and Canon, *Judicial Policies,* 148.

[41]See Pritchett, *Congress Versus the Supreme Court,* 60.

[42]See Michael Ross, "Senate Approves Civil Rights Bill," *Los Angeles Times* (July 19, 1990): A-1; and Steven A. Holmes, "Supporters Vowing to Try Again for Job Discrimination Bill Vetoed by Bush," *New York Times* (Oct. 26, 1990): A-15.

[43]See Neil A. Lewis, "President's Veto of Rights Measure Survives by 1 Vote," *New York Times* (Oct. 26, 1990): A-1.

[44]Paschal, "The Continuing Colloquy": 204; and Solimine and Walker, "The Next Word": 425–27.

The ten decisions were *Patterson v. McLean Credit Union,* 491 U.S. 164 (1989); *Wards Cove Packing Co. v. Antonio,* 490 U.S. 642 (1989); *Martin v. Wilks,* 490 U.S. 755 (1989); *Price Waterhouse v. Hopkins,* 490 U.S. 228 (1989); *Lorance v. A.T. & T. Technologies,* 490 U.S. 900 (1989); *Library of Congress v. Shaw,* 478 U.S. 310 (1985); *EEOC v. Aramco,* 499 U.S. 244 (1991); *Independent Federation of Flight Attendants v. Zipes,* 491 U.S. 754 (1989); *Crawford Fitting Co. v. J. T. Gibbons, Inc.,* 482 U.S. 437 (1987); and *West Virginia University Hospitals, Inc. v. Casey,* 499 U.S. 83 (1991).

The 1991 Civil Rights Act was but part of a larger skirmish extending back to the aftermath of *Grove City College v. Bell,* 465 U.S. 555 (1984) wherein Congress overrode a Reagan veto to pass a bill overturning the *Grove* ruling, which held that a federal ban on sex discrimination in colleges receiving federal aid applied only to the specific program receiving such aid, not to college activities as a whole. See Irvin Molotsky, "House and Senate Vote to Override Reagan on Rights," *New York Times* (Mar. 3, 1988): A-1.

though "only" statutory reversals, the stakes were as high as in many constitutional struggles between the Court and Congress.

In other instances, a single Supreme Court decision, constitutional or otherwise, decided in a period of relative calm in Court-Congress relations, and initially divorced from the mainstream of contemporary policy debate, can become a cause célèbre, sparking near-violent legislative (and executive) reaction. Such was the case in the reaction to *U.S. v. California,* 332 U.S. 19 (1947), in which the Supreme Court (Justice Black) held that title to off-shore mineral (read oil) deposits lay with the national government. The decision evoked a decade of bitter controversy, recessed though not terminated by a congressional reversal of the ruling in 1953. Given the stakes involved—untold billions in oil royalties—the issue attracted the widest possible array of participants, all the way from oil companies to teacher organizations, and from presidents of the United States to local fishing associations. Indeed, a flurry of Court decisions and legislative acts, national and state, was spawned by the initial ruling, illustrating as few cases do that judicial decisions are anything but final policy pronouncements. In the end, Congress and the president won out over a less-than-contrite Supreme Court.[45]

A third exception to these generalizations concerning anti-Court congressional reaction embodies instances in which Congress seizes the opportunity to undermine landmark constitutional rulings by the exercise of its power to pass ordinary legislation, often appropriations bills. Such was the case in Congress's reaction to the controversial ruling of *Roe v. Wade,* permitting abortions within the first trimester of pregnancy. Congress was successful in adopting the so-called Hyde Amendment (Rep. Henry Hyde, R-Ill.), which blocked the use of federal funds for elective abortions.[46] Since a great many such operations had been performed in federally funded abortion clinics, this legislation was said to have had the effect of significantly reducing the number of abortions actually performed nationwide. The Court upheld the constitutionality of the Hyde Amendment in *Harris v. McRae,* 448 U.S. 297 (1980). On the other hand, Congress has been a good deal less successful in the use of its appropriations power to thwart the Court's decisions in areas such as busing.[47]

Finally, as briefly noted, anti-Court and antidecision congressional actions are sometimes joined, as in the case of constitutional amendments attempted or enacted. Though usually aimed at a specific decision, such proposed amendments are often reflections of strong congressional hostility toward certain judicial decisions or decisional tendencies.

Enough has been said to provide the flavor—indeed, a smorgasbord—of possible congressional responses to Supreme Court rulings. Though an important segment of the relationship is cooperative, intense conflict periodically emerges. Given the range of options open to Congress, combined with the strongly negative legislative attitudes toward many judicial policies, we may wonder why more anti-Court legislation is not passed. What prevents Congress from severely restricting the power of the Court and its decisions? Scholarly commentary seems to focus on the following interrelated factors as important in answering the question.

First, a protective cloak of sacrosanctity covers the Court and its decisions. This explanation has been stated in different ways by different scholars, but basically the thesis is that particularly in times of Court-Congress crisis, the Court is protected by its "magic"

---

[45]An interesting account of what came to be called the "Tidelands Oil Controversy" is Lucius J. Barker, "The Offshore Oil Cases," in C. Herman Pritchett and Alan F. Westin, eds., *The Third Branch of Government* (New York: Harcourt Brace, 1963), 234–74.

[46]Johnson and Canon, *Judicial Policies,* 8–10.

[47]Johnson and Canon, *Judicial Policies,* 146–47.

from serious anti-Court congressional action. In explaining the near-complete failure of Congress to punish the Court legislatively for its "procommunist" decisions of the late 1950s, Herman Pritchett argued that

> Basically, the Court was protected by the respect which is so widely felt for the judicial institution in the United States. This attitude is often rather inchoate and not based on a well-formulated understanding of the judicial function. It may grow in part out of unsophisticated assumptions about the "non-political" character of the Supreme Court's role, which are fundamentally in error. But, whether for the right reasons or the wrong reasons, a great part of opinion in the United States holds that the Supreme Court should be let alone, or rather that it should be subject to influence only in the accepted manner, namely, by use of the appointing power when vacancies occur. This sense of the fitness of things was outraged when Franklin Roosevelt proposed to lay hands on an economically conservative Court in 1937 and, in spite of some changing of sides due to the different directions from which complaints against the Court came, the same feeling protected the Court in 1957.[48]

Research to date has not lent much empirical support to the sacrosanctity hypothesis, but Pritchett and other scholars are probably correct that this attitude toward the Court is inchoate and difficult to document, though in all likelihood a powerful influence in explaining the reluctance of Congress to use its full powers to restrict the Court.[49] Even Senator Barry Goldwater, hardly an apostle of liberal Supreme Court rulings, repeatedly opposed attempts to restrict the appellate jurisdiction of the Supreme Court.

Second, because successful attacks on the Court must overcome the "touch-me-not" hurdle, only widespread or very intense negative public (interest group) reaction is sufficient to push Congress into the actual enactment of anti-Court legislation. Conversely, when judicial policies split the Court's opposition, which is much more often the case, anti-Court congressional action is very unlikely. The result is that only very rarely (we might say never) can we expect anti-Court congressional attitudes to result in the enactment of legislation. Rather, the congressional game in this regard is largely bluff, huff, and puff.[50]

Finally, measuring the political effectiveness of congressional response by legislative proposals actually enacted may miss the point, for the threats—the huffing and puffing—may be sufficient to persuade the Court to back down from some of its earlier controversial rulings or to alter a judicial policy path it might otherwise have taken. Again, this is quite difficult to document, for how can we demonstrate that a given congressional response has caused the Court to behave in a certain way? Yet, there exists persuasive evidence of an indirect nature.

After a careful examination of the nine historical eras of Court-Congress conflict, Gerald Rosenberg concludes that "the Court does indeed heed the wishes of Congress under certain conditions."[51] These conditions include the perceived likelihood of successful con-

---

[48]Pritchett, *Congress Versus the Supreme Court,* 119. Other assertions of the sacrosanctity proposition can be found in Stumpf, "Congressional Reversal": 101–03; and Paschal, "The Continuing Colloquy": 179, among other sources.

[49]Johnson and Canon argue that "Making a rigorous test of the sacrosanctity theory is difficult," and in the absence of better explanations, they conclude, "There is some truth to the sacrosanctity argument," *Judicial Policies,* 153–54.

[50]See Ignagni and Meernik, "Explaining Congressional Attempts to Reverse the Supreme Court": 365–69, where the authors argue that public opinion and interest group activity are significant in explaining success of reversal bills. In "Overriding Supreme Court Statutory Interpretation Decisions," Eskridge finds that successful legislation is associated with an ideologically divided Court, the Court's reliance on "plain meaning" reasoning rather than looking into key legislative signals, and/or the Court's rejecting positions taken by federal, state or local governments, 334.

[51]Rosenberg, "Judicial Independence," 44.

gressional action, which, in turn, may depend upon the most recent election returns. When the electorate endorses an anti-Court Congress and a president of similar persuasion, the conditions are ripe for a strategic judicial retreat.

Numerous examples of the Court reversing itself under these conditions can be cited. During the 1858–1869 Court-Congress crisis sparked by the *Dred Scott* ruling, the recession of judicial power was clearly in evidence. The Court's ruling in *Ex Parte McCardle,* which upheld the authority of Congress to withdraw the Court's appellate jurisdiction, was the centerpiece of the judicial retreat of that era. Essentially the same judicial behavior accompanied the New Deal attack on the Court. Following the New Deal electoral victories of 1936, President Franklin Roosevelt set forth his famous Court-packing plan. Though it was never approved by Congress, the threat was sufficient to cause the Court to back down— the so-called switch in time that saved nine. Decisions such as *West Coast Hotel v. Parrish,* 300 U.S. 379; *NLRB v. Jones and Laughlin Steel Corp.,* 301 U.S. 1; and *Steward Machine Co. v. Davis,* 301 U.S. 548, all handed down in the spring of 1937, signaled an unmistakable—indeed dramatic—about-face in judicial policy-making.

Less dramatic but nonetheless convincing evidence of the retreat of the Court in the face of massive congressional threats were Supreme Court rulings in 1958 and 1959, which seemed to set a different tone than did earlier rulings on national security issues. For example, in *Watkins v. U.S.,* 354 U.S. 178 (1957) the Court appeared to set definite limits on the investigatory reach of congressional committees, holding that there existed no right to expose people's lives merely for the sake of exposure. In *Barrenblatt v. U.S.,* 360 U.S. 109 (1959), however, the Court seemed to march back down the hill by upholding the congressional contempt citation of a university professor who refused to answer questions about his past associations. Similarly, on the subject of discharge of public employees for their alleged beliefs, the Court seemed to stand fast for the right of the private citizen in *Slochower v. Board of Education* in 1956 (350 U.S. 551). But in *Beilan v. Board of Education,* 357 U.S. 399, and *Lerner v. Casey,* 357 U.S. 468, both decided in 1958, the Court backed away from this stance by upholding, respectively, the dismissal of a public school teacher and a New York subway employee, both of whom refused to answer questions concerning their past allegedly subversive activities.[52] The variable intervening between the earlier and later sets of decisions was the 1957–1958 legislative threat to withdraw the appellate jurisdiction of the Court in these and similar policy areas (the Jenner-Butler bill). It is this sort of evidence that has led Rosenberg to conclude that

> Arousing substantial opposition to the Court may be enough to dominate it. That is, if the Court is dependent upon political elites for the implementation of its judgments, angering some portion of them may effectively stymie the implementation of Court decisions. Thus, "success" in dominating the Court may occur well before the passage of a Court-attack bill. And that point, or range, may vary with the issue and the members of the Court.[53]

State Legislative Responses

Although state legislatures have no direct control over the national Supreme Court, they can—and do—respond to certain Supreme Court decisions, primarily those directed at state and local practices. The most publicized state legislative reactions within the last several decades have been attempts to modify or thwart the impact of Supreme Court edicts. State legislative responses to *Brown v. Board of Education,* 347 U.S. 483 (1954), outlawing

---

[52]Rosenberg, "Judicial Independence", 30–34.
[53]Rosenberg, "Judicial Independence", 45.

racial segregation in public schools, provide the most notable examples. The strategy of "massive resistance" was in large part imposed by Southern state legislatures. Closing public schools entirely, rescinding state compulsory attendance laws, funneling public funds to "private" (read segregated) schools—these and similar tactics were commonly employed by state legislatures in cooperation with state executives in the 1950s and 1960s. State legislative resistance to the Court's reapportionment and school prayer decisions of the early 1960s is also well known. Memorials and nonbinding resolutions were passed by state legislatures in support of congressional proposals to amend the Constitution to override these and similar rulings. Evasive legislative tactics to delay reapportionment (weighted voting schemes and the like) were also common.[54]

State legislatures, not unlike state supreme courts (see Ch. 10) are also capable of expanding individual rights beyond the minimums set out in U.S. Supreme Court decisions. Thus, in May 1990 Minnesota governor Rudy Perpich beat Congress to the punch by enthusiastically signing legislation passed by the Minnesota legislature that in effect reversed the narrow readings of civil rights law contained in three specific Supreme Court rulings: *Patterson v. McLean Credit Union,* 491 U.S. 164 (1989); *Wards Cove Packing v. Antonio* 490 U.S. 642 (1989); and *Lorance v. A.T.&T.,* 490 U.S. 900 (1989).[55] The *Patterson* ruling interpreted an 1886 civil rights law so as to apply to hiring only, not to racial discrimination at work! *Wards Cove* removed the old requirement that when business screened out minorities and women, they must prove "business necessity." And in *Lorance,* the Court considerably shortened the time limits for suits claiming discrimination. Said Stephen Cooper, former Commissioner of Human Rights of Minnesota, the legislation on these three points is designed "to restore to the people the rights they enjoyed before the Supreme Court took its buzzsaw to them in the last session."[56]

Despite these examples, state legislative resistance to Supreme Court edicts has probably been less common than has compliance. When the United States Supreme Court voids a state law on constitutional grounds, the most frequent state legislative response is to do nothing or to revise state law in accordance with the new rule. Requirements that states supply counsel for indigents have generally met with compliance, as have most obscenity rulings.[57] *Furman v. Georgia,* 408 U.S. 238 (1972), in which the Supreme Court voided death penalty statutes in 39 states, provides an example of the difficulty of labeling legislative responses as compliant or resistant. Following this decision, 37 state legislatures revised their death penalty statutes, ostensibly to comply with *Furman,* but more likely to ensure that the state could continue to impose the death penalty. Ironically, this massive response may have moved the Supreme Court to "comply" with state legislative wishes by upholding the constitutionality of most of the new statutes (*Gregg v. Georgia,* 428 U.S. 153 [1976]).

State legislative reaction to state judicial decisions is less well-documented. State legislatures, of course, generally have the same creative and budgetary control over state courts as does Congress over the federal judiciary. However, the power to confirm judicial appointees and to alter the appellate jurisdiction of state supreme courts is usually lacking at the state level. In Chapter 3, we noted the historic seesaw battle between state legislatures and state courts for preeminence in policy-making, which tells us that the legislative-

---

[54]See, e.g., Harry P. Stumpf and T. Phillip Wolf, "New Mexico," in Eleanore Bushnell, ed., *Impact of Reapportionment on the Thirteen Western States* (Salt Lake City: University of Utah Press, 1970), 207–40.

[55]See William E. Schmid, "Minnesota Rebuts High Court and Widens Job Rights Law," *New York Times* (May 12, 1990): A-7.

[56]Schmid, "Minnesota Rebuts": A-8.

[57]Johnson and Canon, *Judicial Policies,* 158.

judicial relationship in the states is not always serene. At least two factors tend to moderate the legislative-judicial conflict in the states. First, state supreme courts are usually deferential to legislative will; decisions tend to be made on narrow, technical grounds hewing to a strict constructionist approach. Second, state legislatures meet for only short periods of time and typically have limited staff and other resources, which restricts their ability to monitor and respond to judicial policy-making.[58] In general, then, legislature and judiciary tend to give one another a somewhat wider berth at the state level than is the case in Washington.

EXECUTIVE RESPONSES

Generally, the president has the option of joining with Congress in its responses to judicial policies, and as we have noted, the combination of president and Congress is usually too much for the Court to withstand. The president is, of course, a key player in influencing the Court through its personnel; indeed, the president is predominant in this arena. Either implicitly or explicitly, all presidential nominations to the Court are responses to past judicial decisions, as well as statements of presidential preference for future judicial policy. In fact, probably no dimension of presidential or congressional power vis-à-vis the Supreme Court is as important as the president's appointing power in influencing the future direction of judicial decisions.

Occasionally, the president has initiated personnel-type responses to Supreme Court decisions other than via the actual selection of nominees. The classic case was, of course, FDR's Court-packing plan. However, President Jefferson set the precedent for such attacks by working somewhat surreptitiously to have certain lower federal judges removed and to impeach Justice Chase. Although neither of these presidential initiatives met with success in the formal sense, both achieved their ultimate goal of nudging the Court toward policies more in keeping with presidential preferences.[59]

Court packing of the nineteenth-century variety was often a joint executive-legislative venture. For example, President Jefferson pushed hard for the repeal of the Judiciary Act of 1801, which had reduced the number of justices on the Court from six to five. The repeal, in the form of the Judiciary Act of 1802, returned the Court to six members, giving Jefferson an opportunity to appoint an additional justice. Throughout his presidency, Jefferson sought to replace Federalists with Republican judges, thereby reorienting the federal judiciary to an ideological posture more to his liking.[60] Similarly, judicial politics was clearly a campaign issue in the election of 1860 due to the *Dred Scott* decision, and the expansion of the Court to ten members in 1863 was intended to ensure a pro-administration Court.

Because of a variety of formal and informal powers at his or her command, and despite the doctrine of separation of powers, the president is actually the chief legislator of national politics. As such, the president can not only join in but, in fact, initiate any of the legislative responses to the Court. Attempts to amend the Constitution to override Court rulings often have White House sponsorship. Both Presidents Nixon and Reagan had advocated such moves. Presidents must, of course, sign or veto statutory reversal bills, and at times such bills are initially proposed by the White House as a means to modify judicial edicts inconsistent with administration policy.

---

[58]Johnson and Canon, *Judicial Policies,* 157.
[59]*Guide to the United States Supreme Court,* 691.
[60]See Clinton Rossiter, *The American Presidency* (New York: Mentor Books, 1956), 2–23.

In addition to leading Congress in its legislative responses to the Court, the president has at least three weapons which, depending upon whether and how they are used, can shift the balance of power for or against the Court. The first of these can be deployed in the role as chief of state, spokesperson for the American people.[61] In this capacity, the president is in a powerful position to mold and shape public opinion. From the time of Thomas Jefferson's angry denunciation of the federal judiciary through the outspoken criticism by Presidents Nixon and Reagan of certain judicial opinions, presidents have not been hesitant to use the prestige of their office to help shape public opinion for or against certain judicial policies. President Roosevelt's "fireside chats," in which he denounced the Court as "nine old men" out of step with the times and Richard Nixon's criticism of the Court for aiding criminals are clear instances of presidents attempting to add their weight to the effort to modify judicial policy.

More recently, President Clinton led a chorus of criticisms of the Court's ruling in *U.S. v. Lopez,* 63 LW 4343 (1995) wherein the justices, for the first time since 1936, were unable to find in the Commerce Clause sufficient justification for congressional action to regulate local though nationally related commercial activity. Here, the congressional ban on gun possession within one-thousand feet of schools was held unconstitutional, even though such guns moved in interstate commerce, and the educational process involved had countless interstate commercial ramifications. "I am determined to keep guns out of our schools," said the president, and he ordered the attorney-general to come up with ways to accomplish that goal.[62]

At times, such tactics have helped to produce results, though as mentioned earlier, the results are often subtle and difficult to measure. In this instance, there is every appearance of the Court's having moved "back down the hill" in the *Watkins* and *Barrenblatt* tradition. In *U.S. v. Robertson,* 63 LW 4386, decided only a week after *Lopez,* the Court failed even to mention its highly controversial *Lopez* doctrine in unanimously finding the activity (or rather inactivity) of a small, defunct Alaska gold mine to be well within the scope of the commerce power for purposes of applying the federal racketeering law. Noted Linda Greenhouse of the *New York Times,*

> It is possible that, with tempers still raw from the battle over United States v. Lopez, the gun case, . . . the Justices simply decided to disengage and step back from the issue rather than divert energy needed for other hard cases before the term ends in about two months.[63]

But a better explanation might be Rosenberg's: that it is possible to influence (dominate) the Court even without formal legislation or executive action.

Closely linked to the president's power to influence public opinion is his power to enforce or refuse to enforce Supreme Court decisions. A widely cited example of the latter was President Eisenhower's continued refusal to place the weight of his office behind the Court's 1954 decision in *Brown v. Board of Education.* Though he did not publicly oppose the ruling (at least while in office), his reluctance to enforce it was widely believed to have encouraged Southern resistance. In contrast, President Kennedy's verbal support of the initial prayer decision (*Engel v. Vitale,* 370 U.S. 421) at a press conference in June 1962 may have ameliorated some of the intense opposition to that decision.[64]

---

[61]Rosenberg, "Judicial Independence," 5–6.
[62]Todd S. Purdum, "Clinton Seeks Way of Avoiding Ruling on School Gun Ban," *New York Times* (Apr. 30, 1995): A-1.
[63]Linda Greenhouse, "Justices Decline to Expand Commerce-Clause Ruling," *New York Times* (May 2, 1995): A-12.
[64]Lawrence Baum, *The Supreme Court,* 5th ed. (Washington: Congressional Quarterly, Press, 1995), 254.

This discussion should not be taken to imply that the president is completely free to obey or not obey the Court. In cases in which the president's actions are themselves in question, and an adverse ruling by the Supreme Court could not be avoided, executive compliance is the usual response. This is because direct defiance of a Supreme Court ruling by the president would be likely to precipitate a constitutional crisis involving widespread destabilization of the government itself. Thus, in the face of a direct order from the Court to deliver the infamous White House Watergate tapes, President Nixon complied. President Truman responded in like manner when, in 1952, he was ordered by the Court to release the steel mills from federal control and return them to private hands. Had the presidents' initial actions in these two cases enjoyed strong support from Congress and public opinion, however, the outcomes may have been quite different. As has often been noted, the president's power is amorphous and depends more upon his or her capacity to persuade and build support than on legal power to command in the narrow sense.

Finally, the president, through the Solicitor General in the Justice Department, is in a unique position to influence the policy agenda of the Supreme Court. When the United States government is a party to a case (a very large portion of federal litigation in the last several decades), the position taken by the Justice Department can be crucial in the final disposition of the matter. And even when the government is only an interested bystander, the Solicitor General's office may file an amicus curiae brief which can carry considerable weight with the Court. One study found that in cases in which it was a party from 1900 to 1950, the Justice Department won 64 percent of its pleas, while the Court agreed with about 80 percent of amicus curiae briefs filed by the government.[65] Other research has revealed that the Court granted *certiorari* in an average of 71 percent of petitions filed by the Solicitor General over a recent 14-year period, whereas petitions from other litigants were granted at a rate of only 8 percent. In the 1983 term alone, the Solicitor General enjoyed an 80 percent *certiorari* grant rate, while other petitioners succeeded in only 3 percent of their filings.[66]

In short, the president, through the Office of Solicitor General, can exercise considerable influence over the work of the Court. Through the selection of cases for appeal, the filing of amicus curiae briefs, and in other ways, the executive can send signals to the Court indicating support of or opposition to certain judicial policy trends. This can be both an active as well as a reactive process. That is, the Justice Department, which is the president's law firm, can use the Solicitor General either to initiate new judicial policy thrusts or to attempt to deter judicial policy that it opposes. This may be seen as beneficial to a Court whose justices are well aware of the need for executive support in fashioning successful judicial policy. In turn, the president may gain by cooperating with the Court, because judicial endorsement of, or at least neutrality toward, the president's policies can help ensure their success. As with congressional-Court relations, cooperation between the president and the Court can go a long way in raising the comfort index of both branches.[67]

THE JUDICIAL BUREAUCRACY

Judicial policy, at whatever level enunciated, is almost always subject to further judicial "review." This situation is apparent in trial court determinations, because appellate courts exist

---

[65]Johnson and Canon, *Judicial Policies,* 162–63.

[66]S. Sydney Ulmer and David Willison, "The Solicitor General of the United States as *Amicus Curiae* in the U.S. Supreme Court, 1969–1983 Terms," paper presented at the annual meeting of the American Political Science Association, New Orleans, August 29–September 1, 1985: 3.

[67]Ulmer and Willison, "The Solicitor General": 8–9. See also Steven Puro, "The United States as *Amicus Curiae,*" in S. Sydney Ulmer, ed., *Courts, Law, and Judicial Processes* (New York: Free Press, 1981), 220–29.

for the very purpose of reviewing the work of lower courts. Hence, the supervisory process of appellate courts is one arena in which judicial implementation and impact can be studied.

Somewhat less obviously, lower courts may reverse these roles by "reviewing" the work of appellate courts. They are given this opportunity by virtue of their position as implementing or interpreting agencies for courts above. Almost all policy is subject to interpretation and implementation by someone, and in the judicial system, lower courts are formally charged with this task, giving them enormous opportunity to enhance or restrict the scope and effect of appellate rulings. As noted,

> This potential should not be surprising, since bureaucratic resistance in administrative hierarchies is a well-documented fact of life. . . . Not infrequently, a party who wins an appeal to the Supreme Court still winds up the loser on return to the lower court.[68]

We should add that lower courts can as easily expand, amplify, or even anticipate appellate judicial policy-making; noncompliance or evasion is but one type of lower court response.

Although administrative hierarchies involve the possibility of low-level frustration of policy as enunciated from on high, they are even more prominently characterized by norms of cooperation and compliance. Judges are professionals and operate within a framework of professional expectations. Adherence to the rules of law as handed down by upper courts, the reality or at least the appearance (often the same) of intercourt cooperation, honest consideration of relevant precedents, and the like, are included in the professional norm. Indeed, it is on this foundation that the very survival of the judicial bureaucracy rests, and perpetuation of the system is the *ultimate* professional value. Basic to our discussion of implementation and impact within the judicial hierarchy is the fact that in most instances, judges attempt to give an honest rendition of upper court policy; there are very good organizational (political) reasons for doing so.[69]

At the same time, factors moving lower-court judges in deviant directions are many and compelling. Judicial policy, like any other policy, often fails to cover all cases, or in other respects is unclear or poorly communicated, forcing lower-court judges to "shoot in the dark" in implementing the legal rule in question. There is plenty of room for honest misinterpretation of appellate rules, even leaving aside intentional deviation.[70] The Supreme Court's attempts to draw the line between obscene (and therefore illegal) and acceptable books, movies, and the like have left lower court judges confused. If one book is "patently offensive," who is to say how the next book is to be interpreted? And "patently offensive" to whom? This is but one example of many appellate judicial policies in which honest attempts to apply a new rule can lead to quite different lower-court results. The Supreme Court's decisions in areas such as taxation, adherence to due process standards in criminal proceedings, and affirmative action have created similar problems for lower courts.

More widely documented is intentional judicial evasion by lower courts growing out of ideological resistance to the substance of the policy itself. "Lower" courts, to which appellate courts remand cases, are often part of a political milieu encompassing values quite different from those influencing appellate courts. Federal district judges, state supreme

---

[68]Murphy and Pritchett, *Courts, Judges, and Politics*, 284.

[69]See Johnson and Canon, *Judicial Policies*, 33–48, for an elucidation of this important point.

[70]One scholar argues that

> Much lower court leeway is created by the fact that since Supreme Court opinions often represent a compromise among divergent approaches and views of individual Justices, there are sometimes multiple threads running through an official opinion which are inconsistent with the dominant pattern of thought. Even where a judge wishes to hew strictly to the High Court's line he may be left in doubt as to what was dogma and what was dicta.

Walter F. Murphy, "Lower Court Checks on Supreme Court Power," *American Political Science Review* 53, No. 4 (Dec. 1959): 1018.

court justices, or judges of state trial courts, while under oath to obey the law of the land and faithfully implement appellate judicial decisions, nonetheless find themselves heavily influenced by regional or local political thinking which often runs counter to appellate court doctrine. When such forces are stronger than the professional norm, resistance frequently results. Although opposition tactics are usually deployed subtly—narrow interpretations of the new judicial policy, convenient misunderstandings of upper court rulings, or perhaps avoidance of the policy—outright defiance is not unknown. Examples in all categories abound.

Southern federal and state judges, reacting to *Brown v. Board of Education* and similar racial desegregation rulings, as well as in response to certain criminal procedure edicts of the Supreme Court, have not infrequently exhibited overtly defiant behavior. For example, one city judge in Birmingham, Alabama, not only refused to implement Supreme Court rulings ordering the desegregation of municipal facilities, but went so far as to hold the Fourteenth Amendment itself unconstitutional.[71] A New Mexico judge, Caswell S. Neal, came close to doing the same thing in his decision in 1963 implementing the Supreme Court's initial legislative reapportionment decision. He wrote,

> Of course, few people, and particularly this Court, had ever dreamed that the highly controversial Fourteenth (14th) Amendment could be held applicable to cases posing political issues arising from a state's geographic distribution of legislative strength among its political subdivisions. . . .
>
> This encroachment upon the rights reserved to the States and to the people thereof, under the Tenth (10th) Amendment is nothing new. Its insidious growth has culminated more recently in *Baker vs. Carr* . . . and before that in *Brown vs. Board of Education* . . . and many others. The final result in terms of impact upon the future of this nation—its very existence as a democracy—is shuddering to the mind of this Court; and these remarks are made in the hope that at some future time, other judges, in other cases, having the power to halt this great danger to the Republic, will have the courage to do so.[72]

However, Judge Neal ultimately relented by directing the New Mexico Legislature to reapportion, concluding, "Be these things as they may, I suppose it is too late in this the high-noon of the Twentieth Century to dwell longer upon this depressing subject."[73]

In rather obvious defiance of the *Brown* decision, Federal District Judge John Bell Timmerman of South Carolina refused to apply the desegregation principal in *Brown* to city buses in a 1956 ruling. In a slap at the "psychological" aspects of *Brown,* Timmerman observed that "one's education and personality is not developed on a city bus."[74] Overt resistance was also the path taken by some state courts in response to the Supreme Court's ruling in *Mapp v. Ohio,* 367 U.S. 643 (1961), which applied the exclusionary rule (described later) to the states. A year after the decision, a New Jersey Superior Court simply denied the applicability of the *Mapp* rule, reasoning that,

> It cannot rationally be said that the state courts of all the states must necessarily follow every twist and turn of federal decisional law. . . . The case of *Mapp v. Ohio* . . . requires only that the state courts apply the sanction of suppression to property which has been found to have been unreasonably seized.[75]

---

[71]Johnson and Canon, *Judicial Policies,* 40.

[72]Stumpf and Wolf, "New Mexico," 216.

[73]Stumpf and Wolf, "New Mexico," 216.

[74]Murphy and Pritchett, *Courts, Judges, and Politics,* 1st ed. (1961), 590.

[75]David R. Manwaring, "The Impact of *Mapp v. Ohio,*" in David H. Everson, ed., *The Supreme Court as Policy-Maker: Three Studies on the Impact of Judicial Decisions* (Carbondale, Ill.: Public Affairs Research Bureau, Southern Illinois University, 1968), 8.

A federal judge in Alabama was even more blunt in his response to the Supreme Court's prayer decisions. In approving a state prayer law, he argued that in its interpretation of the First Amendment, the United States Supreme Court has "erred."[76] However, the decision was overruled by the United States Courts of Appeals.

Whether labeled outright defiance or disingenuous evasion, the case of *Williams v. Georgia,* 349 U.S. 375 (1955), stands as a clear if shocking example of the power of lower (here, state) courts to evade appellate judicial policy. Aubrey Williams, a young Black man, was convicted of murder in Georgia in 1953 and sentenced to die in the electric chair. However, he had been found guilty by a jury that suffered from de facto exclusion of Blacks in rather clear violation of the Court's holding in both the second Scottsboro case, *Norris v. Alabama,* 294 U.S. 587 (1935), and more specifically, *Avery v. Georgia,* 345 U.S. 559 (1953). The jury that convicted Williams had been selected by the same method declared invalid in *Avery;* the names of prospective white jurors were written on white cards, while those of Black jurors were on yellow cards.

Williams's appeal to the Georgia Supreme Court won him no relief, but the United States Supreme Court granted *certiorari.* The high court held that the defendant had indeed been unconstitutionally convicted and remanded the case to the Georgia Supreme Court. Writing for the Court, Justice Frankfurter concluded that

> The facts of this case are extraordinary, particularly in view of the use of yellow and white tickets by a judge of the Fulton County Superior Court almost a year after the State's own Supreme Court had condemned the practice in the *Avery* case. That life is at stake is of course another important factor in creating the extraordinary situation. . . . We think that orderly procedure requires a remand to the State Supreme Court for reconsideration of the case. Fair regard for the principles which the Georgia courts have enforced in numerous cases and for the constitutional commands binding on all courts compels us to reject the assumption that the courts of Georgia would allow this man to go to his death as the result of a conviction secured from a jury which the State admits was unconstitutionally impaneled.[77]

In reply, Chief Justice Duckworth, writing for the Georgia Supreme Court, states that "We will not supinely surrender sovereign powers of this State." Again holding that the issue of the improperly impaneled jury should have been raised at trial, the court reaffirmed its earlier ruling. Williams's attorney again filed a petition for *certiorari* to the United States Supreme Court, which was denied in January 1956. On March 30 of that year Aubrey Williams died in the electric chair in the state penitentiary at Reidsville, Georgia.[78]

Another successful Southern resistance strategy involved the rather fruitless efforts of Virgil Hawkins, a Black man, to be admitted to the University of Florida School of Law. In 1949, Hawkins sued in state court to obtain law school admission, and after considerable delay, the Florida Supreme Court, in 1952, dismissed the suit. Hawkins then filed a petition for *certiorari* to the United States Supreme Court. In a per curiam order, the Court remanded the case to the Florida court in light of the *Brown* decision. The Florida Supreme Court responded with a complex ruse delaying Hawkin's admission indefinitely. The plaintiff then returned to the United States Supreme Court and the Court for the second time, per curiam, held that he was "entitled to prompt admission under the rules and regulations applicable to other qualified candidates."[79]

---

[76]Baum, *The Supreme Court,* 230.

[77]*Williams v. Georgia,* 349 U.S. 375 (1955), at 391.

[78]This runaround of appeals is detailed in Murphy and Pritchett, *Courts, Judges, and Politics,* 1961, 602–06.

[79]*Florida ex rel Hawkins v. Board of Control,* 350 U.S. 413 (1956).

Returning to the Florida Supreme Court, Hawkins was again denied admission, the Court holding,

> It is unthinkable that the Supreme Court of the United States would attempt to convert into a writ of right that which has for centuries . . . been considered a discretionary writ; nor can we conceive that that Court would hold that the highest court of a sovereign state does not have the right to control the effective date of its own discretionary process. . . . We will not assume that the Court intended such a result.[80]

The United States Supreme Court refused to hear the case a third time but suggested that Hawkins try a United States district court, which he did. However, the federal district court refused Hawkins's request for injunctive relief against the University of Florida, whereupon he appealed to the United States Courts of Appeals. The Appeals Court reversed and remanded the case, whereupon District Judge Devane of the United States District Court for the Northern District of Florida, Tallahassee, held that "Plaintiff failed completely to establish any such right under the law applicable to cases of this character and he will be denied the right to enter the law school."[81] The result was that after nine years of litigation and two favorable Supreme Court rulings, Mr. Virgil Hawkins was never admitted to the University of Florida School of Law.[82]

Resistance of this sort by lower courts is limited neither to Southern judges nor to racial issues. Following the Supreme Court's ruling in *Mallory v. U.S.,* 354 U.S. 449 (1957), that a suspect had to be arraigned as soon as possible after arrest (to help prevent police-coerced confessions) lower courts found numerous ways to avoid the new rule. In fact, one researcher concluded that the response to *Mallory*

> provides a classic example of the power of inferior judges to reshape legal doctrine expounded by the Supreme Court. By means of explaining, limiting, and distinguishing, the district and circuit judges in the District of Columbia [from which the *Mallory* case came] have been able to permit the use in evidence of a high percentage of confessions secured during delays in arraignment.[83]

In one case, Federal District Judge Holtzoff of the District of Columbia refused to apply the *Mallory* precedent to throw out a confession after considerable police questioning, reasoning that "An opinion of a court is not to be treated and read as an essay in determining the rule of law to be evolved therefrom."[84] In the same opinion, the judge made clear the difference between the policy import of *Mallory* (to protect the suspect from police coercion) and his own philosophy on crime (protection of the public—the law-and-order theme):

> Every member of the community has a constitutional right to be protected in the safety of his person and his property. The victim of the crime must not become a forgotten man. His rights are much greater than those of the criminal. When the criminal law ceases to protect the public, it has failed of its purpose.[85]

In other policy areas, a Texas judge in 1958 adamantly refused to implement the Supreme Court's decision in *Wickard v. Filburn,* 317 U.S. 111 (1942), which upheld the power of Congress to establish price support programs for agriculture. For at least four

---

[80]93 So. 2d 354, as cited in Murphy and Pritchett, *Courts, Judges, and Politics,* 611.

[81]As cited in Murphy and Pritchett, *Courts, Judges, and Politics,* 617.

[82]This same type of appellate runaround was employed by the courts of Alabama to continually harass the NAACP. See *NAACP v. Alabama,* 360 U.S. 240 (1959), and 377 U.S. 288 (1964).

[83]Murphy, "Lower Court Checks," 1024.

[84]Murphy, "Lower Court Checks," 1023.

[85]Murphy, "Lower Court Checks," 1023.

years, this judge was successful in preventing the implementation of the program in northern Texas. Similarly, trial courts in several states in the 1940s and 1950s enforced antivagrancy laws in the face of the Supreme Court's insistence on the right to travel of all citizens, indigents or not.[86] Finally, in response to the 1961 *Mapp* decision applying the exclusionary rule to the states, one Philadelphia judge flatly refused to go along, noting that the case had been decided by a six-to-three vote, and he agreed with the dissenters![87]

Impact research tends to mislead in its overemphasis on (usually conservative) lower court evasion or resistance to (usually liberal) Supreme Court rulings. Reactions to Supreme Court decisions provide us with examples of more liberal lower courts refusing to apply what they have regarded as unacceptably conservative Supreme Court holdings. In a similar vein, it is important to document the capacity of lower courts not merely to limit but also to expand appellate court judicial doctrine.

In the first category are instances in which state courts have relied on their own state constitutions to render decisions more permissive or liberal than those handed down by the U.S. Supreme Court. Chapter 10 contains numerous examples of such responses by state courts. Thus, even though the Supreme Court, in *San Antonio Independent School District v. Rodriguez,* 411 U.S. 1 (1973), could find no equal protection reason for requiring states to distribute public educational funds on a per-pupil basis, California as well as other states imposed such a requirement on their state legislatures on the strength of their own state bill of rights.[88] Similarly, the New York Court of Appeals (the state's court of last resort) has held that topless entertainment is protected by its own state constitution's free speech provision, even though the United States Supreme Court had ruled that the First Amendment to the federal Constitution does not protect such expression.[89] Such state court progressivism is not new in the present era, however. At least twenty-two states had adopted the exclusionary rule in order to make meaningful the Fourth Amendment's prohibition against unreasonable searches and seizures long before the Supreme Court did so in 1961.[90]

Instances of lower courts expanding or amplifying appellate court rules are legion. Such tactics are at times anticipatory of later "confirmation" by the relevant appellate tribunals, though more frequently the lower courts are acting in response to ideological (political) pressures in their respective states and communities. Lower courts at times expand doctrine by applying it to different subjects, or they may apply a rule in situations not at all covered by the original ruling. An example of the latter has been the rather widespread enthusiasm of lower courts for the doctrine of the right of privacy. After its application to the right to use birth control devices in *Griswold v. Connecticut,* 381 U.S. 479 (1965), lower courts have applied the concept in upholding the right to wear one's hair as one wishes, to dress as one wishes in places of public employment, and the like.[91]

The technique of expanding a doctrine to cover questionable subjects was exemplified in the busing decisions of several states. In the mid-1970s, the Supreme Court held that lower courts in Detroit, Dayton, and Pasadena went further than was necessary in ordering busing to

---

[86]Both of these examples can be found in Johnson and Canon, *Judicial Policies,* 40.

[87]Arlen Specter, "*Mapp v. Ohio:* Pandora's Problems for the Prosecutor," *University of Pennsylvania Law Review* 111, No. 1. (Nov. 1962): 5.

[88]See Johnson and Canon, *Judicial Policies,* 168. In general, see Richard Lehne, *The Politics of School Finance Reform* (New York: Longman's, 1978).

[89]Johnson and Canon, *Judicial Policies,* 43. See also Robert Pear, "State Courts Move Beyond U.S. Bench in Rights Rulings," *New York Times* (May 4, 1986): A-1.

[90]Bradley G. Canon, "Testing the Effectiveness of Civil Liberties Policies at the State and Federal Levels: The Case of the Exclusionary Rule," *American Politics Quarterly* 5, No. 1 (Jan. 1977): 57.

[91]Johnson and Canon, *Judicial Policies,* 47.

achieve racial integration of schools.[92] The Supreme Court's sex discrimination rulings have also been expanded by some lower courts to extend to subjects (for instance, girls playing on boy's varsity high school sports teams) not initially covered by Supreme Court decisions.[93]

The expansion of appellate court doctrine can take on absurd dimensions, sometimes by taking appellate dicta (parts of a decision not directly relevant to the ruling) too seriously. Thus, Justice Douglas's rather uncharacteristic dictum in an early case upholding "release-time" religious instruction programs in public schools (*Zorach v. Clauson,* 343 U.S. 306 [1952]) that "we are a religious people whose institutions presuppose a Supreme Being" has been used by numerous lower court judges to justify a wide variety of religious practices in schools and elsewhere. In fact, one scholar noted that we could discuss *Zorach* "simply as a study in the misadventures of a dictum."[94] This same researcher reported that one federal judge went so far as to use the Douglas statement to deny a petition for naturalization to an atheist![95]

Appellate courts are not without power to discipline lower-court judges in attempts to bring them into line with extant judicial policy, but the tools available are of limited effectiveness. The use of the writ of mandamus, as with the power to impeach, is more the recognition of a failed policy than it is an effective tool to force compliance, except perhaps where resistance is isolated and idiosyncratic.[96] Most organizations employ the power of hiring and firing to bring underlings to heal, but appellate courts can hardly use this device. The professional norm is an informal and largely voluntary force for compliance; it is not a tool appellate courts can wield at will.

Clarity of appellate rulings, as well as their effective communication, can help, and ploys such as unanimous appellate decisions, perhaps authored by the chief justice, provide added weight to appellate court policies. But at bottom, when the centrifugal forces of localism and judicial federalism, with their attendant detractive political philosophies, result in a noncompliant posture, particularly when such resistance is intense or widespread, appellate courts are probably best advised to go slow, lest their inherent political weakness be revealed.

THE EXTRAJUDICIAL BUREAUCRACY

A number of power centers other than the obvious three branches of government exist to receive, respond to, enhance, ignore, evade, or resist the application of judicial policy. There is no convenient label to cover this conglomeration of agencies, bureaus, departments, and

---

[92]Johnson and Canon, *Judicial Policies,* 47. The cases are *Pasadena City Board of Education v. Spangler,* 427 U.S. 424 (1976); *Milliken v. Bradley,* 418 U.S. 717 (1974) and 433 U.S. 267 (1977); and *Dayton Board of Education v. Brinkman,* 433 U.S. 406 (1977).

[93]Johnson and Canon, *Judicial Policies,* 46–47.

[94]In general, see "The Precedent Expands," in Sorauf, *"Zorach v. Clauson,"* 787–90, particularly 788.

[95]Sorauf, "Zorach v. Clauson," 788–89.

[96]See, e.g., Johnson and Canon, *Judicial Policies,* 80, 92, and 217. In a rather unusual turn of events, state judges took to the lobbying trail in the late 1980s in an attempt to persuade Congress to overturn the Supreme Court's ruling in *Pulliam v. Allen,* 466 U.S. 522 (1984). *Pulliam* was seen as widening the arena of legally actionable practices of judges while on the bench. In his majority opinion, Justice Blackmun noted that " . . . it is up to Congress, not this court, to determine whether and to what extent to abrogate the judiciary's immunity." But to date, state judicial power in the legislative arena has not been sufficient to move Congress to act. Issues raised in *Pulliam* are discussed in Paul M. Bator et. al., *Hart and Wechsler's the Federal Courts and the Federal System,* 3rd ed. (Westbury, N.Y.: Foundation Press, 1988): 1305–07. See also Stephen Wermiel, "Judges Make Little Headway in Seeking Legislative Remedy to High Court Ruling," *Wall Street Journal* (Nov. 13, 1989): B-3.

even private institutions except perhaps the "extrajudicial bureaucracy."[97] We refer here to the almost countless bureaucracies in and out of government usually charged with implementing policies made elsewhere. They range from cabinet-level departments in the executive branch of the national government to street-level bureaucracies, such as local housing authorities, police departments, school boards, and welfare departments. Individuals such as state superintendents of public instruction, district attorneys, or state attorneys general are also at times included in this category. Hospitals, retail stores, bar associations, or other private organizations may also be included, depending upon the judicial policy in question.

Behaving largely in the organizational mode, these entities must interpret the judicial policies pertinent to their operations, search for alternative responses, and adjust their programs accordingly. The policies adopted in these three stages of response are, in turn, determined in large part by factors similar to those affecting the response of lower courts to appellate rulings—the clarity and communication of the judicial policy, the policy setting (political environment) within which the agency operates, and the internal dynamics of the agency itself.[98] Empirical studies in this arena of judicial policy implementation and impact have been quite popular since the 1950s.[99] Although space does not permit complete presentation here of these studies and their findings, a discussion of a few representative policy areas can illustrate the politics at work. Probably no research better represents this line of inquiry than studies focusing on police reaction to key criminal procedure rulings of the Supreme Court or the response of public schools to establishment of religion rulings. We will report some of the findings in each area.

The Exclusionary Rule

On June 19, 1961, the Supreme Court in *Mapp v. Ohio,* 367 U.S. 643, "nationalized" the exclusionary rule—that is, it held that evidence pertinent to an alleged crime gathered in violation of the prohibition against the unreasonable searches and seizures provision of the Fourth Amendment could not be used in state courts. The rule had been in force in proceedings in federal courts since 1914 (*Weeks v. U.S.,* 232 U.S. 383), but in *Wolf v. Colorado,* 338 U.S. 25, in 1949, the Court expressly refused to apply this evidentiary limitation to the states. *Mapp* reversed *Wolf* and was something of a bombshell to local courts and law enforcement officials. Leaving aside the issue of whether the doctrine was effectively rescinded by subsequent Court rulings, our interest here is with the reception of the rule by state and local police officials.[100]

As with most impact research, the evidence for the implementation of *Mapp* is mixed. On the one hand, findings from several early studies tend to support the conclusion that *Mapp* brought about significant changes in police behavior in the desired direction. Senator Arlen Specter (R-Penn.) who at the time of the *Mapp* ruling was assistant district attorney in Philadelphia, concluded that *Mapp* "revolutionized" police practices and prosecutorial procedures in many states. "There can be no doubt," he said, "that the *Mapp* de-

[97]The term used by Johnson and Canon in *Judicial Policies* is "the implementing population" (see their Chapter 3)—although lower courts, which they call "interpreting populations," are among the most important implementers, illustrating once again the seamless web of policy.

[98]These categories are suggested by Johnson and Canon, *Judicial Policies,* 81–86.

[99]See, e.g., Richard M. Johnson, *The Dynamics of Compliance* (Evanston, Ill.: Northwestern University Press, 1967); Kenneth M. Dolbeare and Philip E. Hammond, *The School Prayer Decisions: From Court Policy to Local Practice* (Chicago: University of Chicago Press, 1971); and selected studies cited in Charles S. Bullock III and Charles M. Lamb, *Implementation of Civil Rights Policy* (Monterey, Calif.: Brooks/Cole, 1984).

[100]For exceptions to the exclusionary rule, see *U.S. v. Leon,* 468 U.S. 897 (1984) and *Nix v. Williams,* 467 U.S. 431 (1984).

cision has significantly impaired the ability of the police to secure evidence to convict the guilty."[101] Consistent with the Specter report are data from a study by Michael J. Murphy, former police commissioner of New York, which indicated that although search warrants in New York City were rarely used prior in 1961, from the summer of 1961 through 1965, nearly 20,000 had been obtained by New York police. Said Murphy of the *Mapp* ruling, "I can think of no decision in recent times in the field of law enforcement which had such a dramatic and traumatic effect as this."[102]

On the other hand, the most common ideological posture of the police in America is the one described in the crime control model outlined in Chapter 9. Thus, the police tend to see their principal task as apprehending criminals, and the courts have no business interfering. Given this set of attitudes, police in some jurisdictions found means of sidestepping the real intent of *Mapp,* which was to stop illegal searches and seizures, along with violations of privacy, harassment, and even brutality often accompanying such behavior. One ploy was simply to keep the case out of court. For example, studies in New York and New Haven reported continuing police harassment of suspects—aggressive and sometimes physically harmful home and person searches, hostile and threatening interrogations, and the like— that might lead to incriminating evidence or even confessions, but which seldom came under the scrutiny of police supervisors or judges. The point is, the *Mapp* sanction of the inadmissibility of evidence sometimes failed to achieve the desired result precisely because police were willing to pay the price to achieve a more valued goal—crime control through continued harassment and brutality against society's "undesirables."[103] Civil actions against the police in such situations are always possible, but the victims seldom pursue such remedies.

Further research on the reception of the *Mapp* ruling by police departments was undertaken by Bradley Canon in a pre- and post-*Mapp* study in nineteen cities. Measuring the decision's impact by rates of arrest for search and seizure offenses, Canon found the effect of the decision to be negligible in slightly over half the cities studied. The chief explanatory variable appeared to be the politicolegal stance of police and city leaders. Where resistance, if not defiance, was advocated by the local police chief and others similarly situated, police behavior seemed to be largely unaffected by the *Mapp* ruling.[104]

School Prayers

Few judicial rulings have evoked more comment and resistance, especially at the national level, than have the Supreme Court's so-called prayer decisions. In 1962, In *Engel v. Vitale,* 370 U.S. 421, the Warren Court held that the recitation of a 22-word nonsectarian prayer composed by the New York State Board of Regents constituted an "establishment" of religion in violation of the First Amendment. A year later, in *School District of Abington Township v. Schempp,* 374 U.S. 203, the Court made clear its disapproval of such practices by placing daily public school Bible reading and the recitation of the Lord's Prayer in the same prohibited "establishment" category. The storm of protest and continuing political maneuverings in response to these rulings are described elsewhere.[105] Our central concern here is the response of local school officials to these decisions.

---

[101]See Specter, "*Mapp v. Ohio,*" 42.

[102]Michael J. Murphy, "Judicial Review of Police Methods in Law Enforcement: The Problem of Compliance by Police Departments," *Texas Law Review* 44, No. 5 (Apr. 1966): 941.

[103]See Jerome H. Skolnick, *Justice Without Trial: Law Enforcement in Democratic Society* (New York: Wiley, 1966), especially 211–25. Support for this conclusion may be found throughout the Skolnick book.

[104]Canon, "Testing the Effectiveness": 71–72.

[105]The literature on responses to the prayer decisions is vast. See, e.g., Dolbeare and Hammond, *School Prayer Decisions;* Donald R. Reich, "The Impact of Judicial Decision Making: The School Prayer Cases," in Everson, *Supreme Court as Policy Maker,* 44–81. See also Wasby, *Impact of the United States Supreme Court;* and Johnson and Canon, *Judicial Policies,* passim.

Given the religious diversity of the nation, it is not surprising that school practices bearing on the *Engel* and *Schempp* doctrine varied quite widely both before and after the decisions were handed down. Accordingly, attitudes toward the rulings have ranged from being seen as a legitimizing force to solidify policies already favored within the state (such as in California) to a symbol of further federal encroachment on the rights of citizens in a free society (much of the South and border states). Data from national surveys focusing on the attitudes and behavior of teachers and other school officials have clearly documented a significant degree of compliance with the rulings in all parts of the nation, though strong regional variations were reported. For example, H. Frank Way, Jr., reporting the responses from a national survey of 2,320 public elementary teachers in 464 schools in 1964–1965, found that whereas 60 percent of the teachers had had prayers in their classrooms prior to the Supreme Court decisions, this figure dropped to 28 percent after the rulings. Regarding Bible reading, the percentages changed from 48 percent to 22 percent.[106] A similar 1960–1966 before and after national survey of religious practices in public schools revealed a definite drop in Bible reading (41 percent of school districts reported having the practice in 1960 but only 13 percent in 1966). As to regular devotional services, this same study found that 33 percent of the school districts surveyed reported that all schools in their system had such programs in 1960, whereas the comparable figure for 1966 was only 8 percent.[107]

Seemingly belying these rather impressive compliance figures are extensive regional variations, along with what turned out to be a characteristic school district response pattern—namely, teacher option. Not surprisingly, data from Southern and border states, where religious fundamentalism is more pronounced, revealed high levels of noncompliance. In a 1964 Texas survey of high school and junior high school principals, nearly three-quarters of the respondents reported Bible reading in their schools, both before and after the Supreme Court decisions. Data from surveys in Kentucky and Indiana also revealed low compliance rates: only a little more than one-fourth of the Kentucky school districts had discontinued prayer and Bible reading in response to the judicial edicts, and only about 6 percent of Indiana school boards had altered their policies in response to the Court's decisions.[108]

A familiar pattern of "no policy" emerged in several states. State or local superintendents would frequently issue no directives at all in response to constitutional bans on overt religious practices in their schools, leaving to the principal or teacher the determination of what was to be done. A not-dissimilar policy found in some states or local school districts was one based on a "permissive" interpretation of the Supreme Court's rulings: states may not *require* religious exercises in their schools, but must ensure the free exercise of religion for all. Hence, as long as no overt coercion was involved, schools and schoolteachers were free to do as they wished. In either case—no policy or a permissive interpretation of the Court's ruling—the actual result was often to continue religious practices in the schools as before, except in the unlikely event a local suit required otherwise. In the case of prayer and Bible reading in the schools, passive resistance worked. Doing nothing resulted in a de facto policy of circumvention of the Court's edicts. The national survey results reported by Frank Way, Jr., document the pervasiveness of this policy of no policy. Of the teachers responding to the survey in 1964–1965, 1,011, or 62 percent, indicated that their school had adopted this approach.

A study of the implementation of the prayer and Bible reading decisions in five Indiana communities illustrates the somewhat more subtle evasion of judicial policy that can

---

[106]H. Frank Way, Jr., "Survey Research on Judicial Decisions: The Prayer and Bible-reading Cases," *Western Political Quarterly* 22, No. 2 (June 1968): 190–91.

[107]The original study is Richard B. Dierenfield, *Religion and the Public Schools* (Washington: Public Affairs Press, 1962). The follow-up data can be found in Reich, "Impact of Judicial Decision-Making," 46–52.

[108]Wasby, *Impact of the United States Supreme Court,* 131.

result from a permissive or no-policy stance. The remarks of one school superintendent illustrate the permissive interpretation of the decisions just referred to:

> The way I interpret this is that school boards, state, etc., cannot prescribe a certain religious prayer. I feel that the teacher, on her own volition, may use religious readings, prayer, etc., as long as it is not offensive to a child. In that event, I think the child can be excluded from that portion which is offensive to him. We plan to continue until *forced* to stop.[109]

As this policy filtered down to one teacher, she concluded that "I just accepted the fact that they weren't going to allow prayer." But the person who interviewed this teacher stated that

> She may not have prayers every morning, but she does just about every other thing religious one could think of. She has Sunday School charts up on her walls, . . . stars for . . . Sunday School, . . . Christmas and Easter stories, . . . Nativity scenes.[110]

Concluding, the interviewer quoted her as saying, "I'm not able to be at the church anymore, but I feel I compensate by what I do in school."[111] Finally, another teacher, elderly and a former Sunday School teacher in the local Methodist Church, appeared to pull out all stops: "I consider it my professional responsibility to teach children religion." Students in her classes

> start out every morning with a morning prayer and they start off every afternoon with an afternoon prayer, and they say grace before they have lunch. They sing Sunday School songs, . . . learn new songs on Sunday in order to teach their classmates, . . . [hear] Bible stories every afternoon, [are taught] prayers and religious poems, . . . [as well as being read] Christmas and Easter stories.[112]

Illustrating, if nothing else, the continued defiance of local school districts to the Supreme Court's prayer decisions, a current ploy is to leave religious instruction ostensibly in the hands of students, though with behind-the-scenes official endorsement.[113] Thus, for example, the superintendent of schools in Pontotoc County, Mississippi, argued in 1996 that widespread religious practices in his schools were wholly initiated and operated by students: "The school did not write any prayers or force anyone to say anything," he said. "There has been [only] student-initiated, voluntary activity, controlled by the students. If they had not initiated it, there would have been no prayer."[114]

Nonetheless, Federal District Judge Neal Biggers, Jr., of Mississippi, ruled on June 3, 1996, that the county schools had violated the First Amendment by including in their daily regimen prayers recited each day over the school intercom, more prayers before lunch, Bible classes led by instructors selected and paid by the local churches (a community tradition of fifty years standing), and religious observances. Such practices had widespread support from local as well as national political leaders such as Mississippi's Gover-

---

[109]Dolbeare and Hammond, *School Prayer Decisions,* 42–43, emphasis in original.
[110]Dolbeare and Hammond, *School Prayer Decisions,* 76–77.
[111]Dolbeare and Hammond, *School Prayer Decisions,* 77.
[112]Dolbeare and Hammond, *School Prayer Decisions,* 77.
[113]This approach was probably inspired by the Court's holding in *Lee v. Weisman,* 112 S. Ct. 2649 (1992), which, depending on one's reading of the fractured opinion, held that members of the clergy, in league with school officials, could not compose and deliver prayers at school commencements, implying, perhaps, that student-initiated commencement prayers would be acceptable. This student option seemed to be sanctioned in Texas in 1992. *Jones v. Clear Creek Independent School District,* 977 F. 2d 963 (5th Cir. 1992), cert denied 113 S. Ct. 2950 (1993). See Louis Fisher, *Constitutional Rights: Civil Rights and Civil Liberties* (New York: McGraw-Hill, 1995), 795.
[114]Peter Applebome, "Court Restricts Prayer at Mississippi School," *New York Times* (June 4, 1996): A-7.

nor Kirk Fordice, as well as both U.S. Senators Trent Lott and Thad Cochran, the former being selected Majority Leader of the U.S. Senate to replace Robert Dole.

Children whose parents protested these "non-policies" had earphones placed on their heads and/or were led out of class in front of the other children. One teacher was reported to have said to her class that "children who believe in God stay in Bible class and those who do not, go someplace else." The school superintendent called the federal court's decision "a setback for religious freedom."[115]

These research findings pertaining to the implementation of Supreme Court decisions in the areas of due process in criminal proceedings and the establishment of religion underscore the power of local bureaucracies in ultimately determining the import of judicial policy. It is not too much to say that depending upon the Court decision in question and the tenor of local bureaucratic politics, the semivisible local elites have almost complete power over the ultimate meaning of often-celebrated decisions of the United States Supreme Court. Clearly, as Llewellyn has emphasized, law is less what the rule provides than "what officials do."

INTEREST GROUPS, PUBLIC OPINION, AND THE MEDIA

We conclude our discussion of the implementation of judicial policy with a brief consideration of three residual forces that influence in different ways the ultimate impact of court decisions—namely, interest groups, public opinion, and the media. The first point to be made about these entities, particularly public opinion and the media, is that they are sufficiently amorphous so as to render precise statements about their effects rather difficult. While more sharply defined, interest groups share some of the characteristics of public opinion, it being difficult at times to distinguish between the two. Our knowledge of the role of the media in judicial policy implementation is likewise imprecise, in part because the press and other organs of the mass media behave like interest groups in some situations, while at other times seeming to be the voice of public opinion.

A related point is that these three entities more often than not impinge on judicial policy implementation (and ultimate impact) indirectly, frequently operating through the legislative and executive branches, or even through lower courts, so that to an extent we have already taken account of these in the preceding discussion. For example, as we have shown, Congress responds as it does to Supreme Court rulings in large part because of the activities of political interest groups or the state of public opinion relative to the issue in question. The media, too, are not without influence in this process. Similarly, lower courts may (or may not) implement appellate judicial rulings due to community elite opinion, particularly when that is stronger than the force of professional norms.

At the same time, interest groups, public opinion, and the media can operate directly on the judicial process. Groups, for example, can employ a number of tactics to directly affect judicial policy and policy impact. These tactics may act either to enhance or to retard policy implementation, depending upon the goals of the relevant groups. The implementation of judicial policy favorable to interest group goals can be encouraged and enhanced by a wide range of tactics running the gamut of the judicial process, such as attempting to shape public opinion in a manner consistent with the new judicial policy; joining with other groups to lobby for policy enhancement; pressing for the recruitment of policy-makers likely to facilitate the expansion of the policy in question (and opposing can-

---

[115]Applebome, "Court Restricts." In *Moore v. Ingebretson*, No. 96–331, Nov. 4, 1996, the Supreme Court denied *certiorari,* thus in effect upholding, the Mississippi federal court ruling. See Linda Greenhouse, "Supreme Court Roundup," *New York Times,* Nov. 5, 1996: A-8, section on "School Prayer."

didates for office who may deter the desired policy); and using the tool of litigation itself, including amicus curiae briefs, to achieve further judicial victories calculated to clarify, expand, or enforce policy already in place. Interest groups regularly employ these and similar tactics in response to judicial policy. Conversely, they also employ the opposite tactics to impede the impact of undesired judicial decisions. Some examples in each category follow.

The initial decision of the Supreme Court in the legislative reapportionment revolution, *Baker v. Carr,* 369 U.S. 186 (1962), merely opened the courts to suits by urban political interests who had long been denied equal representation. The decision held that legislative apportionment was a justiciable issue, contrary to the common understanding of the earlier ruling in *Colgrove v. Green,* 328 U.S. 549 (1946), which held legislative apportionment to be a "political" issue beyond the reach of judicial power. Accordingly, numerous local, state, and national political interest groups, both those in existence and those newly formed, filed suit to implement *Baker* and to gain the fruits of greater legislative representation.[116] A similar flurry of litigation followed *Brown v. Board of Education,* with the NAACP and other groups filing suit to implement the decision. Such interest group activity has usually significantly enhanced the effect of these decisions. In contrast, implementation of the school prayer decisions did not appear to be advanced or, for that matter, retarded by interest group activities. In one Indiana study, for example, relevant interest groups, such as teachers' organizations and civil liberties associations, were not found to have taken aggressive action in support of decision implementation in that state, resulting in the "noncompliance by inaction" response pattern.[117]

When interest groups find themselves in opposition to judicial rulings, they can often be effective in nullifying or at least limiting the impact of the decisions. This appeared to be the case in the period immediately following the *Miranda* ruling, which required a suspect in police custody to be informed of his rights. Both local and national police associations, including the FBI, took a stance of seeming compliance but actual opposition, at least to the spirit of the ruling, by offering advice on how the impact of the decision could be minimized or how the requirements of the *Miranda* warnings could be avoided altogether.[118]

Interest groups may also use the more formal route of litigation and related approaches to seek modification or reversal of judicial policies they oppose. Such tactics have traditionally been seen as a way of explaining initial access to the judicial arena—how cases reach courts—but they may also be viewed as an aspect of judicial policy implementation and impact. For example, in the early case of *Corrigan v. Buckley,* 271 U.S. 323 (1926), the Supreme Court held that racially restrictive covenants in housing contracts, because they were entirely private agreements, did not violate the Fourteenth Amendment's Equal Protection clause. This, in effect, permitted racial segregation in housing in large sections of the country. Attorneys for the NAACP sought for twenty years to reverse this decision. Through repeated petitions for *certiorari* and amicus curiae briefs in addition to scholarly law journal articles and books critical of the precedent, they succeeded in keeping the issue before the public and helping to create a climate of opinion favorable to their cause. Finding just the right cases for their purpose, they provided legal counsel and other assistance to black petitioners in five different but similar cases throughout the nation. Winning a grant of *certiorari* in 1945, NAACP lawyers finally succeeded in persuading the Court, in effect, to overturn the *Corrigan* ruling, the new doctrine being that restrictive covenants cannot be enforced in state courts (*Shelly v. Kraemer,* 334 U.S. 1 [1948]).[119]

---

[116]The role of interest groups in implementing the reapportionment decisions has been widely documented. See, e.g., Bushnell, *Impact of Reapportionment,* passim.

[117]See Dolbeare and Hammond, *School Prayer Decisions,* 54–64.

[118]Johnson and Canon, *Judicial Policies,* 168.

[119]A classic study of these activities is Clement E. Vose, *Caucasians Only: The Supreme Court, the NAACP and the Restrictive Covenant Cases* (Berkeley: University of California Press, 1959).

Although not all political interest groups have the resources to sustain such a lengthy litigation crusade, the work of the NAACP in this and other cases illustrates the potential significance of this strategy. A more common litigation approach of interest groups is through lower courts, attempting to persuade them to make narrow or even contradictory interpretations of appellate court rules opposed by the groups. In any case, through tactics ranging from informal pressures on local bureaucracies to formal litigation, including shifting to alternative policy arenas, interest groups have an array of possible tools in influencing implementation and impact of judicial rulings. Even indirect approaches through attempts to mold and shape public opinion are not without success, as the NAACP efforts in this case attest.[120]

In her excellent overview essay on interest group influence on judicial policy-making, Lee Epstein points out the slow start (and some backward steps) in moving political scientists into this fruitful arena of research.[121] Following the publication of David Truman's influential work, *The Governmental Process* in 1951[122] and Jack Peltason's even more pointed theoretical essay on the subject, *Federal Courts in the Political Process* in 1955,[123] scholars in the subfield (with notable exceptions) were slow in following up these important theoretical leads by empirically examining the work of interest groups in this regard. Of late, however, there has been significant renewed interest in the subject. Yet, the focus of this newer research has tended to be on the twin topics of interest group sponsorship of litigation, following the earlier cited Vose study, and participation in amicus curiae briefs, largely before the Supreme Court.[124] Another arena of renewed research emphasis concerns the role of interest groups in judicial selection.[125] Research in all of these areas has been discussed in previous chapters.

Group activity in influencing the judicial process at the impact/compliance stage, notes Epstein, has been much less studied. One way to enter this arena is to inquire into the impact of group sponsorship of litigation. Did such activity ultimately make any difference? One such study, undertaken by Joseph Stewart and James Sheffield, focused on civil rights litigation in the electoral process in Mississippi. Their results show

> litigation being effective in boosting black voter registration and black candidacies for public office. . . . [But as to] promoting [voter] turnout for black candidates and . . . electing blacks to office . . . [group sponsored] litigation does not appear to be directly useful.[126]

Studies of public opinion vis-à-vis the judiciary have largely failed to demonstrate precise links between it and the implementation of judicial decisions. There are several

---

[120]In an interesting piece of research, Joseph Kobylka has shown how interest groups opposed to Supreme Court policy change in the field of establishment of religion—change that seemed sure to come with more conservative Reagan and Bush justices appointed to the Court—have been successful in forestalling change, at least thus far, by the careful fashioning of legal arguments by attorneys representing key liberal civil liberties groups. See his essay "The Mysterious Case of Establishment Clause Litigation: How Organized Litigants Foiled Legal Change," in Lee Epstein, ed., *Contemplating Courts* (Washington: Congressional Quarterly Press, 1995): 93–128.

[121]Lee Epstein, "Courts and Interest Groups," in John B. Gates and Charles A. Johnson, eds, *The American Courts: A Critical Assessment* (Washington: Congressional Quarterly Press, 1991), 335–71.

[122]New York, Knopf.

[123]New York, Random House. See examples of the current application of Peltason's group process orientation in Austin Ranney, ed., *Courts and the Political Process: Jack Peltason's Contributions to Political Science* (Berkeley: Institute of Governmental Studies Press, 1996).

[124]In particular, Epstein cites not only the early Vose work but also her own more recent research, along with that of Sorauf, Cortner, O'Connor, and others. See her essay at 345–49. Recent amicus curiae research cited is that of Caldeira, O'Connor, and Bruer, and others (345–50).

[125]See, e.g., Gregory A. Caldeira and John R. Wright, "Lobbying for Justice: The Rise of Organized Conflict in the Politics of Federal Judgeships," in Lee Epstein, ed., *Contemplating Courts,* 44–71.

[126]Joseph Stewart, Jr., and James F. Sheffield, Jr., "Does Interest Group Litigation Matter? The Case of Black Political Mobilization in Mississippi," *Journal of Politics* 49, No. 3 (Aug. 1987): 780, 795.

reasons for this situation. One factor is that public opinion is so closely entwined with other forces, such as legislative action, executive pressures, interest group activity, and the like, that it is difficult to determine exactly what force produces what implementation outcome.[127] Moreover, public opinion, even in this relatively sophisticated era of polling, is difficult to measure. This is especially so regarding attitudes toward the judiciary, because if there is anything on which polling results in this area agree, it is that only a minority of the public (often called the "attentive public") knows or appears to care very much about the judiciary and its policies. Hence, a study of attitudes toward the Supreme Court in late 1966 revealed that although the mass public was willing to utter opinions about the Court (about 70 percent of the respondents had some views on the subject), very few could support their views with specific information. In fact, fewer than half (46 percent) could recall anything at all the Court had done recently.[128]

Other research has produced similar results. A Wisconsin public opinion poll, again in 1966, reported that when respondents were asked to specify what they liked and disliked about the Supreme Court, fewer than 20 percent could be even as specific as mentioning civil rights or the prayer decisions.[129] In all, public opinion polls have repeatedly demonstrated (1) the low level of public knowledge of the Court, (2) the willingness of respondents to utter opinions in spite of this lack of knowledge, and (3) the importance of the distinction between the "mass public" and the "attentive public" in discussing the role of public opinion in judicial policy-making and implementation. On the third point, one study concluded that the Supreme Court is

> almost exclusively an object of elite attention— . . . elites are more responsive to, more knowledgeable of, and more confident in the Court, and therefore more likely to be channels by which Court-initiated policies become transformed into local practice or at least are acted upon in some way.[130]

If the "attentive public" constitutes the relevant sector of public opinion regarding the judiciary, the next question is, What evidence exists as to the influence of this force on judi-

---

[127]Karen O'Connor, in studying women's interest groups and the judiciary, notes that "studying the impact of prior publicity in evaluating publicity-oriented strategies . . . creates unique problems." See her *Women's Organizations Use of the Courts* (Lexington, Mass.: Lexington Books, 1980), 50. The point was underscored by Lee Epstein, who added that "indeed, disentangling the effect of publicity-oriented strategies [of interest groups] from actual litigation campaigns presents an interesting research challenge." Epstein, "Courts and Interest Groups," 365.

An excellent survey and appraisal of research on public opinion and the judiciary is Gregory A. Caldeira, "Courts and Public Opinion," in John B. Gates and Charles A. Johnson, eds., *The American Courts: A Critical Assessment* (Washington: Congressional Quarterly Press, 1991), 303–34. As to the key research issues involved, the influence of courts on public opinion and the reverse, the impact of public opinion on courts, Caldeira concludes that after a quarter century of work, "we have precious few findings and generalizations planted in solid empirical soil. We possess even less theoretical understanding" (326–27). However, see William Mishler and Reginald S. Sheehan, "The Supreme Court as a Countermajoritarian Institution? The Impact of Public Opinion on Supreme Court Decisions," *American Political Science Review* 87, No. 1 (March 1993): 87–101. There scholars show a congruence of public opinion with Supreme Court decisions over time, though with a divergence in the era of the Rehnquist Court.

[128]Walter F. Murphy, Joseph Tanenhaus, and Daniel L. Kastner, *Public Evaluations of Constitutional Courts: Alternative Explanations* (Beverly Hills, Calif.: Sage, 1973), 111 and passim. Caldeira ("Courts and Public Opinion": 322) termed the Murphy and Tannenhaus research—"one of the best and most carefully planned of the previous studies."

[129]Kenneth M. Dolbeare and Phillip E. Hammond, "The Political Party Basis of Attitudes Toward the Supreme Court," *Public Opinion Quarterly* 32, No. 1 (Spring 1968): 20. These authors go on to remark, "In both national and state samples, far more people express attitudes toward the Court than could be said to have any substantial degree of knowledge about it," 21.

[130]Dolbeare and Hammond, *School Prayer Decisions,* 23.

cial policy implementation? The answer is not very much, or at least not much that indicates a major role for this sector of opinion.[131] Since detailed knowledge about specific judicial decisions is so sparse, even among members of the attentive public, and certainly among the public at large, those charged with implementing judicial policy are seldom either encouraged or restrained by public opinion to any significant degree. The most prominent variable pertaining to this process is probably the extent to which the judicial decision in question is personally felt by the public. However, very few Court decisions fall within this category. Indeed, drawing upon the range of existing research, probably only the abortion, school segregation and prayer decisions qualify. We might, then, expect implementation of decisions in these two areas to be in some way affected by public opinion. Certainly there is a good deal of evidence that this effect was felt in the case of *Brown v. Board of Education,* where both mass and elite opinions strongly opposed the Court's policy. Similarly, Dolbeare and Hammond report that elite opinion was important, at least in a general way, in explaining the local Indiana policy of "do nothing" in response to the school prayer decisions.[132] But in general, the judiciary and its policies are not particularly visible to the public, leaving implementation to be influenced by more tangible and proximate forces.[133]

The role of the media in judicial policy-making in general, and judicial policy implementation in particular, is equally problematic. Press coverage, even of the Supreme Court and its decisions, is not extensive, and available research indicates a certain superficiality in this field of journalism.[134] Only a handful of reporters representing such major news entities as the *New York Times,* the *Washington Post,* National Public Radio, and the wire services, regularly cover the Supreme Court. Reporting can be inaccurate, and the choice of which decisions to headline can lead to underreporting otherwise significant rulings.[135] When Supreme Court decisions were announced only on Mondays, considerable pressure was placed on journalists to report on a large number of decisions in a very short time.

---

[131]Johnson and Canon note that

> Because public opinion about judicial policies is so vague and ill-informed, and because researchers and pollsters rarely ask questions about specific Court decisions, it is difficult to discuss what impact the public may have on the implementation of judicial decisions." Johnson and Canon, *Judicial Policies,* 178.

[132]Dolbeare and Hammond, *School Prayer Decisions,* 23.

[133]The relationship between public opinion and judicial policy implementation is analyzed by Stephen Wasby. See his *Impact of the United States Supreme Court,* 233–42. His summary statements on 242 are particularly useful. See also the discussion of diffuse support for the judiciary in Ch. 13.

For an insightful study of the role of public opinion in and the impact of the abortion decisions, see Gerald N. Rosenberg, "The Real World of Constitutional Rights: The Supreme Court and the Implementation of the Abortion Decisions," in Lee Epstein, ed., *Contemplating Courts* (Washington: Congressional Quarterly Press, 1995), 390–419, and the sources cited therein. Rosenberg reports the very low level of public awareness that the Court had even handed down abortion decisions (403–04), even as much as a decade after *Roe v. Wade* was announced, along with poll data which show that the decisions themselves had very little impact in changing opinion over time. See also Charles H. Franklin and Liane C. Kosaki, "Republican Schoolmaster: The U.S. Supreme Court, Public Opinion, and Abortion," *American Political Science Review* 83, No. 3 (Sept. 1989): 751–71.

[134]On media coverage of judicial subjects in general, see Doris A. Graber, *Mass Media and American Politics.* 4th ed. (Washington: Congressional Quarterly Press, 1993), 327–32. A helpful recent essay on the media and the Supreme Court is Charles H. Franklin and Liane C. Kosaki, "Media, Knowledge, and Public Evaluation of the Supreme Court," in Lee Epstein, ed., *Contemplating Courts* (Washington: Congressional Quarterly Press, 1995), 352–75. On state courts, see Robert E. Drechsel, "Uncertain Dancers: Judges and the News Media," *Judicature* 70, No. 5 (Feb.–Mar. 1987): 264–72.

[135]Graber, *Mass Media:* 330. Graber reports that in a recent term of the Supreme Court, even the *New York Times* failed to report a fourth of its written opinions. She also reports research findings illustrating the inaccuracy of much Supreme Court coverage in a wide sampling of metropolitan daily papers.

Spreading out the announcement of decisions over the week has helped; but still, the piling up of decisions, especially at the end of the term, gives reporters and writers little time to intelligently digest and report Supreme Court opinions.

The dearth of media attention to things judicial is even more clearly illustrated in figures on TV network early evening news coverage of the three branches of the national government. During a twelve-month period in 1990–1991, researchers report that ABC, CBS, and NBC together telecast an average of 131 news stories per month on some aspect of the presidency, 92 stories on Congress, and only 12 on the Supreme Court. As measured by percentage of network time devoted to these three branches of government by the three network evening news telecasts, the presidency on average received 62.8 percent, Congress 36.5 percent, and the Supreme Court only 3.3 percent.[136]

The role of the media is best seen as a two-way street or a link between the judiciary and its public. The media serve as a conduit of information for both parties: the public is informed of recent judicial doings, and the judges receive feedback as to public reaction to their decisions. Evidence that judicial decisions are influenced by media feedback is scant, though in one case—*Gannett v. DePasquale,* 443 U.S. 368 (1979)—press reaction quite possibly influenced the ultimate policy outcome. In that decision, the Court held, or at least implied, that the public's right to free access to trials was not guaranteed by the Sixth Amendment. After highly unfavorable press reaction, the Court appeared to reverse itself in *Richmond Newspapers v. Virginia,* 448 U.S. 555 (1980), by reasserting a First Amendment public right of access to trials.[137]

As to the influence of the media in policy implementation, we have little direct evidence. The media, of course, help to set the agenda, as policy analysts say, for public and elite debate about judicial decisions, and in that capacity obviously play a role in helping to shape public reactions to judicial policy. But precisely what that role is, is not well understood. As Johnson and Canon remark, "Whether the media's accounts of decisions and of reactions to them affect either the originating court or the other responding populations is an unanswered question."[138] In general, either the question of the media's impact on judicial policy implementation is not addressed by researchers, or when it rarely is, no effect is found. For an example of the latter, a study of press coverage of racial desegregation in Louisville and Nashville found that the media seemed to have little effect on the "white flight" response to desegregation rulings.[139]

As the research findings reported in this chapter abundantly demonstrate, policy must be seen as a seamless web, with implementation and ultimate impact just as important as the initial policy-making. The continuing political struggle following the announcement of judicial policy involves a very wide assortment of competing centers of power, where the impact of the initial policy is "finally" determined, if we can speak of finality at all in the circularity of politics. The processes of interpreting, implementing, administering, or even consuming policy are not easily distinguishable one from the other, for pressures on extant policy—which is to say, politics—are ubiquitous.

The discussion thus far has focused on the implementation of judicial policy. But as suggested in the discussion of the judicial bureaucracy, courts can also be seen as agencies that administer or implement policy made elsewhere, particularly congressional or admin-

---

[136]Graber, *Mass Media:* Tables 9–1 and 9–2. More detailed data on media coverage of the Supreme Court may be found in Franklin and Kosaki, "Media, Knowledge," 356–60.

[137]Baum, *The Supreme Court,* 154.

[138]Johnson and Canon, *Judicial Policies,* 175. However, one scholar asserts, without citing empirical evidence, that "widespread adverse publicity about Supreme Court decisions outlawing prayers in public schools has encouraged individuals and entire school systems to ignore that ban." See Graber, *Mass Media,* 331.

[139]Johnson and Canon, *Judicial Policies,* 175.

istrative agency policy. This view of the judicial role is consistent with the earlier (Chapter 2) discussion of courts as multifaceted political agencies capable of a variety of governmental tasks. A particularly insightful case study of courts functioning in this capacity is the recent work of R. S. Melnick focusing on the implementation of the Clean Air Act of 1970.[140] Far from deferring to the expertise of administrative agencies (in this case, the Environmental or Protection Agency), a stance long associated with judicial review of administrative rulings, the federal courts in this instance not only adjudicated claims brought under the Act, but also "legislated" in significant areas of air pollution policy left unclear by the new law. And rather than checking or limiting overly aggressive administrative action, the courts, for the most part, led Congress and the EPA in the development of new doctrines and even new organizational tools and structures in an effort to enhance the effectiveness of the Act. A particularly interesting finding of this research was the tendency of federal district courts to bow to the pressures from state and local interests to dull the cutting edge of the Act, while the Court of Appeals for the D.C. Circuit, because of differences in judicial structure—hence, politics—was likely to lean toward a more aggressive, creative posture in not always successful attempts to further the goals of the legislation.[141] Some observers have been so struck with this new role of the courts as to label these developments the "new era" in administrative law.[142]

The case of the Clean Air Act is but one example of the significant expansion of the judicial role in implementing policy initiated elsewhere. In recent decades, American courts have participated in, if not led, the supervision and administrative reform of governmental activities as diverse as medical care, corrections, public schools, mental health services, housing, and food and drug regulation, among others.[143] In fact, the judicial function in such cases is said to move beyond adjudication in the ordinary sense of hearing disputes and rendering decisions. Courts are now acting more as regulatory agencies or even as top administrators of agencies of government, taking on a role that has been called "political powerbroker."[144]

One issue emerging from the exercise of judicial power of this nature and breadth is the effectiveness of court-devised remedies. Are courts equipped to engage in such institutional reform? This, in turn, raises the larger question of whether the judicial process and judicial institutions carry inherent limitations in this and other policy roles. These issues will be addressed in the concluding chapter as part of an overall assessment of courts in American society.

FURTHER READING

Baum, Lawrence. "Implementation of Judicial Decisions: An Organizational Perspective." *American Politics Quarterly* 4, No. 1 (Jan. 1986): 86–114.

Becker, Theodore L., and Malcolm M. Feeley, eds. *The Impact of Supreme Court Decisions: Empirical Studies,* 2nd ed. New York: Oxford University Press, 1973.

---

[140]See R. Shep Melnick, *Regulation and the Courts: The Case of the Clean Air Act* (Washington, D.C.: Brookings Institution, 1983).

[141]Melnick, *Regulation and the Courts.* Another work that richly illustrates the role of the courts in policy implementation is Robert A. Katzmann, *Institutional Disability: The Saga of Transportation Policy for the Disabled* (Washington, D.C.: Brookings Institution, 1986).

[142]See Melnick, *Regulation and the Courts,* 9–13.

[143]See Colin S. Diver, "The Judge as Political Powerbroker: Superintending Structural Change in Public Institutions," *Virginia Law Review* 65, No. 1 (Feb. 1979): 44–45.

[144]Diver, "Judge as Political Powerbroker," 46.

Caldeira, Gregory A. "Courts and Public Opinion." In John B. Gates and Charles A. Johnson, eds. *The American Courts: A Critical Assessment.* Washington: Congressional Quarterly Press, 1991, 303–34.

Canon, Bradley C. "Studying the Impact of Judicial Decisions: A Period of Stagnation and Prospects for the Future," paper presented at the annual meeting of the American Political Science Association, Denver, Sept. 2–5, 1982.

Dolbeare, Kenneth M., and Phillip E. Hammond. *The School Prayer Decisions: From Court Policy to Local Practice.* Chicago: University of Chicago Press, 1971.

Epstein, Lee. "Courts and Interest Groups." In John B. Gates and Charles A. Johnson, eds., *The American Courts: A Critical Assessment.* Washington: Congressional Quarterly Press, 1991, 335–71.

Eskridge, William N., Jr. "Overriding Supreme Court Statutory Interpretation Decisions." *Yale Law Journal* 101, No. 2 (Nov. 1991): 331–417.

Franklin, Charles H., and Liane C. Kosaki. "Media, Knowledge, and Public Evaluations of the Supreme Court." In Lee Epstein, ed., *Contemplating Courts.* Washington: Congressional Quarterly Press, 1995, 352–75.

Ignagi, Joseph, and James Meernik, "Explaining Congressional Attempts to Reverse Supreme Court Decisions." *Political Research Quarterly* 47, No. 2 (June 1994): 353–71.

Johnson, Charles A., and Bradley C. Canon. *Judicial Policies: Implementation and Impact.* Washington, D. C.: Congressional Quarterly, 1984.

Katzmann, Robert A. *Institutional Disability: The Saga of Transportation Policy for the Disabled.* Washington, D. C.: Brookings Institution, 1986.

Melnick, R. Shep. *Regulation and the Courts: The Case of the Clean Air Act.* Washington, D.C.: Brookings Institution, 1983.

Mishler, William, and Reginald S. Sheehan. "The Supreme Court as a Countermajoritarian Institution? The Impact of Public Opinion on Supreme Court Decisions." *American Political Science Review* 87, No. 1 (Mar. 1993): 87–101.

Murphy, Walter F. *Congress and the Court.* Chicago: University of Chicago Press, 1962.

———. "Lower Court Checks on Supreme Court Power." *American Political Science Review* 53, No. 4 (Dec. 1959): 1017–31.

Paschal, Richard A. "The Continuing Colloquy: Congress and the Finality of the Supreme Court." *The Journal of Law and Politics* VIII, No. 1 (Fall 1991): 143–226.

Peltason, Jack W. *Fifty-Eight Lonely Men: Southern Federal Judges and School Desegregation.* New York: Harcourt, Brace & World, 1961.

Rosenberg, Gerald N. "Judicial Independence and the Reality of Political Power," paper presented at the annual meeting of the American Political Science Association, New Orleans, Aug. 29–Sept. 1, 1985.

Schmidhauser, John R., and Larry L. Berg. *The Supreme Court and Congress: Conflict and Interaction, 1945–1968.* New York: Free Press, 1972.

Solimine, Michael E., and James L. Walker. "The Next Word: Congressional Response to Supreme Court Statutory Decisions." *Temple Law Review* 65, No. 2 (Summer 1992): 425–58.

Stumpf, Harry P. "Congressional Response to Supreme Court Rulings: The Interaction of Law and Politics." *Journal of Public Law* 14, No. 2 (1966): 377–95.

Wasby, Stephen L. *The Impact of the United States Supreme Court: Some Perspectives.* Homewood, Ill.: Dorsey Press, 1970.

13

American Courts

An Assessment

Courts are political agencies. . . . They typically act politically and . . . they are supposed to act politically. [But] a political system encompasses many roles, each qualitatively different from the next and each contributing something different to the political process.

—Martin Shapiro,
"Stability and Change in Judicial Decision-Making"

This is a court of law, young man, not a court of justice.
—Oliver Wendell Holmes, Jr.

It is appropriate to conclude this study of judicial politics by bringing together the various strands of our discussion into an overall assessment of American courts. This evaluation can best be undertaken along functional lines, beginning with a determination of the nature of the judicial role (roles), then proceeding to an estimation of the extent to which the American judiciary successfully performs these tasks. Such will be our approach in this final chapter.

We use the term "estimation" advisedly, for running as an unbroken thread throughout the foregoing analysis of the judicial process is the paucity of empirical research on virtually every aspect of the system. Our lack of knowledge on issues of vital concern ranging from the policy implications of court structure to the variables associated with judicial impact is the central overriding fact in teaching and research on American courts. Derek Bok, former dean of Harvard Law School and formerly president of Harvard University, wrote that

> Legal scholars are rarely trained in the methods of empirical investigation and hence do not devote themselves to explaining the actual effects of legal rules on human behavior.
>
> Our limited knowledge severely inhibits efforts to increase efficiency and access to the legal system.

. . . Law schools have done surprisingly little to seek the knowledge that the legal system requires. Even the most rudimentary facts about the legal system are unknown or misunderstood.[1]

Although, as described in Chapter 2, social science-oriented legal research undertaken by political scientists, sociologists, and the like has tended to fill the void, the resources of most of our nation's law schools are still expended largely not on the study of the critical issues of the operation of our legal system, but rather on what Bok terms "pedestrian forms of research [and] endless picking at legal puzzles within a narrow framework of principles and precedents."[2] With notable exceptions,[3] the continued disdain in most law schools for empirical research having broad social implications is summed up in the remarks of one "witty" law professor who is reported to have said, "All research corrupts, but empirical research corrupts absolutely."[4] One result of such academic ideology is that the current student of judicial affairs must be content with speculative estimates of how well our judicial system is doing in fulfilling its sociopolitical role; our current level of knowledge permits little more.[5]

COURTS AS RESOLVERS OF DISPUTES

Courts are agencies of government: They are created to serve the needs of the regime. No realistic assessment of their performance can overlook this central fact. At least in developed societies, and perhaps even in primitive systems, courts are first and foremost hearers and hopefully resolvers of individual and group disputes. Central policy-making organs of government—legislatures and executives—most directly and expressly perform the broad policy functions of government; but for the most part, they are not structured to handle everyday squabbles and disputes of citizens and groups—with one another and with government. A more specialized, individualized agency is needed for that role. Courts are assigned this task.[6] Therefore, our first order of business is to inquire as to how well the American judicial system is performing in this role, and the first step in that inquiry is a clarification of the dispute processing function in society. For purposes of analysis, the various functions of courts are distinguished, although their close interdependence is an overriding fact basic to an understanding of the judiciary in society.

What need have government and society for domestic dispute resolution and what are the characteristics of successful dispute resolution processes? Put simply, disputes

---

[1]Derek C. Bok, "A Flawed System of Law Practice and Training," *Journal of Legal Education* 33, No. 4 (Dec. 1983): 577, 581.

[2]Bok, "A Flawed System": 584.

[3]Some of the nation's most prestigious law schools are moving away from the Langdellian model, at least in research, and sometimes even in teaching. Examples include Yale, University of California–Berkeley, Northwestern, and Wisconsin. But compare this view with that of Lois G. Forer, *Money and Justice: Who Owns the Courts?* (New York: Norton, 1984), especially Chapter 10, "The Siren Song of Research." See also the Stumpf and Shapiro comments in Harry P. Stumpf, et al., "Whither Political Jurisprudence: A Symposium," *Western Political Quarterly* 36, No. 4 (Dec. 1983): 540, 541. Finally, see an assessment of social science approaches in legal education in Lawrence M. Friedman, "The Law and Society Movement," *Stanford Law Review* 38, No. 3 (Feb. 1986): 763–80.

[4]Bok, "A Flawed System": 581.

[5]See, e.g., the knowledge gaps noted in Jethro K. Lieberman, ed., *The Role of Courts in American Society: The Final Report of the Council on the Role of Courts* (St. Paul, Minn.: West, 1984), passim.

[6]See Shapiro's "root concept" of the classic triad of dispute resolution: A, in dispute with B, seeks a resolution from C. Martin Shapiro, *Courts: A Comparative and Political Analysis* (Chicago: University of Chicago Press, 1981), especially 1–18.

threaten social stability, and one function of government is to maintain that stability. Not only may unattended disputes lead to antisocial and antigovernmental attitudes and behavior (a seething sense of injustice), but disputes by their nature tend to spread, threatening to include ever larger sectors of the populace, posing clear and immediate danger to societal peace and stability. Disputes are a cancerous growth on the body politic; they must be dealt with in the interest of the very survival of the regime. Dispute resolution, therefore, is a vital function of government. Effective, peaceful resolution of citizen-to-citizen and, even more importantly, of citizen-to-government disputes, enhances the credibility of government. It engenders a sense of "justice" and citizen well-being, and promotes harmony among individuals and groups, enhancing the peace of the realm.

A long-forgotten argument of Carl Friedrich nails down the point. "The settlement of disputes," he wrote "is the primordial internal function which a political order has to perform, antedating the making of rules and the application of such rules in administrative work."[7] This function, continues Friedrich,

> corresponds in basic importance to the defending of the political order. Indeed, it constitutes the defense of the political order internally. Through it, justice is continually reinterpreted and recreated. Without it, there can be no internal peace. Time and again, it has served as a unifying agent in efforts to cement a more comprehensive political community and thus as the pathfinder of a more inclusive political order.[8]

The features of successful dispute resolving mechanisms are the same everywhere. At a minimum, they must first lend the *appearance* of fairness and impartiality. Second, they must be readily available and accessible. And third, they must be reasonably efficient. A sense of fairness is essential, because successful dispute resolution depends upon acceptance of not only the process but also the outcome by those involved. Solutions leaving one or more of the parties disgruntled are not solutions at all. On the contrary, they may well exacerbate ongoing conflict. Social agencies for dispute resolution are not serving their purpose if they are distant or otherwise inaccessible in practical terms for the ordinary citizen. Finally, once access is gained, if proceedings are too cumbersome, costly, or otherwise impracticable, the mechanism will fail to serve the needs of the citizenry—and more importantly, of the regime.

Assessed in these terms, the deficiencies of American courts as dispute processors are manifest. Indeed, their shortcomings are notorious, giving rise to the current "crisis" of our judicial system discussed by scholars, practitioners, and citizens alike. Scholarly and professional legal assessments of our judicial system on grounds of fairness are reflected in book titles such as *Unequal Justice*,[9] *The Administration of Injustice*,[10] and *Denial of Justice*.[11] Deficiencies of accessibility have been so acute as to have spawned a serious and widespread movement away from courts altogether, a movement representing one of the chief intellectual and professional developments in the field today. Variously termed "access to justice,"[12]

---

[7]Carl J. Friedrich, *Man and His Government: An Empirical Theory of Politics* (New York: McGraw-Hill, 1963), 57, 423.

[8]Friedrich, *Man and His Government*, 440.

[9]Jerold S. Auerbach, *Unequal Justice: Lawyers and Social Change in Modern America* (New York: Oxford University Press, 1976).

[10]Melvin P. Sykes, *The Administration of Injustice* (New York: Harper & Row, 1975).

[11]Lloyd L. Weinreb, *Denial of Justice: Criminal Processes in the United States* (New York: Free Press, 1977).

[12]See Laura Nader, ed., *No Access to Law: Alternatives to the American Judicial System* (New York: Academic Press, 1980); and Mauro Cappelletti and Bryant Garth, "Access to Justice: The Newest Wave in the World-Wide Movement to Make Rights Effective," *Buffalo Law Review* 27, No. 2 (Spring 1978): 181–292.

"court alternatives,"[13] "informal justice,"[14] or "neighborhood justice,"[15] the movement has been characterized by a general agreement on the unworkability of our formal judicial processes, especially at the lower levels, leading to serious experimentation with arbitration (especially of the court-directed variety),[16] mediation,[17] and similar forms of local, informal dispute processing.[18] Most mechanisms, however, function under the shadow of formal court intervention should the dispute not be resolved.

Not only the lack of fairness and access, but also the absence of efficient procedures has contributed significantly to the movement away from formal dispute processing. Practitioner and scholar alike have commented critically on this aspect of American courts. The tenor of the criticism is seen in titles such as *The Process Is the Punishment,*[19] in which an established scholar seriously argues—and abundantly demonstrates—that proceedings in lower criminal courts have reached a state in which conventional modes of punishment are somewhat beside the point, for exposure to the judicial process is sufficient punishment in and of itself. Other critiques include *Why Courts Don't Work,* written by the Chief Justice of the West Virginia Supreme Court,[20] and *The Death of the Law,*[21] in which sitting judges all but throw up their hands at the near-total breakdown of the system. But these are broad generalizations. What specifically is wrong with American courts as dispute processors? Precisely where and how do they fail along the three overlapping dimensions of fairness (or perceived fairness), accessibility, and workability (efficiency)? And what reforms or alternatives appear most promising?

From the moment disputants contemplate third-party intervention to resolve their differences to the final impact of the appellate decision, the American judicial process is characterized by unfairness; that is, a sense—and often the demonstrable reality—of inequality. This is not to say that all potential or actual disputants view the system in these terms. Participant winners and often nonparticipants—those having no firsthand knowledge of the system—may assess the process as roughly fair and equitable.[22] The preponderance of evidence gathered at the scene, however, points to the contrary. From top to bottom, American dispute processing mechanisms of the formal variety suffer from the class

[13]See, for example, American Bar Association, *Resoloving Disputes: An Alternative Approach* (Chicago: American Bar Association, 1983).

[14]Richard L. Abel, ed., *The Politics of Informal Justice,* 2 vols. (New York: Academic Press, 1982).

[15]See, e.g., Roman Tomasic and Malcolm M. Feeley, eds., *Neighborhood Justice: Assessment of an Emerging Idea* (New York: Longman, 1982).

[16]See E. Allen Lind and John E. Shepard, *Evaluation of Court-Annexed Arbitration in Three Federal District Courts* (Washington D.C.: Federal Judicial Center, 1983).

[17]J. Folberg and Alison Taylor, *Mediation: A Comprehensive Guide to Resolving Conflicts Without Litigation* (San Francisco: Jossey-Bass, 1984).

[18]See Paul Wahrhaftig, "An Overview of Community-Oriented Citizen Dispute Resolution Programs in the United States," in Abel, *Politics of Informal Justice,* Vol. 1, *The American Experience,* 75–97; and Larry Ray, ed., *Dispute Resolution Program Directory* (Washington, D.C.: Public Services Activities Division, American Bar Association, 1983). Probably the best brief overview of the dispute-resolution movement and literature on the subject is Jonathan B. Marks, Earl Johnson, Jr., and Peter L. Szanton, *Dispute Resolution in America: Processes in Evolution* (Washington, D.C.: National Institute for Dispute Resolution, 1984).

[19]Malcolm M. Feeley, *The Process Is the Punishment: Handling Cases in a Lower Criminal Court* (New York: Russell Sage Foundation, 1979).

[20]Richard Neeley, *Why Courts Don't Work* (New York: McGraw-Hill, 1982).

[21]Lois G. Forer, *The Death of the Law* (New York: David McKay, 1975).

[22]See Yankelovich, Skelly, and White, Inc., *The Public Image of Courts* (Williamsburg, Va.: National Center for State Courts, 1978). Repeated here is the finding reported elsewhere that the public's satisfaction with courts varies inversely with citizen-court experiences (p. 1). A similar finding was reported in the *Missouri Bar Prentice-Hall Survey: A Motivational Study of Public Attitudes and Law Office Management* (The Missouri Bar, 1963), 105, 178.

bias characteristic of American society as a whole. Not only does the substance of our law reflect this bias,[23] but judicial proceedings themselves—more germane to our discussion here—are likewise slanted in favor of the "haves," over the "have-nots." Our survey of small claims practices in Chapter 8 clearly illustrates this point; so does the description of the criminal process in Chapter 9, as well as aspects of the appellate process.

What Marc Galanter termed the "haves" in our society—established, wealthy, culturally dominant interests—enjoy enormous advantages over the "have-nots" in obtaining resolution of disputes favorable to their cause. Possessing superior resources, in the broad sense of that term, "have" parties can structure the hearing itself to their advantage. They have the luxury of time, they have the advantage of community status, and as repeat players, they have superior knowledge of the process and can benefit from economies of scale.[24] These are but a few advantages enjoyed by "have" interests. If law and courts are political, and if politics has to do with the distribution of advantages and disadvantages, then it is hardly surprising that officially established mechanisms for dispute resolution operate to the advantage of the "haves" in society. Indeed, it is axiomatic.

What is true on the civil side is equally true of criminal courts. It can hardly be seriously contended that the resources of the defense in most plea-bargaining situations are equal to those of the prosecution. No one knows this better than "have-nots" ensnared in the process. Opting out by simply not appearing in court or lumping grievances all together (Chapter 8) are common methods of coping in civil disputes. Default judgments in small claims and similar proceedings are but one indication of the frequency of this type of behavior. However, avoidance is not as easy in criminal proceedings. Reflecting the wisdom of a Black youth in San Francisco in the 1960s, Ed Lewis, a Hunter's Point poet, succinctly summarized the role of law in society as seen by the "have-nots":

> I arrest you in the name of the law.
> What law?
> Our law.
> What law?
> Our law.
> What law is our law?
> Our law is our law, boy.
> I figured that.[25]

Evidence cited in Chapter 9 indicates that the critical decisions of arrest, prosecution (including plea bargaining), and sentencing reflect political realities. That is, the operation of the criminal justice process, and its accoutrements, mirror the views of the dominant elements of society toward crime and punishment. Fairness—equality of treatment for all caught up in the criminal "justice" system—is not a dominant societal value, except symbolically.[26]

---

[23]See, generally, Jacobus ten Broek, ed., *The Law of the Poor* (San Francisco: Chandler, 1966); and Harry P. Stumpf, *Community Politics and Legal Services: The Other Side of the Law* (Beverly Hills: Sage, 1975), especially Ch. 3, "The Law of the Poor," and the sources cited therein.

[24]See the insightful article by Marc Galanter, "Why the Haves Come Out Ahead: Speculations on the Limits of Legal Change," *Law and Society Review* 9, No. 1 (Fall 1974): 95–160. Galanter reexamines and reasserts his own conclusions in "Afterword: Explaining Litigation," *Law and Society Review* 9, No. 2 (Winter 1975): 347–68.

[25]Ed Lewis poem cited in John Hurst, "The Wide Gulf Between Police and Residents," *San Francisco Examiner,* (May 30, 1968): 1.

[26]See Stumpf, *Community Politics,* Ch. 9, "Legal Services: A National Perspective." See also the insightful work by Stuart A. Scheingold, *The Politics of Rights: Lawyers, Public Policy and Political Change* (New Haven: Yale University Press, 1974), especially Part 1, "The Myth of Rights."

A central ingredient—some have argued *the* central ingredient—of inequality in the American judicial process is inequality of access. To the extent that access is controlled by the legal profession, our findings reported in Chapter 7 explain the source of the problem. *Gideon v. Wainwright,* 372 U.S. 335 (1963), and its progeny hardly guarantee equality of legal representation for the poor in criminal cases. Although that may have been the Supreme Court's intent, reality—law in action—tells a different story. It is a story of unfulfilled promises, of defense lawyers lacking both time and resources (or no representation at all), resulting in underdefended if not altogether unrepresented indigent criminal defendants. It is a story so well known as to have become standard textbook fare in the field of criminal justice.[27] On the civil side, the availability of legal representation is even further from the American ideal of justice for all. At its peak funding of $321 million annually in the late Carter years, the Legal Services Corporation could provide little more than a drop in the bucket of the need of the poor for legal representation.[28] At this writing, even the program's current budget of $283 million (FY 97) is facing total elimination by the Republican Congress.[29] As long as Americans peg the availability of legal services to the ability to pay for them, equal access to the fruits of formal dispute resolution will remain largely a myth.

Efficiency and practical workability are among the least descriptive terms for America's courts. Delays of many years in obtaining the resolution of relatively simple disputes, huge case backlogs, adversarial processes oriented more to technicalities than to the core of the dispute—these features more accurately characterize our formal dispute processing mechanisms. Simple and speedy dispute resolution is, by and large, unavailable in our society. This is especially true for those of modest means. For a society's "haves," delay and inefficiency may work to their advantage in wearing down their less affluent adversaries, illustrating once again the abject class bias of the American judicial process. Yet, there is now evidence that even "have" interests are growing weary and are no longer as willing to pay the price of the gross inefficiencies in the system. Those with financial means are showing increasing signs of moving to less expensive legal representational forms or to purchasing their own private dispute processing mechanisms.[30]

Two points emerge from this discussion. First, unfairness—inequality due to class biases—is not simply one among many characteristics of formal dispute processing in our society. Rather, it seems to be the *central* feature of the process. This is so because access is, at bottom, a resource issue, as is the efficient working of the system once access is gained. Hence, (and this is the second point) whether fairness, access, or practical workability is present or absent is largely dependent upon one's perception, one's economic resources, or if you will, which side of the regime one is on. A good case can be made that for those of means, our courts as dispute processors are more than adequate. Things could be better, perhaps, but from the viewpoint of the "have" interests, our formal dispute processing forums can still be used, if somewhat ineffectively, to enhance their status or to work out their differences. But for those who wish to employ dispute processing agencies

---

[27]See, e.g., George F. Cole, *The American System of Criminal Justice,* 6th ed. (Monterey, Calif.: Brooks/Cole, 1995), Ch. 9.

[28]See Stumpf, *Community Politics,* 273–81; also Anthony Champagne, "Legal Services: A Program in Need of Assistance," in Anthony Champagne and Edward J. Harpham, eds., *The Attack on the Welfare State* (Prospect Heights, Ill.: Waveland Press, 1984), 131–48.

[29]See Champagne, "Legal Services," 142–45. See also "Legal Services Survives, Barely," *New York Times* (Editorial, May 6, 1996), A-14; and William Booth, "Killing the Lawyers," *Washington Post National Weekly Edition* (June 10–16, 1996): 32.

[30]See Bok, "A Flawed System", 578. Also see Robert Gnaizda, "Rent-A-Judge: Secret Justice for the Privileged Few"; and Robert Coulson, "Rent-A-Judge: Private Settlement for the Public Good," *Judicature* 66, No. 1 (June–July 1982): 6–13.

to alter the balance of power as it affects them, to achieve *genuine* redress for their grievances, the deck is stacked against them. As we said, fairness—equality—must *appear* to be a significant ingredient of the process. If appearances hold up, all is well for the regime. But if the process creaks from age and gross inefficiency, and its inequities and other shortcomings can no longer be hidden, then reform is in the offing.

It is, of course, misleading to cast the judicial dispute resolution process entirely in the mold of "have" versus "have-not" social interests. American courts expend a great deal of time and other resources in resolving disputes between "have" interests. In fact, celebrated court decisions resolving these clashes, often in the form of bargains struck within the shadow of the law, become the raw material for legal scholarship—the National Labor Relations Board pitted against the Jones-Laughlin Steel Corporation in the 1930s, the Texaco-Penzoil clash in the Texas courts in 1985, the breakup of American Telephone and Telegraph by the Justice Department, and so on. But as suggested before, if inequality of access or the imbalance of resources of the disputants does not plague such proceedings, then the issue of efficiency may loom large as a reason to avoid such confrontations and to seek alternative means of handling one's affairs.

The literature on American courts abounds with proposals for change, running the gamut of the entire judicial process. Reforms directed to improved structure, enhanced access, simplified procedures, the reduced costs, speedier trials, more equitable sentencing, better court management, delegalization, improved legal services, and even (some would say especially) more realistic and relevant approaches to legal education—all have been proposed and widely discussed. Many of these and other reforms have been tried, though few have resulted in lasting change of any great significance. Many more have remained merely in the realm of debate, reflecting the stiff resistance of the system to innovation.

In either case, many scholars and practitioners have concluded that reform of the existing system is all but hopeless. Indeed, by the late 1970s, the leading edge of the reform effort of American courts had shifted from reform itself to a search for court alternatives. This movement to informal or semiformal methods of dispute resolution became the order of the day. Although dispute resolution, broadly defined, includes proposed reforms of existing judicial machinery (for instance, systems for directing cases to informal forums in the early stages of the process, in-court settlement conferences, improved management techniques), an emphasis on nonadjudicatory processes of resolving disputes became the core of the movement. Court-annexed compulsory arbitration, a variety of mediation systems, the ombudsman approach, and multifaceted neighborhood justice centers designed to enhance access to informal, inexpensive, participatory forms of problem-solving and dispute processing exemplify the movement to informalism.[31] There are several theoretical as well as practiced problems with the move to dispute resolution as we have defined it. A full critique is not possible here, but we can make some of the points of such an assessment.[32]

First, we may ask why overt moves to less formal, less structured mechanisms are needed at all when, as we have shown, a chief characteristic of formal processes is informal bargaining in what has been called the shadow of the law. Since we already have informalism in practice, why are we experiencing formal moves to informalism? The point

---

[31]See Marks, Johnson, and Szanton, *Dispute Resolution,* 10. A useful bibliography covering dispute resolution and the informal justice movement is provided by Christine Harrington, "Selected Bibliography on Dispute Resolution," American Political Science Association, *Newsletter,* Law, Courts and Judicial Process Section 3, No. 2 (Spring 1986): 1–7. The entire *Judicature* issue of Vol. 69, No. 5 (Feb.–Mar. 1986), is devoted to alternative dispute resolution.

[32]There are several good critiques of informalism. See, e.g., Richard L. Abel, "The Contradictions of Informal Justice," in Abel, *Politics of Informal Justice,* Vol. 1, *The American Experience:* 267–320; and Christine B. Harrington, *Shadow Justice: The Ideology and Institutionalization of Alternatives to Courts* (Westport, Conn.: Greenwood Press, 1985).

was well expressed by a group of scholars associated with the Civil Litigation Research Project of the University of Wisconsin:

> If in the world of ordinary litigation judges rarely reach formal decisions on the merits, the parties negotiate albeit "in the shadow of the law," judges actively intervene to encourage settlement, and settlement is the rule, not the exception, then perhaps the whole reform debate falls wide of the mark. Perhaps the right approach is not to reach for wholly new institutional alternatives to a hypothetical process of adjudication, but to understand the nonadjudicative dimensions of litigation, to see how and why they work, and to seek to make this dimension of the litigation process even more central and effective.[33]

Second, is not a logical outcome of informalism the diversion of "lesser" cases from formal adjudication into "people's" forums, resulting in a "second-class" system of justice for the poor? And further, was this not the very problem that the access to justice movement of the 1960s (the Legal Services Program of the Office of Economic Opportunity, the public interest law movement, and so forth) was intended to remedy? Among the earliest analyses of the "law of the poor," leading up to the creation of the legal arm of the War on Poverty, was that of Jerome Carlin. Writing in 1966, he argued that people's courts, such as juvenile, family, and small claims courts, are characterized by loose procedural standards, overwhelming caseloads, and a tendency to delegate decision-making power to administrative "experts." In addition, Carlin argued that these courts

> tend to be staffed by the poorest trained, least experienced, and least competent judges having the lowest salaries and the shortest tenures; and they are usually served by the lowest ranking, least competent, and least responsible attorneys.[34]

Informalism may well result in the resurrection of the poor people's justice of an almost bygone era under a new name—forums in which the due process safeguards of formalism, meager though they may be for "have-not" interests, are further eroded.[35]

Finally, based on the foregoing analysis of the politics of courts generally, as well as the specific characteristics of American dispute processing, the central question to be posed concerning informalism is, Who benefits? Reform for whom, for what purpose, to what ends? Who is to dominate the process? As with most reform movements concerning law and courts (as well as with most other subjects), euphemizing abounds. Reform is usually proposed and undertaken in the interests of the "common man" to achieve "fairness," "increase efficiency," and the like. These and similar symbols are invariably employed to enlist support for the movement.[36] But what is the outlook?

First, we should stress that informalism is not a new phenomenon in the history of dispute processing.[37] And at least its recent history raises questions as to the ends sought and achieved. Small claims courts, some say, have not merely been captured and dominated by interests hostile to those they were said to serve; an examination of their roots shows that the original purpose of these tribunals was to enhance the ability of dominant community entities (hospitals, department stores, collection agencies) to collect debts.[38] The same can be

---

[33]David M. Trubek et al., "The Costs of Ordinary Litigation," *UCLA Law Review* 31, No. 1 (Oct. 1983): 122.

[34]Jerome E. Carlin, "Courts and the Poor," paper presented at the American Political Science Association meeting, New York City, September 6–10, 1966; see also Stumpf, *Community Politics,* 93.

[35]This and other points in this critique were suggested in the Marks, Johnson, and Szanton work, *Dispute Resolution,* 51–53.

[36]On the ideology of informalism, see Abel, *Politics of Informal Justice,* Vol. 1, *The American Experience,* 7–9.

[37]See Christine B. Harrington, "De-legalization Reform Movements: A Historical Analysis," in Abel, *Politics of Informal Justice,* Vol. 1, *The American Experience,* 35–71.

[38]See Barbara Yngvesson and Patricia Hennessey, "Small Claims, Complex Disputes: A Review of the Small Claims Literature," *Law and Society Review* 9, No. 2 (Winter 1975): 226.

said of housing courts, which became an important adjunct for real estate interests.[39] A third historical example of informalism is the "independent" regulatory agencies established mostly in the New Deal period to simplify governmental regulation. Almost without exception, they fell under the control of those they were ostensibly intended to regulate.

That the informalism movement may be yet another attempt to extend the control of already dominant interests is at least suggested by the type of interests sponsoring and funding the National Center for Dispute Resolution in Washington, D.C. Even a partial list of sponsors gives us pause: American Telephone and Telegraph, the Prudential Foundation, the Exxon Educational Foundation, General Motors Corporation, Aetna Life and Casualty, the Chrysler Corporation, and so on.[40] What stake do such organizations have in dispute processing reform? It may be that they see informalism as a more effective, less costly means of dominating dispute processing in their own interests. The history of informalism is replete with just such uses of the technique. By "cooling out" "have-not" grievants—mollifying their resentments through informal, participatory mechanisms—dominant socioeconomic interests may reduce mounting threats to the status quo. As Abel suggests,

> Informalism is a mechanism by which the state extends its control so as to manage capital accumulation and diffuse the resistance this engenders. Its objects are not randomly distributed but rather are concentrated within the dominated categories of contemporary capitalism: workers, the poor, ethnic minorities, and women.
> . . . help is always extended downwards—the very relationship of helping is inherently unequal. Because the personnel of informal institutions are of relatively low status, those whom they help must be even lower.
> Informal institutions control by disorganizing grievants, trivializing grievances, frustrating collective responses. Their very creation proclaims the message that social problems can be resolved by fiddling with the control apparatus once more, that it is unnecessary to question basic social structures.[41]

Reform movements, including informalism, deserve a full hearing—and trial. The deficiencies of the present system are too great to ignore. The alleged benefits of the dispute resolution movement—reducing overcrowding, lowering costs, increasing access to dispute processing forums, better dispute resolution—may be realizable, and empirical research is needed to answer the question. But enough has been said to raise doubts about the dispute resolution movement as a viable alternative to present structure and processes, though this, of course, depends on one's perspective, which is to say, one's politics. As suggested in foregoing chapters, the form of the reform is perhaps less important than the result, the actual consequences of new forms. As with the substance of legal rules, structural and procedural change should not be taken at face value; the realities of "law in action" apply to them as well.

By the 1990s, most publicly and vocally with the advent of the Republican Congress in 1994, "informalism" had been largely replaced by a new "reform" movement, usually referred to as "tort reform." The literature on and critiques of this political movement are now voluminous indeed, much of this covered previously in the chapter on civil justice. What is interesting for the present discussion is that the same societal interests backing informalism (as well as the elimination of federally funded legal services) are now on the tort reform bandwagon, and for the same reasons.

---

[39]See Mark H. Lazerson, "In the Halls of Justice, the Only Justice Is in the Halls," in Abel, *Politics of Informal Justice*, Vol. 1, *The American Experience*, 119–63.

[40]A list of sponsoring organizations for the National Institute for Dispute Resolutions can be found in most of the institute's literature, such as the *Dispute Resolution Forum* published several times a year.

[41]Richard L. Abel, "Introduction," in Abel, *Politics of Informal Justice*, Vol. 1, *The American Experience*, 6–7.

JUDICIAL POLICY-MAKING, CONSTITUTIONAL DEMOCRACY, AND SOCIAL CHANGE

In the course of processing and attempting to resolve disputes in accordance with existing law, courts inevitably fashion new rules. It is this policy-making function, much more than dispute resolution, that has plunged the American judiciary into controversy. This is somewhat curious, since judicial decision making in common law systems has always provided a creative, incremental thrust to law.[42] The American doctrine of separation of powers, with its emphasis on specialization of function, probably has helped spark the great debate over the "problem" of judicial policy-making. Each branch of government, separate and distinct, has its assigned role. Stepping out of that role constitutes institutional aggrandizement; it is seen as a usurpation of the power of coordinate branches of government. Although this view of governmental functions contradicts the history of governments in general, and our own political institutions in particular, such misconceptions, nonetheless, have fueled the Great American Debate over the nature of judicial power.[43]

A second reason for the persistence of this controversy was detailed in Chapters 1 and 2: the internal contradictions inherent in Blackstonian judrisprudence. Americans have never decided what role (roles) they wish their judges to play, whether that of oracles of revealed truth, semi-independent policy-makers, or legitimizers of extant policy. The persistence of the myth of judicial objectivity tends to infuse the debate with hypocrisy and high-sounding "principled" arguments, which cloak raw value preferences. The student of American courts must get past a great deal of hyperbole and obfuscation in order to undertake a realistic assessment of the policy role of the judiciary in our society. As in our analysis of the judicial dispute processing function, it is useful to first ascertain what roles the courts actually play in the determination of policy, then to assess this role in terms of generally acceptable criteria of democratic policy-making.

What is the precise character of judicial policy-making in America? If we are to believe some commentators, our courts have run amok, usurping the legislative function in area after area of policy, coming dangerously close to destroying the nation.[44] The foregoing analysis of the American judicial process at all levels does indeed describe a policy-making mechanism of imposing proportions. Since law is an important political resource, courts are capable of significant redistribution of values in the polity. And merely an introductory survey of this process demonstrates that American judges have not been shy in using this power to redirect societal advantages and disadvantages. Thus, the extent and nature of American judicial power has been amply demonstrated. But what of limits on that power?

Our coverage of compliance with and implementation of judicial decisions in the foregoing chapter reveals an array of forces capable of imposing significant checks on the policy-making power of our nation's courts. To recall briefly, judicial decisions regularly evoke a number of possible negative responses, any of which can severely restrict, if not

---

[42]See Martin Shapiro, "Stability and Change in Judicial Decision-Making: Incrementalism or Stare Decisis?" *Law in Transition Quarterly* 2, No. 3 (Summer 1965): 134–57.

[43]This debate is discussed in Lieberman, *Role of Courts,* passim. There it is cast in terms of the Traditionalist versus the Adaptionist view of the judicial role. Briefly stated, Traditionalists see courts as having special attributes that severely limit their role, whereas the Adaptionist view is much more flexible.

[44]See, e.g., Nathan Glazer, "Towards an Imperial Judiciary," *The Public Interest* 41 (Fall 1975): 104–23; Lino A. Graglia, *Disaster by Decree: The Supreme Court's Decisions on Race and Schools* (Ithaca: Cornell University Press, 1976); and Raoul Berger, *Government by Judiciary: The Transformation of the Fourteenth Amendment* (Cambridge, Mass.: Harvard University Press, 1977). But see a critical review of the Berger book by Walter F. Murphy, "Constitutional Interpretation: The Art of the Historian, Magician, or Statesman?" *Yale Law Journal* 87, No. 8 (July 1978): 1752–71.

entirely undermine, the import of initial judicial decrees. Statutory reversals, anticourt legislative thrusts, proposed constitutional amendments, the selection of fresh judicial personnel—these and other congressional powers represent an important set of limits on judicial policy-making. As discussed, executive efforts can supplement those of Congress in nullifying or circumscribing judicial policy. Furthermore, executive power can be used semi-independently, as in the nominating process or the veto power, to limit the policy role of courts. When we add to these potentially important constraints, the inertia imposed by lower courts, the drag of state and community (not to mention federal) bureaucracies charged with implementing judicial decisions, as well as limits imposed by public opinion and interest group reaction, we can build a case that more than sufficient countervailing power exists within the formal and informal political process to check judicial power.

Such limits constitute one possible answer to the perennial question of how we can reconcile judicial policy-making with the requirements of political accountability usually seen as necessary for governments to be labeled constitutional democracies. Although nonelected (or perhaps elected for life) judiciaries would seem to lack the required political accountability, that is true only formally; informally, the larger political system of which the judiciary is a part can avail itself of a number of options for effectively checking the possible excesses of judicial decision making. Thus, as often argued, the apparently nondemocratic institution of judicial review is rendered democratic in practice.[45]

More than purely external checks are at work in holding judicial policy-makers within limits. Judges are not politically naive. At bottom, they understand the need for survival, for conducting themselves in their relations with other power centers in American society in such a way that their power and prestige are enhanced, or at least not destroyed. Only a nodding acquaintance with American judicial history, presumably possessed by most or all judges, points to discretion as often the better part of valor—that self-imposed limits might well enhance judicial prestige in the long run. Thus, a tradition of judicial self-restraint, born of painful political experiences as well as common law conceptions of the judicial role, exists as yet another set of limits on American courts.[46]

Examples of the use of judicial self-restraint are scattered throughout the history of American judicial decision making. They include the following:

1. The self-imposed limits on the types of cases that judges will decide (Chapter 12);
2. The widely cited guidelines set out by Justice Brandeis in *Ashwander v. T. V. A.*, 297 U.S. 288 (1936), which include a presumption of the constitutionality of legislation, the rule that decisions be fashioned as narrowly as possible, and the like;[47]

For a more recent set of arguments that the American federal judiciary is dangerously assertive, see "Symposium: The End of Democracy: The Judicial Usurpation of Politics," *First Things*, No. 67 (Nov. 1996): 18–42; and "The End of Democracy: A Discussion Continued," *First Things*, No. 69 (Jan. 1997): 19–28. Further commentary on these essays is found in Peter Steinfels, "Beliefs: A Symposium that questions a 'government by judges' provokes a squabble that takes some divisive religious nuances," *New York Times*, Dec. 14, 1996: A-14; and Jacob Heilbrunn, "Neocon v. Theocon," *The New Republic*, Dec. 30, 1996: 20–24.

[45]This is the argument used by Victor G. Rosenblum in *Law as a Political Instrument* (New York: Doubleday, 1955).

[46]A useful essay on this subject is John P. Roche, "Judicial Self-Restraint," *American Political Science Review* 49, No. 3 (Sept. 1955): 762–72.

[47]A brief but useful discussion of the *Ashwander* rules and the concept and practice of judicial self-restraint may be found in Glendon A. Schubert, *Constitutional Politics: The Political Behavior of Supreme Court Justices and the Constitutional Polices that They Make* (New York: Holt, Rinehart & Winston, 1960), 206–16. For a somewhat more extended discussion, see Henry J. Abraham, *The Judicial Process: An Introductory Analysis of the Courts of the United States, England, and France,* 6th ed. (New York: Oxford University Press, 1993), Chapters 8 and 9.

3. The willingness of courts to "reconsider" rulings and perhaps refashion those that have met with strong political resistance;
4. The complete avoidance of issues thought to be too politically explosive; and
5. A willingness to develop approaches to implementation consistent with perceived current public, or at least elite, opinion.

These and similar patterns of judicial behavior reveal the cognizance of judges that their power is not unlimited. Hence, a combination of what we might term the "internal" and the "external" limits on judicial policy-making presents a strong case for the democratic character of judicial review. In fact, with this impressive array of checks on judicial power in America, we might ask, what is left? On balance, how can we characterize the policy role of courts in American politics?

In an influential essay written many years ago, Robert Dahl suggested that judicial power, at least as exercised by the United States Supreme Court, is best seen as a legitimizing force; it places a stamp of approval on broad policy proclivities already set out by Congress and the president. Far from being the guarantor of individual and minority rights that it is often said to be, the Court actually joins what Dahl calls the current "law-making majority" in helping it to rule.[48] As American politics is characterized by long-term one-party dominance, so the Court tends to fall into line, adopting policies that are generally consistent with, or at least not in significant opposition to, the policy preference of this ruling coalition of interests.

Although the early years of the coalition's reign may bring judicial opposition, this is usually because there are justices carried over from the old regime. The president's power to nominate and appoint new justices (on the average of every twenty-three months) enables the current law-making majority to counter hostile judicial action. Thus, writes Dahl, "The policy views dominant on the Court will never be out of line for very long with the policy views dominant among law-making majorities of the United States."[49] Though the Court may occasionally delay the executive–legislative will, sometimes (rarely) for long periods, he continues, "National law-making majorities—e.g., coalitions of the president and a majority of each house of Congress—generally have their way."[50]

However, more than mere rubber-stamping is involved in Dahl's view of the judicial role. The Court is a partner in governing with the other branches. When the ruling coalition is not united or is indifferent on certain policy issues, the Court can move in with important policies of its own. But at best, such policies are likely to be consistent with the general political philosophy of the governing coalition. Dahl based his analysis largely on the outcome of congressional policies vetoed by the Court within a four-year period, presumably when the "law-making majority" remained vital.

A number of other scholars in their own analyses of the role of the judiciary in our society would seem to be in fundamental agreement with the "legitimizing" thesis set forth by Dahl. Two examples are Charles Black in his widely cited work *The People and the Court*,[51] and Charles Press and Kenneth VerBerg in their survey of state politics.[52] It is es-

[48]Robert A. Dahl, "Decision-Making in a Democracy: The Role of the Supreme Court as a National Policy-Maker," *Journal of Public Law* 6 (Fall 1957): 279–95. A somewhat revised version of this classic article may be found in Robert A. Dahl, *Pluralist Democracy in the United States: Conflict and Consent* (Chicago: Rand-McNally, 1967), 154–70.
[49]Dahl, *Pluralist Democracy,* 156.
[50]Dahl, *Pluralist Democracy,* 163.
[51]Charles L. Black, *The People and the Court: Judicial Review in a Democracy* (New York: Macmillan, 1960).
[52]See Charles Press and Kenneth VerBerg, *State and Community Governments in the Federal System* (New York: Wiley, 1979), Ch. 9.

pecially interesting to note the similarity of the Dahl thesis with the notions of Woodrow Wilson. In his classic work, *Congressional Government,* published nearly seventy-five years before Dahl's analysis appeared, Wilson wrote,

> The national courts are for the most part in the power of Congress. . . .
> This balance of judiciary against legislative and executive would seem . . . to be another of those ideal balances which are to be found in the books rather than in the rough realities of actual practice; for manifestly the power of the courts is safe only during sessions of political peace, when parties are not aroused to passion or tempted by the command of irresistible majorities.[53]

Jonathan Casper has challenged the "relatively policy-impotent" theory of judicial power. Noting the frequent judicial vetoes of state actions by the Supreme Court, as well as the many instances in which the Court has held acts of Congress unconstitutional after Dahl's four-year cutoff, Casper argues that the Court's policy-making clout is much greater than Dahl's analysis would suggest.[54] Also, argues Casper, Court vetoes are not the only way to exercise judicial power; the imposition of the Court's policy preferences has also been a very important aspect of Supreme Court policy-making. Finally, Casper cites the complexity and the nuances of the policy process as reasons to question the simple "winners and losers" method of determining relative institutional power used by Dahl. Casper does not deny the legitimizing function of the Court; his concern seems to be with demonstrating that judicial policy-making is more lively and impactful than Dahl's analysis seemed to admit.

A careful reading of these two competing theories of judicial power suggests that they may not be entirely inconsistent. Dahl does not rule out the important interstitial law-making role of the Supreme Court. Within the parameters of the dominant policy-making majority (as represented in president and Congress), the Court has a great deal of latitude for creative policy-making. The Dahl analysis simply asserts that when push comes to shove, when the two entities clash, judicial power tends to come out second best. At bottom, it seems that this is not necessarily inconsistent with Casper's conclusions. Dahl's analysis emphasizes the limits of judicial power, while Casper stresses the broad possibilities short of those limits.

In sum, judicial policy-making may be likened to the conscience of the realm or, as Dahl puts it, a "guide" or "pioneer." Judges are saying, in effect,

> When elected political decision makers permit, or more precisely, to the extent that they do not disagree, and in further consideration of our own values as well as our common law traditions, we set forth *this* view of things; we recommend (decree) *this* course of action. All things considered, it is the policy that best reflects our sociolegal values as those have evolved over the centuries. If you accept the decision, it will be our contribution to the resolution of an important political dispute, as well as a modest advance in the articulation of the values underlying our democracy as we see it. If you do not agree, then, of course, we defer to the judgment of others. We realize that judicial power is a delicate instrument, often, ironically, most efficacious when it is least used. We have learned from our own judicial history that such power must be very carefully employed. On the large issues of the day, or when passions run high, we bow to the superior political power of others. But there are many times when there is no agreement among other policy-makers; when, for one reason or another, others cannot act—when, indeed, they prefer not to act—or when the ruling coalition is in disarray. It is in such situations that judicial policy-making is appropriate.

---

[53]Woodrow Wilson, *Congressional Government: A Study in American Politics,* reprint ed. (New York: Meridian Books, 1973). Wilson completed his classic work on American politics in 1884.
[54]Jonathan D. Casper, "The Supreme Court and National Policy-Making," *American Political Science Review* 70, No. 1 (Mar. 1976): 50–63.

This view of the policy role of American courts does not appear inconsistent with the conclusions reached by scholars who have studied implementation and impact. Thus, Johnson and Canon conclude that

> Historically the Supreme Court has seldom prevailed when its policies in major areas have been in direct conflict with those of Congress and the president. [However], the Court does make considerable policy in areas where Congress and the president are not so directly concerned.
> . . . Courts cannot make policies that stand in opposition to prevailing economic trends or doctrines. When courts try to do so, as the 1937 crisis proved, the judicial policies will be overridden.
> . . . On occasion, . . . [courts] will initiate fundamental changes in public policy. More often they will legitimize, enhance, or more fully develop policies made by other governmental agencies or by non-governmental institutions.[55]

If this is a roughly accurate view of the nature, extent, and limits of judicial policy-making in America, how are we to assess our courts in this regard? How well is the judiciary functioning in its policy-making role? If the criterion used to answer this question is that just suggested—namely, the requirements of constitutional democratic government—then we may conclude that our courts are performing reasonably well in one sense, though on a second dimension, their work is open to serious question.

Democracy requires that policy-makers and policy-making in process, outcome, and fact be accountable to policy recipients, whereas the constitutionalism of constitutional democracy requires that real, effective checks be placed on government to safeguard fundamental rights. While the common view of the judicial role in America is that courts score high in protecting fundamental rights and liberties but low in political accountability (witness the current—and recurring—attacks on our courts for their deviation from their assigned path of interpreting the law in the light of the original intent of the framers), the opposite is closer to the truth. That is, the informal but effective restraints on judicial power circumscribe judicial policy-making within relatively broad but politically tolerable limits. However, these same political checks have the effect of channeling judicial policy into popular paths, pleasing to the political elite but often detrimental to "have-not" interests. That such constraints operate to denigrate the judicial role of protecting minority rights was a central point of the Dahl thesis. Dahl himself put it best when he wrote,

> To the extent that the Supreme Court accepts the policies of law-making majorities, . . . it retains its own legitimacy and its power to confer legitimacy on policy; yet to that extent it fails to protect minorities from control or regulation by national majorities. To the extent that it opposes the policies of national law-making majorities in order to protect minorities, it threatens its own legitimacy. This is the inescapable paradox of judicial review in a democratic political order.[56]

Gerald Rosenberg reached essentially the same conclusion in his study of Court-Congress relations. While noting that "To lay people, lawyers, and social scientists alike, . . . [t]he independence of the federal judiciary from political control is a hallmark of the American legal system," he concluded that "Depending on the Court . . . to defend unpopular minorities or opinions against political hostility is misplaced." And he termed "dangerously wrong" the conception of courts as the "ultimate guardians of our fundamental rights."[57]

---

[55]Charles A. Johnson and Bradley C. Canon, *Judicial Policies: Implementation and Impact* (Washington, D.C.: Congressional Quarterly, 1984): 268–69.

[56]Dahl, *Pluralist Democracy,* 170.

[57]See Gerald N. Rosenberg, "Judicial Independence and the Reality of Political Power," paper delivered at the annual meeting of the American Political Science Association, New Orleans, August 29–September 1, 1985: 1, 45.

Implicit in this view of the judicial policy role is the notion that law and courts are not likely to be in the vanguard of social change. Rather, they more often reflect change initiated elsewhere. This is an important point requiring some elaboration.

The pervasiveness of judicial power, especially in the United States, and especially in our era, has raised the specter of courts as important instruments of directed social change. *Brown v. Board of Education* in 1954 is undeniably the model reflecting this view of the judicial role. Following *Brown*, "have-not" interests came to see in the judiciary a real hope for fundamental social, economic, and political reform in America. Civil rights groups (indeed, by the 1960s, they represented a social movement) pressed for further gains in rights for the legally unrepresented, the criminal suspect, the underrepresented urban voter, racial minorities, and so forth. And hope was raised that the legal (hence, social and economic) lot of the poor as a class could be substantially improved through litigation. The Legal Services Program of the Office of Economic Opportunity, created in 1964, vigorously pursued this goal.[58] What have been the results?

As for the policy fallout of *Brown* itself, the results were not encouraging. That the lot of Blacks and other racial minorities is considerably improved over that of thirty years ago cannot be denied. But of itself, *Brown* met with little compliance. It was not until Congress and the president moved forcefully with economic and other disincentives to racial segregation in education and other areas of American life that any real gains were made. Though *Brown* could be seen as a catalyst for such change, it was probably little more than that.

The analogy of *Brown* for the poverty lawyers was ill-drawn. At least (and probably at most), *Brown* carried with it the moral conscience of the American people. That gross, overt racial discrimination was seen as "wrong" significantly enhanced the impact of the 1954 ruling. Thus, the moral suasive effect of the decision helped to nudge Congress and the White House, and it was the combination of these forces that can be credited with the changes that eventually came about. In contrast, public opinion has never held that poverty is morally repugnant, nor that its social, political, and legal manifestations are legally correctable. On the contrary, the problem is widely viewed psychopathologically— it is the victim's fault.[59] Hence, when poverty lawyers sought social change through litigation, the results were quite limited. Even when they won judicial victories, the countervailing forces of implementing (or rather nonimplementing) populations often obliterated the impact of the legal gains.[60] The lesson from the legal theater of the War on Poverty was that the relationship between law and social reform is complex and indirect. To attempt to employ legal change to bring about more fundamental change in society is probably to put the cart before the horse. Law is more reflective of social values and behavior than the reverse. At best, law—legal change through judicial policy-making—must be joined with a host of other forces if directed social change is desired. And until those more fundamental forces head in the direction of change, legal reform itself can achieve only very modest results.[61]

Adding fuel to this long-simmering debate on the role of law, especially judicially made law, in social change, is Gerald Rosenberg's book-length treatment of the subject,

[58]See Stumpf, *Community Politics and Legal Services,* Chs. 1, 4, 8, and 9.

[59]See Stumpf, *Community Politics and Legal Services,* Chs. 1, 2, 8, and 9.

[60]Stumpf, *Community Politics and Legal Services,* 273–81. Several of the points made in this discussion were suggested by Geoffrey C. Hazard, Jr., in "Social Justice Through Civil Justice," *University of Chicago Law Review* 36, No. 4 (Summer 1969): 705–07.

[61]For a more complete discussion of these issues, see Stuart S. Nagel, ed., *Law and Social Change* (Beverly Hills, Calif.: Sage, 1970); Joel B. and Mary H. Grossman, eds., *Law and Change in Modern America* (Pacific Palisades, Calif.: Goodyear, 1971); and a more highly focused work by William K. Muir, Jr., *Prayer in the Public Schools: Law and Attitude Change* (Chicago: University of Chicago Press, 1967).

published in 1991.[62] There, he directly confronts the questions, "To what degree and under what conditions, can judicial processes be used to produce political and social change?"[63] He begins by positioning two contrasting views of judicially induced change, which he calls the Dynamic Court view and the Constrained Court view. Undergirded by the "myth of rights," fostered by the law schools and by American liberalism, the Dynamic Court view holds that American courts have produced, can produce, and do produce dramatic social change. The Constrained Court view, however, harks back to Hamilton's "least dangerous branch" prediction—that having the power of neither the purse nor the sword, and hemmed in by the more powerful democratically elected branches, judicial power is felt, if at all, mainly along the edges of policy-making, with only minimal or indirect impact on social change.

After a near-exhaustive examination of a wealth of empirical evidence in the areas of racial segregation in education, abortion and other women's rights, environmental regulation, reapportionment, and criminal law, Rosenberg concludes that

> . . . [C]ourt decisions are neither necessary nor sufficient for producing significant social reform. . . . [T]he Constrained Court view more closely approximates the role of the courts in the American political system. While . . . courts can be effective producers of significant social reform, . . . this occurs only when a great deal of change has already been made.[64]

Due in part to the significance of the issue, as well as Rosenberg's starkly stated conclusions, the book has engendered a good deal of critical comment.[65] Interestingly, however, even some of his critics concede that Rosenberg

> . . . combines an elegant analytical scheme and extensive empirical evidence into an impressive study that convincingly demonstrates the huge gap between the alleged promises and actual achievements of liberal reform litigation.[66]

And again,

> . . . Rosenberg succeeds in shifting the burden of proof to those who claim great powers for the courts. . . . It is now incumbent on those who believe that courts can and do effect significant social change to marshall evidence to support their claims.[67]

In any case, the reader will note that the central thrust of the Rosenberg thesis is not at variance with that of other scholars, most notably Dahl, Johnson and Canon, and Hazard, discussed previously, along with Stuart Scheingold's argument in *The Politics of Rights*,[68] and the notions of David Adamany, set forth in the 1970s.[69]

Thus far our discussion of judicial policy-making has focused on that sector of the policy process that could be called *policy enunciation*. But as suggested in Chapter 12,

---

[62]Gerald N. Rosenberg, *The Hollow Hope: Can Courts Bring About Social Change?* (Chicago: University of Chicago Press, 1991).

[63]Rosenberg, *The Hollow Hope*, 1.

[64]Rosenberg, *The Hollow Hope*, 35.

[65]Probably the best critique and rejoinder is "The Supreme Court and Social Change," *Law and Social Inquiry* 17, No. 4 (Fall 1992): 715–78. The reviewers are Professors Michael W. McCann and Malcolm M. Feeley. See also Susan E. Lawrence's review of the Rosenberg book in *American Political Science Review* 86, No. 3 (Sept. 1992): 812–13.

[66]Michael W. McCann, "Reform Litigation on Trial," *Law and Social Inquiry* 17, No. 4 (Fall 1992): 716.

[67]Malcolm M. Feeley, "Hollow Hopes, Flypaper, and Metaphors," *Law and Social Inquiry* 17, No. 4 (Fall 1992): 746–47.

[68]New Haven: Yale University Press, 1974.

[69]David Adamany, "Law and Society: Legitimacy, Realigning Elections, and the Supreme Court," *Wisconsin Law Review* 1973, No. 3 (1973): 790–846.

American courts have also increasingly involved themselves in the complex process of *policy implementation*. The implementation of *Brown v. Board of Education* in the late 1950s and early 1960s served as an early model illustrating this role.[70] But more intense and more complex tasks of this genre were assumed by judges in subsequent decades, giving rise to a wide-ranging discussion centered on the competence of courts to perform adequately these essentially administrative or, as one observer put it, "powerbroker" tasks.[71]

One side of the debate argues that structural reform—the design and supervision of major changes in the administration of governmental service delivery systems such as hospitals, schools, prisons, and the like—is not a feasible judicial function. The reasoning here is that the traditional administrator, being closer to the functioning institution, can employ intuition gained from experience, is better able to proceed incrementally with step adjustments if needed, and is in a position to use the techniques of education, psychological and financial inducements, and the like to move personnel toward politically mandated reform. Ordinary adjudication, on the other hand, with its tendency toward bipolar solutions and the use of authority to achieve reform, is ill-suited to the supervisory role needed to guide these public service institutions into making reforms.[72]

This restricted view of the judicial function is grounded in a sharp distinction between a political or a bargaining (powerbroker) role for courts and that of traditional adjudication. Since the latter is said to be oriented to dichotomous, authoritarian solutions based on "principle," it is inherently unsuited to the more flexible bargaining or exchange approach required in the type of policy implementation that reallocates power through a continuous supervisory judicial process. In these new tasks, writes Diver, there has occurred a

> profound transformation in the institutional role of litigation and the courts. The demands of structural reform have magnified the explicitly political dimensions of litigation. . . . Rather than an isolated, self-contained transaction, the lawsuit becomes a component of the continuous political bargaining process that determines the shape and content of public policy. . . . The judge comes to rely, for his influence, far more on exchange than on coercion and, for his mode of operation, far more on bargaining than on adjudication. He uses his central position in the lawsuit to wield influence far beyond the immediate boundaries of the case before him, assessing and weighing the impact of outcomes within the courtroom on the distribution of influence outside it. The judge assumes the role, in essence, of political powerbroker.[73]

A contrary view, outlined in Chapter 2 and adopted as a paradigm for this book, posits a more fluid, flexible judicial role. Rather than dichotomous, authoritative decision making based on principle, a genuinely political view of courts implies, first, empiricism (a systematic examination of how courts actually function) combined with a willingness to reorient our thinking in the light of the results of our empirical inquiry. What we find is, of course, that bargaining—powerbrokering, if you will—characterizes adjudication in American courts from top to bottom, whereas dichotomous, authoritarian, "principled" decision making exists more in the minds of normative legal theorists than in the real world.[74] This would seem to suggest that, as governmental agencies, courts can play many political roles

---

[70]See Jack W. Peltason, *Fifty-Eight Lonely Men: Southern Federal Judges and School Desegregation* (New York: Harcourt, Brace & World, 1961).

[71]See Colin S. Diver, "The Judge as Political Powerbroker: Superintending Structural Change in Public Institutions," *Virginia Law Review* 65, No. 1 (Feb. 1979): 43–106. See also Abraham Chayes, "The Role of the Judge in Public Law Litigation," *Harvard Law Review* 89, No. 7 (May 1976): 1281–1316; and Donald L. Horowitz, *The Courts and Social Policy* (Washington, D.C.: Brookings Institution, 1977).

[72]Diver, "Judge as Political Powerbroker": 62–63.

[73]Diver, "Judge as Political Powerbroker": 45–46.

[74]This is the conceptualization suggested by Martin Shapiro in *Courts*, especially Chapter 1.

and, in fact, do so in going about their daily tasks. Courts are probably as inherently capable as any other organ of government of assuming the administrative, supervisory tasks needed to reform governmental service institutions. At the very least, no convincing empirical data have been marshaled to show otherwise. That "litigation is a social institution inherently dichotomous in nature,"[75] the touchstone of Diver's abjectly apolitical view of courts, is empirically false.

Whether engaging in dispute processing, policy enunciating, or the various styles of implementation, courts are inherently political, which signifies that they must function in accordance with the needs of the regime. It is unrealistic to expect them to do otherwise. However, the tasks of government are many and not always consistent with one another. Thus, as we have shown, regime maintenance requires both the *reality* of substantive policy support (including enunciation, implementation, and administration) from the judiciary, as well as the *appearance* of detached, neutral dispute-processing involving the promise of justice for all, especially for minority and "have-not" interests in society. How can the judiciary, or any other institution, play both roles? The answer, some suggest, lies in a third function performed by law and courts, a function that may be their most important sociopolitical role.

COURTS AS PURVEYORS AND SUSTAINERS OF MYTH

Governing involves more than the exercise of raw power. Politics consists largely of the ability to persuade. Brute force, or threats of force, have never been sufficient to govern. Regimes regularly face the problem of how to convince the governed of the legitimacy of the system. Indeed, this may be the central problem of government: how to justify the rule of one person or group over others.

A longstanding tool employed by those in power to legitimate their rule is the creation and diffusion of myth, usually through the manipulation of symbols. Indeed, "law" and "justice" are among the symbols most frequently used to these ends. Thus, courts are established not only to resolve disputes and help govern through policy enunciation and implementation, but also to fulfill the closely related purpose of legitimizing the regime through the diffusion of the myth of equal justice under law. Although other social institutions, public and private, share in this task, courts are most closely associated with this important regime-maintaining function.

Essentially, we believe what we wish to believe, which is to say, what is comfortable. Since we have a need to believe in the basic fairness of our polity (the "ours is best" syndrome), law and courts exist to lend credence to this belief. The human need for a secular deity (itself a contradiction) creates that deity, and the icons of law and courts in turn feed this need. In this role, appearances are paramount, confirming some of Machiavelli's notions about successful regime maintenance. What often matters is not what law and courts are, in fact, but what they seem to be. As discussed in Chapter 2, this is the familiar use of myth to bridge the gap between what is and what is desired, helping to create a sense of security and stability. As Thurman Arnold so insightfully wrote more than six decades ago,

> No one should be surprised because there is so little similarity between the ideals of the law and what the courts actually do. It is part of the function of the "Law" to give recogni-

---

[75]Diver, "Judge as Political Powerbroker": 106. For a broader discussion of dichotomous models of adjudication, see Meir Dan-Cohen, "Bureaucratic Organizations and the Theory of Adjudication," *Columbia Law Review* 85, No. 1 (Jan. 1985): 1–37.

tion to ideals representing the exact opposite of established conduct. Most of its complications arise from the necessity of pretending to do one thing while actually doing another. It develops the structure of an elaborate dream world where logic creates justice. It permits us to look at the drab cruelties of business practices through rose-colored spectacles.

The principles of law are supposed to control society, because such an assumption is necessary to the logic of the dream. Yet the observer should constantly keep in mind that the function of law is not so much to guide society as to comfort it. . . .

"Law" is primarily a great reservoir of emotionally important social symbols. . . . It ordinarily operates to induce acceptance of things as they are. It does this by creating a realm somewhere within the mystical haze beyond the courts where all our dreams of justice in an unjust world come true. . . .

From a practical point of view it [law] is the greatest instrument of social stability because it recognizes every one of the yearnings of the underprivileged, and gives them a form in which those yearnings can achieve official approval without involving any particular action which might joggle the existing pyramid of power. It permits the use of an argumentative technique by which powerful institutions can be defended on the ground that taking away privilege from them would take away freedom from the poor.[76]

How well are American courts performing in this important sociopolitical role? Though difficult to assess, the answer would seem to be a tentative very well, again depending on one's perspective. One way to answer the question would be through an examination of the crucial relationship between law and courts, on the one hand, and public opinion, on the other. Although available data are skimpy and, perhaps more importantly, subject to varying interpretations, recent polling results would seem to indicate the following. First, the courts and the legal system are woefully lacking in salience for the public. That is, the general public knows very little about courts and judges, few respondents have had contact or experience with courts, and thus what substantive opinions are expressed may be open to question (see Chapter 12).[77] Second, poll results have repeatedly shown a negative correlation between experience with law and courts and support for these institutions.[78] And third, despite—or perhaps because of—the factor of low salience, courts tend to enjoy a rather high level of public support, especially of the diffuse variety. "Diffuse support" refers to generalized attitudes not particularly sensitive to transient policy issues, hence more important in measuring enduring attitudes toward the regime as a whole.[79] For example, the legal needs survey by the American Bar Foundation in the mid-1970s indicated that roughly three-fourths of the respondents were of the opinion that judges are honest and fair in deciding cases. Even multiple users of courts agreed with this assessment at a rate of 74 percent, while 78 percent of nonusers agreed.[80] Similarly, nearly 90

---

[76]Thurman W. Arnold, *The Symbols of Government* (New Haven: Yale University Press, 1935), 33–36. The mythology and symbolism of law and legal institutions has been discussed in a wide variety of books and articles. A particularly useful work is Sheingold, *The Politics of Rights:* especially Part 1, "The Myth of Rights." See also the near-classic essay by Max Lerner, "Constitution and Court as Symbols," *Yale Law Journal* 46, No. 8 (June 1936): 1290–1319. Finally, for a more general and philosophical view of law and myth, see Peter Fitzpatrick, *The Mythology of Modern Law* (London: Routledge, Chapman and Hall, 1992).

[77]A very useful summary of survey research dealing with law and courts is Austin Sarat, "Studying American Legal Culture: An Assessment of Survey Evidence," *Law and Society Review* 11, No. 3 (Winter 1977): 427–88. See also Thomas R. Marshall, *Public Opinion and the Supreme Court* (Boston: Unwin Hyman, 1989); and the discussion of public opinion and courts in Ch. 12.

[78]Yankelovich, Skelly, and White, *Public Image of Courts,* 1.

[79]On the subject of diffuse support, see Barbara Luck Graham, "Institutional Popularity of the Supreme Court: A Reassessment," paper delivered at the annual meeting of the American Political Science Association, New Orleans, August 29–September 1, 1985: 1–9, and the sources cited therein.

[80]See Barbara A. Curran, *The Legal Needs of the Public: The Final Report of a National Survey* (Chicago: American Bar Foundation, 1977), 236.

percent of the respondents agreed with the statement, "If you, yourself, were accused of a crime, you could expect to get a fair trial."[81]

In an extensive analysis of the findings of public opinion studies concerning law and courts, Austin Sarat drew similar conclusions. For example, he found that most surveys reported a "general, if not intense, support for local courts." And as to the Supreme Court, Sarat found,

> Though neither knowledge nor approval for specific decisions [of the Supreme Court] is very high, many people, including substantial numbers of those who disapprove of specific decisions, accord the Court high level of diffuse support; respect for the institution seems not to be based on approval of its decisions.[82]

It is true that the findings from public opinion polls concerning attitudes toward our legal system are mixed, with some studies reporting high levels of dissatisfaction with the system. A report of a poll of attitudes toward state and local courts in the mid-1970s concluded that public confidence in these tribunals was only moderate to low.[83] But a closer examination of these data illustrate the difficulty in interpreting poll results. Although some courts were rated by the public as fair or poor (minor civil and juvenile courts received less than 50 percent support), five out of seven local courts were rated as excellent, very good, or good by an average of 64 percent of the respondents.[84] The question often comes down to whether the proverbial glass is half empty or half full. And in view of the many reasons why the American judicial system should not attract the support of the public, what seems most striking is not the lack of public support but rather the relatively high level of public approval of our judicial system, particularly of the diffuse variety.

Assuming the foregoing conclusions to be generally correct—that American courts at all levels enjoy public approval probably out of proportion to a realistic assessment of their work—the question is, why? What is the basis for such support? Again, public opinion polls provide an answer. Several surveys have pointed to the persistence of the myth of judicial objectivity as the reason for continuing diffuse support for the judiciary.[85]

Gregory Casey has shown that some 60 percent of the respondents in his survey describe the work of the Supreme Court in mythic terms—what Casey calls "in the glow of symbols and credenda."[86] Moreover, Casey found that viewing the Court in terms of the traditional legal myths of American law (Chapter 2) is not a function of ignorance or low levels of education. In fact, he concluded,

> Those who accept the judicial myth are disproportionately from the more advantaged strata of society—socially, politically, and educationally. Acceptance by these influential societal sectors undoubtedly gives the myth its cultural dominance and explains the emphasis on the Court in the (only superficially effective) civics curricula of grade schools.[87]

---

[81]Curran, *Legal Needs of the Public,* 235. Nonusers of courts agreed with the statement at the rate of 87 percent, while one-time users agreed at an even higher rate, 90 percent.

[82]Sarat, "Studying American Legal Culture": 439. In several early public opinion surveys of attitude toward the Supreme Court, that tribunal seemed to evoke a relatively low level of public support. But these findings have been rather persuasively challenged. See Graham, "Institutional Popularity of the Supreme Court": 8–9.

[83]Yankelovich, Skelly, and White, *Public Image of Courts,* 81 and passim.

[84]Yankelovich, Skelly, and White, *Public Image of Courts,* 81–82, 96.

[85]Much of this research is cited and discussed in Sarat, "Studying American Legal Culture," especially 338–41.

[86]Gregory Casey, "The Supreme Court and Myth: An Empirical Investigation," *Law and Society Review* 8, No. 3 (Spring 1974): 398.

[87]Casey, "Supreme Court and Myth": 402.

In attempting to explain the roots of the diffusion of the judicial myth in American Society, Casey writes that

> The overall social environment is crucial: high political interests, middle class identification, daily newspaper readership, and some college experience admit people to a social world for which the cult of the Supreme Court is real. This social world appears better able to transmit and sustain the myth than formal institutions of education.[88]

If these findings and conclusions are correct, the important function of our courts as purveyors of the myth of justice is being performed quite well. The persistence of the myth among both the more and less knowledgeable, as well as over time, tends to support this conclusion.

This discussion is not unrelated to our earlier coverage of law, judicial decisions, and social change. If the symbols and myths of law and courts can help maintain the status quo, can they also be important forces inducing social change? In *The Politics of Rights,* Prof. Scheingold argues in the affirmative. If correct, this view of legal action may portend a more optimistic view of the role of courts as catalysts for change than that set forth in the Rosenberg analysis.[89]

Our overall assessment of the American judicial system comes to this: as multifaceted, flexible agencies of government, our courts will inevitably reflect—indeed, enhance—the values and policy preferences of the government of which they are a part. And even when these values are at cross purposes, courts play the important role of making the paradox of American judicial power seem nonparadoxical. In the final analysis, whether the system is performing well or poorly in its dispute processing, policy-making, and myth diffusing roles must depend upon the perspective of the observer. A search for neutral grounds in assessing the judicial system is as fruitless along the dimensions of structure and function as it is in the area of policy output. For as political instruments, law and courts exist to distribute societal advantages and disadvantages in accordance with the values of those who control them. At the same time, with a polite nod in the direction of the constitutive view of law, the foregoing account of the American judicial process is replete with evidence of law, courts and their accoutrements speaking for themselves in influencing the outcome of political-legal disputes.[90]

FURTHER READING

Abel, Richard L., ed. *The Politics of Informal Justice,* 2 vols. New York: Academic Press, 1982.

Arnold, Thurman W. *The Symbols of Government.* New Haven: Yale University Press, 1935.

Berger, Raoul. *Government by Judiciary: The Transformation of the Fourteenth Amendment.* Cambridge, Mass.: Harvard University Press, 1977.

Casey, Gregory. "The Supreme Court and Myth: An Empirical Investigation." *Law and Society Review* 8, No. 3 (Spring 1974): 385–419.

---

[88]Casey, "Supreme Court and Myth:" 403.

[89]This perspective is argued more fully by Malcolm Feeley. See his "Hollow Hopes, Flypaper, and Metaphor": 751–52.

[90]The appeal of the "constitutive" view of law is covered by Martin Shapiro in his essay, "Courts of Law, Courts of Politics," in Austin Ranney, ed., *Courts and the Political Process: Jack Peltason's Contributions to Political Science* (Berkeley: Institute of Governmental Studies Press, 1996), 108–113. See also Michael McCann, "It's Only Law and Courts, But I Like It," paper presented at the annual meeting of the American Political Science Association, Chicago, 1995.

Dahl, Robert A. "Decision-Making in a Democracy: The Role of the Supreme Court as a National Policy-Maker," *Journal of Public Law* 6 (Fall 1957): 279–95.

Diver, Colin S. "The Judge as Political Powerbroker: Superintending Structural Change in Public Institutions." *Virginia Law Review* 65, No. 1 (Feb. 1979): 43–106.

Friedman, Lawrence M. "The Law and Society Movement." *Stanford Law Review* 38, No. 3 (Feb. 1986): 763–80.

Galanter, Marc. "Why the Haves Come Out Ahead: Speculations on the Limits of Legal Change." *Law and Society Review* 9, No. 1 (Fall 1974): 95–160.

Horowitz, Donald L. *The Courts and Social Policy.* Washington, D.C.: Brookings Institution, 1977.

Lieberman, Jethro K., ed. *The Role of Courts in American Society: The Final Report of the Council on the Role of Courts.* St. Paul, Minn.: West, 1984.

Marshall, Thomas R. *Public Opinion and the Supreme Court.* Boston: Unwin Hyman, 1989.

Muir, William K., Jr. *Prayer in the Public Schools: Law and Attitude Change.* Chicago: University of Chicago Press, 1967.

Nader, Laura, ed. *No Access to Law: Alternatives to the American Judicial System.* New York: Academic Press, 1980.

Rosenberg, Gerald N. *The Hollow Hope: Can Courts Bring About Social Change?* Chicago: University of Chicago Press, 1991.

Sarat, Austin. "Studying American Legal Culture: An Assessment of Survey Evidence." *Law and Society Review* 11, No. 3 (Winter 1977): 427–88.

Scheingold, Stuart A. *The Politics of Rights: Lawyers, Public Policy and Political Change.* New Haven: Yale University Press, 1974.

Shapiro, Martin. "Courts of Law, Courts of Politics," in Austin Ranney, ed. *Courts and the Political Process: Jack W. Peltason's Contributions to Political Science.* Berkeley: Institute of Governmental Studies Press, 1996.

"The Supreme Court and Social Change." *Law and Social Inquiry* 17, No. 4 (Fall 1992): 715–78.

Name Index

Abel, Richard L., 60n, 237,
244n, 248n, 251, 253–254,
256, 258, 263, 264n, 269,
270n, 275, 291n, 452n, 455n,
456n, 457, 469
Abraham, Henry J., 46n, 81n,
82n, 86, 106n, 109, 118n,
119n, 125, 135n, 191n, 194n,
195n, 197n, 200n, 201n, 204n,
205n, 206n, 211n, 215, 301n,
389n, 390n, 402n, 459
Abrahamson, Shirley S., 366n,
370n
Acheson, Eleanor D., 190
Adamany, David, 464
Adams, John, 8n, 96, 226
Addison, Alexander, 134
Addler, Stephen J., 160
Aguilar, Robert P., 213, 214n
Ahmad-Taylor, Ty, 220n
Alfini, James J., 143n, 165n
Allison, Garland W., 187n
Alsop, Joseph H., 19n, 416n
Altman, Andrew, 34n
Anderson, Burnett, 389n, 390n
Anderson, James E., 54, 56n,
411n
Andrews, Lori, 293n, 294, 295,
296n
Apple, R.W., Jr., 195n
Applebome, Peter, 130n, 152n,
251n, 440n, 441n
Aquinas, Thomas, 6
Arkes, Hadley, 8n
Armstrong, Scott, 200, 391n,
406n

Armstrong, Virginia, 400n
Arnold, Thurman, 32, 34, 49n,
50, 64, 466–467, 469
Ashman, Allan, 90n, 140n, 143,
148n, 156n
Ashman, Charles R., 165n
Aspin, Larry T., 145n, 167
Atkins, Burton M., 151, 152n,
379n
Atkinson, David N., 419n
Auerbach, Jerold S., 226n, 230,
233, 234n, 240, 243, 258,
270n, 451n
Aumann, Francis R., 71n, 74n,
88, 93, 358n
Austin, Arthur, 42n
Austin, John, 8, 9, 234

Baer, Judith A., 38n, 41n
Baker, Bob, 291n
Baker, Leonard, 421n
Baker, Thomas E., 103n
Ball, Howard, 53n, 385n, 389n
Balzer, John, 149n
Banks, Arthur S., 221n
Banks, Taunya L., 373n, 374n
Barbanel, Josh, 164n
Barber, Sotorius, 45n, 46n, 64
Barker, Lucius J., 424n

Barr, Carl, 80n
Barrow, Deborah J., 209n, 210n,
215
Bator, Paul M., 94n, 125, 358n,
436n
Baum, Lawrence, 27, 108n,
119n, 140n, 149n, 152, 351,

357n, 366, 376, 381, 381n,
389n, 391n, 395n, 397n, 404n,
408, 413n, 429n, 433n, 446n,
447
Beasley, Dorothy Toth, 373n
Beck, Paul Allen, 130n
Becker, Theodore L., 49n, 413n,
447
Beer, Lawrence W., 46n
Begue, Yvette, 164n, 165n, 167
Bell, Derrick A., Jr., 42
Bender, Leslie, 40n
Bensman, Joseph, 218
Bentham, Jeremy, 7
Bentler, Arthur F., 21n, 22
Berg, Larry L., 144n, 151n, 416n
Berger, Raoul, 284n, 458n, 469
Bergerson, Peter J., 140n
Berke, Richard L., 194n, 196n
Berkson, Larry C., 90n, 91n,
157n, 179n, 181n, 215
Berle, Adolph, 227, 228, 229
Berman, Larry, 125n, 171n, 215
Berns, Walter, 38n
Bernstein, Nina, 249n, 277n,
392n
Besharov, Donald J., 244n, 248n
Best, Arthur, 287n
Bigger, Neal, Jr., 440
Billings, Rhoda B., 149n
Birch, Jonathan, 226
Bird, Rose Elizabeth, 130n, 145,
149n, 367
Bishop, Katherine, 214n
Biskupic, Joan, 195n, 213
Black, Charles L., 460

471

Black, Hugo, 109n, 170, 196, 198, 203, 211, 424
Black, Jeremiah, 131
Blackmun, Harry A., 196, 199, 201, 206, 209n, 405, 436,
Blackstone, William, 7, 9, 10n, 19, 226, 458
Blake, Fanchon, 267n
Blakenburg, Erhard, 271n, 298
Blasi, Vincent, 37n, 368n
Blaustein, Albert P., 204n
Blumberg, Abraham S., 300, 303n, 312n, 313n, 325n, 327n, 344
Blumberg, Mark, 301n, 313n
Bok, Derek, 26n, 258n, 449–450, 454n
Boland, Barbara, 318, 319
Booth, William, 249n, 454n
Bork, Robert H., 38n, 131n, 184, 192, 193, 194, 202, 207, 386, 412
Botein, Stephen, 71n
Bousche, Beverly, 149n
Bowen, Catherine Drinker, 13n, 209n
Bowen, Lauren, 252n
Bower, Francis, 217n
Boyce, Joseph N., 236n
Boyd, Gerald M., 192n
Brace, Paul, 177n, 365, 377
Brandeis, Louis D., 12, 13, 20, 130, 131, 193, 198, 200, 201, 204, 205, 206, 207, 210, 228, 388, 459
Brandon, Mark E., 45n
Brennan, William J., 38, 49, 69, 194, 199, 210, 229, 369n, 370, 375, 376, 377, 402n, 405
Brereton, David, 337n
Brest, Paul A., 31, 36, 37
Breyer, Stephen G., 109, 196, 197, 199, 205, 209, 392
Brigham, John, 42n, 43n, 48n
Broder, Josef M., 91n, 194,
Brody, Jane E., 294n
Bronner, Ethan, 131, 193, 215
Brown, David J., 355n
Brownell, Emery A., 245n
Bryce, Lord, 228
Buchanan, James, 96, 131
Bulger, Roger J., 293n
Bullock, Charles S., III, 437n
Bumiller, Kristin, 276n
Burbank, Stephen B., 214n
Burger, Warren E., 38, 111, 113, 191, 192, 193, 194, 199, 206, 211, 271, 284, 358, 391n, 400, 405
Burgess, John W., 18
Burgess, Susan R., 45n

Burnett, Warren, 145n
Burstin, H.R., 296n
Burton, Harold H., 398
Bush, George, 113, 125, 132, 173, 175, 177, 178, 179, 180, 181, 182, 183, 184, 185, 186, 187, 188, 189, 190, 194, 195, 202, 204, 207, 215, 248, 271, 311, 357, 358, 406n
Bushnell, Eleanore, 213n, 427, 442
Butler, Gregory Brian, 271n
Butler, Pierce, 20, 130n
Butterfield, Fox, 309n, 334–335
Byrd, Robert, 185
Byrnes, James F., 198, 211n

Cain, Patricia, 40n
Calabresi, Guido, 37, 42
Caldeira, Greg A., 131n, 353, 355n, 366n, 398n, 402, 443n, 444n, 448
Callow, Keith M., 149n
Campbell, Colin, 173n
Campbell, James S., 84n
Cameron, Benjamin, 385
Cameron, Charles M., 387, 408,
Cameron, James D., 146n
Canon, Bradley C., 144, 153, 155, 156, 164, 167, 357n, 366n, 368n, 412, 413n, 414n, 417n, 423n, 424n, 425n, 427n, 428n, 430n, 431n, 432n, 435n, 436n, 437n, 438n, 442n, 445n, 446n, 448, 462, 464
Cannon, Mark W., 389, 402
Cappelletti, Mauro, 46n, 451n
Caplan, Gerald M., 248n
Carbon, Susan, 90n, 91n, 179n, 181n, 215
Cardozo, Benjamin N., 12, 13, 14, 15, 20, 198, 206, 357, 404
Carlin, Jerome E., 245n, 291n, 456
Carlson, Christopher D., 84n, 287n, 288n, 290n, 298
Carnes, Edward E., 186
Carp, Robert A., 166n, 184, 190n
Carpenter, William S., 87n
Carrington, Paul D., 35, 36n, 355, 360n
Carson, Clara N., 159n, 220n, 221, 222n, 223, 224, 258
Carswell, G. Harrold, 130n, 185, 190, 201, 202, 206
Carter, Jimmy, 173, 175, 178, 179, 180, 181, 182, 183, 184, 187, 188, 189, 191, 196, 208, 212, 212, 214, 216, 217, 253
Carter, Lief, 43n
Carter, Robert M., 343

Cartwright, Bliss, 349n, 351n, 359,
Casey, Gregory, 468, 469
Casper, Jonathan D., 337n, 461
Casper, Gerhard, 65n
Castberg, A. Didrick, 30n
Catledge, Turner, 19n, 416n
Cavanaugh, Ralph C., 298n
Celebrezze, Frank D., 149n
Champagne, Anthony, 149n, 162n, 167, 248n, 301n, 454n
Chang, Robert, 42
Chapper, Joy A., 349n, 377n
Chase, Harold W., 170n, 171n, 176n, 215
Chase, Samuel P., 108, 211, 421, 428
Chayes, Abraham, 465n
Chisum, James, 149n
Choate, Rufus, 227
Choper, Jessie, 37n
Church, Thomas, 329n
Cicero, 6, 217
Claiborne, Harry E., 212, 213
Clark, David C., 287n
Clark, Leroy, 320n
Clark, Thomas C., 198, 200, 211n, 405
Clark, John H., 198, 211n
Clary, Mike, 164n
Cleveland, Grover, 174, 175, 195
Clifford, Nathan, 210
Clinton, William J., 19, 124, 163, 173, 180, 181, 182, 183, 187, 188, 189, 190, 195, 196, 204, 206, 208, 209, 214, 248, 249, 311, 429
Clune, William H., 70n
Coates, Dan, 264n
Cochran, Thad, 441
Cohen, Morris, 9, 12, 13
Cohn, Beverly, 249n
Cole, George F., 301n, 304n, 305, 314n, 317n, 323n, 325n, 336n, 343n, 344, 454n
Collins, Robert F., 214
Comte, Auguste, 8
Conley, John M., 290n
Conti, Samuel D., 92
Cook, Beverly Blair, 153n, 157n, 159n
Cook, Rhonda, 163n
Coolidge, Calvin, 175
Coons, John E., 70n
Cooper, Phillip, 389n
Cooper, Stephen, 427
Cooter, Robert, 38n, 64
Cortner, 443
Corwin, Edward S., 6n, 7n, 10n, 18, 21n, 22n, 24, 46, 49, 241n
Costanzo, Mark, 301n

Coulson, Robert, 454n
Countryman, Vern, 258
Cousins, William, Jr., 138n
Couzens, Michael, 309n
Cox, Archibale, 192
Coyle, Marcia, 202n
Cramton, Roger C., 247, 248n
Crites, Laura, 153n, 159n
Cruikshanks, Randal L., 165n
Culver, John H., 70n, 93, 130n,
    139n, 145n, 149n, 165n, 237n,
    251n, 270n, 286n, 349n, 358n,
    367n, 375, 376n, 377
Curran, Barbara A., 157n, 159n,
    220n, 21, 222n, 223, 224,
    244n, 258, 467, 468n
Currie, George R., 247n

Dahl, Robert A., 24, 460–461,
    462, 464, 470
D'Alemberte, Talbot, 373n
D'Amato, Anthony A., 402n
Dan-Cohen, Meir, 466n
Danelski, David J., 21n, 27, 130n
Daniels, Stephen, 274n, 276n,
    293, 294, 295, 296, 298, 359
Davies, Thomas Y., 352n, 354,
    355, 377
Davis, David, 201
Davis, Robert R., Jr., 214n
Davis, Steven, 142n
Davis, Sue, 373n, 374n, 377,
    379n, 381n, 405n, 408
Dawson, Thomas A., 267n
Decker, John F., 306n
Delgado, Richard, 42, 64
Derge, David R., 217n
Deukmejian, George, 367,
Dewey, John, 14, 22
DeZee, Matthew R., 394n
Diamond, Shari Seidman, 17n
Diamond, Stuart, 317n
Dierenfield, Richard B., 439n
Diver, Colin S., 447n, 465, 466,
    470
Dolbeare, Kenneth M., 55n, 412,
    437n, 438n, 440n, 442n, 444n,
    445n, 448
Dos Pasos, John, 227
Dole, Robert, 441
Doud, Maureen, 195n
Douglas, William O., 52, 108,
    109n, 170, 198, 203, 209, 210,
    211n, 404, 405, 417n, 421,
    436
Downes, William, 190n
Downing, Ronald G., 138n,
    139n, 141, 142, 145n, 168,
    254n
Doyle, Stephen P., 252n
Drechsel, Robert E., 445n

Drecksel, Paul C., 251n
Dryfus, Rochelle Cooper, 119n
Dubois, Philip L., 140n, 148n,
    149n, 152, 167, 353n
Duffner, John, 172
Duffy, Shannon P., 113
Dutter, Lee E., 388n
Dworkin, Ronald, 37, 54n

Eastland, James O., 172
Easterbrook, Frank, 386
Easton, David, 31, 56, 57
Edelman, Martin, 46n
Edelman, Murray, 49n
Edwards, George C., III, 414n
Edwards, Harry, 385
Egan, Michael J., 179
Egger, Daniel, 386n
Ehrlich, Eugen, 11
Eisenhower, Dwight D., 175,
    194, 200, 201, 202, 429,
Eisenstein, James, 57, 113n,
    303n, 317n, 324, 325n, 326n,
    344
Elazar, Daniel J., 46n
Eldridge, William B., 343n
Elter, Jon, 46n
Elwell, Suzanne E., 84n, 287n,
    288n, 289n, 290n, 298
Ely, John H., 37
Emerson, Deborah Day, 320n
Emmert, Craig F., 138n, 140n,
    144, 147, 153, 154n, 155, 167,
    372
Engel, David M., 276n
Epstein, Lee, 23n, 47, 55n, 108n,
    110n, 114, 115, 125, 131n,
    329n, 387n, 390n, 395n, 401,
    402n, 407n, 408, 443n, 444n,
    445n, 448
Escovitz, Sari S., 138n
Eskridge, William N., 419n,
    425n, 448
Esler, Michael, 372n
Esser, John, 48n
Eulau, Heinz, 217n
Evan, William M., 17n
Evans, Evan A., 175
Everson, David H., 432n, 438n
Ewell, Miranda, 214n

Fairchild, Erika, 301n
Farber, Daniel, 94n
Farrand, Max, 95n
Farris, Juli E., 84n
Febbjajo, Alberto, 48n
Feeley, Malcolm M., 91n, 304n,
    329n, 344, 363n, 413n, 447,
    452n, 464n, 469n
Feinstein, Dianne, 173
Feldman, William B., 287n

Felstiner, William L., 263n,
    264n, 269n, 270n, 298n
Fesler, James F., 69n, 357n
Field, Stephen J., 204, 209
Fillmore, Millard, 131
Fine, Erika S., 252n
Finifter, Ada F., 23, 27, 64, 298n
Finman, Theodore, 258,
Finn, John E., 45n
Fino, Susan P., 363n
Fish, Peter G., 121, 123n, 125
Fisher, Louis, 118n, 440n
Fisher, William W., III, 14n
Fiss, Owen, 33, 34, 35, 37, 39,
    61, 64
FitzGerald, Jeffrey, 272
Fitzpatrick, Collins T., 214n
Fitzpatrick, Peter, 467n
Flango, Victor E., 92n
Flanigan, James, 70n
Fleming, James E., 46n, 64
Flemming, Roy B., 317n, 320n,
    324n, 326, 328n, 344
Flynn, Leo J., 151n
Folberg, J., 452n
Foote, Caleb, 320n
Ford, Gerald, 175, 178, 183, 188,
    189, 210
Ford, Richard T., 42n
Ford, Stephen D., 5
Fordice, Kirk, 441
Forer, Lois G., 450n, 452
Fortas, Abe, 199, 201, 206,
    207n, 211, 212, 405, 421
Foss, Edward, 133n
Frank, Jerome E., 15, 16, 24, 27,
    66n, 217n, 346
Frankel, Marvin E., 336n, 337
Frankfurter, Felix, 52, 95, 97n,
    107n, 109n, 119, 125, 176,
    177n, 198, 203, 406, 418, 433
Franklin, Charles H., 445n,
    446n, 448
Freed, Daniel J., 340n, 342n
Freeman, Andrew D., 84n
Freund, Ernst, 56n
Freund, Paul A., 111
Friedelbaum, Stanley H., 358n,
    369n, 370n, 374n, 377
Friedman, Lawrence M., 26,
    61n, 63n, 72, 76n, 93, 225,
    226n, 231n, 232, 233, 240n,
    241n, 273, 349n, 351n, 356,
    359, 368n, 450n, 470
Friedman, Milton, 38
Friedrich, Carl J., 28, 46, 60n,
    451n
Fritsch, Jane, 251n
Fuller, Melville, 192
Fyfe, James J., 301n, 303, 313n,
    345

Gaius, 6
Galanter, Marc, 86, 220, 221, 222n, 258, 262n, 264, 265, 267, 269n, 271n, 272n, 273, 275n, 279n, 282n, 283, 285n, 288, 291, 296, 297, 298, 299, 351, 453, 470
Galie, Peter J., 358n, 368n, 371n, 373n, 375n, 376n
Gallas, Geoff, 67n, 90
Garcia, Chris, 158n
Gardner, James, 372
Garmel, Julie, 162
Garrow, David J., 113n, 124n, 192n
Garth, Bryant, 451n
Gates, John B., 23n, 27, 38n, 45, 49n, 55, 64, 141n, 167, 171n, 402n, 408, 412, 443n, 444n, 448
Gaynes, Elizabeth, 322n
George, Robert P., 45n
George, Tracey E., 407n
Gerhardt, Michael J., 214n
Gerstein, Richard E., 320n
Gibson, John, 356
Giles, Walter I., 19n
Gilligan, Carol, 41n
Gillman, Howard, 38n, 44n
Gilmore, Grant, 14n, 18n, 27
Ginger, An Fagan, 241n
Ginsburg, Douglas H., 194, 199
Ginsburg, Ruth B., 196, 199, 204, 252, 392
Gizzi, Michael C., 103n
Glazer, Nathan, 284n, 458n
Glick, Henry A., 53n, 92, 93, 138n, 139, 140n, 142n, 144, 146, 147, 148n, 150, 151n, 153, 154, 155, 167, 350n, 363n, 364, 386n
Gnaizda, Robert, 454n
Goerdt, John A., 285n, 287n
Gold, Nan, 138
Goldberg, Arthur J., 109, 405
Goldberg, Carey, 367n
Goldman, John H., 294n
Goldman, Sheldon, 30n, 171n, 172n, 173n, 174, 175, 176n, 177, 178, 179n, 181, 183, 184n, 186n, 187n, 188, 189, 190n, 202n, 215, 343n, 363n, 381n, 385n, 403n, 404n, 408
Goldschmidt, Jona, 139n
Goldstein, Candice, 164n, 165n
Goldwater, Barry, 422
Goodnow, Frank, 18
Gorai, Patricia, 221
Gordon, Margaret S., 245n
Gordon, Robert, 72
Gorman, John P., 418n

Gorton, Slade, 186
Gossblat, Martha, 157n
Gottlieb, Scott, 277n
Graber, Doris A., 445n, 446n
Graglia, Lino A., 458n
Graham, Barbara Luck, 160n, 161n, 163n, 167, 467n, 468n
Granfors, Mark W., 241n
Gray, Jerry, 249n
Green, Justin J., 144n, 385n
Green, Mark J., 233n
Green, Wayne E., 130n
Greenberg, Douglas, 26n, 46n
Greenhouse, Linda, 99n, 113n, 124n, 159n, 163n, 191n, 192n, 193, 196n, 202n, 212n, 213n, 234n, 252n, 390n, 392n, 402n, 406n, 421n, 429
Grier, Robert, 209
Griswold, Erwin N., 32, 236
Grodin, Joseph, 145, 367
Grofman, Bernard, 413n
Gross, Bertram, 21
Grossman, Joel B., 30n, 49n, 53n, 54, 56n, 60, 151n, 172n, 173, 206n, 215, 270n, 276, 277, 299, 463n
Grossman, Mary H., 463n
Grotius, Hugo, 6
Gruhl, John, 344
Grutman, Roy, 217n
Gryski, Gerald, 209n, 210n, 215
Gunther, Gerald, 421,
Gulick, Luther, 57, 58, 59
Gumplowicz, Ludwig, 11
Gunther, Gerald, 86n, 125,n, 421n
Guttmann, Diane S., 366n, 370n

Hacker, Andrew, 233
Hain, Paul L., 217n
Haines, Charles Grove, 21n, 22, 88n, 356n
Hakman, Nathan, 246n
Haley, John O., 272n
Hall, Andrew, 322n, 323n
Hall, Jerome, 16
Hall, Kermit L., 71n, 108n, 135n, 167, 211n, 356, 390n
Hall, Margaret E., 12n, 404n
Hall, Melinda Gann, 363n, 365, 376
Hall, William K., 145n, 167
Hallian, Joseph T., 293n
Halliday, Terrence C., 241n
Halpern, Stephen C., 26, 235n, 406n
Haltom, William, 193n, 405n
Hamilton, Alexander, 96
Hammond, Philip E., 437n,

438n, 440n, 442n, 444n, 445n, 448
Hammurabi, 63
Hansen, Mark, 113n
Hanson, Roger A., 349n, 377
Haq, Kathy, 164n
Harding, Warren G., 175
Harlan, John M., Jr., 52, 109n, 402n, 405
Harpham, Edward J., 248n, 454n
Harrell, Mary Ann, 389n, 390n
Harrington, Christine B., 48n, 177n, 455n, 456n
Harris, Joseph P., 170n, 215
Harris, Richard, 130n, 206n, 215
Harris, William F., II, 45n, 46n
Harrison, Benjamin, 175, 191
Harrison, Cynthia, 389n
Hart, Henry, 30n, 32, 34, 94n, 95n, 96n, 97n, 98n, 99n, 109n, 113n, 116n, 118n, 120n, 125
Harvey, Steve, 163n
Hastings, Alcee L., 212, 213
Hatch, Orin, 173
Haveman, Robert H., 247n
Hawkins, Virgil, 433, 434
Haydel, Judith Ann, 140, 141n, 161n, 167
Haydock, Roger S., 251n, 252n
Haynes, Evan, 133n, 134n, 135, 167
Haynsworth, Clement, 199, 201, 202, 205, 206, 207
Hazard, Geoffrey C., Jr., 240n, 244n, 252n, 258, 463n, 464
Hazeltine, H.D., 11n
Headen, Susan M., 293n
Heflin, Howell, 193
Heilbrunn, Jacob, 459n
Heinz, John P., 254n, 256, 257n, 258, 354n
Heller, Matthew, 83n, 384n
Hellman, Arthur D., 125, 383n, 384n, 408
Helmes, Jessie, 422
Henchen, Beth, 142n, 416n
Henderson, Bancroft C., 148n
Henley, R.G., 140n, 149n
Hennessey, Patricia, 84n, 286n, 287n, 289n, 290n, 456n
Henry, D. Alan, 322n
Henschen, Beth M., 142n, 416n
Hensler, Deborah R., 271n, 276, 292n, 297
Hensley, Thomas R., 24n, 25n
Hepperle, Winifred, 153n, 159n
Herndon, James, 148
Heumann, Milton, 329, 344
Heussenstamm, F.K., 315n
Hill, Anita F., 195, 207
Hirsch, H.N., 48n

Hobbs, Douglas S., 30n
Hobel, A.E., 3
Hobson, Charles F., 51
Hoffman, Daniel N., 384n
Hoffman, James R., 159n
Hogarth, John, 343n
Hojnicki, Marie, 149n, 152n
Holland, T.E., 8
Hollingsworth, Ellen Jane, 247n
Hollingsworth, Robert J.,287n, 288n, 290n
Holmes, Oliver Wendell, Jr., 6n, 13, 14, 21, 27, 57, 62, 194, 196, 200, 209, 210, 261, 333, 389, 404, 449
Holmes, Steven A., 242n, 423n
Holt, Wythe, 34n
Hoover, Herbert, 174, 175, 200, 205, 210
Horowitz, Donald L., 217n, 465n, 470
Horwitz, Morton J., 14n,, 24n, 72n, 74n
Houseman, Gerald L., 38n
Howard, J. Woodford, Jr., 174, 177, 215, 378, 379n, 380n, 383n, 385n, 386n, 387n, 388, 407n, 408
Howard, Jan, 245n
Howe, Frederich C. 216
Howell, Ronald F., 32
Hruska, Roman, 111, 172, 206
Hughes, Charles Evans, 20, 52, 78, 192n, 198, 205, 210, 211n, 404, 405
Hume, David, 7, 8
Hurst, James Willard, 74, 93, 120n, 131, 132n, 219, 226n, 227n, 231n, 232, 243n, 244
Hurst, Ward, 210
Hutchinson, Allan C., 34n, 35n, 37n, 38n
Hyde, Henry 424

Idelson, Holly, 196n, 213n
Ifill, Gwen, 196n
Ignagi, Joseph, 416n, 425n, 448
Irish, Marian D., 18n, 27
Irons, Peter H., 403n

Jackson, Andrew, 131, 134
Jackson, David W., 84n, 93n
Jackson, Donald, 172n, 176n, 215, 367n
Jackson, Robert H., 19, 109, 198
Jacob, Herbert, 53, 54, 56n, 65, 75n, 87n, 89n, 93, 134n, 143, 144n, 218n, 237, 240, 256, 298n, 303n, 314n, 324, 325, 344, 382n
Jacobs, James B., 303n
Jacobs, Margaret A., 278n

Jacobs, Mark D., 84n
Jacobsohn, Gary J., 46n
Jacoby, Joan E., 318n
Jahnige, Thomas P., 30n, 172n, 174, 178n
James, Howard, 83n
James, William, 14
Jay, John, 108
Jefferson, Thomas, 7, 10n, 134, 226, 393, 421, 428, 429
Jeffries, John Calvin, Jr., 124n
Jellison, Nancy L., 159
Jenkins, William Jr., 145n, 146n
Jesilow, Paul, 309n, 310n
Johnson, Andrew, 131, 191,
Johnson, Charles A., 23n, 27, 44n, 45n, 64, 141n, 149n, 167, 171n, 368n, 400n, 402n, 412n, 413n, 417n, 423, 423n, 424n, 425n, 427n, 428n, 430n, 431n, 432n, 435n, 436n, 437n, 442n, 443n, 444n, 445n, 446n, 448n, 462, 464
Johnson, David T., 272n
Johnson, Dirk, 237n
Johnson, Earl, Jr., 447, 452n, 455n, 456n
Johnson, Lyndon B., 173, 175, 178, 183, 201, 213, 246
Johnson, Richard M., 437n
Jonas, Frank H., 70n
Jones, Harry W., 69n

Kagan, Robert A., 275n, 346, 349n, 351n, 359, 360, 363, 377
Kahlenberg, Richard D., 233n
Kahn, Ronald, 48n
Kairys, David, 30n, 34n, 48, 64, 217n
Kales, Albert, 138, 229
Kalven, Harry, Jr., 331n, 333n
Karst, Kenneth, 37, 320n
Kassoff, George, 190
Kastner, Daniel L., 444n
Katz, Ellis, 373n
Katzmann, Robert A., 88n, 447n, 448
Kauder, Neal B., 273, 274n, 279n, 280, 281n, 283n, 286n 289n, 299, 311n, 350n, 352n, 360n, 361n, 362n, 377
Kaufman, Herbert, 130n
Kawashima, Takeyoshi, 277n
Kaye, Judith S., 369n, 372n, 373n, 374n, 375n, 377
Keiter, Robert B., 70n
Keefe, William J., 88n
Kelly, Michael J., 255n
Kelman, Mark, 34n, 39n, 64
Kelson, Hans, 9

Kennedy, Anthony M., 163, 194, 199, 204, 207, 252, 392
Kennedy, Duncan, 254, 255n
Kennedy, Edward, 172, 192, 193
Kennedy, John F., 173, 174, 175–176, 196, 201, 429
Kent, James (Chancellor), 356
Kessler, Mark, 249n
Keys, Clinton Walker, 6n
Kilborn, Peter T., 248n
Kinkaid, John, 46n
King, Gary, 177n
King, Rodney, 303n, 332
Kirchhof, Paul, 46n
Klare, Karl E., 235
Klein, Fannie J., 63n
Klein, Stephen P., 243n
Klonoski, James R., 55n
Knight, J.T., 221n, 272n
Kobylka, Joseph, 443n
Kolbe, John, 146n
Kommers, Donald P., 46n
Kornhauser, Lewis, 39, 267n, 298n, 299
Kosaki, Liane C., 445n, 446n, 448
Kramer, Paul A., 373n
Krislov, Samuel, 413n
Kritzer, Herbert M., 270n, 298n, 299
Krivosha, Norman, 138n
Kronman, Anthony T., 228n, 234n, 258
Kurland, Fred, 138n
Kurland, Philip B., 51n
Kuykendall, Mae, 349n, 350n

Labaton, Stephen, 124n, 190n, 271n
Lacey, Micola, 302
Ladinski, Jack, 142n, 254n
LaFollette, Robert M., 205
LaFree, Gary D., 336n
Lamar, Joseph R., 198
LaPiana, William P., 233, 258
Lamar, Lucius Q.C., 195
Lamb, Charles M., 363n, 385n, 403n, 406n, 408, 437n
Landon, Donald D., 255n
Landis, James, 95, 96n, 9n, 107n, 119, 120n, 125, 176, 177n
Langdell, Christopher Columbus, 18, 231, 232, 233, 235
Laski, Harold, 138
Lasswell, Harold D., 31n, 217, 218n, 220n
Latzer, Bary, 371, 371, 372, 372
Laumann, Edward O., 254, 256, 257n, 258, 354
Law, Sylvia, 293n

Lawrence, Susan E., 246n, 350n, 464n
Lawton, Anne, 166n
Lay, Donald P., 338, 340, 342
Lazerson, Mark H., 291n, 457n
Lee, Richard E., 123
Lee, Robert B., 247n
Lehne, Richard, 70, 369n, 435n
Lehnen, Robert G., 306n
Lempert, Richard, 26
Lermack, Paul, 146n
Lerner, Max, 13, 50n, 64, 467n
Leuchtenburg, William E., 19n
Lev, Dan, 220n
Levin, Martin, 130n, 303n, 343n, 344
Levine, Felice J., 17n
Levine, James P., 86, 87n, 306n, 331n, 333n, 344
Levinson, Sanford, 31n, 46n, 389n
Levy, Leonard W., 38n, 320n
Lewis, Ed, 453
Lewis, Neil A., 173n, 186, 187, 190, 196n, 202n, 217n, 271n, 423n
Lieberman, Jethro K., 271n, 450n, 458n, 470
Lincoln, Abraham, 124, 201, 204, 209, 226, 236
Lind, E. Allen, 452n
Linde, Hans A., 88n, 374
Linowitz, Sol M., 228n, 234n, 258
Lipscher, Robert D., 92n
Lipsky, Michael, 411
Litan, Robert E., 86n, 274n
Littleton, Christine A., 41n, 72
Llewellyn, Karl N., 14, 15n, 16, 26, 27, 229, 258, 297, 301, 441
Lloyd, Dennis, 7n
Locke, John, 6, 7
Lodge, Henry Cabot, 197, 200
London, Robb, 149n
Lott, Trent, 441
Lovrich, Nicholas P., 141n, 149n, 151n, 152n, 167
Low, Peter W., 124n
Lowe, R. Stanley, 150n
Lubet, Steven, 165n
Lucey, Patrick, 156n
Luhman, Niklas, 48n
Lurton, Horace H., 197, 198, 200
Luskin, Mary Lee, 83n, 92n
Lutz, Donald, 372

Macedo, Stephen, 45n
Machiavelli, Niccolo, 466
MacIver, R. M., 48, 49n
Maddi, Dorothy L., 146n
Maggiotto, Michael A., 413

Mahenna, 318, 319
Mahoney, Dennis J., 320n
Maine, Henry, 11
Mainman, Richard J., 298n
Maitland, Frederick William, 11, 62n
Maltese, John A., 197n
Manion, Daniel, 132n, 185, 186, 206n, 412
Mann, Coramae Richey, 303n
Manning, Bayless, 270n
Manwaring, David R., 432n
Maraniss, David, 19n
March, James G., 44n
Marcus, Frances Frank, 214n
Marcus, Maeva, 89n, 95n, 125, 371n
Margolick, David, 251n, 271n
Marks, F. Raymond, 228n
Marks, Jonathan B., 452n, 455n, 456n
Marshall, John, 9, 21, 51, 52, 88, 108, 204, 228, 347, 356, 406
Marshall, Thomas R., 204n, 467n, 470
Marshall, Thurgood, 194–195, 199, 204, 210, 303n, 343n, 405
Martin, Joanne, 274n, 295, 298
Martin, Luther, 227
Marvell, Thomas B., 349n, 350n, 352, 353n, 362n
Masaro, John, 205n
Mason, Alpheus T., 18, 24, 44n, 368n, 392n
Mather, Lynn, 55n, 56n, 298n
Maule, Linda, 149n, 167
Mayer, Andrew C., 217n
Mazzola, Jean-Claude, 162n
McCann, Michael W., 38n, 48n, 464n, 469n
McCloskey, Robert G., 389n
McClennan, John L., 172
McCoy, Candace, 328n
McCree, Wade H., 355n
McDougal, Myres, 217, 218n, 220n
McEwen, Craig A., 298
McFadden, Douglas, 206n
McGee, Frasier, 250
McGuigan, Patrick B., 131n, 193n
McGuire, Kevin T., 398n
McIntosh, Wayne V., 273, 298n, 299
McIntyre, Lisa J., 250n, 258
McKay, David, 83n
McKean, Dayton, 241n
McLaughlin, William P., 125
McLeish, Archibald, 52n
McKinnon, Catherine, 41, 64

McReynolds, James C., 20, 198, 200, 406
Meador, Daniel J., 360n
Meernik, James, 416n, 425n, 448
Meese, Edwin, III, 37, 38n, 124, 125, 184
Meinhold, Stephen S., 276n
Melamed, A. Douglas, 42n
Melnick, R. Shep, 447n, 448
Meltzer, Daniel J. 94n
Mendelsohn, Robert, 55n
Menkel-Meadow, Carrie, 40n
Menninger, Karl, 336n
Mensch, Elizabeth, 30n, 37n
Merrill, Frederick R., 246n
Merritt, Gilbert S., 389n
Mersky, Roy M., 204n
Meskill, Thomas J., 172n, 380n, 384n 389n
Metrailer, Rosemary, 402n
Michelman, Frnak, 37
Middleton, Martha, 164n
Mikva, Abner, 385
Miller, Arthur S., 28, 32, 33n, 61n
Miller Benjamin K., 166n
Miller, Brian David, 271n
Miller, Herman P., 245n
Miller, Mark C., 91n
Miller, Merle, 200n
Miller, Richard E., 263n, 264n, 265n, 266n, 267, 268, 269n
Minda, Gary, 38n, 39n, 40n, 41n, 64
Minier, David D., 83n
Minnow, Martha, 41n
Minton, Sherman, 198, 418
Mishkin, Paul J., 94n
Mishler, William, 444n, 448
Mnookin, Robert H., 84n, 267, 298n, 299
Moll, Richard W., 217n, 237n
Moll, Walter L., 11n
Molotsky, Irvin, 423n
Monahan, Patrick J., 34n, 35n, 37n, 38n
Moody, William, 198, 200
Moog, Robert, 142n
Moore, Frederick W., 11n
Moore, John Bassett, 18
Moore, Underhill, 22
Moore, Wayne D., 45n
Morris, Gouverneur, 97
Morris, Norval, 336n
Morrow, Sue, 164
Mosk, Stanley, 374n
Mowbray, John, 164n
Muir, William K., Jr., 463n, 470
Muraskin, Matthew, 400n
Murdock, Margaret Maier, 158n
Murphy, Frank, 198

Murphy, Michael J., 438
Murphy, Walter F., 18, 27, 29,
    30*n*, 46, 52, 53*n*, 55*n*, 64,
    125*n*, 171*n*, 176*n*, 191*n*, 215,
    368*n*, 378, 393*n*, 400*n*, 404*n*,
    406*n*, 407, 408, 413*n*, 415*n*,
    416*n*, 431*n*, 432*n*, 433*n*, 434*n*,
    444*n*, 448, 458*n*
Musheno, Michael C., 306*n*

Nader, Laura, 270*n*, 275, 299,
    451*n*, 470
Nader, Ralph, 293*n*
Nagel, Robert F., 394*n*
Nagel, Stuart, 301*n*, 363, 416*n*,
    463*n*
Nardulli, Peter F., 317*n*, 324*n*,
    326*n*, 344
Navarro, Mireya, 83*n*
Neal, Caswell S., 432
Neal, David, 337*n*
Nedelsky, Jennifer, 45*n*
Neeley, Richard, 452*n*
Neff, Alan, 179*n*, 181*n*
Nelson, Robert L, 222*n*, 228*n*,
    372*n*
Neubauer, David, 276*n*, 301*n*,
    305–306, 322*n*, 323, 324*n*,
    345
Newman, Frank, 370
Nixon, Richard M., 51*n*, 172,
    175, 178, 183, 188, 189, 191,
    192, 201, 204, 205, 296, 428,
    429, 430,
Nixon, Walter L., Jr., 213
Noble, Kenneth B., 192*n*, 193*n*
Norris, George, 205
Norton, W.W., 193*n*
Novak, Viveca, 242*n*
Nufter, Harold F., 117*n*

Oakley, John B., 383*n*
O'Barr, William N., 290*n*
O'Brien, David M., 27, 31, 43,
    44, 109*n*, 124*n*, 171*n*, 172*n*,
    173*n*, 201*n*, 215, 389*n*, 392*n*,
    394*n*, 399, 394*n*, 402*n*, 403*n*,
    408
O'Callaghan, Jerome, 144*n*
Ogul, Morris S., 88
Ohlin, Lloyd E., 300
Olsen, John P., 44*n*
Olson, Walter, 277*n*
Oskamp, Stuart, 301*n*
Osthus, Marlin O., 349*n*
Ostrom, Brian J., 65*n*, 66*n*, 67*n*,
    159, 273*n*, 274*n*, 279*n*, 280*n*,

281*n*, 283*n*, 286*n*, 299, 311*n*,
    350*n*, 352*n*, 360*n*, 361*n*, 362,
    377
Overby, L. Marvin, 195*n*

Pacelle, Richard L., Jr., 65*n*,
    395*n*
Packer, Herbert L., 304, 306*n*
Palay, Thomas, 222*n*, 258
Palmer, Barbara, 398*n*
Palumbo, Dennis, 306*n*
Paonita, Anthony, 149*n*
Parker, Isaac, 73, 130*n*, 231
Parker, John J., 200, 202, 205,
    421
Parker, Richard, 173*n*
Parness, Jeffrey A., 90
Parrish, Elsie, 50
Partridge, Anthony, 343*n*
Paschal, Richard A., 416*n*, 420*n*,
    421*n*, 423*n*, 448
Pataki, George, 376*n*
Patrick, Gordon, 413*n*
Patterson, Dennis, 40*n*
Patterson, Edwin, 13, 14*n*, 27
Patterson, Samuel, 187
Paul, Jerry, 300, 315*n*
Paul, Kevin C., 40*n*
Paxton, Tom, 216
Pear, Robert, 248*n*, 249*n*, 369*n*,
    435*n*
Peireson, James E., 217*n*
Peller, Gary, 31*n*, 64
Peltason, Jack W., 15*n*, 21, 22,
    23, 24, 35, 39*n*, 55*n*, 130*n*,
    131, 132*n*, 261, 267*n*, 275*n*,
    392*n*, 394*n*, 411, 412, 443*n*,
    448, 465*n*, 469*n*
Penrod, Steven, 264*n*
Pepinsky, Harold E., 309*n*, 310
Percival, Robert V., 273*n*
Perez-Reilly, Mario, 107*n*, 170*n*,
    198–202
Perpich, Rudy, 427
Perry, H.W., Jr., 398*n*, 408
Phelps, Glen, 38*n*, 49*n*
Phelps, Timothy M., 195*n*
Pitney, Mahlon, 198
Plucknett, Theodore, 62*n*
Polan, Steven, 293*n*
Pollock, Frederick, 11, 62*n*
Pollock, Ellen J., 160
Porter, John F., 91*n*
Porter, Mary Cornelia, 70*n*, 93,
    357*n*, 358*n*, 359–360, 363,
    364, 365, 366*n*, 370*n*, 377
Porter, Russell, 417*n*
Posner, Richard A., 36, 38, 65*n*
Post, C. Gordon, 62*n*
Post, Robert C., 369*n*
Pound, Roscoe, 5, 11, 12, 14, 15,

26, 27, 56, 75*n*, 90, 136, 137*n*,
    233*n*, 297, 358
Powell, Lawrence, 332,
Powell, Lewis F., Jr., 192, 199,
    211, 369, 405
Powell, Michael J., 241*n*
Press, Charles, 460
Pringle, Henry F., 210*n*
Pritchard, E.F., Jr., 52*n*
Pritchett, C. Herman, 18, 21*n*,
    22, 24, 25, 26, 27, 30*n*, 52*n*,
    53*n*, 378, 392, 393*n*, 400*n*,
    401*n*, 404*n*, 407, 415*n*, 416*n*,
    421, 422, 423*n*, 424*n*, 425,
    431*n*, 432*n*, 433*n*, 434*n*
Provine, Doris Marie, 80*n*, 81*n*,
    82*n*, 83, 93, 282*n*, 398*n*, 400*n*,
    408
Pruet, George W., Jr., 363*n*
Purdum, Todd S., 429*n*
Purnick, Joyce, 167*n*
Puro, Marsha, 140*n*
Puro, Steven, 140*n*, 430*n*
Pyne, Thomas, 164*n*

Quale, J. Danforth, 271

Radin, Max, 3
Rafter, Nicole Hahn, 303*n*
Rakove, Jack N., 38*n*
Ranney, Austin, 15*n*, 39*n*, 275*n*,
    443*n*, 469*n*
Rawls, John, 37*n*, 64
Ray, Larry, 452*n*
Reagan, Ronald W., 10, 113*n*,
    125, 132*n*, 173, 175, 175, 176,
    177, 178, 179, 180, 181, 182,
    183, 184, 185, 186, 187, 188,
    189, 190*n*, 191, 192, 193*n*,
    194, 204, 207, 215, 247, 248,
    311, 358, 386, 428, 406*n*, 428,
    429
Reed. Stanley F., 198, 404–405
Reed, Thomas, 14*n*
Reeve, Tapping, 231
Reeve, Henry, 217
Rehnquist, William H., 21*n*,
    38*n*, 49*n*, 99*n*, 108*n*, 109,
    113, 124, 163, 169, 191, 192,
    194, 196, 199, 201, 204,
    379*n*, 386, 392, 402*n*, 405*n*,
    406*n*
Reich, Donald R., 438*n*
Reid, Traciel V., 38*n*
Reidinger, Paul, 195
Remmington, Frank J., 300*n*
Reskin, Barbara F., 331*n*
Reynoso, Cruz, 145, 367
Rhode, Deborah L., 240*n*, 244*n*,
    252*n*, 258, 298*n*
Richardson, Richard J., 55*n*,
    65*n*, 95*n*, 96, 98*n*, 126, 174,

Richardson, Richard J. *(cont.)* 175, 177, 353, 382*n*, 385*n*, 387*n*, 388*n*
Riddlesperger, James W., Jr., 367*n*
Ritter, Halstead, 212
Roane, Spencer, 356
Robel, Lauren K., 384*n*
Roberts, Albert R., 301*n*
Roberts, Owen J., 10, 20, 198, 404
Roberts, Steven V., 194*n*
Robertson, John A., 80*n*
Robinson, Laurie O., 320*n*
Roche, John P., 459*n*
Rockman, Bert, 173*n*
Rodino, Peter, 212
Rohde, David W., 403*n*
Roll, John M., 138*n*, 167
Roosevelt, Franklin D., 19, 20, 21, 22*n*, 170, 175, 176, 184, 191, 200, 202, 209, 210, 211, 425, 428, 429
Roosevelt, Theodore, 175, 197, 200, 243, 404
Rorty, Richard, 48
Rose-Akerman, Susan, 39
Rosen, Daniel, 400*n*
Rosenau, Pauline Marie, 40*n*
Rosenbaum, Judy, 90*n*, 91*n*
Rosenberg, Julius and Ethel, 108*n*
Rosenberg, Gerald N., 419*n*, 420*n*, 425*n*, 426, 429, 445*n*, 448, 462, 463, 464, 470
Rosenberg, Maurice, 360*n*
Rosenblum, Victor G., 21, 22, 24, 30*n*, 69, 70*n*, 219, 234, 254, 255, 256, 258, 357*n*, 459*n*
Ross, H. Laurence, 261, 267, 297, 299, 303*n*, 336*n*
Ross, Michael, 423*n*
Rossiter, Clinton, 428*n*
Rostow, Victoria P., 293*n*
Rowland, C.K., 184*n*
Rubin, Alvin, 389*n*
Rubin, H. Ted, 84*n*
Ruffin, Jane, 152*n*
Ruhnka, John C., 84*n*
Rumble, Wilfred E., Jr., 14*n*, 27
Russell, Peter H., 60*n*
Rutledge, John, 94, 95
Rutledge, Wiley B., 109, 198
Ryan, John Paul, 140*n*, 148*n*, 156*n*, 157*n*, 167
Ryskamp, Kenneth L., 186

Sabine, George S., 6*n*, 7*n*
Sack, Kevin, 161*n*, 162
Sacks, Albert, 30*n*

Sahid, Joseph R., 84*n*
Saffell, David C., 413*n*
Saks, Michael J., 271*n*, 292*n*, 294*n*, 297, 299
Saks, Richard, 161*n*, 167
Sales, Bruce D., 140*n*, 148*n*, 156*n*
Salmond, J.W., 8
Samborn, Randal, 244*n*
Sampson, Kathleen M., 138*n*
Sander, Richard H., 237
Sanders, Joseph, 26
Sanford, Edward T., 198
Sarason, Matthew D., 189*n*
Sarat, Austin, 27, 35*n*, 60, 263*n*, 264*n*, 265*n*, 266*n*, 267, 269, 270*n*, 276, 277, 299, 343*n*, 363*n*, 381*n*, 403*n*, 404, 408, 467*n*, 468*n*, 470
Savage, David G., 248, 369*n*
Savell, Lawrence, 217*n*
Savigny, Frederick Karl von, 11
Saxe, John Godfrey, 3, 4
Sayer, Wallace S., 130*n*
Scalia, Antonin, 38*n*, 191, 192, 194, 196, 199, 201, 204, 392
Scheb, John M., II, 146*n*
Scheff, Thomas J., 291*n*
Scheingold, Stuart A., 247*n*, 453*n*, 464, 467*n*, 469, 470
Scheppele, Kim Lane, 17*n*, 26*n*
Schick, Marvin, 400*n*
Schlegel, John H., 233*n*
Schlesinger, Joseph, 318*n*
Schmid, William E., 427*n*
Schmidhauser, John R., 24, 26*n*, 30*n*, 144*n*, 197*n*, 200*n*, 203, 207, 208, 215, 347*n*, 416*n*, 448
Schmitt, Richard B., 276*n*, 385*n*
Schneider, Ronald S., 144*n*
Schneyer, Theodore, 244*n*, 258
Schotland, Roy, 152*n*
Schubert, Glendon A., 14*n*, 18*n*, 22, 23, 24, 27, 28, 29*n*, 30, 31*n*, 56*n*, 218*n*, 400*n*, 403*n*, 413*n*, 459*n*
Schumer, Charles, 303*n*, 309*n*
Schur, Edwin M., 9*n*, 11*n*, 17*n*, 54, 55*n*
Schwartz, Bernard, 109*n*
Schwartz, Herman, 176
Schwartz, Ira M., 84*n*
Scrivner, Ellen, 301*n*
Scruggs, Ann M., 162*n*
Segal, Jeffrey A., 23*n*, 114, 115, 365*n*, 387*n*, 403*n*, 408,
Seidman, David, 309*n*
Sessions, Jefferson B., III, 185, 186

Shaman, Jeffrey M., 165*n*
Shapiro, Daviad L., 94*n*
Shapiro, Martin, 3, 15, 16, 21*n*, 22, 23, 24, 25*n*, 26*n*, 27, 30*n*, 31*n*, 37*n*, 39*n*, 40–43, 44*n*, 45, 48*n*, 49*n*, 54*n*, 58–59, 60, 64, 262, 267, 269*n*, 298*n*, 346, 347, 348, 356, 366, 381*n*, 382*n*, 449, 450*n*, 458*n*, 465*n*, 469*n*, 470
Shaw, Lemaul, 356,
Sheehan, Reginald S., 401*n*, 444*n*, 448
Sheffield, James F., Jr., 443*n*
Sheldon, Charles H., 88*n*, 141*n*, 149*n*, 151*n*, 152*n*, 167, 357*n*, 358*n*
Shenon, Philip, 132*n*, 185*n*, 186, 212*n*
Shephard, John E., 452*n*
Sherrill, Robert, 117*n*
Sherry, Suzanna, 94*n*
Shogan, Robert A., 212*n*
Shuit, Douglas P., 296*n*
Sickels, Robert J., 353*n*
Sierra, Christine Marie, 158*n*
Sigler, Jay A., 311*n*
Sikes, Bette H., 157*n*
Silberman, Linda J., 80*n*, 82*n*
Silver, Carol Ruth, 246*n*
Silverstein, Lee, 245*n*, 246*n*
Simon, James F., 51
Simon, Rita James, 17*n*, 331*n*
Simpson, O.J., 84, 333
Sinclair, T.C., 148*n*
Singer, Linda R., 252*n*
Sinks, Dwight B., 165*n*
Skocpol, Theda, 44
Skogan, Wesley G., 306*n*, 309*n*
Skolnick, Jerome H., 301*n*, 303, 309*n*, 313*n*, 314*n*, 315, 345, 438*n*
Slagstad, Rune, 46*n*
Sloan, Frank A., 292*n*, 299
Slonim, Shlomo, 46*n*
Slotnick, Elliot E., 145*n*, 149*n*, 152*n*, 168, 171*n*, 172*n*, 173*n*, 181, 183, 187*n*, 215, 366*n*
Sloviter, Delores K., 99*n*
Smathers, Webb M., 91*n*
Smigel, Monroe, 18
Smith, Christopher E., 67*n*, 99*n*, 126, 244*n*, 386*n*
Smith, Joseph H., 73*n*
Smith, Monroe, 18
Smith, Nancy J., 162
Smith, Reginald H., 245*n*
Smith, Rogers, 34*n*, 35*n*, 44, 45, 64
Smith, Walter F., 322*n*
Smith, William French, 125*n*

Smothers, Ronald, 161n, 163n, 251n
Snider, Anna, 42n
Solimine, Michael E., 419n, 423n, 448
Solomon, Rayman L., 174n, 228n
Songer, Donald R., 184n, 190n, 379n, 381n, 385n, 387, 401n, 408
Sorauf, Frank J., 130n, 413n, 436n, 443n
Souter, David H., 113n, 194, 199, 204, 252, 392
Spaeth, Edmund B., Jr., 349n
Spaeth, Harold J., 23n, 24n, 49n, 114, 115, 355n, 365n, 391n, 403n, 405, 406n, 408
Specter, Arlen, 193, 194, 435n, 437, 438
Spence, Gerry, 217n
Spencer, Herbert, 241n
Sperlich, Peter, 34n, 43
Spohn, Casia, 344n
Sporkin, Stanley, 213
Sprague, John D., 217n
Spriggs, James F., III, 210n
Squire, Perveill, 211n
Stanberry, Henry, 131
Stang, David P., 84n
Steele, Eric H., 286n
Stefancic, Jean, 42n, 64
Steinfels, Peter, 459n
Stephenson, Donald Grier, Jr., 44n, 368n, 392n
Stern, Philip M., 217n
Stevens, Amy, 276n
Stevens, John Paul, 108, 109, 162, 199, 209n, 210, 392, 397
Stevens, Robert, 233n, 258
Stewart, Joseph, Jr., 443n
Stewart, Potter, 124, 191, 199, 211n
Stidham, Ronald, 166n, 184n, 190n
Stone, Alec, 46n
Stone, Christopher D., 42n, 43
Stone, Harlan Fiske, 20, 109n, 198, 229
Stone, Michael, 332
Stone, Theron G., 229, 230n
Stookey, John A., 197n, 201n, 215
Story, Joseph, 231, 356
Stover, Robert V., 235n
Stow, Mary Lou, 355n
Strong, Theron G., 229, 230
Strum, Philippa, 394n
Stumpf, Harry P., 18n, 23n, 25n, 26n, 27n, 48n, 55n, 60n, 70n, 93n, 130n, 233n, 237n, 244n,

246n, 247n, 250n, 251n, 255n, 270n, 286n, 349n, 358, 376n, 377, 416n, 417n, 418n, 419n, 420n, 425n, 427n, 432n, 448, 450n, 453n, 454n, 456n, 463n
Sugarman, Stephen, 70n
Sullivan, Joseph F., 267n, 270n, 370n, 373n
Sullivan, Ronald, 162
Sutherland, George, 20
Sykes, Melvin P., 451n
Szanton, Peter L., 452n, 455n, 456n

Taft, William Howard, 120, 137, 175, 197, 198, 200, 210, 311
Taggart, William A., 394n
Tannehaus, Joseph, 18n, 27, 29, 46n, 400, 444n
Taney, Roger B., 51, 123, 131, 192n, 203, 204
Tarr, G. Alan, 70n, 79n, 93, 350n, 357n, 358n, 359–360, 363, 364, 365, 366n, 369n, 370n, 373n, 374n, 376n, 377n
Tapp, June L., 17n
Tate, C. Neal, 26n, 46n
Taugher, Mike, 145n
Taylor, Alison, 452n
Taylor, Stuart, Jr. 125n, 183n, 193n
Taylor, Zachary, 191
Teger, Stuart H., 406n
Teir, Robert, 371n
ten Broek, Jacobus, 453n
Tesitor, Irene A., 165n
Teubner, Gerald, 48n
Thielemann, Greg, 149n
Thomas, Bill, 217n
Thomas, Clarence, 8, 132n, 184, 187, 191n, 195, 196, 199, 202n, 204, 207, 208, 392
Thomas, Clive S., 158n
Thomas, William, 217n
Thompson, Mark, 249n
Thompson, Robert S., 383n
Thornberry, Homer, 199
Timmerman, John Bell, 432
Tobin, Eugene M., 241n
Tocqueville, Alexis de, 217, 389
Todd, A.L., 201n
Tomasi, Timothy B., 176n
Tomasic, Roman, 17n, 452n
Tonry, Michael, 336n
Tribe, Lawrence, 37, 125n, 215
Trubek, David M., 48n, 228n, 265n, 456n
Truman, David B., 443
Truman, Harry S., 22, 175, 200, 202, 204, 430

Tushnet, Mark, 34n, 35n, 36, 37n, 64
Tuttle, Elbert, 385
Tydings, Joseph D., Jr., 121

Uhler, Lewis K., 247
Ulen, Thomas, 64
Ulmer, S. Sydney, 363n, 430n
Unger, Roberto M., 34

Vallimder, Torbjorn, 26n, 46n
Valvel, Lawrence, 242
Van Alstyne, Scott, 254n
Van Alyssstyne, William, 37n
Vandenberg, Donna, 159
Vanderbilt, Arthur T., 284n
Vander Kolk, Kenneth J., 293n, 235
Van Devanter, Willis, 20, 198, 210
Van Dyke, Jon M., 331n
Van Horn, Carl E., 366n
Van Loon, Eric E., 233n, 235
Van Natta, Don, Jr., 249n
Vazquez, Martha, 173
Velona, Jess A., 176n
VerBerg, Kenneth, 460
Verhovek, Sam Howe, 293n
Vidich, Arthur J., 218
Vidmar, Neil, 84n, 287n, 292n, 293n, 299
Vile, John R., 107n, 170n
Villamoare, Adelaide, 60
Villinder, Torbjorn, 26n
Vines, Kenneth N., 55, 65n, 75n, 93, 95n, 96, 98, 126, 134n, 174, 175, 177, 218n, 353, 364, 382n, 385n, 387n, 388n
Vinson, Frederick M., 109, 198, 400
Visher, Christy A., 331n
Volcansek, Mary L., 166n, 213n, 214n
VonMehren, Arthur Taylor, 277n
Vose, Clement E., 442n, 443n

Wahrhaftig, Paul, 452n
Wald, Patricia, 385
Waldo, Dwight, 329n
Walker, James L., 419n 423n
Walker, Samuel, 301n, 304n, 306n, 310n, 311, 313n, 314n, 323n, 327n, 328n, 329n, 336n, 343n, 345
Walker, Thomas G., 114, 115
Wardell, Walter F., 217n
Wallace, James G., 129
Warren, Charles, 72n, 123n, 226n
Warren, Earl, 109n, 121, 199,

Warren, Earl *(cont.)*
200, 202, 203, 358, 400, 402,
405, 406
Wasby, Stephen L., 206n, 213n,
298n, 384n, 389n, 392n, 394n,
398n, 399n, 400n, 401n, 402n,
405n, 408, 413n, 438n, 439n,
445n, 448
Washington, George, 96, 393
Wasserstein, Bruce, 233n
Watson, George L., 197n, 201n,
215
Watson, Patti, 193n
Watson, Richard A., 138n, 139n,
141, 142, 145n, 168, 254n
Way, H. Frank, Jr., 439
Webster, Daniel, 227, 228
Wechsler, Herbert, 31–32, 33,
34, 37, 94n, 95n, 96n, 98n,
109n, 116n, 118n, 120n, 121n,
125n
Weiler, Paul C., 292n, 294n, 299
Weinreb, Lloyd L., 451n
Weinstein, Henry, 249n
Weintraub, Bernard, 185n
Weisberg, Herbert, 187n
Welch, Susan, 344n
Weller, Stephen, 84n
Wellington, Harry, 37
Wells, Richard S., 30n, 49n,
53n, 54, 56n
Wenner, Lettie McSpadden,
388n

Wermiel, Stephen, 373n, 386n,
436n
West, Luther C., 117n
West, Robin, 41n
Westin, Alan F., 424n
Weyrich, Dawn M., 131n,
193n
Wheeler, Russell, 93n, 389n
Wheeler, Stanton, 349n, 351n,
359
White, Byron R., 69n, 86, 109,
113, 195, 196, 199, 201, 211
White, Edward D., 198
Whittaker, Charles E., 199, 405
Wice, Paul, 244n
Wicharaya, Tamasak, 337n
Wightman, Linda F., 240n
Wilkins, Leslie T., 343
Williams, Aubrey, 433
Williams, Douglass, 237n
Williams, John Sharp, 177
Williams, Lena, 185n
Williams, Patricia, 42
Williams, Robert F, 372n, 373n,
376n, 377
Williams, Thomas D., 167n
Williamson, Robert B., 247n
Willison, David, 430n
Willson, David, 430
Wilson, James Q., 107, 226,
312n, 315, 316
Wilson, Woodrow, 18, 46, 131,
200, 201, 461

Winfield, P.H., 11n
Winternitz, Helen, 195n
Winters, Glen R., 138n
Wisdom, John Minor, 96n, 385
Wissler, Roselle L., 290n
Witt, Elder, 375n, 376n
Wold, John T., 130n, 145n,
149n, 353, 355n, 364n, 367n,
376n
Woldman, Albert A., 226n
Wolf, T. Phillip, 70n, 427n,
432n
Wolff, Robert P., 49n
Wood, Arthur L., 217n
Woodward, Bob, 200n, 391n,
406n
Wright, Eric Q., 336n
Wright, John R., 131n, 398n,
402, 443n
Wythe, George, 356

Yngvesson, Barbara, 48n, 84n,
286n, 287n, 288n, 289n, 290n,
456n

Zane, J. Peder, 290n
Zawitz, Marianne W., 306, 435
Zaug, Mary E., 162n
Zeisel, Hans, 331n, 333n
Zeitsoff, Michael L., 10
Zemans, Frances Kahn, 219,
234, 255, 256, 258
Zane, J. Peder, 290n
Zuk, Gary, 209n, 210n, 215

Case Index

Ableman v. Booth, 12 How. 506 (1859), 123n

Alabama Power Co. v. Ickes, 302 U.S. 464 (1938), 393

Alexander v. Holmes County Board of Education, 396 U.S. 19 (1969), 401

Argersinger v. Hamlin, 407 U.S. 25 (1972), 250

Ashwander v. TVA, 297 U.S. 288 (1936), 459

Avery v. Georgia, 345 U.S. 559 (1953), 433

Bakelite Corp, Ex Parte, 279 U.S. 438 (1929), 116

Baker v. Carr, 369 U.S. 186 (1962), 50, 162, 393, 432, 442,

Barreblatt v. U.S., 360 U.S. 109 (1959), 426n, 429

Bates v. State Bar of Arizona, 433 U.S. 350 (1977), 252

Batson v. Kentucky, 476 U.S. 79 (1986), 331

Beilan v. Board of Education, 357 U.S. 399 (1958), 426

Brown v. Board of Education, 347 U.S. 483 (1954), 33, 50, 54, 125, 162, 386, 426, 429, 442, 445, 463, 465 432, 433, 442, 445, 463, 465

Burch v. Louisiana, 441 U.S. 130 (1979), 330

Bush v. Vera, 64 LW 4726 (1996), 163

Chandler v. Judicial Council of the Tenth Circuit, 398 U.S. 74 (1970), 214

Chicago & Southern Airlines v. Waterman Steamship Co., 333 U.S. 103 (1948), 393

Chisholm v. Georgia, 2 Dall. 419 (1793), 420

City of Greenwood v. Peacock, 384 U.S. 808 (1966), 124

Colegrove v. Green, 328 U.S. 549 (1946), 393, 442

Coleman v. Miller, 307 U.S. 433 (1939), 393

Coleman v. Thomas, 11 S.Ct. 2546 (1991), 124n

Cooper v. Aaron, 358 U.S. 1 (1958), 123n, 124

Corrigan v. Buckley, 271 U.S. 323 (1926), 442

Crawford Fitting Co. v. J.T. Gibbons, Inc., 482 U.S. 437 (1987), 423n

Dayton Board of Education v. Brinkman, 433 U.S. 406 (1977), 436n

DeFunis v. Odegaard, 416 U.S. 312 (1974), 371, 393

Dred Scott v. Sandford, 19 How. 393 (1857), 389, 420, 426, 428

Drink, Inc. v. Babcock, 421 P.2d 798 (N.M. 1966), 70n

EEOC v. Aramco, 499 U.S. 244 (1991), 423n

Engle v. Vitale, 370 U.S. 421 (1962), 420, 429, 438, 439

Erie Railroad v. Tompkins, 304 U.S. 64 (1938), 71

Federal Maritime Board v. Isbrandtsen, 356 U.S. 481 (1958), 418

Felker v. Turpin, 64 LW 4677 (1996), 124n, 421n

Flast v. Cohen, 292 U.S. 83 (1968), 393n

Florida v. Meyers, 460 U.S. 380 (1984), 401

Florida ex rel Hawkins v. Board of Control, 350 U.S. 413 (1956), 433–434

Frothingham v. Mellon, 262 U.S. 477 (1923), 393n

Furman v. Georgia, 408 U.S. 238 (1972), 391n, 427

Gannett v. DePasquale, 443 U.S. 368 (1979), 373, 446

Gibbons v. Ogden, 9 Wheat. 1 (1824), 347, 389

Gideon v. Wainwright, 372 U.S. 335 (1963), 250, 417, 454

Gitlow v. New York, 268 U.S. 652 (1925), 368

Glidden v. Zdanok, 370 U.S. 530 (1962), 116

Goldfarb v. Virginia State Bar Association, 421 U.S. 773 (1975), 252n

Gompers v. U.S., 233 U.S. 604 (1914), 62

Gordon v. Justice Court, 525 P.2d 72 (Calif. 1974), 82

Gregg v. Georgia, 428 U.S. 153 (1976), 427

Gregory v. Ashcroft, 111 S.Ct. 2395 (1991), 164*n*

Griffin v. Illinois, 351 U.S. 12 (1956), 351

Griswold v. Connecticut, 381 U.S. 479 (1965), 435

Grove City College v. Bell, 465 U.S. 555 (1984), 423*n*

Guss v. Utah Labor Relations Board, 353 U.S. 1 (1957), 418

Gyuro v. Connecticut, 393 U.S. 937 (1968), 87

Harris v. McRae, 448 U.S. 297 (1980), 424

Hayburn's Case, 2 U.S. (2 Dallas) 409 (1792), 371, 393

Hurtado v. California, 110 U.S. 516 (1884), 87*n*

Independent Federation of Flight Attendants v. Zipes, 491 U.S. 754 (1989), 423*n*

Jay Burns & Co. v. Bryan, 264 U.S. 504 (1924), 12

J.E.B. v. Alabama ex rel T.T., 114 S.Ct. 1419 (1994), 331

Jones v. Clear Creek Independent School District, 977 F. 2d 963 (5th Cir, 1992); cert. denied 113 S. Ct. 2950 (1993), 440*n*

Laird v. Tatum, 409 U.S. 824 (1972), 192

Lee v. Weisman, 112 S.Ct. 2649 (1992), 440*n*

Lerner v. Casey, 357 U.S. 468 (1958), 426

Library of Congress v. Shaw, 478 U.S. 310 (1985), 423*n*

Lloyd Corp. v. Tanner, 407 U.S. 551 (1972), 370

Local 1976 v. NLRB, 357 U.S. 93 (1958), 418

Lorance v. A.T. & T. Technologies, 490 U.S. 900 (1989), 423*n*, 427

Lujan v. Defenders of Wildlife, 504 U.S. 555 (1992), 394*n*

Luther v. Borden, 7 How. 1 (1849), 393

Mallory v. U.S. 354 U.S. 449 (1957), 434

Mapp v. Ohio, 367 U.S. 643 (1961), 432, 435, 437, 438, 439

Marbury v. Madison, 1 Cranch 137 (1803), 356, 419,

Martin v. Wilks, 490 U.S. 755 (1989), 423*n*

Maryland v. Garrison, 480 U.S. 79 (1987), 374

McCardle, Ex Parte, 7 Wall. 506 (1869), 421, 426

McCarty v. McCarty, 453 U.S. 210 (1981), 418

McCulloch v. Maryland, 4 Wheat. 316 (1819), 51, 52, 347, 389

Meyer v. Nebraska, 262 U.S. 390 (1923), 368

Michigan v. Long, 463 U.S. 1041 (1983), 370

Miller v. California, 413 U.S. 15 (1973), 374

Miller v. Johnson, 63 LW 4726 (1995), 163

Milliken v. Bradley, 418 U.S. 717 (1974), 436*n*

Miranda v. Arizona, 384 U.S. 436 (1966), 374, 414, 442

Mobile v. Bolden, 446 U.S. 55 (1980), 161

Moore v. Ingebretson, No. 96–331, Nov. 4, 1996, cert. denied, 441

Muller v. Oregon, 208 U.S. 412 (1908), 12

NAACP v. Alabama, 360 U.S. 240; 377 U.S. 288 (1959), 434*n*

NLRB v. Bildisco and Bildisco, 465 U.S. 513 (1984), 418

NLRB v. International Rice Milling Co., 341 U.S. 665 (1951), 418

NLRB v. Jones-Laughlin Steel Corp., 301 U.S. 1 (1937), 21, 426

New Jersey Coalition Against the War in the Middle East v. J.M.B. Realty Corp, 650 A.2nd 757 (N.J. 1994), 370

Nix v. Williams, 467 U.S. 431 (1984), 437*n*

Nixon v. U.S., 113 S.Ct. 732 (1993), 213

Norris v. Alabama, 294 U.S. 587 (1935), 433

North v. Russell, 427 U.S. 382 (1976), 80

Northern Pipeline Construction Co. v. Marathon Pipe Line Co., 458 U.S. 50 (1982), 116*n*

Oregon v. Mitchell, 400 U.S. 112 (1970), 420

Osborn v. Bank of the U.S., 9 Wheat. 738 (1824), 392, 9–10, 392*n*

Pasadena City Board of Education v. Spangler, 427 U.S. 424 (1976), 436*n*

Patterson v. McLean Credit Union, 491 U.S. 164 (1989), 423*n*, 427

Pollock v. Farmers' Loan and Trust Co., 158 U.S. 601 (1895), 420

Price Waterhouse v. Hopkins, 490 U.S. 228 (1989), 423*n*

Pruneyard Shopping Center v. Robins, 447 U.S. 74 (1980), 370, 373

Public Citizen v. Department of Justice, 491 U.S. 440 (1989), 202

Pulliam v. Allen, 466 U.S. 522 (1984), 436*n*

Richmond Newspapers v. Virginia, 448 U.S. 555 (1980), 446

Robins v. Pruneyard Shopping Center, 592 P.2nd 341 (Calif. 1979), 370, 371, 373

Robinson v. Cahill, 62 N.J. 473 (1973), 369

Rodriguez v. San Antonio Independent School District, 337 F. Supp 280 (W.D. Tex., 1971), 369

Roe v. Wade, 410 U.S. 113 (1973), 50, 389, 424, 445

San Antonio Independent School District v. Rodriguez, 411 U.S. 1 (1973), 70, 369, 371, 435

Schenck v. Pro-Choice Network, No. 95–1065 (argued October 16, 1996), 402*n*

School District of Abington Township v. Schempp, 374 U.S. 203 (1963), 438, 439

Seminole Tribe v. Florida, 64 LW 4167 (1996), 379*n*, 392

Serrano v. Priest, 487 P.2d 1241 (Calif. 1971), 70, 369

Shapiro v. Thompson, 394 U.S. 618 (1969), 347

Shaw v. Reno, 509 U.S. 630 (1993), 163

Shelly v. Kraemer, 334 U.S. 1 (1948), 442–443

Slochower v. Board of Education, 350 U.S. 551 (1956), 426

South Carolina v. Katzenbach, 383 U.S. 301 (1966), 161*n*

Southern Burlington County NAACP v. Township of Mt. Laurel, 336 A.2d 713, N.J (1975); and 456 A.2d 390, N.J. (1983), 375*n*

Southern Pacific Co. v. Jensen, 244 U.S. 205 (1921), 13*n*

Steward Machine Co. v. Davis, 301 U.S. 548 (1937), 426

Swift v. Tyson, 16 Pet. 1 (1842), 71

Thomas v. Winchester, 6 N.Y. 397 (1852), 357

University of California v. Bakke, 438 U.S. 265 (1978), 401

U.S. v. Butler, 297 U.S. 1 (1936), 10, 404

U.S. v. California, 332 U.S. 19 (1947), 424

U.S. v. Cannelton Sewer Pipe Co., 364 U.S. 76 (1960), 417

U.S. v. Galloway, 943 F.2d 897 (8th Cir. 1991), 342*n*

U.S. v. Leon, 468 U.S. 897 (1984), 374, 437*n*

U.S. v. Lopez, 115 S.Ct. 1624, 63 LW 4343 (1995), 21*n*, 379*n*, 429

U.S. v. Robertson, 63 LW 4386 (1995), 429

Wards Cove Packing Co. v. Antonio, 490 U.S. 642 (1989), 423*n*, 427

Watkins v. U.S., 354 U.S. 178 (1957), 416, 426, 429

Weeks v. U.S., 232 U.S. 383 (1914), 437

West Coast Hotel v. Parrish, 300 U.S. 379 (1937), 426

West Virginia University Hospitals, Inc., v. Casey, 499 U.S. 83 (1991), 423*n*

Wickard v. Filburn, 317 U.S. 111 (1942), 434

Williams v. Florida, 399 U.S. 78 (1970), 330

Williams v. Georgia, 349 U.S. 375 (1955), 433

Wolf v. Colorado, 338 U.S. 25 (1949), 437

Zorach v. Clauson, 343 U.S. 306 (1952), 436

Subject Index

Abortion (*see Roe v. Wade*, Implementation of judicial decisions

Act to Improve the Administration of Justice (1988), 110

Administrative agencies, 103, 219, 380–382, 457

Administrative Office of the U.S. Courts, 120, 121

Administrative role for courts, 59–60, 304–306, 329, 333, 353–356, 378, 382, 388–389, 446–447

Afro-American (Black) (*see* Lawyers; Judicial selection, state; judicial selection, federal)

Alabama, 136, 137, 162, 162n, 185, 186, 339, 341, 359, 359n, 362

Alaska, 85, 136, 137, 139, 140, 159n, 328, 339, 341, 350n, 351, 361, 372n, 429

Alternative dispute resolution (*see* Dispute processing)

Amherst School, 47

Amicus curiae (*see also* U.S. Supreme Court, *Amicus curiae*), 348, 401, 402

Analytical jurisprudence (*see* Positivist jurisprudence)

Anti-Terrorism and Effective Death Penalty Act of 1996, 124, 421n

Appeal (*see also* Appellate courts): functions of, 346–349, 350–352, 346–348

Appellate courts (*see also* specific courts, Judicial selection, Jurisprudence): 346–408; and appeal to Privy Council, 73, 88, 347; and case method, 18–19, 25, 26, 29, 231–233; caseloads, 66–69, 103–104, 106–107, 111–116, 350–352, 360–362, 379–381, 394–397, 398–399; functions of, 346–349, 356, 378, 389; history of, 65–66, 71–75, 85, 94–98, 102–115, 356–360; legislatures as, 72, 88; and perceived superiority, 24, 66, 74, 171, 346, 389, 412; procedures on, 348, 352–356, 360–363, 382–385, 390–392, 397–399, 401–403; in states, 66–70, 346–377; structure, 76–79, 85, 87–93, 102–104, as subjects of study, 9–12, 18–19, 24, 25, 26, 29, 30, 50–58, 378; U.S., 19–21, 50–53, 94–115, 378–408, 436

Arizona, 136, 137, 140, 146, 161, 339, 341, 351, 363

Arkansas, 123, 136, 137, 162, 162n, 163, 163n, 339, 341, 362

Attitudinal model (*see* Behavioral jurisprudence)

Austinian jurisprudence (*see* Positivist [Analytical] jurisprudence

Bail (*see* Criminal judicial process)

Bankruptcy, 67, 99, 102, 103, 116, 381

Bar associations (*see* Lawyers, Legal education, Legal services to the poor)

Behavioral Jurisprudence, 22–23, 24, 28, 405

California, 67, 68, 70, 75, 76, 82, 83, 93, 130n, 136, 137, 138–139, 144, 145, 149n, 152, 161, 162n, 165, 194, 204, 213, 220, 247, 248, 328, 337, 339, 341, 343, 350n, 351, 354–355, 359n, 360, 361, 362, 363, 367, 369, 374, 435

Catholics (*see* Roman Catholics)

Civil judicial process, 261–299; caseflow (type and number of filings, 273–274, 278–285); and grievances, 263–270; informal dispute processing, 276–278; and litigiousness, 270–276; medical malpractice cases, 291–297; small claims processes, 285–291, 297; on state appellate courts, 354–355

Civil (Roman) law, 61, 63

Civil Litigation Research Project, 265–270, 274–275, 298, 456
Colonial (U.S.) courts, 71–74
Colorado, 136, 137, 140, 159n, 161, 287n, 339, 341, 362
Columbia University, 18, 231
Common law (English), 11, 13, 61–63, 72–74, 88, 132
Comparative law and jurisprudence, 11, 25, 46
Compliance with judicial decisions (*see also* Impact of court decisions, Implementation of court decisions), 55, 411–448
Conflict resolution (*see* dispute processing)
Connecticut, 136, 137, 166–167, 229, 287, 339, 341, 362
Constitution (U.S.): amendment of, 392, 393, 420, 424, 428; Article III, 94, 99, 371; Article VI, 94; Bill of Rights, 86, 285, 368; Commerce clause, 20–21, 429; Due Process clause, 20; Eleventh Amendment, 392, 420; Equal Protection clause, 50, 369, 435; Fifth Amendment, 20, 87; First Amendment, 373, 435; Fourteenth Amendment, 20, 50, 420, 432; Fourth Amendment, 374, 435, 437; imprecise language of, 51–52, 94, 107; intent of framers, 37–38, 52; interpretation of (*see* specific schools of jurisprudence); judicial appointment provisions, 169–170; and *laizzez faire*, 20; Sixteenth Amendment, 420; Sixth Amendment, 446; and Supreme Court jurisdiction, 109, 421–422; as supreme law of land, 10, 123–125; as symbol, 7, 49; Taxing clause, 20; Tenth Amendment, 432; Twenty-Sixth Amendment, 420
Constitutional law, (U.S.): 18, 19, 21, 22, 23, 24, 25, 26, 44, 368–370; (state): 368–376
Constitutional theory (and jurisprudence), 24; (*see* Princeton School)
Constitutive View of Law, 47–48, 469
Court unification (state), 75, 89–93
Criminal judicial process, 300–345; arrests, 312–317; bail, 320–324; case flow, 307, 311,

318, 319; crime statistics, 306–311, 313, 317; expenditures on, 310–311; implementation of appellate decisions, 412, 414, 432, 433, 437–438; juries, 320, 330–332, 333; models of, 304–306; plea bargaining, 305, 316, 318–329; and political science, 300–301; and the political system, 300–303; prosecutorial discretion, 303, 316–329; public defenders, 326; and race, 303, 314–315, 331–332, 333, 334, 343, 343n, 344, 344n; sentencing, 333–344; on state appellate courts, 354–355; trials, 318, 329–333
Critical Legal Studies, 34–36, 38, 39, 40, 42, 48, 61
Critical Race Theory, 42

Defense attorneys (*see* Criminal judicial process)
Delaware, 136, 137, 339, 341, 343, 351
Democracy: and the Princeton School, 46, 47; and judicial selection, 131, 134–135, 147, 151–152; and judicial policy making, 458–466
Dispute processing (settlement) (*see also* Civil judicial process): 2, 58–61, 263–270, 450–458
District of Columbia, 85, 220, 338, 339, 341

Equity, 62, 63

Federal Court Improvement Act of 1982, 119
Federal Judicial Center, 121
Federalism (*see* Judicial federalism)
Feminist jurisprudence, 40–41, 42
Florida, 136, 137, 140, 146n, 162, 161, 162n, 164, 186, 206, 212, 220, 339, 341, 351, 362
Georgia, 134, 136, 137, 162, 162n, 163, 186, 339, 341, 343n, 362

Habeas corpus, 124, 397
Harvard Law School, 11, 18, 194, 231–232, 449
Harvard Medical Malpractice Study, 294–296
Hawaii, 136, 137, 159n, 339, 341, 342, 350n, 351, 361, 362, 374
Hispanic (*see* Critical Race The-

ory; Lawyers; Judicial selection, state; Judicial selection, federal)

Idaho, 136, 137, 339, 341, 359n
Illinois, 136, 137, 138n, 145n, 146n, 162, 166, 220, 339, 341, 343, 359n, 362
Impact of judicial decisions (*see also* Compliance with court decisions, implementation of court decisions, 30, 58, 411–448
Impeachment of judges (*see* Judicial removal and retirement)
Implementation of judicial decisions (*see also* Impact of judicial decisions, Compliance with judicial decisions), 23, 57, 261–262, 348, 411–448; of abortion rulings, 412, 420, 424; and policy, 56–58, 458–459; and civil judicial processes, 262; and Congress, 414, 415–426, 441; of criminal procedures decisions, 412, 432, 433, 437–438; as focus of study, 411–415; and interest groups, 441–443; of legislative apportionment rulings, 413, 420, 427, 432; by lower courts, 430–436; and the media, 445–446; and obscenity rulings, 431; and the police, 414, 437–438; and the president, 414, 428–430; and public opinion, 443–445; and racial desegregation rulings, 412, 420, 426–427, 432, 433, 435–436; of school prayer rulings, 412, 420, 427, 433, 438–441
Implementation of policy by courts, 59–61, 446–447, 465–466
Indiana, 134, 136, 137, 162n, 185, 339, 341, 350n, 351, 439
Informalism, 276–278, 451–452, 455–457
In forma pauperis petitions, 110, 112, 395–396
Interest groups and courts, 22–23, 87, 401–402, 441–447
International law, 6, 18, 25
Iowa, 136, 137, 144, 159n, 287n, 290n, 339, 341, 361, 362

Jews, 154, 196, 201, 204
Judicial administration, state, 92–93; federal, 119–122
Judicial Code of 1911, 98

Judicial Conference of the U.S., 120–121

Judicial Councils Reform and Judicial Conduct and Disability Act of 1980, 214

Judicial discipline (*see* Judicial removal and retirement, state, federal)

Judicial federalism, 65–66, 89, 94–98, 123–125, 366–376

Judicial removal and retirement: state, 163–166; federal, 208–215

Judicial review (*see also Marbury v. Madison*): growth of doctrine, 88; as Supreme Court policy, 51, 123

Judicial selection, federal (*see also* Judicial selection, general; judicial selection, state): 169–215; and the American Bar Association, 171, 172, 178–179, 180–183, 190, 197, 200–202, 207; Carter reforms, 179, 181, 184; characteristics of judges selected (tables), 180–183, 207–208; constitutional provisions, 169–170; for federal district and appellate courts, 171–190; and gender, 180–184, 187–190, 204; general criteria of selection, 174–179, 197, 200–205; and interest groups, 171, 185–186, 200–201, 205, 206; localism, 176–177; and party affiliation, 174–175, 197; and political ideology, 175–176, 197, 200; and professional merit, 177–179, 201–204; and race, 179–184, 187–189, 200, 204, 206; U.S. Supreme Court, 190–208; U.S. Senate, 171, 172, 184–187, 201, 205–208

Judicial selection, general (*see also* Judicial selection, federal; Judicial selection, state): and democracy, 131, 134, 147, 151; in England, 132, 133–134; and interest groups, 130–131, and policy making, 132, 155–156; political culture of, 130–133; and political parties, 130, 151, 154, 155, 156; significance of, 58, 129–130

Judicial selection, state (*see also* Judicial selection, federal; Judicial selection, general): 133–167, 367; appellate court selection plans, 136; and the bar, 135, 138, 141, 142, 143, 144, 146, 147, 149; and court unification, 92; explaining state choice of, 140–141; executive appointment, 133–134, 150; and gender, 153, 154, 156, 157, 158, 158; general trial court selection plans, 137; influence of jurisprudence on, 132–133, 147, 151; judges' backgrounds, 143–144, 153–158; judicial elections, 134–135, 136, 137, 147–153; judicial elections and race (*see* "and race," below); legislative selection, 133–134, 150; "merit" selection, 92, 131, 135, 138–141, 150, 151, 163; "merit" selection analyzed, 141–147, 150; and race, 154, 156, 157, 158, 159–163; retention elections (*see* "merit" selection); and state legislatures, 87, 135

Judiciary Act of 1789, 65, 88, 94–96, 107

Judiciary Act of 1801, 97, 428

Judiciary Act of 1802, 97, 428

Judiciary Act of 1891 (Evarts Act), 98, 109

Judiciary Act of 1925 (Judges Bill), 98, 109

Juries, 16, 62, 71, 85, 86–87, 101, 274, 293n, 295–296, 320, 330–332–333, 348

Jurisprudence (*see also* specific schools of jurisprudence): defined, 4–5; and judicial selection, 132, 147, 150–151; origins, 5; significance, 1–6; schools of, 5–6; subject of study, 18, 26

Justices of the Peace (*see* Trial courts, limited jurisdiction)

Juvenile courts (*see* Trial courts, limited jurisdiction)

Kansas, 75, 77, 136, 137, 139, 140n, 339, 341, 350n, 351, 359n, 361, 362

Kentucky, 136, 137, 339, 341, 351, 362, 439

Law and Economics movement, 38–39, 40

Law and Language Movement, 42–43

Law and Society Association, 25

Lawyers (*see also* legal education, legal services to the poor): 216–258; advertising, 252; certification for practice, 241–243; and civil litigation, 267, 269, 270, 272; in colonial America, 72–73; and court unification, 91; criticism of, 216–217, 225, 227–230; as focus of study, 58, 217–220; in government, 223; practice specialities, 255–257; in pre-Civil War America, 225–230; organization of the bar, 240–244; in private practice, 222–223, 227; professional ethics, 227–230, 234–236, 243–244; professional ideology, 227–230, 234–236; professional stratification, 225–230, 227–230, 254–258; and public interest law, 240, 250–254; racial minorities, 223–224, 236–237; roles of, 217–220; socioeconomic background, 237, 240; statistics regarding, 220–225, 237–239; training of (*see* legal education); transformation of the bar, 227–230; women lawyers, 157, 159, 223–224, 236–237

Legal education, 16, 25–26, 26n, 35–36, 43, 49, 225–226, 230–240, 254–256, 449–450

Legal services to the poor, 233, 233n, 244–253, 275, 454

Legislative apportionment (*see Baker v. Carr*, Implementation of judicial decisions, Judicial selection, state—"and race")

Legislative courts (*see also* specific courts), 115–116

Louisiana, 63, 123, 136, 137, 160, 162n, 339, 341, 361, 362, 364

Maine, 85, 136, 137, 339, 341, 342, 359n

Maryland, 72, 85, 135, 136, 137, 148, 339, 341

Massachusetts, 72, 85, 136, 137, 159n, 231, 242, 288, 339, 341, 360, 361, 364, 374

Mediation and courts, 59, 60, 262–263, 276–278, 281–282, 289–290, 304–305, 455–456

"Merit" judicial selection (*see* Judicial selection, state)

Michigan, 136, 137, 328, 339, 341, 350n, 351, 359n, 362, 363, 374

Minnesota, 75, 78, 136, 137, 165, 206, 248, 339, 341, 359n, 361, 362, 427

Mississippi, 134–135, 136, 137, 162n, 165, 195, 213, 339, 341, 361, 374, 439–440

Missouri (for Missouri Plan, see Judicial selection, State, "merit" plan): 136, 137, 138–139, 162n, 165, 339, 341, 350n

Montana, 136, 137, 339, 341, 361

Myth as related to law and courts, 15, 16n, 33, 48–50, 59, 66, 171, 346, 390, 412, 443n

National Court of Appeals, proposed, 111, 113, 400

Natural law, 6–8, 17, 31; attacks on, 7–8; natural rights, 6,7; and founding fathers, 7; and Supreme Court decisions, 8; as symbol, 7

Nebraska, 135, 136, 137, 138n, 339, 341

Neutral principles of law, 31–34, 37, 43, 48–50, 52, 58, 61

Nevada, 136, 137, 164n, 212, 339, 341, 359n, 361

New Hampshire, 136, 137, 159n, 249, 339, 341

New Institutionalism, 44–45

New Jersey, 136, 137, 159n, 165, 248, 339, 341, 350n, 351, 359, 359n, 363, 364, 369, 373, 374, 375

New Mexico, 70, 81–2, 135, 136, 137, 145n, 158n, 162n, 164, 174,

339, 341, 350n, 362

New York City, 160, 162

New York (state), 75, 79, 85, 88, 134, 136, 137, 139, 152, 161, 162, 162n, 164, 220, 339, 341, 357, 362, 374, 376n, 435

Norm-enforcement as a judicial function, 53–56

North Carolina, 136, 137, 149n, 152, 162n, 163, 163n, 225, 339, 342, 359n, 361

North Dakota, 136, 137, 148n, 339, 342, 361, 362, 373

Ohio, 85, 136, 137, 149n, 152, 162, 162n, 287–289, 340, 342, 350n, 351, 359

Oklahoma, 136, 137, 149n, 162n, 195, 340, 342, 350n

Oregon, 12, 81, 136, 137, 340, 342, 343, 359n, 361, 362, 374

Pennsylvania, 81, 87, 107, 134, 136, 137, 162n, 220, 340, 342, 350n, 362, 364, 373

Plea bargaining (see Criminal judicial process)

Police (see also Criminal judicial process): 301, 303, 304, 307–310, 312–316, 320, 328

Policy making (see also specific courts and policy making, specific schools of jurisprudence): as appellate function, 50–55, 347, 379, 382, 386–387; assessment of, 458–466; and behavioral research, 405; conceptualization of, 50–58; and constitutional values, 36–38; and Critical Legal Studies, 34–36; incrementalism in, 54; and intent, 53–54; and judicial myth, 49–50; and judicial selection, 130–133; and judicial self-restraint, 458–460; and lawyers, 217–219; limits on, 458–460; and neutrality, 31–33, 48–50; and norm enforcement, 53–56, 56n; police, 56–57, 312–316; political jurisprudence, 17–22; and social change, 458–466; and state courts, 68–69; and state supreme courts, 369, 363–367; U.S. Courts of Appeals, 104, 378–379; U.S. Supreme Court, 19–22, 50–53, 394, 403–407

Political jurisprudence (see also Policy making, Political science): 5, 6, 17–31, 35, 38, 44, 47, 58, 59–60

Political science, study of law in (see also Political jurisprudence, 5, 6, 17–27; and Post-Realism, 43–48;

Positivist jurisprudence, 5, 8–11, 17, 19, 25, 28

Post Modernism, 40

Post-Realism, defined, 34; and political science, 43–48, 61

Princeton School of Jurisprudence, 18, 45–47

Probate courts (see Trial courts, limited jurisdiction)

Probation, 101

Public choice and law, 39

Public opinion and courts, 301–302, 316, 335, 343, 441–447

Race (see Critical Race Theory; Lawyers; Judicial selection, state; judicial selection, Federal)

Realist jurisprudence, 5, 13–17, 18, 21, 22, 25, 26, 28, 35, 42, 43, 50, 54, 55, 60, 61, 233, 346; sociological-realist differences, 14–16

Rhode Island, 136, 137, 157, 159n, 340, 342, 359n

Roman Catholics, 154, 204

Salaries of judges, 80, 85, 99, 108, 422

Small claims courts, 83, 279, 280, 281, 285–291

Social change and law, 463–464

Sociological jurisprudence, 11–13, 17, 18, 21, 22, 25, 26, 28, 35, 42, 54, 55, 60, 61, 404; sociological-realist differences, 14–16

Sociology and law, 11, 12, 17

South Carolina, 136, 137, 157, 163n, 340, 342, 351, 361, 362

South Dakota, 136, 137, 148, 163n, 340, 342, 359n, 361

State courts (see specific courts)

State intermediate appellate courts (see also Appellate courts): 349–356; appellate ratios, 69, 349–351; caseloads, 67, 352; civil cases, 354–355; creation of, 85, 349, 359–360; criminal cases, 354–355; dissent, 353; procedures, 352–356; structure, 76–79, 85

State judges (see specific courts; Judicial selection, state; Judicial removal and retirement, state)

State supreme courts (state courts of last resort) (see also Judicial selection, state; Appeal; Appellate courts): caseload, 67, 359–363; decision making on, 360–367; dissent, 363–365; evolution of, 71–74, 87–88, 356–360; and expansion of judicial doctrine, 435–436; importance of, 68–71, 356; justices, 356; policy making, 68–71, 88, 356–360, 364, 367–376; research on, 88, 359–360; role of, 94, 356; structure, 74, 76–79, 85, 359–360; versus state legislatures, 87–88, 95, 366, 427–428

Tennessee, 136, 137, 149n, 162, 162n, 340, 342, 359n, 361, 362

Texas, 81, 85, 130n, 136, 137, 148, 149n, 152, 161, 162, 161,

162n, 163, 163n, 165, 185n, 200, 220, 294–295, 340, 342, 350n, 361, 362, 367n, 369, 434–435, 439

Trial courts (*see also* specific courts, Judicial selection, state; Judicial selection, federal; civil judicial process, criminal judicial process), 25; caseloads, 66–68, 273–274, 278–285, 311; and fact-finding, 16; federal (*see* U.S. District Courts); of general jurisdiction (state), 68, 84–85; 273–274, 278–281; importance of, 68–69; limited jurisdiction (state), 75, 78–84, 281–282, 350; number, 69; and policy-making, 53, 55–56; as subject of study, 16, 17

U.S. Court of Federal Claims, 100, 117–118
U.S. Court of International Trade, 100, 118
U.S. Court of Military Appeals, 100, 117–118
U.S. Court of Veterans Appeals, 100, 117
U.S. Courts of Appeals (Circuit Courts) (*see also*, Appellate courts): 102–104, 378–398; caseload, 66, 103–104, 379–382; decision making, 102, 384–389; dissent, 385; *en banc* decisions, 102, 385; procedures, 102–103, 382–384; history, 95–99, 101; jurisdiction, 96–98, 103; policy making, 103. 378–379, 386–387; presiding (Chief) judge, 103; retirement/removal of judges, 208–211; selection of judges, 103, 171–190; structure, 95–99, 100, 102, 105, 106; and three judge panels, 102, 103, 383–385
U.S. Court of Appeals for the Federal Circuit, 119
U.S. District Courts: caseloads, 101–104, 273–274, 282–284; civil cases, 99, 103, 282–284; criminal cases, 99, 104, 311; history of, 95–99; impeachment of judges, 211–215 jurisdiction, 96, 99; local orientation of, 96, 97; number, 68; selection of judges, 99, 169–190; structure of, 95–99, 100

U.S. Magistrates, 67, 99
U.S. Supreme Court (*see also* specific decisions, justices, Appellate courts, Judicial selection, Jurisprudence), 19–21, 22, 24; *amicus curiae*, 401–402, 430; and Brandeis brief, 12; budget, 108; caseload, 65–67, 98, 109–115, 394–397; as centralizing force, 65, 97, 98, 104, 107, 347; *certiorari* 109–110, 113, 115, 391, 394, 397–401, 402, 407, 430; chief justiceship, 108, 391; and circuit riding, 96–97, 108; conferences, 391, 398; and Congress, 109–110, 415–426 (*see also* Judicial selection, U.S. Supreme Court, structure); constitutional establishment, 75, 94, 104, 107–109, 169; decisions (*see* specific decisions); dissent, 391; docket, 110, 394–397, 397–398; implementation of decisions, 412, 414–447; importance of, 24, 389, 407; and Judiciary Acts (*see* specific acts); jurisdiction of, 94–99, 109–110, 421–422, 426; law clerks, 108–109, 397–398; membership, 107–108, 420–421, 428; and natural law, 8; New Deal, 10, 19–21, 419, 421, 426; and news media, 391–392; opinions, 110, 111, 391–392–395, 401, 403; oral argument, 110, 113, 391, 401–402; and policy making, 394, 460–466 (*see also* Jurisprudence, Policy making, Political jurisprudence); precedent in decision making, 12–13, 15, 52–53, 404; procedures on, 109–111, 390–392, 394–395, 397–399, 401–402; and public opinion, 429, 443–445, 462; retirement/removal of justices, 208–211; reversal rate, 407; review of state courts, 65, 66, 347, 368–376; rules of access, 392–394; selection of justices, 108, 169–170, 190–208; and social change, 463–464; staff, 108–109; and state legislatures, 426–428; statutory interpretation, 52–53, 395, 416–419, 424; structure, 94–95, 97–98, 104, 107–108; voting blocks, 405; writ of appeal, 110

U.S. Tax Court, 100, 117
Utah, 136, 137, 140, 340, 342, 361, 362

Value enunciating jurisprudence, 36–38, 43, 44, 61
Vermont, 134, 136, 137, 340, 342, 350n, 351, 361, 361
Virginia, 81, 136, 137, 159n, 340, 342, 350n, 361, 361, 375
Voting Rights Act of 1965 (and attendant legislation), 161–162

Washington (state), 136, 137, 149n, 162n, 186, 340, 342, 351, 362 373, 374
West Virginia, 85, 136, 137, 340, 342, 359n, 361
Wisconsin, 136, 137, 152, 156n, 162n, 248, 340, 342, 351
Women (*see* Feminist Jurisprudence; Lawyers, gender; Judicial selection, state; Judicial selection, federal)
Wyoming, 135, 136, 137, 140, 148, 340, 342, 351, 361